Listen to Your Heartsense

Ask Thelma 2004-2014

Thelma Domenici
with Melissa W. Sais

Library of Congress Control Number: 2017960250

ISBN-13: 978-0-9995897-0-0

Contents

Preface

When I began to organize the weekly *Ask Thelma* newspaper columns into this book, I immediately knew we had more than just a series of etiquette questions and answers to compile. We had a 10-year continuing education course in kindness, respect and love to share.

I invite you to start at the beginning. The columns are presented in the order in which they appeared in the *Albuquerque Tribune* from March 2004 to October 2007 and in the *Albuquerque Journal* from November 2007 through December 2014. Reading from the beginning takes you through the seasons of each year and hits specific relationship questions that don't necessarily fit in a specific category of manners. Reading through also shows how Thelma's relationship with her readers developed over almost 11 years of weekly communication. Reading through will remind you to be kind all the time and will make you smile. If you do find yourself with a particular etiquette issue to address, there is an index to guide you.

So what is *heartsense*? It's a word Thelma created to express that common sense of the heart, an internal awareness that leads you to what really is the right thing to do. Thelma would say heartsense has no boundaries, no prejudices, it lives the present moment, it does not judge others, and it wakes up every morning grateful for that day.

To me, heartsense is the essence of Thelma Domenici, my mentor and my friend, who has no boundaries, no prejudices, lives the present moment, does not judge others, wakes up every morning grateful for that day, and who never goes out of style.

Melissa W. Sais
December 2017

Ask Thelma 2004
It's Not Just Which Fork to Use

Dear Thelma: Are good manners really that important in this day and age? Shouldn't people just accept me for who I am?

A: People with the very best manners will accept you for who you are. But really, you can do better than that. It isn't hard.

Etiquette is not just which fork to use. It's the respect and courtesy we offer each other that make life run smoothly. It's about building strong and lasting relationships by making those around us feel at ease.

There are simple ways to incorporate etiquette into our everyday lives. Say please and thank you to everyone from your boss to the waiter who serves your lunch. Use these words often around your children. Always be on time, and call if you can't be.

Don't talk with your mouth full and keep your elbows off the table. Turn off your cell phone and give your full attention to your lunch or dinner companion. Double check that you have turned it off before you enter a religious service or a theater.

Hold the door you've just passed through for the person behind you, whether you are a man or a woman. If you must smoke, do so outside.

Respond to invitations by the requested date whether or not you will attend. Bring a gift for the host or hostess when you're invited to someone's home. Send a handwritten thank-you note after attending a party or receiving a gift or favor.

The world may be changing around us, but remember, good manners never go out of style.

Dear Thelma: A friend and his wife invited my wife and I out to dinner. The host knows my fondness for good wine and asked me to select the wine. I didn't know how much he intended to spend and was embarrassed to ask. I ended up ordering just above the cheapest bottle. What should I have done?

A: The host put you in a difficult spot, but not a disastrous one. As a general rule, it's appropriate to spend about as much on a bottle of wine as you would on one person's complete dinner.

When ordering wine for a group it's always proper to ask what others at the table prefer and what they are planning to order for dinner. If you and the hosts were planning to order dishes best paired with a red, and your wife chose a lighter entrée, she could order an individual glass of white wine while a bottle of red was shared at the table.

Dear Thelma: My coworkers threw me a baby shower just days before my daughter arrived. I've got a crying newborn and 22 thank-you notes to write, address, find stamps for and send. Can I just email them?

A: A handwritten note on stationery or a note card is always appreciated by any gift giver and is essential for casual acquaintances and those you don't know well. But your closest friends will be pleased to hear from you even in electronic form.

The purpose of a thank-you note is to express your appreciation in a sincere and timely fashion. Email may be the best way for you to do that with this group.

Each email should be personal. Be sure to mention the gift and how you will or are using it. If several people pooled their funds to buy you a large gift, you should send a personalized message to each of them.

Technology may take us to new places, but good manners never go out style.

Dear Thelma: I have some questions about caller ID. Since I know who's calling when the phone rings, should I answer as though I know who's on the line? And if someone calls and doesn't leave a message, should I call back since my caller ID shows that they called?

A: I don't think you should ever short circuit courtesy in favor of technology. Caller ID does have a fun yet courteous side, but remember that conversations should always start with a polite greeting exchange.

My niece often answers my calls with a polite, "Hi, Aunt Thelma." To which I can respond with my own hello.

However, I am so disarmed when I make a call and the person answering picks up the phone and simply says, "Thelma" or begins the conversation without a greeting. It makes me uncomfortable, and it's just not a normal way to begin a telephone conversation.

So, should you answer as though you know I'm calling? Perhaps so, if you know me very well. Otherwise, opt for a standard greeting of "Hello" or "Chavez residence."

As for whether you should call back those you've captured on caller ID but who did not leave a message, the answer is no. If the person wants you to call back, they should leave a message asking you to do so.

There are reasons the person did not leave a message. They may know they are going to be unavailable for the rest of the day and intend to call you again when they have time to talk. Or perhaps they dialed your number by mistake. The courteous thing to do is let the caller contact you again when they are ready.

Callers who do not leave a message should not expect a call back, although I know many do. This practice is just not practical. If you want a callback, leave a message.

Even if we're in the know, good manners never go out of style.

Dear Thelma: The mother of a business colleague recently passed away. Should the office, as a group, send a sympathy card or should individuals just send cards? If we send a group card, should everyone sign it or simply state, "from your friends at the office?"

A: A sympathy card should stay incredibly individual and very personal. In the case of grieving, I don't think a group response is appropriate.

This is not a case of just manners. It's hard to get a group message to feel as meaningful as an individual response. The person grieving will appreciate receiving single notes from whoever sends them. Each should be a heartfelt and personal message, even if it is short.

Dear Thelma: I have recently attended some banquets at hotels where the ballrooms are situated with round tables. The tables are usually set for 10 people, while it appears they're better suited for eight. Each place setting seems to merge into next. So which coffee cup is mine?

A: I've been at those tables too, and invariably, people begin asking one another your exact question. The answer: My coffee cup is always on the right side of my plate.

A simple rule to remember: food on the left, beverages on the right. In a place setting, all glasses and cups – whether for water, wine or coffee – are placed to the right of your plate. Your bread-and-butter plate and salad plate, if there is one, are set to the left of your dinner plate.

If your neighbor takes possession of your cup, let it go. It wouldn't be proper to point it out. Simply ask a server to bring you another.

Dear Thelma: I work in a cubicle. Since I have no door to close, co-workers stop by to chat whenever they need a break. I've considered wearing headphones to give me an excuse to ignore them, but that seems unprofessional. How can I get my work done without being rude?

A: There is a polite and appropriate way to convey the message that at certain times you need to focus fully on your work, particularly if you have deadlines to meet.

I've found that humor goes a long way in creating comfortable and functional offices. I suggest you create a humorous road sign – DEADLINES AHEAD: Please Come Back Later. Let your co-workers know in a gentle way that when the sign is out you need to focus fully on your work.

You also can try arranging your desk to face away from the cubicle opening so you're not catching the eye of every passer-by. And if someone's chat has gone on too long, stand up or move toward the opening while saying you need to make a copy or get something off the printer.

Note that you shouldn't keep the sign up continuously or try to avoid all contact with co-workers. You don't want to create a permanent barrier to building relationships with your colleagues. You do have to make time for personal interaction and relationship building in your workplace.

We can't function successfully in the work world without personal interaction, but we also can't allow that interaction to take the place of performance. But be sure to remember, even on deadline, good manners never go out of style.

Dear Thelma: When I call my best friend, her 8-year-old son usually answers the phone. Unfortunately, he has very little phone etiquette. He either shouts into the phone to call his mother or shows no interest in taking a message. Should I mention this to my friend? I have a 5-year-old daughter. What is the best way to teach phone manners to children?

A: If this woman is in fact your best friend, there is an appropriate and kind way to talk to her about it. Mention that you worry about whether she is receiving your messages accurately or receiving them at all. It's likely she would rather hear it from you than offend an acquaintance or miss a vital call.

I believe moms are the best teachers of telephone etiquette. You might suggest getting together with your friend to teach your daughter and her son the finer points of answering calls and taking messages.

Make it a game. Use your home phone and a cell phone to make actual calls and role-play several calling scenarios with each child. When answering, stress the use of a greeting like "Hello" or "Daly residence." Make sure they understand how to speak clearly.

Pretend the person the caller seeks is available. Practice saying, "One moment, please." Or, "May I ask who's calling." Tell them not to shout out, "Mom, the phone's for you!" Instead require them to find you in the house and give you the phone quietly or tell you the phone is for you.

Then pretend the person is unavailable. "She's unavailable. May I take a message?" Set up a magnetic marker board on your refrigerator or standard spot in the house where a pen and paper are available for messages. The message they take must include the caller's name and phone number. Require the child to repeat the message back to the caller to double-check the facts.

Remind children of rules about strangers. If an unknown caller asks, "Who's this?" tell your child to say, "Who are you trying to reach?" Instruct your child that she should never tell anyone that she is home alone. Tell her that if she is scared or uncomfortable by anything a caller says, hang up and tell you about it. This also is a good time to teach children about dialing 9-1-1 in an emergency. Even our children should know, good manners never go out of style.

Dear Thelma: I'm in the final stages of interviewing for a new job. The next step is a lunch interview with the top manager. Why do they want to interview me over a meal? How do I answer questions and eat at the same time?

A: This company knows that strong interpersonal and social skills equal business success.

Management has seen your résumé, checked your references and heard your answers to interview questions. Now the person at the top wants to observe your comfortability in a social setting.

An interview over a meal is a very appropriate way to do that. The manager can observe your dining etiquette, along with your ability to make conversation in a setting outside the office walls. From this meeting, the manager will learn much about the confidence you have in yourself and how you will fit in to the company.

Prepare yourself for this meeting as much as you prepared for initial interviews. Be ready for informal conversation by keeping up with current events or sports topics. Critique your own table manners and table posture and brush up accordingly. Confidence in proper dining etiquette will help you be more relaxed and polished, exactly what the interviewer is going to observe.

Arrive at the restaurant on time with your cell phone or pager already silenced. Follow the manager's lead on when to open your menu. Stick to a non-alcoholic beverage, you want to keep your mind sharp and clear. When it's time to order, select a mid-priced meal that will be simple to eat. Avoid hard-to-handle foods and foods that you eat with your fingers.

The manager understands the challenges of eating and responding to questions at the same time. He or she may say, "Let's eat for a few moments and then we'll get to the interview."

During the meal and informal conversation, the manager will be doing some talking too, and you'll have the opportunity to eat then. Take small bites that are easy to chew and swallow when the conversation turns back to you.

It's understood that the manager who invited you to the meal is the host and should pick up the tab. You don't need to make a ceremonial attempt to help with the bill. Leave with a gracious thank-you for the meal and a comment that you look forward to meeting again in the future or can answer further questions by phone. Follow up the next day with a handwritten thank-you note. If you're looking to land the job you should know, good manners never go out of style.

Dear Thelma: My wife and I are taking a seven-day cruise this spring. It is our first vacation together since our kids left home and our first where we'll be dealing with people expecting tips. Can you give me some advice on tipping? How do I decide who to tip and how much?

A: Cruise tipping is different than general travel tipping. Most cruises tell you what's appropriate for tipping in the literature they send you before the cruise. It may suggest a percentage or an amount per day. One thing to remember is that you don't generally do your tipping during the cruise, but at the end of the cruise, before you leave the ship.

When you are at the airport or hotel before or after your cruise, it's appropriate to tip the skycap or bellman who handles your baggage at least $1 per bag. Tip more if you have a lot of luggage. At home or abroad, good manners never go out of style.

Dear Thelma: My daughter is graduating from high school this spring. A debate is raging on who should receive an announcement. Her list is very short, including only very close family and friends. I contend that an announcement is just that, an announcement of a major life milestone, and therefore, that would broaden the range of people who would be pleased to learn of the event. Which one of us is right? Also, how soon before graduation is the appropriate time to mail the announcements? We are also planning a party. Is it alright to include the party invitation in with the announcement?

A: A graduation announcement is a great way to stay connected with family and friends. Your daughter may be worried that people receiving announcements will believe that she expects gifts from them. Assure her that receiving an announcement does not obligate the receiver to send a gift. It would be appropriate to send her a card to congratulate her and acknowledge that they received the announcement, but a gift is optional.

Announcements should be sent at least one month before the event, six weeks is even better. If your hands are tied waiting for the announcements to arrive from the school, send them out as soon receive your order.

Proper etiquette calls for your party invitations to be sent separately, and invitation to the graduation party does require a gift unless otherwise stated.

Dear Thelma: What is the best way to squelch office gossip around the proverbial water cooler?

A: This is a prevalent and harmful problem. Gossip most frequently turns into critical judgment of others and affects morale. Ending it depends on your reaction to the gossip while it is taking place.

As an individual you must first make a conscious decision that you won't participate in gossip, then act accordingly. I think that by your example you can speak more strongly than trying to convince others with words. When gossip begins, walk away or say, "I don't wish to participate in this conversation."

Don't allow gossip to take the place of respect and trust in the workplace. Healthy work environments do not promote gossip, so be comfortable in making a conscious decision to make your feelings about gossip known. Whatever you do or say, express yourself calmly and politely. Taking a stand in this area takes courage, but it is necessary to build a healthy work environment, where good manners never go out of style.

Dear Thelma: I recently attended the Symphony Ball. Not all of my guests knew each other, so I thought that using place cards would assure interesting conversation partners and make the act of finding one's seat more convenient. As I placed the cards I realized that I was not sure of the seating rules which may apply to a round table function. What is the proper way to seat a table of 10 in that situation?

A: Keep in mind the basics of seating guests around your dinner table in this situation. You as the host and your co-host sit opposite each other. The guest of honor should be seated to your right; at the Symphony Ball this may have been your daughter. Other honored guests would be seated to your left and to the co-host's right and left.

Seats of honor should be based on rank in a business or political situation. At your table at the Symphony Ball those deserving honor might be grandparents or an out-of-town guest.

Assign the remaining seats to the rest of your guests. Taking the time to do a seating arrangement for this type of event and not seating spouses next to one another creates the opportunity for the most socialization. It provides an opportunity to meet new people and focus on conversation, as being near someone you don't know well motivates you into discussion. Try to alternate men and women if the make up of the group allows.

It's also a good idea to use place cards at the table so that the guests don't have to wait for you or the co-host to arrive at the table to seat them.

In a very formal setting, it is appropriate for a guest's title and last name to appear on a place card. However, if your guests have never met, include their first names so they can refer to each other's cards if they've forgotten names during conversation.

An issue often faced at events like these is what to do when guests don't show up, leaving empty spaces at the table that create instant conversation barriers. If it happens, ask the wait staff to clear those place settings and invite your guests to adjust themselves to fill in that space. It's worth the shuffle to foster conversation and enjoy the evening.

And final note to guests: It is terribly rude to arrive at a table with place cards and rearrange them to your own liking. The results of a thoughtful seating arrangement will tell you, good manners never go out of style.

Dear Thelma: What's the standard for tipping at a restaurant these days? I've heard it has gone up from 15 percent to 20 percent? What if the service is bad? Is it right to punish the server by withholding the tip?

A: An appropriate tip amount for a small group remains 15 percent of the bill before tax is added. A party of six or more should tip 18 percent. If you want to reward your wait staff for excellent service by leaving a larger tip, that is your decision. The amount is totally up to you.

Many servers are paid less than minimum wage and rely on tips as part of their income. But despite restaurant bills that offer tip calculations of 15 and 18 percent or 15 and 20 percent, a tip and its amount are not guaranteed.

If the service is poor, I don't advocate withholding the tip, but it is appropriate to tip less than you normally do. Keep in mind what part of the problem was within your server's control.

Dear Thelma: I often meet with clients in different parts of the country in very formal and professional situations. Being from New Mexico, I am often compelled to dress in a way that shows a Southwest flair. Would it be appropriate to dress in a Santa Fe skirt with concho belt or some other Southwest style? Or should I stick to a business suit?

A: In business it is always best to meet the client at the client's level. So in professional situations it's wise to dress as a professional rather than in attire that demonstrates a geographical part of the country.

A professional man or woman never makes an attire mistake if he or she is dressed in a business suit.

For men, a dark business suit – navy to dark gray – worn with a long-sleeved dress shirt and tie is most appropriate. A belt and matching dress shoes with over-the-calf socks are necessary accessories.

For women, pantsuits or dress suits are standard professional attire. Choose skirts that are no shorter than three inches above the knee. Hosiery that is your skin color or darker is required with skirts at all times. Choose dress shoes that have comfortable heels no taller than 2 inches.

If part of meeting your clients includes dinner in the evening, I would encourage you to wear your Santa Fe skirt then. It will give you a great opportunity to bring up our unique Southwest culture as dinner conversation. Fashion changes; good manners never go out of style.

Dear Thelma: I am to be honored at a retirement dinner next month. I've been to these types of dinners before and people always end up toasting the honoree. What should I do if I'm toasted?

A: When you are toasted, you do not take a drink with the others. Doing so would mean you are toasting or honoring yourself. Simply smile and nod or say, "Thank you." Hold on to your glass, but leave it on the table.

After you have been toasted, you should respond by returning the toast and thanking the host of the dinner. You might say something like: "It has been an honor to have worked along side of you for these many years and it's an honor to be with you tonight. I'm sure everyone here would like to join me in thanking our hosts, John and Mary, for a wonderful evening. To John and Mary!"

As you conclude a toast, look the person you're toasting in the eye and raise your glass high. Then take a sip and set your glass down.

Clinking glasses after a toast is a very old custom and many people thoroughly enjoy it, but in today's etiquette world, instructors teach that you should just raise your glass. They reason that clinking is not necessary and is hard on glassware. If someone does extend a glass in an obvious effort to clink, don't hold your glass back. Doing so would be unkind.

Dear Thelma: My husband and I just frequented a restaurant where the tables allowed you the option to sit at one side of the table in a chair, or on the other side on a booth style cushion. Where is it appropriate for the woman to sit? My husband thought it didn't matter which side, but I thought the woman should sit on the cushion side. Is there a right or wrong way? Where would you suggest?

A: There's no rule to follow here, but I believe on a date the man should ask the woman where she prefers to sit. Etiquette rules revolving around gender have changed in recent decades, but the basic rules of politeness remain. We should be gracious to each other every chance we get and when someone extends a courtesy to us, we should thank him or her. Good manners never go out of style.

Dear Thelma: I was at a symphony concert the other evening and was embarrassed for the musicians because people clapped before the entire number was played. What guidance can you give to people who attend such concerts?

A: It is considered proper concert etiquette to clap after a piece of music is complete. In classical music, there are places within the piece that sound like endings, but aren't. Before the concert begins, refer to your program. It will list the piece and its movements. There will be a 15- to 30-second pause after each movement, during which time there should be no clapping.

If you keep track of the movements, you'll know when you're hearing the last one and can clap after that. If you lose track, watch the conductor's hands. They will remain up between movements and will be lowered at the end of the piece. Still in doubt? Wait for the rest of the audience to applaud before you begin to clap.

Other courtesies to remember: Turn off cell phones, pagers and watch alarms before you enter the concert hall. Arrive early so you are in your seat when the performance begins. When the music starts, don't talk or whisper and don't get up from your seat.

If you're worried about coughing, open up some cough drops and place them in a handkerchief before the music begins. Someone rummaging through a purse or the sound of crinkling wrappers can be more distracting than the cough.

Most performances depend on silence from the audience, so refrain from humming, singing and tapping your feet. Conducting along with the music will also be distracting to others.

Dear Thelma: A friend of mine has a daughter who is two years older than my daughter. Over the past school year, she has shared with us the most beautiful, outgrown dresses, nightgowns and play clothes. My daughter loves them all. I could never repay her for the hundreds, if not thousands, of dollars in clothes she's given us, but I would like to show her my appreciation. What sort of thank-you gift would you suggest?

A: A gift for such a friend is absolutely in order. I would suggest something specifically for her. If you know her quite well, maybe you know she likes wine or cook books, you can give her something very personal to match her interests. If you're not sure what to give, restaurant gift certificates are always appreciated and flowers are a timeless thank-you gift.

Just like flowers, good manners never go out of style.

Dear Thelma: My two young sons are actively involved in sports and other after-school, weekend and summer programs. Because of this, they have a very large circle of friends -- not all of them close friends. Over the summer it is likely that we will be invited to at least a few birthday parties each month. We can't make it to all of these parties. If we don't attend, are we obligated to send a gift?

A: I know that parents work so hard making sure their kids have good friends and that those relationships are important to your children and to you.

It sounds like you may have some tighter circles of friends within a large group or several groups of friends. If your circle is a cohesive, tight-knit one, you want to make sure that connection stays in tact. And if it's a close friend's party you have to decline, you and your children will probably want to give a gift and should do so.

It is certainly a very gracious gesture to send a gift to every child's birthday you're invited to and can't attend, but it's not a requirement.

Dear Thelma: I love it when I check out at a grocery store and the clerk looks me in the eye and says hello. I hate it when I approach the check out stand and the clerks force me to interrupt their conversation about their weekend just so I can make my purchases. What's even worse is when they don't even stop their conversation. They just continue it while scanning my items and offhandedly mentioning my total price. Talk about feeling invisible. Besides hoping all grocery clerks will read this letter, what can I do to let them know how rude they are being?

A: What I hope is that all managers will read this letter. Attention to customers should be the top priority of store cashiers and should be part of their training.

This is a prevalent problem that I myself have experienced. I have handled it in different ways. I've gently asked them to pay attention to what they're doing for me, which does cause them some embarrassment but focuses them back on their job. I've also spoken to store managers about it, who have sometimes become defensive but have taken care of the problem.

I see nothing wrong with saying something about the problem, but it doesn't have to be done rudely. Your voice shouldn't betray the anger you're feeling inside.

Even in frustrating situations, good manners never go out of style.

Dear Thelma: I have a daughter who just graduated from high school and is planning a graduation party. We received an invitation to a friend's graduation party, which is on the same day ours is planned for. My daughter was not planning on inviting this particular friend to her party, but wants to let her friend know why she can't go to his party. What is the appropriate response?

A: It doesn't sound like this is a close friend and so there's no reason to offer a detailed explanation. Don't leave him wondering if you're going to accept the invitation. It is important to respond quickly that you have a conflict and won't be able to attend. It would be unkind to say you're having a party of your own and that he is not invited.

Dear Thelma: I'm getting married this summer. My fraternal grandparents split up when I was very young and I grew up very close to my grandmother, not my grandfather. Now my grandfather is publicly with his girlfriend for whom he left my grandmother. I don't want to invite my grandfather's girlfriend to my wedding, but she has made it clear that my grandfather will not come if she is not invited. What is the right thing to do?

A: In this situation it's important to turn the focus to what kind of consideration you want to show your grandmother. If you are very close to her, you should discuss with her how the presence of your grandfather and his girlfriend would make her feel. Let how you feel about that conversation guide your decision.

If your grandmother is going to be there regardless of who the other guests are, then you need to decide whether you want your grandfather there badly enough to endure his girlfriend.

If he hasn't been a part of your life to this point, you don't have to invite him. You won't be any closer to him because of the wedding. If you do decide to invite him and his girlfriend, she doesn't have to be catered to or brought into the family that day.

You are the bride and whom you invite to the wedding is your choice. The key is showing consideration for those who are most important in your life. When we care about those closest to us, good manners never go out of style.

Dear Thelma: I just graduated from college and have an interview in two weeks. Can manners help me get the job? What is the best way to prepare?

A: Good manners can help you get the job. When you are comfortable with how to handle your self, you come across as confident.

Go into the interview prepared. Know your skills, achievements and qualifications. Speak confidently about your strengths and weaknesses. Be prepared to answer questions about your goals and why you are considering this job.

Don't go in blind. Research the job and the organization on the Internet. If you can, talk to people who work there. Know the company well and have questions of your own ready for the interviewer.

When you meet the interviewer, put out your hand, make eye contact and say his or her name. It's better to be formal rather than casual: "Ms. Jones, thank you for taking the time to see me." A handshake should be held for three to four seconds. Remember to smile.

Don't take a seat until the interviewer motions you to sit. Sit attentively in the chair. Sit up straight, don't cross your legs or your arms, and keep your legs still.

During the interview, it is more important to hear what the interviewer has to say than it is to articulate what you want to say. Use active listening techniques like eye contact, head nods, an appropriate "Hmmm," and ask questions.

Address your strengths and weaknesses at the appropriate time. Stay positive about previous employment, prior supervisors and professors. Don't be afraid to assert yourself. Tell the interviewer that you have great respect for the company and would be very proud to join the team. Or that you are a very hard worker and are enthusiastic about the company's future.

When the interview ends, shake hands. While shaking, make eye contact, smile and say the interviewer's name. Establish a date for following up with the interviewer and get his or her business card so that you can send a thank you follow-up letter 24 to 48 hours after the interview.

Dear Thelma: As a vice president of my company, I frequently attend cocktail parties and fundraisers. These are usually held during the dinner hours and are my only opportunity to eat an evening meal. Is it appropriate to do so?

A: As a vice president, you are an ambassador for your company and the primary reason you are at these events is to represent your company. So you really can't look at these times as opportunities to eat.

You've heard that you only have one chance to make a first impression. These events may be your only chance to make an impression about your company. Make it a good one by being available to meet people and talk with them about your company without being hampered by hands full of food and drink keeping you from offering a proper handshake and introduction.

It is especially important that if you do partake of the evening's offerings, choose to eat or drink, but don't do both at the same time. In the preliminary stages of a reception, it's easier to have a drink rather than eat when you are trying to meet people. Keep your drink in your left hand so your right hand is free for shaking hands.

When you think you're done with introductions, choose an hors d'oeuvre that you can place in your mouth and chew quickly so you're not caught with your mouth full when someone approaches you to ask about your new product.

Dear Thelma: Until four years ago I lived in Albuquerque. We have since moved to Boulder to be closer to our family. Our grown children were astounded that we tipped 15 percent. I think in a place like Albuquerque 15 percent may be OK, but believe it or not, there is another world out there. Maybe you ought to let your readers know that in the world of New York, Boston and even Denver, 15 percent is looked upon as a "cheap" tip.

A: I contend, and other etiquette and restaurant resources out there agree, that 15 percent remains the tipping standard for good service at the majority of restaurants. At an exclusive, expensive restaurant,

20 percent may be expected. But at such an establishment, first-class service, deserving of more than 15 percent, is expected as well.

At such a place you'd also be tipping the coat-checker $1 per coat, the maître d' $10 to $100, the wine steward at least $3 to $5, the restroom attendant $1 and the parking attendant $3.

Big city or small town, good manners never go out of style.

Dear Thelma: My 10-year high school reunion is coming up this summer. I do want to go because I have some friends I'm really looking forward to seeing. But there also will be some people there who were really awful to me in high school. How should I react or respond to them? Can I spend the whole weekend ignoring them?

A: You definitely should go to your reunion. It's going to be a great chance to reconnect with those people you've missed seeing over the years.

Go with an open mind and heart, willing to say to everyone, I'm glad to see you here. You don't have to seek out the people who did you wrong, but don't ignore them. A lot can happen in 10 years. Time has changed things for you and for them. As you've matured, some of those differences you experienced in high school will have disappeared.

Be gracious and confident in your self, and you may find it all to be more comfortable than you expect.

Dear Thelma: My neighbor has a peach tree that hangs over the fence and into my backyard. When they are ripe, would it be all right for me to pick and eat those peaches that are on my side?

A: Yes. If the peaches hang over onto your property, it's fine. It wouldn't be proper for your neighbor to come into your yard and pick the fruit, so it's all right for you to take care of it.

Because they are on your property, you really don't even have to tell your neighbor. But you could reach out in graciousness and say, "Those peaches are delicious this year."

Dear Thelma: What do you do if you discover you have made an error in the addressing (i.e., the titling or actual name) of a business executive in a letter? Should you communicate your awareness or leave well enough alone?

A: If this is a business executive who you want to continue communication with, you should acknowledge that you made an error. Most executives have an administrative assistant. Contact that person as soon as you discover the error and make your apologies. The assistant should pass it along.

If you're already scheduled to meet with the executive, make your apologies in person at that time: "I apologize for the error I made in your title in the letter I sent." If it's a business relationship you want to continue, you must take care of it quickly. For keeping relationships right, good manners never go out of style.

Dear Thelma: I will be attending a wedding next month and am having a difficult time finding a babysitter for my 5-year-old. He is a good kid and I don't think he'd be any trouble. Is it appropriate to bring him to the ceremony? The reception? Both?

A: It is only appropriate to bring him if he's been invited, and don't assume he is. Look at how the couple addressed their wedding invitation for guidance. The children will be mentioned if they are welcomed to attend: Mr. and Mrs. Charles Baca and Family or Mr. and Mrs. Charles Baca and Diego and Alex.

All invitations should be addressed very specifically and guests should honor them. If the invitation does say "Family," that means the immediate, nuclear family. It does not include your in-laws and favorite cousin.

If you're still unsure, you must ask the couple, and honor their wishes. They may not have invited children because they are taking great care in ensuring a ceremony with no distractions. Your son may be cute and well behaved at the dinner table, but asking him to sit through an hour-long ceremony may push him over his limit. The couple also may have a reception budget that limits their guest list.

Dear Thelma: My husband has very little experience with appropriate table manners. And, to tell you the truth, he drives me crazy. Last weekend we were at a banquet and he ate from the wrong bread plate and drank his neighbor's water. There was nothing I could do to stop him without causing a scene. What's the best way to handle this situation when seated at a large table with acquaintances?

A: The most gracious thing you can do is to not make a fuss at the time. If it's your water that has been seized by your neighbor, discreetly ask the wait staff to bring you another glass. If your neighbor notices and asks, "Oh, did I take your water? I never know which is mine." You can say, "A good rule to remember is solids, like bread plates, are on your left and drinks are on your right."

Talk to your husband after the event. Again, don't make a fuss while you're there. Remind him of the right and left rule, and suggest taking a class on manners together or investing in an etiquette book. Handle it gently and he's more likely to listen.

You're never too old to learn good manners never go out of style.

Dear Thelma: I am hosting an open house and have mailed out a large number of invitations. Is there a rule of thumb to use in guessing the percentage of invitees who will not attend?

This party is a casual affair, a swim party and barbecue, so most of the invitations were addressed to families. This makes estimating a correct headcount even more difficult since I do not know if some or all of the children will attend with their parents. My invitation requested that the guests RSVP and indicated a cut-off date. It is a few days before that date and I have heard from only a hand full of people. I need a headcount for the caterer, should I call those who have not responded?

For my last party, I asked for "regrets only" and got even less of an accurate accounting. Could you please explain when is it appropriate for a host to select between regrets and RSVP requests?

A: Let me first speak to the guests you've invited to your party. It is terribly rude to ignore any RSVP request. Whether it's a formal gala or a 5-year-old's birthday party, the host has honored you with an invitation. It is your responsibility to respond.

You should respond within a week of receiving the invitation and let the host know whether or not you will attend. That means, even if you can't make it, you must respond.

A lack of respect for the RSVP is epidemic in today's society, making it ever more difficult to host a successful party. People today have become very casual with their responses to invitations and almost indifferent to the fact that someone is working to create an occasion for their enjoyment.

I suggest that you seriously consider reviewing your guest list to identify the people who have caused this inconvenience and consider not inviting them next time. Perhaps if enough of the RSVP-ignorers stop receiving invitations, we won't have such problems getting accurate headcounts and they will be so excited to be invited to anything, they will respond immediately.

On to your questions. A good rule of thumb to use in estimating a headcount for any event, big or small, is that 10 percent will not attend.

It is perfectly acceptable to call those guests who have not responded and ask whether they will attend and how many from their household will accompany them.

Using a "regrets only" line generally only works if you've invited a small group of close friends. Otherwise, stick with the RSVP request.

Especially when you're a guest, good manners never go out of style.

Dear Thelma: I will be attending a funeral on Saturday. Funerals make me so nervous. I don't know what to do or say. Do I have to wear black? What is the most appropriate sympathy gift? What should I say?

A: Although funerals can be difficult to attend, don't avoid them. The family will truly appreciate your presence and your expression and support.

Black is the traditional color of mourning, but it is no longer required dress at a funeral. You should definitely avoid bright colors and attire that calls attention to you or makes fashion statement. It is best to dress very modestly.

If you feel the need to send something, flowers sent to the funeral home are most appropriate. It's important to pay attention to the family's wishes expressed in the obituary. If it asks for donations to a charity in lieu of flowers, honor that request.

A reception often follows the services giving family and friends a chance to connect and recall fond memories of the person who has passed away. If you are very close to the family, it would be appropriate to send a meat tray or an appetizer tray to the home for use at the reception or during the days of mourning and receiving visitors that may follow the funeral.

Comforting someone who is grieving is hard for everyone. The best thing to do is to express sincere regret for their loss. It can be as simple as saying, "I am so sorry," or "I deeply regret your loss." If you are close to the family, you might say, "If I can help you in any way, please know that I am here."

Dear Thelma: The small firm I work for is owned and operated by a man who is one of the best IT people around. However, he is very frequently not a good people manager. After three years of observing and being on the receiving end of public criticism and ridicule, I'm calling it quits. I may not wait to have another job lined up before turning in my resignation. My question is on job interviews; how do I politely answer the question of why I left my previous employer without making myself look bad?

A: Find an honest, credible and positive statement you can use when you are asked why you left. You don't have to go into great detail, but you must be positive about your former place of employment.

You might try something like, "My former firm is a leader in the field of information technology. I learned so much from working in that environment, but the time was right to begin seeking greater career advancement opportunities."

Never bring even a hint of negativism into a job interview. Don't bring up the problems you faced or your assessment of your boss. You don't want the interviewer to ever feel that you would have a negative attitude coming into her organization.

If you keep a positive attitude and your stellar skills, strengths, qualifications and achievements in front of the interviewer at all times, the reason you left your last job will become a footnote.

Dear Thelma: In many restaurants now, bread is served with pats of butter individually wrapped in foil. I don't like to slather all that butter onto one piece of bread and I don't like dealing with the foil on my bread plate. So, I usually take my bread knife, move the butter from the foil onto the plate, and then apply the butter bit by bit onto the bread as I eat it.

Does this sound right or wrong? And if it's OK, what do I then do with the scrap of buttery foil?

A: You are correct to move the butter to the plate and to butter your bread bit by bit. As for the foil, the most important thing to know is that you don't put it on the table. Secondly, if there's a dish holding several wrapped pats of butter, you don't put your foil back on that plate. Instead, fold the foil up neatly and place it on the edge of your bread plate or put it on the edge of the saucer holding your coffee cup. The polite diner knows good manners never go out of style.

Dear Thelma: How does one know whether or not birthday gifts are appropriate for adult birthday parties? I've had three incidents lately that have left me feeling socially inept.

First birthday: The invitation said, "No gifts, please, your presence is the best gift." I did not bring a gift and was very embarrassed to be literally the only person without a gift.

Second birthday: The invitation said, "no gifts", but after my previous experience, I decided to bring a gift. This time I was literally the only person to bring a gift and felt inept.

Third birthday: No mention of gifts on the invitation. Again, I brought a gift and was embarrassed to be the only person with a gift.

What is the correct thing to do in these situations?

A: Don't feel graceless. In two out of three instances, you did the right thing.

Birthdays are an important celebration in anyone's life – adult or child – and birthday gifts are appropriate for any age. If the invitation makes no mention of gifts, then a gift is appropriate. You were a social star at the third birthday party.

However, if the invitation specifically says, "no gifts," then the invitees should honor that. It is absolutely appropriate not to take a gift in that instance, and you can feel confident in your decision to do so. There's no need to apologize or make reference to the fact that the invitation said no gifts. Just walk into that party, arms free, and have a good time.

At the first party, although I know you felt embarrassed, there was really no reason to be. You had done the right thing.

If you are still unsure, it is always acceptable to contact the person who sent the invitations and inquire about gift giving.

Dear Thelma: When is it too late to send a thank-you card?

A: It is always best to send a thank-you note within 24 hours of attending an event or receiving a gift. You should never let it go longer than a week.

But if a week or weeks go by, you're not off the hook. You still must send the thank-you and be very apologetic about the delay. Be sure that you don't do so much explaining about how busy you are that your thank you leaves the giver feeling unappreciated. This is not a making-excuses note; it's a thank-you note.

Keep a stack of thank-you cards on hand so you are always ready to respond to another's kindness in a timely fashion.

Whether you're giving or receiving, good manners never go out of style.

Dear Thelma: A friend of mine asked me if I were invited to an engagement party would I automatically expect to be invited to the wedding. She had heard from relatives that it was unacceptable to invite people to an engagement party without also asking them to the wedding.

Her daughter has decided to have a very small wedding and three engagement parties. One party will be in the city where her parents live, another where his parents live and a third where she lives now. I told her that sounded like a fun practical way to include everyone, but you are the expert, what is "etiquettely" correct?

A: The key here is that the couple has decided to have a very small wedding. There is nothing wrong with a couple wanting to have an intimate ceremony and wedding day designed for the people closest to them.

How gracious that they also want to share their happiness with all their family and friends by bringing the celebration to them. These parties are a convenience to their guests and give all the opportunity to spend time with the happy couple. It is not a requirement that guests at an engagement party be invited to the wedding.

The bride might consider sending out wedding announcements to the party guests on the day of the wedding. In wording and design similar to her wedding invitations, the announcement tells when and where she was married.

Those receiving announcements are not expected to send gifts, but it is proper to send a note of congratulations.

Dear Thelma: I just completed a first round of job interviews with a company. Should I send a thank-you note to everyone I met? What should I say?

A: If you participated in a team interview, each member of that team considers him or herself valuable. Responding to each of them with a thank-you letter makes a good impression. If you met and interviewed one-on-one with several individuals, you definitely should send letters to each of them.

An essential part of the interview is asking for the business card of the person you meet. That gives you the correct spelling of his name and his job title. With cards in hand, you can write and send your thank-you letters immediately after the interview.

In your letter, thank the interviewer for the time she spent with you. Write about how impressed you are with specific aspects of the company and the great contributions you could make. Ask her to call if she has additional questions. End with how you're looking forward to hearing from her. Type the letter on good-quality stationery and sign it by hand. Send it within 24 hours of the interview.

Follow-though is part of that first impression' you leave with interviewers. And as we all know, you only have one opportunity to make a first impression.

Dear Thelma: I recently received a "hold that date" card. What a great way to let people become aware of an upcoming special occasion. With this information I'll be able to take advantage of advance ticket purchase prices, have plenty of time to make other travel arrangements, and even ask for vacation time off well in advance. Are hold-the-date cards appropriate for all occasions?

A: Hold-the-date cards are typically created for major business or community social events or fundraisers. The guest list for these types of functions usually is filled with people whose calendars fill very quickly. If you are planning a major event, get the date into your guests' calendars months ahead of time.

Save-the-date cards also are sent if you are inviting many out-of-town guests to a special occasion, like a wedding, for just the travel-related reasons you've mentioned.

The card text should announce the event, the host and the date, and end with a line saying, "Invitations to follow" or "Details will follow." The cards should be sent months in advance.

For most events, you should mail your invitations sufficiently far in advance of the event so that your guests have time to make arrangements. Four to six weeks serves well in most situations.

In the art of inviting, good manners never go out of style.

Dear Thelma: The founder of our company died. He was a wonderful man who gave me a great career. The family has asked for donations to a choice of three organizations in lieu of flowers. Because he was such a special person and gave so much to me and many others, I would like to make the largest donations I can to a couple of the organizations. I do not want to do anything inappropriate or out-of-line in the amounts. Due largely to this family's generosity, I am now a millionaire myself. Can you help me with the amounts I can give appropriately?

A: Since you are in a position to recognize the generosity of this man and what he's done for you with a large donation, I don't think there is a limit to the amount you can give. Your sincere giving is an opportunity to express your great respect and appreciation for his generosity to you and others.

You will make your memorial contributions directly to the organizations. Be sure the organizations know you've made the gift in his honor. Generally, organizations send the family a list of those who have made contributions, but they don't provide the amounts of individuals' gifts.

Although the family will be notified of your gift, it is still important that you express your reasons for making the donation because of the personal relationship that existed. In a personal note, let the family know how much you appreciated him and that his generosity serves as a model for you. It's not necessary or appropriate to provide information about the amount you've given to the selected organizations.

Using the sincerity you've expressed in your question, you will make your tribute with grace and it will be received with gratitude.

Dear Thelma: A friend's daughter is getting married and her fiancé wants to invite all his friends to the rehearsal dinner. Not everyone is happy about this. Who traditionally gets an invitation to that event?

A: The traditional guest list for a rehearsal dinner includes the wedding party; the couple's parents, grandparents and siblings with their spouses or significant others; the officiate and his or her spouse; and any one else required to be at the rehearsal, like those doing readings. Spouses or significant others of the attendants are often included. Beyond that, out-of-town guests may be invited and just about anyone else the host – typically the groom's family – so desires.

Guest lists can cause friction, but good manners never go out of style.

Dear Thelma: Is it still the rule that a man should not shake a woman's hand until she offers it? And is it still the rule (and is it not awkward) for a woman to wait a significant amount of time until a man opens a door for her?

A: This old-school gallantry is no longer the standard. But that's not to say that courtesy and respect are no longer required and admired.

The business etiquette of today began to replace the chivalry of the

30

past in the 1970s when women began to demand equality in the workplace. While the focus on gender ended, the importance of civility and consideration for each other expanded. We each have a responsibility to treat others with consideration and to help whoever is in need, whether we are a man or a woman.

Courtesies that may have been one-sided in the past are now inclusive. Stand and extend your hand during any introduction or greeting. Whoever is the first to the door should hold it open for others. Carry a package for anyone who needs help. The person at the front of the elevator exits first. A professional stands for a visitor to his or her office and remains standing until the visitor is seated. The person who invites another to dinner picks up the tab.

This new spin on the old rules doesn't negate the need for men and women to be gracious to each other. A man should not be afraid to hold a door for a woman and a woman should not be offended by his gesture. Being graceful means knowing how to offer common courtesies meant to show care for the other person's comfort or safety and how to accept those courtesies graciously.

Dear Thelma: When addressing something to a married couple, where you want to use the first names of each, is it proper to list the husband or the wife first?

A: When addressing a letter or invitation to a married couple who use the same last name it is correct to write Mr. and Mrs. Charles Preston. You list their first names only if the woman uses her maiden name or a hyphenated name. In those instances, you list the man first and write Mr. Charles Preston and Ms. Sandra Howe or Mr. Charles Preston and Ms. Sandra Howe-Preston.

However, if a woman outranks her husband, her name comes first, as in The Honorable Judy Miller and Mr. Jeff Miller.

Etiquette evolves with society, but good manners never go out of style.

Dear Thelma: In the U.S. there is a protocol for eating with a knife and fork (hold the fork with your left, cut with your right, then transfer the fork to your right to bring the food to your mouth). In Europe, the protocol differs – I think you cut with your left hand. For me, it feels more natural to cut with my left and hold with my right. How hard and fast are these rules and can I use the European approach as long as it is close to what feels more natural? And how set are these rules? How about if we just look civilized when we dine?

A: First, let's clearly define and describe the two basic methods of using silverware at a meal.

In the American style, you hold your fork in your left hand with the tines down to steady your meat and your knife in your right hand. Cut one bite of meat and place your knife on the plate with its cutting edge facing in. Switch the fork to your right hand with tines up, pick up the food, raise it to your mouth and eat. Switch hands again when you're ready to cut another piece.

In the European style, more widely known as continental style, you hold your fork in your left hand and your knife in your right hand throughout the meal. Cutting is done the same way as in American style. After you've cut one bite of meat you may add other food by pushing it onto the fork with the knife. Then raise the fork to your mouth with the tines down, twisting your wrist and forearm slightly toward you as you place the food into your mouth.

When you're eating and not cutting, keep the knife in your right hand and the fork, which you may turn tines up or keep tines down, in your left. Use the knife to push the food away from you and onto the fork.

When eating salads or desserts where no knife is used, hold the fork in the right hand with the tines up.

It's important that you get comfortable with one style or the other. Either is appropriate, but don't dance between the two at a meal and don't create a hybrid version. Learning and using the finer points of dining etiquette is easy to do and shows that you care about polite behavior and good manners, which brings advantages in the business and social worlds.

You've heard me say it before: Good manners never go out of style.

Dear Thelma: What are the rules for married/maiden names? If a woman married, divorced and then remarries, can she keep using her last married name with a hyphen to her new married name?

A: The importance of your name becomes clear when you consider changing it, doesn't it?

If you have strong name recognition in the professional world, you don't want to lose that. If people in your business community know you by your maiden or first married name, it makes sense to keep it as a middle name or add a hyphen and your new married name. To make sure a middle or hyphenated name sticks, you'll have to use it every time you introduce yourself and in all correspondence.

Children may also be a consideration when making a name change. A woman may keep her children's surname as part of her name to keep confusion with schools or doctors to a minimum.

Be sure to stay in communication with your fiancé or new husband when considering your options and in making your decision.

There may be confusion when you do make a change. Remember your good manners when people address you incorrectly.

Dear Thelma: Is eating soup still done with the spoon in an outward rather than inward motion?

A: Yes, spoon your soup away from you and toward the center or top of the bowl. As you come to the end of your soup course, it is acceptable to tilt your bowl or soup plate away from you to scoop up the last spoonful.

Many manners guides state you should sip the soup from the side of the spoon, but to me the word sip is misleading, inferring that you shouldn't take the spoon into your mouth. I can't eat soup that way. It's exhausting and messy and I may end up slurping.

On the other hand, don't plunge the spoon, point-first, into your mouth. Do place the edge of the spoon near the point into your mouth and take the soup from there.

If your soup bowl has two handles, you may lift it and drink the broth after you have eaten any vegetables, pasta pieces or meats with your spoon.

Between spoonfuls, leave your spoon in your bowl. When you are finished, place the spoon on the plate under your bowl. If there is no plate beneath your bowl, leave the spoon in the bowl; never return it to the table.

On the subject of soup, good manners never go out of style.

Dear Thelma: If someone is dominating the conversation at a dinner party, how do you politely get the conversation turned?

A: It is the host's responsibility to make sure all their guests enjoy themselves and to keep conversation flowing. That sometimes may require the host to cut off someone who has taken control of the conversation.

When a topic is exhausted, inappropriate, upsetting to someone, or if too few of the other guests have knowledge or interest in it, it is perfectly acceptable for the host to step in.

To do so politely is important. You may try interjecting and inviting another guest to offer her opinion – "Let's hear Irene's opinion on that." – with the hope that Irene takes the opportunity to steer the conversation in another direction. Humor and a light touch also can go far in keeping the poor conversationalist from feeling ill-treated.

The situation sometimes may require a more direct statement paired with another subject to keep the conversation flowing – "I think we may have exhausted this subject. And before the night's over, I want to hear what our resident runner Carl thought of the Olympic men's marathon."

The host may also utilize a tradition that began in the early 19th century, in which conversation partners around a dinner table switch after each course. After the first course is brought out, the host would turn to speak to the guest at his right. Conversational parings then form to the right around the table. When the second course is brought in, the host turns to his left and everyone else switches accordingly, and so on throughout the meal.

If guests don't catch on and leave someone with no one to talk to, the host can direct the conversational traffic with humor.

I've been to parties with chronic conversation hogs, who I find it hard to believe don't know they're guilty of this impoliteness. Afterwards people say, "Can't we do something about that?" As a group we've decided to take them on and work together to steer the conversation elsewhere. The saddest thing I've found is that they may not be invited back because they've made parties so uncomfortable.

We can all stand to improve our conversation skills. Before attending a party or event, think about what a good conversationalist does. She can talk about a broad range of subjects and shows sincere interest in other people and their pursuits and pastimes. He can sense when he is boring people by their glassy stares and fidgeting feet and is quick to change the subject or launch the ball into another's court.

Whether host or guest, good manners never go out of style.

Dear Thelma: I understand that if you are invited to a wedding reception, and you will be attending, a gift is required. However, if you are not planning to attend, is a gift still required? And, to complicate matters, the bride never acknowledged our generous high school graduation gift check of several years ago. We are not close to the bride; she is the only daughter of a business partner. Thank you for your guidance.

A: If you've been invited to a wedding reception, a gift is required regardless of whether you will attend.

At their heart, social functions are about relationships. If it is important to you to maintain your relationship with your business partner, then you will want to act with the utmost grace and courtesy.

The bride's failure to thank you for your last gift to her is not excusable, but you can't use her lack of manners as a guide for your behavior. You still must do what you know is right.

Dear Thelma: At a dinner out recently I ordered a delicious gumbo. My problem was the huge shrimp included in the dish. They were too big to eat in one bite and hard to cut in the slippery bowl of gumbo. So, I spooned them out onto my bread plate, cut them up and put them back into the bowl. This didn't feel quite right. What should I have done?

A: Your best option would have been to pierce the shrimp all the way through with your fork to steady it, and then cut it with your knife, one bite at a time. This may have been difficult at the bottom of a bowl of dark stew, but I think you could have done it. You then could alternate between your fork and spoon to scoop up the broth and vegetables.

It sounds quite possible that you didn't have the correct silverware for the task. If you were not given a knife and fork, or if your fork was taken away with your salad, it would have been perfectly acceptable to ask the waiter for the utensils you needed.

While eating, use the plate under your bowl to place the utensils you are not using at the time. When you are completely finished, put all the utensils on the plate. You had no plate? Keep them all in the bowl or on a bread plate. After the silverware is taken up from the table it never returns.

Even when faced with culinary challenges, good manners never go out of style.

Dear Thelma: My neighbor recently lost a very public job. It was headline news in our community. I see him in his yard a time or two a week and always speak to him. My question is, do I bring up the loss of his job and offer sympathy, or just pretend I'm unaware of his situation?

A: It is appropriate to offer an expression of being sorry, and it would be very wrong to ignore it completely.

Keep your comment sincere and brief – "I'm sorry to hear about your situation." – and offer it in a way that shows your neighbor that you don't expect him to expound on the issue or make it a conversation topic.

If your neighbor chooses to deal with it longer, you should be attentive. Your listening ear may be what he needs at that time.

Dear Thelma: I've been frustrated recently by people who don't seem to know how to show proper respect during the Pledge of Allegiance or the national anthem. Can you share proper etiquette for honoring the flag?

A: By showing proper respect to the United States flag, we honor our nation, our fellow Americans, our past and our future.

The Pledge of Allegiance at a civic meeting should be recited while standing at attention, facing the flag and saluting by placing your right hand over your heart. Hold the salute from the first word of the Pledge through its last line. So, yes, you must stop your conversation with your tablemates for a brief moment and focus on the flag.

In 1943, the U.S. Supreme Court ruled that no one could be forced to say the Pledge of Allegiance. If you choose not to say it, you must remain silent and respectful during it.

When the national anthem is played or sung, stand at attention and salute with your right hand over your heart. Place it there at the first note of the anthem and hold it there through the last note. Face the flag if it is displayed. If a flag is not present, face the source of the music.

Men should remove their hats. A woman will need to make a judgment call. If her hat is a very casual one – a ball cap or a bucket hat – she should remove it. Women wearing dress hats as part of their fashion ensembles can keep them on during the anthem.

If a flag passes you in a parade, stand at attention and start your hand-over-heart salute as it enters your area. End it when the flag has passed you.

When it comes to our flag, good manners never go out of style.

Dear Thelma: Ankle bracelets seem to be all the rage these days. I can't decide when they are appropriate. What do you think?

A: Ankle bracelets are appropriate in a purely social setting. Especially at a time of year when it is acceptable to go without pantyhose, a delicate gold chain ankle bracelet can be an attractive part of your accessorized look. I've spotted some very sophisticated, very-well dressed women wearing them at social events.

However, ankle bracelets should not be worn with nylons, and they are not appropriate in a professional setting. They have no place in proper business attire. Also, tattooed ankle bracelets should be avoided at all cost.

Dear Thelma: While I'm no barbarian, I didn't grow up using formal manners. The local steakhouse with the giant steer statue outside the door was the swankiest place my family ever went to eat. Now I'm moving up in the professional world and finding myself in unfamiliar territory. Where do I start my etiquette education? And will the truly refined spot me trying to be mannerly from a mile away and just laugh?

A: You've already made the right start. You realize you are moving to a new level professionally and socially, and now you have a responsibility to learn what you need to know to operate in those arenas.

Continue by realizing that respect for others is at the heart of all business and social etiquette. Absorb that realization and become very comfortable with yourself and your ability to incorporate courtesy into all areas of your life.

You could join a class or sign up for one-on-one coaching, but there are also many resources available at libraries, bookstores and on the Internet to guide you.

Then go out and practice what you've learned. Make a point to try out your conversation skills at a business reception rather than hanging back with your regular circle of associates. Go to dinner with a friend at a fine restaurant to test your silverware savvy. Assess your look in the mirror each morning. Is it professional?

As you learn and practice, these skills become a part of you, not something you turn on or off as you go about your day. As your comfortability in social and business situations rises, so does your self-confidence. With an improved self-image you can ditch the label of feeling or looking out of place.

Through your own refinement you'll learn that those with the best manners always go out of their way to make others feel comfortable and confident. And you'll know good manners never go out of style.

Dear Thelma: I work in a hospital and am constantly using elevators. It seems like every day I encounter some kind of rudeness – whether it's a loud cell phone conversation or someone ignoring my obvious effort to get to the elevator door before it closes. I realize that a hospital brings together diverse people with many different things on their minds, but maybe if we treated one another better, we'd feel better too. Our world needs a dose of elevator etiquette. Can you help?

A: Riding in an elevator presents an aspect of life we're not all comfortable with. After all, the amount of personal space most people require is equal to about the size of an elevator. So we are no doubt trespassing on one another every time we enter an elevator.

Taking the time and making the effort to be courteous can make the trip between floors more comfortable for everyone.

When the elevator arrives, stand back and let those getting off exit before charging in to claim your space. If you have entered the elevator and see someone rushing to catch it, hold the open-door button for him and make room.

Face the elevator doors as you ride. Facing the riders rather than the doors will make everyone uncomfortable as you invade their personal space further by forcing them to look you in the eye.

In a crowded elevator everyone at the front should get off when the doors open, even if they are not at their floor, to allow those behind them to emerge. After the car has emptied, get back on and proceed to your floor. If you are going to the top floors of a building, make an effort to find a space in the back to stand.

Exit the elevator quickly and to the side to make it easier for those behind you to get off. Whoever is at the front of the elevator should get off first, regardless of gender. If the elevator is not crowded, it's a fine gesture to allow ladies or those who outrank you to exit first.

It is fine to smile at people as they enter and give them a nod goodbye when they leave. If you accidentally push against someone in the elevator, give a quick and sincere "I'm sorry" or "Please excuse me."

Keep talking to a minimum and stick to a generic topic, like the weather. Never speak loudly and avoid subjects that are personal or confidential – you never know who may be riding with you. And save your cell phone conversation for later.

Especially in small spaces, good manners never go out of style.

Dear Thelma: I often attend luncheons and functions with business associates and potential clients. I also wear a hearing aid. In a crowded room it's often difficult for me to hear all of what an individual speaking to me is saying. Should I ask the person to speak up or just go along catching what I can?

A: There's nothing wrong with saying, "I'm sorry. It's very loud in here and I don't want to miss anything you're saying, so could you please speak up?"

It would be impolite and awkward to let the person continue talking at a level that you can't hear and for you to miss something important.

If a person mentions wearing a hearing aid or it is visible, do what you can to make the conversation flow most easily. Face the person directly, speak clearly and at a moderate pace. Do not shout; shouting distorts sounds received by a hearing aid.

If a group is gathered and one person mentions having trouble hearing the conversation, everyone should pay attention to that and be sure they are speaking clearly and so that everyone can hear.

Communication is key in all relationships. We should always make every effort to help it flow effectively.

Dear Thelma: I recently attended an outdoor, tent-type event, an art auction fundraiser with food and music. The invitation said something like "black-tie and Southwestern glamour appreciated." I wore a black cocktail dress, my husband a dark suit. Someone showed up in faded jeans and a western shirt. There was one man in a tux. What's a girl to do?

A: Well, after you get there, nothing. If you've dressed as the host requested, you should feel perfectly comfortable. You should always dress according to what's designated on the invitation. Always.

The host has every right to decide the ambiance of his or her own party. And a considerate guest will respect the dress request.

As society gets more casual about everything and propagates an attitude of "it's all about me," more and more people are ignoring the dress designation in favor of their own contentment. This is unacceptable, especially when someone has gone out of their way to create an atmosphere and an event for your enjoyment.

Of course you never point out to the shirker that they're dressed improperly, whether you're the host or a fellow guest. And don't make anyone feel uncomfortable with judgmental looks or side comments. That would be improper and unkind.

If you'd like to be invited back, remember, good manners never go out of style.

Dear Thelma: The head of our swimming club is rude, humiliates children and is obstructive to attempts to communicate with him formally or informally. I approached him and politely but persistently asked for a parent's meeting, which he did not like. We are now being asked to leave the club for being rude and disruptive. How does one deal politely with rudeness?

A: Our own kindness, respect and courtesy in the face of rudeness are the best response we can give. Our controlled conduct will serve to highlight the poor behavior of the rude individual and keep us above the fray.

Children should not be subjected to humiliation or rudeness. And any adult in a leadership or teaching position should know he is a constant role model for behavior and must act accordingly. When you became concerned about the head of your club's attitude toward your children, it was absolutely appropriate for you to ask politely for a meeting.

If this person is not the highest authority at the club, then it is important that you do go to the ultimate decision maker or decision-making board to express your concerns.

If you've gone to the top and the club doesn't care that it's representative is rude to its membership, then maybe this is a club you don't want to belong to.

Dear Thelma: I'm a college freshman and live in the dorms. My roommate is nice but really messy. I almost feel like it's too late to bring it up. Is there anything I can do about this now?

A: It's not too late to open up the lines of communication and that's where you've got to start. You've said your roommate is nice, so it shouldn't be too hard to pick a time when you'll both be in the room or make plans to go out for coffee and a talk.

Before you approach your roommate, think about the specific issues you can address. Don't say, "We've got to talk. You're too messy." Instead say, "It's hard for me to get from the door to my side of the room without tripping on your shoes." Or "The refrigerator is starting to smell. Can we cut a deal to clean out our own leftovers once a week?" Keep it light and be sure to ask if there's anything you can do to make your roommate's life any more pleasant.

The successful sharing of such a small space depends on communication and compromise, by both of you. Your roommate will probably never be as neat as you, so appreciate any attempts made.

Especially in cramped quarters, good manners never go out of style.

Dear Thelma: I'm hosting Thanksgiving for my family and I want to make it very special. Can you give me some ideas for setting the table and for convincing my husband that paper plates and plastic forks are not very special?

A: If you really want to make people feel special, you should use the best you've got.

Setting an elegant table changes the entire atmosphere of a celebration. People truly feel honored when you've made an extra effort for them.

I once hosted a dinner that included two children. I set their places with china and silver. Their grandfather called the next day. "No one ever lets the kids use the china," he said. "You served them on it and did you see how well behaved they were?"

When you bring out your best for people, even little people, they give their best to you.

For your celebration, start with a pretty tablecloth and a centerpiece. At each seat set a dinner plate flanked by a knife and tablespoon on the right and a salad fork and dinner fork on the left, placed in order of use from the outside in.

Set a small bread plate above and to the left of the forks with a butter knife placed across it. Glasses sit to the right of the place setting above the knife. Place a simply-folded cloth napkin to the left of the forks or on the dinner plate.

I'm confident your extra effort will highlight the happy memories of the day.

Dear Thelma: Today I was invited to an engagement party that will be held at a restaurant. The invitation included the per-person cost for catering, and the host/organizer is collecting money in advance. I have always heard of engagement parties being paid for by the party's host and scaled accordingly. However, since I am not from New Mexico I may be unacquainted with local customs. Is it customary here for engagement parties to be paid for by the guests?

A: No, it's certainly not customary for guests to foot the bill at any party. And I'm taken aback by the situation. It just shouldn't be done.

If you are organizing a group planning a get-together, it's fine to ask that group to share in the cost and responsibilities. But that has to be communicated and agreed to by all those you're asking to chip in. If someone is simply being invited to a party, they should never be asked to pay to attend.

From the invitation, you've been given two options: pitch in or pack up. Not exactly a gracious appeal.

Those extending invitations should remember, good manners never go out of style.

Dear Thelma: I have a New Zealand friend who says the correct placement of the knife and fork at the end of a meal is vertically in the center of the dinner plate. I was taught to place the knife, with cutting edge in, at approximately 11 o'clock and 4 o'clock and the fork next to the knife on the inside, tines down. What is the correct placement of the knife and fork on the dinner plate when one is finished eating?

Is it ever correct to rest the knife or the fork on the edge of the dinner plate, with the handle of either utensil on the table? My New Zealand friend does this. In my family we called this gang planking, and like elbows on the table, it was not allowed.

A: The two most common dining styles used in business and social settings are continental style and American style. I'd advise everyone to learn and stick to one or the other.

In both styles when you are finished with your meal, you place the utensils across the center of the plate at what we call 10:20. If your plate were a clock face and your utensils hands, the tips sit at the 10 and the handles at the 4. The utensils are placed close together, with the knife on the right with the cutting edge facing the center of the plate and the fork on the left. In the continental style the fork is placed with the tines down. In the American style, tines face up.

As for what you call "gang planking," the most improper place to set the silverware you're eating with is back on the table, even just the handles. Once you have picked up your utensils they should always be placed on your plate when you're resting between bites.

When resting your silverware in the continental style, imagine the face of the clock again. Rest your knife, cutting edge in, at 10:20. Place your fork, tines down, across your knife with the tip facing the 2 and the handle facing the 8. In American style, rest by placing your cutlery in a modified 10:20, spacing them wider apart and slightly higher on the plate.

Placing our silverware in a specific spot is not a nonsensical rule. It signals the server that she may remove our plate. Conventions like these make our meal and our interactions flow more smoothly.

The most important manners lesson we can learn is that our words and actions should always show consideration for others. Even when dining with a misinformed friend, good manners never go out of style.

Dear Thelma: Who should I send holiday cards to?

A: The holidays are the one time of year we have a concrete way of staying connected. Greeting cards give us a real opportunity to maintain relationships with family, friends and business associates.

Everybody has their own personal card list, which changes over the years as we meet new friends and lose touch with others. At a minimum, I expect you will include your family and close friends. Your list may include people from your past – a college roommate or childhood friends – with whom this may be your once-a-year correspondence. You also might include those colleagues and business associates with whom you have a personal connection.

Do I think you should send a card to everyone in your office? No. It's a nice thought if you're using it as an opportunity to say something nice that comes from your heart. But it's not required.

Over the past several Christmases, I've been sending a Christmas letter. Since your cards aren't going only to those closest to you, it's nice to use them to let people know what's been happening this year. You can be selective with whom you send the letter to, choosing not to include it with strictly professional contacts. Be sure to sign it personally.

Keep the holiday letter positive and work to make it more than a litany of your latest successes or travels or kids' accomplishments. Let it convey the spirit of season – that you're thankful for your blessings, which include their friendship.

Dear Thelma: My husband and I recently bought our first house. We've finished upgrading and decorating and now we want to share it with our family and friends. Can I give my own housewarming party or is that something someone else should throw for you?

A: Yes, you can give your own housewarming party.

With the work you've done and the excitement of being new homeowners, of course you want to share it, and your family and friends are eager to see it.

Your party can be anything from a simple open house with drinks and hors d'oeuvres to an elaborate dinner party. Plan to offer tours of your new home or allow people to wander through.

People may bring gifts, which you can open as they're given or after the party. If everyone attending has brought a gift, you can open the presents as part of the celebration.

As you're making out your guest list, consider including your new neighbors. Like such gestures of goodwill, good manners never go out of style.

Dear Thelma: I'm not close to any of my fellow workers and don't really care to spend any extra time with them. But the holiday office party is coming up. Am I obligated to attend? Will it look bad if I don't?

A: To go to party for obligatory reasons defeats the purpose and spirit of a party. And to be honest, if I were hosting the party or even just attending it, I don't think I'd want you to be there.

You act as you think. Your negative attitude toward the party and your coworkers is going to show through in your body language, your conversations and your demeanor.

If you do go, you have to manifest that you're glad you're there, otherwise just don't go. Attending with a negative party attitude may be even worse for your career than not showing up to the festivities.

Interpersonal and relationship building skills are integral parts of career success. It seems you've missed the relationship building process in your organization. Realizing that, it's important that you take the steps now to begin that process. And I hope that by next holiday season, you'll be ready for the party.

Dear Thelma: Recently I was invited (in a round about way) to a Christmas party hosted by someone I had met only once. This acquaintance invited me by asking my very good friend, Chris, to call me. Since I enjoy Chris's company, I agreed to attend. As the date for the event drew near, no party information (where, when, attire, etc.) was relayed to me nor was a formal invitation from the host ever given. It is now five days before the event, and I have received an invitation for the same date to a party I really want to attend with many of my friends. How do I get out of this mess?

A: Don't go to the party you weren't ever properly invited to. Tell

44

Chris you have a conflict and go to the other party.

Since Chris is a "very good friend," you can tell him or her that you feel uncomfortable at never receiving an actual invitation from the host. Chris should understand.

Generally, the only valid reasons for changing your response to an invitation is a truly unavoidable conflict or an emergency. An invitation to a better party doesn't fall into those categories. However, this seems to be a very casual affair to which you were never officially invited.

Your concern over this situation shows you already know good manners never go out of style.

Dear Thelma: Last year everyone in my department – staff and managers –exchanged Christmas gifts, except me. While I received gifts from everyone, I didn't give any. Considering the size of my family, I have enough gifts to buy. My budget and common sense tell me that buying gifts for my 10 co-workers and managers is not necessary. Is this going to hurt my career?

A: A decision to give no gifts probably won't end your career. But a lack of interest in sharing in the generous spirit of the holiday season points to a problem with relationship building, which can hold you back professionally.

Studies show that relationship building is a vital part of the culture of an organization. Professionals coming into career positions sometimes aren't retained if they don't build relationships or learn how to represent the organization internally and externally.

You'll help your career by establishing relationships with the people working with you. Then the thought of giving gifts won't feel so obligatory to you.

Thoughtfulness, kindness, sensitivity and inclusion should direct the spirit of your gift giving. The holidays are not a time for leaving anybody out. If you are very close to some of your co-workers and have special gifts for them, give them outside the office.

Stationery, soaps, gift certificates for books or dinner, and baked goods – home baked or store bought – are always appropriate and appreciated gifts for colleagues.

The gifts you give your co-workers don't have to be expensive or elaborate, just thoughtful and kind. A festive bow on their favorite candy bar and a holiday card with a personal message shows you've thought of them and shouldn't break the bank.

Dear Thelma: It never fails, every year someone gives me a Christmas gift out of the blue. It's always someone I'm friendly with, but never considered exchanging gifts with. So should I run out and buy a gift to present to them the next day? Or should I just say thanks and let it drop?

A: If you don't have a gift to present right then – like an emergency supply of baked goods – you shouldn't go out and buy one. Just be sure to give a very gracious thank you and then think about how you can be thoughtful in some other way. You might say you'd like to take them to lunch during the holiday season – a gift of a good meal and good company.

When sharing the holiday spirit, good manners never go out of style.

Dear Thelma: Every year our family hosts a holiday open house. I serve on several boards and also belong to a reading group. I have developed friendships with some of my fellow members but not everyone. I feel compelled to invite everyone if I invite anyone. I do not want to be rude by not inviting everyone, but if I do the party becomes too large to manage. How do I best handle this awkward situation?

A: A guest list for a holiday party should center on relationship not necessity. Focus on "friendships" and let go of the feeling of being "compelled."

As you consider each potential guest, think through how your action will affect your relationship with that person.

If your relationship doesn't go beyond the boardroom, not including them on your list shouldn't create a problem for you or them. Realize though that they may become aware of your party from others. Some may even ask you why they weren't invited. Kindly and gracefully explain that space considerations or a big group of family members attending kept you from extending your guest list. And then keep them in mind for another gathering or next year's open house.

Dear Thelma: I come from a large family of diverse political opinions. Typically, we enjoy engaging in political discourse, but the recent election season and the discussions that ensued left many of us feeling battered and reluctant to participate anymore. We'll be gathering again with family and friends during the holidays and the topics of politics, winners and losers are bound to come up. Is it proper

46

to discuss politics in mixed company? And is there anything I can do to temper this post-election political climate?

A: Many groups of family and friends find themselves in the same uncomfortable situation because of the division that has lingered since the election.

I believe we suffer from a kind of "sound-bite" thinking that has influenced the way we speak to one another. Rather than thoughtfully engaging, our political conversations become a string of 10-second declarations.

To bridge the divide we have to stop thinking and talking that way. We can change by dedicating ourselves to and encouraging others to embrace the idea that conversation is about listening respectfully to others and allowing for polite give-and-take. We've got to turn the tables on the attitudes that have deprived us of the opportunity to comfortably express ourselves and be listened to. We must bring respect back into our conversations that have a political focus.

I like what former President Bill Clinton said at the dedication of his library in Little Rock: "Today, we're all red, white and blue." We've got to, as individuals and as a nation, adopt that attitude and move forward.

Because of strong opinions and emotions tied to political issues, many believe they should be avoided as topics of conversation. I believe talking about them when we can is an important part of our democracy.

Make your best judgment of a group before you launch into political discourse. If your family has a history of discussing politics, then it's likely an acceptable topic. Be more cautious in a group you don't know well.

Once the conversation has started stay alert. If you feel yourself becoming too emotional or sense a strong emotional reaction from someone else or if you're the host witnessing a heated exchange, make a decision to move to another topic with a statement like, "I don't think we're going to come to agreement on this one. Let's talk about something else."

The political waters ebb and flow; good manners never go out of style.

Dear Thelma: The gift my mother-in-law gave me for Christmas is a sweater that I do not like and will never wear. I want to return it, but need the receipt. Should I try to get the receipt or should I just live with it?

A: The most important factor in deciding to return any gift is consideration for the giver. Most gifts are given in love and with thought and joy behind them. If you can receive them in that same spirit, then what to do with them afterwards may not cause you as much worry.

It is always acceptable to exchange a gift for a different size or even color, and you may not need a receipt for that. But if you're going to get something completely different, you must respect the giver. That means communicating with your mother-in-law that you would like to get something else and asking for the receipt.

If you feel that request would hurt her feelings and impact your relationship negatively, then it's better to keep the sweater. If your family talks openly about gifts and giving and expresses the freedom to exchange or return gifts, then you shouldn't feel badly about asking for the receipt.

Make your decision based on your own family, remembering that you never err when you're being considerate and gracious.

Ask Thelma 2005
Relationships that Thrive

Dear Thelma: I have a small business and have hired a college student to help with clerical matters. I have noticed that she is lacking in professional attire, and at meetings she sits with her legs tucked under her. Any ideas on the best way to address this?

A: There's only one way to address it. That is to sit down and talk to her about it.

It's perfectly acceptable for you to say, "We're in a professional environment and there are certain professional standards we adhere to that include attire and posture."

Help her to fully understand that she is helping to represent your small business. You have one opportunity to make a first impression; it has to be a good one. In a small business the opportunities for first impressions are more limited and you have to take full advantage of them.

When it comes to posture, advise her to look comfortable, not stiff or slouched. Cross legs at the ankle rather than the knee. Her posture should show that she is attentive.

Tell her that business suits, pantsuits or dresses are the standard professional attire for women. Dress skirts should be no shorter than 3 inches above the knee. Hosiery, the wearer's skin color or darker, is required with business skirts at all times, along with dress shoes with heels no taller than 2 inches.

In a business setting, conceal all tattoos and body piercing. Limit jewelry to no more than five pieces. Consider a wedding ring, one pair of earrings, one necklace, a bracelet and a wristwatch.

Dear Thelma: How does one eat Brie correctly? The white rind on the cheese isn't very tasty, but I haven't figured out a way to gracefully remove it. Should it be removed before serving the cheese or by the individual who cuts off a slice?

A: The rind on Brie is not removed before serving. Whether or not you choose to eat the rind is a matter of personal taste. It is edible and is very often eaten, but if you don't like it you don't have to eat it.

If you're eating a cheese course as part of a meal, you'll be using your knife and fork and can cut away the rind. If the Brie is served as an hors d'oeuvre, as you bite into the cheese avoid as much of the rind as you can and leave it on your plate when you're finished.

In business or social settings, good manners never go out of style.

Dear Thelma: My young son's basketball team experienced a terrible display of sportsmanship last Saturday. When the opposing coach disagreed with the call of a referee, he pulled his entire team off the court with more than half the game still to play and left. What's the best thing to say to my son about this?

A: Approach the subject with kindness. It's important to stress that while you don't condone the behavior that was seen publicly, you also have to realize and help your son realize that there may be circumstances behind the behavior that no one but the coach is aware of.

Of course, getting up and storming out set a bad example for the children on both teams, and it's important to say to your son that what the coach did is not a good way to handle problems. But it's also important to explain to him that we don't always know why some judgments are made.

Talk to your son about what he saw and help him think about other ways the coach may have handled himself. If he truly felt the problem was so big that he needed to get his team off the court, perhaps he could have called time out, composed himself and said to the other coach, "I'm sorry but we have to leave."

Impress upon your son how respectful communication might have helped avoid the trouble or minimized the irritation felt by his team.

Dear Thelma: What should you do when you're out to eat and split the check with your dinner companion and then he tips terribly? I feel bad for the server, but I've given my portion of the tip. Since I feel bad about it, do I have to cover my friend's tip too? Should I worry about offending my friend?

A: If you are paying cash and you see that the tip isn't fair, generally you wouldn't say anything to your friend. Then it becomes a matter of conscience.

What would I do? I'd slip a few more bills onto the table. If my friend is offended and says so, then I'll have the chance to tell him that the standard tipping rate is 15 to 18 percent, or more in upscale restaurants.

If this is a close friend and someone I'm going to split the check with again, I might look for the opportunity to talk about appropriate tipping before we go out again.

In all our relationships, good manners never go out of style.

Dear Thelma: My husband and I have attended four very nice weddings over the past year, two of good friends' children and two family weddings. We have yet to receive a thank-you note from any of the couples for the gifts we sent. I would really like to know if they received our gifts (several were ordered from reputable stores online). I don't know if I should contact the couples or if I should follow up with the stores involved. Is there any way I can find out without embarrassing any of the parties?

A: It is absolutely appropriate to ask in a polite fashion if they received your gifts, telling them you shipped the items and want to make sure they arrived safely. If contacting them directly feels to confrontational to you, send notes to them.

If they received the gifts and have let more than three months go by without acknowledgement, then they may feel embarrassed at their unkindness, but they should.

Failing to thank the giver of a gift is inexcusable. You put time and thought into selecting the gifts; the receivers need to acknowledge your effort with the same care.

If the gift has come by mail, there's a greater responsibility to respond promptly so that the giver doesn't have to wonder. When you receive a gift in the mail, acknowledge it within a few days with a thank-you note or with a phone call or email followed by a thank-you note.

Don't shy away from contacting the couples directly. The more we make people aware of the need for thank-you notes, the more it will become part and parcel of receiving a gift. Part of giving a gift is sharing in the joy it brings to the receiver. A thank-you note lets the giver share in that joy.

Dear Thelma: My mother works at a couples resort. When taking reservations, they use the first names of the couples informally without any titles. Should the couple be addressed as John and Jane Smith or Jane and John Smith? As a team, they would like to use the same order consistently but they do not know which is proper.

A: There's no contemporary rule to follow here. I find it most natural to follow the conventional form listing the husband's name first: John and Jane Smith. However, the team wouldn't be incorrect in listing the wife's name first, a form often used in addressing informal notes.

Some rules hold fast, others don't; good manners never go out of style.

Dear Thelma: I have three young children, ages 6, 4, and 18 months. My husband and I enjoy eating out and like to include our children sometimes, but we often get looks from wait staff and other diners that say we are not welcomed. Our children are generally well mannered and if they aren't or if the meal is moving too slowly for the baby, then one of us takes those who can't behave out of the restaurant. Is it wrong to take children to restaurants for sit-down dinners?

A: Your first concern really must be the comfort of those dining and working around you.

You can't predict even the best-behaved children. So it's important to be cautious and wise when deciding to take your young children out into in any unfamiliar environment that is not designed with kids in mind. If you fail to be thoughtful about it, you may be setting up your family and the people around you for a less than enjoyable experience.

Consider carefully the restaurant you're choosing. Is it the type of place couples go for an adult evening away from their own kids? If it is, you'll understand neighboring diners' frustrations if they've paid for a sitter, yet still have to deal with the playful antics of children or the fussing of a baby.

Will the pace of the meal be too slow for young children who are used to being served soon after sitting down and expect to be excused promptly when finished? Long wait times may lead to misbehavior born out of boredom and frustration.

Do you want to force your children in to what is essentially an adult experience? There are plenty of kid-friendly restaurants, where neither you nor the children will have the tension of watching and being watched so closely. Connect with your kids in an environment that is best suited for them.

If it's very important to you to provide a fine dining experience to your kids, pick an appropriate time for it. Choose brunch, lunch or very early on a weekday evening when the establishment may be less crowded and the meal's pace may move more quickly. Before you go, let them know what to expect and what will be expected of them. Practice proper table manners at home first.

I believe kids should have the opportunity to enjoy a kid's life and adults should be allowed to enjoy an adult's. But whether young or old, good manners never go out of style.

Dear Thelma: Am I obligated to throw a buck into those tip jars you see on every counter these days?

A: No. Contributing to a tip jar is completely optional.

If you feel a counter person has gone out of his way to extend you some added services and want to leave a tip, go right ahead. But you needn't feel guilty for choosing not to tip. Unlike full-service restaurant wait staff, counter workers' wages and taxable income are not based on the expectation of tips.

If you do choose to tip, the ordinary restaurant tipping guidelines of 15 percent for good service to 20 percent or more for exceptional service do not apply. Generally, at a buffet restaurant, where a server may refill your drinks or bring clean plates, an appropriate tip is 10 percent. It's up to you do decide where your friendly counter worker's level of added service falls.

Don't let the deluge of tip jars cause you to forget that any tip is a gesture of reward from the giver and should be merited.

Dear Thelma: Please tell me what to do with my knife and fork once I have the food in my mouth and I am chewing it. Do I put the knife and fork on the plate or do I hold them in my hands? What happens if there is a conversation going on at the table? What should one do with the cutlery in the meantime?

A: Although it may not be between every bite, you're always at liberty to rest your utensils while dining.

If you are eating American style – zigzagging your fork from the left hand to cut to the right hand to eat -- rest your knife cutting edge in across the upper right rim of the plate and your fork at the same angle nearby.

If you are eating continental style – lifting your fork, tines down, with your left hand and keeping your knife in your right – rest your utensils in an inverted V. Place your knife diagonally across the right half of the plate and your fork across the left half close to or overlapping the tip of the knife.

It's important to note that while you have your utensils in your hands, never use them to illustrate or punctuate your conversation.

When you are finished, imagine your plate as the face of a clock. Place your utensils in the 10:20 position with the tips at 10 and the handles at 4.

When it comes to dining style, good manners never go out of style.

Dear Thelma: I've been dating a woman for a couple of months. I'm thinking of sending flowers to her at work for Valentine's Day. Is that proper?

A: Yes. It's a sweet gesture, and that kind of thoughtfulness is usually very appreciated.

If you've received flowers, it's fine to show your pleasure at receiving them, but it's not necessary to make a big fuss or act embarrassed. Be sure to give a call to thank the sender and let him know the flowers arrived.

Dear Thelma: How do I tell a man that I no longer want to date him?

A: Honesty in any relationship is essential. Don't promote something you don't feel is real.

If you've just started to date, it would be wrong to continue after a couple of dates if you knew it wasn't going to work. Politely say this just isn't right and I don't think we should see each other any more.

If you have been dating for some time, but you realize the chemistry isn't correct, explain that realization and say I don't think we should date anymore. Be honest when you break up and be able to say up front why you don't want to date the person.

You will have to deal graciously with whatever feelings he expresses. When you surface how he feels, do more than listen. It's important to respect his answer and respond kindly, but be firm in your intention to end the relationship. Wavering could give false hope.

Dear Thelma: Two acquaintances, although they speak English well, always speak in their native language to each other. They do this in my presence, knowing that I do not understand a word they say. Is this proper etiquette?

A: When you are in a social or a business setting and English is the language spoken by the entire group, that fact must be respected.

Speaking in another language puts the person who can't understand the conversation in a judging situation, making him or her feel suspicious and uncomfortable. And it decidedly leaves people out, which is never a kind thing to do.

I've been in this situation and it always makes me want to say, "Hey, what are you talking about?"

Instead, I gently say, "I don't understand what you're saying. Can you share your conversation with me?"

I doubt your friends intend to be rude. Speaking their native language may simply be a behavior they fall into when they're together. It's alright for you to remind them you'd like to participate in the conversation too.

Dear Thelma: I work part-time from my home office. How do you suggest that I answer my phone?

A: During business hours, especially if you are expecting client calls, answer with your business name and your name: "Thelma Domenici & Associates, Thelma speaking."

A home office that shares a line with the family is a good place to use caller ID. With the ability to differentiate between clients and your mother you'll always answer appropriately.

With any caller, the tone of your voice should show you appreciate the call. Even a simple hello said incorrectly can convey something negative. Don't sound distracted or preoccupied. Do indicate that you are totally attentive and glad they called.

Also, if you receive business calls while your family is in the home, try to make sure you're the one doing the answering. It's unsettling for a person making a business call to be greeted by young child or anyone else who clearly is not accustomed to answering such calls.

If your home and home office share an answering machine or voice mail, greet callers by listing your home first: "You have reached the Colby residence and the home office of Michael Colby. Please leave a message and we will return your call."

Above all, whether in person or over voice mail, be sure you have a smile in your voice. Your caller will appreciate it.

In all manners of communication, good manners never go out of style.

Dear Thelma: Recently I held an art showing at my house for a friend of mine who is an artist. We agreed that we would split the expenses. Fifty people attended the showing, it was a great success and my friend made a nice profit. It has been three months and I have not even received a thank you, let alone reimbursement for expenses. I have emailed her and left a message mentioning my desire to "close the books" on the event and again have received no response. Should I just leave it alone?

A: From a manners standpoint, the artist's actions are wrong. Any agreement made, especially involving money, should be honored and at the very least discussed if there is a problem in holding up one end of the deal.

But the key word I find in your question is "friend." If you are close enough friends to have done this for her, then there's a connection between you that should allow you talk openly with each other.

You are absolutely correct in saying point blank, "This is what is owed." As a friend, I expect you will be willing to listen to her and work something out if there is a problem.

Perhaps your next message to her should be, "I haven't heard from you since the show. Are you OK?" Approaching her that way may open the door to discussion.

Dear Thelma: My cell phone rang at a funeral. What should I do? Send a formal apology?

A: First things first. Make it a habit that anytime you go into any large public gathering or a gathering with an expectation of reverence attached, turn off all noise making devices – cell phones, pagers and even watch alarms. If you are someone who is officially "on call," set your phone or pager to vibrate mode.

Secondly, learn your phone. Know how to instantly stop it from ringing and send the call straight to voice mail. And finally, keep the phone accessible, not at the bottom of your handbag.

If you turned the phone off immediately, people will assume you simply forgot to turn it off and will forgive. If you let it ring and took the call, or even left to take the call, then you should send a note of apology to the family of the person who died.

In uncomfortable situations, good manners never go out of style.

Dear Thelma: I am 23 and working as a waitress at two different places to make the ends meet. I have been told millions of times that I am a great waitress. I work almost everyday of the week and see the same thing everyday. People come in to eat and are nice. Then when the bill comes, they become mean and tip 10 percent – if I'm lucky. I always thought that 15 percent was for a good job and 20 percent for a great job. What's the deal?

What gives with the 4 percent to 9 percent tips? I work my butt off beyond what my tables see and only get paid $2.13 per hour. Believe me, I am very gracious to all of my customers and never let them know how I really feel about their tips.

I am just fed up with, for example, a $76 ticket on 6 people and only getting a $2 tip, when I ran my butt off for them. What gives?!

A: It should be no shock to people that in a restaurant there is a tip due good service. It's been communicated so universally that tipping rates are 15 to 20 percent that no one can claim ignorance.

What people may be unaware of is the importance of the tip to a server. Diners may feel like the tip is something extra, a perk. A closer look reveals that tipped employees may work under a special, reduced minimum wage, which varies from state to state but is set at a federal minimum of $2.13 an hour. The server, restaurant owner and the IRS expect that tips from diners will make up the difference. Servers are required to report their tips, which are taxed and subject to federal withholding. Servers may even end up with $0 pay stubs after taxes and withholdings, making tips all they have to take home.

While a growing number of restaurants are beginning to follow the European model of including a service charge on the bill – in which case no tip is expected – the majority of servers in the United States rely on their customers' tips.

If we as diners are accustomed to good service, then we should be accustomed to tipping at least the standard 15 percent. If we expect good service and receive it, then our consciences should bother us greatly if we leave a poor tip or tip a flat amount no matter where we go or what we order.

Good manners are behind a gracious tip, and good manners never go out of style.

Dear Thelma: I took a bridal/wedding gift to the shower. Do I need to bring a gift to the wedding?

A: While gift-giving is never mandatory, weddings are one of those times when gifts are customary – even if you have already given a shower gift.

Generally, and especially if it's a question of budget, shower gifts can be less costly and less elaborate. For the wedding you can focus on a long-lasting gift for a new couple setting up their first home.

If you've already given a substantial gift at the shower, think about something more personal or creative you can share with the couple for a wedding gift – a book, a CD or a special photo album. The point of your gift is to let them know you share in their happiness and wish them well for the future.

Dear Thelma: When is it correct to address an envelope to a couple with Mrs. first and then Mr.?

A: I don't see any time when you would address an envelope Mrs. and Mr. When sending correspondence, Mr. and Mrs. is the traditional and most natural way to address it.

When a woman outranks her husband, her title and name are listed first on an envelope: The Honorable Sara Cline and Mr. Robert Cline or Major Anna Garcia and Lieutenant Dan Garcia.

If it is informal correspondence you're sending and you are not going to use courtesy titles, it's fine to list the woman's name first: Jessica and Carl Rogers.

Dear Thelma: What is the difference between round and oval soup spoons? Is there a difference in their lengths?

A: In 21st century America both the round and oval spoons are used for soup. However, traditionally and currently in many other countries the oval spoon is used as a fruit and dessert spoon.

Based on the traditional use of the round spoon for soup, we've learned and taught that it's proper to eat soup by sipping it from the side of the spoon. But when we try to transition that teaching to an oval spoon, the task becomes difficult. Because of the oval shape, it's more difficult to sip the soup delicately from the side.

Rather than slurping or spilling while trying to use the oval spoon like a round one, I recommend taking the soup from the tip of an oval spoon instead of from the side.

As far as spoon lengths are concerned, that's up to the designer. Silverware design is a lot like fashion, it can change with the seasons.

Designs change; good manners never go out of style.

Dear Thelma: Is it still a rule that you are not to wear white shoes until after Memorial Day?

A: Absolutely not. You may wear white clothing, shoes and accessories on any day of the year. While the weight of the fabric or the shoe material may change based on the season, the color does not have to. Designers know this; that's why you see white clothing and accessories sold year round.

The origin of the prohibition of white shoes between Labor Day and Memorial Day has a few theories. Some suggest it may have begun as a class issue, instituted as part of a set of rules for the nouveau-rich attempting to fit into high society. Another theory suggests that white shoes reflect light and heat, making the wearer of white colder in winter.

In the American South, the rule allows for white shoes after Easter. In the Northeast, Memorial Day is the line of demarcation. These differences lead me to believe the rule and its adaptations are based the weather, as they should be.

Base your own switch between summer and winter styles in white on your weather, rather than an antiquated code.

Dear Thelma: A friend of mine enjoys having people over for dinner, but she always starts doing dishes before we've left. While I'd like to be enjoying the company of all the guests, I feel guilty and end up in the kitchen with her. What should I be doing?

A: A host's role is to put guests at ease. Your friend is failing to do that and putting you in an awkward situation.

Clearing the table for dessert is one thing, but cleaning the entire kitchen before the guests have left is another. Cleaning up is not part of being invited. Guests should enjoy themselves, and the host sets the tone for that by creating an ambiance of enjoyment and relaxation.

Your friend probably doesn't intend it, but she is creating an atmosphere of anxiety. Guests may feel compelled to get up and help only to be told to sit down and enjoy themselves, or they may feel badly to be enjoying themselves while the host cleans up.

I believe every time I dine with others it's a celebration, and enjoying the company is part of that celebration.

Help your friend by setting the example at reciprocal dinners or by gently encouraging her to come back to her guests and offering to help out when the night ends.

Especially when nurturing friendships, good manners never go out of style.

Dear Thelma: I want to set up an on-line wish list that I can direct friends to for my birthday. My sister finds the idea appalling. What do you think?

A: The fact that you want to set up this list is not appalling. The way you spread the word about it and what you expect out of it may be.

A survey released last September by the USC Annenberg School Center for the Digital Future shows that 75.9 percent of Americans now go on-line. Of adult Internet users, 43 percent make purchases on-line.

Along with driving communication and purchasing patterns, new technology creates new opportunities to apply civility to new situations. Technology also prompts us to look at and apply what we find at the core of good manners: respect and consideration.

While we want to embrace the efficiency and ease provided by technology, we also want to build and maintain strong relationships. Your family and friends may find your on-line list of desired gifts a convenient time-saver, a consideration to their busy lives. Others, your sister included, may feel that gifts should be voluntary and by creating a list you're creating a disrespectful expectation of receiving gifts.

The manner in which you present the list will go a long way in influencing how it is received. It is not something you would note in an invitation, broadcast generally to a group or even mention to someone like your sister who you know it would offend.

If family members or close friends genuinely inquire as to what you would like for your birthday, it's fine to mention the Web address for your list.

Your on-line list is similar to a bridal or baby shower registry, which no one finds distasteful. We just either use them or we don't.

I would suggest that you include items in a variety of prices ranges. I wouldn't advocate that every time you think of something you add it to the on-line registry. Spending too much time and effort on it may send the message that gifts are the only things important to you.

No one should ever feel obligated to use the list or feel that another gift he put time and effort into selecting for you would be unappreciated. Make sure you place the person and your relationship with her ahead of your concern over the gift she selected.

Technology may drive us into new territory, but even there good manners never go out of style.

Dear Thelma: A friend emailed me an invitation to her birthday party at a tea room. She's a busy mom like me and our circle of friends communicates regularly through email, so it's not all that surprising. But is it proper to extend an invitation via email?

A: It is perfectly fine to offer an invitation via email. The important thing to note is that you must put the same content, quality and creativity into any invitation you send.

All invitations call for the same basic elements: the host's name, the occasion, the date and time, the location, guest attire, reply instructions and clarity as to who is invited, an element that would be addressed by the envelope in a traditional mailing.

Structure your email to evoke in your guests the same feelings of style and grace they get from card stock. Just as in any invitation, the sender is responsible for molding the message in a way that honors the receiver.

Composed this way, email becomes a substitute for postage but not for the grace behind extending the invitation. While there will always be a place for handwritten, printed and engraved invitations, the polish and honor abundant in them can, and in our contemporary times will, be expressed via email.

Email loses its grace when it becomes obvious that the sender has used it as a quick fix. While email is a time saver, we can't let brevity or a "hurry-up" state of mind rule our interactions with it. Any invitation for a large event should be made four to six weeks ahead of time. Invitations to a casual dinner party should go out one to two weeks ahead. Even when a spontaneous get-together arises, the host must thoughtfully consider the best way to reach all the guests with all the information in the timeliest fashion.

Along with the respect inherent in proper timing, it is also important to respect your entire guest list by sending all of the invitations in the same format. If there are some guests who don't use email, you should send all the invitations by traditional mail.

When extending an invitation you should never lose sight of being on-time, kind and gracious, no matter the medium you choose to use. While the written invitation may have been seen as the only gracious invitation in the past, it's up to us to make technology come through with same graciousness. Email does have a heart – it's yours.

Even electronically, good manners never go out of style.

Dear Thelma: My sister is preparing to graduate from college and is conducting much of her job search on-line. She's forgoing cover letters and résumé paper for electronic communication. She has great qualifications and experience, but I'm worried her email address – lovebunny44@isp.com – could be found unprofessional. Could a hiring decision be influenced by something like that?

A: You've heard it before: You only have one chance to make a first impression, make it a good one. When shared with others as a means of contacting you, your email address is somewhat of a calling card. Its qualities and personality reflect yours. Your email address is your first opportunity to project an image of yourself.

Unlike a company account where email addresses may be standardized, your personal email account allows for creativity. In certain fields a creative address may be appreciated, but don't get so creative that you run the risk of not being taken seriously. Something that comes across as clever to your friends could put off a potential employer.

Digital résumés are the primary contact medium for 70 percent of today's employers. By selecting keywords and skills descriptions with care you'll be more likely to pass unhindered through corporate screening filters. At the same time, research the position and include material that demonstrates your success and accomplishments pertinent to the job you seek. Online résumés can work for you if you use clear, concise language describing tangible skills that motivate the reader to interview you.

When foregoing cover letters and résumé paper, remember, the medium may change, but quality must not. The attention to detail that you would put into a paper document – whether it is a résumé, a memo, or a quick note to a friend – should be present in your electronic communication as well.

Dear Thelma: My husband and I are having a debate. How do you know which shaker is for salt and which is for pepper?

A: If salt and pepper shakers are unmarked, it is most appropriate for the salt to be placed in the shaker with fewer or smaller openings. Salt, with its robust flavor, should be taken in sparing amounts so as not to deviate too far from the chef's intent. Pepper can be enjoyed as liberally as one prefers.

Additionally, pepper consists of larger flakes accommodated best by larger or more holes. Salt is heavier and flows smoothly making it easier to shake out too much salt unless the flow is restricted.

From technology to the table, good manners never go out of style.

Dear Thelma: I've heard that there is a specific way you are supposed to properly introduce people to one another. What is it?

A: The way we meet and greet individuals makes a first impression and leaves a lasting one. Introductions must always demonstrate great consideration and respect. Remember two essential points: introductions must be made and there is an order in which to make them.

Business introductions are based on rank. It is proper to present a person of lesser authority to a person of senior authority. You will do it correctly if you say the more important person's name first, as in the following examples: "Ms. Montoya, I'd like you to meet our new account rep Mr. Steve Blackwell. Ms. Carla Montoya is our Chief Financial Officer." Or, "Mayor Alexander, please meet our new summer intern John Carter."

In the case of a client, the client always occupies the position of most importance: "Dr. Chavez, this is Ms. Ann Honeywell, our chief executive officer. Dr. Dominic Chavez is our client from Phoenix."

When introducing people of equal rank, present the person you know well to the one you don't know well: "Diana, I'd like you to meet Jerry Carlson. Jerry is a partner in my firm. Diana Smith is a partner at the Hurst Firm."

Provide professional titles where necessary, such as judge, doctor, or ambassador. Finally, always give some information about each of the people you've introduced to help inspire conversation between them.

Dear Thelma: I've recently attended several fundraising events and seen many of the same people. Unfortunately, I can't always remember their names. How do I handle this?

A: Everyone has forgotten a name along the way. Exhibiting good manners when our memory slips simply means remaining poised. When someone's name has left your brain, stay calm and state just that, "Forgive me, but I've just drawn a blank. Please remind me what your name is." Then gracefully move on to more interesting conversation.

You may wish to reintroduce yourself, "Hello, we met at the museum function. I'm Sue Edwards, nice to see you again."

To help the memory, some people imagine the name of the person stamped on their forehead. Others repeat the person's name several times during the course of conversation.

Requesting a business card is appropriate and will provide a visual reference for the name. Later, you can write a few notes on the back to jog your memory as to your conversation or what the person looked like.

Dear Thelma: I have been retired for many years, but I remain active in the community on boards and committees. My problem is the world seems to run on technology, but I have no interest in having email or voice mail. I feel they are intrusive and I don't want my life run by them. People complain because they can't dash off a quick email to notify me of a meeting or can't get an instantaneous response from me. Isn't it their responsibility to find a way to reach me?

A: If you are active on community boards and committees, you are probably missing much of the decision-making process by resisting the introduction of email into your life.

Email is a very effective means of communication, especially on issues that need immediate response from a group of busy people volunteering their time to a cause. Questions are asked, ideas are offered and decisions are made over email during the amount of time it might take to schedule a meeting around conflicting schedules and active lives.

If you want to participate but are unable to use the communication tools favored by the group, you will have to discuss with the organization or your fellow board members the best way to communicate with you.

If the only way to reach you quickly is by phone, then to be an effective member you must have an answering machine or voice mail. If the rest of the group is communicating through email, then decisions are being made quickly. The group must be able to reach you or leave a message for you with the same efficiency with which it can reach the rest of the members.

Decision-making documents that may be attached to emails will have to be picked up by you or come to you through the postal service. That delay will put pressure on you to respond immediately if you want your opinions considered before a decision is made.

Don't complain when you don't receive information first or at all. When your own stand on technology leaves you without the tools to communicate, it is bound to happen.

Finally, if you are set on being a deliberate resister because you don't want the intrusions, then you should reconsider your membership in groups in which frequent communication to and from you is a requirement.

Technology changes things, but good manners never go out of style.

Dear Thelma: I've noticed the inconsideration of many cell phone users. I am a check-out clerk at a grocery store and often get ignored when these people remain on the phone even when I'm trying to tell them their total and give them change. How rude can you get?

A: Cell phones are a mainstay of our society but they don't have to be heartless, eliminating any and all face-to-face interaction. A savvy cell phone user wisely picks and chooses when and where to dial up.

In this fast-paced society where multi-tasking is the norm, the gracious person reserves multi-tasking for safe, appropriate and considerate moments. We should all know to avoid cell use when driving, in elevators, doctors' offices, auditoriums, theaters, restaurants, or small confined spaces like buses or subways.

Yes, there are a handful of people who must take calls no matter where, no matter what, for instance, mothers, law enforcement, heads of state, and expectant fathers. However, everyone can resort to turning on the vibrate option or allowing voicemail to take the message.

Unless it's an emergency, no cell conversation should take precedence over the opportunity to communicate in person. Whether it's ordering a latte, standing in line to purchase tickets or paying for your groceries, the gracious cell user defers all calls to voicemail and addresses the matter at hand. It's time to dial down on all the rude cell chat and remember our manners.

Dear Thelma: I was at a casual benefit auction conversing with a business person whom I'd just met. We were standing up and an appetizer rolled off my plate, onto the floor. I left it there and she proceeded to pick it up. I felt like a clod. What was the proper way to handle the situation?

A: Receptions offer a special etiquette challenge because of the awkward nature of dining while standing. Traditional protocol recommends that whenever something is dropped on the ground, wait staff should be attentive enough to pick it up. However, during receptions, wait staff is usually busy serving hors d 'oeuvres and beverages.

While kicking the fallen item under a buffet table when no one is looking may be tempting, it is most definitely out of the question.

If you are unable to rally a server to your rescue, it is most considerate to discretely pick up the item with a napkin, and dispose of it to prevent guests from stepping on it.

Just like respecting those around us, good manners never go out of style.

Dear Thelma: I work closely with the guy who sits in the half-wall cubicle next to mine. We often collaborate on projects and we get along well. However, I'm put off by the fact that he constantly wants to dialog over email. I'm sitting four feet away from him. At least occasionally he could just stand up and ask me a question rather than filling my inbox. Shouldn't he?

A: Yes, he should. When used correctly, email is a good tool for building strong relationships, but when you are in that close proximity there is no reason to always pass up in-person contact in deference to the speed or convenience of email.

An organization is only as healthy as the relationships that exist within it. It is important that as members of an organization we make the effort and take the time to build those relationships.

That may mean making an active choice to sometimes sacrifice the efficiency of email for a personal connection. Spending time in conversation is time spent building relationships, and that is time well spent. Our inboxes are full, so if there is something we can pass along in person, we should.

It's also important to note that about 65 percent of the information we receive during an in-person conversation comes from body language, while 28 percent comes from voice, pitch and tone. That means only 7 percent of what we receive actually comes from what is said. Send an email and you've just lost 93 percent of your tools for communicating.

By completely ignoring the opportunities for face-to-face communication, your fellow cube-dweller falls into a career damaging behavior pattern. He may move from an attitude of "I can communicate this quickly by email," to "I don't really feel like getting up and talking. I'll let the computer do it for me;" to "I don't want to deal with people."

You can help pull him out of this pattern by stopping by to answer some emails in person or by scheduling a time to talk. Knowing that conversation is important to you, he may follow your lead and do the same. And even if he still prefers to email, you'll be doing your part to build a face-to-face relationship.

Over the ether or face-to-face, good manners never go out of style.

Dear Thelma: We will be visiting family and friends this summer and staying in their homes. What are some simple rules for being a good house guest?

A: Before you pack your little black suitcase, it is important to consider some basic houseguest rules.

First, provide your two-week notice. Remind your intended host of your arrival and departure dates two weeks in advance. A three- to four-day visit is more than enough when your vacation accommodations are at the home of loved ones.

Throughout your stay, pick up after yourself. Make your bed and keep your living space clean. Be sure to bring your own toiletries. It is poor form to rely on your host like you rely on your local drug store.

Finally, help with the household chores where appropriate. Offer to make dinner for your hosts or treat them to a nice restaurant. Offering to pay for the groceries is another courteous option.

When you depart, leave behind a note thanking the hosts for their generous hospitality. The most organized among us bring a small gift to leave as a token of appreciation. A gift also may be sent after you've arrived back home. Paying attention to these details will help ensure many happy returns.

Dear Thelma: My family – me, my husband and our two biological children – adopted a baby from China. We are getting asked a lot of personal questions: Why did you choose to adopt? Can't you have any more? Is she yours? Are they siblings? How much did she cost? I want to say, "It's really none of your business." What's a better way to let people know I'd like to preserve my privacy without being rude?

A: Adoption is a personal and wonderful choice for many families all over the world. Don't let others' curiosity diminish the joy and love brought about by raising children, regardless of their birth circumstances.

Peoples' curiosity may often reflect their personal experience in raising children, an appreciation for your beautiful family or the joy that children bring wherever they are.

The simplest and most gracious way to answer confused on-lookers is to simply state, "We are blessed with three wonderful children that reflect the diverse world in which we live. Adoption has been a terrific option for our family."

Failing to address the more intrusive inquiries may go unnoticed, or better yet might hint at the inappropriate nature of the questions.

If all else fails, you could always respond "Why? Are you interested in adopting too?" It might actually get them thinking.

Adopting good manners never goes out of style.

Dear Thelma: I have a friend who has never emailed me a personal message, but sends at least four or five "inspirational" forwards every week. I guess I'm glad she's thinking of me, but I need to get out from under her constant forwards. What can I do?

A: First, take a deep breath and realize that she's probably not sending these forwards just to annoy you. Preserve your feelings of friendship by taking gentle action to let her know how you feel.

Send her an email message that includes the lines: "Dealing with time constraints, I limit myself to opening business and personal email and generally don't open forwarded messages. I would love to hear from you though, so write when you can." She should consider more carefully when she knows how you feel.

With the inbox overload faced by many, all email users should carefully consider the forwards they send. Before you forward to your entire address book, ask yourself if each person really needs that clever quip or word or wisdom. Also ask yourself if each person would appreciate this forward or has the time to appreciate it. You can make the choice easy by emailing your friends and asking if they like to receive jokes or inspirational stories. Then honor their requests.

In addition, concern yourself with the content. When it comes to off-color jokes or inappropriate images, let them stop with you. Sending them on could offend or create personal or professional problems for the receiver.

Dear Thelma: I received an invitation to an event billed as "creative black tie." What does that mean?

A: An invitation that designates the event as "creative black tie" asks that guests put a creative twist on their formal dress.

"Black tie" means men are to wear a black tuxedo jacket and matching trousers with a formal piqué or pleated-front white shirt. A black bow tie and matching black cummerbund along with black patent shoes and black dress socks complete the look. For "creative black tie" combine the tuxedo with something trendy like a black shirt or wear a colored or patterned bow tie and cummerbund.

For women, a "black tie" event means a floor length evening gown or a short, dressy cocktail dress. "Creative black tie" adds dressy separates to the list of options and encourages colorful jewelry and whimsical accessories like a colorful shawl or even a feather boa.

Whether classic or creative, good manners never go out of style.

Dear Thelma: I am a frequent business flier. As the summer kicks into high gear, so do vacation plans. Can you offer travelers basic in-flight etiquette to help make us all a bit more comfortable as we jet across the wild blue yonder?

A: Consideration for other travelers can be difficult when flying in the cramped quarters of an airplane, but consideration is the key to comfort.

Minding your own and others' personal space is of the utmost importance. Keep your hands, feet, knees and belongings in your own area. Avoid hogging the armrest and bin space.

Some people look forward to making new friends or business opportunities. Some don't. Learn to recognize both. If you prefer to avoid a chatty seat mate to sleep or work, it is appropriate to graciously say so.

Children can be an in-flight challenge for passengers and parents alike. Little can be done about a child's excited squeals of delight when boarding or the cries that come from the pressure change at take off and decent. However, parents can keep kids' feet and hands off the back of the seat in front of them. Instruct children to leave the tray tables alone and attempt to keep excited noise under control.

Inconsiderate behavior that disturbs your neighbors is also to be avoided. Refrain from pulling on the seatback of the person in front of you and avoid slamming the tray table closed. Keep the music on your MP3 or Walkman down. Not everyone wants to hear a mini-concert. Don't hold business meetings in the aisle. If you must, modulate your voice to low tones so other passengers aren't forced to become party to your conversation. Besides, you never know when a competitor is listening.

Finally, a little kindness goes a long way. Accommodate split parties. Be open to changing seats so the newlyweds or a father and son can sit together. If you notice someone struggling with their luggage, help them. When deplaning, allow the people in front of you to move into the aisle first. Your kind restraint will make the exit more pleasant for everyone.

Dear Thelma: I am a professional woman. As summer approaches, I dread the thought of having to wear hosiery to the office. What is the proper business attire?

A: Professional attire is no longer dictated by a dark suit and hosiery. It is both appropriate and professional to go without hosiery, but do make sure your feet and legs are well groomed.

Fashion fluctuates; good manners never go out of style.

Dear Thelma: I was at a business lunch last week. I am naturally a slow eater and found that I was the only one left eating during the lunch. The wait staff had removed everyone's dishes but mine. I stopped eating and left the luncheon feeling uncomfortable and hungry. What is the best way to handle this situation?

A: Business lunches can be a bit tricky. It is the host's responsibility to set the pace for the meal. It is diners' responsibility to match that pace. If you lag behind, skip a course. Slow down if you notice that you are eating faster than your companions.

Choose simple, easy-to-eat meals. Take small bites so you can comfortably maintain conversation without others having to wait for you to finish a large bite of food.

Wait staff must refrain from clearing plates until the entire party has finished their meal. Early removal can make guests feel they need to stop eating or finish quickly. It is perfectly appropriate to remind servers to wait until all the guests at the table have finished eating before removing empty dishes.

Dear Thelma: I recently interviewed with a company that I'm very interested in working for. What is the best way to follow-up and show my desire to get hired?

A: You have passed the first phase of the job selection process with your interview. A proper thank-you note is the next step to creating that lasting and positive impression.

Surveys show that very few applicants send thank-you notes, so a well-crafted letter is a great way to set yourself apart from the crowd and send positive signals about the kind of employee you will be.

Send your thank you within 24 to 48 hours of your interview. A prompt letter conveys that you have a good sense of business protocol and timeliness. It also shows you understand the value of an active, professional follow-up.

Keep your letter short, concise and clear. Describe something specific that will place you solidly in the reader's mind and reiterate your interest in the company and the position. Keep your letter to fewer than 150 words.

The only thing worse than not sending a thank-you note is to send one with the interviewer's name, title or organization misspelled. This is where the business cards you collect during your interviews come in handy. They provide a tremendous resource in preventing potential spelling errors.

Finally, note that you will follow-up within the next week to check on the status of the position. And then, do just that.

Dear Thelma: With the Fourth of July coming up can you share some information on flag etiquette?

A: While many people bring out the stars and stripes every day in honor of our national heritage, there is an abundance of flag-flying on Independence Day. If you are displaying a flag on an angled or horizontal staff from the front of your home, the blue field of stars, called the union, should be at the peak of the staff.

You may also hang the flag vertically from a window or a roof eave with the union to the observer's left. If you are displaying the flag horizontally against a wall, the flag also is positioned with the union to the observer's left.

The flag customarily is flown from sunrise to sunset. If you choose to display it at night, it should be illuminated to the point that its stars and stripes can be seen from a reasonable distance, which may be possible with your porch light.

The flag should not be permitted to touch the ground, a floor or water. Special care should be taken to protect the flag while it is in storage.

Your flag should be in good condition. Have it dry cleaned and mended if necessary; however, it should not be hemmed to the point that it becomes disproportioned. The flag serves as a symbol of our country. When it becomes too worn to serve as a proper symbol, it should be destroyed by burning in a dignified manner.

If your flag is made of all-weather material, it may be flown during rain or other inclement weather, but if the weather will damage the flag, it should be brought down.

When a flag passes in a parade, men and women should stand at attention with their hands at their sides or with their right hands over their hearts. A man wearing a hat should remove it and hold it to his left shoulder with his hand over his heart. A woman wearing a baseball cap or other unisex hat should do the same.

Another upcoming time to display the flag will be Sept. 11, when flags are flown at half staff to honor the victims of the terrorist attacks of 2001. To indicate such honor and mourning on a flag flown from a pole extending from your home, attach two black ribbons the length of the shorter side of the flag to the top of the pole and allow them to fall naturally. When honoring our country, good manners never go out of style.

Dear Thelma: I was driving my niece to her friend's house. When we arrived, I walked around the car to open the door for her and received a glaring look of disapproval. As a man growing up in the South, this was what one did for the opposite gender. Is chivalry dead?

A: We have seen a lot of changes in the last 40 years with regard to gender roles in society. Of course the old school rules of chivalry still apply today, but women are now sharing the role of gallantry more commonly known as courtesy.

Today's contemporary rules of courtesy are non-gender specific. The first to arrive at the door should hold it open. Whoever is at the front of the elevator gets off first. The man or woman who invites a client to dinner picks up the tab. A woman stands for any visitor to her office and remains standing until he or she is seated, just as a man would do for a client.

Finally, to anyone who offers you a kindness or respectful action, greet it with a gracious thank you.

Young or old, good manners never go out of style.

Dear Thelma: My husband and I are invited to several barbecues in the coming months. What is your advice for properly eating things like ribs, watermelon and corn-on-the-cob? Or is it best to avoid them?

A: Sharing a meal with friends is always a celebration, so don't plan to avoid anything you're served.

Barbecues are outdoor events where the dining and the dishes prepared are usually informal. When you are outdoors, it is fine to pick up ribs or chicken with your fingers. Be sure you have several napkins close by to keep your fingers and face clean. Eat as neatly as you can, taking small bites and using your napkin often.

Corn-on-the-cob is also meant to be picked up with your fingers. It is often presented with corn skewers placed at the ends of the cob before serving. Butter and season a few rows of corn at a time as you eat from one end of the cob to the other. Avoid buttering the entire cob, as you're likely to end up with a dripping mess. Corn served a formal dinner should be cut off the cob and seasoned before it is served.

Eating watermelon depends upon how it is served. You can hold in your hands a slice with the rind and eat it bite by bite. Since at this point it is a finger food, remove any seeds from your mouth with your thumb and forefinger and place them on the edge of your plate.

You also may eat such a slice with a fork. Remove the seeds with the fork tines and move them to the side of the plate. Use the edge of your fork to cut the melon into bite-sized pieces. If the melon is served cut into chunks, remove the seeds in the same way and use your fork. If you find a seed in your mouth, bring your fork to your mouth and move the seed with your tongue onto your fork. Then place it on the edge of your plate.

If you are picnicking in a public place, remember to always thoroughly clean up the area before you leave. Dispose of or pack out all paper goods, aluminum cans and cigarette butts. Leftover or spilled food and drinks will attract animals and insects, so pack it out and clean it up. If you've started a fire or used a grill, make sure the coals are doused with water and rake the ashes to make sure the fire is completely smothered.

Even in the informal outdoors, good manners never go out of style.

Dear Thelma: An ex-boyfriend asked for a necklace back he gave me as a Christmas gift. I am completely taken aback. I know that this is completely wrong, but he seems to think that it is fine. What is the exact etiquette protocol for this situation? And how can I make sure he knows what he did is wrong?

A: You are right; a gift-giver should never ask for a gift back. And if he does, you don't have to give it back. Once you have received a gift, it's yours to do with what you wish.

If a gift is to be given back, it is always the prerogative of the receiver to offer it, never for the giver to ask for it back. When a relationship ends, you may not want to keep that reminder and can feel comfortable giving it back soon after the breakup.

The choice is yours in this situation. You may tell him, "I chose to keep this gift you gave me," or you may decide to return it and make a clean break. If you're determined to educate him in the etiquette of gift-giving, send it back to him with a copy of this column and say no more.

Dear Thelma: I am expecting my first baby in December. Since my husband and I have spread the news, we are getting boxes and bags full of all kinds of hand-me-downs, everything from furniture to baby clothes to maternity clothes. I appreciate the kindness, but some of it is old stuff that I don't want. Should I just accept it all and then get rid of it or tell them I want to buy my new baby some new things?

A: You should be honest with those offering hand-me-downs. If you don't need what they're donating, be truthful about it and say no thank you. Don't feel obligated to accept anything.

If you have items to pass along to a new parent, ask if they need them before you show up with overflowing bags. They may plan to buy those items new or may have already received them.

Also, be thoughtful in your giving. Go through the items carefully beforehand to make sure they are clean and only gently used. A stained t-shirt with a stretched-out neck worn by your first, second and third baby may not appeal to first-time parents. On the other hand, a tiny, almost-new dress with once-worn patent leather shoes may be much appreciated.

In all manners of giving, good manners never go out of style.

Dear Thelma: My wife's step-sister (who joined the family after my wife moved out of the home) just got married. She has been living with her boyfriend for over three years and their gift registry was filled with "homemaking" items. Our feeling was that the gift giving for a wedding is related to building a home, which was already established. We did give a gift for the bridal shower, but opted not to give a gift at the wedding. Our drive to the wedding was significant and the time commitment and expenses required to share the day with them seemed to be enough. Were we wrong?

A: Yes, you were wrong. Although gifts, by definition, are never mandatory, wedding gifts are always in order when you have received a wedding invitation – even from your step-sister-in-law whose registry doesn't meet your approval.

The point of a wedding gift is to let the couple know you share in their happiness and wish them well for the future. Let your gift reflect that.

A gift registry is a list of what the bride and groom have decided together that they need and want. It's a decision they have every right to make for themselves.

Remember that the registry is a guide for guests, not a mandate. It is perfectly acceptable to buy a gift outside the registry. Choose something more personal or creative or something that your time being married has taught you it is important.

Your position of, "We've done enough, a gift is not in order," isn't acceptable. The gift and getting to the wedding are always two separate things. Your travel shouldn't be subtracted from the honor due the bride and groom.

Dear Thelma: If you have a friend who always insists on paying for a meal, how do you wrestle the check away from him without making a scene?

A: Tell your friend before the meal begins that you will take care of the bill. Let the wrestling take place then, not after the meal when it's too easy for him to grab the check and make a run for it. Say to him, "I'm getting it now; next time you treat."

If he still goes for it at the end, just put your credit card down with his and ask the server to split the check in half. That will show how serious you were and next time he might just let you pick up the tab.

On either end of a gift, good manners never go out of style.

Dear Thelma: I am traveling to a large city and plan to spend several days there. On all my previous vacations I've put my camping fee in the box at the entrance to the campground and gone off to pitch my tent. From what I've heard, with this trip I will have to tip virtually everyone. What exactly are the standards for hotel tipping?

A: Don't worry. You won't be handing out bills to everyone you meet. The key is to focus on the service that the person has provided for you and reward them for their effort.

The more expensive the hotel is, the more you can expect

opportunities to tip as the level of service and the variety of people available to serve you will increase. Many in the service industry rely on the tips they receive as part of their income. However, a tip should always be merited and should be decreased if the service offered is poor or indifferent.

A hotel doorman is not tipped for opening the door. He does deserve $1 to $2 a bag if he unloads them from or loads them into your car or taxi, and $1 to $2 for hailing a cab for you or for asking the garage to bring your car.

Tip a bellhop $1 to $2 a bag depending on the size and weight of the luggage and $1 to $2 for delivering something to your room.

If the concierge provides you a special service like recommending a restaurant and making reservations, tip $5 to $10. For extra-special service, like obtaining hard-to-get theater or sporting event tickets, tip 10 percent to 20 percent of the cost of each ticket. If the concierge makes a strong effort but isn't able to get the tickets, still offer a tip of 5 percent to 10 percent of what the tickets would have cost.

Tip your housekeeper $1 to $2 a night. Add $1 to $2 if the housekeeper provides any extra service, like fetching extra towels.

If you order room service, check the bill for "gratuity." If it's included, then you needn't add a tip. However, if the bill only includes "room-service charge," which is not the same as gratuity, then include a tip of 15 percent to 18 percent of the bill before taxes.

Tip valet parkers $1 to $2 when the car is brought back to you.

Take a stack of one dollar bills on your trip so that you are prepared when an appropriate time to tip arises.

A gracious traveler knows good manners never go out of style.

Dear Thelma: Growing up in a Hispanic family in New Mexico there were always tortillas on the table as part of every meal. My favorite way to eat a meal with tortillas is to scoop a little bit of my meal into a piece of tortilla then take a bite of the tortilla. This is a tradition I have grown up with my entire life and it is the best way to eat Mexican food. Frequently I find myself wondering if this is proper etiquette in a restaurant setting, particularly when dining with business associates. Please advise.

A: The use of a tortilla with Mexican food, especially in New Mexico, is a cultural tradition that you need not leave at the restaurant door. You can feel comfortable and confident in using pieces of tortilla in the way you describe.

However, don't transfer your entire plate into a tortilla for your own version of el burrito grande, and avoid wiping your plate clean with your tortilla no matter how good the red chile is.

Dear Thelma: I recently came from staying two days as one of 10 guests invited to a summer home. I took the host a gift. Although he opened other guests' gifts, he never mentioned opening mine. It made me wonder what he thought of it. Also the host presented each of the guests with a gift. I wasn't sure whether to open it there or after I got home. I opened mine and thanked the host, but a fellow guest didn't think it proper to open the gift. What do you think of these situations?

A: To keep guests at ease, a host should open all of the gifts and offer sincere thanks or open none of them at all. If there is worry that someone who didn't bring a gift would feel awkward, gifts can be opened in private and the giver thanked during a private conversation.

You didn't err in opening the gift the host presented to you. By doing so you were able to thank the host in person for the specific contents of the gift. I'm sure the host was pleased with your reaction. A host might help guests avoid confusion by inviting them to open the gifts before they leave.

I prefer to open gifts I receive in the presence of the giver so that I can offer an appropriate and specific thank you.

Don't forget that a thank-you note is still appropriate when you return home -- for the gift and for the stay.

Gifts and good manners never go out of style.

Dear Thelma: I read your column on hotel duty and tips and was grateful for the information. I travel to Washington, D.C., once a year and stay at a very nice hotel not far from the White House. My question is: How do I make certain the right housekeeper gets the tip? Do I leave the tip on the bureau or table daily? Or should I hand it directly to the person? I usually leave it at the end of my stay but can't be certain the right person gets it because I leave on a Saturday.

A: Tipping the housekeeper is often forgotten because their work isn't out in front of us like that of a restaurant server, bellhop or taxi driver. So I'm glad to hear that you make a habit of it.

There are several ways to make sure your housekeeper gets your tip. The first is to tip $1 to $2 daily, as the person who has kept your room for several days and deserves your tip may be off on the last day of your stay. Handing the tip directly to the housekeeper is the best way to make sure it gets to the right hands.

If you aren't able to hand it to the person, leave it in the room with a note or in an envelop designating that it is for the housekeeper. Employees are trained never to take anything out of a room. Including a note will ensure that the tip isn't overlooked and it will protect the employee.

If you aren't able to tip daily, you may call the desk and ask the name of your housekeeper. Then leave the tip with the front desk in an envelope marked with his or her name. You also may mark the envelope "Housekeeping" and include your room number and dates of your stay.

Dear Thelma: What does RSVP mean?

A: RSVP is an acronym for a French phrase meaning "respond, if you please." More importantly, its use in an invitation signals to you as a guest that you should respond within one or two days with a decision to accept or decline the invitation. You must respond whether or not you will attend.

When you receive an invitation, acknowledge that someone is attempting to create an event for your enjoyment and respond quickly. While it is acceptable for a host to phone those guests who haven't responded and ask for an answer, don't waste their time with that. Your host will love you for it.

When honored with an invitation, good manners never go out of style.

Dear Thelma: What is the best way to react to people who are rude to you at parties? These people know me but continually act as if they do not and snub me when we encounter each other. Should I be gracious or return their snub?

A: You absolutely should not return the snub. A kind greeting is always in order for anyone you meet. Despite the offenders' lack of good manners, yours should never falter. Make your greeting and move on to greet other party-goers.

It will be best to avoid these people who are rude to you as much as possible at the parties you attend. Seeking them out will only make you and everyone else uncomfortable. If you do find yourself in a group with them, you must be polite and attentive to the conversation until you can make a polite exit.

If you feel there's a chance that they just don't remember you or have forgotten your name, you could make a comment like, "Haven't we met before?" However, a party is not the place to be confrontational. If it's a once-close relationship that has gone sour, have a private conversation with them on your own time.

There's always more than one person at a party. Concentrate on those with whom you can share a conversation and make it a point to enjoy their company.

Dear Thelma: I have a friend who is getting married soon and has decided to keep her maiden name. I have also kept mine, and we have a disagreement about how ladies like ourselves should be addressed. I have always used "Ms. Sally Smith," whereas she thinks the proper address is "Mrs. Sally Smith." I have always thought the latter was for a divorced woman who kept her married name. Which is correct?

A: Both forms of address are correct for a married woman.

Traditionally, courtesy titles were tied to marital status and closely to the husband. Times dictated that a married woman should only use the title "Mrs." in connection with her husband's name. Miss Sally Smith married Mr. Daniel Jones and became Mrs. Daniel Jones. During those times, a woman's first name appeared in an address only if she were a divorcée – Mrs. Sally Jones.

With the introduction Ms., titles have lost their vital connection to marital status. Sally Smith who married Daniel Jones can properly and graciously be called Mrs. Daniel Jones, Ms. Sally Smith or Mrs. Sally Smith.

Conventions may change with the times, but good manners never go out of style.

Dear Thelma: I recently attended the most incredible opera performance of my life. The performers were amazing and the production was beautiful. What I cannot get over, however, is the rudeness displayed by many in the audience during that performance. In-depth conversations taking place during the show was one thing, but members of the audience leaving the house as soon as the curtain dropped, failing to recognize the effort of the cast, floored me. Can you offer opera audiences a manners lesson?

A: Offering your applause and encouragement at the end of an opera performance is a vital part of thanking that cast. Walking out before the cast has been properly acknowledged is rude.

Opera goers should be aware that most operas last two to three hours. Plan to arrive early as latecomers often are not permitted to go to their seats until after the first act. Then plan to stay for the entire performance, including the final bows.

During the performance, which begins with the first note of the overture, there should be no talking among companions, singing, humming or tapping out the tune, all of which are distracting to other audience members. Open cough drop or candy wrappers before the performance. Silence all electronic devices before entering the performance space.

If you are unsure of when applause is appropriate, take your cues from the rest of the audience.

Dear Thelma: My husband and I have a son-in-law and a daughter-in-law who address us by our given names. When signing individual greeting cards or correspondence directly to them, it's an obvious choice to use our given names. However, when signing general occasion or joint occasion cards that also are addressed to our daughter and son, I believe we should just sign them "Mom" and "Dad." My husband thinks we should sign them either both ways--- "Mom and Dad"/"John and Mary" or just "John and Mary." I think signing four names is awkward, and I don't care to sign my given name for our own children. I would very much appreciate your opinion on this.

A: This is not a case to decide based on what is right or wrong, but rather on your personal feelings about it. Use your own common sense and make a decision that makes sense for you. If you and your husband can't agree, then when you sign cards do it your way, and when your husband signs, let him do it his. Regardless of the name you use, I'm sure they will know the sentiment is from you.

Just like common sense, good manners never go out of style.

Dear Thelma: Can you provide some pointers on how to end small talk at a mingling type reception and move on to meeting other people? Also, how do you enter a conversation with a group that is already established?

A: The ability to exit a conversation graciously is an important skill to possess. When done properly, you remain comfortable and confident in your self, and the group or person you're leaving feels respected and remains at ease.

Never try to just slip away. Always excuse yourself with a statement like: "It was lovely speaking with you. Please excuse me, my boss just arrived and I should greet her."

When looking to join a conversation, it is the responsibility of someone in the group to welcome you, introduce you and fill you in on the topic of conversation, which those in the group should look for the opportunity to do.

If you know a member of the group, you may approach that person and quietly ask to join the conversation. Then make sure that person introduces you to the rest of the group.

Dear Thelma: I work in an old, established law firm. Although we are informal with each other, I am surprised that the lax behavior has now extended to cell phones. Several of our partners answer their cell phones during meetings and some actually send text messages or read while we are meeting. I find this very disruptive and disrespectful to the group, even though we may not be partners. Am I being too straight laced?

A: No, you are not being straight laced and are right to be concerned.

At the core of good manners are respect and consideration, principles that don't change with the latest advance and that should be observed whether with those above or below you on the ladder.

Anyone with a cell phone should realize and remember that the people in the room with you are always your first priority and deserve your undivided attention. When going into a meeting, silence the phone's ringer. Once the meeting has begun only take vitals calls after excusing yourself and leaving the room. If you are expecting a call that you must take, it is most courteous to announce that fact at the beginning of the meeting and then excuse yourself and leave the room to take the call.

The ever increasing popularity of text messaging and wireless handheld computers brings new behavior challenges. Use these capabilities quickly and discreetly in meetings for crucial correspondence only. Announcing to the group, "I'll text Charles for those figures," is a far cry from spending the entire meeting checking your email under the guise of "efficiency."

Good manners strengthen our relationships and improve our personal and professional lives. Build those relationships by thoughtfully applying the standards of grace and courtesy to the new options available. And remember that technology does have a heart – it's yours.

Dear Thelma: A colleague's emails to me always come up very strangely on my end. His message begins in the subject line and then continues in the regular message portion of the email. I assume it's because he's sending them from his PDA. So I start reading the message and it makes no sense because it starts in the middle of a thought. Then I have to backtrack to the subject line. I think he could be more conscientious in composing his messages. Can I mention this to him? Can I do it by email?

A: You can mention to him by email that his messages are confusing to you. Try to understand from him if he composes messages that way out of necessity or out of a lack of consideration. If he clearly lacks consideration, send him what follows.

The etiquette of technology doesn't deviate from etiquette standards we all know. Etiquette and manners are about thinking of others before ourselves and treating them with respect and courtesy in all our actions – even those dominated by technology.

When using a personal digital assistant or a wireless handheld, respect the conventions of email and proper correspondence. Do all that you can to send an intelligent and clear message, even when faced with the limitations of a handheld.

Given the on-the-move nature, miniature keyboards and stylus functions of handhelds, you may be tempted to use abbreviations or your own form of shorthand to get your message out quickly. By doing so, you run the risk of confusing your receiver, which will waste time rather than save it. Some abbreviations are fine, but don't make your message of string of them.

If you plan to use the subject line for your message or part of your message, let people know that's how you plan to operate. By establishing subject line protocols with those you email regularly, you will avoid causing the receiver to delete your message in confusion or email you back for clarification, neither of which is an efficient use of technology designed to make us more efficient.

Finally, especially if you are using your handheld for business purposes, realize that the disclaimer at the end of your email, "Sent from my wireless handheld device," is not a license to use poor grammar and spelling, or juvenile abbreviations. You send a message about yourself with every message you send. Make sure the message you send is a proper reflection of you.

In the embrace of new technology, good manners never go out of style.

Dear Thelma: I recognize that discretion is key when using the cell phone, particularly in airports. I travel a great deal and often must conduct business over the phone while on the road. I get frequent dirty looks. What is appropriate airport cell use etiquette?

A: The appropriate use of a cell phone in the airport is discreet use. Cell users must realize that if not kept in check, their conversations cause true frustration for others – something we know in our hearts should strive to avoid creating.

Imagine someone sitting next to you at the airport reading a book – out loud. You may want to concentrate on your own thoughts, which are interrupted by the engaging story or the monotonous delivery or sheer confusion. You may have some interest in the story, but you obviously can't snuggle up beside the reader or ask to see the pictures. So there you sit, at his mercy.

Now imagine that he is reading every other paragraph out loud. All you can concentrate on is filling in the blanks. As you struggle to reconcile the dissonance, a dirty look appears on your face. Without even inserting judgment on the notion of why this odd-ball is reading out loud, you are frustrated, irritated and ultimately mad.

The moral of his story: keep conversations conducted in close quarters short and quiet. If you really must conduct business, find the bank of telephone booths -- usually situated to provide space between phone conversations and waiting passengers -- and stand there to make your call. No one will question your manners there.

Dear Thelma: We recently learned that my husband's brother and his wife are divorcing. Due to family connection, I realize that my loyalties must lie with my brother-in-law. However, my sister-in-law was a good friend to me and a good aunt to my children. I can't decide if staying in contact with her will be more painful than letting that relationship end. Is there a proper thing to do?

A: My best advice is that if a genuine relationship exists, a conversation should take place between the two of you. That conversation will inform your decision to stay in contact.

It may, in fact, be too painful. Each party involved in a divorce does need a support system at that tumultuous time. There is no sense in maintaining that relationship if you're not going to be a support for her in some way.

In every relationship, good manners never go out of style.

Dear Thelma: Could you please offer some words of advice on car and designated-driver etiquette?

When one person in a group of friends does a disproportionate amount of the driving and provides the vehicle as well, is it proper for the rest of the passengers to pay for their share of gas or other costs? Or is the driver a "host" who should assume all financial responsibility?

If a passenger makes a mess in the car, is it acceptable for the driver to ask him to clean it up? In the case where a passenger routinely "forgets" to clean up after himself or to pay his way, how can the driver politely correct the situation and avoid being used?

A: Those regularly sharing in the ride should always share in the responsibilities.

Anytime you officially accept to carry the driving responsibilities for a group, it's important to discuss guidelines and responsibilities with your passengers immediately. If you've suddenly found yourself in the driver's seat most of the time, have the same discussion as soon as you realize your role.

If you are sharing rides often, then it's likely you know each other well. Talk to the entire group to establish guidelines that include sharing expenses, cleaning up and being on time.

Friends who depend on a particular driver and his car for going out on the town should reimburse him for fuel and parking costs on a regular basis. Together you can come up with a fair rate that each passenger should pitch in when the evening begins – not when it ends and everyone is out of cash. Use humor to keep collections from feeling awkward, but don't use so light a touch that riders ignore their responsibility.

In a weekday carpooling situation, maintenance costs should be figured in to the reimbursement as well and a plan to compensate the driver weekly or monthly should be established.

Adults really shouldn't have to be told to clean up after themselves, but some may. It is perfectly acceptable to ask your passengers to pack out everything they've packed into your car. Providing a container for trash may help. Or stop the car at a gas station trash barrel at the end of the evening and don't take anyone home until the car is clean.

Decide on a maximum wait time. If you're carpooling for work, five minutes may be the best limit. If you're going out for fun, you may decide to offer more leeway.

When you discuss them up front – so to speak – good manners never go out of style.

Dear Thelma: I recently received a wedding invitation with a separate card enclosed that said, "Money Tree Available." Am I supposed to give a wedding gift and money, or will money alone suffice?

A: Money alone will suffice. The statement "money tree available" is a very nice way of telling you that money is an appreciated gift. However, it does not obligate you to give money as a gift.

In many pockets of society it is absolutely inappropriate to mention gift preferences or registries in a wedding invitation. In other communities it is less of an issue. If you do wish to let you guests know of your preference, do use a separate card mailed with the invitation. Do not list your desire for money on the invitation itself.

Dear Thelma: At one point in my career I worked in an office in which we always used initials to address or sign off on internal written communication. I've since left there, but still just use the first letter of my first name to sign off emails to people I correspond with regularly. Is this poor form?

A: The signature style you use has a long history of use in informal correspondence. It is perfectly proper and sheds the professional formality of a full signature in black and white.

However, don't let yourself fall into a habit of using your initial exclusively. Do use your full signature or a least your first name in an email to someone you don't yet know well or where a higher level of formality is appropriate.

Dear Thelma: I'm adopting a baby. Four different people have offered to throw me a baby shower, but I don't need four showers. How do I get out of this without offending anyone?

A: The people who are offering to throw you a shower are friends and you can communicate with them as friends. It is possible to keep the friend connection and not spend a month of Saturdays at showers without leaving anyone out.

As the honoree of the shower, you have the opportunity to create the guest list. Shuffle your guest into one or two lists and then connect the individuals who want to help to each other. They can then work together to host the shower or showers.

Adopting a child is a beautiful act of generosity. People want to support you and assist you in that generosity. Do what you can to include them all.

When giving and receiving, good manners never go out of style.

Dear Thelma: Is there such a thing as playground etiquette? Are there rules about how long you can stay on the swing when there's a line? Is it okay to play with the toys someone else has left in the sandbox?

A: All etiquette revolves around treating those around us with care and respect. The playground is the perfect place for children to learn and practice those important lessons.

Just because a line forms for the swing does not mean your child must jump off immediately. Think about how long you and your child would be willing to wait for a swing. Then announce to your child and the group, "We will swing for five minutes and then it's Jessie's turn."

The playground is a place for community play. With that in mind, children and parents should choose toys to take to the playground that they won't mind sharing. It's always proper to ask those nearby if you can use a toy that's not your own. But if no one is around or interested in the pail and shovel at the moment, build your castle. If you've brought toys that you're not willing to share, put them in your bag near your bench if your child is no longer using them.

Parents should remember that the playground will be an environment for learning proper social manners, which are sometimes hard for small children to adopt. Parents should expect ups and downs as these lessons are learned and should do their best to model these manners.

Dear Thelma: I've been invited to a "black tie optional" event. What does that mean?

A: I love black tie optional because more of your closet comes alive with this dress designation. You can dress it all the way up to a formal, floor-length evening gown, stand somewhere in the middle with a short, dressy cocktail dress or chose your favorite dressy separates.

Many of the men attending will wear dark suits rather than

tuxedos, so the event won't feel as formal as a black-tie evening. If you're worried about feeling overdressed, go with a dressy cocktail dress and sparkling jewelry.

By using the black tie optional designation, the host lets you know that this is an occasion for dressing up, as formally as you wish. It also lets guests know that this isn't a casual event. If you do choose separates, make sure they are dressy fabrics and accessorize to enhance an elegant look. Khakis and loafers will not do.

Ballroom or playground, good manners never go out of style.

Dear Thelma: Last weekend I fell into someone's lap while trying to get to my seat in the movie theater. What's the best way to navigate a darkened, crowded theater aisle?

A: The very best thing to do is to arrive well before the lights go down. That will make your actions less of an inconvenience to your fellow movie-goers. If you must move through a crowded aisle to get to your seat, a plan and controlled movements will help you avoid accidents.

If you arrive to a darkened theater, take a few moments to adjust to the lighting before you move to the aisle and begin maneuvering. Chose a seat that getting to will inconvenience the least amount of people possible. If you spot your very favorite seat in the theater open but blocked by a long line of bodies, pick another and remember to arrive early next time if you want the best seat.

When moving into an aisle, start by saying "Excuse me," to each person you must pass. Continue by saying "Thank you," to anyone who moves for you. Face the screen as you move down the aisle. Yes, your backside will be to the row you are passing, but that way you can steady yourself with the chair backs in front of you. If you do stumble, it is much better to sit on someone's lap rather than land face-to-face. If you do land on someone, get to your feet as quickly as you can and apologize.

Hold anything you're carrying high above the people around you. Shuffle your feet to avoid stepping on anyone's toes. If you do step on someone, apologize, but keep moving.

For those in the theater being passed, even if you are annoyed, turn your knees in the direction the person is moving so they may slide by you more easily or stand if it's convenient.

Dear Thelma: Do I tip the pedicurist?

A: Tipping those who provide a personal service – including pedicurists – is customary. A good rule of thumb for tipping manicurists or pedicurists is 15 to 20 percent or a minimum of $2.

Such tips should always be deserved. Tips can be reduced proportionally if the service is poor or rude; however, if you are unsatisfied and leave no tip at all, the service provider may just think you're forgetful or cheap and your point will be lost. Taking dissatisfaction to the extreme of leaving just a few coins places you in the category of rudeness.

Wherever we maneuver, good manners never go out of style.

Dear Thelma: I've encountered some pretty rude people while trick-or-treating with my children in years past. Can you offer them some etiquette rules regarding this tradition?

A: The rules for Halloween are the same as those for any day of the year: Be respectful, courteous and considerate. Since there are more people out and about on this day, there are plenty of opportunities to practice.

The first thing trick-or-treaters should remember is that if a house's porch light is off, they should not knock or ring the bell. Just move on to the next home. If there are people inside, they may be out of candy or they may not participate in the tradition.

When you approach a home with the light on, ring the doorbell or knock and wait patiently for the answer. Give the person at the door a smile and say your line: "Trick or treat!" Always say thank you for whatever you have been given – even if it's something you don't like.

If you are a teenager and wish to partake in the fun of trick-or-treating, then you must wear a costume, and no, you cannot dress as "a teenager in a sweatshirt."

Be courteous to other trick-or-treaters out for the evening. Give them space on the sidewalk, and move out of the way once you've received your candy so they may step up to the door.

When walking up to a house or leaving it, stay on the sidewalks and out of the landscaping, and don't disturb the home's jack-o-lanterns or other decorations. While walking through the neighborhood, keep your voice at normal level. While you don't have to whisper, shouting and screaming will be disturbing to others.

End your trick-or-treating outing by 8:30 p.m., so as not to disturb small children who have been put to bed or people settling in for the night.

For those at home who choose to participate, answer your door with a smile and comment on the revelers' costumes if you wish. Don't act as if it is an imposition to have them at your door. If it is, turn off your light, but realize that it won't be a truly quiet evening.

Clear out your porch or entry way so the trick-or-treaters can reach your door safely, and don't go out of your way to scare young children.

Offer candy to all who come to your door, even parents. And, yes, even the "teenager in a sweatshirt." His lack of Halloween manners needn't tarnish yours.

Even on Halloween, good manners never go out of style.

Dear Thelma: Have you heard of these "push presents?" It's some British custom that has crossed the Atlantic where you give your wife expensive jewelry after she gives birth to your child. My wife's due in December and says she's expecting much more than a baby boy. What do you think of this trend?

A: Giving a gift that celebrates a life-changing experience is a beautiful and appropriate act, but where is the joy for giver or receiver in any gift that's purchase has been dictated or demanded.

Such a gift should be more of a spontaneous gesture given with great love and affection, not added pressure during a time that is stressful for everyone.

As for the gift, jewelry may be fitting, but so also are a heartfelt poem or letter, flowers or a gift certificate for a massage or pedicure. Even better, support your wife and new child with love, care, time, and your active participation rather than an expensive bauble that most likely will end up covered in spit up.

Of course you know your wife better than anyone and in her delicate condition she may not be interested in the good manners of gift giving. If so, chalk it up to high maintenance and for the sake good labor relations do your best at the jewelry counter.

Dear Thelma: My brother is planning his wedding. I was somewhat dumbfounded when he stated that in the invitation he is asking for money to help pay the cost of the honeymoon. They are both previously married and health care professionals. He said he didn't need any bowls, silver or crap. He needed money. I asked him to reconsider his wedding present request, but he is adamant on sending the invitation as he prepared it. Is this proper manners?

A: Any reference to gifts should not be part of the text of the wedding invitation. Your brother's inclusion of the preference for monetary gifts in the invitation places the emphasis on gifts rather than on celebrating the union, which can easily offend guests.

If he must include the reference to wedding gifts, it should be done on a separate card mailed with the invitation. Otherwise, information on the couple's preference could be spread by word of mouth. When people ask about a registry or gift ideas, it's fine to say, "If you like the idea of giving money as a gift, we'd use it to help pay for the cost of the honeymoon. But we'll really appreciate whatever you choose."

In sticky gift situations, good manners never go out of style.

Dear Readers: Compared to 20 or 30 years ago, do you think people are more rude, less rude or about the same?

A: According to an Associated Press-Ipsos poll released in October, 69 percent of you believe people are ruder than ever. You blame this increased rudeness on the examples set by celebrities, athletes, public figures, parents, TV shows and movies. You frequently encounter people who use their cell phones annoyingly, speak offensively, drive recklessly and lose control of their children.

However, you yourself rarely participate in these behaviors. In the last few months, only 8 percent of you have used your cell phone loudly, and only 13 percent of you have made an obscene gesture at another person while driving a car. Twenty-three percent of you admit to getting impatient with someone and speaking rudely to them and 37 percent fess up to swearing in public.

What these disconnected perceptions say to me, is that we all need to take a close look at our own behaviors if we want politeness to improve in our world.

The next time your cell phone rings, consider the person or people you're with before you take the call. If it's your dinner companion, send the call to straight voice mail. If you must answer, ask your companion's forgiveness and tell the caller you will return their call later. If you're with fellow waiting airplane passengers, move away to a secluded spot so they aren't annoyed hearing your one-sided conversation. If it's the grocery cashier, put the phone down so she doesn't have to interrupt your conversation to give you your change.

You know what offensive language is. Make it a habit not to use it in public, despite what you hear around you. Be especially aware in areas where children are likely to be listening and avoid all obscenities and crude language in their presence.

Put on a gracious attitude even in the seclusion of your car. Yes, people will drive badly, but your loss of emotional control and composure will not make them use their turn signal or climb out of your tailpipe. They'll probably just report to me that you are the poor and rude driver.

Put thoughtfulness and consideration for others ahead of your own ego as often as you can. With one selfless deed, you may start a chain reaction that turns around the day for a long string of people. As our manners improve, so do our relationships and our worlds.

Despite the trends, good manners never go out of style.

Dear Thelma: How long should a cocktail reception be when it is connected directly to a dinner? They seem to go on endlessly and make the evening so long. What is the proper timing?

A: While there is no standard time frame to be followed for cocktails and visiting or networking before dinner, a thoughtful host when planning will consider an appropriate time for the evening to end and work backwards from there. The host then will work to keep the evening on schedule.

When planning, consider the schedules and lifestyles of your guests. Be aware of their work schedules or if they are parents of young children. Consider the day of the week. Most guests are willing to stay out later on weekends, but want to get home and settled earlier on week nights. Time changes may also play a role. A party may begin a little later during daylight savings time than it would during darker months.

Also consider how well your guests know each other. A long cocktail hour for a group like an organizational board that spends a lot of time working together isn't really necessary as they will likely feel comfortable continuing to network and visit during dinner. A group of strangers may enjoy a longer opportunity to meet each other before dinner begins.

During the evening, it is up to the host to direct the flow of the event. If in your mind, you've determined that cocktails will end at 6:30, then with a small group you may announce at 6:30 that dinner is served. With a larger group, begin approaching groups of people and invite them to the dinner table. Enlist good friends to help you encourage people to move to the table.

When the evening is drawing to a close, send a signal to guests, such as "Would anyone like some coffee?" Then as guests begin to leave, walk each guest or couple to the door to say your goodbyes. Even guests who are having the time of their lives should be aware of these signals and move to the door as the host approaches you to offer goodbyes.

If the signals have gone unnoticed by some guests, feel free to subtly nudge by offering their coats. If they're still parked on your couch, tell them pleasantly: "This can last ten more minutes. I've got to get up in the morning."

From the party's beginning to end, good manners never go out of style.

Dear Thelma: When cutting meat and the fork is transferred between hands, should the piece of cut meat be left on the tines or should the empty fork be transferred and the meat speared again?

A: In the American style of dining, which you describe in your question, you do not take the meat off the fork to re-spear it. Simply switch the fork and move the bite to your mouth. Neither do you re-spear the meat in the Continental dining style. Doing so in either style is an unnecessary extra step that would in no way make you more mannerly.

Dear Thelma: What would be an appropriate gift to take to the hosts of a cocktail party?

A: A gift of appreciation for the host is always fitting. A bottle of wine, candy, a fruit basket, or homemade treats make wonderful host gifts, but don't expect them to be served at the party. The host will enjoy them later.

A flower arrangement also makes a nice gift, but ask the host about the party's color scheme beforehand so you can choose something complementary. Don't bring a bouquet without a container; the host won't have time to find a vase and arrange flowers in the midst of the party. Another option is to send a flower arrangement and note the day following the party.

Books make lovely gifts. Choosing one can depend upon how well you know the host's interests and tastes. A cookbook for a food lover or a beautiful coffee table book may be just the thing.

Dear Thelma: Do you have advice on how to offer a toast?

A: Toasting is a wonderful way to honor a special guest or a gracious host. Before you begin, make sure glasses are filled. Any beverage will do when making this gesture of friendship.

You may sit or stand to give your toast. Do what comes naturally and makes the most sense. The person being toasted should remain seated. Others may also stay seated, unless asked to stand by the person giving the toast.

When giving the toast, face the person you're honoring, directing your words directly to her. Make your toast simple, and rehearse it beforehand so your thoughts are clear and you don't stumble over the delivery.

When your remarks are complete, look the person in the eye, raise your glass towards her and say "To Ann," and take a sip.

When you are toasted, you do not take raise your glass or take a drink with the others. Doing so would mean you are toasting yourself. Simply smile and nod or say, "Thank you."

When toasted, respond by returning a toast: "It's an honor to be with you tonight. I'm sure everyone here would like to join me in thanking our host, Chris, for a wonderful evening. To Chris!"

While simply raising your glass is the most proper way to toast, clinking glasses is a very old custom and many people thoroughly enjoy it. If someone does extend a glass in an obvious effort to clink, don't hold back. Just be careful with the glassware.

Like all heartfelt goodwill, good manners never go out of style.

Dear Thelma: The streets and parking lots were so busy over the holiday. Can you remind the impatient among us how to behave on the road?

A: First, respect safety and the law. Next, lose the 21st century mentality of getting there faster is better. Finally, keep the same courtesy you use face-to-face when you're bumper-to-bumper.

Using your turn signal properly, driving at or under the speed limit, respecting traffic signals and following other cars at a safe distance are all required by law to keep you and other drivers safe. Also, it's simply considerate to let the driver behind you know you're going to turn. You would appreciate such a gesture from the car ahead of you.

It is inconsiderate to zip around other cars with obvious disdain or speed through neighborhoods and parking lots. It is absolutely rude to tailgate and to rush your left turn through the intersection after the signal arrow has turned red just because you know oncoming traffic will not pick up speed fast enough to hit you. Stop doing these things now.

Horns are reserved for emergency use only, not to express your frustration. Although you may be willing to risk your life crossing three lanes of traffic to make your left turn, the driver ahead of you may place more value on the lives of the three children in her car. Honking at her will not change that.

Parking lots are designed for slow and cautious driving. Follow the traffic direction markings and be attentive to pedestrians. Do not illegally take a handicapped parking space.

Do not have your passenger jump out of your car to stand in the space you want but can't get to. It is unsafe. To claim a space that someone is backing out of, give the person leaving adequate room and use your turn signal to stake your claim. If you see someone near a space you want who has turned on his signal, consider the space taken. Do not attempt to race him for it.

Once you've found a space large enough for your vehicle – remember that SUVs are not considered "compact" – park with care and consideration. Center your car between the lines. Be careful with your doors getting in and out of your car.

Finally, when drivers break these rules, don't take it personally and don't allow it to cloud your own judgment in making courteous driving decisions.

Even behind the wheel, good manners never go out of style.

Dear Thelma: My family is out of control. Between my parents, my two brothers and their families, on Christmas Eve you can't even walk through the living room because of all the gifts. Present opening is a three-hour marathon. Is there any way to change this situation?

A: Honest communication well beforehand is the best way to resolve your unease. This year you won't have time to make any changes. However, after your marathon might be a good time to thank your family members for their wonderful generosity, and then ask if they feel things are getting out of hand.

Come to the conversation with ideas for solutions. You might suggest drawing names. Another option might be for each family to give a group gift to each of the other families. Gift ideas might include family games or gift certificates for a dinner and movie outing. Giving your time to one another – a regular coffee or lunch date – also makes a great gift.

If someone comes to you with these concerns, hear them with an open heart and mind. In large families the ability to give usually varies. Some may feel they can't live up to the high material standard.

Dear Thelma: My family has decided to draw names this year instead of everyone exchanging Christmas presents, but I love gift giving and I want to buy something for everyone. Can I?

A: Yes, you can, but you must not inconvenience or stress others by your giving. You should let your family members know individually that you plan to buy them gifts, but that you don't expect anything in return. Do not give your gifts during the family gift exchange, at which time everyone will be expecting to give and receive just one gift. Deliver your gifts individually at a separate time.

Dear Thelma: My sister, who lives in another state, always mails one Christmas package to me and expects me to deliver the gifts in it to our extended family. Is this polite?

A: It is most proper to mail individual gifts to their recipients. It adds to the thoughtfulness of the gift giving.

I suspect that in the beginning your sister asked if you would do this for her. You agreed then, but now it has become an inconvenience and upsets you. If that's the case, let your sister know well in advance of the holidays that it is hard to find time to do all the delivering and that you would appreciate being relieved of this duty.

Like clear communication, good manners never go out of style

Dear Thelma: How do you know if you should give holiday gifts at the office? Who should you give them to?

A: Giving gifts should be a joyful extension of good feelings we hold toward our fellow human beings.

In the workplace, give gifts to those to whom you want to show appreciation or gratitude, whether a boss, coworker, vendor or client. However, only give your boss a gift because you have a sense of sincerity and appreciation, not because you feel obligated. If you think you have to, it's the wrong reason to give a gift.

If you give a gift to an individual and do not have gifts for everyone else in your immediate area, give the gift outside of the office. Workers who don't get gifts when others do end up feeling left out, neglected, and not appreciated. As a manager, you never err when you are totally inclusive with workers in holiday celebrations and gifts.

Accept a gift in the spirit that it's given and receive with joy, even if you don't have a gift for the giver. Gift-giving is not meant to be a material exchange, it's an expression of the warmth we feel for certain people who bless our lives.

Always send a thank-you note. It can be a thoughtful email, or it can be a note of thanks added to that holiday card you were planning to send out anyway.

Dear Thelma: How do you handle holiday get-togethers when both spouses have family in town and can't have one get together for everyone?

A: Realize and respect that everyone wants to share special holiday time together. Then communicate thoughtfully and considerately how you can get that done.

As a family, you should try to discuss holiday plans well in advance and work together to schedule and create enjoyable time together.

I know of one couple who asks their children and grandchildren to save New Year's Day for their holiday celebration. That way the children and their spouses can celebrate with their own families or their spouses' families on Christmas without guilt or conflict. They also say that way they can do all their gift shopping at the after-Christmas sales!

If your families insist on holding events at exactly the same times, keep an open mind and heart as you work out with your spouse ahead of time how you will schedule yourselves. You can even plan host your own event for one side of the family at another time.

Among family and friends, good manners never go out of style.

Dear Thelma: What is the best way to handle planning and attending holiday work parties and gatherings?

A: In planning holiday office parties, your top concern should be creating an event that is inclusive, not exclusive. Holidays should be happy times for everyone who works together. All should feel equally honored by the invitation – from the entry level to the top.

Careful planning is important. In the invitation, clearly define the details that matter to others: time and place, attire, and gift exchange parameters. Be sure to note if it is a potluck or cost-sharing occasion. Do include an RSVP request, which should help in the planning.

Be thoughtful in everything you plan. If gift giving has been a custom, be sure it does not cause a financial problem for some of the workers. Holiday work parties should not only be inclusive but thoughtful, friendly and considerate toward all staff. If you decide gift giving is not appropriate at the party, this does not mean that there cannot be a gift exchange among individuals on their own time.

For those invited to the party, realize that the event is the company's way of celebrating the season with you. It may be being planned by an individual coworker or group of volunteers. Respect their time and effort by responding to the invitation promptly and attending with a festive attitude.

Holiday work parties should be an excellent opportunity for internal networking – getting to know people better, mingling, and discovering wonderful things about your coworkers. Make it a point to chat with people you don't typically spend time with at work or introduce yourself to someone in the company you haven't met. This is a time when people's hearts meet and share, and reach out to each other. Relationship building is a wonderful outcome and a lasting one.

By all means celebrate, but celebrate with respect for others and for yourself. The workplace holiday party is not the time to cut so loose that only the designated driver knows how you got home. Do concern yourself with what others will remember from the party. Conduct yourself in a way that you can be assured that tomorrow you will have no reason to be concerned about tonight's behavior.

As at any party, when you leave thank your hosts – both the senior level people whose decision it was to fund the party and those who did the party planning. Your gracious comments will be appreciated. Especially during the holidays, good manners never go out of style.

Ask Thelma 2006
Common Sense of the Heart

Dear Thelma: While traveling through airports over the holidays, I found that people have an increasing lack of consideration for each other. What's the best way to handle the hassles of air travel?

A: Start you trip with a dose of respect. Before you leave the house, decide you will treat those you meet and who serve you with consideration. Expect to face the unavoidable snags with courtesy and a positive attitude.

When you arrive at the airport and are faced with computer terminals to handle ticketing, don't be afraid to seek out the airline personnel for help if you need it. That will help things run more smoothly for everyone.

When standing in line, don't crowd those ahead of you and be prepared for what's next. When you reach the screeners, have your ID ready, your shoes off and your jewelry and change ready to dump into the plastic tray.

Take the luggage restrictions seriously. Check with the airline beforehand on size limits and number of pieces allowed. Don't try to get away with fudging on the size rules for carry-ons.

Carry your bag in front of you as you board the airplane and place it carefully in the overhead bin above your seat. If you see someone struggling with a bag, do help them.

Treat elderly or infirm passengers with patience and respect, and be helpful when you can.

Away from home, good manners never go out of style.

Dear Thelma: I participated in a potluck recently where the planning committee would not let people take home their own leftovers and required that everything be brought in disposable dishes so that all food could be stored for an impromptu leftovers lunch the next day. The committee also controlled the size and quantity of dessert portions in order to ensure a supply of desserts for the next day. Is this the wave of the future: Adults fighting over custody of homemade pumpkin pie?

What is the protocol for a potluck at work? If someone puts a lot of effort into a special dessert and it isn't served at the original potluck, is it tacky for him to retrieve it and take it home to his family? Does all food that comes in the door become the property of the planning committee?

A: We should take our work potluck protocol from what's proper at a potluck hosted in a home. While a host may ask you to bring a dish for a potluck meal, he would never require you to provide him with leftovers for the next day. On the contrary; in a home you are expected to take home any food you brought that wasn't eaten, along with its container. This frees the host or hostess from a mountain of clean-up, overflowing leftovers and the effort to return each guest's container.

Transfer that to the work environment. The host – the planning committee – should not require you to leave your food for the next day's leftovers luncheon. Once people have had their fill and the potluck is over, it is proper to take your leftovers home to eat and your containers home to clean. When you're ready to leave, do let the host know that you plan to do so.

Dear Thelma: I disagree with your reply to the expectant mother and her query about hand-me-downs. If the hand-me-downs are presented as a gift they should be accepted. It is easy to donate, recycle or dispose of them. I believe this is the appropriate manner to receive a gift. If the hand-me-downs are presented with a question, such as, "I have some old baby things, would you like them?" then it would be appropriate to turn them down. My Grandma taught me to never look a gift horse in the mouth. This means to accept all gifts without judgment.

A: You are correct in believing such about gifts. Always accept any gift in the spirit that it's given.

However, I interpreted the expectant mother's question differently than you did. I didn't find that these bags stuffed full of hand-me-downs were presented as gifts. Her question read more like well-meaning friends and family, people she knew
well, oversupplying her with used items. When the relationships are that close, I believe she can be truthful about what she needs and wants and whether she will be able to use the items.

Communication and good manners never go out of style.

Dear Thelma: I have a girlfriend at work who would get along great with a guy I know well. I'd love for them to meet, but I worry they might feel weird about being "set up." What's the best way to initiate that relationship?

A: To invite a group of friends to lunch at this time of year to celebrate Valentine's Day would be a natural way to introduce the two of them. It might be just the three of you or a larger group if you prefer. There's more comfort and less stress in a casual meeting of friends than a blind date or even a double date. Then let the relationship progress from there.

Dear Thelma: My teenage son wants to start dating soon. I'd like to have some standards for him to follow, but in today's world, does dating etiquette even exist?

A: The bottom line of all etiquette is respect, something that definitely should be taught by parents to their children and especially to teens beginning to date.

If you've determined your teen is responsible and respectful enough to date, first set and communicate your own rules of dating – curfew or nights of the week acceptable for dates – and the consequences for breaking those rules. The manners you must communicate that you expect your teen – boy or girl – to show on a date come next.

When asking someone out, extend the invitation as far in advance as possible. Two days may be fine for a movie date, but asking someone to the prom should be done at least a month in advance.

Accept or turn down a date as soon as possible – preferably within a day. If you choose to turn down a date, thank the person for asking and politely tell him or her no.

Especially on a first date, whoever has done the asking typically pays for what has been planned for the date. Once you've established a relationship you might decide to go Dutch treat or alternate who pays the full cost.

When making a date, be clear about your plans. Be on time to pick up your date or be ready when your date arrives. Go into your date's home and meet his or her family. Greet parents with a handshake and a smile. Answer their questions and ask your date's curfew. Respect it as well as your own.

Finally, honor your commitments. If you've made a date, the only acceptable reasons for breaking it are family emergencies or genuine illness. When socializing at any age, good manners never go out of style.

Dear Thelma: I am the chairperson of an anniversary committee for an organization. The group's active members' only request was that they wanted to be involved in the invitation list and were very adamant about who they wanted to invite.

After the invitations went out I received an email from a member stating that an invitation needed to be sent to an individual. This name was not approved by the membership. I took this issue to the officers and to the committee and everyone felt we should adhere to the original wishes of the voting membership.

The committee has since found out that the RSVPs that have not been returned (it is past the date) are in fact being held as negotiating tools until this one individual receives an invitation. This problem goes beyond etiquette. At this point, I'm so distraught that I'm not sure what my question is.

A: Perhaps you do not have a direct etiquette question, but it most assuredly has etiquette implications. I say that because there seems to be a lack of respect for the individuals organizing the event and for the guidelines that have been established regarding the invitation list.

I do know what it is like to get caught in these situations because I have chaired these kinds of events. When things like this happen it frequently damages the genuine spirit of the event and affects the openness and trust of those who work together.

It seems that if you want attendance at this event, dialogue with the parties involved must take place and someone is going to have to compromise in order to move forward. Approach the discussion with your active listening skills finely tuned. Don't assume that you know exactly what a person is saying or will say. Clarify the meaning and intent of what the person is saying by asking questions. Confirm that you are listening by paraphrasing their words. And seek out shared goals arrived at during your dialogue to keep the conversation solution oriented.

It will be difficult to tie things back together, but I do encourage you to talk with each other respectfully and jointly decide what is best for the event. It is so necessary to listen to each other without prejudices, be kind to one another and respect the results of your discussion. I wish you well and add that communication from the heart frequently removes barriers. When dealing with conflict, good manners never go out of style.

Dear Thelma: Some new friends have invited me to a fondue party. While I understand the concept of fondue, I'm wondering if there is anything special I need to know about how to participate properly.

A: The No. 1 rule of fondue: No double-dipping.

In the first and last courses, you'll likely be sharing a bowl of melted cheese and melted chocolate, respectively. Never take a bite and then dip back into the bowl for more sauce. Why? While we do want to share your company, we don't want to share your cold.

It's also best not to eat off of your fondue fork – the long-handled fork designed for dipping into the pot – for the same reason. Some try to take the bite off the fondue fork without letting the lips or mouth touch the fork, but using your dinner fork to slide the cheese-covered bread or chocolate covered strawberry onto your plate and then eat it is a better bet.

Spear the bread or fruit with your fondue fork and dip it into the pot. You may swirl it around to coat it completely. Then hold the piece over the pot while the excess drips back into the pot and the bite cools. Then remove it to your plate and eat.

The meat course likely will begin with a bowl of cubed raw meat being passed around. Spoon out several pieces you plant to eat. If you are given two plates, use one for the raw meats you are waiting to cook and the dinner plate for the cooked meats. Spoon the sauces available for the meat onto your dinner plate.

Skewer a cube of meat onto your fondue fork with the fork tines protruding. Plunge the meat into the pot of hot oil or broth to cook. The protruding fork tines will keep the meat from sticking to the bottom of the pot. When the piece is cooked, remove the meat from the fondue fork – which will be very hot –with a dinner fork to your dinner plate. Cut it into bites with your knife and eat it while your next piece is cooking.

If you drop a piece of food into the pot, do your best to retrieve it. Traditions differ on the penalty for dropping a piece of food into the pot. Some hold you have to pay for a round of drinks, others say you have to kiss the person next to you, and still others say you have to kiss everyone at the table.

Even when paying the penalty, good manners never go out of style.

Dear Thelma: I sent my estranged father a weekend getaway hotel package for Christmas, which included a dinner certificate. He sent back the hotel stay stating that he won't be able to fit in a vacation this year. He kept the dinner certificate. I think it's tacky to send a gift back. I think it's especially tacky to send back half of the gift! What do you think?

A: The main responsibility of a person who receives a gift is to issue a prompt and heartfelt thank you to the giver. Beyond that the gift is theirs to do with what they wish, including gracefully refusing something they feel they can't accept.

The responsibilities of a gift giver are to choose an appropriate gift for that specific individual and to give the gift unconditionally as an expression of affection or regard for that person.

If your father did properly thank you for the gift, he did fulfill his responsibility. At that point he could choose to use the gift, give it away, or not use it all.

Perhaps he did the most considerate thing by keeping the part of the gift he could use – enjoying the dinner you wanted him to have – and returning the portion that he knew was a great expense for you but that he would not be able to use.

Dear Thelma: A friend has entered the hospital and will be there for an extended period of time. I want to show support, but don't want to be a pest. I'm not sure how often to visit him or how long to stay.

A: Do visit to show your support, but you should not stay long. It takes great energy to see visitors. Show your support and do what you can, but respect his need for rest and recovery.

During your first visit talk to your friend about what he needs. If he's surrounded by family much of the time, he may appreciate a new companion once a week or so. If he's alone much of the time, he may ask you to come more often or stay longer.

What may be more important is to be helpful in taking care of things for him at home and to be available to him after he gets home. If there's anything you can anticipate that he will need when he arrives home, take care of it. And when he's at home recovering, call to check in on him, ask when you may visit and what help he may need.

Compassion and good manners never go out of style.

Dear Thelma: What are the most important phone etiquette rules when talking to a client on the phone?

A: The first thing to consider in client phone etiquette is first impression. Since you don't know who might be on the line, always answer your phone in a manner that makes a great first impression. Put a smile in your voice as you offer a greeting, state the name of your business or your department, and identify yourself. "Good morning, Accountants Inc., this is Melissa."

Next, be sure your tone of voice shows that the caller has your attention, your consideration and that you are absolutely listening. Achieve this by giving your total attention to the caller and his needs. People can tell when you're multitasking, so save it for another time.

Then show that you are listening by asking questions, restating what the client has said, and answering her questions. Make sure your client has the opportunity to clearly state her expectations; reiterate them to ensure that you've fully understood.

If you find it necessary to put a client on hold so that you may find his file or pull up computer data, ask him if you may do so, explain why you need to and thank him before you put him on hold. Don't put him on hold to answer another call or leave him on hold for more than a minute.

Finally, be fully aware that communicating over the phone to your clients is a large part of relationship building, so use that telephone time wisely. Even by phone we must be thoughtful and give our communications the respect and friendliness of an in-person encounter by their style and quality.

Dear Thelma: We are having a wedding and want to know who gets invited to the rehearsal dinner. Are out of town guests invited to go?

A: The traditional guest list for a rehearsal dinner includes the wedding party; the couple's parents, grandparents and siblings with their spouses or significant others; the officiate and his or her spouse; and any one else required to be at the rehearsal, like those doing readings. Spouses or significant others of the attendants are often included, as are out-of-town guests.

I would encourage you not to slight out-of-town guests. If they have taken the time to travel to attend your celebration, you should show respect and courtesy to them by inviting them to the dinner. Otherwise, they are likely to spend the evening alone for the night in their hotel rooms. When building any relationship, good manners never go out of style.

Dear Thelma: I feel like we are the middle of a baby boom. Maybe I am just at "that age," but I feel like I am going to baby showers all the time. I am wondering if it is appropriate to have a baby shower for any or all children after your first?

A: A baby shower is people's way of welcoming the new little one into this wonderful world of ours. For most, it's a happy opportunity to share in the building of community for that child. That celebration is appropriate whether the child is first in line or bringing up the rear.

While showers for a first born often seem focused on equipping the new parents with the latest and greatest in baby gear, showers for babies following the first born tend to take on a different personality. They tend to focus even more on celebrating that new life and new addition to the family and the world.

For a second or later shower, it is appropriate to be very specific about the kinds of gift items you need. A diaper shower theme, in which diapers and baby wipes are suggested gifts, might be right. If you have boys and now are expecting a girl, people will want to know so they can shop for tiny rosebud prints and lace.

While you wouldn't host a shower for yourself, you shouldn't refuse those who want to host showers for you. While close relatives and very close friends will most definitely be included on the guest list, other guests might include people who didn't attend your first shower.

In my view, having a baby is a lot more reason to celebrate than other reasons people have for throwing parties.

Dear Readers: I was recently in line at the grocery store behind one other customer.

She was eating a muffin and drinking coffee while trying to unload groceries from her cart to the conveyor belt. Crumbs flew and coffee spilled.

Her cart was full of loose fruit, which she hadn't gone to the trouble to bag or separate as she put it onto the belt. The clerk was forced to sort a jumble of oranges, lemons and potatoes.

Then she learned that if she had selected six bottles of wine instead of four, she would get a discount. She sent an employee to the back of the store for two more bottles.

When it was time to pay, she wanted to put the bill on two different credit cards, but she could only find one of them. She went to her car to get the other. I waited in line behind this customer for 28 minutes.

Having a full basket and several coupons to use is one thing. A complete lack of concern for everyone around you is another. Always be aware of how your actions affect others, or your bad behavior may end up in print.

Dear Thelma: What is proper buffet line etiquette?

A: When you are in any buffet line – cocktail, dinner or restaurant – show the same courtesy and respect you expect to receive.

Do not look for someone in line with whom to strike up a conversation and use that as an opportunity to avoid taking your rightful place at the back of the line. Also, don't encourage friends who walk by to join you in line. It is unfair to those behind you.

As you progress, remember those following. Use the serving spoons properly, returning them to their proper dishes after you have served yourself. Do not switch the spoons or leave them out of the dishes.

Move away from the buffet to continue or start conversations. Do not block the line or access to the table by setting yourself up in a place that is awkward for those trying to get to the food.

If you are taking a second trip to the buffet, leave your first plate and utensils on your table and get fresh ones.

Finally, while it may be a buffet, it needn't appear that you're never going to eat again. Judge how much you should take by the size of your plate. If food is beginning to pile up or fall off your plate, step away from the buffet.

Consideration and good manners never go out of style.

Dear Thelma: A dear friend's mother passed away. Her funeral is to begin at 10:30 a.m., but I have a meeting I must attend at 11:15. Can I go early to hug my friend, then stay near the back and leave at 11 even if the service has not ended?

A: Never plan to leave a funeral service early. Be there for the entire service or don't go at all.

If you can't commit yourself to the entire service, send a flower arrangement or other condolences. Call or email your friend right away to say that you can't attend the funeral, but that you will see her as soon as possible.

There is not usually a lot of time for hugging before the service. If there is a visitation before the funeral, there might be time for a quick show of support, but after the internment and most assuredly at the reception is the best time for greetings.

Plan to visit with your friend when you are not rushed. Offer to help in any way you can and stay in contact with your friend over the coming days and weeks.

When we pay our last respects we must keep the idea of "respect" first in our minds. A funeral is time to be somber, reflective and respectful in our dress, our conversation and our behavior.

Black is the traditional color of mourning, but it is no longer required dress at a funeral. It is best to dress very modestly. Avoid bright colors and attire that calls attention to you.

Flowers are always an appropriate way to honor the person who has died. It is important though to pay attention to the family's wishes expressed in the obituary. If the notice asks for donations to a charity in lieu of flowers, honor that request.

Offer comfort by expressing sincere regret for the loss. It can be as simple as saying, "I am so sorry," or "I deeply regret your loss." If you are close to the family, you might add, "If I can help you in any way, please know that I am here."

A reception often follows the services giving family and friends a chance to connect. If you are very close to the family, it would be appropriate to send a dish or a dessert to the home for use at the reception or during the days of mourning and receiving visitors that may follow the funeral.

When giving honor due, good manners never go out of style.

Dear Thelma: I work in a small, private retail boutique that is connected to a large professional organization. I understand and accept that cell phones are a large part of my clients' business; however, I have yet to find an acceptable and polite way of dealing with people who are having an in-depth (and often very personal) phone conversation while trying to conduct business with me.

I have tried going on to the next customer while the first one finishes his or her conversation, but that is often met with a hissed "I was here first." I have also tried to continue working on something else while waiting for the client to finish his conversation, but that is often met with a rude remark for making them wait.

Thelma, I would never be so rude as to pick up my phone while I was completing a transaction with a client. How should I deal with those who refuse to extend the same courtesy to me?

A: To those who deal with discourteous cell phone users, you are perfectly within your right to say: "Pardon me, but I feel uncomfortable being in the middle of your conversation. Until you finish your conversation, I'll be working with another customer. I'll come right back to you when I've finished with them."

Although those you say this to may react negatively, you are entitled to be charge of the situation.

To those who insist on using phones while trying to conduct a retail exchange, your behavior is rude to the clerk and rude to other customers waiting behind you. It shows a lack of respect for the service the clerk is providing and for the time of everyone around you.

At the core of good manners are respect and consideration, principles that don't change with the latest technology and that should be observed whether you're dealing with your boss or the cashier at a store.

Times when you are face-to-face with someone are not times for multitasking. Unless it's an emergency, no cell conversation should take precedence over the opportunity to communicate in person. Whether it's paying for your groceries or sitting in a meeting, the gracious cell user defers all calls to voicemail and addresses the matter at hand.

Cell phones are a mainstay of our society but they don't have to be heartless, eliminating any and all face-to-face interaction. A savvy cell phone user wisely picks and chooses when and where to dial up.

Technology changes; good manners never go out of style.

Dear Thelma: I recently experienced what I would call a hostile job interview. The interviewer asked demeaning and non-job related questions and acted as though he was upset at being made to call me. How do you bow out of a hostile interview without being upset or angry yourself? Or how do you politely set them straight?

A: It is not your responsibility to set the interviewer straight. Since you don't know where you'll come in contact with that person again, it's important to remain completely professional and polite.

Receiving such treatment from an interviewer would show me that this is not a place I want to work. If you have changed your mind about seeking the job mid-interview, do your best to get through to the end. Answer questions in a calm, non-assertive way, and don't get into long, involved answers. Be brief and be on your way. That will signal the interviewer that you're no longer interested.

When you want a job you've interviewed for, it's always important to send a written thank-you note to the interviewer. In your particular case, not sending a thank-you sends the clearest message that you're not interested in the job.

Dear Thelma: What should I do at a job interview when everything that the interviewer is proud of in his operation is antiquated? He has problems that he doesn't even seem to know about, and I've fixed problems just like his at previous jobs.

A: During an interview is not the time to tell a prospective employer what is wrong with his company. It is the time to highlight your experience and find out if it is welcomed by this employer.

The interviewer will ask about your skills and previous experience. Talk then about upgrades you've implemented and seen through at other companies. That will give him the opportunity to say "That's our next step," or "We're not ready to go there."

It is important to find out if the company is interested in using your experience and skills. If they're not, you'll be frustrated working there.

A good question to ask is, "What are your future goals for the company and how can someone in the position you're seeking to fill further those goals?"

His answer will tell you if they entertain change or want to stick with the status quo. In a professional manner you can let them know you have worked through change and would be an asset if the company is moving in that direction.

Professionalism and good manners never go out of style.

Dear Thelma: I usually go for light lunches so if I'm out with colleagues for an office lunch, I have lot of leftovers - more than half given the size of servings in the restaurant. Is it OK to get the leftovers packed to take with me?

A: If you are with friends, you've each paid for your own meals and it is the type of restaurant that provides take-home containers, it is fine to ask for one and take the leftover food with you.

If it's a business lunch with a host who has paid for all the meals, leave the leftovers behind.

It also is acceptable when ordering to ask if the restaurant can serve you just half the order, which I often do myself. Restaurants often can give you half and will charge you less than the full amount.

Dear Thelma: If a table of people at a restaurant is being so loud that I can't carry on a conversation with the person across from me, should I ask them to quiet down?

A: Since the table causing the commotion is likely disturbing more than just your party, it's right to ask the waiter to speak on behalf of the restaurant. Also the waiter should be able to ask in a friendly and customer service-oriented way, which may bring better results.

Dear Thelma: Is it proper to sample food from someone else's plate?

A: I believe it should be avoided. You definitely should not spear anything off another diner's plate and you should not accept a mouthful of food off another's fork.

If you do choose to accept an offer of food or offer a taste, discreetly move the food from the original plate to the taster's bread plate or the edge of his dinner plate.

Dear Thelma: When I'm done with a meal, can I put on lipstick while still at the table?

A: If you can do it inconspicuously, then it is acceptable. However, you should not pull out a mirror or a compact. If you need a mirror to apply it, excuse yourself to the ladies' room.

In our society, professional women are very attentive to their appearance. I know that I can tell you immediately when I need lipstick and I feel self-conscious without it. I've learned to dip down into my bag and slip it on in almost one motion.

For any primping beyond lipstick, do excuse yourself. And both women and men should never comb, arrange or even touch their hair at the table.

When eating out, good manners never go out of style.

Dear Readers: My recent advice concerning leaving a funeral service early because of a work commitment was this: "Never plan to leave a funeral service early. Be there for the entire service or don't go at all."

My stance on the issue met with disagreement from some readers. One said, "An appearance of any sort is better than a no show and will be immensely appreciated by the grieving parties. It is the quality of your presence, not the quantity of time that you spend that is important."

Another offered: "I can't imagine the family objecting [to a person slipping out], if they see it at all, though it is my experience that their attention will be directed entirely in the opposite direction. Since most funerals are held during working hours, people understand about the press of business."

And another said, "I believe that I would appreciate my friend coming even if it was for only a few minutes."

These readers most certainly have their hearts in the right place. Their intention is to honor the person who has died and console the family as best they can.

However, in the fast-paced, multitasking-friendly world we now live in, we run the risk of believing that our time is too valuable to spend sitting quietly and motionless for an extended period of time to honor a life lived. If we operate under the assumption that leaving a funeral early is just fine, then we are less likely to even consider attempting to resolve our schedule conflicts and give those grieving our full attention. When we set our standards low, our behavior meets them there.

As each person is at his or her own discretion in all matters of manners, use what I call heartsense – that feeling of right and wrong at the core of you – to inform your judgment. Consider very carefully and deeply how your presence, absence or early exit will be felt by others.

If your heartsense tells you that your presence there – even if it's abbreviated – will be part of the family's healing process, spend the time you can. Be certain that your behavior is discreet. Do not give the appearance of being in a rush or tell anyone that you are. Sit at the very back, on the aisle, near the door and time your exit to coincide with natural breaks in the service. Slip out silently.

Giving your best and good manners never go out of style.

Dear Thelma: Are there any rules for wearing patent leather shoes? I've been told they are only to be worn during the summer months. Is that true?

A: Patent leather shoes only in summer falls into the realm of fashion rules that have become fashion folklore. If designers are making and selling patent leather accessories year-round, then it's appropriate to wear them year-round.

I bought a pair of patent leather shoes trimmed in white this winter – two supposed faux pas in one pair of shoes.

The prohibition against white before Memorial Day and after

111

Labor Day is also a myth. White is appropriate all year in fabrics and in shoes. While the weight of the fabric or the shoe material may change based on the season, the color does not have to.

Sandals and slides also are sold and worn year-round, so they're not just for summer anymore.

And while some people wait for warmer weather to go without silk hosiery, many now go all year without it. That's not to say that it's improper to wear hosiery, most of us probably should, but your manners are intact either way.

Dear Thelma: Is it appropriate for women to wear hats to the breakfast at a business conference?

A: I don't think wearing a hat creates any kind of controversy. It's the kind of hat you choose, where you wear it and if it disrupts your connections to other people that can cause problems. Hats must be selected carefully and tailored to the occasion.

I imagine your business conference room to be a mass of round tables in a hotel ballroom with a front podium for a speaker. When selecting your hat, you must be sure that it doesn't keep people from speaking to you because they can't see your face and that it doesn't obstruct the view of others. A hat becomes problematic if people can't see around you to speak to others at your table or can't see the speaker.

If you choose to wear a large hat, you should remove it if it appears that it may obscure other people's view or becomes very distracting.

At a cocktail hour or a wedding reception, where there is a lot of moving around and you are not formally seated, is a great place to wear a hat that doesn't hide your face.

Fashion stays in flux; good manners never go out of style.

Dear Thelma: A business acquaintance sent a broadcast email as a wedding invitation, asking for gift certificates instead of gifts since they were moving out of state. We sent our regrets. Then I got an emailed shower invitation asking for gift certificates to a particular store. I sent my regrets by email, just checking a box. There was no address to send a formal regrets note. I do not socialize with this person and both times I felt like nothing more than a name on an email list. I am happy that she found someone to share her life with, but I really feel no personal connection to her. I did not send a gift and now I am wondering if I should have.

A: Although weddings are occasions when gift-giving is customary, gifts of any kind are never mandatory.

However, if you do work together, it's important to define your relationship before deciding not to give. Look at the need for that relationship in a business setting and decide if a wedding gift is important to it. Is this a relationship that needs to grow? Will giving a gift help it to grow or strengthen your connection? Let these answers guide you.

Another thing to ask yourself is whether your attitude toward gift-giving and attending would have been different if the invitations had come by regular mail. As email takes over the bulk of our daily communications, expect more and more invitations to be issued electronically.

It is perfectly fine to offer an invitation via email. The important thing to note is that the same content, quality and creativity should be put into any invitation sent. Since the main information you took from these emailed invitations was what kind of gifts were being wished for, it seems the couple and the shower hostess may have failed at issuing gracious invitations. Gifts should never be the focus of an invitation, and should rarely even be mentioned.

Email invitations should be structured to evoke feelings of style and grace, just as cardstock does. The sender is responsible for molding a message in a way that transmits friendliness and that honors the receiver.

Composed this way, email becomes a substitute for postage but not for the grace behind extending the invitation. While there will always be a place for handwritten, printed and engraved invitations, the polish and honor abundant in them can, and in our contemporary times will, be expressed via email.

Even electronically, good manners never go out of style.

Dear Thelma: My daughter is getting married and I have questions about invitation etiquette. My mother's brother, my uncle, is divorced from his wife, who was a wonderful aunt for 24 years. I feel we should invite my uncle and his children, but not my "ex-aunt." However, the children live with their mother. Can I include the children on the invitation sent to my uncle and exclude my "ex-aunt?"

A: It is very important that we not disregard kindness in these kinds of situations. While compiling any guest list is the prerogative of the host, it's very important to consider how your actions will affect important relationships.

The first person to look to is the bride. Will the invitation or exclusion of the former aunt cause her discomfort?

In your invitation situation, the next most important people to consider may be the children. How will your exclusion of their mother affect their relationship with you?

Personally, I believe an invitation which includes the children should be made to both their father and their mother. Let them know in a separate note or a phone call that they are all invited and that you will leave it to them to decide with whom the children will attend.

By extending both invitations, your caring and kindness remain intact and set the tone for their behavior. Depending upon the state of their post-divorce relationship, they may both be able to comfortably attend with their children, or following the example of your kindness, your "ex-aunt" may be kind enough to decide to not attend.

Dear Thelma: I gave away an important family heirloom to a friend before I knew what it was, and now I realize that I shouldn't have. My family is likely to ask to see it and will be upset when they learn I've given it away. I feel terrible about having to ask for it back, but will feel an even greater disservice will be done if I don't. How can I go about asking for it back?

A: If your relationship is one of friendship, then I have no problem with you asking for the heirloom back.

I encourage you to give a full explanation to your friend and apologize for having given the item away without thinking through the ramifications. A true friend will hear your explanation and will give back the item in the name of friendship.

Led at all times by kindness, good manners never go out of style.

Dear Thelma: If I'm tight on time and not interested in where a conversation is going, how do I interrupt or stop the person who is talking on and on without being rude or curt?

A: I think some people would like my answer to be "Just stamp your feet and walk away!" Of course, that is not my answer.

Regardless of how quickly you might wish to exit a conversation, you must always do so politely and considerately. When the first opportunity arises, use a positive statement to end the conversation in a pleasant and genuine way.

At a cocktail reception or event like it, it's fine to exit a conversation with:

"Please excuse me. An old friend just walked in and I'd be remiss if I didn't greet her."

"It's been lovely speaking with you. Please excuse me, my boss just arrived."

"Oh my, look at the time. Please excuse me. I must call to check in with the babysitter."

Or at the office, politely end a discussion with:

"I'm sorry; can we continue our conversation later? I'm expecting a client's call and need to get back to my desk."

"Please excuse me. I'm on deadline and must get back to work."

It is never appropriate to display any kind of personal displeasure at being in that conversation whether through body language, facial expression or negative comments.

Dear Thelma: I was told on several occasions that informally written correspondence should include the woman's name first dealing with a married couple, for instance, addressing Kathy and John Jones on the outside envelope in lieu of more formal addressing. That the "man's first name is never separated from his last name" unless children are being addressed. Is this because I was married to a Jr. and one wouldn't address John and Kathy Jones Jr.?

A: I am asked this question quite often. Informal correspondence is traditionally addressed as you describe, with the wife's first name listed first: Kathy and John Jones. However, there really is no contemporary rule to hold you to that.

Personally, I find it most natural to follow the conventional form taken from the formal address of Mr. and Mrs. John Jones and list the husband's name first: John and Kathy Jones. Either way, your letter will find its recipient, and it's quite possible they will be so happy to have received a letter that they won't notice how it's addressed.

Traditions may change, but good manners never go out of style.

Dear Thelma: Please address tipping for a hairdresser. Is there a difference if the hairdresser is the shop owner?

A: Contemporary manners hold that if the salon owner cuts your hair, it is proper to give the standard hairdresser tip of 15 to 20 percent of the bill. Those salon owners who charge more for cuts may not accept tips and will let you know. It also is appropriate to ask the receptionist if the owner accepts tips for styling hair.

This has become confusing for many because in the recent past customers generally did not tip a shop owner who cut their hair. But if you think of any tip as a reward for good service, it makes sense to offer that appreciation to whoever styled your hair. Conversely, if the service is substandard, it is appropriate to decrease a tip proportionally.

In a salon where you are attended by several people during your visit – a separate colorist, stylist and manicurist – and you've received good service, give each person 15 to 20 percent of the cost of their particular service to you. Or give 10 percent of the total bill to the person who spends the most time serving you and split 10 percent between others who help. Don't tip anyone less than $2.

Dear Thelma: I'm a working mom with a child in school and one in day care. I like to keep my cell phone on at all times so that if there is a problem or an emergency no one will have any trouble reaching me. I don't want to be rude to clients or co-workers, but I need to attend to that phone. I feel I have to settle for offending some in order to care for my own. What do you think?

A: Proper discretion with the cell phone and its polite use are where you need to place your focus. Keep your phone close to you and silence the ringer when you can, especially during meetings with clients or co-workers.

If a call comes in and you see that it is from the school or day care, excuse yourself from the meeting – "Please excuse me, I really must take this call." – walk away from the table and answer the call. Calls from numbers other than those possible emergency numbers should be left to voice mail while you attend to the people and the matter at hand.

Such behavior will not give offense and you will remain a responsible colleague and a caring mother.

Good sense and good manners never go out of style.

Dear Thelma: I am very dismayed to read your response to the question of hosiery for summertime business attire. As a woman with more than 20 years of experience in the business world, I assure you that a woman in bare feet and legs (i.e., sans hosiery) is no more well-thought of than the man who shows up without socks. Trendy, maybe, but no heavy-weight.

A: As a woman with more than 30 years of experience in the

business world, I assure you that the fashion dictates I followed at the beginning of my career have changed dramatically over the years and they will continue to change.

Every time we get dressed our choices should show self-respect and consideration to those around us. If in your work environment and in your position, hosiery remains a part of showing that respect, then continue to wear it. You are perfectly polite in doing so. But we should not be surprised or become judgmental as the pull of fashion changes that rule we considered unbreakable a generation ago.

Wearing hosiery is no longer a matter of manners. While it may not be your choice if you're going for the most conservative of looks, it is a personal choice. Of course we must focus on the aspects of self-respect and consideration when going bare-legged by making sure our feet and legs look their very best.

As for dressing differences between the sexes, women's clothing choices for business will always be more influenced by fashion than men's. The simple fact is that men and women do dress differently and different standards do apply. While there may be men out there willing to stuff their bare feet into dress shoes for the sake of fashion, a man in a suit sans socks is still a no-no. Sorry, guys.

Dear Thelma: On the RSVP card included with an invitation that I received, the center line has "M_____" Am I supposed to put my name on that line?

A: Do put your name on that line, beginning with your title. Complete the preprinted "M" with Mr., Mrs., or Ms. If you use a different title, like Rev. or Dr., draw a line through the "M" and write the proper title. If you are replying as a couple, complete the preprinted M as "Mr. and Mrs. John Clark" or "Ms. Kathryn Stevens and Mr. Greg Garcia."

Faced with the traditional or the fashion forward, good manners never go out of style.

Dear Thelma: Should a divorced mother expect her boyfriend to pay for her child's activities, trips, etc.? How financially involved should a boyfriend or fiancé be before there is a permanent relationship, such as a wedding?

A: Your question is a pertinent one because of the prevalence of situations like yours that arise today. It also is a question that involves more than simply manners.

On the manners end, it's not proper to expect your boyfriend to pay your kid's way.

If he invites you and your child on an outing and clearly intends to play host to the two of you, it's fine to accept. However, if you bring the child along instead of hiring a babysitter or you simply spend a lot of time doing things as a group rather than a couple, it's politest to pay your child's expenses.

In any dating relationship, the person who asks generally pays for the date he or she has planned. If the person invited suggests adding an activity or brings along someone, that person covers the extra expense.

By covering your child's expenses, you're more than just minding your manners. You're teaching your child that you take ultimate responsible for him.

If the relationship grows and the man becomes your fiancé, it will be important to discuss finances and make decisions about family responsibilities before you say, "I do."

Dear Thelma: My daughters and I are having tea at the Ritz in London late in June at 5:30. Is that too late for a hat? If not, what style would be best? I am a young 60 and my daughters are in their 30s.

A: Time is not the decision-maker for a hat. Tea is an incredibly appropriate time to wear a hat and the time of day doesn't matter.

In today's social world where hats are becoming the accent piece of choice for many, an individual can and should choose a hat that complements her own style. I'd suggest you and your daughters make a day of shopping for hats and advise each other on what works best for each of you.

As I've said before, when choosing a hat and where to wear one, avoid a hat that can obstruct another's view at an event like a concert or a movie where someone would have to see around you to see the action. That shouldn't be a problem at the tea room.

Good manners never go out of style.

Dear Thelma: A couple, who my husband and I consider close friends, has asked that our family join them on a family vacation this summer. Their children and ours play together often and we generally all have a good time together. I think we'd have fun, but I'm a little concerned about how an extended stay together could affect our friendship. Do you have any tips that could help make this work?

A: Throughout the planning and taking of a joint vacation, communication and consideration are your keys to a great trip.

Before you agree to a joint vacation, the first thing to do is to honestly assess with your husband whether your families will get along for an extended period. Are the children close in age and do they enjoy similar activities? Are you flexible enough to accommodate another family's likes and dislikes on your vacation? Discuss the issues you believe could arise and how you would handle them.

Next, meet with the couple to openly discuss what each of you expects out of a vacation. Do the adults have similar attitudes and interests when it comes to vacationing – does one family love to ride every coaster at every park within 50 miles while the other likes most days consumed with lying on the beach?

Discuss the times you get up in the morning and go to bed at night, when you eat, and if you schedule naps for the kids into your activities. Find out where each family wants to stay and what they want to do. Do your vacationing styles mesh?

If you decide to travel together, continue the communication. Plan as much as you can and make your compromises before you leave. Talk beforehand about any activities your family might plan to skip.

Discuss expenses to be shared or handled individually, the need for individual family time, and sharing of duties or babysitting. Once on the trip, if costs are split, pay your share promptly.

It's also important to talk to your kids about what behavior you expect from them and what they should expect during the trip. Talk to them about how your families will share time and decision making. Prepare them to participate in the other family's interests and activities. Plan to discipline only your own children's misbehavior during the trip.

Once the vacation begins, be flexible, courteous and keep communicating. If difficulties arise, remember that these are your friends and strive to treat them with the kindness and respect that made you friends in the first place.

When sharing, good manners never go out of style.

Dear Thelma: Recently I was introduced to someone by a colleague when I ran into them in a restroom. What is the proper way to acknowledge the introduction under that slightly awkward circumstance? A polite nod or wash hands and extend a handshake or something else?

A: A heartfelt introduction from a colleague or close friend in any location typically should be properly acknowledged with a handshake. Consider that if you are introduced in the restroom, you'll both have the easy opportunity to wash your hands before you leave.

But also let heartsense guide you. If the sanitation factor paralyzes you or if the other person doesn't seem comfortable shaking hands, it would not be unkind to say, "Let me wash up so I can properly greet your friend," or simply give a genuine smile and nod. If you react to the situation with kindness, the actions you take won't be wrong.

Introductions are very important in honoring and building relationships and they take place everywhere. We should always follow our heart to respond to them with utmost respect and courtesy, and most importantly always be prepared to meet someone new.

Genuine kindness and good manners never go out of style.

Dear Thelma: I have many business relationships where my clients are quite friendly with me; however, we do not socialize outside of work. I sometimes take them to lunch. If one of these people makes the suggestion that we have lunch or meet for a drink after work, should I still pay for everything?

A: No, you shouldn't be expected to. The person who makes the invitation, even if they are the client, is considered the host and should be prepared to pay for the meal or drinks.

As a client in that situation, it's important to say something like, "I'd like to take you to lunch," or "Drinks are on me this time," to make it clear that you intend to pay. If a client says, "Let's have lunch together," that may indicate that he'd like to share the expense. No one should ever invite a person to lunch expecting that his guest will cover the bill.

If you're unsure about the intention of your client's invitation but accept it anyway, it's fine to say, "Can I help with the check?" or "Would you like to split the cost?" before the meal begins. A good host will say, "No, I'm taking care of the bill today."

If the check comes and it's clear the client expects you to pick it up, go ahead and do so, and remember that the next time that client makes an invitation. Make your decision on whether to accept based on the realization you will likely – despite the impropriety – be expected to pay.

When you know your clients well and have established strong relationships with them they will want to reciprocate the kindness you've shown to them. Accept their genuine invitations graciously and let them honor you with a lunch or a drink.

Dear Thelma: What are a parking valet's duties? Is he to open door for the lady or does she wait for her husband or date to come around and open it for her upon arriving and leaving an establishment?

A: The parking valet should open the car door for the lady. The husband or date would then thank the valet for doing so. If the valet fails to open the door, the date should come around to open it or the woman may step out of the car on her own if she wishes.

Standard tipping for a parking attendant is $1 to $2, given to the driver when the car is brought to you, rather than when you arrive.

Dear Thelma: My church has dinner clubs of about eight people who take turns hosting dinners for each other over the course of a year. A woman in our group (I'll call her Tammy) lives in the same area that I do, so the group leader decided we should pool our date have the dinner hosted by the three of us.

Here's the problem: Tammy told the group leader that she wanted to fix a Slovakian meal at her house for all of us. That would be fine if I did not know what I do about Tammy and her cats. Her litter box is a few feet away from the countertops. Her cats go directly from the litter box to the counters and Tammy thinks nothing of it. I honestly do not want to go there, but I do not know what to do. I would rather us all go to a restaurant. Should I confide in the group leader my reasons for not wanting to go?

A: Since this particular meal is designed to be a group effort between you, Tammy and the group leader, you should feel comfortable and Tammy should expect that you will be planning it together. As a partner in the process, you should have ample opportunity to lobby for the ease and practicality of going to a restaurant. If she is set on cooking a special meal, tell her you want to do your part too by hosting the cooking and dining at your home.

If she won't allow for your suggestions and you don't feel your relationship is strong enough for you to talk with her about the cats, then go to the leader and tell her your concerns.

At that point it will be the leader's decision whether or not to speak to Tammy. The easier issue to address would be importance of cooperation in the process. Addressing the sanitation issue, she might say, "It's been brought to my attention that some members of our group are uncomfortable with house cats. Is it possible to remove the cats and their box from the kitchen before our gathering?" However, that still may mean moving the cats and not the dinner.

At that point it becomes a personal decision for you. If you've been eliminated from the planning and hosting process then you could opt out of attending, saying, "I'm just not able to make it this time."

Before you make that decision you should weigh the importance of your friendship with Tammy and the rest of the group with your own comfort level. If I were in that situation, I would look at it as a one-time sacrifice to strengthen the relationships I've built and get through the dinner as best I could.

Dear Thelma: Three friends gave a bridal shower. They spent a great deal of time and money in order to prepare for the event. After the shower, the bride-to-be said, "Thank you." That was all.

The ladies who gave the lovely shower and gave gifts also thought the bride-to-be should have given each of them a "hostess gift." Should a hostess gift have been given, or is this asking too much?

A: It is very important that the honoree at a bridal or baby shower show proper appreciation to the people who have made the effort to host the shower on her behalf. More than just a verbal thank you is due these hostesses.

Hostess gifts for those who planned and orchestrated the shower are a very appropriate way for a bride or mother-to-be to express thanks and honor due. Even a small token that shows you understand and appreciate the lengths others have gone to to honor you will be heartily felt.

Sometimes brides and mothers-to-be don't think of these things. They can become so focused on their own planning, that they forget the small acts of appreciation and kindness that close friendships deserve. Showers take a ton of time and planning, and they are not an easy thing to pull off. Those who do it should be well-thanked.

Stationery, a candle, flowers, or a package of their favorite cookies – something that shows you thought of them while they were thinking of you – given before or after the guests arrive will make they memory of your shower a good one for your hostesses.

Even if I'm just invited to dinner, I always take a hostess gift. It's a neat way to express that you appreciate the effort that has been made for you.

Dear Thelma: I recently read an article about emerging iPod etiquette. Is there such a thing?

A: What matters most is that we apply the manners we already know to the use of technology. That means giving our full attention to the people we meet face-to-face. Don't make them question whether or not you are really listening; take off both ear buds and focus.

Also, don't let the technology isolate you from the people around you. Your career life and social life are about building relationships. If you are constantly unavailable due to your MP3 player, you create a permanent barrier to starting and building those relationships. Digital portable music players may be hot, but disregarding the world around you in favor of your favorite tunes is not.

Even when embracing technology, good manners never go out of style.

Dear Readers: Many of you are preparing your children or grandchildren for a new school year. You're buying new shoes and that first-day-of-school outfit, checking to see if the backpack needs to be replaced this year, and stocking up on crayons and glue or spiral notebooks and pens.

I hope that while you're on those shopping trips, you take the opportunity to reconnect with your children and have some important conversations. Back-to-school time is a natural time to talk about the consideration and respect we want to have as part of our lives and our kids' lives.

Stress courtesy while you're shopping. Stores are a great place to model respect and kindness toward other shoppers and toward sales clerks. Kids will notice how you respond to long lines, shoppers that take up much of a clerk's time, and crowded parking lots.

Review the summer. As a family, were you as courteous to each other as you should have been? Talk about the times you yelled orders from the kitchen when you could have walked to your son's room to list his chores for the day. Think about poor behavior toward one another or habits that may have crept in over a summer in close quarters – a pesky little brother's antics answered by a screaming older sister. Now's a good time to say, "This is not the way we want to treat each other as a family. Let's start fresh at school and at home." Then communicate and model the positive behavior you want everyone to achieve. Start with "please" and "thank you."

Talk about heartsense. Yes, it's a word I made up, but it properly describes that feeling of knowing in your heart, although you're not quite sure how, that your behavior is right or wrong. Refresh your kids' memories about respecting adults, especially their teachers, and about respecting other students. There will be new friends to make and opportunities to involve others in their playground games. Ask them to think about how their actions or words can affect others. Tell them you expect consideration for others from them, and knowing that they're a good friend and a good student is what makes you proud.

Discuss first impressions. Let them know that taking care of themselves, their clothes, and their school work shows self-respect and respect for those around them, as does being on time. Show them that these things are important.

Make manners an important lesson to learn this year. After all, unlike that pair of pants you just bought, good manners never go out of style.

Dear Thelma: I am hosting a family picnic/pool party for about 15 guests. One of the guests is my 25-year-old son's girlfriend who will be coming to our home for the first time. My question concerns my sister-in-law (I'll call her Donna) who always comes dressed for a pool party in a bathing suit top that barely covers her.

I am afraid that my son's girlfriend will feel uncomfortable sitting at the same table with Donna. Do I have the right as the hostess to ask Donna to wear a T-shirt or something over her bathing suit while we eat? My husband thinks I am being a prude, and my own mother doesn't think I can say anything, because a person can wear anything they want to my home. Is that true?

A: Asking guests to come dressed for dinner is perfectly within your right as the hostess of the party.

Further, I believe that your concern over your new guest's experience is valid. A person's choice of revealing clothing does have an effect on how others relate to them. It may make a person uncomfortable enough to avoid being sociable and unwilling to communicate with the scantily clad, who may actually be the nicest person in the room.

It sounds like you are a family that has fun getting together. You should try talking to one another too. Have a very sincere conversation with Donna, explaining that as a new guest in your home you consider your son's girlfriend the guest of honor at the party. You don't want her to feel at all uncomfortable and so you're planning to ask everyone at the party to come to the dinner table wearing their t-shirts and cover-ups. Talk to everyone else invited too and let them know you'd like them all to "dress for dinner" as well.

As we've said before, you have only one chance to make a first impression. In this case it's a family effort to make a first impression on someone joining them for the first time. Work together to make it a good one.

Dear Thelma: Is there a guideline for giving monetary gifts when it comes to events such as bridal showers, weddings, graduations and birthdays or do most people just give what they can afford?

A: The amount spent on a gift or given as a gift is always at the discretion of the giver. Base your decision on how well you know the person and what you can afford to spend. Be considerate in your giving, but know that it's a personal choice.

Like gracious gift-giving, good manners never go out of style.

Dear Thelma: A friend of mine and I have applied for the same position in another area of our company. She has told everyone she has applied and been granted an interview. I have also been granted an interview but I have not even told anyone that I applied. I feel this is my own business, and I don't want to put myself into competition with anyone else. Is this correct or should I mention it to her? Office politics are the pits!

A: I would not mention it. You are under no obligation to share that personal information with anyone and you are right that those kinds of revelations create an element of competition in a workplace that is not necessary.

If you do end up with the job and your friend asks why you didn't share, you can say, "Since we all get along so well, I didn't want to create an uncomfortable or competitive atmosphere in our department."

Dear Thelma: I just got engaged and am starting to plan for a wedding and reception next spring. Are there set rules as to who pays for what? And how do I go about bringing up that kind of thing with my fiancé and his family?

A: There are many great wedding planning guides available to help you answer your first question, but what it will come down to is what works and is comfortable for you and your situation.

More than a beautiful wedding and a fun-filled reception, the wedding planning process will be an important time to further develop your communication skills with your future husband and his family. Start your conversation about funding the wedding with your fiancé and let him take the lead in discussing it with his family.

Keep all your communication with your new family friendly, sincere, honest and open, but remember that communication involves more than speaking and being heard. It also requires active listening. Asking questions, reading body language and thoughtful consideration of another's thoughts and feelings are as important as getting your own point across. True listening goes beyond just hearing the words that are said; it's absorbing what is said with a bias towards the person you love and it's understanding what might not be said.

Such communication will provide wonderful ways to grow relationships with your spouse and his family. It's the opposite – poor, self-centered communication – that keeps us from knowing and understanding one another.

Dear Thelma: I recently attended the memorial service for the family member of a close friend. Is it required that I also send a card to the family? Is the visit enough or is it better to do both?

A: If sincerely expressing your sympathy is important to you, you should take the time to send a card as well. I'm sure your friend and his or her family will appreciate the sentiments that a card will give you the additional opportunity to express. The card frequently is something that is read after the emotional intensity of the memorial during more peaceful and quiet moments. In life's most joyous and most difficult times, good manners never go out of style.

Dear Thelma: I have a neuromuscular disease and use a wheelchair and a service dog. I also live in a small town. No matter how many times I say it, people can't seem to understand that petting the dog and talking to him when he's in harness – without the handler's permission – is not "being friendly." It is a very unwelcome distraction.

It is never appropriate to interfere with an assistance animal, and most states have laws on their books regarding such interference. The dog needs permission every time to interact with someone else. If people can't resist, they can ask first, but they shouldn't be disappointed if they are told, "Not right now, the dog is working."

If people truly respect and admire these working dogs and the wonderful tasks they do, then folks can be quiet, keep their hands off, and let the dogs do their job! Could you please help me make your readers aware of this?

A: Thank you for writing so clearly on the subject of service dogs and allowing me to spread the word.

Assistance dogs include guide dogs for people who are blind and visually impaired, hearing dogs for those who are deaf and hard of hearing, and service dogs for people with disabilities. Some assistance dogs may be identified by a cape placed around their midsection or a special harness. Never touch, pet, feed or talk to dogs that are in service to a person.

While it's very tempting to interact with these intelligent and beautiful dogs, it is proper to remember that they have an important job to do and allow them to do it without distraction.

Dear Thelma: We are staying at a hotel that charges $38 a day for parking and only has valet parking. Are we supposed to tip the valet every time he brings the car up? We are in and out several times a day.

A: Some people equate a daily charge for parking at a hotel with a monthly garage rental, in which it is not necessary to tip the attendant each time your car is brought to you.

However, I feel it important to reward a hotel parking attendant for good service with a tip and would offer $1 to $2 when the car is delivered.

Unless the establishment posts a sign saying tips are not necessary, tips may be an important part of the attendant's wages and an important way to show appreciation for a personal service. Merited tips and good manners never go out of style.

Dear Thelma: I attended an inside concert this evening starring Clint Black and many of the audience members wore cowboy hats. Two people in front of me wore cowboy hats and obstructed my view. Would it have been proper etiquette to ask them to remove their cowboy hats during the performance?

A: Yes, you could have politely said, "Would you consider removing your hat?" – provided that you realized you might have to take no for an answer.

The proper and courteous thing for any hat-wearer to do is to remove the hat indoors and especially at an event where people will need to see around the hat to enjoy the action on stage.

Otherwise, hat-wearers should be sensitive to the wishes of those around them, especially if the problem has been called to their attention. If someone asks you to consider removing your hat, realize that they probably truly cannot see the concert and it would be most kind of you to not obstruct their view.

In any venue, it's likely that you will contend with people who will ignore or just not realize the courteous thing or choose their accessory over manners. That's when you must keep your own manners about you.

Dear Readers: For some time now, I've been thinking about the service industry and how the word "service" seems to be fading from the job description.

Lately I've felt like an intruder into the private lives and private time of many in the profession. Maybe you too were subject to this conversation at a popular lunch spot: "You were supposed to come today with a tattoo. What happened? You know if everyone who works here has a tattoo, then the boss can't make us cover them ... Oh, can I help you?"

Or this one at the pharmacy: "I didn't get my break yet today. Did you get your break? I'm closing this line now. They have to give me a break. That'll be $10."

The lack of attention to the customer at many establishments borders on absolute discourtesy. Employees can hardly help you because they're so involved in their own conversations. On top of being an annoyance, the lack of attention creates opportunities for mistakes to be made, further frustrating the customer they've been hired to help.

My favorite organic grocer is an exception. Its clerks are truly attentive to customers and outright helpful. They strike me as outstanding. But are they? Or is everywhere else just so bad that basic customer service seems outstanding?

To all those in customer service, be aware that your customers hear everything you say. We all hear about your tattoos and your date last night and your lack of a break. It's obvious to us when you are not concentrating on the job you've been hired to do. So I'd like to gently remind you, you're not in a bubble with your peers, hanging out at the coffee shop. You work there.

Dear Thelma: My mother passed away recently. Should I send an acknowledgement card to her brothers and sisters for the flowers they sent?

A: Yes, do send those cards. Since they are members of the family who are also in mourning, their added thoughtfulness deserves your recognition and attention.

Like thoughtfulness, good manners never go out of style.

Dear Thelma: Next year our mother turns 80 and my two sisters and I want to host a party to celebrate her life. My sister's son also will be graduating from nurse anesthesia school. This will be his third advanced degree, and there has been a party with each of them.

My sister wants to have a joined party at the country club, putting his name on the engraved invitations, as well as inviting his friends and having a display table of his achievements. Since many family members will be coming from out of town, I suggested a gathering the night before in his honor, but both sisters feel that this is unnecessary.

After 80 years, I feel that Mom is entitled to her own party. I love my nephew and am proud of his accomplishments but feel this should be Mother's party. My biggest question for you is should my nephew be sharing the party time with Mom?

A: There is no doubt that both events are worthy of celebrations. However, I would not unite the two celebrations.

When planning for a party, there are several things that should be considered initially. First, it is essential to know why you are having a party. Second, it is important that the invitation list be planned to honor the reason for the party. Third, the guests should be connected to the celebration.

It doesn't seem to me that there is compatibility in the guest lists required for a joint party. I may not completely understand your family, but in my own family the people who would be invited to celebrate an 80th birthday would be different from those invited to celebrate receiving a degree.

I just hosted a graduation party for a niece and nephew (siblings in the same family). One graduated from high school and the other from college. I will say that even that had two distinct groups of people enjoying the food at my home but not celebrating together. Would I repeat that? No, I would not.

Next is the question of an 80th birthday celebration. How many individuals really have the gift and privilege of celebrating an 80th birthday? No too many. This should be a very special celebration and one that sincerely honors the birthday mother. There are many memories attached to celebrating an 80th birthday and it is a wonderful time to remember those and to show appreciation for a life beautifully lived. Eighty years of life deserves its own celebration.

For a sincere celebration, good manners never go out of style.

Dear Thelma: At my college I have suite mates in a co-ed dorm building. There are two of us in each room, sharing a bathroom in the center. We also share a balcony. My roommate and I are girls, our suit mates are guys.

The problem I am having is that one of my suite mates feels that we are more than friends. He feels we are an "item" or that I am his girlfriend. The way he treats me, everyone else thinks this too.

I consider him a very good friend, but not a boyfriend. I have discussed this with him over and over. But he is just not getting it. He is in my room when I come in from classes. If I go on the patio, he goes on patio. If I get online on my computer, he does too. I feel trapped. I do not want to lose a friend, but I am ay my wits end. What do I do to get this situation to where I have some privacy and peace?

A: Whether the relationship is platonic or romantic, a true friend would not invade your privacy in this way. No one should intrude in another person's space without an invitation. That's rude.

You indicated that you have discussed the depth of your relationship with him, but how firm have you been? If you have made your feelings crystal clear by word and by your own actions, then there should be no question in his mind as to where he stands with you.

It sounds as though you need to tell him clearly that you are not interested in a romantic relationship with him. Next tell him that your privacy is important to you and that he should only enter your room if he's invited. Then make sure your actions back up your words: don't flirt with him, don't show up in his room uninvited, and lock your bathroom door so he can't just walk on through to your room.

If clear communication has failed to get your message through, then you'll need to consider whether this is a friendship that you can afford to keep. Pull back by spending more time with other friends in your room or by spending less time in your room. Seek out a resident advisor if it becomes an issue you can't work out on your own. And next year, avoid the co-ed dorm. Like a healthy respect for privacy, good manners never go out of style.

Dear Readers: Over recent weeks the experiences I've had at two events I attended have prompted me to share with you what seems to me to be a neglect of manners and respect for others.

I attended an elegant, thoughtful and exceedingly well-planned celebration with about 300 guests. Unique and beautiful centerpieces adorned each table along with individual favors for each guest. During the sit-down dinner the hosts visited each table. Every detail was an expression of their graciousness and gratitude.

"RSVPs" were requested for this formal occasion in the invitation, yet as I looked around the room there were empty places and even empty tables. Empty seats and empty tables either mean that people responded and didn't attend or that they didn't respond at all. In this situation we find yet another example of the rampant neglect of the RSVP.

Where is our thoughtfulness and respect for those who plan such memorable events? Food, favors and place settings are planned according to our responses. If something occurs and your "yes" becomes a "cannot attend," the thoughtful thing is to let the hosts know as soon as possible.

When I teach business etiquette classes, one of the first requests made by employers is that I teach the necessity of responding to an invitation. Businesses often sponsor tables for charitable events, and one of the universal problems is the time that is spent calling the employees who received an invitation and have not responded.

We may be distracted and busy, but neglect in this area truly earns a person the label of inconsiderate.

For the record, when you see "RSVP" on an invitation, you are to respond as promptly as possible whether your answer is yes or no. Simply not responding at all is not a clear signal to your host of your intentions.

The second major event I attended brought to mind that if you find yourself in the limelight as a master of ceremonies, realize that it requires preparation and a full understanding of the role. Introducing yourself to the audience is essential and sets the stage for the audience to be attentive and to listen to you. Being an MC requires that you fully understand the purpose of the event and act accordingly. Finally, in most situations it is important to remember that the MC is not a key speaker, but one who maintains the tempo and quality of the event.

Whether you are an official host or an honored guest, the value you place on respect and kindness shown to others is directly connected to your manners. Your manners, in essence, show who you really are all the time. And good manners never go out of style.

Dear Thelma: Please clarify the proper etiquette for women wearing hats during an outdoor flag ceremony if the hat is clearly part of their dress. There has been considerable conversation about scarves, baseball caps, and hats for sun shade. The subject evokes considerable emotion from both sides.

A: Over the decades as women's fashion has changed, the etiquette of wearing a hat has changed along with it.

If you are a woman or a girl wearing what is unmistakably a woman's formal fashion accessory hat, then the rules of the past apply and a woman's hat remains on her head during a flag ceremony.

But with the casual hats worn most often today – including baseball caps or other very informal, unisex hats – contemporary rules are applied to both genders. Without question, always remove your unisex hat to show respect during the playing of the National Anthem, the passing of the flag in a parade, or in a cemetery or other monument to the dead.

It is appropriate for men and women to wear casual hats in public areas like a store or a building lobby that you are just passing through. Once you reach your destination – a restaurant, a person's office, a home, or a church – removing your cap shows respect to those around you or to the sanctity of the place you've entered.

Hat etiquette also requires that you always take off your casual hat at a meal in a home or in a restaurant. Again, a woman's hat that is clearly part of her dressy ensemble remains on in a restaurant or a formal tea but generally is removed when dining in a home.

Dear Thelma: My son's girlfriend of five years is pregnant. They eventually will be getting married, probably after the baby is born. She has asked me to have a shower for her and I gladly said yes. Now a coworker has said it is inappropriate for a grandma to give a shower. Who is right?

A: Contemporary etiquette does allow family members to host showers in celebration of the new life. You can feel perfectly correct in doing so.

There was a time when it was not considered proper for a family member to host a shower. Because the point of a shower is to provide the honoree with gifts it appeared self-serving if an immediate family member hosted. However, those ideas, and the rules along with them, have changed. Enjoy hosting the shower and the new grandchild.

Dear Thelma: My son will be getting married out of town where his fiancée's family lives. I know that very few of our family members and probably none of our friends will be able to attend the wedding. Therefore, we plan to have a celebration locally, sometime after the wedding, to introduce the couple to our friends in town. This celebration may be six to eight months after the wedding because of their school schedules.

Our family and closest friends will be invited to the wedding, regardless of whether they are expected to attend. However, I'm unsure of whether to invite our local friends to both the wedding and the later celebration, or if they should just be invited to the later celebration. What is the proper etiquette in this situation?

A: If it's within your means to do so, I believe that all of them should be invited to both celebrations. Even if they cannot attend, people enjoy hearing first hand of the blessed event and the honor of a wedding invitation.

Make it clear by the wording and style of your second invitation that this event is an introduction and not a second, very-late wedding reception. Present the celebration as a time to gather together and enjoy the company of the newly-married couple. If it is not made clear, guests may feel it necessary to bring gifts as they would at a reception, which shouldn't be the purpose of this gathering.

Any gifts wedding guests choose to give should be given as close to the time of the wedding as possible.

Gracious hosting and good manners never go out of style.

Dear Readers: As the holidays approach I begin thinking about opportunities for celebration. For me, hosting a dinner party is a happy responsibility. Here's how I go about it.

The first thing I consider is the "why" of having a dinner party. The reason I cherish most is to bring together an intimate group of people who I want to celebrate as being my friends. Creating an occasion for these wonderful people get to know each other is a delight for me.

My second consideration is the guest list. The ultimate success of the evening is very much dependent on the combination of people I invite. Most frequently I try to limit a dinner party in my home to eight people. This size of group creates the most opportunities for everyone to connect.

I work to develop a list of people who will enjoy being together. My thought process behind creating the mix changes for each dinner I plan, so why I include certain individuals and leave others for another fun evening remains for me to decide. When planning a list, I must be considerate of those invited and not put anyone in an uncomfortable situation.

I enjoy sending my guests a handwritten invitation. I believe the sentiment indicates I'm planning an extra-special evening for them and it heightens their anticipation and festivity.

Once my guests have responded, I create place cards for them and arrange their seating at the dinner table. The cards eliminate the need for me to stand at the table and say, "You sit here and you sit there." They also are an essential ingredient for a fun and conversational dinner party.

I like to arrange the seating so that husband and wife do not sit next to each other – when you're sitting next to someone you don't know well, you're more motivated to socialize and it provides the maximum opportunity for everyone to get acquainted.

As host, I sit at the head of the table. From that spot I can initiate or consolidate the conversation if necessary. If two tables are used I ask in advance for a particular guest at the second table to exchange places with me at some point in the meal. I select someone I know will be comfortable doing this and plan it with him or her privately ahead of time.

I also plan for my time to be spent with my guests and not spent entirely in the kitchen.

Too much time in the kitchen creates an atmosphere where the guests begin to think that they should help and then they become not guests but helpers for the evening. Good hosts, good parties and good manners never go out of style.

Dear Thelma: What is the polite way to tell friends you no longer want to exchange Christmas gifts with them?

A: A conversation has to take place in this instance. It is important for your friends to know the reason for ending the exchange so that they don't feel slighted or that you're interested in ending the relationship along with the exchange.

Tell your friends honestly that due to a need to simplify or financial constraints you would like to end the customary exchange. If possible, ask if they'd like to plan to do something together instead. The gift of time is often the best gift of all.

Dear Thelma: My daughter in-law recently invited my husband and myself to our twin grandsons' 1st birthday and addressed the card to Maria and John. I am very upset at the way it was addressed. Am I being too sensitive even when she knows how this bothers us? We have a very good relationship with them but I do feel out of respect for us Nanny and Popi should be used.

A: Your daughter-in-law has addressed the invitation correctly. Loving nicknames are not generally used in addresses on envelopes. In addition, the invitation is coming from the host of the party – your daughter-in-law, who probably calls you Maria and John – not from your grandsons. You are being too sensitive.

Dear Thelma: What should I do if I am hosting a dinner party and guests are late?

A: Latecomers to a small, intimate dinner should always notify you in advance that they will be late and how late they will be. If they know ahead of time, they should let you know as soon as they are aware of it. If something detains them that evening, they should call as soon as possible.

Waiting 30 minutes prior to seating everyone is more than sufficient. This pre-dinner time is usually reserved for guests to have drinks, greet one another and be introduced to new friends. When these activities start to dwindle and the food is ready to be served, it is fine to start dinner without the tardy guests.

Seating can be quickly rearranged if you make your own call and discover the latecomers won't attend, or you may leave it as is so they have places when they do arrive. After graciously accepting their apologies and welcoming them to the table, start them with the course the rest of the group is being served. However, if you've already progressed to dessert, offer to serve them the main course.

Gracious entertaining and good manners never go out of style.

Dear Thelma: Receiving guests – whether I know them or not – is stressful. Do you have any tips on how I can help me and our guests feel more at ease?

A: First off, you need to want to have guests. If you are in some way resentful or even just ambivalent about your guests, that will show and create feelings of unease in every one. Next, do all you can to properly plan for having guests. If you're not prepared for them, you will be stressed and your guests will feel it too.

Wanting to have guests translates to wanting to make them feel welcome. Make your home and the activities you plan comfortable and inviting.

You should be a part of what you plan for guests. Don't give them the car keys and say here's where I've planned for you to go. Time spent with your guests is an important ingredient to making them feel they are welcome and are not an imposition.

When you view receiving guests as giving the gift of your time as much as anything else, you'll be more likely to truly set it aside. That will help you avoid the anxiety created when you really aren't taking the time to connect with your guests.

Dear Thelma: I recently sent out invitations to a 50th wedding anniversary dinner. Space was limited so we had to select guests carefully. We would have loved to include everyone. My question is what do you do when people send back the RSVP card with additional guests listed that were not invited? I don't want to cause hurt feelings; however, space is very limited.

A: What your invitees have done is out-of-line. Invitations always list exactly who is being invited to an event. They may read "Mr. and Mrs. Garcia," "Mr. and Mrs. Cline and Children," or "Mr. Sam Jones and Guest." The wording in these cases is very clear. A guest inviting additional people is wrong.

As the host, I believe it is in your power to call these guests and politely explain the situation: "We have very limited space for this event and our guest list is tied directly to that space. Although we would have liked to invite more guests, we're just not able to accommodate additional people. I hope you understand our situation."

This communication should be in person or by telephone and should allow for the invitee to express why he or she felt the need to add the uninvited. If it is important enough, you may look for a way to work the guest in, but don't feel you have too. Your list is entirely up to you.

Guest relations and good manners never go out of style.

Dear Readers: It's the time of year that places much of our focus on giving gifts. I encourage you to use your heartsense as you consider your gift-giving list.

A gift should show that you are thinking of the receiver and that you value their place in your life. But the perfect gift doesn't have to be wrapped up and tied with a bow. Often, time spent with a person can be the most valuable gift you can give.

A friend of mine took this advice to heart this year. Her family's tradition with another family was to exchange gifts for the children. Knowing each other well, and knowing the full toy boxes at each home, gift ideas were harder to come by.

My friend realized that what the children enjoy most is spending time together. So rather than exchanging toys, she proposed that they take a family outing together. Minus the wrapping paper and bows, the 10 of them will spend a day ice skating together during winter break – a day to remember.

There are many ways we give and show that we're thinking of someone. While it may come from a catalog or a department store, it doesn't have to – but it does have to come from the heart.

Dear Readers: I've been thinking about children and the holidays. Much of the focus of the season is placed on letters to Santa and grabbing up the hot new toy to please a child. Perhaps it's time more energy was placed on creating opportunities that allow children to give.

I know one family that sat down as a group and decided how they would give this year. Together they chose to sponsor a family that couldn't afford much for Christmas. Their 11-year-old had $20 saved and ready to commit to the cause. Her six-year-old brother had $5.

By participating in the discussion from the beginning the children were able to make helping those in need a focus of their own holiday celebration.

Whether you plan to head to the nearest Giving Tree or even try to get your kids to come up with gifts for each other, talk them beforehand. Encourage them to understand why giving is important and rewarding. Given the opportunity, I think they'll love having the chance to give.

Dear Thelma: My job often requires me to attend social events with leaders of various religious denominations, especially during the holiday season. As a protestant, I am not overly familiar with forms of address for these individuals. Can you offer a quick referral guide when addressing Catholic bishops and priests, Jewish rabbis and pastors of protestant faiths other than my own? I don't wish to offend these individuals, and am unsure if it is appropriate for me to address them in the way a member of their faith would.

A: It is always polite and appropriate to use a person's official title when greeting and speaking with them. Pay special attention when you are introduced to a person with a religious title; a proper introduction will give you the immediate information you need.

Address a Catholic archbishop or bishop as "Your Excellency" or "Archbishop Sheehan." If he prefers that you call him "Archbishop Michael," he will tell you. A Catholic priest is properly addressed as "Father Sanchez," or if he prefers "Father Steve" or simply "Father." A Catholic nun is addressed as "Sister Margaret" or "Sister."

A Jewish rabbi is addressed as "Rabbi Rosenblum" or simply "Rabbi."

Reverend, Pastor, Dr., Mr. and Ms. are used among protestant faiths. Again, take note of how the clergyperson is introduced to you and use that title. And if you're still unsure, it's never wrong to ask the person how they prefer to be addressed.

A sincere heart and good manners never go out of style.

Ask Thelma 2007
Growing in Gratefulness

Dear Thelma: I attended cocktail parties and hosted my own party this holiday season and found the martini glass to be very awkward. What is the proper way to hold it? Is it supposed to be held by the stem or by the base? It can be quite unmanageable.

A: Martini glasses are designed so that you can consume the cocktail as it was meant to be consumed – while cold. People go to great lengths – chilling the shaker, the liquor and the glasses – to be sure the drink is cold. The glass is designed to keep it that way while you sip.

If you place your hands around the glass itself, heat from your hands will affect the temperature of the drink. Hold the glass by its stem close to the bottom of its triangular bowl. This will give you a solid hold, but you will avoid warming the drink. Holding the glass by its base or at the stem near the base is too cumbersome. Its top-heavy bowl may tip and spill.

Remember that during cocktail hours when you would expect to greet friends and meet new people, hold any drink you have in your left hand. Doing so will leave your right hand warm, dry and free for shaking. Also, it is best to eat or drink, rather than tying your hands up by doing both at the same time. If both your hands are full, you won't be able to give a proper handshake.

Dear Thelma: In your column discussing the differences between American and Continental dining styles, do the same rules apply to those who are left-handed or should one use the opposite hands?

A: As a left-handed person, hold your utensils in the opposite hands of those described previously for your right-handed dinner companion. That means hold the knife in your left hand, the hand with which you have the most control, and the fork in your right hand.

Also, if you are the host of a dinner out or of a dinner party at home and you know that a guest is left-handed, seat that person at the left corner of a table so that elbow bumping with a right-handed neighbor won't be a problem. If you're left-handed and invited to a dinner, it's fine to let the host know so that he or she can seat you most comfortably.

Handling things properly and good manners never go out of style.

Dear Thelma: In line at a store, I was privy to a cell phone conversation involving raised voices and foul language. It was very disturbing. I was ready to put my purchases down and leave the store. What is the appropriate way to handle such a situation?

A: The least gracious and possibly the most unsafe thing to do is to elevate the situation by causing a confrontation between yourself and the person who has offended you.

If you feel you must intervene, start by contacting the store manager or other personnel and ask that person to speak with the cell phone offender.

If that's not possible and you feel compelled to intervene personally, place special attention on what you say and by your tone of voice. With a calm voice and a friendly face you might say, "Excuse me, I can't help overhearing your conversation. Would you be able to lower your voice?"

If the person has an interest in graciousness and simply let himself or herself get caught up in the conversation, he or she may honor your request. However, be prepared for the fact that some people don't understand or don't care about phone boundaries or manners and may ignore your request or even lash out at you. Respond graciously by simply leaving the situation as best and as quickly as you can.

Dear Readers: I'd like you to consider starting the New Year off with a commitment to the good manners of technology.

With technology changing so quickly and people embracing it at so many different levels, how do we know what are the good manners of technology? We know by remembering that manners are about thinking of others before ourselves and treating people with respect and courtesy in all our actions – even those dominated by technology.

That means giving your full attention to the people you meet face-to-face, whether it's your boss running the staff meeting or the grocery store clerk. It also means considering how your technology use affects those around you. At the airport, in a store, on the other end of that email message, pay attention to the effect your technology use is having or will have on other people.

My top five techno-etiquette standards are:

5. The iPod should never isolate you. Its constant use will create a permanent barrier to starting and building important relationships. Be sure to take off both ear buds when someone needs your attention.

4. The disclaimer at the end of your PDA email – "Sent from my wireless handheld device" – is not a license to use poor grammar and spelling. You send a message about yourself with every message you send. Do all that you can to send an intelligent and clear message, even when faced with the limitations of a handheld.

3. The person before you always takes precedence over a cell phone conversation. Unless it's an emergency, the gracious cell user defers calls to voicemail and addresses the matter and the person at hand. That includes your dinner companion as well as the coffee shop cashier.

2. Carefully review every email and text you send. Verify your recipients, check the spelling, and read it with an eye for its clarity and tone.

More than 90 percent of face-to-face communication comes in the form of body language, facial expression, and voice pitch and tone. Less than 10 percent comes from the words spoken. Without the benefits of facial expressions and voice tone, subtleties can be lost and sarcasm misunderstood. For successful and efficient electronic communication, messages should be clear and concise with obvious meaning.

1. Your cell phone conversation should absolutely never make others uncomfortable or be a distraction to them. Keep conversations conducted in public short and quiet. Cell users must realize that if not kept in check, their conversations cause true frustration for others, and that's just not nice.

In the embrace of new technology, good manners never go out of style.

Dear Readers: Recently I went to the pharmacy in a hurry. I took out my wallet and left my handbag in the car.

When I stepped out of the store, my car was in full view and I saw a woman standing next to it. Her ragged clothes and unkempt look startled me, and I didn't want her near my car. She caught my glance and motioned me over with a wave of her hand.

On my guard, I approached her and she said to me: "I don't want you to be concerned about me, but I saw that your car was unlocked and I saw two men walking around it. I noticed your purse inside thought I should stay nearby."

Well, I thanked her for her kindness, but felt terrible about the prejudgments I had made. While we do have to be cautious in our current times and protect our selves and our property, we must also take time to assess before leaping to conclusions.

The dictionary defines prejudgment as the act of judging a person, issue or case before sufficient evidence is available. Are we really aware of how much we prejudge people or situations even of the most innocent and simple kinds? Negative prejudgments often are made in working and family relationships and in friendships.

When we prejudge, we place a label on a person. Often times, that label prevents us from clear communication, causing us to focus on the label rather than on the content of a conversation. None of us is free of this and it's something we can work to avoid if we seek healthy communication as a part of our lives.

Dear Thelma: What would you suggest is the appropriate response to a child who has not received a card or gift, much less a phone call from their biological mother during the holiday?

A: I would say that this is a time to avoid prejudgment.

Children have a great capacity to love and to forgive, if we allow them to use it. By keeping our own prejudgments about the situation or the person to ourselves, we can help that child to preserve the good feelings he or she has concerning that important relationship.

You don't say that the child is upset about this situation, only that he or she may need an explanation. I would suggest a response like this: "For some reason your mom hasn't been able to contact you. We don't know why that is, but we have to keep in mind what we do know, and that is that you love each other. We'll hope together that you do hear from her soon."

Like preserving good relationships, good manners never go out of style.

Dear Thelma: I recently attended an event that included many high ranking government officials and dignitaries. What interested me were the different ways people positioned their hands during the posting of the colors, the Pledge of Allegiance, and the national anthem. These were people who should know the proper salute, but they did so many different things. What are the proper postures for honoring our nation?

A: I have seen the same confusion at official events I have attended, and you are right in saying that these are people who should know the proper protocol for civic functions. Unfortunately, many may not have learned correctly or have forgotten. Perhaps we can help.

I have found the National Flag Foundation to be the best resource for information concerning proper treatment and attention to our flag and have relied on its expertise for the answers to your question.

Before the ceremony begins, all guests should be called into the banquet room and seated so that they are ready to give proper respect to the flag. When the posting of the colors begins all present stand and direct their attention to the flag as it approaches its place of honor. As the flag passes you, place your right hand over your heart, just as a member of the armed forces would salute as the flag passes. Once the flag has passed, you may remove your hand but remain at attention. Keep focus on the flag until the bearers have put it into holder and completed their salute.

While reciting the Pledge of Allegiance face the flag and place the right hand over the heart with the first word of the pledge. Hold that salute through the pledge's last word. If you are not a U.S. citizen or choose not to recite such a pledge, stand as a sign of respect but do not repeat the words or offer the salute.

During the singing or playing of "The Star Spangled Banner," citizens should stand, face the flag, and salute by placing the right hand over the heart. Hold that position from the start of the national anthem to its final note. You may sing if you wish; however, if you don't choose to sing you must remain quiet. If a flag is not displayed during the anthem, salute and face the source of the music. Those who are not citizens should stand.

In honoring the spirit of our country, good manners never go out of style.

Dear Thelma: I've been struck recently by the poor customer service I've received at institutions that are supposed to be all about service. I can't tell if individual workers just have no sense of how to treat people and that translates into their work or if the businesses just don't make it a point to instruct their workers on proper service. Don't manners and customer service go hand-in-hand?

A: Customer service is a business term for using good manners with your customers. The basis of the two is the same: respect and consideration for those you encounter during your day.

In a hurry to prepare for a trip I stopped at the bank thinking I could pick up some traveler's checks. I asked the teller for them and she told me shortly, "Banks don't handle things like that."

"Can you tell me where I can get them?" I asked.

"I don't know," was her short reply.

As I walked away, marveling in the complete lack of service I had just been provided, a woman next to me approached.

"You can drive up this street to AAA," she said. "They'll take care of it for you and they're really nice." She was right on all counts. I'll always treasure the kindness of the woman who went out of her way to help someone in need.

On the other hand, I will always remember that bank and its teller's lack of respect for me and for her position in customer service. Even if she couldn't provide the product I needed, she could have shown an interest in me as her customer, taken the time to point me in the right direction, or found someone else to help me.

Today's consumer has many options from which to choose. Businesses that make an effort to hire people with good manners and that train and expect strong customer service are at an advantage when customer word-of-mouth recommendations are important. Customers notice and remember when an effort is made on their behalf. An emphasis on courtesy and respect to the customer and to colleagues also makes for a more pleasant place to work.

Customers should also remember that they are not off the hook when it comes to good manners when receiving a service. The words "please" and "thank you" are wise to use in any situation, and treating another person with courtesy and respect will help you receive the same consideration in return.

On either side of a transaction, good manners never go out of style.

Dear Thelma: I've finally gone and done what my younger co-workers say is a must for dating in this day and age: I put my profile on an online dating service. How does etiquette fit in here?

A: The most important thing to remember is that good manners have as much place online as they do in every other aspect of life. If you are serious about meeting people and establishing a special relationship, etiquette gives you a framework for putting your best foot forward in any venue.

Focus on the fact that you are communicating with a living,

breathing human being. That person should receive the courtesy and respect due any relationship.

Start by being honest in your profile and posting recent photos of yourself. Personalize your email messages. Respect the privacy of new friends and don't press for personal information. Allow a person to respond to a message before sending another.

Use email etiquette when communicating with new online friends. Start your message with a greeting (Dear Sam, Hi Pat) and end with a closing (Sincerely, Cheers) and your name. Review you message before you send it, watching out for sarcasm or humor that can be misconstrued. Use spell check.

Do your best to reply within one week to those who contact you. Although some online dating advocates say not responding when you aren't interested is acceptable, the truly polite thing to do is to reply with a short "Thank you, but I'm not interested," message.

If you decide to meet face-to-face with someone you've met online, start with a short date in a public place. Meet for coffee or lunch. Follow-up with an email thanking the person for meeting you. Depending on your feelings, that email may be a "thanks, but I don't think we're a match" or a "thanks, I had a great time" message.

If you've seen someone a few times and have decided a romantic relationship is not in the future, let that person know as soon as you realize it. You'll be tempted to end it with an email message, but a conversation by phone or in person is much more sensitive to their feelings.

Using an online dating service allows you to meet many people who are also interested in meeting many people. So how do you know when it's time to take down your profile and focus on one special person? Have a face-to-face conversation with that person to share your interest in an exclusive relationship and find out if he or she feels the same.

Like clear communication – online and in-person – good manners never go out of style.

Dear Thelma: Wedding etiquette normally suggests that the father of the groom host, pay for, and participate in the planning of a rehearsal dinner, and the bride's father handle the wedding reception. My son and his bride inform me that they have made all arrangements themselves, including deposit for caterers and for venue. It is her second marriage. He is a millionaire.

I know that they are underwriting the reception perhaps to relieve her family of the expense. Should I insist on reimbursing my son for the rehearsal dinner – knowing that he will refuse and regard the overture as a hollow gesture or worse, a putdown on his own style?

A: The customary ways of dividing wedding costs – based more upon tradition springing out of necessity than etiquette – do not always fit the situation in today's world. Many couples marrying today are well-established wage earners and it's very common for them to fund their own weddings. There should be no sense of impropriety surrounding the practice.

Insisting upon reimbursing your son is not necessary and, according to your own words, may damage your relationship. You don't want anything you choose to do to be viewed as a hollow gesture or a putdown. It's important to follow your heartsense in a decision like this. The success of your son is something to be proud of. Accept his decision to take care of the costs on his own because you respect and love him. Don't do something that will hurt him because you feel it's "proper."

While dispensing with the monetary tradition, you shouldn't be barred from participation in the planning and hosting of the event. Talk with your son about taking an active role in making the occasion special and handling other traditional roles filled by the father of the groom like greeting guests as a host at the rehearsal dinner. You definitely should not be treated as a guest at your own son's wedding but as a participant in the in this joining of two families.

The independence of young people who have money is hard for some of us to accept. When we focus instead on accepting one another's intentions graciously, we find it possible to grow in love and respect.

Like tradition respected out of love rather than obligation, good manners never go out of style.

Dear Thelma: I recently attended a fundraising event that included a dinner and dance. The dance floor was small and sometimes very crowded. That didn't matter to a number of couples who seemed to believe they were auditioning for "Dancing with the Stars." Are my partner and I to make way for them or are they obliged to tone it down when the floor is crowded?

A: Common courtesy and common sense tell us that when the dance floor is crowded, everyone should make an effort to keep their dancing compact and their elbows in close. It may even require you to alter your style until more space is available or to move to a more open area if there is one. Respect those around you by doing so.

If you bump into someone or fling your partner into another couple, do apologize and take note of any alterations you need to make to avoid it happening again.

Of course if a couple is oblivious to this need for dance for courtesy, give them room if only to protect yourself.

Dear Thelma: A manager at work invited me and my husband to attend a benefit dinner as guests at a table purchased by our company. The evening also includes a silent auction to raise funds for the organization holding the benefit. Am I obliged to purchase a silent auction item in exchange for the free evening?

A: You are not obliged to purchase a silent auction item. However, there are two points to remember – it is a company table so use your best representational skills and be pleasant to everyone.

While the manager may have invited you because of your interest in the organization or the cause benefiting from the auction to allow you the opportunity to support it, there is no requirement to do so.

Do express your thanks for the evening by sending your manager a letter or email within three or four days. Describe what you enjoyed most and thank him or her for the invitation and the fun evening you shared.

Dear Thelma: If I'm low on cell phone minutes, can I ask people to call me back on a "land line"?

A: If you gave them the cell number, then you should expect their calls at that number. It would be rude to ask them to call you back. However, you may ask if you may call them right back, and then you can switch to the land line.

Even during the daily buzz, good manners never go out of style.

Dear Thelma: My brother is getting married for the third time. This is his fiancée's first marriage. Should I send a wedding gift? I feel I have given already since he has kept the items from the other marriages.

A: Although you may be frustrated with your brother, the point of a wedding gift is to let the couple know you share in their happiness and wish them well for the future. If you decide not to give a gift, what message will that send about the importance you place on your relationship with your brother and your new sister-in-law? Will withholding a gift damage those relationships? Will giving a gift help strengthen your connection? Let these answers guide you.

You may choose to give something more personal or creative than the household items they may register for – something that shows your interest in the success of their marriage or something that your own relationships have taught you it is important.

Gifts of any kind are never mandatory, but wedding gifts are customary and are always in order when you have received a wedding invitation – even a third wedding invitation.

Dear Thelma: Why do people bring their young children to restaurants that are clearly focused on serving adults? No one seems to enjoy themselves in these situations, not the parents, not the children and certainly not the other diners. Even the wait staff often seems annoyed. Wouldn't it be kind for parents be more discriminating in their dining choices?

A: I believe kids should have the opportunity to enjoy a kid's life and adults should be allowed to enjoy an adult's. And I agree that parents should think carefully – with the children in mind – when making choices about dining out.

The first concern should be the comfort of those dining around you. If the restaurant you are choosing is the type of place couples go for an adult evening away from their own kids, you must understand their frustrations if they've paid for a sitter, yet still have to deal with the playful antics of children or the fussing of a baby. Be sensitive to others when deciding whether to take your children to a fine restaurant.

Be sensitive to others, but also be sensitive to your children. Consider whether you really want to force your children into what essentially is an adult experience. The pace of a fine meal may be too slow for young children who are used to being served soon after sitting down and expect to be excused promptly when finished. The bill of fare also may lack desirable tastes for young palates. Long wait times and dissatisfied tummies may lead to misbehavior born not out of ill-mannered children, but out of understandable boredom, hunger and frustration.

If it's important to you to provide a fine dining experience to your kids, especially as they reach a new level of maturity, pick an appropriate time for it. Choose brunch, lunch or very early on a weekday evening when the establishment may be less crowded and the meal's pace may move more quickly. Before you go, let the children know what to expect and what will be expected of them. Practice proper table manners at home on a regular basis first.

Until they are ready for that outing, there are plenty of kid-friendly restaurants, where neither the parents nor the children have the tension of watching and being watched so closely. I encourage parents to connect with kids in those environments that are best suited for them. Like making sensitive choices, good manners never go out of style.

Dear Thelma: My daughter is expecting a baby in August. She told me today that her friends shouldn't have to pay for the baby shower and that I should pay for it. What is customary? My other daughter's friends held a baby shower for her and the issue never came up. I have always tried to make sure that we treat all the children equally.

A: The duties of any host or hosts include paying for the expenses of the celebration. If your daughter's friends do not have the means to pay for the shower, then they should not offer to host one.

Customarily you accept someone's offer to host a shower for you, you do not ask them to hold a party in your honor and you especially do not demand it. If your daughter would like you to host a shower for her, then she should ask you in a more respectful and kind way. If she's having a child, it's time to grow up.

Dear Thelma: Please remind your readers that customer service etiquette goes both ways. Service people are human and deserve to be treated with respect, rather than face imperious demands and have things thrown at them, which I witnessed at a grocery store. Don't grunt at service people when asked a question, which I witnessed at a bank. The people helping you are exactly that, people.

A: You're right. We must demand courtesy and respect of ourselves if we expect to receive it.

Along those lines I've found a disturbing trend facing the service industry: Customers who do not respect the appointments they have made. Whether it's a doctor visit, a dinner reservation or a salon appointment, if you cannot make the appointment do give as much notice as possible so that your appointment time can be given away. We must respect the service provider and his or her time just as we expect our time to be respected.

On the flip side, it also shows respect for the client when appointments are kept on schedule by the provider. Recently my own scheduled doctor's visit was not kept. I was kept waiting for over an hour and left upset before seeing the doctor. My respectful physician called me later that day and apologized for the problem, showing me that he did care about my time, my needs and my respect for him.

It's an old rule, but still the best: treat others as you want to be treated.

Dear Thelma: Spring break season is upon us and that means more traveling families and college students. Can you publish some airplane etiquette tips for us?

A: Considering that the amount of personal space that the average person needs to feel comfortable is roughly the size of an elevator, airline travel causes us to trespass on one another every time we enter a plane. Consideration for each other is the key to comfort.

Start with what you choose to wear on your trip. Dress in your own style, but in a way that respects the sensitivities of other travelers. Need further guidance? Consider whether what you've chosen would scandalize the 11-year-old and his grandmother traveling together. Also pay attention to your personal grooming. Don't overdo the perfume, but don't go deodorant-free.

Carry your bag in front of you as you board the plane being very careful not to bump already those already seated. Place it carefully in the overhead bin above your seat and offer to help anyone you see struggling with a bag.

Mind your own and others' personal space – what little there is of it. Keep your hands, feet, knees and belongings in your own area and avoid hogging the armrests.

Some people look forward to making new friends. Some don't. Learn to recognize both. If you've been chatting with someone and now are ready to stop, simply tell them you're going to do another activity: "I think I'll do some reading now." If someone is politely engaging in your conversation, read any non-verbal signs they give that they'd like some quiet time. Once they take out a book, computer or headphones, respect their need for privacy.

Children can be an in-flight challenge for passengers and parents alike. Little can be done about a child's excited squeals of delight or the cries that come from pressure changes. However, parents can keep kids' feet and hands off the back of the seat in front of them. Instruct children to leave the tray tables alone and attempt to keep excited noise under control.

Avoid behavior that's likely to disturb. Refrain from pulling on the seatback of the person in front of you or slamming the tray table closed. Keep the music coming from your headphones down. If you must hold a business meeting in the aisle, use low tones so other passengers aren't forced to become party to your conversation.

When deplaning, allow the people in front of you to move into the aisle first. Your kind restraint will make the exit more pleasant for everyone.

Airline travel may test our manners mettle, but good manners never go out of style.

Dear Thelma: How should a coach handle parents disgruntled over minor issues especially when said parents do not have knowledge of the game or what it means to play on a team?

A: Volunteer coaches are often put into a position of spending much of their time thinking about and dealing with parent issues. It seems to come with the territory.

It's best to handle disagreements with parents as unemotionally as possible. All parents feel an intense desire to see their child appreciated and cared for and kept from harm – whether it's physical or emotional harm. If you can take the emotion out of your response to their complaint, the volatility of the situation should be cut in half.

Truly listen to the grievance. Then make a comment that lets the parent know he or she has been heard. If it's appropriate for you to apologize, then do so sincerely. If time is needed to let emotions cool, you might consider a response like: "I've heard what you've said. I will think about it and get back to you tomorrow." Then follow through.

Work to maintain good communication with parents throughout the season so that they understand your methodology. Their concerns may be put at ease if they can see your entire strategy.

As for parents, it's important to keep at the front of your minds that these coaches are volunteers spending their valuable time providing instruction for your children. They aren't paid experts in a particular sport or in child psychology. They need your help to model what being a team player means. They need your help to motivate your child to get the most out of practice by paying attention and giving her best.

Parents should realize that the most important part of a child's athletic experience will take place at practices. That's where all the instruction takes place and all the learning is done. You should spend most of your time watching what goes on at practices. Observe the instruction so you can reinforce it at home. Study how your child behaves and whether he needs motivation from home. If your child runs a lot of laps during practice, it's most likely because he is not paying attention to what's being taught or said. Discuss that with him.

Games are the test at the end of the week. If your child has prepared well in practice she'll be able to do her best at the games. If she's arrived late, missed practice or not paid attention during it, it will show at the game in how well she does and in what opportunities she is given.

From the field of play to the sidelines, good manners never go out of style

Dear Readers: An interesting evening began as we parked our car at a restaurant that boasts "the world's greatest hamburger." We waited to open our door while the SUV parked next to us unloaded three children and three adults.

When we reached the restaurant two boys – both age 7, I learned later – were holding the door for us. As we thanked them they took time to greet us with smiles that welcomed us right in.

These little boys so intrigued me that I decided I had to meet them. I introduced myself to their mother and asked if I could talk to them to see why they held the door open and why they seemed like such happy kids. She allowed me to.

By this time the three boys were all seated together at a table waiting for their order. Picture a total stranger asking to sit down and talk to them for a few minutes. Stone, Jadin and Andreus greeted me, shook hands with me and were very comfortable with my joining them. Two of these boys are brothers and one a very good friend. My question to them was: "Why did you hold the door open for us?"

The conversation that followed would fill anyone's heart with joy. They held the door open because at home they are taught to be nice to people and respect people by doing even little things for everyone whenever they can.

They informed me that every evening at dinner they talk about what the best thing and the worst thing was that happened at school that day. They said the best things are always fun and the worst thing is talked about so that their parents can help them learn what to do make that particular situation better if it comes up again.

These three boys love talking with their parents because to quote one of the boys: "Mom and Dad teach us to be better people and to be good people all our life!"

The key statement of the conversation for me was this: "We are taught that we need to love each other at home so we can love everyone else all the time." My thanks to Mom and Dad for teaching love by living lives of loving each other.

I was blessed with the privilege of meeting three happy kids, the kind of kids that will always do their part to keep the world wonderful and to make it better and better.

These kids know good manners never go out of style.

Dear Readers: My community recently marked the passing of a local institution – a private dinner club where the city's business elite met for 51 years. Some bemoaned its passing as the end of an era in which business networking was marked by fine dining in your finest attire with the finest of friends.

But the tone of some tributes to the place left me with that feeling that some of the lamenters were being critical of today's younger professionals. It seemed to convey that because they didn't want to dress up for a two-hour lunch they were less than professional.

That is not the case. Networking has become a much more spontaneous part of what professionals do all the time. They do accomplish all they need to do in representing their companies, yet they use different venues and different means than were employed 50, 30 or even 10 years ago. They are still going somewhere to establish relationships, but they are connecting more informally in a variety of places.

Relationship-building is a skill to develop and an expectation of performance to meet. With the more casual and spontaneous approach, professionals must be even more skilled in knowing what their organization is about and truly representing it all the time.

While there will always be a place for fine dining in business relationships, don't limit yourself by thinking it's the only place.

Dear Thelma: My parents request my wife address them as Mom and Dad, but she thinks she should call them by their first names. Believing in formal manners, my parents abhor their daughter-in-law (or son) to use their first names. They say she can call them Mr. or Mrs. if she doesn't like using Mom and Dad. Who is correct?

A: Your question moves beyond correctness and into an area I like to call heartsense. Your parents' respect for your wife as part of the family shows in their request that she call them Mom and Dad. They are not attempting to distance her by requiring her to call them Mr. and Mrs. They've used their heartsense to create choices for her that don't go against their own upbringing and sense of decorum.

Your wife now must use her heart to choose the address that will show her respect for them and allow her to feel comfortable. Addressing them as Mom and Dad may feel too intimate or Mr. and Mrs. too distant, but if she makes a reasoned choice and begins to use it, it will soon feel natural.

Dear Thelma: My sister and I want to give a baby shower for our sister-in-law. Our mother thinks she needs to be involved and throw the shower also. Our problem is that she doesn't have any finances to help with the shower and we don't know what to tell her. She gets her feelings hurt very easily. Any ideas to tell the grandma-to-be in this situation?

A: The kindest thing would be for you to include her despite her lack of finances. Can she help decorate? Can she prepare food? Can she help clean up afterwards?

I have written recently that the duty of the shower host is to pay for the expenses of the celebration. But in this situation it sounds like you and your sister are the hosts and are willing to take on those expenses. Excluding your mother in the planning and the operation would simply be unkind.

If in the planning her ideas outweigh your pocketbooks, just say, "Sorry, Mom, our budget can't cover that," and go on to the next idea. Grandmothers are important people; love her enough to find a way to include her.

Dear Thelma: Thank you for your recent column on dining out with children. We are a military family, and are serving in the Diplomatic Corps overseas. There are many reasons to expose children to habits and customs of cordial, fine dining. There have been times when our family has been invited to dinner in the home of business associates. Despite the word "casual" on the invitation, we are expected to behave with a certain level of decorum. I am delighted when my children display proper etiquette at the table. They would not have this awareness had we not exposed them at an early age to public dining manners with adults.

We do take them early to fine restaurants, and have even called the establishments ahead of time to tell them of our intentions. The staff is usually delighted to be a part of the subtle and important task of incorporating manners and etiquette into the life of a child.

I agree that as a family we should choose off-peak hours. Children are often hungry early in the evening, and become restless when taken out too late. We have gradually worked up to standard evening hours so that the children see all environments of fine dining. After all, how did the adults of today learn to practice good manners? Someone, hopefully a parent, exposed them so that they established good habits. Children learn best when they are surrounded by, and praised for, good manners.

A: Your children will know good manners never go out of style.

Dear Thelma: I am a high school teacher. I know the tradition has always been to remove hats in the classroom out of respect. The question students ask that I really don't have an answer for is this: Who are they disrespecting when they wear their ball caps in class?

A: Students disrespect no one person in particular when they do not remove their hats in class. What they are rejecting are societal norms that spring from a historical tradition that has much to do with respect and reverence for authority in general.

This tradition is said to stem from medieval times. A knight lifted his face guard with his hand to show who he was, originating the military salute. Knights returning from battle entered the castle and took off their helmets as a sign of reverence before the king. These military traditions are thought to have been adopted by nobility and their households and carried on through the centuries to become a part of the etiquette of modern culture.

At the turn of the 20th century, hats continued to be functional. No longer armor for a battle, they now were part of good hygiene, serving as protection from industrial dirt in the cities and the outdoor work of rural life. Hats continued to be tipped or removed when meeting someone to show respect or friendliness – like the knights of old lifting a face guard or a military salute. Hats were taken off indoors to show a higher level of civility or respect for what goes on inside. In times of old, hats served their purpose outdoors.

Perhaps with the exception of baseball players and working cowboys, most hats today are more fashion than function. I doubt most pitchers and ranch hands want to wear their sweaty, dirty hats at the dinner table, but for most students, hats are simply an accessory – part of their look for the day. Viewed as such, the need for hat etiquette can seem unnecessary and even nonsensical. While there's nothing particularly bad about wearing a hat inside, taking it off shows your level of respect for the society that you live in and its traditions of civility.

Along with serving as a place to learn academics, school is a place to learn to function in our society. It's important we learn the standards expected of us. And in our society, for now, tradition calls for the removal of hats in the classroom.

Asking good questions and good manners never go out of style.

Dear Thelma: My company recently consolidated its two large local offices into one huge, new building. Some people seem to be having trouble with elevator etiquette. It's difficult to get on and off when you need to, and cell phone use seems acceptable to some and annoying to others. Can you tell us what we need to know?

A: Elevators make many of us uncomfortable. Riding with people who don't care to use the ride as a time to show consideration for others can make it even more difficult. However, if each of us makes the effort to be courteous, the trip between floors becomes more comfortable for everyone.

The amount of personal space most people require is equal to about the size of an elevator. In these close quarters, it's important to keep additional ventures into the personal space of others at a minimum.

When the elevator arrives, stand back and allow the riders to exit before charging in to claim your space. If you have entered the elevator and see someone rushing to catch it, hold the open-door button for him and make room.

Finish your cell phone conversation before you enter the elevator. Once on, if you decide to talk with other riders, stick to a generic topic, like the weather. Speak quietly and avoid subjects that are personal or confidential.

Face the elevator doors as you ride. Doing the opposite may be entertaining for you as you watch people's reaction, but it really does make everyone uncomfortable as you invade their personal space further by forcing them to look you in the eye.

In a crowded elevator everyone at the front should get off when the doors open – even if they are not at their floor – to allow those behind them to emerge. After the car has emptied, get back on and proceed to your floor. If you are going to the top floors of a building, make an effort to find a space in the back to stand.

Exit the elevator quickly and to the side to make it easier for those behind you to get off. Whoever is at the front of the elevator should get off first, regardless of gender. If the elevator is not crowded, it's a fine gesture to allow ladies or those who outrank you to exit first.

It is fine to smile at people as they enter and give them a nod goodbye when they leave. If you accidentally push against someone in the elevator, give a quick and sincere "I'm sorry" or "Please excuse me."

Especially in small spaces, good manners never go out of style.

Dear Thelma: What is the proper way to thank a host for being so hospitable in letting you stay in their home for a few days? I want to do something really nice, and really show my gratitude.

A: A sincere note thanking them for their hospitality and a thoughtful gift are the best way to show your gratitude at the end of your stay, along with an invitation to a stay at your home if that's possible.

It's great to think ahead in a situation like this. Once you are in the home and spending time with your hosts, you may not have the opportunity to shop for a gift. If you can, purchase the gift and wrappings before you leave home, and take with you the card and envelope you'll need to write the note at the end of the stay.

Since they've opened their home to you, I assume you know them fairly well. When considering a gift, think about their hobbies or things they enjoy. Do you know they enjoy wine? Add a bottle to their collection. Are they planning a trip? A book on their destination would be appreciated. Do they like to attend live performances? They might enjoy tickets to an event.

Even if you don't feel you know their personalities that well, you can come up with a thoughtful way to express your appreciation with a household item they can use, gift certificates or a basket of goodies.

If you aren't able to purchase a gift before or during your stay, have a flower arrangement or a potted plant delivered to them the next day.

Aside from a gift and note to express your gratitude, being a well-mannered guest is the best thing to do to show your thanks. Contact your hosts two-weeks before your stay and remind them of your arrival and departure dates. A three- to four-day visit is the most you should spend under typical circumstances.

Throughout your stay, pick up after yourself. Make your bed and keep your living space clean. Bring your own toiletries rather than relying on your host for such.

Finally, help with the household chores where appropriate. Offer to make dinner for your hosts or treat them to a nice restaurant. Offering to pay for the groceries is another courteous option. Paying attention to these details will help ensure many happy returns.

When counting on the kindness of others, good manners never go out of style.

Dear Thelma: I belong to a few organizations that this other person belongs to. She is very active in the community, but she is the rudest person I have ever met. She will cut down speakers at meetings. She will cut down owners of businesses at Chamber functions. She talks during events when speakers are talking. The list goes on and on.

It is a small town and people just say, "Oh, 'Sally' is just being 'Sally,'" but she has caused people to leave organizations and people don't join others because of her. Any suggestions?

A: The key words for me in your question are "small town." In a small town, community service organizations and opportunities are limited in number. By necessity everybody belongs to the same organizations. Yours sounds like a case in which there probably isn't room to avoid her and there may not be abundant options for community involvement and networking away from her.

If your town is that small, she should be made aware of how her actions are affecting others, and it can be done in a positive way. If I were in that small town, I would keep track of specific examples of times she is rude or ignores good manners. In a personal and private conversation I would tell her: "People were offended when you criticized the banquet speaker," or "I feel I must let you know that people are leaving the chamber because they heard your negative comments at the meeting last month."

There is nothing wrong with making those kinds of honest comments when the poor behavior is affecting so many people.

Dear Thelma: There is a question going around our office about whether or not a baby shower should be a surprise for the mom-to-be or not. Please help to settle this.

A: I don't see anything wrong with planning a surprise shower for a mother-to-be. Deciding to throw a surprise party for most any occasion is fine if that's what the group wants to do.

There is a lot of fun and emotion to put into planning a surprise. A successful surprise always takes a group of people working together to get it done and it could be fun for an office to do. It gets people working together and creates another opportunity in the office for relationship building.

So, unless there's a real chance that such a surprise as this could put her into early labor, I think you can proceed with surprise plans. It's no surprise; good manners never go out of style.

Dear Thelma: I received my master's degree this month. Being an older, returning student, I didn't see the need at the time send out invitations to the graduation. That seemed more geared to the younger graduates. Now I wish I had sent out something to share the news. Can I?

A: A printed graduation announcement is a great way to stay connected with family and friends and share your news. An announcement, as opposed to an invitation, is strictly what it says it is: an announcement of the accomplishment.

It is likely that your university has printed announcements available for you to purchase. These may have space in which you may neatly hand write your name and your degree. If the announcements are not designed with space for your name, you may have your own social card printed with your name and degree or you may write it by hand on a plain card and include it with the announcement. Send them as soon as possible.

Those receiving announcements are not obliged to send a gift. It would be appropriate to send a card of congratulations, but a gift is not expected.

Dear Thelma: Our daughter is getting married and she and her fiancé need to restrict the number of people who attend the wedding and reception. Is it proper to send invitations to those who they really want to attend and announcements to other friends and not-so-close family? If so, should the announcements be sent after the wedding?

They don't want it to look like they are just trying to get gifts from the uninvited. They truly want to share their good news, but cannot afford to have all of them at the festivities.

A: A wedding announcement is designed to do just what you're asking it to do. It is the best way to share the news with those you aren't able to include on the guest list.

The formality, style and wording of the announcement should match that of the invitations and include the date and place of the wedding. Replace the line that says "request the honor of your presence at the marriage of," with "have the honor of announcing the marriage of."

Unlike wedding invitations, announcements do not carry an expectation of gift-giving. Those who receive announcements may choose to send a gift, but they are never expected to. Sending a note or card of congratulations is proper.

Prepare the announcements for mailing before the wedding takes place so they are ready to send immediately after the event. You may have an attendant or friend mail them the day of the wedding or mail them yourself within a few days after the wedding.

Happy news and good manners never go out of style.

Dear Thelma: Summer pool season is upon us. Please remind your readers of proper manners for the pool – especially those readers with children.

A: As with all manners, respect and consideration for others are key to creating an enjoyable experience for everyone – children and adults alike. Everyone should make use of "please," "thank you" and "excuse me" as they enjoy the water.

On your walk or drive to the pool, talk to your children about the pool's safety rules and your own rules for their behavior. Remind them it is important to walk in swimming areas to avoid slipping and collisions, to obey the lifeguards and to steer clear of rough play that can become dangerous. Ask your older and bigger kids to be aware of and watch out for younger and smaller children.

If you are visiting a pool with a very shallow area designed for toddlers and young children, tell your bigger kids to leave that area to the little ones or to keep their splashing or aggressive play out of that area. If lanes are designated for lap swimming, make sure your children understand people are using them for exercise and that kids should stay away from that area.

If the cannonball is your child's next swimming feat, encourage her to execute it in a location where other swimmers will appreciate it. Balls, noodles, and diving toys are great fun, but make sure kids have enough space to use them to avoid hitting innocent bystanders. If the pool is very crowded, leave large pool toys out of the water.

When claiming tanning space, occupy only one lounge chair per person. Keep your belongings in a confined space so everyone has room to enjoy the pool deck.

For lap swimmers, Dr. Phillip Whitten, author of "The Complete Book of Swimming" offers some good points of pool etiquette, including that when lanes are designated as slow, medium or fast, be sure to choose the lane that best fits your speed.

If two swimmers are sharing a lane they may decide to each keep on their own side of the lane. However, if three or more are sharing, they must circle swim, which in the United States means to stay to the right. To pass a slower swimmer, tap him on the foot to indicate you intend to pass and then pass on the left.

Wait until other swimmers have made the turn and pushed off before entering the water. If you need to stop, squeeze into the corner to the right of oncoming swimmers so they'll have room to turn. Finally, push off underwater to avoid sending waves into oncoming swimmers. Even when wet, good manners never go out of style.

Dear Readers: I keep receiving email messages from many different senders who refuse to begin sentences with capital letters or observe other writing standards. An actual example:

after giving this some thought i have the following recommendation to make. I think we should take traveler checks with us and not ALL cash. i did not see any emails that the vouchers were wrong--so i will approve them tomorrow morning. in addition--the decision about the driver in Rome. do we want to keep him?

Obviously, this sender's shift key does work as there were capitals used at times. So, why the disregard by an educated and intelligent person for the standards of writing?

When communicating in any form, our goal should be clarity. By ignoring standards of composition, we muddy the waters. The writer may have been able to tap out his message two seconds fasters, but now the reader must add back that precious time and more to decode the poorly composed message.

The loss of capitalization and punctuation in standard email may stem from the use of wireless handhelds and personal digital assistants with their tiny keyboards and styluses. Users of such devises sometimes feel that the disclaimer at the end of their email, "Sent from my wireless handheld device," is a license to use poor grammar and spelling. It's not. We should always do what we can to send an intelligent and clear message, even when faced with the limitations of a handheld.

But the above message was sent via standard email, not a handheld. So it doesn't even qualify for that excuse.

I find it difficult to accept the idea that people are so busy that they cannot use proper writing conventions when using email. Most of us learned to type using those conventions and it would seem to take an additional effort to retrain that muscle memory. So why do it?

While email may be a more relaxed form of communication, we should not lose our sense of responsibility to others when using it. Good manners are about thinking of others before us and treating them with respect and courtesy in all our actions – even those dominated by technology.

Users of email must remember that you send a message about yourself with every message you send. Make your best effort to ensure the message you send is a proper reflection of you.

In the embrace of new technology, good manners never go out of style.

Dear Thelma: I'm on a very restricted diet for my health. I have to know what the food ingredients are in every meal. I have severe reactions, including loss of breath and other symptoms, to most food ingredients, including preservatives.

My problem is that our friends and family members know that I'm on this restricted diet for my health. Not being able to breathe is pretty severe, wouldn't you agree? However, most people still get offended when I politely decline get-togethers that include food. This includes going to a restaurant to eat, going to a coffee bar, going to a friend's for dinner or potluck dinners. I usually explain because of health reasons, I must politely decline their offers.

I feel that my refusal is given with courtesy and politeness, but friends and family members are offended. I feel that it's much better than asking if I can see the ingredients listing of every dish served before I partake of it.

Is there a better way to refuse these get-togethers?

A: I feel it is important for you to avoid defining all get-togethers that involve food as events to be avoided. By doing so, you deprive yourself of the opportunity to cultivate and sustain relationships and run the risk of becoming reclusive because of this problem.

You must make the effort to stay connected. They have offered the invitation and made the effort to connect with you. You should find a way to honor that invitation.

One choice is to provide for yourself what is needed. To an invitation to dinner party or barbecue you might say something like: "I enjoy your company and want to stay connected with you, but because of my allergies would you mind if I brought my own dish?" Make enough to fill you up and share with others.

Many hosts these days even invite you to share your dietary requirements by asking in the invitation for those with special needs to contact them. It would be fine to identify the restrictions and provide a list of them to the host.

Depending upon your diet, wise choices at a restaurant may be a possibility. You can even eat your main meal at home before you go and then order a simple dinner salad. It wouldn't even be terrible to pull out your own salad dressing from your bag when the alternative is to deprive yourself of that relationship.

Finally, don't focus on the food itself as your reason for attending the event. Focus instead on the relationships and the opportunity you have been given to share time with your friends and family. You may leave with an empty stomach, but not an empty heart.

Relationship building and good manners never go out of style.

Dear Thelma: I have a question pertaining to being invited to a certain wedding. The wedding will be in a church and the reception will be at a day camp. This wedding and reception are supposed to be a "casual" setting and on the invitation it was printed that you are to bring a plate of cookies or a pasta salad for the reception. Have you ever heard of anything of this nature? I was dumbfounded when I read that you are supposed to supply food. Is this tacky or bad etiquette or just plain unheard of?

A: I've never been invited to such an event or heard of it really happening. However, knowing now that it has been done in your situation, I have to assume that only very close family and friends are invited to that particular wedding – people the bride and groom are very close to and who would fully accept and want to bring the food.

A couple can't send this kind of invitation/request to someone they barely know and not expect them to react negatively. And given the standards followed for most important events we attend and hold in our lifetimes, even close friends may be caught off-guard.

A casual setting for a wedding and reception is fine, but creating a casual atmosphere doesn't mean the graces of being a good host are left behind. Whether it's a formal gala or a backyard barbecue, being a host means taking care of the needs of those invited. If a family or a couple is financially unable to care for those needs, then they must rethink the size of the guest list or the cost of the food chosen. A better option they might have chosen would be to ask select, close family or friends who've offered their assistance if they would like to help with the food. I feel asking every guest to provide a dish veers to the bad etiquette and just-plain-unheard-of side.

But now the ball is your court. Whether or not it is the most gracious invitation, it is their invitation. You have to decide whether these relationships are important enough to you to participate in the event. You also must follow the directions given on the invitation or don't go.

I hope that you can put your shock aside, grab your pasta salad and go for the relationship's sake.

Having a heart and good manners never go out of style.

Dear Readers: I recently returned from an incredible trip to Italy that was filled with very treasured memories. What I want to share with you happened in an unlikely place, but is the most treasured of all.

In the Dallas airport on the final travel leg of my journey home, I was changing concourses when over the public address system a voice said: "Attention. The airport manager would like to speak to you. In just a few minutes a group of our troops returning from Iraq is going to deplane. If you look up you'll see a glass wall. That is the walkway you'll see them going through. Please join us in welcoming our soldiers back home."

As I looked up the doors opened and for the next 25 minutes these men and women moved through that walkway above us and for 25 minutes the applause never diminished. We couldn't hear each other, but the energy of connection was there. They threw back hugs and kisses and we waved and cheered. We could feel them and they could feel us.

It was the most profound, grateful, heartfelt, absolutely spontaneous reaction I've ever experienced. It gave me an incredible sensation as a cross-section of America sitting in this airport stood in unison to applaud our troops. In the entire concourse, no one was sitting and the applause never stopped or even faltered. I was so amazed I had to share it with someone close, so I dialed my sister in Virginia and held out the cell phone.

"What is that," she asked.

"It's all of us clapping for the men and women coming home right now!"

Then, after the last soldier went by, there was absolute silence. Finally, the person next to me spoke: "Wouldn't it be wonderful if this were all of them."

Going though our own busy lives we don't always have the chance to realize how grateful we are to them. To be able to be there when they were there and to thank them was remarkable. It was beautiful to be able to show them how much we appreciate the sacrifice they're making and the sacrifice the American family is making.

I realize there may be a lot of differences in our ideas about many things, but when we have the chance to say thank you, it is in unison.

Thank you from all of us to all those who have answered the call to serve.

Dear Thelma: A good friend passed away unexpectedly. Her memorial service is planned for the day after my family is scheduled to leave town on vacation. I just don't know what to do and nothing seems right. I'm hoping you can help me sort out my decision.

A: Thank you for the question and know that others have had the same concern. I attended a memorial service last week for a very dear friend only to learn that two of the deceased person's closest friends could not be there because they had just left for vacation.

They talked to the family and the family was most sincere in wanting them to remain where they were. I know it is not exactly the same, but in some way it is because it involves plans that have been made and includes more than you. Also I do know that in situations like these more often than not the friends need you more after all quiets down and yet another stage of grieving begins.

There really is no right or wrong way to answer you, but from the sensitivity expressed in your question I know that all will be well. Our heart frequently gets called on to react in many directions at the same time. Sometimes we must simply do our best to answer its calls.

Dear Thelma: I found your website online because I wanted to find out the proper etiquette of who to introduce first in a certain situation. I did find your article that says to "present a person of lesser authority to a person of senior authority (and to) say the more important person's name first." Now I know this is for business introductions, but who would I introduce first if I were introducing my sister (a very important person) to my boss (another very important person)?

A: In the type of situation you propose, a good rule of thumb is to present the person you know best to the person you don't know as well. In this case introduce your sister (whom I expect you have the longer relationship with) to your boss.

The order of the introduction would go like this: "Ms. Bennett, I'd like you to meet my sister, Cheryl Clarkson. Cheryl, this is Ms. Ruth Bennett, the CEO of Bennett Industries."

In most everyday situations, the order of introductions is not likely to be scrutinized. The biggest blunder to make is to fail to make an introduction when the opportunity arises.

An honest effort and good manners never go out of style.

Dear Thelma: The state of New Mexico recently enacted legislation making the bolo tie the state's official tie. I might consider wearing one if I knew how. I have many questions, including when to wear it, how to wear it, and is it acceptable with a dress suit?

A: Wearing your bolo tie in New Mexico and Arizona (where it is also the official state neckwear) can be done with confidence as our Southwestern roots find their way into our fashion. Now that it is New Mexico's state tie, I believe New Mexicans have even more liberty to wear it many places.

At a recent formal western themed social event I attended in Santa Fe, men in sharp dress suits wore the bolo tie at the top of the collar, where the knot of a traditional tie would be.

While state legislators may be able to wear bolo ties during their official duties, other men may need to check with their company dress codes if considering wearing a bolo tie to work. Also, use your common sense. If dress outside the traditional, conservative norms would detract from the business at hand, then save the bolo tie for social events.

Outside the Southwest, men will need to look at local customs and attire to determine whether a bolo tie would be appropriate. Worn at the wrong place at the wrong time it might relegate you to the fringes.

Dear Thelma: This is regarding your 'Potluck Wedding' invitation column. I have presided over the wedding of friends who had a potluck reception. It was one of the more enjoyable and relaxing weddings I have been to. A wedding is a creation of a family, and families eat together. They pitch in and help one another. What better way to celebrate than to bring food and enjoy it with your friends? Maybe I am old fashioned, or just an old hippie, but eating in a hotel ballroom is not my idea of a healthy environment. All I can think of is how much debt is there going to be when this is over.

A: A potluck supper among friends is a perfectly fine way to celebrate any occasion – the key word being "friends." If everyone invited to the wedding is a friend who the hosts would ask to attend a potluck at their home, then most of the guests will feel as you do.

However, most weddings include some people you'd like to honor with an invitation, but who you may not be very close to. They are those who will wonder at the honor of a potluck invitation.

Reading the crowd and good manners never go out of style.

Dear Thelma: I've seen this happening before and it has never bothered me too much, but I suppose today I'm not in a forgiving mood. Should a person be brushing their teeth in the company bathroom? It just seems to me it's like when someone brushes their teeth using the kitchen sink. Maybe my gag reflex is heightened today.

A: These days many of us are being told that brushing our teeth after every meal is important part of keeping teeth healthy. I have been encouraged by my dentist to do it. So what you describe is happening; I've seen it.

However, I don't think it has to be done in front of an audience. If it is important to do, choose a time when the restroom will not be crowded and the fewest number of people will be made uncomfortable. If you enter and there are a lot of people around, wait to start your teeth bushing until they leave. If someone happens to walk in during your hygiene time, all you can do is finish as neatly and quickly as you can.

Healthy consideration for others and good manners never go out of style.

Dear Thelma: My son is getting married in April. Both he and his fiancé will be moving to London after the wedding and will live there for two years. They are selling most of what they have here in Iowa including their condo.

What should we do about wedding gifts? They both have good jobs and are financially fine, but they'd like to request money for wedding gifts for convenience's sake. They just don't know where they are going to end up in two years due to business reasons. What are your thoughts on this please?

A: Giving money as a wedding gift has become commonplace throughout much of the country. It is a fine way to present your good wishes to a couple and help them start a nest egg, or travel or purchase what they want and need.

However, couples and their families must understand that it is not appropriate to include their wishes for cash in their invitations. Invitations are meant to "request the honor of your presence," not to tell you what we expect out of your attendance. While gifts are customary, they are not mandatory.

The quandary becomes, how does the couple let people know their preference? The best way is through parents or members of the bridal party who will be asked where the couple is registered. The answer can be: "They are registered at ABC Store, but I know that since they're moving to London they are hoping to move as few items as possible. They're saving up to buy what they need when they get there."

Because many people don't feel comfortable giving money as a gift, your son and his bride should register, thinking carefully as they do so about what they'd enjoy having in London with them or what might be particularly useful to them as they move or travel.

Dear Thelma: If a couple is married and the wife outranks the husband, how are they addressed? Is it Mr. and Mrs. or Mrs. and Mr.?

A: Mr. and Mrs. are social titles and don't indicate any sort of rank. They are always listed as Mr. and Mrs., as in Mr. and Mrs. Jerry Alexander.

However, if the couple chooses to use military, professional or elected titles or if one of the two uses such a title, the person of higher rank or the person using a title is listed first. Examples include Commander Marissa O'Neill and Major Dominic O'Neill, Dr. Isabella Witt and Mr. Justin Witt, and Senator Christina James and Mr. David

James.

Dear Readers: The transition from summertime to school days presents a unique opportunity to have many important conversations with your children – including one centered on good manners, courtesy and respect.

Begin the conversation as the return to school becomes a reality, maybe as you're making those back-to-school purchases of school supplies and fresh tennis shoes or as the final days of summer vacation begin to pass.

Operating within any group – whether a fourth-grade classroom or an adult workplace – requires a set of social skills that differ from what children may have experienced over a summer in the yard with siblings and neighborhood kids. No one really has the option to take their ball and go home.

Remind kids of school-specific manners that may have dwindled during the summer, and tell them that what's important to you is that they be a good student and a good friend.

What is a good student? A good student respects the teacher by following the class rules, by focusing on the lesson, by working neatly, by being responsible for supplies and assignments, and by being kind. A good student respects himself by preparing for the day with a good breakfast, brushed teeth, washed face and combed hair, and by coming to school ready to learn.

What is a good friend? A good friend is friendly to all, even the annoying person who sits behind you. While you may not spend recess together, you can still help her pick up spilled papers and listen respectfully when she gives an answer. Tell your children that you expect them to care for people who are hurt or sad or are in need of a friend.

Energize for the coming change by talking about and writing down specific goals for this school year. If your son was disappointed that handwriting grade ruined a perfect report card last year, have him neatly write down his goal to slow down a bit and use that extra time to focus on carefully-formed letters. If your daughter missed the talent show last year for lack of a great idea, have her write down her goal and what it will take to prepare for and perform in the show this year.

It's also a good time for parents to think about their own goals for this school year. Maybe it's carving out 30 minutes a day to sit with the kids at the table while they do homework to be available for questions or casual conversation, or maybe it's even just getting out of the house on time. Share all your goals as a family and work together to make them happen.

Family focus and good manners never go out of style.

Dear Thelma: My daughter and son start their soccer and football seasons this month. I almost dread it because of the stress created on the sidelines by overzealous parent-fans. The yelling – positive and negative comments – can easily get out of control. I even have to admit that I have to keep myself in check a lot of the time. Can you remind us how to behave?

A: The first thing to do, even as you are approaching the field, is to remind yourself that the other team's players, their parents and coaches, and the referees are not your enemies. Make a point to look at people as you approach – see a dad tying his kid's shoe or a mom sneaking in a quick kiss before the player hits the field. Seek out the good and what you have in common.

In any kind of competition there is a degree of "us versus them," but keep it in perspective. These are families and people who, just like you, are going to take their kids out for ice cream after the game, and who over the course of a season are going to laugh and high five one day and need hugs and a shoulder for tears another.

If you're a yeller, think seriously about whether it's really helping your child and his team or could it cause confusion. If you truly have something to add to a team's experience, find out what it takes to become a coach or assistant. Then you can offer your instruction during practice and see its results on the field.

Ask your kids what they think of the way you express your support. If they tell you you're embarrassing them, you should listen and make some changes. You can also get a sense of yourself by watching a video of a game taken by yourself or someone standing near you. If you'd be annoyed as a fan watching nearby, changes are in order.

Try this exercise: Decide for one game that you will silence yourself. Simply watch the game, enjoy the game, clap or cheer with the entire group when appropriate. That kind of focus may give you the chance to observe some precious moments you may have missed before. It also may help you break the yelling habit.

If you know you should but just can't seem to control it, sit yourself as far back from the field as possible. There, if you choose to yell, your yelling won't bother other fans or players. With such positioning, you may find yelling pointless and won't even want to do it.

Sportsmanship and good manners never go out of style.

Dear Thelma: I see in the death notices of a funeral home in a nearby town where it is no longer necessary to go to the funeral home to pay your respects. One can merely send your respects through their websites. What are your thoughts on this?

A: I don't understand this streamlined sympathy, especially if it is the only offer of condolence that you make. All it says to me is, "I read the obituary, but I don't have time to really connect with you."

For me it's a matter of heartsense. The sincerest way to show your sympathy if you can't get to the services is by sending a card. A card with a sincere note shows that you took the time to go to the store, buy the card, write the note, find a stamp and send it. It shows a higher level of attention and care.

A message in an online guest book would be fine if it's in addition to funeral attendance, a card sent to the home or flower arrangement sent for the services. However, don't make it your only communication to the grieving family.

Dear Thelma: Recently my father passed, and I am unsure if and how I respond to friends that have sent sympathy cards.

A: Respond to handwritten notes of condolences with your own note of thanks as soon as you're able. It is also important to respond to those who have sent flowers, made contributions, and provided meals or other special help. A pre-printed sympathy card with no personal message does not require a written thank-you.

Dear Thelma: It has been over a year since my loved one died. Is it too late to acknowledge expressions of sympathy?

A: The grieving process is different for everyone. As I suggest above, acknowledgments should be sent at soon as you're able. If for you that meant a year's time has passed, then the time for you is now.

I must assume that you have expressed thanks to those closest to you who grieved with you. Now it seems you are beginning to want to reconnect with friends. By taking the time to write a note acknowledging their support, you let them know that it's a good time to reestablish the relationship.

In difficult times, good manners never go out of style.

Dear Thelma: Many grocery stores offer a service in which an employee will walk you to your car and load up your groceries. Is this a tipping occasion, and if so, what amount is appropriate? Does one also tip the grocery bagger?

A: I do not consider having groceries loaded or bagged tipping occasions and some stores even prohibit tipping such employees. In fact, I once tried to tip the nice kid who took my groceries to the car and my tip was turned down. I asked, "Isn't it appropriate to tip you?" He said, "No, we're already taken care of."

Some internet sites that offer charts of standard tipping amounts say that grocery loaders may be tipped anywhere from $1 to $3 depending on the size of the load. However, unlike restaurant wait staff who are often paid less than minimum wage and are expected to make up the difference in tips, grocery loaders should be adequately compensated by the store for their contribution to the customer experience.

While tips are a gesture of reward for good service received, not every service provided must be met with a tip.

Dear Thelma: My daughter is expecting a baby soon. Her stepmother declined a shower invitation from our family, and she is planning a baby shower for my daughter to which I am apparently not invited. There has not been a relationship problem with her prior to this. Am I out of line in thinking that this is very poor etiquette?

A: Being the hostess, it is her prerogative to choose who is and is not on her guest list. Any host of any gathering has this privilege, just as any guest may accept or decline any invitation.

Although it is natural for you to feel hurt by her refusing your invitation and by not issuing one to you, looking deeper into the situation may ease that pain. Perhaps she didn't want to cause discomfort to anyone on your daughter's special day with you and your friends and family. She also may have a group of her own friends and family that she wants to share the happy expectations with that she didn't feel she could ask you to include on your guest list.

You've said there have been no problems between you in the past; don't count this as a problem either. Just count it as more blessings and love for your daughter and your new grandchild.

Healthy relationships and good manners never go out of style.

Dear Thelma: Are birthday gifts expected at adult birthday

172

parties? Sometimes I feel uncomfortable inviting people to celebrate my birthday because I don't want them to feel like they have to bring me a gift. Other times, I'm invited for a night out with friends to celebrate a birthday and wonder if on top of the $100 I'll spend on my and my husband's portion of the meal and festivities, am I expected to bring a gift too.

A: It's always gracious to give a birthday gift. Birthdays are an important celebration in anyone's life – adults included. However, gifts are never mandatory. While they are customary for occasions like weddings and birthday parties, no one should ever feel they are somehow entitled to a gift. A gift by definition is voluntary.

For your own birthday, don't let your discomfort over gifts stop you from celebrating. It is perfectly acceptable to print "No gifts, please" on your invitations. A guest who receives an invitation noting that no gifts are expected should honor that instruction. It indicates that the issuer of the invitation is only interested in your company at the party. If it's a close friend for whom you've already found the perfect gift, present it to the honoree at a time away from the party or save it for another occasion.

When going out to celebrate a friend's birthday and everyone is expected to cover their own expenses, a gift in addition to those expenses should not be expected. While bringing a gift is perfectly acceptable, a person who does not bring one should not feel they've acted inappropriately. On the other hand, if you've been invited to a celebration out that is being hosted and paid for by someone else, selecting a gift for the honoree would be most kind.

If you are invited to an actual birthday party and no mention of a desire for no gifts has been included in the invitation, it is best to honor the person whose life is being celebrated with a gift.

On a final birthday note, I recently received a call from a woman concerned about selecting birthday gifts for a set of twins to whose party she was invited. She said she knew one of the brothers better than the other and asked if it would be appropriate to get the one she knew best a more personal gift. I advised her to get them similar gifts – games or puzzles – to avoid any kind of jealousy or rivalry.

"But they're turning 40," she replied.

We laughed over that one, and then decided she could buy the one she knew best a more personal gift.

Thoughtful gift-giving and good manners never go out of style.

Dear Thelma: I would love to host a small party to celebrate the birth of a friend's new baby, but I can't afford to invite all the guests and pay for it. I want it to be very casual dinner and drinks; just to hang out. How do you ask the guests to pay for their own dinners? Or better yet, is it right to do so? The few invited would not care, I'm sure, but I hate to look cheap.

A: There's no way to issue a standard invitation for such a party, tack on at the end that you want the guests to pay their own way, and not look cheap. You can't pretend that you are actually hosting a party, and then not live up to the responsibilities of a host.

What are the responsibilities of a host? A host should issue an invitation that would make each guest feel honored to have been included and should plan and carry out an event that fits the occasion.

I see you having a few options here. The first is to contact a few of the honoree's closest friends, explain what you'd like to do and the situation, and ask if they'd like to host the party with you – meaning the small group of you would cover the costs of all the guests.

Another is to craft your party according to what you can afford. Have people over for dessert rather than a meal and have on your guest list only as many people as you can afford to serve.

The other option is to make a more casual invitation for a night out. Call up your friends and say, "A group of us is meeting for dinner with Carmen to celebrate her new baby. Would you like to join us?" The ambiguity of this invitation is a signal to those attending that they should be prepared to cover their own expenses. However, you should plan to at least pay for Carmen's meal, as she is the honoree.

Deciding to host any event should be a decision made with care. Being a host does not dictate the need for formality or holding a party that doesn't fit your personality, but it does mean you've decided to take on the responsibility of planning an experience for your guests. Whether it's a backyard barbeque, a child's birthday party or a complicated dinner party, your focus as host should be on the needs and comfort of your guests.

Recipients of any invitation should feel honored to be invited, not burdened by the responsibilities of the host. If your invitation doesn't covey that sense of honor, reconsider issuing it.

In extending any invitation, good manners never go out of style.

Dear Thelma: My children are in fifth and second grades and parent-teacher conferences are around the corner. Usually my children are doing fine, so that is what is said and that's the end of the conference. What should I be doing to get the conversation flowing?

A: The best way to approach a parent-teacher conference is to do your homework. Make a true effort yourself to prepare for the conference and be ready to stimulate a dialog between you and the teacher.

Prepare by observing your children doing their homework. Make of note of which types of assignments excite them and which types send their minds wandering. Listen to them talk about school and about what they like or dislike.

Also, ask your kids if there is anything they'd like you to ask or to tell the teacher. Talk with them about the conference and assure them that they shouldn't feel anxious or worried about it. If they seem overly worried, try to engage them in a conversation that will bring out their fear or a problem at school that they haven't yet shared with you.

Before each conference, write down your questions, concerns and observations. Add to your list any significant changes or events in each child's life that it would be important for the teacher to know that you haven't already shared – things like an illness or death in the family, a move, or a divorce.

Also list questions you have about what the teacher observes while your child is at school. Is he focused? What types of assignments does she seem to like most? Are there any behavioral issues the child is working on that you can reinforce at home?

By writing down your list of items, you'll be less likely to forget something. You also can refer to it if the conversation comes to a halt but you still feel the need to continue the dialog.

On conference day, be on time for your scheduled appointment and be ready to give your attention to the task at hand. If you bring your child with you, be sure that her presence doesn't keep you from focusing.

Listen carefully to the teacher's assessment of your child and look carefully at any work samples they have from your child. Use these as the springboard for your conversation. Refer to your list when necessary. Do watch the time and make every effort not to let your appointment stray into the next parent's time slot. If you have more to discuss, make an appointment then with the teacher to further the conversation. Solid communication and good manners never go out of style.

Dear Thelma: I read your last column regarding parent-teacher conferences and hoped you could address a follow-up question. I don't agree with some of the teaching and discipline methods my daughter's teacher uses. For example, during a science project, she gave an entire group an F because of one of the member's misbehavior. The same misbehaving student was told several times to raise her hand and be acknowledged before speaking out. She did not change her behavior and the entire class was told to write 100 times: "Susan will raise her hand before speaking."

I want to voice my concerns because I don't feel this approach adds anything to my daughter's educational experience and it doesn't seem to faze the offender, but I don't want to cause any problems for my daughter. Is there a proper way to approach this?

A: If you can take your emotion out of this situation, there is a way to approach it in a way that expresses your concerns, opens dialog with the teacher and keeps things positive.

Make an appointment to meet with the teacher one-on-one. If she asks why you want to meet, tell her that you'd like to discuss some experiences in the classroom that have been difficult for your daughter.

Approach the meeting with a desire to learn why the teacher uses the methods she does and how you can work together to help your daughter achieve success. Write down your values, expectations and concerns, and be ready to express them without sounding accusatory or defensive.

Once in the conference, let the teacher know you are there because you value your daughter's education and appreciate that the teacher is an important part of your daughter's life. Explain your values and expectations, and then describe the methods that you find troubling. Ask the teacher if you've understood the situations and the resulting discipline correctly from your daughter, and ask the teacher to explain the use of the methods.

Listen to the answers and make an effort to engage in a conversation that helps you understand where the teacher is coming from. Be prepared for the possibility that your conversation will not change the way she disciplines. Don't accuse her of causing difficulty, but express that you want to know what you can do to help accomplish what is best for your child.

At the very least, the conversation should help you understand the reasons behind the methods and help you explain them to your daughter if they come up again.

Keep the conversation non-confrontational and highly respectful. This is the person you trust to watch over your child for the majority of the day. She deserves your respect and consideration, even if you disagree with the discipline. When asking the tough questions, good manners never go out of style.

Dear Thelma: My husband and I have been invited to a quinceañera by some neighbors who we don't know well. We would like to give an appropriate present to the honoree. I read a little and see a strong religious emphasis on gifts, but it is not my faith and I would feel uneasy about guessing what would be good. Would a cash gift be acceptable?

A: As more quinceañeras are now celebrated in the United States, more questions are being asked about them. A quinceañera is a rite of passage typically celebrated by Hispanic families to honor a daughter's 15th birthday symbolizing the end of her childhood and beginning of her life as a young woman.

Many of the gifts you see mentioned with the strong religious emphasis are the traditional symbolic gifts given by family and godparents. They can include a tiara symbolizing the girl being a princess before God; a ring representing commitment to God; a religious medal as an expression of faith; a bible to keep the word of God in her life; earrings as a reminder to listen to the word of God; or a scepter representing the young woman's authority and responsibility for her own life.

Outside of the religious and cultural emphasis of the quinceañera, the event is also a 15th birthday party. You can select your gift with that in mind, and as you know, most 15-year-olds do appreciate cash. A gift certificate also would be a good choice.

Dear Thelma: My family recently received in the mail a pre-printed postcard announcement of the impending birth of a cousin's first child. The baby is due in 2008 and we live in the same city as the expectant parents and see them several times a year.

While pleased that they are expecting, I find the announcement of a baby through a pre-printed postcard to be rude, impersonal and tacky. They couldn't take five minutes to pick up the phone and tell us? My husband's view is "at least they told us" and he thinks I'm making too big a deal out of the postcard announcement. The couple is in their early 20s. Is this a new trend among young people?

A: You should be pleased you didn't receive the announcement via text message. I suspect the excited first-time parents wanted to inform a large number of people simultaneously. They also cared enough to design and mail a postcard when they could have sent out a mass email. In this modern age our social networks are huge and communication often is expected to be instantaneous. I think they did their best. I'm with your husband on this one.

Accepting the good news for what it is and good manners never go out of style.

Dear Thelma: I am leaving a company that I have been with for more than 15 years. That's a long time and it's a difficult move for me. What is the proper way to resign?

A: Keep respect, consideration and courtesy at the forefront as you leave any job. A focus on these elements will help keep your decisions and actions at a highly professional level and keep important relationships intact.

The nuts and bolts of leaving a job are fairly standard. Give at least two-week's notice so that plans can be made to replace you or shuffle the workload. Check your company handbook in case a longer notice is required. Provide a written letter of resignation stating what your last day of employment will be. After resigning with your supervisor, inform your staff as a group and thank them for their efforts. Next, let your co-workers know.

During this period, be positive. If you are leaving a bad situation, let all your discussions focus on the future rather than the past. Even if asked to provide constructive criticism, resist any temptation to be petty or resentful. It's important to leave any position on good terms, preserving relationships and your professional image for the future.

Be as helpful as possible by completing as much work as you can in your final weeks or training your replacement. Leave your office and any pending projects in a state that the next person can step into as easily as possible.

Above the mechanics of leaving are the emotions of making this break. It is difficult to leave an organization you've been with for a long time. When I left my position as CEO of a health care company after 14 years, I thought seriously about how to do it well. I realized I should not focus on my exit, but on helping those I worked with transition to new leadership roles.

I thanked the people I worked with for making the organization as strong as it was. I wanted to leave the staff feeling good about themselves. I wanted to make sure they knew they had a vital role to play in the continued success of the organization. And I wanted them to know how much I respected them and that I trusted them to continue the work we had started.

At the core of exiting gracefully is the knowledge that you don't abandon the relationships you have formed. Those connections should stay intact and remain important. Ten years later, I run into people who I left at the health care company and they still say, "We miss you." I think much of that stems from the way in which I left.

Like a graceful exit, good manners never go out of style.

Dear Thelma: I am hosting a retirement party for my husband. My invitation requested that the guests RSVP and indicated a cut-off date. The cut-off date has passed, the party is days away and I have heard from very few people. I need a headcount for the caterer. Can I call those who have not responded?

A: The host of a party should not have to issue an invitation and call to see if it is accepted, but she can feel perfectly mannered if she must do so.

Those who are receiving invitations are really who we must speak to in answering this question. Whether it's a formal gala or a 4-year-old's birthday party, the host has honored you with an invitation. It is your responsibility to respond within a week of receiving the invitation to let the host know whether or not you will attend. That means, even if you can't make it, you must respond.

A lack of respect for the RSVP is epidemic in today's society, making it difficult to host a successful party. People today have become very casual with their responses to invitations and almost indifferent to the fact that someone is working to create an occasion for their enjoyment. In defense of more successful parties, I suggest that we all consider reviewing our guest lists to identify the people causing this inconvenience and consider not inviting them to our next event. Perhaps if enough of the RSVP-ignorers stop receiving invitations, we won't have such problems getting accurate headcounts and they will be so excited to be invited to anything, they will respond immediately. Especially when you're a guest, good manners never go out of style.

Dear Thelma: Last year, I attended a holiday party for a group of friends. For some of us, a slightly uncomfortable situation arose when a few people started exchanging and passing out gifts. We were not aware this was going to be happening. Additionally, the hosts were unaware and extremely embarrassed.

This year I am throwing a holiday party and am inviting several different groups of friends including those from the party last year. I am not asking our guests to bring anything (food or drink), and was wondering if there is a polite way to include a note asking people to not bring gifts for others attending the party to avoid any uncomfortable situations during the event? All I want is to have is an enjoyable night with friends.

A: I relate quite well to your question because I was placed in a similar sensitive situation. I was included in a holiday celebration where exchange of gifts was planned in advance and a select few were never told. I even received gifts yet had none to exchange. I admit that it was a very embarrassing and emotional situation for me. It is difficult to conceal one's surprise and embarrassment and yet attempt to graciously accept what is occurring.

I decided at that very moment that when I next had the opportunity of being the hostess for a holiday celebration I would clearly state the intentions of why I was planning the party. Your doing so for your party is not only appropriate but will eliminate that potential awkward situation.

The intentions for the celebration should be expressed in your invitation. Find a way to say exactly what you stated in your question: "This evening is a time for us all to enjoy each other's company – time together is our gift to each other."

If people bring gifts for you as the hostess graciously accept them and place them away from the party setting and open them after the guests leave. If you observe gifts being brought for others politely request that they be given as guests leave. If the invitation is clear and gracious the guests should act in like manner.

Dear Thelma: Because our family has become so large, this year it was decided that the adults would have a white elephant gift exchange, where each person buys one gift, the presents get opened one at a time and then when it's your turn you can exchange an unopened gift you've been given for something someone else already opened.

Anyway, I love gift-giving, and I want to buy a present for everyone. How do I go about getting a gift for the exchange, but then giving individual gifts too?

A: Think carefully about how your family will react before you decide to take this path. There's probably a reason your family decided to do the gift exchange this way, whether it's because they feel the season has become too commercial or because some family members are not as financially comfortable as others. You don't want your actions to show disrespect for the decision or situations of your family members.

Use your heartsense – that common sense of the heart – and what you know about your own family as you proceed. If you decide to give the individual gifts, do what you can to make sure your giving doesn't stress or inconvenience others. Speak to your family members individually and let them know that you plan to buy them gifts, but that you don't expect anything in return. Realize that some of them will feel pressured to give something in return, and you may in a round-about way undermine the gift-exchange decision.

Everyone will be expecting to give and receive just one gift at your family exchange, so give your individual gifts at a time separate from the main event and to the individuals alone rather than at another group gathering.

Dear Thelma: It seems that every year someone I am not expecting to exchange gifts with gives me a Christmas gift. What does one do in that situation? Should I buy them a gift to give soon thereafter? Or should I just say thanks and move on?

A: The most important and appropriate thing to do is give a very gracious thank you for the person's thoughtfulness. That is all that's really required, but it can leave you with a funny feeling.

Some people have an emergency supply of gifts to exchange in such a situation – baked goods or other all-purpose gifts. Instead, I like to think about how I can be thoughtful in some other way. I might offer to take them to lunch during the holiday season – the gift of a good meal and companionship.

Dear Readers: As you're making your gift list and checking it twice, I encourage you to use your heartsense when giving. A gift should show someone that you value their place in your life and that you're thinking of them. But the perfect gift doesn't have to be wrapped up and tied with a bow. Often, time spent with another can be the most valuable gift you can give.

Plan to give the gift of a lunch date with at least one friend or family member this season. Even children would appreciate an outing – or should have the opportunity to learn to appreciate one – to a unique place or experience. One family I know swapped their kids' usual gift exchange with another family for the opportunity to spend the day together bowling and having lunch. It's a day they're all looking forward to again this year.

I encourage you to use the season to show you care and to celebrate the relationships in your life. Gifts from the heart and good manners never go out of style.

Dear Thelma: Do you have a suggestion for how to downsize gift giving at Christmas for family members? Our family is about 26 people representing six family units with children. Most of the family members live scattered about the U.S. and we don't visit very often. In the past we have sent gifts for everyone and basically never heard back from any of them. All of the family groups would like to change how we give gifts but don't know how to do it. Give just to adults? Give just to kids (even if you don't know them well)? Give just to the 'family' group? Can you help?

A: Your question states that "all of the family groups would like to change how we give gifts." If you absolutely know this to be true, then you've already begun the most important part of resolving the issue: honest communication.

If you feel you have enough time to make the change this year, start communicating with all the family groups as soon as possible. Email may be an effective way to poll the heads of the families on their preferences. Mention the options you've listed in your question and indicate your favorite. Telephone any who don't use email regularly. Work together to decide what's best for you all.

Ultimately, the decision on how you give will be up to you. All of the ways you've mentioned are acceptable. Another family of six siblings I know decided to simply exchange family photos each Christmas, which allowed them to keep up with the changes in each other's families and children. It became a gift they all anticipated each year.

For those families in which the subject has yet to be raised, you may not have time to make changes this year. However, shortly after

Christmas would be a good time to thank your family members for their wonderful generosity in the past and to ask if they feel a change is necessary. Be honest about your feelings and approach the conversation with your ideas for solutions.

If someone in your family comes to you with these concerns, hear them with an open heart and mind. Although such a change may feel drastic and foreign based on your past giving traditions, new ways of sharing our love with each other can take hold quickly if we allow them to.

Dear Thelma: This has not been a good year for me at work. I'm annoyed with my boss and some of my coworkers, and I just don't feel like going to the holiday office party. Am I obligated to attend? Will it cause problems if I don't?

A: Attending a party for obligatory reasons defeats the purpose and spirit of a party. Through your demeanor, conversations and body language you run the risk of casting a negative cloud over the event. It's highly likely that your attitude toward the party and your coworkers will show through, and that could be more harmful to your career than if you simply didn't attend.

On the other hand, if you decide it's time to make a fresh start, the party may be the place to do it. Interpersonal and relationship building skills are integral parts of career success. If you go, decide that you will approach the situation with a positive attitude and use the time to connect on a personal level with as many people as you can. Keep this in mind for the rest of the year and you should be ready for the next holiday season.

A festive spirit and good manners never go out of style.

Dear Thelma: I'm conflicted about buying Christmas gifts for my co-workers. Is it really necessary? I don't really have the budget to get all 8 of them something really nice and I don't know if what I can afford is really worth giving.

A: You've lost sight of the true purpose of a gift during this time of year. The holidays are a natural time to show our appreciation for one another and to honor the time spent together over the past year. They're the perfect time for building relationships.

Studies show that relationship building is a vital part of the culture of an organization and important to professional success. Professionals coming into career positions sometimes aren't retained if they don't build relationships.

If you've established those relationships with the people working with you, giving a token of thanks and your interest in them should feel natural. If those relationships are not solidified, use this time to start the process.

Thoughtfulness, kindness, sensitivity and inclusion should direct the spirit of your gift giving. The holidays are not a time for leaving anybody out. If you are very close to some of your co-workers and have special gifts for them, give them outside the office.

Gift certificates for books or to their favorite lunch stop, stationery, soaps, and baked goods – home baked or store bought – are always appropriate gifts for colleagues. Include a holiday card with a personal message of appreciation for the past year and warm wishes for the new one.

The gifts you give your co-workers don't have to be expensive or elaborate, just thoughtful and kind. A festive bow on their favorite candy bar and a holiday card with a personal message shows you've thought of them and shouldn't break the bank.

Accept any gift in the spirit that it's given and receive it with joy. Gift-giving is not meant to be a material exchange, it's an expression of the warmth we feel for people who bless our lives.

Dear Readers: I received a response to the column on changing gift-giving traditions that I choose to share with you for its example of the heartsense on which I like to focus. By thinking and communicating with the mind and the heart, a new family tradition emerged and is now cherished.

Dear Thelma: Your gift-giving column raised an issue my wife and I dealt with several years ago. We received Christmas gifts from a few close friends who lived elsewhere, and we also received birthday, Mother's Day and Father's Day gifts from our two adult children. As we grew older and had fewer needs, we found it harder to reciprocate creatively and we knew our friends and children had the same problem.

We solved the problem with our friends by writing them and informing them we were going to make a donation in their honor to a charity we knew was important to them. We have continued this practice with satisfaction on both sides.

With our children, we asked them to make a donation in our honor to a charity important to them. This removed the problem of determining "What the heck does dad need?" while making all of us feel good. We continue to give our grandchildren modest gifts for birthdays and Christmas, but the significant gift for them is an addition to an education fund for each of them.

Reader, I agree with your suggestion to communicate. It is the key. Warm giving and good manners never go out of style.

Dear Thelma: How do you feel about regifting? It doesn't really seem proper, but sometimes it makes a lot of sense to me.

A: Ever since the television show "Seinfeld" brought the term "regifting" into popular culture, much has been made of the practice. But it's really nothing new. A friend remembers Christmas 30 years ago when his father wouldn't let the family open the cheese and cracker gift package they received so they would have a spare gift to exchange if needed. Oh, how that 7-year-old boy longed to try that little wheel of cheese.

Done carefully, regifting is an acceptable way to make the most of something you've received and shown thanks for but can't use. Done improperly, it turns the giving into something that doesn't feel very gracious.

Any gift you plan to recycle should be kept unused and in its original packaging and labeled immediately with the original giver's name and the situation in which it was given. Do not trust yourself to remember this information. You do not want to take any chance that the gift could find itself back to the original giver or someone closely connected to the person or the event at which it was given. That would show that you were not thoughtful in your giving.

Think carefully about the gift and who will receive it. Be certain it is something that the receiver would really like. Don't regift just to get rid of something. If it's an item that you don't like and can't imagine anyone you know liking, do not give it as a gift. Instead, find a charity you can donate it to for the group's use or for sale at a fundraiser.

As a receiver, accept any gift in the spirit of love and generosity in which it is presented. If you suspect it to have been recycled, look to the signs that point to the fact that the giver thought of you and your needs in selecting the gift.

Ask Thelma 2008
Treasuring Connections

Dear Thelma: I recently attended an indoor luncheon with cloth table covers and napkins attended by about 100 people. Some women in attendance wore cowboy hats. The men in hats wore cowboy hats, baseball caps and engineer hats. None of the wearers of engineer hats removed their hats during the invocation or the meal. Only one of the baseball caps was removed for the invocation and meal. The men in cowboy hats did remove their hats for the invocation and the meal. None of the women removed their hats at any time.

I questioned the lack of courtesy and was told by one of the women wearing a cowboy hat that the "Code of the West" out here differs from "back East" rules, and that "out West" the men are only required to remove their hats in church. According to manners books at my local library there is no differentiation for East and West. What is currently correct in the West?

A: East or West the way to respectfully wear a hat remains the same. Common hat courtesy requires men to take off their hats to show respect during the playing of the National Anthem, the passing of the flag in a parade, during a prayer, or in a cemetery or other monument to the dead. This is done a sign of reverence.

A man may wear his hat in public areas like a store, a hallway or building lobby he's passing through. Once he reaches his destination – a restaurant, a museum, a theater, a person's office, a home or a church – he removes his hat to show respect to those around him or for the sanctity of the place he's entered. He also removes his hat during a meal at home or in a restaurant.

These norms may have grown out of times when hats were functional and served as protection from the industrial dirt of the cities and the outdoor work of rural life. Hats served their purpose outdoors and were taken off indoors to show a higher level of civility or respect for what goes on inside.

For women, hat etiquette has changed as their use of hats has changed. In times past, a fashion hat was a regular part of a woman's ensemble for the day. It matched her suit or dress perfectly and was pinned on her head. Today, fashion hats are not the norm. Most women wear hats that are casual in nature and are often informal unisex hats or baseball caps.

So, a woman must decide what type of hat she is wearing and follow the rules for that hat. A woman's hat that is unmistakably a formal fashion accessory and part of her dressy ensemble remains on in a restaurant or a formal tea but generally is removed when dining in a home. It also stays on during a flag ceremony or a prayer.

Any other type of hat should be removed at the same instances and places that a man's hat is removed.

Perhaps with the exception of baseball players and working cowboys, most hats today are more fashion than function. I doubt most pitchers and ranch hands want to wear their sweaty, dirty hats at the dinner table. For the rest of us, hats may simply be a casual accessory – part of an informal look for the day. Viewed as such, the need for hat etiquette can seem unnecessary; however, taking off your hat shows your level of respect for the society that you live in and its traditions of civility.

Respectful hat wearing and good manners never go out of style.

Dear Thelma: People complain about the newbies who show up at the gym at this time of year, but I think a lot of the regulars could use a good dose of gym etiquette. From the sight of them you'd think they would know by now how to behave, but they often don't. How about a refresher course?

A: Like any public place, a gym is a place where consideration for others should rule our actions. Sometimes we have a tendency to forget this because what we do in a gym is so personal. It's about taking care of our bodies and our health. However, if we are going to do those things in public, then we have to take others into consideration.

In general, it's best to be quiet in a gym. Not that a gym is a quiet place, but hearing loud conversations, the oblivious treadmill runner singing along with her tunes and the startling clatter of weights dropped from too high all cause uneasiness.

Depending on your gym's specific rules, leave behind or turn off your cell phone. Do not carry on cell phone conversations during your workout. If you are expecting a vital call, silence your ringer before you enter the gym and go to a lobby or parking lot to take the call.

Avoid other behaviors that disturb and distract. Don't use foul language, and keep personal conversations personal. Dress appropriately for your workout in clothes that are clean, odor-free and that adequately cover you. Also, use good personal hygiene before you arrive at the gym. Smell clean, but don't overpower us with perfume or cologne.

Show respect by sharing. Honor the time limits set for cardio machines. If you're using a weight machine for multiple sets, offer to let a waiting person work in during your rest periods.

Clean up after yourself. Bring along a towel to wipe your sweat from the
equipment you've just used. Also return the weights or plates you've just used to their proper place so that everyone can find what they need in the gym and so the machine is ready for the next person.

In the locker room, cover up with a towel and be considerate in the time you take using the facilities. Trying to keep yourself from looking at a naked person hogging the mirror is uncomfortable.

If you find you can't bring yourself to use these manners at the gym, buy a treadmill and some weights and work out in your garage naked while you talk on your cell phone.

Dear Thelma: I went to a friend's bridal shower and her wedding as well. Is it proper to give a gift for each occasion? If so, is there a proper gift to give at each occasion?

A: Yes, it is customary to give a gift for each occasion. Showers are specifically gift-giving occasions. You're there to shower the bride with good wishes and with items the couple may need in their new home. If you don't attend the shower, you are not obligated to send a gift. It is tradition that those invited to a wedding – whether or not they attend – send or bring a gift.

Generally, and especially if it's a question of budget, one of the gifts can be less costly and less elaborate – possibly something more personal or creative. For the other gift, you can focus on something long-lasting for a new couple setting up their home. Both gifts should let the couple know you share in their happiness and wish them well for the future.

Dear Thelma: Why do so many people, particularly women, chew gum in public and the work place. Isn't that unprofessional?

A: Men and women who want to be considered completely

professional in their actions and appearance should always avoid chewing gum in meetings, social gatherings and even conversations at work.

It really is one of the things I observe so often and find to be such a distraction. We all know not to chew food and talk at the same time; the same rules should be considered when chewing gum. Those around you can hear the gum, and they can see the gum and the chewer's tongue. They really shouldn't have to. Choosing to sit across from you in a meeting doesn't mean I want to know you and your gum that intimately.

I have personally observed a CEO whose professional attire is impeccable and whose business manners are close to perfect, but I have yet to see this person not chewing gum faster than the speed limit. There is no relaxation in the face; all attention is on chewing this piece of gum that you know has been gnawed flavorless. The gum is the first thing I think of when this person comes to mind.

In a professional setting, a business meeting or a cocktail reception, gum should not be a part of your professional look. If you like, chew it in the car on the way to freshen your breath, but don't forget to take it out before you enter the meeting or event. Better yet, use breath mints.

A long-time friend of mine aptly describes it with this poem:

What is the difference between a gum-chewing person and a cud-chewing cow?

What is the difference? I know now.

The thoughtful look on the face of the cow!

Dear Thelma: Could you please tell me how to address an issue with an employee who has bad breath. Two employees told me that one of the employees that I supervise has bad breath. What should I do?

A: This is a very sensitive issue to handle because it is so personal, but it can't be ignored. Ignoring it will create a situation in which the employee could become isolated, and you don't want that. Ignoring it also could bring about criticism of your performance as a supervisor.

As the supervisor you have the ultimate responsibility to assess and handle the situation. The best way usually is to conduct the conversation yourself. The employee needs to know that this view you're expressing exists within the group. Begin with: "This is a difficult thing to say, but it has been brought to my attention that you may want to consider the freshness of your breath more carefully. I don't want you to be in any way isolated because of this and so that's why I wanted to let you know."

Encourage breath mints and tooth brushing, rather than gum-chewing.

Dear Thelma: I ran into a friend I had not seen in years. I asked her when her baby was due. She informed me she was not pregnant. Yikes!

A: When this statement came to me, I have to admit, I giggled. It has happened to many and will continue to happen as well-meaning people make mistakes. All you can do is express how very sorry you are for being so daft and remember to never again comment on a woman's pregnancy until she herself has told you she is pregnant.

When faced with sticky situations, good manners never go out of style.

Dear Thelma: Recently, while running late for an appointment, I ran into a traffic slow down on a four-lane road. Upon passing some of the cars, I realized that I was passing a funeral procession. I felt terrible. I seem to remember having read somewhere that passing is improper in this situation. What would be the right thing to do in this situation?

A: You're right, it is improper to pass. A funeral procession, also called a cortege, is usually signaled by a line of cars with headlights on or hazard lights flashing. The respectful thing to do when you encounter one is to pull over to allow the line of cars to pass, hold up traffic even when you have a green light to let the line pass through the intersection, and avoid passing the procession.

On a four-lane road it was an honest mistake. Once you realized you were passing a procession, you needed to do whatever was safest. If you were near the end of the line it may have been possible to slow down and move in behind the procession; however, if you realized as you approached the family's limousine or the hearse it may not have been safe to drop back to the end or stay in the passing lane.

The fact that you realize your mistake shows your heart is in the right place. So, forgive yourself and from here forward, stay aware on the road. Heartsense and safety can get you down it smoothly.

Dear Thelma: Friends have asked my new husband and me what we need for the house as a wedding gift. I feel awkward when I get asked this question because I don't know what their price range is, and it just feels funny. I usually say not to get us anything because we have a lot of stuff, but they still want to get us a gift. What am I supposed to say to this question? If I don't say anything, then I might get something I don't want or need, but if I do is that rude?

A: I think many people go through this kind of dilemma, but know that you can handle it gracefully. First, if a person is asking for gift ideas, it is because he wants to honor you and your husband and your decision to marry. He wants to celebrate with you by giving a gift. You shouldn't feel rude by answering his honest question. If he can't afford to give you a gift or if he just doesn't want to give a gift, it's unlikely he'd ask what you would like.

Next, when times like a wedding, a baby shower or even a birthday come around, create a "mental registry." You probably registered for wedding gifts at a department store and did a service for the people who wanted to give you what you needed and had chosen. This "mental registry" is the same idea. In your head have some ideas in mind to offer when people ask you what you'd like. Not a greedy list of things you expect, but a range of options to offer if someone asks.

If you know a person well, you can probably give an answer that fits his price range. You may really want a crystal chandelier, but you know that salt and pepper shakers would be a better option for him. Let him know how much you need those shakers. If you don't know him well, keep your answers in a range that you consider an affordable gift.

Thoughtful consideration and good manners never go out of style.

Dear Thelma: I am having a "no gift" birthday party for my 3-year-old daughter. Our gift to her is opening a college fund/savings account. Is it acceptable to put this on the invitations in case someone wishes to give her something?

A: It is perfectly fine to host a "no gift" party and note on your invitation that it is a "no gift" party. You should then not expect any gifts. If guests don't follow your wishes and do arrive with gifts, those will be of the guest's choice.

You shouldn't note on an invitation that you would like contributions to her college fund. That will make people feel obligated to contribute, and that $15 they would have spent on a doll now looks trivial as a contribution to her higher education.

Some people holding "no gift" parties give an option of donating to a charity to teach children about selfless giving, but your daughter's college fund is not a charity. If you think her grandparents or other relatives might be genuinely interested in contributing to the fund, then you can mention plans for your gift to her. They may decide on their own that they want to participate.

Finally, if you are invited to a "no gift" party, honor the host's request. Although it may go against your nature to show up without a gift, it's more important to follow the directions on the invitation, which were put there for a reason. If it soothes your soul, bring a card so you won't feel empty handed.

Dear Thelma: I am having a retirement party for my husband at the Albuquerque Museum of Art. How much should I tip the caterer serving hors d'oeuvres and the bar serving beer and wine? Also, how do I tip a caterer for a small group dinner?

A: Caterers and bar services most often include the gratuity in their bill. If you see a "service charge" listed on your bill, that is the tip. You are not required to tip anything above that. It is then up to the service company to distribute that amount among its staff members.

It is perfectly acceptable and preferable to ask beforehand if the tip will be included in the bill. If you are told that it will not be included, then you should be prepared to tip 15 percent to 20 percent of the bill. Some people tip on the pre-tax cost; others calculate the tip from the total bill. That's up to you. The tip is typically given with the total payment and it is up to the management to distribute it to the staff.

If there are individual members of the staff who you feel really went out of their way for you, you can tip them individually. That tip will be above the tip given on the total bill.

Be aware that the days of tipping 10 percent for restaurant meals and food services are gone. Restaurateurs I know tell me that 18 percent is now the standard average.

Follow up: I felt a reader's comments on the recent chewing gum question were worth sharing. She writes: Chronic bad breath can be caused by a number of medical maladies. A supervisor needs to be aware that tooth decay, sinus infections, and digestive problems can cause dreadful breath, and the employee may be working with his/her doctor to identify the cause. A breath mint and daily tooth brushing won't help in these cases.

She's right, but again it is important to bring it up so that the employee can address it and avoid being isolated by co-workers.

Sensitivity and good manners never go out of style.

Dear Readers: I get many comments and questions on the negative impact of communication technology like email on relationship building and etiquette. We all know that technology is here to stay. What we must realize is that technology does have a heart – your heart.

That means as respectful and caring people, we've got to use our heartsense to turn email into something that reflects the same respect, friendliness and decorum as an in-person conversation, a letter or a business memo. Used properly, it can bring great efficiency along with real connections and even joy.

I discovered that joy last month as I celebrated a milestone birthday. My family is scattered across the country and had already gathered a couple of times for important events last year. So I decided to hold what I will now call "email birthday parties."

On the eve of my birthday, I sent an email to every family member who had an email account and printed out copies for the few who didn't. In this email I toasted my family, thanking them for the love and support they've shown me throughout my life. My goal was to convey what was in my heart to all these people living across the country. After I created my toast I questioned whether I should really continue with this email birthday party, but finally I pushed "Send."

The next morning emails came back and hearts connected in a very real and joyful way. All day long the messages kept coming. I heard from every single person in my family. It was an incredibly loving and heartfelt experience for this special birthday.

By hitting the "Reply all" button, the emails were shared with everyone, and it was like being in the same room together experiencing each person's personality and nuances and energy. I wanted to be sure that I connected with all of them and it ended up that we all connected with one another. It was a beautiful birthday, made possible by technology.

Dear Thelma: I recently attended what was clearly a networking event for about 300 people; however, the music from the band hired for the evening was so loud that networking was nearly impossible. We practically had to scream our conversations. It was uncomfortable and, in the end, pointless. At these kinds of events I don't think music is even necessary. What do you think?

A: Great care should be taken when planning any event and the ultimate purpose of the event must be kept at the front of the planner's mind. That purpose changes from event to event. A fundraising dinner featuring special entertainment is one thing; a professional networking reception is another. Event planners have to think carefully about the atmosphere they are trying to create and select accordingly.

The point of a networking event is to build relationships. Entertainment can be a distraction and a barrier to creating those relationships. We only have one opportunity to make a first impression and social events provide us with that opportunity. When we need to struggle to be heard or become uncomfortable during conversation, we have lost that first-time opportunity.

Networking is the initial step in relationship building, and creating the atmosphere for networking when planning an event is essential. While the selection of music can help to set a mood or create an atmosphere, it should not take center stage for the entire evening. The extracurricular noise should never drown out the conversations that relationships are built upon.

Good first impressions and good manners never go out of style.

Dear Thelma: Is it appropriate for someone to have a social gathering in the evening and invite all co-workers (both male and female) but no spouses or significant others?

A: The answer to your question depends upon the purpose of the gathering. A reception or event that is clearly held for work-related reasons or for relationship-building purposes within the organization can properly serve as an employees'-only gathering.

The waters get muddier as you move away from that scenario. A party held at someone's home or planned for an exclusive venue tends to be more social and people expect to bring their social companion when socializing.

As the host of a party you do have control of your own guest list; however, when it comes to partying, couples usually are a packaged-deal.

Dear Thelma: In the fall we were guests at a wedding for my son's best friend. He was the best man. We are now well into the new year and we still have yet to receive a thank-you note from the couple. Is it appropriate for us to ask them if they received our gift of money? Maybe it was lost in the shuffle of the evening? We don't know. I just would like to know if they received it or not.

A: It is perfectly acceptable for you to ask the couple if they received your gift. Be sure to ask respectfully and keep it from becoming a judgmental question. Explain that you are worried that it may have been lost in the shuffle of the evening and would like to know if they received it. If contacting them directly feels too confrontational to you, send them a note.

Thank-you notes should always be sent as soon as possible after receiving any gift. Extra special attention should be paid to those gifts that givers may question whether you've received.

Gracious receiving – be it cards, guests or gifts – and good manners never go out of style.

Dear Thelma: I am an avid men's Lobo basketball fan. For many, many years I have been a season ticket holder and sit in the same seats as my great uncle before me. I attend every game and cheer along with the crowd. One of the reasons I am so devoted is the unique setting of The Pit. The sixth man is alive and well in Lobo Country, and I believe that the cheering of the crowd has helped pull games out in a clinch. I like being a part of that energy.

Unfortunately, we have a long-term ticket holder, a woman, occupying seats behind us who constantly screams, complains, swears and is so obnoxious that some of my family members will not go to games and I will not take my child.

When did holding a ticket to a game become a license for rude behavior? And how do I get her to tone down?

A: What I would like to say, hoping that this intrusive individual hears me is: "Shame on you. Your selfish behavior has ruined an entertainment opportunity for individuals and families. We don't need people like you at games."

Sports continue to be an important leisure and relaxation activity for adults. And in today's world, they also have become an integral part of how families spend their value time together. By attending games together, parents teach children what it means to be on a team and how to cheer for a team. The game itself, along with the energy that surrounds it, can be an enjoyable experience for all ages.

The horrible example set by this woman destroys the kind of unifying experience families are seeking and individuals desire. To be barraged with obscenities and constant running commentary is uncomfortable for everyone.

This kind of behavior is nothing new and is not necessarily surprising, but it is time to call it what it is, and that is rude. This fan is unwilling to control her words and behavior. She has no concern for the fact that she's ruining the experience for the twenty people sitting near her. That is rude.

Buying a ticket to a game doesn't entitle anyone to such disrespect. It doesn't give a right to cheer in any manner you wish or to offend the captive audience around you with foul language or obnoxiousness.

While we can see that she is being rude, she probably would not describe it that way. She might even be annoyed with you for not showing enough support and for trying to silence her.

I suggest you try talking to her before the game begins. Approach her as a friendly, fellow fan: "Hello, I was wondering if I could talk with you for a minute." Explain that you understand that she wants to support the team and enjoy the game. Then ask her if she can avoid using foul language and avoid directing her yells directly over your shoulder and explain why without displaying your own anger and frustration. If enough of us do this, perhaps we can make an impact.

I don't know if this will work with this particular person. If you can't resolve the issue, I suggest you contact the ticket office. I'm told they can move you to a comparable seat. I understand these are your long-time seats and you don't want to be run out of them, but you may find that you can be much happier elsewhere. I most definitely would move so that the family could go to the games again and so could your child.

Every sports fan needs to know good manners never go out of style.

Dear Thelma: My 6-year-old daughter came home from school crying a few times last week. Her problem was not that people were being mean to her, but that they wanted her to be mean to others – not allowing certain people into a playground game. It's not in her nature to be that way and it hurt her to be put in that situation. We talked over what it means to be a good friend and to be a good person. She seemed to have new resolve to stand up to her "friends," but it worries me? She's with them for seven hours a day. What more can I do to help her stay true to herself?

A: I detect this as a form of bullying on the part of her friends, and it's their effort to pull her into a bullying situation. We talk about bullying more with older kids, but this is where it starts. It's important for you to identify it as such now, so that you continue to take it seriously.

When you take something seriously, you're more likely to monitor it regularly. For you, that may mean having a detailed conversation once a week with your daughter about school and friends. Ask questions about how things are going with her attempts to be inclusive. Ask if she was put into a situation that week that forced her to exclude someone. Ask how these things make her feel and encourage her empathy. Continue to reinforce the values of respect for others and friendliness to all. Praise her for good decision-making in those areas and help her sort out things that didn't go quite right.

If you can keep this conversation going throughout her school days, you'll continue to have good opportunities to influence the decisions she makes when it comes to respecting others.

Dear Thelma: I completely forgot my hair appointment last week and realized it about an hour later. I called immediately and apologized. My stylist graciously accepted my apology and rescheduled me. I feel so bad. Is there anything more I should do?

A: You did the right thing. Owning up to that kind of a mistake right away is always the best thing you can do. Your call also let your stylist know that you do value her time.

I spoke to my own stylist about how he feels when a client cancels an appointment and doesn't give notice. He said: "When people do that, it's like stealing money from me. When it happens regularly I really do not want them to return. However, I am very understanding with clients when the last-minute call is for a good reason, and if I am running late, I try to notify my clients."

He added that clients expect respect from the person providing their personal services, but that respect must be mutual. We go to these professionals –to style our hair, perfect our nails, or care for our skin – because they are experts. We should treat them with the esteem they deserve.

I'm often asked to comment on tipping the owner of a salon or nail studio who provides the service. In the past, that sort of tipping wasn't the norm. But in today's service-oriented society, those tips are appropriate. My manicurist says customers don't necessarily need to tip, but she always appreciates when they do.

I really appreciate my hair stylist and my manicurist. I like that consistency they provide in my life. These people are important parts of our lives. It's important that we treat them that way.

Proper respect and good manners never go out of style.

Dear Thelma: My daughter is getting married and doesn't want children at her wedding or reception. Her fiancé is worried that the people he is asking to come from out of town or in town for that matter may not come if children aren't included. Is there a way to handle this so everyone is happy?

A: This is just the beginning of the compromises required in a marriage and this is the best time to begin using those communication skills that will help a marriage last. Your daughter and her fiancé must work out the issue of inviting children to the wedding together. They must respectfully and lovingly express their feelings on either side of the issue to each other. They must listen to each other with their ears, minds and hearts and even listen with a bias toward their beloved. By openly discussing the issue and making the decision together, they have the chance of making the outcome feel like a shared decision rather than a compromise in which one person has had to give in to keep the peace.

It sounds as though you are leaving the guest list up to the couple. If that's the case, then it's important that you let them make this decision together. This is your first chance to show what a wonderful, unobtrusive mother-in-law you will be.

As we move into the traditional wedding season, those receiving invitations should know that those invited to the wedding will be specifically listed on the invitation, usually on the inner envelope. If the invitation is made to "Mr. and Mrs. Torres and Family," then your children are welcomed to the celebration. If it simply says "Mr. and Mrs. Torres," then the invitation is to the couple only. If "Ms. Evey and Guest" are listed, then she may bring a guest. If only "Ms. Evey" is listed, she should come alone.

Hosts of a wedding make these distinctions for many reasons, whether it's the size of the accommodations or desire for an adult-only evening. As hosts, the guest list is their prerogative. Guests should always take those distinctions seriously and not deviate from them.

Dear Thelma: I have to admit, I haven't done a very good job of instilling in or expecting table manners from my children, ages 7 and 9. So far, it's taken all my energy just to get them to eat what I serve. Is it too late for us?

A: It's never too late. This is a great time of year for such lessons as opportunities arise for extended-family gatherings and parties. If there is an Easter dinner you'll be attending or a spring tea party you've always wanted to host, use those events to motivate yourself and your etiquette students.

Good manners are important skills children can develop when they are young and benefit from for a lifetime. Parents play an integral role as up-front models for proper table behavior.

Present the basics and then practice at a meal – even practice one element at a time until they become habitual. Start by teaching your children to place napkins on their laps and to use them to dab the corners of their mouth. Tell them that if they need to wipe their entire faces with the napkins, that's a sign that they're not eating with proper control.

Remind your children to eat slowly and to take small, easily managed bites. Taking bites that are too big is unsafe and also rude. Show them how to eat with her mouths closed. Help them to remember to keep their free arms and elbows in their laps while eating and not to rest them on the table.

Say "please" and "thank you" when you want something to be passed to you. Your kids will follow suit. Remind children to refrain from making negative comments about what they are served. They may choose not to eat what's on their plate instead.

And finally, wait for the entire family to finish eating before anyone leaves the table. Then encourage the kids to help you clean up. Even toddlers can learn the habit of taking their cups and spoons to the sink. Young children can help load the dishwasher, put away leftover food or wipe the table.

Start with these basics and you'll have a good foundation to build upon.

Dear Thelma: It seems like text messaging is the preferred method of communication for some people, like they'd rather text me than actually speak to me. Isn't that rude?

A: It can be. Users of any technology must take care to avoid replacing all in-person contact in favor their favorite device. They must also avoid choosing the device over the people around them.

The most important text etiquette point for me is that texting be done outside of your time spent with others. The person you are with face-to-face should always take precedence over a text message. If you are expecting something urgent, you can inform that person that you may have to attend to a text during your time together and apologize beforehand. Apologize again when the message comes through and use your response to end the exchange until you are no longer occupied.

Most truly important matters shouldn't be handled by text. Text messages are informal and should be brief and concise. Anything more you have to express should be handled in a phone call or in person.

The most basic manners of texting include selecting an alert tone that doesn't disturb and keeping its volume as low as possible – even silent in some instances. Don't confuse your reader with less than obvious abbreviations and double check the number before sending. Finally, for safety's sake, don't text while driving. Even when embracing technology, good manners never go out of style.

Dear Thelma: Regarding the reader who wanted college contributions in place of gifts at her child's birthday, is it me, or are party intentions out of control. Recently, I was asked to contribute to a pot-luck wedding shower, plus asked to make contributions for the honeymoon. Also, my daughter is thinking of asking for contributions on her baby shower invitations for the purpose of buying a car. I am hosting the shower and am appalled and embarrassed at what my relatives and friends will think about this. In our day we paid for our own honeymoon and bought our own cars. Whatever happened to the old fashioned idea of shopping for gifts? Am I too old fashioned, or do I need to get with the program?

A: There is nothing old fashioned about realizing that gifts really should have meaning behind them and shouldn't be dictated by the receiver. Gifts are voluntary, and part of the joy in gift-giving is choosing something carefully and seeing the receiver's reaction.

Tell your daughter that a shower is about more that gifts or money. It's about the honor people want to bestow upon her and the new life she carries inside her. And it's about being a gracious receiver, rather than what could be perceived as a greedy one.

Dear Thelma: I have a comment for the reader who asked if there was a way to handle the situation of children being invited to her daughter's wedding or reception. My best friend was married in California, and my children were in the wedding. Children were invited to the ceremony, but the reception was adult-only. After the ceremony, a few teenagers who were at the ceremony took the children to a relative's house and they had their own pizza party with games and movies. It was a great compromise and worked out well for everyone.

A: Thoughtfulness and good manners never go out of style.

Dear Thelma: When I'm a guest at a party how do I communicate with people whom I do not know anything about?

A: Having a handle on the art of conversation seems natural to many people, but it really is something that you can prepare yourself for and practice.

Most people like to talk about themselves, so ask as question to break the ice. It can be as simple as, "Have you tried the stuffed mushrooms?" to "I heard you say you are originally from California. What part?"

You can also use a compliment as an icebreaker; however, keep it neutral and appropriate for either gender: "That's an interesting button on your label. What does it mean?" or "I really like your glasses. Where did you get them?"

Keep up the small talk with current or cultural events. Scan the newspaper before you go out for the evening for topics of conversation. Find something upbeat, interesting or unusual. "Did you read that the University of Connecticut's women's basketball team closed the New York Stock Exchange yesterday? They are only the second women's team to ever do that." Or "Have you seen what's coming next to Popejoy Hall? I really enjoyed seeing Phantom of the Opera last season." Sports are also usually a fine topic of conversation in any setting: "Did anyone see the game last night?" or "Do you follow the NBA?"

Use active listening skills to keep the conversation flowing. Eye contact is the glue of a conversation. It illustrates that you are interested in the person and the conversation's content. The well-placed "Hmm" or head nod indicates that you understand and follow the conversation.

Your body language should show that the person you're speaking with has your full attention. Do not let your eyes wander around the room. Never show signs of impatience or boredom like tapping fingers, looking up at the ceiling, or sighing. Folding your arms in front of yourself can be a sign of rejection. It is best to keep your arms relaxed, hold a beverage, clasp your hands or put them in your pockets.

If you think more about asking questions and giving others the opportunity to talk, the conversations has the potential to flow nicely.

Regardless of how quickly you might wish to exit a conversation, always do so politely and considerately: "It's been lovely speaking with you. Please excuse me."

Dear Thelma: Do you wear an anklet over or under your stockings and on which ankle?

A: Ankle bracelets should not be worn with nylons. You can choose either ankle, but you should wear them only in purely social settings. Especially at a time of year when it is acceptable to go without nylons, a delicate gold chain ankle bracelet can be an attractive part of your accessorized look for a social outing.

In most office environments appropriate jewelry for women includes one earring per ear, one ring per hand, a watch, and either a bracelet, or a brooch or a necklace. All the pieces should add to a woman's professionalism and should complete a look rather than creating distraction.

Dear Thelma: I just read your column about forgetting hair appointments. I hate to admit that I have done this. When I do, I insist on paying my hairdresser for the missed appointment, including the tip. If I don't, that's income that she misses out on. If I missed a doctor's appointment, you can bet she would charge me for it. My hairdresser is harder to get an appointment with than my doctor. She deserves the same respect.

A: Good for you for knowing good manners never go out of style.

Dear Thelma: If writing a check for a wedding gift who should the check be made out to – the Bride, Groom, Mr. and Mrs., or other?

A: From a manners standpoint, it doesn't matter. I would use both the bride and groom's full names. Simply write it in such a way that they can cash it and that they know it's for them to share.

Dear Thelma: I read with interest the letter from the reader whose 6-year-old daughter was coming home from school crying because she was feeling pressured to be a bully. In response to what has happened in schools across the country as a result of bullying among students many schools now have "bully prevention" programs. The family may want to contact the school principal, counselor or social worker to find out what is available. They need to know what is going on and the little girl may be able to learn skills she can use throughout her lifetime.

A: Thanks for your insight and advice to this family. Encouraging healthy relationships and good manners never go out of style.

Dear Thelma: My son is getting ready for the prom. Can you give us a crash course in prom etiquette?

A: For teens who take the formality of the evening to heart, prom can be a wonderful opportunity for them to have a great time while practicing the social savvy that will carry them forward in the adult world.

Assuming you already have established how much you can afford to spend and have asked a date, don't be afraid to communicate openly about expectations, plans and expenses. Whoever made the invitation to the prom – guy or girl – should be prepared to pay for at least the prom tickets. You also may want to pay for dinner if that's part of what you have planned for the date. That can be discussed along with things like prom pictures or renting a limousine. Together you can decide to share some expenses or dispense with them all together. The person who asked for the date should be prepared to pay for the basics of the date. If the person asked wants to add to the date, he or she should be prepared to pay for the additions.

If you haven't yet, take the time to meet your date's parents before the night of the prom. This shows courtesy and respect toward your date and his or her family. Prom night will be a rush of getting ready, pinning on corsages and snapping photos. Families will appreciate having met you beforehand rather than during your rush to get to the event. It may also make the pre-prom activities more comfortable for you.

Dress appropriately for a formal evening. That typically means girls in formal evening dresses and guys in tuxedos. Respect the atmosphere being created by following the dress designation called for by the prom planners. Traditional prom accessories of corsages and boutonnieres are pinned on the wearer's left shoulder or lapel. Place wrist corsages on the left wrist.

Proper planning shows your good manners. Make your reservations for dinner and transportation and place orders for corsages or boutonnieres as soon as possible. Arrive on time to pick up your date or be ready when your date arrives for you. Be on time for your dinner reservation and at the end of the meal tip your server 15 percent to 20 percent of the bill.

With a focus on the formality of the occasion, a guy should open the car door, make sure his date is in safely and then close the door for her. He also should open restaurant and other building doors for her and let her enter first.

When we're all dressed up, the need for restaurant table manners feels magnified. Remember to place your napkin on your lap when you sit down, use utensils positioned furthest from the plate first and work your way in with each course. At a table set for more than two, keep track of your own drink and bread plate by remembering that your drinks are at your right and solids to your left. Use your napkin to dab the corners of your mouth and never talk with your mouth full.

Once at the prom, remember that you are there with a date. While you don't have to command each other's full attention constantly, never leave one another out if you find yourself in a group and do be sure to spend time together dancing or talking.

Most importantly, respect yourself and your date by refusing to use alcohol or drugs during this special evening. Make the evening about enjoying each other's company and the company of your classmates safely. Good prom memories and good manners never go out of style.

Dear Thelma: You recently wrote that now is a season when it is acceptable to go without nylons. What, exactly, are the standards of nylon wearing? If I never, ever wear nylons am I considered ill-mannered?

A: Unless you are violating your company's dress code, it is now always acceptable to wear a dress or skirt without nylons. It's now less a case of the season as it is a case of fashion that sets the standard. Even in areas of the country not blessed with the mild winter weather we have, women still go without nylons throughout the year in the name of fashion.

So choose your look depending upon the standards required by your profession, then by your own preference. I would not advocate company's making major changes to their conservative dress codes, but I do like the fashion standard because it's more comfortable. Some people will always stay in nylons because of untanned legs or age spots they think they shouldn't show. They don't have to abandon their nylons, but it's OK if they do.

So, while it's not ill-mannered to go without nylons, it is important that if you do choose the fashion standard, you should choose it completely. That means your feet and legs must be well-groomed, which involves shaving, moisturizing and caring for your nails so that you look your best.

Dear Thelma: My nephew met a girl when he got out of prison, and they fell in love and decided to get married. She found out she was pregnant before the wedding had been planned. The family decided to push for a quicker marriage since funds would be very slim for them for quite some time. Wanting to keep the wedding budget as low as possible while still giving them beautiful wedding memories, we opted for a small, close-family affair. We thought we would send out marriage announcements, once the dust settled.

When I spoke to my sister about it she told me she thought it was a "tacky" idea to send out announcements. I told her our nephew thought it would be rude to not formally advise the family of his marriage and I agreed. "You might as well just send out letters asking for gifts!" she argued. Is she right?

It's been one full month since they were married. Have we waited an inappropriate period of time to send announcements?

A: If you're glad he's out of prison, glad he fell in love and glad he decided to get married, then why not send out announcements?

Any new marriage is a time for celebrating the new couple and helping them get started. The circumstances surrounding this wedding make it no different. There's nothing "tacky" about responding graciously and thinking kindly.

Your nephew is certainly correct that it would be rude to not inform the family. A wedding announcement is designed to share the news with those you aren't able to include on the guest list. The style and wording of the announcement should match that of the invitation and include the date and place of the wedding. Replace the line that says "request the honor of your presence at the marriage of," with "have the honor of announcing the marriage of."

Those who receive announcements may choose to send a gift, but they are not expected to. Sending a card of congratulations is proper.

Typically, announcements are prepared for mailing before the wedding takes place so they are ready to send immediately after the event. In your case, I'd get them out as soon as you can.

Kind thinking and good manners never go out of style.

Dear Thelma: Graduation season is here and we need some help. What is an appropriate graduation gift? Is money the best for friends and family? What amount is appropriate? My daughter has a part-time job to cover some of her expenses, but we will need to help her with graduation gift giving. Some of the invitations are to her only from graduates we know casually, and some are to our whole family from graduates we love dearly. Is cash all these kids need or want at this point in their lives? I love giving something tangible, but is that not ideal?

A: This is one question that I am answering purely from my own personal preference. I always relish and treasure opening a gift when I know someone has actually taken the time to think about what I might like and selected it for me. That gives me great joy. There is a heartfelt connection there.

On the other hand, I also have appreciated – particularly reflecting on my graduation from high school – when money was given to me because I knew it was to help me accomplish my next step in education.

Both are appropriate as a graduation gift. As the giver, you have the opportunity to choose the gift that best expresses your own sentiments. The cost of the gift or amount of money you give also depends upon you as the giver and your gift-giving budget. If you are going to give money, have it at least equal the amount you would have spent on a gift.

The essence of gift giving is connection to the person, which can be made in many ways and in all amounts.

Dear Thelma: What is the correct manner in which to show appreciation for a meal or food a friend brings over (without being asked) during illness. It seems as though "Mom" always said you should not return a dish empty. Of course I always write a thank you and see that the container is returned. But, if I felt well enough to prepare or obtain something to return in the dish I would not need the food in the first place.

A: You don't have to return the dish with something in it. The error would be in not returning the dish at all and in not expressing your thanks.

The person who brought you the meal did it to be kind. If when you are well you want to reciprocate, you may choose to. You also may choose to "pay it forward" as they say, extending the same kindness to someone else in need.

Dear Thelma: When typing a letter to a married couple as Mr. and Mrs. John Smith in the envelope address, in the salutation should it read "Dear John and Karen" or "Dear Karen and John?" And in the case of a married couple where the wife uses her maiden name only, whose name should come first in the address line and the salutation.

A: I'm pleased when I see that personal, handwritten correspondence delivered to a mailbox still exists in this world.

Interestingly, this is the question I am asked most often. And in my estimation, in this day and age it really makes no difference at all.

I prefer "John and Karen" because it sounds more natural and more in line with "Mr. and Mrs." However, traditionally, informal salutations and addresses have been written as "Karen and John."

When the woman does not take her husband's name, the traditional address is "Ms. Karen Simpson and Mr. John Smith."

Something besides bills in the mailbox and good manners never go out of style.

Dear Thelma: When we go out to dinner with friends of ours, the husband starts off before appetizers are even served by ordering and drinking two doubles of single-malt scotch and then has another during dinner. His wife orders a bottle of Champagne even if no one will share it with her and then drinks it by herself. My husband and I might have one or two glasses of wine during the evening, but nothing more and we do not order premium drinks. When we go out we often take turns buying or we split the bill in half, but we are beginning to feel uncomfortable as the alcohol bill continues to climb.

Because it is so costly, we try to only entertain at the home and trade off to each other's home, but they are pushing to go out for dinner again. I don't want to keep paying $100 or more in alcohol for casual dinners. What can I tactfully do?

A: Everyone who goes out with friends with the intention of splitting the bill should stay aware of how their orders match up with their companions. Use your heartsense – that common sense of the heart that steers you right from wrong. Of course no one wants to get stuck with more than their fair share of the bill. If you ordered prime rib and your friend ordered a salad, don't fool yourself into thinking that he'll find it acceptable to simply split the bill down the middle. If you drank a bottle of Champagne and your friend had water with lemon, no, she doesn't want to pay for half of your bubbly.

If your expenses total greatly over half of the bill, then you – the person who ordered the most – should contribute more than half or ask the waiter for separate checks. Don't expect the friend who's been finagled to voice a concern – he's in a socially excruciating position. You yourself must realize that it's a concern and take care of it. That is the courteous thing to do.

To those stuck in a pattern of paying more than your fair share with no end in sight, you must start a conversation with your friends that will resolve the issue so that you do remain friends. Before your next dinner our, say to your friends, "We need to discuss how to handle the expenses for our evening out. Tom and I aren't planning to order more than one drink each this evening, so I thought we'd ask the waiter before the meal to give us separate checks. Is that OK with you?"

Once you've had this one-time conversation, you can simply ask the waiter for separate checks before every meal. It should become your new pattern and may go a long way to enhancing and extending your friendship.

Dear Thelma: My sister- and brother-in-law are renewing their vows for their 50th anniversary. What is the protocol for giving a gift?

A: Although gifts are always voluntary, an anniversary celebration typically is a gift-giving occasion. Use your heartsense to choose something to memorialize this special couple's 50 years together or to honor their commitment. What to give is up to you.

Some celebrating such a milestone indicate "No gifts, please" at the bottom of the invitation. If they have made such a note, do honor it. If you have something special you'd like to give them, bring it to them at another time, rather than to the party.

Loving respect for one another and good manners never go out of style.

Dear Thelma: Is it appropriate for people to lapse into another language (which you do not understand) in your presence? What should you do? Ignore it? Ask for a translation? It has happened more than once and I am not sure what to do. I don't want to embarrass the speakers, who are in-laws, but last time they were apparently making some comments about me – indicated by one of them pointing at my clothing while speaking. Maybe they were saying something positive, but it was pretty humiliating.

A: When you know two languages, it is never appropriate to begin speaking a language not understood or spoken by the entire group assembled. It is rude, inconsiderate and a source of discomfort for those left out by the language barrier deliberately created. It's natural for that person to become curious and self-conscious and then make the assumption that they have become the conversation piece.

If they are your in-laws, then they obviously know that you don't understand them. You should not ignore it. You can bring the problem to light without causing them to become overly embarrassed, although a little embarrassment is probably in order. When they lapse into their other language say, "Oh, I'm sorry, I didn't understand what you said. Can you translate it for me?" By doing this consistently, they will get the picture that you don't want to be left out of the conversation and that you expect them to act courteously. If they need to have a private conversation, then they should go to private place to have it.

Dear Thelma: I have heard that in today's business world, one should not clink the glasses with the others seated at the table after a toast. Can you tell me if this is just proper business etiquette, or does it carry over into personal etiquette as well?

A: For me, clinking glasses is a traditional social custom that I don't believe is going to disappear. I grew up in an Italian family where you said "Salute!", clinked your glasses, and loved the sound of it. It is a happy family tradition and there's no reason to let it go.

In your business dealings, read the group. If someone extends his glass for a clink, offer him one. If nobody extends, you can stay reserved with the rest of them. However, when you're among friends let yourself celebrate with the melodious "ting" of happy glasses if it pleases you. Just be gentle with the stemware, of course.

Dear Thelma: Our daughter is a medical doctor and our son-in-law is an attorney. We normally address their letters Mr. Mike and Dr.

Amy Moon. How should we do it when both of them have graduate degrees that would allow them to be addressed as Dr.? Amy is an MD (Medical Doctor) and Mike is a JD (Jurist Doctor).

A: Traditionally, your doctor daughter and husband would be addressed as Dr. Amy and Mr. Mike Moon. I'm most pleased that you are actually writing a letter and less concerned with how you address it.

Mike may be a JD, but most lawyers do not address themselves or each other professionally or socially as doctor. It would not be proper to address the couple as "The Drs. Moon" or "Drs. Amy and Mike Moon," as is traditional for couples who are medical doctors.

You could address him as Mike Moon, Esq., but that's usually only used in business correspondence among attorneys and wouldn't be used when writing to the two of them.

Dear Thelma: My college-age daughter has a summer internship with a company away from home. I've told her that dressing for work in the business world is different than dressing for class on a college campus. She assures me that she knows what she's doing. I dread the thought of her showing up that first day in flip flops. Can you help me help her?

A: Your daughter will be taken most seriously and feel most comfortable if she's dressed in a way that meshes her personal style with the expectations of the company. If the company hasn't already let her know their dress code, encourage her to contact the human resources department for guidance. If they don't have a specified code, they should be able to tell her as what's most suitable.

In many offices, women are expected to wear business suits, pantsuits or dresses. Even for an intern, dress pants, a dressy top and dress shoes are likely the norm. Skirts should be no shorter than three inches above the knee and heel height should not be extreme.

Your daughter's goal should be to avoid distracting those around her, which may mean concealing tattoos and body piercing and limiting jewelry to a ring, one pair of earrings, one necklace, a bracelet and a wristwatch. It also means covering cleavage and making sure all undergarments remain concealed by clothes that fit properly.

If you have the opportunity, make a shopping trip of it. Look at her favorite stores for a few basic pieces that she can work with and a pair of shoes that fit her style as well as an office environment.

Let her know that until she really knows what flies in the office, save flip flops – even her dressiest pair – for the weekends.

Dear Thelma: Sometimes it seems like transitions are tough on my kids' manners. A few weeks into summer it feels like all they know about being polite to one another and everyone else around them has flown out of their heads. How do I even things out and keep them on the right track?

A: School is now out for most kids and the slate of summer programs is set to begin. This is a natural time to repeat any manners lessons you've been working on and offer reminders. As your children make this transition and you talk with them about the safety aspects of their new environments, also take the time to remind them of the manners that will be expected of them.

Entering a program for the summer, whether it's swimming lessons or an art camp, usually means meeting new people. Let your child know that a warm smile and a friendly hello show that you are open to making a new friend. If your child is attending a program with children she already knows, encourage her to look for kids who may be new to the group or look like they need a friend. Just being friendly may help another person get through a difficult day. Express how proud you are of her when she relates how she's put these lessons to use.

Your child also will be working with new authority figures. Remind him to show those adults proper respect. Explain to him before he begins the program the behavior you expect from him – listening attentively and following direction.

Finally, take the time to remind them of the behavior you expect in your own home – even during the summertime.

The spirit of summer fun and relaxation is only heightened when we treat one another kindly and with those good manners that never go out of style.

Dear Thelma: I often attend large luncheon meetings for organizations giving awards or making presentations. The attendees are all like me, business people attending to support the organization and to network with others. Some of these luncheons are very well organized, but others are not and drag out well past the lunch hour. People end up having to slip out before the program is finished or sacrifice valuable work time. Can you offer some guidelines to those organizing these luncheons?

A: I believe the most successful luncheons happen when planners appreciate that professionals use their lunch time to come to these events, value that time, and organize accordingly.

Work backwards from the time the event needs to end. The next important slot of time is probably for a keynote speaker. Once those slots are set, add in the other events necessary to the program and limit their time accordingly.

The welcome should begin as soon as the room is seated. The program may start while lunch is being served and eaten. Some menu items may be pre-set to cut down on wait staff traffic. Ask that during a long set of introductions that applause be held until the end. If proclamations have been issued, print them in the program and refer to them rather than reading them to the group. Set a time for the keynote speaker or awards ceremony to begin and stick to it even if the entire room has not finished their meals.

If you set and follow your own protocol, nothing will be shortchanged. The attendees will have time for networking, your special guests will be honored, and everyone will enjoy the hour without checking their watches and agonizing over getting back to the office.

Dear Thelma: I am newly married. My husband's niece, who has been away to college and who I hardly know, wants me to host her wedding shower. It will be a huge event. I have a small condo and I am reluctant to invite a lot of people I do not know and then pay for a place to entertain them. I also think showers are tacky, like begging for gifts, but I do not want to offend my new sister-in-law's family. What should I do?

A: I believe the first discussion you must have is with your husband. Find out from him what his expectations for this shower really are. Is this a very special niece that he has a particularly close relationship with? Does he see this as the first opportunity for you as a "newly married" couple to participate in an important family celebration? If these things are important to him, he may not have thought through the issues of space and cost that you are struggling with. Talking it out with him is important.

Outside of that conversation, you must speak openly with your niece and sister-in-law. Explain the type and size of celebration you are willing and able to provide. In that conversation you may find out that they are not counting on you to plan and fund the entire event.

Other family members may be willing to help.

I don't agree that showers are tacky. I believe they are an opportunity for friends and family to gather to express their desire to help the new couple get started. If you can look at the celebration as a way to express love for your new family, it may help you find some joy in the planning and the party. Use your heartsense – that common sense of the heart – to make the most of your opportunity to honor and support. Opening your heart and good manners never go out of style.

Dear Thelma: I went camping last weekend and was really bothered by the actions of many people. They were loud, messy and outright rude. Being courteous at a campsite doesn't seem like rocket science to me, but some campers are clueless. Can you help advise them?

A: Camping is a great summer pastime, but the good time can be ruined by the inconsiderate actions of a few. While you're camping, everything you do should point to respect and consideration for those around you and those to come after you.

Camping also provides a great opportunity to let kids participate in planning and preparing for a trip. I encourage families to assign tasks to the children based on their ages and abilities and to give them jobs they can work on together. From filling the cooler with soda cans and ice to carefully cleaning the camp site when it's time to leave, there's a sense of camaraderie and accomplishment created that seems intensified by the great outdoors.

As far as manners go, camping opens doors for such lessons for children and adults. First and foremost, read and follow the campground's rules. They are designed to make your stay, as well as your fellow campers', as safe and as comfortable as possible.

Introduce yourself and your family to your campsite neighbors, then smile and greet them when you have the opportunity. Use it as an opportunity to teach your children how to be friendly without being intrusive.

Everyone in the family should clean up after themselves and each other throughout the stay, which includes each doing his or her share to keep the campground's shared facilities like bathrooms or showers in good order.

Keep the noise level appropriate for the time of day and the proximity of other campers. Watch the volume on your radio and even ask your neighbors if they find it too loud.

Never walk through another group's campsite. It is an intrusion into their space and privacy. Help your children think about how they would feel seeing someone stomp through their area.

Know the rules for fires and follow them. If drought conditions exist, fires may be banned. Bring wood or find out the area's rules for collecting it. Only burn wood and paper in your fire and nothing else, even if you are tempted to throw that Styrofoam cup into the flames. Extinguish your fire properly when you are sleeping or leave the campsite.

Dispose of trash and leftover food in the campground's bins promptly so you don't attract unwanted critters while you are sleeping or are away from your site. Clean up spills on picnic tables for the same reason.

Don't chop at standing trees or nail anything to them. Use ropes to hang things instead. And clean your site thoroughly even down to the last bottle cap before you leave. It's always appropriate to leave your campsite better than you found it.

Dear Thelma: I invited some new neighbors over for dinner. I asked the woman if there was anything she didn't eat. She said she was a vegetarian. Can I serve meat to everyone else and provide a different option for her or does everyone have to eat the vegetarian meal?

A: You can serve meat to the rest of your guests, but you must have something for her. You were wise to ask when you made the invitation so that you were able to take care of her needs in advance, rather than discovering them during the meal. Thinking ahead, thoughtfulness and good manners never go out of style.

Dear Thelma: Every year in our small town there is a Fourth of July parade that we attend. The parade rightly begins with marchers carrying the American flag and New Mexico state flag. During the rest of the parade, other groups have marchers carrying the flags as well. Do we stand for all these American flags presented throughout the parade?

A: No, it is appropriate to salute only the first United States flag that passes during a parade, according to the National Flag Foundation. All parade-goers along the route should show their respect for our national emblem at the flag's first passing by standing at attention facing the flag with their right hands over their hearts. Those in uniform deliver their formal salute.

A man wearing a hat should remove it and hold it to his left shoulder with his hand over his heart. The National Flag Foundation notes that a woman may keep her hat on during the salute of the flag; however, I encourage a woman wearing a baseball cap or other unisex hat to remove her hat as well.

Dear Thelma: This summer my desert-dwelling family will be taking a beach vacation. We've never been to the beach before. Is there beach etiquette we should know about?

A: The beach is like anywhere else. Show respect and consideration for those around you and your beach manners should roll into place.

Start with how and where you select a space to settle in to for the day. If the beach is not crowded, give lots of space between you and the next group. If it is crowded, try to find a spot that allows you at least five feet, about the length of a beach towel, between you and your neighbors. If you've arrived ahead of the crowd, realize that the view and the privacy you had early in the day is likely to change.

As far as views go, be considerate when putting up an umbrella and avoid placing it directly in the line of sight of someone who's already established their position on the beach. Likewise, keep your noise level reasonable. Although it's not a library, it's only polite to keep your music and voices at a level that won't blatantly disturb others. Also, don't use foul language as it's likely to offend those around you.

When organizing a game of Frisbee or football, move to an area in which you won't risk stomping on a child's sand castle project or launching the projectile into the back of someone's head. Be very aware of the people around you when playing these games of catch or when skim boarding along the edge of the tide. Enthusiasm for the activity sometimes causes collisions with innocent bystanders.

In the water, have your fun but be considerate of those around you by controlling your splashing and yelling when others are near. Also, keep everyone around you safe by keeping a good hold on boogie boards, surf boards and other toys that can hurt if released into the waves.

Get all your trash to the garbage can as soon as you can; otherwise, secure it so that it doesn't blow away and litter the beach. Pack it out when it's time to go. Also, find an open space downwind or well away from others in which to shake the sand out of your towel.

Finally, go over all these things with your children and help them to understand why they are important. Supervise them and remind them of what's appropriate when they forget. The beach is a great place for lessons in courtesy and respect.

Dear Thelma: How do I introduce my employers, whom I know by their Christian names, to my friend who is meeting them for the first time? Do I say "Mr. Clark, this is my friend Jim?"

A: Introductions call for the full names of both parties being introduced, regardless of how you typically address them. Depending upon your relationship with them, they may or may not include social titles like Mr. or Ms. Professional titles, like Dr., usually are included.

It sounds like in your situation, it would be fine to say: "Anthony, I'd like you to meet a good friend of mine, Jim Peterson. Jim, this is Anthony Clark, the president of ABC Electric." You may then tell the two of them something about the other to help get a conversation started.

The person with the highest rank or the person whom you know the least receives the introduction; therefore, you speak his name first and present the other person to him.

Dear Thelma: I've seen you address vacationing with other people before, but how about when those other people are extended family members? My husband, our three school-aged children and I have invited my brother-in-law, sister-in-law and their 2-year-old son to join us at a beach-front condo. We enjoy spending afternoons together, but this will be four days of constant connection. We love these people and want to keep it that way. What do you suggest?

A: A deliberate focus by all on communication and consideration during the planning and during the travel will be vital for a successful trip. The difference between traveling with friends and with family is that with family you may be more likely to let your guard down in these areas. Avoid losing sight of the importance of communication and consideration to encourage that good time you're expecting.

Since you've invited them I assume you've honestly assessed how you'll all get along for that extended period and that you are flexible enough to accommodate another family's likes and dislikes on your vacation.

Next, it will be important that you meet to openly discuss what each of you expects out of a vacation. Do the adults have similar attitudes and interests when it comes to vacationing – does one family like most days consumed with playing on the beach while the other loves to ride every coaster at every park within 50 miles? Discuss the times you get up in the morning and go to bed at night, when you eat, and if you schedule naps for the kids into your activities. Talk about how you can mesh your two family's needs and vacation styles into one trip.

Plan as much as you can and make your compromises before you leave. While you normally may like to leave room for spontaneity, when trying to plan something with another family it's best to avoid surprises. Talk about any activities that are "must dos" for your family or any activities that you might plan to skip. By planning such things beforehand, you can avoid hurt feelings or pressure to do something you don't really want to do while the trip is underway. Do make a point to plan some activities to do together, otherwise, there's little point to traveling as a group.

You must discuss expenses before the trip. Decided what will be shared or handled individually, and stick to it. If you've decided that everyone will cover their own meals, don't grab the check to treat your fellow travelers. They'll feel confused over your straying off course and feel the need to reciprocate. Also, if you are sharing the cost of meals, don't eat or drink extravagantly and then expect to split the bill in half. If you ordered steak and a bottle of wine, don't expect your companion who ordered salad and a glass of water to cover more than his share. Although you may rationalize that it all equals out in the end, someone nearly always feels shortchanged.

There is a wide age range between your kids and the toddler, and parental expectations will be different. It's important to talk to your kids about the behavior you expect from them and what they should expect during the trip. Talk to them about how your families will share time and decision making. Prepare them to participate in their little cousin's interests and activities. Plan to discipline only your own children's misbehavior during the trip.

Once the vacation begins, be flexible, courteous and keep communicating. If difficulties arise, remember how important these people are to you. Strive to treat them with the kindness, respect and love they deserve.

When traveling with anyone, good manners never go out of style.

Dear Thelma: Colleagues at work always bring junk food. My office is in a common area where the food gets placed. I end up eating too much of it. How can I ask them to park it somewhere else?

A: You're perfectly correct to ask them to park it elsewhere. State that you are trying to stay on a healthy diet and their tempting offerings are doing you in. Even suggest another spot that might be more appropriate.

So much attention is now being paid to the health threats caused by obesity, wanting to get rid of junk food is not a bad goal.

In all areas of communication, good manners never go out of style.

Dear Thelma: My son in New York is getting married in California and wants to invite many to travel east to west. My fear is most won't travel and it will look like he is just fishing for gifts. Are there any guidelines?

Dear Thelma: What is proper etiquette if you are invited to but not attending an out-of-town wedding? Is it proper to send a wedding card? Is a gift required? I did attend a local wedding shower with a shower gift. I just don't know proper etiquette on not being able to attend the wedding.

A: As you can see, people fret over this issue from both sides, and it's a question that has been asked in its various forms numerous times.

Tradition holds that everyone who receives a wedding invitation should send a gift; however, gift-giving by definition is a voluntary action. The giver makes the choice of whether to give and what to give. The reader's engaged son can certainly invite casual acquaintances or people he hasn't had contact with in years to share in his happy news, but they shouldn't be expected to send a gift.

People close to the couple generally will be honored at receiving a wedding invitation. Even if they are not able to travel across the country to attend, they appreciate being included in the plans for celebration and will want to share in their happiness. In our culture we bring or send wedding gifts to celebrate the couple and the new family they've created by their commitment.

Such gifts can launch or strengthen relationships with the new couple – even years later. A friend of mine kept many of the wedding cards she received with the gifts they accompanied. Later, when she took down a serving platter kept in its box and found the card inside, she would marvel at the relationship she'd developed with that member of her husband's family since their marriage or wonder at someone's kindness that she didn't quite appreciate years before while opening wedding gifts.

This is yet another time to use our heartsense. Givers and receivers should all let go of the notion of "fishing for gifts," which should never be a part of our attitude. If we can view wedding gifts as joining in the celebration of a beautiful, life-changing event, we are more likely to appreciate the opportunity to give or to receive them.

As to the question of a local shower gift and an out-of-town wedding gift, again, use your heartsense. I've said it's customary to send a gift when you've received a wedding invitation; however, if you've given a costly shower gift because you knew you wouldn't attend the wedding, then you have properly honored the couple. A wedding card or a small gift would be fine to send before the ceremony.

Let proper honor and an eye toward growing and building relationships guide you as you send and receive this season's invitations.

Dear Thelma: You've had several questions and answers regarding tipping, but is it still true that you do not have to tip the owner of a beauty shop if she does your hair?

A: In recent years the common practice of not tipping the owner of a salon who styles your hair has gone through a change. The thought in the past was that an owner of a business may set the prices and enjoy the business' profits, while also receiving a fee from other stylists working in the salon. Tips were reserved for those who didn't share in the ownership.

Today's tipping etiquette focuses more on service. If you think of a tip as a reward for good service, it makes sense to offer that appreciation to whoever styled your hair. A standard hairdresser tip is 15 to 20 percent of the bill. Conversely, if the service is substandard, it is appropriate to decrease a tip proportionally.

Salon owners who charge more for their services may not accept tips and will let you know. It also is appropriate to ask the stylist or to ask a receptionist if the owner accepts tips for styling hair.

In a salon where you are attended by several people during your visit – a separate colorist, stylist and manicurist – and you've received good service, give each person 15 to 20 percent of the cost of their particular service to you. Or give 10 percent of the total bill to the person who spends the most time serving you and split 10 percent between others who help – avoiding giving anyone less than $2.

One thing that is important to remember is that while tipping is customary in the United States, it is not mandatory and it should always be deserved.

Dear Thelma: What is up with restaurant tipping these days? The percentage seems to be growing. It used to be 15 percent, but now I've seen 18 percent and 20 percent thrown out there. Everyone deserves their due, but where does it stop?

A: It should be no shock to people that in a full-service restaurant in this country there is a tip due good service. The standard for that tip ranges from 15 to 20 percent of the cost of the meal. Some diners choose to calculate that pre-tax, others just go by the total.

People have become more aware of the tip's importance to a restaurant server. A close look reveals that tipped employees may work under a special, reduced minimum wage, which may be little more than $2 an hour. The server, restaurant owner and the IRS expect that tips from diners will make up the difference. Servers are required to report their tips, which are taxed and subject to federal withholding.

Restaurant sources confirm that 15 to 18 percent has become the tipping standard for good service at the majority of restaurants. At an exclusive, expensive restaurant, 20 percent may be expected. But at such an establishment, first-class service, deserving of more than 15 percent, is expected as well.

If we as diners are accustomed to good service, then we should be accustomed to tipping at least the standard 15 percent. If we expect good service and receive it, then our consciences should bother us greatly if we leave a poor tip or tip a flat amount no matter where we go or what we order.

Again, we must remember as consumers that a tip should always be deserved. Any reduction of your tip to less than 15 percent should be due to truly poor service.

A well-earned tip and good manners never go out of style.

Dear Thelma: School is back in session and the crosswalks are in use. As drivers we are continually made aware of the need to slow down through them by flashing lights, crossing guards with whistles and even police officers ready to issue tickets. I'm for all of that.

However, isn't anyone instructing the children and teenagers on how to cross the street carefully and respectfully? They don't pay attention, they run wherever and whenever they please, or they amble across slowly. No one wants kids to get hurt. They should be made aware of rules to keep themselves safe too.

A: I agree. Students should take responsibility for crossing the street safely, efficiently and quickly. We must depend on parents and teachers to instruct their students to stay safe and show respect for the drivers who have stopped for them by walking with purpose to the other side of the street. That means concentrating fully on getting to the other side of the street quickly in a way that allows drivers to see crossers clearly and to fully understand their path and their intentions. It's the safest and best-mannered thing for everyone.

Dear Thelma: I greatly enjoy the opera and am glad to see attendance increasing with the availability of electronic translators for the audience. However, with this increased attendance, rudeness also has increased. People don't seem to understand the courtesy that is due to the performers and to the rest of the audience. People talk during the performance and then rush to leave during the curtain call. Can you introduce them to proper behavior at the opera?

A: I appreciate your question because I too experienced some disheartening behavior at the opera this season. At the time when we as an audience are to applaud and communicate our appreciation to the cast, people start to crawl over one another to get out. I was even shoved back into my seat by a person adamant about getting out of the parking lot first.

The opera presents an opportunity to enjoy the talent of a group of incredible performers – a group like no other – and we are willing to pay a hefty price for the experience. Being attentive and offering our applause and encouragement at the end of the performance is a vital part of thanking that cast for their effort and their talent.

Everyone attending the opera should be aware that most operas last two to three hours. When planning your evening, build in enough time to enjoy the performance and to behave properly. Arrive early as latecomers are not permitted to go to their seats until after the first act. Plan to stay for the entire performance, including the final bows. Realize that you will have to sit in traffic for a while as everyone is leaving at the same time.

During the performance, which begins with the first note of the overture, there should be no talking among companions, singing, humming or tapping out the tune, all of which are distracting to other audience members. Open cough drop wrappers before the performance and be absolutely sure you have silenced all electronic devices before entering the performance space.

All of these conventions are simple acts of respect and courtesy to the performers and our fellow audience members. Our heartsense should tell us as much.

If you cannot spend an evening following these basic manners, then you should rethink your decision to attend the opera next season. And if you must be the first to bolt out of the theater, make an effort to buy aisle seats so you don't have to bowl me over.

At all performances, good manners never go out of style.

Dear Thelma: I attend a lot of events that include guest speakers. Many times I pay the fee to go to certain events because of the particular speaker. However, lately I've been very disappointed with the effort put forth by some of these speakers. I've definitely not gotten what I've paid for. Can you offer some guidelines for these speakers and let them know what's expected of them?

A: Anyone who accepts an invitation to speak anywhere should be completely prepared to put in the effort it takes to deliver an engaging and informative address tailored to the audience. If you as a speaker do not have the time or the inclination to do so, you should politely decline.

A friend recently attended a fundraising event for the Special Olympics and described the guest speaker, a popular college coach, as perfect. He expressed a true connection to the organization. He described his introduction to it as a U.S. Olympic athlete making a guest appearance at the Special Olympics and his continued support since then. He showed his financial support and encouraged others to follow suit by purchasing some of the event's silent auction items and handing them out on stage to Special Olympic athletes he had visited with that evening. He provided those sports fans who had come particularly to hear him speak with a first-hand assessment of the upcoming season and added some good-natured ribbing of the rival college team. It was obvious that he understood his role as a speaker at this fundraising event and that he took it seriously.

He's a good example for other speakers. A speaker should only accept if he or she truly feels qualified to address the topic or is committed to the particular cause. Following that assessment, the speaker should properly prepare by gathering a profile of the audience and preparing for them. Respect the audience by arriving well-groomed for the event and by making an effort to connect with them. A speaker should always stay on the advertised topic and should never come through as "winging it." Stay conscious of time limits set by the organizers and be respectful of the audience members' time.

Speakers using visuals should make sure they will be viewable for everyone in the room. Always test out the speaker system before the event begins.

Finally, speakers should arrive early and take time to mingle with audience members before the event begins. Even though you won't meet every one of them, it shows you take your role seriously and may even give you an opening line for your speech that will sincerely connect you.

Dear Thelma: Toothpicks used at the dinner table or in a restaurant drive me crazy. Would you address the appropriate use of them?

A: Toothpicks drive me crazy too. They simply should not be used in the presence of somebody else. That means not at the dinner table in the home or in a restaurant, even on your walk out the door. No one wants to see you picking at your teeth.

If you do get food in your teeth at the table, try to dislodge it by drinking water. If you can't, excuse yourself from the table and take care of it in the restroom. Even in the restroom it's not time for a full-on dental cleaning, but a simple extraction of whatever is bothering you, usually one bit of food between two teeth.

Other than that, save the toothpicks for testing cakes, propping avocado pits over glasses of water so they'll sprout, or building marshmallow molecule models.

Dear Thelma: We travel to Albuquerque several times a month. We enjoy going out to dinner with some of our close friends. They often ask us to join them at one of the chain Italian restaurants and we always decline since we cannot stomach the terrible food they try to pass off as "Italian." My Italian grandmother would turn over in her grave if we ever stepped into one of these places. How do we continue to turn down the invitation without coming off as snobs?

A: If these truly are close friends, then you can feel comfortable suggesting another restaurant while not disparaging their choice. You could say something like, "We've been planning to eat at Guido's. Would you mind going there with us?" You might also take it upon yourself to do the inviting and make the initial restaurant suggestion yourself.

Simply turning down an invitation shouldn't be construed as snobbish, but if these truly were my friends I wouldn't want to continue doing so. For the sake of our friendship I'd find a way to invite them and introduce them to my favorite Italian places – of which there are several excellent local restaurants to choose from in Albuquerque.

I too had an Italian grandmother and an Italian mother and father as well. You probably grew up in the same environment I did, where we made the pasta and the sauce and readily enjoyed our home-cooked Italian food. So, while I do understand the difficulty of being fully satisfied with Italian food that doesn't meet those standards, I believe that relationships with friends would mean the most to my grandmother, as they do to me.

Dear Thelma: I definitely agree with your recent column about children making haste in crosswalks, but what about parental courtesy at bus stops? I live in a neighborhood where the bus stops every few houses and at each stop parents feel the need to either talk with the driver or hand them a cup of coffee. Sometimes it's even several parents conversing with the driver and continually holding up traffic with the bus's stop sign out and red lights flashing.

If bus drivers must personally converse with parents after children are boarded and seated, they should pull to the side and stop holding up traffic for those of us who need to get to our jobs to support our families. All parents should show courtesy to drivers waiting patiently at bus stops.

A: I agree with you. These parents are acting impolitely if it is their morning routine to delay the bus with conversation. A wave and a hello as the children board should be sufficient courtesy to the bus driver. Detailed conversation with the driver should be in an emergency or scheduled for another time.

Dear Thelma: When addressing a sympathy card to a married person should the envelope be addressed to Mr. and Mrs. or only to the person whose family member is deceased? What about the inside salutation, should it be to the family member only?

A: I thought about your question and came up with this: It depends. It depends upon your relationship to the person or to the family. Is one of the two a close friend to whom you will want to express a very personal sentiment? Is your relationship with the couple and is it more natural to address them both?

Follow your heartsense. If it still leaves you wondering, include both in the address and the salutation. They will both be grieving and will appreciate your kind thoughts.

Utmost kindness and good manners never go out of style.

Dear Thelma: I recently attended a summer picnic at my daughter's home. All the picnickers were in-laws and family. After five hours of picnicking, I went off under a tree with my lawn chair to close my eyes for a few minutes. I'm 57 and have heart problems. I sometimes just need a rest. My wife announces this to be poor etiquette, awakens me in front of onlookers and declares that we "must go home now!" Is the nap poor etiquette or just a nap?

A: The nap is poor etiquette because the people around you may have read your actions as displaying sheer boredom on your part and felt insulted by that. If you really did need a nap, and after five hours I'm not surprised you did, it would have been better to excuse yourself from the party and nap at home. Being among family, your wife even could have stayed if she wished and you could have returned to pick her up later.

There is more to this question that disturbs me. Your wife's behavior was just as problematic as yours. She should not have drawn any attention to you and your blunder. It would be most polite to approach and awaken you in a very subdued fashion without the attention of anyone. Her declarations and behavior were embarrassing for both of you.

Dear Thelma: We have two events coming up this month. I responded affirmatively to both invitations that my husband and I would attend. Now my dad will now be visiting with us from his home 1,000 miles away when these events occur. We would like to include him in the festivities. He is known by the host of one event. May I ask if we can bring him along and offer to pay for his dinner or is it better not to ask and rescind our affirmative RSVPs?

A: Your consideration of your father should be your top priority in these situations. It is obvious that your heartsense tells you that spending time with him is most important. First be sure he would be comfortable attending the events. Then contact the hosts. Explain the situation and ask if he may be included. You may offer to pay for his dinner, but most hosts really may not want that. It will be the host's prerogative to decide if he may accompany you. Don't take it personally if the host can't accommodate your extra guest. This will allow you to rescind your affirmative response to the invitation.

This is also an instance when simply rescinding your response is allowable. While not an emergency situation, it is a time when being a host to your father takes precedence over being another's guest.

Dear Thelma: Over the years, I have given numerous gifts for baby showers, weddings, birthdays, anniversaries, and other special events. Seldom have I received a written thank-you for these gifts. I feel it is exceedingly rude not to send a written thank-you. Is it appropriate to mention this lack of manners to gift recipients?

A: A written thank-you note is generally expected for all gifts not opened in the giver's presence and not thanked in-person. Shower and wedding gifts require a written thank you even if the giver has been thanked in-person. Now, is it appropriate to mention this to your recipients? No. Calling attention to another's lack of manners is just as impolite, if not more so.

Make your point about thank-you notes by being a prolific writer of them yourself. Perhaps others will be inspired to match your grace and style.

Being a fine example and good manners never go out of style.

Dear Thelma: I am a sensitive young man with a serious leg injury that happened under embarrassing circumstances. I walk with a limp and sometimes use a cane or brace. I do not wish to discuss my condition or answer curious questions concerning my injury, especially from strangers in public places. How can I deflect these inquiries firmly, but politely?

A: When a person meets someone with a disability it is absolutely impolite to question them about it. It should never be a topic of conversation unless offered as one by the person with the disability. Everyone must take to heart that simply being curious does not amount to a right to know.

It is disappointing that you are faced with too many impolite inquiries. You are under no obligation to explain your injury. I believe using your sense of humor is the best way to deflect these questions. With it you can put your foot down without getting upset while making it clear that you will say no more.

A mysterious grin and a "That's classified" will probably do more to keep the mood light but move the conversation along than anything else. If pressed, simply say, "I don't discuss it."

Dear Thelma: At work we are having a discussion on the most appropriate way to introduce the person you are living with, but are not married to. The couples are over 40, so we feel "boyfriend/girlfriend" is not appropriate, and that "partner" does not indicate the depth of the relationship. Do you have any suggestions?

A: Most government entities define you as domestic partners or as living in a common-law marriage. "May I introduce my common-law husband," doesn't sound quite right to me. "Lover" is too intimate. And from there it just gets sillier: My best friend in the whole wide world, the love of my life, my roommate.

If you need a label that reflects the deepest of commitments in our society, seriously consider marriage. Otherwise, I think you'll have to stick with partner.

Dear Thelma: When newlyweds send the son's father or mother a birthday or any other greeting card should it be written to "Dear Mother" or "Dear Dad" even if the daughter-in-law is writing it out? I feel just because my son is married now doesn't mean that his parents' are no longer recognized as such. How do you feel?

A: I feel it's a shame you have to quibble over this. Be happy that your daughter-in-law has taken the time to send you a card. She's not asking your son not to call you "Mom and Dad." She's simply taking the responsibility for sending the greeting, which you may not have even received if not for her effort.

Being open to kindness and good manners never go out of style.

Dear Thelma: You know that old saying about "never discuss politics or religion." Should we stay out of political conversations as course of good manners?

A: I've often been asked this question in recent months and my question back is: How we can avoid them?

It is absolutely an opportune time to be involved in the political process. We have a right and a duty as Americans to be involved. What we must avoid are conversations imbued with caustic judgment directed at candidates as personalities and their supporters.

While we have the right to judge in a critical sense the opposing sides of the issues or opposing platforms, it shouldn't lead to showing disrespect for people, whether they are the candidate themselves or the supporter engaged in conversation.

All who choose to enter political conversations should be well informed so that they might represent their cause well, and they should be ready to listen. Every party to the conversation must be willing and able to listen long enough to hear what the other person is saying. No one should have an agenda ready with which to interrupt. It's the interruptions that cause those emery board conversations that grate upon us so.

If you feel yourself becoming too emotional or sense a strong emotional reaction from someone else, make a decision to move to another topic with a statement like, "I don't think we're going to come to agreement on this one. Let's talk about something else."

After a political conversation, ask yourself: How do I feel? Did I learn from them and them from me? Was I respectful of all views even when disagreeing? Did I criticize the person or focus on the issue? Do I feel exhausted and battered from the exchange? Use your answers to make adjustments for next time.

We have become an incredibly emotional society and have allowed those emotions to make us become as judgmental with the people in our own lives as we are with a face in a campaign advertisement. If we tend toward judgment and hostility, friends and family may not wish to interact with us long after the election.

Dear Thelma: We will be attending an adoption ceremony in the courthouse as my cousin adopts two teenagers. The teens are brother and sister and are really great kids. What, if anything, should we do as far as gifts? Should they be individual or should we give a family gift for all since he has a teenage son already?

A: You seem to know this family well, so use your heartsense to make a decision about gifts as there's really no right or wrong answer here.

This is definitely a time to celebrate family and the fact that these kids are officially joining yours. So doing something for the entire family would be very appropriate. That might be a family game you know they would enjoy, tickets for the group to a local sporting event, or a gift certificate for a particular outing like bowling or the movies.

Dear Thelma: How do you not spoil your kids so that they have some sense of responsibility while still providing for their wants and needs?

A: Parents tell me it's definitely something you have to think about early and often when raising children today. Materialism in our culture makes it more and more difficult for parents to avoid overindulgence and for children to be satisfied.

I have the opportunity to spend time with a mother of three elementary school children who thinks about this issue often and works with her husband to make it a priority. What I've learned from her is a pattern that instills responsibility and quashes attitudes of entitlement.

These parents work to make sure that their children know that responsibility is part of living in a household. That responsibility begins with respecting their parents as the leaders of their home. How do Mom and Dad teach it? By accepting nothing less. That means when a 10-year-old sasses his mom when she assigns him a chore, she points out his disrespect and cuts the amount of time he has to complete the chore in half. Are the children perfect, do their never sass? No, but it's nipped it as quickly as possible and the children clearly know what is expected.

Their next responsibility is to each other. They are expected to take care of one another. They spend time together, they attend each other's functions, and they celebrate each other's victories. Do they still find occasion to fight and annoy one another? Yes, but it's then their mom can say, "What is your job in this house?" To which they answer "To take care of each other." Then they're expected to follow through.

They also have responsibility to themselves, which involves putting in their best efforts at school and with homework. If someone falls into a pattern of missing math problems out of laziness, he spends time during the weekend redoing the week's worth of missed problems, even if the teacher doesn't require it.

Their final responsibility is to their living space. Even as young as 3, 6 and 8, they had scheduled time to complete assigned chores. The 3-year-old ran a dust rag across baseboards, while the 5-year-old mopped the bathroom and the 7-year-old vacuumed. No, their work is not perfect, but responsibility is taken and effort is made, and as they grow older more is expected. Were there battles and whining at the beginning? Yes, but after two years of routine, they typically just get the job done.

It's only after assessing their performance in all these areas that allowances are considered. The kids know that allowances can be rescinded for ignoring or balking at their responsibilities. They also know that taking care of their "wants" outside of birthdays and Christmas falls to them.

At $1.50 to $3 a week, they complain they will have to save forever and sometimes they do. Dad lets them shine his shoes to earn a little extra. They save to buy themselves toys or videogames, and they even buy gifts for each other. Mom buys clothes and books – things she considers needs – and celebrates a good week with ice cream for everyone.

What goes on in the core of a family can set the stage for life to come. Every time my dad gave me or any of my siblings a quarter, he asked, "How much are you going to save?" And he expected us to answer and to carry through on it. He taught us that responsibility and it stayed with us.

Instilling responsibility in children is not any easy task, but it's worth every effort.

Responsible kids and good manners never go out of style.

Dear Thelma: Nowadays is it considered impolite or improper or even ungentlemanly for a boy or man to stand with his hands in his pockets? I see that so frequently that I wonder if now it is acceptable. What do you think?

A: This falls into the category of body language that sends a negative message. Just as crossing your arms in front of you when someone is speaking to you conveys rejection or boredom, placing your hands in your pockets can indicate the same as well as that you are nervous or tense. Frequently when someone stands in this position, you can see his fingers moving in his pockets, another sign of nerves that is less than dignified.

A gentleman really should not stand with hands in pockets; however, boys are rarely taught this aspect of social behavior anymore and as they move into the adult world and careers, they've adopted the stance out of habit.

What should a professional do with his or her hands while

standing to meet someone or at a reception or other public event? Well, it can be difficult if it doesn't come naturally. You don't want to stand with your arms stiff at your sides, as if you were at attention. The best I've found is to place one hand in front of the other and place them both in front of you.

Other postures that leave observers wondering about your seriousness or professionalism include standing with one foot crossed over the other in a toe point or leaning up against a wall. Women should avoid absentmindedly playing with their jewelry or hair.

Anyone in a social setting, from a child to an adult, should always put their best foot forward. That means using good posture, looking others directly in the eye, and being aware that their body language is being read.

Dear Thelma: I, too, have been the victim of bridal, baby, birthday, and anniversary party honorees who never send a thank you note or give a call. Now, along with the gift or check, I include a very nice packet of fine quality thank-you notes. It may wake them up!

A: A gentle nudge and good manners never go out of style.

Dear Thelma: During the course of each day I receive several political emails, usually bashing my candidate of choice. It seems that my friends and family believe that I am a supporter of the other candidate and send me emails accordingly. There are even times when family members, who know my political views, send emails counter to them in an attempt to dissuade me. I am really annoyed! What should I do? Ask them not to send me any political emails? Tell them that they have assumed incorrectly and that I support the "other guy?" Ignore them. Actually I find myself junking all emails sent with a hint of politics, without even reading them.

A: When I first read your inquiry I thought it was something I might have written myself, as I've faced the same questions the past several weeks. I'm sure the entire reading audience has faced the emails and phone calls that use every strategy in the book to sway us one way or the other. I think we've all deleted or hung up and found ourselves thoroughly annoyed.

The question remains: Should we participate in these dialogs or not? Having received your question, I made a decision to pay more attention than I previously had to these emails and calls. Personally, I have not been too enlightened by them.

I consider myself as one of countless Americans who are concerned about the state of the nation. I am making every effort to better understand how each candidate would begin to address or resolve the issues our country faces so that the emotion of fear within our society is diminished. I have chosen to remain focused on what the candidates themselves say about the major issues. I am continuing to gather information and I will responsibly vote on Election Day.

Over email is not a productive avenue for debate, and so ignoring the political mail that is forwarded is often the best way to handle it. However, if you believe someone has assumed something about you or your choice incorrectly, it would be fine to let them know where you stand on an issue or your choice of candidate. You don't have to go into detail, but state your position and ask them to take you off their political mailing list.

Perhaps your best option is to take advantage of early voting. Once you've voted send a message to those who regularly email you with political arguments and let them know your vote has been cast and no amount of continued persuading will change it.

Dear Thelma: How should staff handle the departure of a manager when the circumstances of that departure are clouded and that manager is angry and saying untrue things about the organization and related parties?

A: As difficult as it may be, the staff members must do their best to avoid becoming emotionally involved in the situation. They should avoid the conversations in which the manager is making untrue or damaging statements. If they find themselves in such a conversation, they should have the courage to say, "I do not want to be involved in this discussion." This doesn't mean anyone has to be unkind, just firm.

Staff should also realize that upon the departure, that person's impact should be gone and no cloud should be left behind that continues the judgmental conversations. When the manager goes, every negative thing connected with that person should be let go.

It is well known that critical judgment of other people's behavior results in serious morale problems and diminishes trust in an organization. Every attempt should be made to avoid it.

Clear communication and good manners never go out of style.

Dear Thelma: The other day I walked by a group of young teenage girls, whom I knew, and thought I heard one of them call me an inappropriate name. I kept on walking but was unsure on how to address this situation. Did I do the right thing or should I have stopped and interrogated them one by one? Should I contact their parents?

A: In situations such as these, it is important to keep your head. It's when people react emotionally without thinking things through that true problems arise.

You say you thought you heard one of them call you an inappropriate name. You must ask yourself before reacting how sure you are. Did she look you in the eye and say it or was something mumbled in passing? Do you know which girl actually said it? Could it have been a different word? You say you know these girls, is this in or out of character for them?

If you've taken the time to think these things through, you're in a better position to respond maturely. If this is a one-time thing or a group of kids you're never again going to come in contact with, it's best to let it go. Chalk it up to misunderstanding or teenage silliness. Don't let your emotions or your ego get the best of you.

If you know the girl and her family well and are sure that what she said was a direct attempt to show you disrespect or it is part of a pattern of disrespectful behavior, you can approach her parents as a concerned friend rather than as an accuser. You must remain the adult in this situation. Let them know you wanted them to be aware of the situation. Explain it and let it end there. They will be the ones to discipline or to correct their child.

You must realize that bringing up the problem may not turn out positive for you. People are very protective of their children and will place them above well-intentioned friends. Before you proceed, ask yourself if this incident is important enough to risk damaging or even losing this friendship.

When all is assessed, it seems to me you did the right thing by simply walking on.

Dear Thelma: Regarding your column on unwanted political emails, I also was getting unwanted emails from a 'friend' in another state. I emailed and politely asked her to quit sending me stuff, that my email box was too full (not true). I then inquired about her family, trying to be nice about this. About a week later she responded by sending me a really hateful and degrading email about one of the candidates. She did not write a note in the email, it was just a forwarded nasty thing. So I blocked her email address. I thought I had won that battle. Well, yesterday I got a couple more emails from her from another email address she has. I have now blocked another email address for her. Now what?

A: You've done all you can do. Let it end there and hope that the aggressive behavior ends with the election. The ball will be in her court to mend the relationship.

Dear Thelma: I told my daughter in-law I would throw a baby shower for her. She sent me a list with 120 people on it. What do I do?

A: Be honest and tell her you can only accommodate 30 people – or whatever number you can. Mention that multiple showers hosted by other family or friends may be a good option for her.

In all types of uncomfortable situations, good manners never go out of style.

Dear Thelma: Recently we received a wedding invitation from my husband's niece. Only my husband's name appeared on the envelope (only one envelope was used). Am I justified in not going to the wedding? My husband says I am invited, but I feel having only his name was inappropriate.

A: If your niece did in fact intend to invite you to the wedding, including only your husband's name on the invitation was inappropriate. Invitations should always be addressed to exactly who is invited to the celebration, which means writing Mr. and Mrs. Donald Garcia, or Ms. Amanda Lewis and Guest, or Mr. and Mrs. Carlos Hoover and Family on either the outer envelope or on the inner envelope if one is used.

Taken at face value, the invitation indicates that only your husband is invited. However, this is your family. If your husband has inquired and found that the invitation was intended for both of you, then you should let it go and chalk it up to an over-loaded bride who made a mistake. Refusing to attend is unlikely to have the affect of teaching her some kind of lesson and instead may result in a string of damaged relationships.

Dear Thelma: You answered the mother-in-law about how to put a cap on the number of people who could be invited to the baby shower for her daughter-in-law and expected grandchild. Since when has it become appropriate for a family member to host a shower of any kind? I'm appalled!

A: I can't tell you exactly when things changed, but contemporary etiquette does allow family members to host showers in celebration of the new life. In times past, a good friend or maybe a relative outside the immediate family were considered the only appropriate hosts for showers. It appeared self-serving for immediate family members to host an occasion that strictly revolved around gift-giving.

However, those ideas, and the rules along with them, have relaxed. Today it's common for the close relatives of the child's mother or father to be involved in the shower planning, especially when individual circumstances, such as a family separated by distance, makes traditional showers impossible. Wedding showers have seen the same trend, as more mothers and sisters of brides are now hosting. Today's typical guest doesn't seem to mind. She's most interested in celebrating the new child or the new couple and a shower is a great place in which to do that.

You might also be interested to know that while traditionally a shower was only held for a woman's first child, today "encore showers" are common. Typically, the guest list for a second or third child shower includes just the closest of friends and family and guest who weren't invited to the previous showers.

Dear Readers: I have been thinking about the coming holidays and the children in our lives. The holidays provide a great opportunity to teach kids and teens important lessons about life and good manners. These holidays remind us to be thankful and generous and caring. Establishing or even simply recognizing the importance of standing holiday traditions helps us solidify that thankful, generous and caring spirit to which good manners call us.

Researchers say that family rituals and traditions help make family life predictable and provide the opportunity to reconnect with one another. Rituals also teach children what it is that the family values. The respect and courtesy on which manners are founded should be an important part of all of these rituals.

I'll be sharing more in the coming weeks. I invite you to share with me holiday traditions celebrated as a child that impacted your adult life and your efforts to establish and perpetuate rituals with your own children.

Together we can show how family tradition and good manners never go out of style.

Dear Thelma: The Thanksgiving tradition in my family is to eat red chile on turkey and mashed potatoes. This year my parents and siblings will be celebrating Thanksgiving with my wife's family. Her family has never tried red chile for Thanksgiving. Would it be alright for my mom to bring her red chile to the dinner?

A: First, let me say how wonderful it is that your families can come together in this way to share this day. It truly is a blessing for which you can be thankful.

As for adding your traditional dish to the celebration, you must approach it with care and respect. If everyone invited is contributing to the dinner, then you may tell the host that a dish you'd like to contribute is the red chile. You may need to explain how it's used, but at a potluck type meal everything typically is welcomed.

If the dinner is a more formal affair, with the host doing all the cooking, expectations may be different. Since this is family I think it would be fine for you to speak to the host of the dinner, probably your mother-in-law, about the menu. You may tell her about the red chile tradition in your family and ask if you might bring it. She will decide if she thinks the addition will fit with what she has planned and if she's willing to accommodate it. As host, it is her prerogative.

If she doesn't choose to add the chile to her menu, you must understand. Hosting a big family dinner takes effort and coordination. Trying to accommodate many individual wishes can be overwhelming. Taking on the responsibility of hosting means making the final decisions, and that should be respected.

If you need your red chile fix, make some to eat with leftovers. Then consider playing host to next year's celebration.

This question brings up the importance of traditional foods at times of celebration. For you, red chile is right because it's part of the ritual of the season established by your family. Without it something's missing.

Children especially love predictability and the holidays are a time they look forward to for ritual and traditions, which they carry into adulthood. If you don't already have a holiday dish that the family can help prepare, find one this year to make together and share. If you already have a traditional dish, make a point this season to talk about it. Share why it's important to each of you or how it started in your family. It may open a great conversation filled with things remembered and new memories made.

236

Dear Thelma: While I love my family, I do not like several of its members. They are loud, rude, and often mean spirited. Can you give me any advice on getting through the holiday meals, which have the potential of being miserable events?

A: Since it is family and the guest list won't be altered to not include these intrusive people, you should talk with them about it beforehand, especially if you are the host of the meal. As the host you have the right to say, "I don't want 'mean-spirited' behavior here."

I myself have found the occasion to say, "We're going to have a happy time. We're not going to pick on each other. Got it?" If confronted, they may say, "Then I'm not coming." And that would be their choice.

Consider bringing out games you can play together after the meal. From cards and dominos to the modern party games, these may help you focus on something other than someone else's faults. It may also start a new, enjoyable family tradition.

Seeking kindness during the holidays and good manners never go out of style.

Dear Thelma: I work for a non-profit company where we have many female donors. Since the woman is the primary donor, what is the proper way to address her if she is part of a married couple? With her as the primary giver, it seems insulting to leave out her first name. For example, if Jan Smith is the primary donor and her husband's name is Josh Smith, it seems that it would be insulting to address correspondences to them as Mr. and Mrs. Josh Smith.

A: First, I will say that there is nothing insulting about being addressed as Mr. and Mrs. Josh Smith. It is the customary formal address for all couples. If the donation is coming from the couple, even if the wife has initiated it, then they should be addressed formally as such.

During the cultivation period of a donor, the details of who is giving the gift and who should be recognized for the gift should be established. The contact person in the organization needs to find out at the outset of the relationship what the donor expects. If the donor has a problem with the way he or she is currently addressed, that donor will let the organization know.

Dear Thelma: The holiday office party will be held this week. It has been a rough year for my industry, and I'm not sure I really feel like a party. I certainly won't be buying a new dress. I'm considering skipping it, but I feel obliged to go. What's your advice?

A: Despite the downturn, the holiday office party is still one of the best places to connect with colleagues on a personal level and build relationships that are an integral part of career success. While the feel might not be as festive as in a profitable year, there still exists the opportunity to share your companionship with and your appreciation for the people who have worked alongside you or for you this year.

Make a point to focus on the personal side of the people you encounter. Ask questions about their interests outside of work and be ready to share yours. Use the opportunity to get to know people you don't typically spend time with or to meet someone in the company you haven't yet met. Approach the chance to make these connections with a positive attitude and use the time to build the bonds that last through the good times and the bad.

The holiday office party is an important tradition to continue even when times are tough. While the event may have to be scaled down or thought about differently, it's still important to give people the opportunity to connect outside of the office in an atmosphere that is open to celebration. It's a tradition that gives business leaders and employees the chance to remind themselves that the organization's biggest assets are the people sitting next to them.

Dear Readers: The importance of tradition continues to circulate for me this holiday season, as it has for many of you. Friends have shared their childhood memories of "spending the night" with brothers and sisters on Christmas Eve awaiting the magic of the morning, and how their own children have adopted the practice.

During my childhood, Christmas was cookie-making time. The special Italian cookie that my family made only at Christmas time was cenci. We worked together to roll the sweet pastry dough very thin, cut it into strips and tie it in bows. Then we deep fried it golden brown and dusted it with powdered sugar.

Everyone had to work together on the hours-long project and most of the cookies had to be given away. As we spent those hours making them, we talked about who we were making them for and why. My mother was great at creating a spirit of family and tradition through cooking. The process of cooking for us was an integral part of learning and enjoying being together.

The cenci tradition has never been discontinued. My sister has maintained it, setting a time each year when the extended family can come together to make cenci. The beauty of it is how it brings the entire family closer together and allows time for conversation, sharing and love.

So, why spend all those hours cooking and cleaning up when you could probably go out and buy something just as good? Because you can't package love, you must experience it. Thinking about cenci, I realize there is a certain amount of love that's at the core of every tradition. Even now, if I don't go to help make cenci but am on the receiving end of it, I just glow because I know the love that went into it. I hope you'll look for the love in your traditions this season.

Love and good manners never go out of style.

Dear Thelma: I've been reading your focus on holiday traditions with interest. My kids are approaching the teen years. I'm afraid this may be the last Christmas that holds some magic for them. How do I make sure traditions aren't replaced by friends and dates and everybody doing their own thing?

A: Don't sell your kids short. The holiday traditions are probably more important to them than you realize. And while negotiating through adolescence towards independence those ties to defining "who I am" and "where I fit" may become even more precious for them.

Start cementing family traditions now. Offer each of your children a tradition for which to be responsible. Offer help when it's needed, but do your best to let them embrace the responsibility and be an important part of carrying the tradition forward.

This may be a year when you can sit back and really enjoy your traditions while someone else covers the logistics. On the other hand, it may create more work for you this year, but the payoff will come when as teens they're ready, able and enthusiastic about doing their part. A friend's 10-year-old son has been in charge of assembling the family's Christmas tree for the last two years, directing younger siblings and Mom and Dad. This year, his mother expects to sit back and watch until it's time to string the lights.

For families with teens, you know you can't eliminate their need to spend time with friends, but you can let them know that they are an important part of the family celebration. Treat them more like adults than children as you plan for the holidays. Respect their plans, but also ask and expect them to make time for family plans as well.

Talk about the responsibility they can take for your traditions. If you have a kid who loves to bake, put him in charge of cookie making. If you have a new driver in the house, ask her to chauffer the traditional Christmas light tour.

The holidays are a magical time because they make all of us – young and old – more open to and aware of sharing our love.

Dear Thelma: When has it become the norm to think that all of your children are invited to a child's party when only one name is on the invitation? It seems to have become the norm also to not respond but to just show up. It is getting expensive to have parties at venues and when more children are dropped off than were invited it puts a financial burden on the hosts. Due to these problems, we are holding our last big party (seven children invited) at a pizza/game place. Three children still have not yet responded. Can you address this situation?

A: Invitations are very specific and should be read by receivers – or in this case, parents of receivers – in that way. Exactly who is invited is covered by the invitation. If your child and all his siblings are invited, then they should all be listed on the invitation. If they are not, then they should not attend. Responding to every invitation – with either a yes or a no – is always required. Ignoring either of these standards is absolutely rude.

I hope you'll reconsider continuing to host parties for your children. Parties are an important place for them to learn the social rules of hosting a party and attending one. They also provide a great opportunity to connect with your kids as you discuss who to invite and what they want to do for the party. Parties don't have to be extravagant or have long guest lists, but there should be shared fun and excitement in the planning and carrying out those plans.

Fun parties and good manners never go out of style.

Dear Thelma: I'm considering emailing holiday greetings this year. My mom thinks it is a terrible idea, but it makes a lot of sense to me. What do you think?

A: Most people really do enjoy getting the mail at this time of year, when it's more likely they'll get a colorful holiday envelope along with the bills and credit card offers. Because of this, I opt for the traditional card, and I enjoy being the one to add a pop of color into my friends' mailboxes.

However, done properly, an emailed holiday greeting to people

240

who use email regularly can also be very gracious. For the communication to arrive with a fitting sentiment, you must mold a message that comes across as gracefully as a holiday card. You must put the same content, quality and creativity into your message that would be contained in an envelope, and your communication should not seem hurried or like a last-minute fix.

This can be a challenge, but if you are serious about spreading the joy of the season you should be able to accomplish it. Composed properly, the email becomes a substitute for postage but not for the grace behind the greeting.

You should try to limit your email greeting to people's personal email addresses, rather than business. And for those on your list who you don't communicate with regularly by email, you must opt for a card.

Dear Thelma: I've been one of your readers for quite some time, and while this may not be a direct etiquette question, I think it may be appropriate commentary for our cynical times and I'd just like to know: What does Christmas mean to you?

A: With everything going on in the world today, from war and politics to poverty and hunger, and with all the information fed to us through so many different – and often so critically judgmental – sources, we seem to have lost our sense of awe.

Awe, that potent mixture of amazement, respect and fear, is often what keeps us striving to be our best selves. Losing that sense of awe does push us toward the cynical. A scan of my online dictionary and my desk version helped me form the following descriptor: Someone who is cynical believes the worst in people, has a sneering disbelief in the selflessness of others, and is doubting or contemptuous of human nature or of the motives, goodness or sincerity of others.

Some people seem to pride themselves on being cynical. But after a close look at the word I can't imagine who really would want to be described as believing only the worst, or exhibiting sneering disbelief and contempt for goodness.

To combat the cynicism even her own young children absorb from the culture, one mom I know takes her three kids to the toy department during Christmas with an assignment to think of others. Each of them must purchase a present for a kid just like themselves who may not have any other Christmas gift this year. They have to put aside their own selfish wants and wishes for a moment and think carefully about someone else.

That's why it's good to be faced with Christmas once a year. Given the chance, Christmas can return us to a calmness and goodness inside ourselves. As we relive our childhood traditions or strive to create that sense of wonder for our own children, the importance of respect, kindness and goodness comes into focus.

The opportunity to highlight the importance of that respect and kindness is why I do what I do. Developing and exercising those qualities make them a part of you all the time. They are not a show you put on to impress the boss or to influence people. Learned correctly they become a part of you. Used wisely they can generate the feelings of generosity and peace we get at Christmas all year long. Properly formed, manners become who you are all the time.

I heard someone once say that it would be wonderful if we could credit to others the good will that we ourselves want to be credited with. Look for opportunities as the season comes to a close to find the goodness, sincerity and selflessness in others. Maybe they'll find these qualities in you too. Then let the practice extend past Christmas and you'll make a positive impact year-round.

Dear Thelma: I have three young children who all believe in Santa. My oldest, a 10-year-old, is being told by classmates not to believe anymore. She comes home talking about it and it's ruining the fun for all my kids. Shouldn't those kids at school just keep their mouths shut?

A: Well, we can't really control that, can we? You'll have to figure out how to handle it in your own family. One mom had a mantra, "You have to believe to receive." The magic continues in that house. Another mom sat down with her oldest and shared the secret he was about to discover on his own. She charged him with keeping the magic alive for everyone who still believed.

Santa and good manners never go out of style.

Dear Thelma: Is it polite to ask people what their New Year's resolutions are?

A: Resolutions are often very personal. So I feel the answer to your question depends upon your relationship with the person you're asking. If you are very close and often share personal details of your lives, it's probably fine to ask. If it's someone you know casually or a work colleague, it's better to let them offer to share rather than to ask.

I have a challenge for all of us during this resolution-making time of year. Many of our resolutions focus on health. We want to get back to exercising regularly or eating healthy foods and those are positive things. Along with care for our physical heart, I'd like to add a focus on the heart of good manners and see more of us resolve to exercise and build our heartsense this year. We've talked about heartsense before. It's that feeling of right and wrong at the core of you that informs your judgment. We all should have it; it's often just a matter of deciding to follow it.

At the core of heartsense and at the heart of good manners are courtesy, kindness and respect. If you keep these at the top of your mind at all times, then your decisions in relationships and answers to your own etiquette questions come easily. When you find yourself in an etiquette dilemma, ask yourself, "What is the kindest thing I can do?" What you come up with from your heart is probably the right answer.

If I could start an epidemic it would be an epidemic of kindness. The thing about kindness is that it is one thing that people receive that they instinctively want to repeat and to create in someone else the feelings that a kindness shown brought to them.

Let's resolve to avoid judging one another critically this year. Let's make an effort show more kindness and respect to all those in our lives. Let's start that epidemic of kindness and see where it takes us individually and culturally.

And go ahead and share your kindness resolution with anyone who asks. Perhaps they'll be inspired to add it to their list of resolutions too.

Dear Thelma: Are there different ways you are supposed to hold different kinds of glasses, like say red wine versus white? Martini glasses are kind of awkward too. How do you hold them?

A: There are different ways to hold different glasses, which are based on keeping the drink at the right temperature. The narrow shapes of champagne flutes and white wine glasses are designed to enhance the flavor and preserve the chilled temperature of the drinks. Hold these by their stems and away from the bowls. By doing so you'll avoid warming the champagne or white wine with your hands and maintain their chilled temperature.

A red wine glass's wide bowl allows more air to circulate and allows the drinker to enjoy the wine's aroma. Hold the glass at the stem at the very base of the bowl or by the bowl itself. Red wine is meant to be served at room temperature, so keeping the wine away from you hand is not as important as with a chilled wine.

With martinis people go to great lengths – chilling the shaker, the liquor and the glasses – to be sure the drink is cold. Hold the glass by its stem close to but not touching the bottom of its triangular bowl. This will give you a solid hold on the top-heavy glass, but you will avoid warming the drink.

Drinking responsibly – in all senses of the phrase – and good manners never go out of style.

Ask Thelma 2009
Technology's Heart

Dear Thelma: Do you have any etiquette tips for users of social networking sites like Facebook? I recently joined and have received a lot of "friend requests" from people I knew marginally in high school 20 years ago. I am inclined to ignore them. How do I handle this with tact and not come across as rude?

A: Facebook and similar sites do provide a great way to keep in touch and to reconnect with friends, but they do come with their own etiquette issues. I think many people have wondered what to do about a puzzling "friend request" or even how to get rid of a friend they accepted and regret doing so.

As I always say, at the core of good manners are respect and consideration, qualities that don't change with the latest advance in technology. Facebook seems to know this at some level. When you chose to click "Ignore" to a friend request, which is basically rejecting someone's interest in connecting with you, there are no bells and whistles, no formal announcement made. The same is true when you de-friend someone. There is no notification made to the former friend. If that person has a long list of friends, it's likely she will not notice your absence. If she does notice that her friend list down to 286 from 287, she may have a hard time figuring out who's missing.

Facebook reports having more than 140 million active users and that the average user has 100 friends on the site. Now some of those people are what most would truly define as "friends" – your sister, your college roommate, your best friend from high school, your fishing buddy. Rejecting or deleting those "friends" could result in social fallout for you.

Others on your friend list are casual acquaintances, people from your past, or people you enjoyed touching base with but now have nothing to say to. I even would venture to say that everyone has at least one "friend" on their list who they absolutely have no idea who that person is.

Because of the fluidity of relationships built on Facebook, people popping into each others' lives with a click of the mouse, the development of manners there is important. To get us started, I propose the following basic Facebook etiquette points:

- "Friend" only people you actually know. That means in making a friend request and in accepting a request.
- If you get an unwanted friend request, ignore it. That is the most honest thing you can do and you won't have the need to undo anything later.
- It is acceptable in Facebook to de-friend people, especially if you really have no connection to them even virtually or if you find their views and the items they post on your wall to be offensive. If they discover it and ask you about it, say that you wanted to create a more manageable list.
- It is fine to make a friend request to someone you've just met; however, don't be upset if they ignore it. Along those same lines, don't be offended if you find yourself removed from someone's list of friends. They're not trying to offend, just creating a more manageable list.
- Keep your Facebook site personal, and only accept friends with whom you want to share your personal life. For your work life, create a LinkedIn account. Direct professional contacts there if they request to befriend you on Facebook.
- For safety's sake, take a close look at your privacy settings, especially if you have a lot of marginal "friends." There's really no need to share your telephone number and email address, among other things, with everybody.

Even virtually, good manners never go out of style.

Dear Readers: Often there is much complaint in the manners world over new technology. How do we make the new technology's users behave properly? Is technology too isolating? Will this newest advance be another excuse to let politeness slip?

Well, spending time with my own extended family this holiday season I saw a tremendous opportunity for families to connect by way of new technology. Through a popular and innovative video game system given as a Christmas gift to three siblings, I saw three generations of family come together to laugh, play and truly enjoy their time together.

The game provided a perfect opportunity for the adults to play with the children and to take an excited interest in what was fun and entertaining to the kids. The kids loved involving the adults in their fun. I saw a team spirit among the family grow as we all played together.

The games – most involving virtual sports – had a way of leveling the playing field so that we all achieved, whether we were the little brother or the great-aunt. The play also brought lessons in sharing, conflict management and sportsmanship. Best of all it brought smiles and laughter.

While we could have achieved these lessons and experiences in a non-technological way through cards or board games or sports contests in the driveway, we were all inspired by the newness and innovation of this technology and we wanted to be a part of it. Experiencing and learning it together made it that much more enjoyable as we let the technology pull us together.

Whether you have a new video game or not, don't let these cold weather months and their opportunities to gather around an activity together pass you by. They are a great time to reconnect as a family, learn something new about one another and just play.

Dear Thelma: I was married for 28 years to a wonderful man. He passed away 5 years ago. I never thought I would find another relationship such as I had, but I have met another great guy and we are about to get married.

Here is my question for you: When I took my first husband's last name (let's say Smith), I kept my maiden name (Let's say Jones) for my middle initial. So my name was Lucille J. Smith. When I marry again do I keep my maiden name for my middle initial or do I take my first husband's name for my middle initial? Will I be Lucille J. Johnson or Lucille S. Johnson?

A: The two options you propose are both correct for a widow when she remarries, so the decision is up to you. Some women retain the last name they previously went by as a middle name to make the transition simpler. They may be well-known professionally by the former name or have children with the name. Keeping a connection to it helps avoid confusion for people who know the woman professionally or helps others understand the woman's connection to the children.

Since it sounds like you will be using just the initial, I think it's clearly a matter of personal preference for you. Perhaps you want to honor your 28-years of living by that name by keeping a part of it. Or maybe it's time to turn the page. Only you can say.

I would suggest that you think about it and discuss it with your fiancé, as his feelings should be taken into account as well. It would be a good decision for the two of you to make together as you start your marriage and life together.

Names may change, but good manners never go out of style.

Dear Thelma: I am a teacher. The mother of one of my students sent a friend request to my Facebook site. I get along with her and have had dealings with her outside of school, but I really want to keep my personal life out of my work world. How do I get out of this one?

A: Even though your Facebook site is likely an honest reflection of who you are, it is very personal and you have the right to keep it separate from your work. You probably don't want to broadcast in your status line and therefore to your student's mother that your class is driving you crazy or that you need a glass of wine, which you might feel comfortable expressing to friends in your personal world. A constant stream of pictures of your adorable baby on your site may not be what you want that parent looking at while wondering how much you're concentrating on her student.

I believe you should set a standard for yourself from here on out. Develop a statement that describes from whom you accept friend requests, something like "My friend list is based completely on personal contacts." Then, judge each request according to your statement. You are free to make exceptions, but you also give yourself the power to make choices that are right for you. Also, if the student's mother asks why you haven't accepted her request, you can say quite honestly, "My friend list is based on personal contacts, rather than professional connections."

You may want to consider setting up a LinkedIn site for professional contacts. Then you can direct that parent to your LinkedIn profile.

Dear Thelma: When serving and clearing dishes, what side is used in both. And if water glasses are placed on the right, where do you refill from?

A: Waiters should serve plates from the diner's left side and remove them from the right side. Plates should be cleared between courses when all the diners have finished the course. All used utensils should be taken with the plates. Utensils for later courses should

248

already be set at the table. The dessert utensils should be placed above the plate or can be brought out with the dessert course.

As you've noted, drinks are placed on the right side of the setting and so drinks are served from the right. You wouldn't want to cross over the diner's plate to refill his drink.

Dear Thelma: What is the proper hat etiquette for a woman singing in a church or other public gathering? On or off?

A: I hope that this woman singing in church is wearing a formal fashion hat that perfectly matches her dress and is pinned on her head. If this is the case, she may wear it to sing, just as she may wear a formal fashion hat in a restaurant or to a formal tea. Her hat also remains on during a flag ceremony or a prayer. It generally should be removed when visiting or dining in a home.

A woman who wears a hat that is casual in nature, like a baseball cap or other unisex hat, must follow the rules for informal hats. Show respect during the playing of the National Anthem, the passing of the flag in a parade, during a prayer, or in a cemetery or other monument to the dead by removing the hat.

Informal hats may be worn in public areas like a store, a hallway or building lobby, but upon reaching the destination – a restaurant, a museum, a theater, a person's office, a home or a church – the hat is removed.

Proper respect and good manners never go out of style.

Dear Readers: I'm confident that you have heard the time-worn expression that "My heart is full and my tongue can't speak." It fully describes my emotional frame of mind as I watched our 44th president take the oath of office and make his inaugural address. Watching this on live TV I saw the crowds experience such a heartfelt connection and the happiness and sincerity of the moment.

As I left this audience and got in my car to go to an appointment, I turned on the car radio thinking that the coverage would continue when I heard that the station would return to its normal broadcast. The first words were from a nationally-broadcast, ego-centric talk show host who clearly identifies himself as affecting the lives of millions of people on a daily basis. His first words went something like this: "This inauguration was clearly one of the most hyped up in history, and while I want to hear from you after the break, I do want to say that it WAS CLEARLY A DOWNER and most obviously a continuation of the campaign rhetoric of this administration."

This man's attitude and comments left me feeling a responsibility to share with you again the importance of respect, civility and courtesy in all our public and private communications. While I realize that, more than anything, he is paid to entertain and to produce ratings that lead to advertising revenue, I fear too many people are adopting his disdainful methods of communication, interaction, and viewing the world.

There are many who voted for President Obama and many who did not, but now our willingness to use heartsense in our everyday behavior can work to heal and bring harmony. The good manners of individuals can go a long way to show that we are willing to contribute to the greater good and not remain focused on the derision that politics today creates.

In addressing world leaders who cling to power through corruption and deceit, Obama said: "...we will extend a hand if you are willing to unclench your fist." We should take that image to heart as well and extend our hands to one another. The handshake of good manners will show that we have courage and a happy heart to become part of this country's great potential.

Our conversations have to change as well. I believe we sometimes suffer from a kind of "sound-bite" thinking that influences the way we speak to one another. Rather than thoughtfully engaging, our discussions become a string of 10-second declarations.

To bridge the divide we have to stop thinking and talking that way. We can change by dedicating ourselves to and encouraging others to embrace the idea that conversation is about listening respectfully to others and allowing for polite give-and-take. We've got to turn the tables on the attitudes that have deprived us of the opportunity to comfortably express ourselves and be listened to. We must bring respect back into our conversations that have a political focus.

Healing our nation may seem like a task to big for us individually, but if each of us can truly embrace heartsense and join in a journey of renewing America in our own corner of it, I believe we can have an effect. As Obama has repeatedly stated, to return America to its origins each person must take responsibility. Part of that responsibility lies in treating each other with the civility and respect that we all deserve.

The spirit of America and good manners never go out of style.

Dear Thelma: I agree that polite conversation and thoughtful exchange of ideas is ideal. However, I seem to sense from your column and other articles in the media that we should usher in a new tone of support and trust toward the new administration without any criticism. That seems hypocritical from a press that had boundless criticism and vile comments for our former president on a daily basis.

The "peaceful, loving crowds" at the inauguration were singing a familiar 'in-your-face-tune:' "Na, na, na, na. Na na na nuh. Hey, hey, hey, GOODBYE!" as President Bush flew off toward Edwards Air Force Base.

Is it simply OK to be ugly toward one administration and polite and supportive of another? Where is your criticism of the members of the crowd who booed the mention of President Bush when he was introduced?

A: In my viewing of the inauguration I missed the rudeness shown to President Bush, but when told about it later I was just as appalled as you were. Several people have either contacted me personally or written emails to call my attention to the neglect that is so clearly expressed in the question you have posed.

Disagreement is likely in our system and criticism can be warranted, but blatant disrespect toward the leader – past or present – of our nation is never acceptable. To boo President Bush was absolutely rude and uncivilized. To show disrespect with a song sung at college basketball games by rabid fans was absolutely immature and embarrassing to our nation.

As Americans we are blessed with the freedom to voice our opinions. I hope that more of us will follow our heartsense – that core inside us that tells us what is good and right – and choose to express ourselves with respect and courtesy towards our fellow citizens and our leaders.

Dear Thelma: When my father died several years ago, an acquaintance donated money for a Mass to be said in his name. However, my father was not Catholic and probably would not have wanted the money to be used in this way. Would it be appropriate to use the money for another purpose in this case? If so, should anything be said to the donor?

A: When a Catholic requests a memorial Mass for someone who has died, it is done with great reverence and caring. Typically, the person makes the request directly to a parish and pays a small stipend, usually around $10. A notification of the Mass day and time and the name of person requesting the Mass is sent to the family of the deceased.

In your situation, I would contact the donor, explain that you are not Catholic and ask if he would like to make the arrangements to use the donation for a Mass. If the donor will not, ask if he would like donation returned or if you can use the donation for something else. Have the alternate memorial in mind to present to him at the time you talk.

Dear Thelma: Is it proper to pick up sushi with your fingers? A friend told me it was, but it just doesn't seem quite right to me.

A: Yes, sushi may be picked up with your fingers or your chopsticks. However, sashimi – thinly sliced, raw fish served without rice – should be picked up with chopsticks or a fork.

If you've picked up a piece of nigiri sushi – a slice of fish pressed onto a pad of rice – with fingers or chopsticks, dip the fish side into your dish of soy sauce, rather than the rice side, which will crumble. Also, avoid obliterating the delicate sushi flavors with too much sauce.

Either way you pick it up, you should put the whole portion into your mouth, rather than biting it in half. If you choose to use a knife and fork, you may cut it into manageable pieces.

In addition, the sliced ginger served with sushi is used as a palate cleanser between pieces of sushi, so you really shouldn't flop a piece of it onto your sushi.

Enjoying unique cultural traditions and good manners never go out of style.

Dear Thelma: As grandparents of many, we send cards on all special holidays and presents at Christmas and birthdays. Half of our grandchildren send thank you cards, the other half call before a holiday but never contact us after they receive their gift. We tried sending along self-addressed envelopes, hoping for a response but are ignored. When we call them, asking if they received their gifts, they always sound appreciative, but we won't hear from them again until right before their next birthday or Christmas. These grandchildren range in age of 6 months to 21 years. The older children are the worst offenders. They do not send presents or cards to us.

Should we continue to send presents and cards to all and suck up the inappropriate social skills or should we discontinue sending to the older grandkids who show no consideration to us?

A: This is an interesting question and one for you to consider carefully. The gift-receiving etiquette is clear. Anyone who receives a gift is obligated to show their thanks, whether in person, by phone or in a thank-you note. For some reason, the parents of half of your grandchildren are not teaching this lesson.

Not knowing the dynamics of your individual family, I can't tell you whether or not to take up the issue with your own children. If the relationships are such that you can feel comfortable bringing it up, then I would encourage you to talk gently with them about it. Mention that you feel your gifts present a good opportunity for the grandchildren to practice the good manners that go with receiving a gift.

The fact that your older grandchildren do not send thank-you notes is not all that surprising. The teen and young adult years can be very self-centered. If thank-you notes are not a part of what they did under the watchful eyes of mom and dad, it's not likely they'll be taking it up on their own at this point. For the same reason, to expect them to send you presents may be asking for disappointment.

It sounds as though you are very generous gift-givers, but that your joy in giving is diminished when you're not properly thanked. That's understandable, but I'm not sure eliminating gifts for the offenders would bring you any joy either. Before crossing anyone off my list, I would try to make a shift in my attitude. I would picture them receiving my gift and how very grateful they must be even though they don't take the time to let me know. I would encourage myself to dwell on the thank-yous I do get.

As a gift-giver, your selection of recipients and of gifts is entirely up to you. If you want to taper off the giving and still preserve all your relationships, base it on the age of the kids rather than the level of their apparent gratefulness. Continue to send cards and well-wishes as often as you can.

Dear Readers: I received a telephone call asking me to consider commenting in this column on Capt. Chesley Sullenberger, the pilot who safely landed a full passenger jet in the Hudson River after a collision with a flock of birds disabled the plane.

I agreed with the caller that Sullenberger's response to the reaction of the public to his life-saving deeds and his journey to that response has taught us a great lesson in the joy of giving and receiving.

Sullenberger wrote in the Feb. 23 issue of Newsweek magazine: "It's been a difficult adjustment, initially because of the 'hero' mantle that was pushed in my direction. I felt for a long time that that wasn't an appropriate word.... That was why initially I decided that if someone offered me the gift of their thankfulness, I should accept it gratefully – but then not take it on as my own.

As time when by, though, I was better able to put everything in perspective and realize how this event had touched people's lives, how ready they were for good news, how much they wanted to feel hopeful again."

Sullenberger came to realize that the gifts of people's thankfulness and joy expressed to him were as important for the givers as they were for him.

That is true with any gift. The giver of a gift takes the time and thought to select and purchase something they believe the receiver will enjoy and that will relay a message about their relationship and its value. For all of that sentiment to be conveyed, the receiver must be open to it. She must accept the gift and thoughtfulness behind it.

A receiver who doesn't know how to accept a gift runs the risk of distancing himself from those who want to show their affection and love. Received indifferently, a gift given in joy can become a source of hurt feelings and damaged relationships.

Since the river landing, Sullenberger and his crew have had to come to terms with the realization that simply by doing their jobs – following their training and valuing the lives on that plane – they became heroes to the people their actions saved and to the rest of us. That even in accepting the thankfulness and attention of the public, they can remain true to themselves. "That accepting it isn't selling out," Sullenberger wrote.

We all should realize that when it comes to giving, heartsense must be present on each end of the exchange.

Dear Thelma: I realize that computers and email make the business world run these days, but I worry about its use for socializing. Do we risk losing our ability to interact face-to-face?

A: I spent about two weeks recently without my computer and have come to some new realizations. If I had any doubt or negative feelings on using the computer to communicate or fears about lack of respect conveyed through it, they're gone.

I missed my computer terribly. I felt I lost real contact with people who are in my personal world. With it I've created a tangible network of people who are important to my life, but who, like me, are busy. We rarely are available at the same time for a phone chat and we schedule our lunch dates weeks in advance. Via email I feel I really can express my heart, be spontaneous in connecting and truly stay in touch.

Face-to-face contact will always be vital to relationships and the only choice for confrontation and real-time dialog in which you need the benefit of body language and voice tone to fully understand. But for the day-to-day and in-between times, email keeps the lines of communication open and flowing.

Like clear connections, good manners never go out of style.

Dear Thelma: I see what I would call a sense of entitlement among teenagers. That worries me. What kind of adults are these kids going to become if they have such high expectations of what they need and deserve?

A: This is an issue that I've struggled with as well, especially after a scene I witnessed last summer in a coffee shop. A group of teenage girls were ahead of me in line chatting away about moving into their college dorms. One spoke about an expensive piece of furniture her mom was buying for her. "And that's not all I'm getting," she assured the group.

Another girl spoke up, "Don't you have to earn any money or help pay for it somehow? My mom and dad would help me, but they expect me to earn some money too."

The others laughed and the first girl was appalled. "What are you talking about? Of course not."

The attitude the girl displayed was very disturbing to me. And a sense of entitlement is a good descriptor for it. It was clear that she believed that anything she wanted was hers for the taking.

That scene made me worry like you are worried now. But I recently had an in depth conversation with the single father of two teenagers that relieved me of some of that concern.

His daughter is a high school senior with early admission to Brown and his son is in 11th grade.

From what I see, they have all gadgets they could want. I asked him, point blank, if he felt his kids were entitled to all the technology that's out there.

His answer: "My kids are entitled to what they need to grow up to be effective and successful in a modern world." He saw equipping them in this way as his responsibility and an effort to groom them for the leadership roles he hoped they would have someday.

He convinced me that with the right attitude of parents, teens could be well-equipped and still develop a healthy attitude of gratefulness and respect. He showed me that having what you and I might consider luxuries for the young doesn't have to preclude kindness, respect and heartsense.

In the end, it goes back to the family. Much of this behavior – on one side of the coin or the other – is developed by the attitudes expressed and expectations kids find in their homes. I encourage parents to help their kids avoid becoming self-focused by expecting and requiring them to think of others and to help them develop an appreciation for the things they have and the people who provide them.

Dear Thelma: Some long time friends seem to have been avoiding us for about the past year. They used to be a constant at all our parties and we used to get together regularly. Now they come up with strange excuses and even lies to get out of accepting our invitations, which isn't necessary as we thought our friendship was such that we could move in an out of each other's lives without drama or stress. My question is if we've all moved on, should we continue to invite them and just not expect them. Or should we keep the lines open?

A: It's true that lives do move on and people and their situations change. When those changes happen in a friendship, one side often feels rejected, and rejection is one of the most difficult emotions with which to deal.

In a sense, those excluding themselves or rejecting you have made a choice. You've got to make a choice too. You can let rejection take you down the path that many take, that of getting angry and making judgments and excuses. But better for you might be to think kindly, stay peaceful and work to avoid that stress in your life.

Look at the situation objectively. Has something that once bonded you been removed from the picture – like similar professional lives or children with common interests? Have other activities or people entered your lives that have changed the dynamics of your friendship? You may realize too that while your friendship doesn't have to end, it may be time for change.

While they may not be handling their end of the change with the best manners – lying and strange excuses are not necessary, a simple "We can't make it" will suffice – you can do your best to stay gracious.

Your guest list is always your own choice. If you don't feel moved to invite them anymore, that's fine. If you do want to keep the opportunity open, do so, but don't attach the negative thinking of "we'll just not expect them" to your invitation. That's not a gracious invitation. It will leave you feeling uncomfortable and may be sensed by them.

Dear Thelma: I really do enjoy your column, but I was disturbed by that single father's attitude of: "My kids are entitled to what they need to grow up to be effective and successful in a modern world." And that it was his responsibility to provide it.

The concern you expressed about kids today growing up with a sense of entitlement is very justified and the attitude of that single father is not helping his teenagers at all. Our country was built up and made strong and prosperous by people following the notions of individual hard work, individual self-determination and working for what you wanted.

Fostering the idea among the current younger generation that they are entitled to these things and that somebody somewhere owes all these things to them is far from healthy for them or our civilization. It removes from them their responsibility to provide for themselves their wants and needs. It is not good for society that they be allowed to shift this burden of being responsible off themselves and onto others.

I feel (or at least hope) that most young people are being brought up with the right attitudes. But there is a growing sense of entitlement out there among the younger generation. So I would urge parents not to follow the attitude of that well-meaning but seriously misguided single father and teach their children that they are not entitled to things and that their success in life is due in a large part (most of the time) to the amount of work, initiative, and effort they are able and willing to put into it.

A: I appreciate your response to the column on entitlement among kids and teens today. I think that many people are concerned, as you and I both are.

Bringing up kids with the right attitudes is key and that task falls to parents. Expecting children to contribute in the home and for things they need and want is a good way to help them develop those notions of hard work and self-determination and a good way to combat the sense of entitlement. Expecting children to be grateful and thankful for what they have also is vital.

Sensing a disturbing attitude of ungratefulness – a precursor to entitlement – in her 6-year-old son, a mother I know completely cleared his room. She packed up his toys, books and posters and left just the bed and dresser. She explained to him that he would have a week to figure out how to be grateful. After that he could begin earning back his things one at a time. There was crying and pleading, but she stood her ground. After a few days she did see a major shift in his attitude which has lasted well past the lesson. At 10 he still remembers it, as does his younger sister. But Mom stays alert anyway and is not above repeating the lesson.

By fostering and even demanding these kinds of attitudes in the home, I think many parents, including the single father I mentioned, can and do inspire children to work for what they want and still equip them with the things they need. It takes more effort and thought than does just handing over the latest and greatest, but it is well worth it.

As you have made clear, it is the previous generation's duty to pass on the notions of individual hard work, individual self-determination and working for what you want upon which our country is built. Let us as parents not shy away from that duty.

Healthy attitudes instilled by parents and good manners never go out of style.

Dear Thelma: A friend of mine is very ill. I hate to risk calling while she is sleeping and I don't want to be another in a string of calls asking her the same questions, but I feel like I should be there for her in some way. I would love to pay her a visit, but it's just so hard to know what to do and what to say. What is the etiquette in situations of illness?

A: Remember first that this is your friend. Recognize that this is a person with whom you have a shared past and common interests. While the point of your call is to show support in her time of illness, the call will include conversation coming from both sides. It may even help your friend feel a moment of "normalness" in a time of turmoil.

It's all right to call and say, "I don't know what to say, but I want you to know I'm here for you." People are touched when someone reaches out to them with concern and respect. They can feel your sincerity, and those calls, in almost every instance, are viewed as support.

During your conversation it would be very appropriate to say, "Would you appreciate visitors?" Then she can tell you whether or not to come and when is the best time. You also can ask what help she may need or if you can make a trip to the store for her. If there's anything you can anticipate that she will need, take care of it for her.

If you do visit, you should not stay long. It takes great energy to see visitors. Show your support and do what you can, but respect her need for rest and recovery. Take something like a card or small gift that you can leave behind for your friend to look at later or to leave if she is sleeping when you make your visit. You may also think about sending her cards periodically. They are great for brightening anyone's day.

Dear Thelma: During cold and flu season there is an acquaintance of mine who will not shake hands with anyone. He has a logical reason for doing so – a desire to avoid illness – but I think he comes across as rude. How do you respond to this?

A: When meeting anyone new or greeting an acquaintance or colleague, my spontaneous reaction always is to offer my hand. If I met the person you describe and he refused my handshake, I'd be careful to avoid showing my disappointment. I'd let my hand drop slowly rather than pulling it back defensively, and I'd make a "nice to see you" comment.

Handshakes are important to building relationships. Genuine positive energy can be exchanged through a handshake. It's the first contact we make to connect with another person. Handshakes are very telling. A good handshake conveys trustworthiness, openness and willingness to listen. A poor one or refusing one may show the opposite.

Do I think it's appropriate for a person to make it a general rule to refuse handshakes? No. Refusing a handshake puts the other person in an awkward and embarrassing situation. If there is a serious medical reason that you must avoid a handshake – a compromised immune system or an illness of your own that you want to protect others from – do all you can to put the other person at ease immediately with a comment like: "I apologize for not shaking hands. I've been ill. But it is a pleasure to meet you."

Despite illness and sometimes because of it, good manners never go out of style.

Dear Readers: I've been asked many questions recently related to what are being called "recession manners." Things like what to do when someone loses a job or asks to borrow money and what to do about gift-giving when money is tight.

Manners should be about who you are all the time, in good times and in bad, in sickness and in health. Manners are about using your heartsense – that common sense of the heart – to decide what is the most respectful and courteous thing you can do. If you've formed this part of yourself properly, "recession manners" are already a part of you.

When someone has lost a job, particularly a friend, there is a lot of emotion involved in such a devastating situation. As a friend, you should be able to be honest about your concern and your support. As soon as you find out about the situation, you should make that call or visit to let your friend feel your support.

People wonder what to say when a friend has lost a job. "I'm sorry you're going through this difficult time," is one way to start the conversation. Show that despite difficulties, your friendship and its importance remains.

If you've heard there have been layoffs at the company of someone you know well and you are concerned about them, it's fine to ask, "How are things going at XYZ Company?" They may appreciate the opening. On the other hand, don't push even someone you know well to reveal a personal situation they're not ready to publicize and don't go fishing for gossip.

If you are in a position to help a person in their search for a new job, you can offer assistance. But don't offer it if it's not something you are comfortable doing or if it's not within your realm to do.

The area of lending money is a very personal situation that must be handled on an individual basis. If you don't have the money, can't spare it, or you worry about the loan's negative effect on your relationship, it is perfectly appropriate to say "I'm sorry, but that's just not something I can do." If you can and want to lend money, you can and should ask for something in writing regarding its repayment so that everyone understands what is expected. If the money is a gift, make sure both sides are completely clear on that as well.

Since the change in the economy, people seem to be doing a better job of focusing on how they spend time connecting with one another rather than on what they spend on one another, and that's a very positive thing. With indiscriminate gift-giving a thing of the past, people are showing their love and friendship in more creative ways.

When the selection of a material gift is important, choose gifts from the heart. Send more cards and personal notes. Purchase fun items in bulk that you can assemble into small gift baskets. If the list of people you give gifts to stretches far and wide, it's fine to trim it down to those closest to you. It's nothing you have to announce, just let those extraneous gift-giving occasions pass without a gift.

Recession doesn't require us to hang our heads and put on sad faces. We can still find happiness in life and share it with each other. Recession also doesn't change the respect and courtesy we should always have for each other. As in any economic time, act with true caring and you'll not go wrong because, as you know, good manners never go out of style.

Dear Thelma: I was laid off and now I am interviewing for a job for the first time in many years. Besides needing a refresher in interview skills, I also need to know how to handle the issue of the loss of my last job. Is there a way to minimize the perceived implications of that?

A: Congratulations on landing the interview. The first thing to remember is that you're not alone in your situation. Many share it and it's not something that will be shocking or deal-breaking for recruiters or interviewers. Keeping as positive an outlook as possible and thinking carefully beforehand about the questions that will arise in your interview are good strategies for any interview.

Review your skills, achievements and qualifications and rehearse the best ways to articulate them. Practice speaking confidently about your strengths and how you utilize them and about your weaknesses and how you overcome them. Be prepared to answer questions about your professional goals and why you are interested in this job.

Realize that you'll likely be asked to explain why you left your last job. Explain that you were part of a company-wide layoff and have an answer ready for questions about what led to your individual layoff. Prepare an explanation that will lead to you sharing your strengths and experience and why they are important to the job you're seeking.

If you've been unemployed for an extended period of time, you may be asked about it. Explain how you've been looking for the right fit or how you've used the time to take a class and expand your skills.

Keep all your observations or comments on your former employer positive. You may feel like venting, but don't. It may cast you in a negative light. Think as objectively as you can about your former employer and develop a positive statement you can honestly make regarding the organization or the knowledge you gained there. Use it if asked.

Along with analyzing yourself, analyze the organization and the position you're seeking. Use the Internet to research the company or talk to people who work there. Know the company well and have questions of your own ready for the interviewer. This will highlight your serious preparation and interest.

When you meet the interviewer, smile, put out your hand, make eye contact and say his or her name. It's better to be formal rather than casual: "Ms. Jones, thank you for seeing me." Don't take a seat until the interviewer motions you to sit. Sit up straight and attentively, don't cross your legs or your arms, and keep your legs still. When the interview ends, shake hands and use the interviewer's name. Establish a date for following up and get the interviewer's business card so that you can send a thank-you letter 24 to 48 hours after the interview.

Dear Thelma: There is a social pressure out there pushing me to be sure that my kids' summer is chock full of intellectual, cultural and athletic pursuits. We've been so busy this year I feel like doing the bare minimum, and yet friends seem appalled to find out I didn't stand in line for hours to get into the "right" summer program. What can I say to get them to stop shaking their heads at me?

A: All you should need to say is, "This is our choice for our family this year." And that's where it should end. You certainly know your family and your children better than anyone. Your choice and reasons for it are not up for debate.

As parents plan for the summer I encourage them to take it as an opportunity for dialog and interaction with their children. Use this time to explore with your kids where they are in life, how certain goals have been met or have changed, and how to use the summer to learn and grow as well as to relax and create their own fun.

Parents who work full-time outside of the home will have to find meaningful and safe activities that accommodate their schedules, but all parents can use the process of summer planning to give their kids the opportunity to think about what they'd like to do or try. All their ideas may not be practical or in their best interest, but they can be open for discussion, consideration and even just dreaming about together.

And as you go through the process, consider the gift of time this summer – time to hang out together, time in which there's "nothing" to do, time to learn to relax. In our overscheduled, fast-moving world, we could all benefit from learning a little more of that. And if someone disapproves, just tell them you're advancing their behavioral and social education.

Dear Thelma: I work in a small office. There are two types of employees among the 11 of us, those employed by the company and those employed by a contract agency. Occasionally lunch is catered into the office. Those of us who are contract are rarely asked to join in the meals being provided even though we all eat at the same time and in the same room.

On occasion the contract employees will be offered the leftovers, but only after we have eaten what we brought. There are also times when they hide the fact that they will be bringing in food. My question is, are we just being petty in being upset over this or is this truly bad manners to not include everyone and then eat in front of us?

A: This situation is rude and inconsiderate, and it borders on destructive. It creates a work environment that is not unified and that fosters a culture that supports critical judgment and lack of trust.

I appreciate this question as it brings back a similar situation in my own career in administration. My advice in this case is to the company. I appeal to its leaders to work for the unity that is required to ensure quality performance. This is one company with people working together toward one mission; its workers should be treated as one.

This situation fosters blame, gossip and prejudgment. These are impediments to relationship building, and an organization is only as healthy as the relationships that exist within it. It takes just a little bit of heartsense to realize that people thrive on being treated with dignity and respect no matter how they're classified by the human resources department.

Healthy work environments and good manner never go out of style.

Dear Readers: I visited Washington, D.C., recently and attended a national board meeting of medical professionals. I went to introduce myself to one of the doctors in attendance and put out my hand for a handshake. He proceeded to offer me his elbow.

"This is what we're doing now," he said, encouraging me to bump my elbow to his rather than shake hands.

Now, I realize that we don't want to cause anyone to be sick or to become sick ourselves, but this is not something I will encourage or promote. You will not become sick just by touching another person's hand. If you are concerned, keep your hands away from your eyes, mouth and nose to avoid germs entering your system, and wash your hands every time you have a chance. If you are sick, stay home.

The connection created by a handshake is important. The bump of an elbow just doesn't seem like a universal substitute.

Dear Thelma: We recently attended a graduation ceremony at Popejoy Hall. When we made our way to what looked like a large unoccupied row and sat down, a woman informed us that the seats were saved. Several of the seats next to her had papers and programs on them and we did not take those.

When the rest of her group arrived just as the ceremony was beginning, a young man with them became very aggressive and nasty about us taking "their" seats. I have even witnessed confrontations over saving seats become violent over the years. The practice of saving seats has bothered me for years. So, who is "out of line," me or the savers?

A: You are not out of line. One person saving a whole row of seats is not acceptable. Seats may be officially reserved by the organizers of the event, but an individual does not have the authority to hold blocks of seats.

It is especially frustrating and inconsiderate when the seat saver's companions show up just as the event begins. It leaves those who are considerate enough to come early and find a seat very annoyed. Everyone else had made an effort to arrive on time, and yet the savers allow their guests to barely make it.

Now, I see nothing wrong with a person saving a seat on either side is his or her own seat, but any more than that borders on being inconsiderate and possibly rude.

Finally, such an event is certainly never a time for any kind of confrontation. If one escalates, extract yourself from it quickly.

Dear Thelma: Has saying "You're welcome," gone out of fashion? I have noticed over the last decade but more so recently, that anytime you thank someone they respond by saying, "Thank you." I was taught that when you are thanked you should always say, "You are welcome." What is with this trend? Am I supposed to be grateful when shown gratitude? Should I, when being thanked for thanking, then say, "You're welcome," or continue the thanks giving? If I receive a thank you card, should I send one in kind? Where does it stop?

A: I don't think "you're welcome" has gone out of style. When someone says "thanks," you receive and accept their gratitude by saying "you're welcome." You're then free to thank them for their kindness as well, but the initial exchange is complete.

It could be an easy thing to get silly about, and I guess it could go on forever if you let it. Instead of focusing on that, focus on the fact that people are trying to be kind. I could never get enough of that.

Kind words and good manners never go out of style.

Dear Thelma: This is the most ill-mannered city in which I've lived. Very few people RSVP at all, and if they do, it is at the last minute. If you have to call them, you endure the "dog ate my homework" excuses, which continue the insult. One friend told me it's because everyone waits to see if something better comes up. Will you please comment on why you think this occurs, and what to do about it?

A: While the problem of guests who don't respond to invitations exists across the country, there does seem to be a very real perception in Albuquerque that the RSVP is optional, creating frustration for hosts of large events and private parties.

RSVP is an acronym for a French phrase meaning "please respond." It is the way for the host to say, "Let me know if you're going to come so that I can plan accordingly." Although guests really should respond immediately, hosts even now give a date by when they should respond. Guests must respond whether they are going to attend or if they must decline. This is information the host needs.

The problem of unresponsive invitees surfaced for me recently. I agreed to co-host a brunch at my home to further a cause for a nonprofit organization. About 70 invitations went out that included an RSVP deadline. We received about 35 responses declining the invitation, which while we would have liked them to attend, we were happy to have their responses. A "no" to a host is equally important as a "yes." We received about six acceptances. From the other 25 invitations we received no response at all. While etiquette would allow me to call all those who did not respond and ask them personally if they were planning to attend, I did not want to do that.

When I was no longer able to hold off the caterer, I had to consider the 25 "no responses" as "nos." My co-host and I decided to cancel the event because of lack of interest. This left us the task of calling the 30 people who had responded "yes" or given no response to tell them of the cancellation.

We made an effort to speak personally with all who had responded "yes," but most of the rest received a voice mail explanation. Truthfully, I was happy that I didn't have to speak personally to them. I didn't want to embarrass them, but I also did not want to inconvenience them by having them show up at a party that had been cancelled.

I'm sure most of us have hosted some kind of party and know the planning and effort that it entails, and yet many people still treat an invitation as something they can ignore indefinitely.

I believe it is a behavior pattern that may be a product of our busy lives. People have fallen into a habit of setting invitations aside. Perhaps they feel they don't yet know what their schedule will demand on that date four weeks from now or the demands of the moment interfere with their ability to make a phone call or send back a response card. That may have been the case a time or two, leading them into the bad habit of ignoring the RSVP and causing a crisis in planning for hosts, brides and event planners everywhere.

To avoid this problem in my own busy life, I've made an effort to develop a habit of responding immediately to invitations so that I don't forget or get so busy that the deadline passes with the invitation under a pile of "to dos" on my desk. I encourage everyone to make this effort with me. The hosts of the world will thank us.

A prompt response and good manners never go out of style.

Dear Thelma: My husband and I have a new friendship with a couple who we really like, but we're a little vexed about something that happened recently and don't know how to get past it. The four of us were planning to attend a concert and the other couple offered to purchase the tickets on their credit card with the agreement that we would pay them back for our two tickets. We promptly paid them the $200 that our tickets cost. We found out later that they'd received the set of four tickets free from a co-worker, and then turned around and charged us.

One of my lifelong pet peeves is cheapness. It's not the monetary amount that bothers me, as I would have spent that much had we bought the tickets ourselves. I can't help but feel hurt and a little taken advantage of though.

I like these relatively-new friends well enough and would like to move past this, assuming this isn't a red flag for our future relationship. How do I go about handling this tactfully?

A: If you are absolutely certain these "friends" received the tickets for free, it is definitely a red flag. These people have taken advantage of the situation and of you. Their conduct is unethical and unfriendly.

I wonder sometimes what people mean by the word "friend." The people in our lives fall into different categories, those who are a natural part of our every day routine on down to acquaintances we might stop to chat with in the grocery store. Different things are expected of the different groups of people in our lives.

A person who is really my friend and who valued my friendship would never do something like this to me. I would not nurture this relationship. Once I find something that diminishes my trust, it's very difficult to leave that person on my list of true friends.

I don't believe challenging them about it would improve the relationship. I would move past this by moving on. When opportunities to come in contact again arise, I would politely decline. They may realize that they were caught in their misdeed, and let the relationship go. If they confront you and want to know why you don't socialize with them anymore, it's fine to be honest. Tell them that you were hurt by what you learned occurred with the tickets.

When something like this occurs, it affects that relationship in a way that usually prevent it from returning to the level it was before. Even if you decide to continue the friendship, it's likely that this event will remain just below the surface for you. It will keep you on your guard and prevent the level of trust that comes with a true friendship.

Good manners support a relationship, manners this bad undermine it.

Dear Thelma: I get more and more requests from family, friends and acquaintances to donate to various organizations. The latest one is from a niece soliciting money to support her and her organization in a worthy cause. I'd like to support my niece, but am feeling somewhat taken advantage of. The message seems to be that I must demonstrate social solidarity by making a contribution to a cause of someone else's choosing.

I have my own pet organizations for which I budget donations. Do I need to budget for these other randomly received requests, and just chalk it up to the expense of maintaining good relations?

A: You do not have to make any donation, large or small, that you do not feel inspired to make or to a cause that you don't fully support. You certainly don't want to give what sounds from your question like a significant amount of money grudgingly or with a feeling of regret. That could taint your relationship with your niece.

However, in the case of family, you can't just say no. It will be important to explain to your niece, and to her parents if she is a child or teen, that while you love her and are happy to see her involved in community service, you've already thought carefully about your charitable contributions and budgeted them for this year. Tell her about the organizations that are important to you and why you support them. Explain that you don't feel right about taking what you've set aside for them to support another.

If her organization is something that you can see yourself supporting in the future, ask if she'll be raising funds for it again. Tell her that you'll consider it in your planning for next year.

To parents of children and teens involved in fundraising for organizations – whether it's their school cookie dough sale or building homes for the poor of Latin America – this presents an incredible opportunity to explain what it really means to contribute to a charitable organization. It's a chance for a kid to understand that people work hard to earn their money and take time to think out how they spend it. Explain what it means to support an organization and that the people they are asking have a choice. As a parent you also must require that for any donations they do receive they must show real appreciation at the time the donation is made and later with a thank-you letter.

Another good lesson parents should teach is that if you are raising money for an organization, the first dollars to go into it should be your own. Every kid willing to stand outside of their local Wal-Mart asking for donations for the cause of the day, should put their own into the hat when the day begins.

I do like your idea of budgeting for new causes that may seek your support over the course of the year. It would give you more freedom to consider those extra solicitations. But I still believe that you must have some interest in the organization and the person soliciting the donation for the exchange to be healthy.

Dear Thelma: We ate at an expensive restaurant with a gift certificate. We had to pay more than the certificate paid for. What do you tip on – the price of the whole dinner or the amount you had to pay out-of-pocket?

A: Your tip at any restaurant is based on the price of the entire dinner. The wait staff had to offer the same service whether you were paying or using a gift certificate or cash, so the tip of 15 to 20 percent is based upon the total bill.

Money matters and good manners never go out of style.

Dear Thelma: Since I've been riding the train there is a controlled mad rush to get on it, people and bikes alike. I asked what the correct boarding etiquette was and the rider carrying his bike just shrugged his shoulders and said you go first. So is there a correct way to board the train?

A: In New Mexico, using public transportation is a new concept for most of us. While the manners surrounding it may sit somewhere in the back of our minds, we haven't taken the time to sort them out. Here are the basics for train commuters.

Boarding the train follows the same rule as an elevator. Stand to the side so that those leaving can exit efficiently, then board with concern for those around you. While you should move ahead with purpose, there is no need to push or even pressure those ahead of you. Keep briefcases, shopping bags, backpacks and handbags in front of you and under control so that no one is bowled over by them. If you are loading with a large item like a bike, let the crowd board before you. Your fellow traveler's instincts were right.

Once on the train, find a seat for yourself. Don't take up a seat with your bags or save a seat for someone getting on later. Seats fall into the first-come-first-served category. Once you've secured a seat, look around. Out of concern and respect, seats should be offered to elderly passengers, pregnant women and riders with physical disabilities. Both women and men are expected to provide a spot for someone who needs the seat more than they do.

While riding public transportation, do your best to avoid intruding on other people, as you'd like the same in return. Limit your phone calls to short, vital-information-only exchanges in quiet tones. If you are using headphones, be sure they are not so loud as to negate the need for them. When you're in conversation with another rider, keep your voices controlled.

On exiting the train, use the same courtesy as when you boarded. Be respectful, do not shove or push, and keep your bags or bikes from knocking into others.

Dear Thelma: My son is in the Army and was engaged. He and his fiancé moved up their wedding date due to his unexpected deployment and were married quickly. Then, as the Army goes, deployment was postponed. We were planning to have a late wedding shower, but now she is pregnant. They plan on renewing their vows after the baby is born.

This is their first marriage and things just didn't go as planned. I hate for them to miss out on special events because of the special circumstances. My question is can we do both a wedding shower and a baby shower at the same time or which one should we do?

A: I would concentrate on the baby shower because that's where they are at this point in their lives and they will need the support and assistance a baby shower provides.

Everyone's relationship and wedding story is unique. Just because they haven't had the typical events you hoped for doesn't diminish their love for each other or the love of their family and friends. There's no reason to try to go back in time and create that for them. They fell in love, were married and created a new life. It's important to honor them where they are now.

You mention a renewal of vows. If that will include a reception that they didn't have when they first married, it is then that guests will have the opportunity to honor them with wedding gifts.

Honoring the moment and good manners never go out of style.

Dear Thelma: Today's restaurants serve too much food and my husband and I are always wasting food. So now, we each order a salad and split the dinner in half. What is the right way to ask to do this? Should we half the plate or ask them to? Is it offensive to restaurants to ask them to do this?

A: I agree that portions are often too big for one person and I also have found the need to split a dinner at times. If the meal is something that is easy for the kitchen to split, like a pasta dish or a meal-sized salad, most restaurants will bring it to you split if you ask your server. It is fine to ask.

If you have ordered something that's not easily split, like a steak and baked potato, ask for an extra plate and split it yourself at the table. A polite request and good manners never go out of style.

Dear Thelma: I recently went to a government office on business. When I arrived I was addressed by an employee as "young lady," obviously referring to the fact that I am not young. She observed that I was irritated at her manner of addressing me. I asked her why she did so, and she thought it was "cute." I did not find it so.

I did not expect to find myself patronized and insulted in an office whose function is to serve the public. There is no reason why anyone should be addressed in any manner that refers to age, gender or physical attributes, or that veers from the office's function.

I, and many in my age group and circumstances, would appreciate a column on the necessity for those bureaucratic offices dealing with the public to be scrupulous in their manners when carrying out their duties.

A: I'm sorry you've experienced this because I have found some of the sincerest and most selfless individuals in my encounters with officials. However, bureaucrats are stereotyped as lacking respect and courtesy and as feeling they have license to be impatient, indifferent and rude. That stems from somewhere.

To combat that view, public officials must create a work environment for their employees that demonstrates the highest levels of respect and service for the public and for each other. From the office's top official to the receptionist, their commitment must be to serve. That is the expectation of the public, and given proper focus, it's an easy one to meet.

I don't believe the employee you met intended to be rude, but her misguided attempt to be light and friendly did not create the proper level of service and respect. Government employees in direct contact with the public must be very deliberate in their manners and keep respect for the person they are dealing with at that moment as the driver for everything they do and say. That may be a challenge, but as a public servant, service always comes first.

Dear Thelma: I am going to my 20-year high school reunion and haven't seen most of my classmates for 20 years. I'm really worried about forgetting someone's name or not recognizing an old friend. What do I do if someone walks up to me and I just can't recall his or her name?

A: Ask them. You're all in the same boat. Twenty years is a long time and there's nothing wrong with saying I forgot your name.

If you realize a classmate doesn't remember your name, remind him: "Remember, I'm Thelma." It's more polite to settle it right away, rather than avoiding the name or the person, or running around to try to find out their name from someone else at the party.

The big hair of 1989 is out, but good manners never go out of style.

Dear Thelma: I often go to the post office or customer service department at my local supermarket to purchase a money order. When I am at the counter invariably I have noticed that an individual instead of standing behind me in line will stand next to me at the counter.

I have been the victim in the past of credit card fraud and feel that it is extremely rude for someone to stand next to me while I have my credit card displayed or when I am presenting large sums of cash to the customer service clerk.

I believe it should be the clerk's responsibility to enforce others to stand in line until it is their turn to be served. Should I be the one to say something to that individual or should the customer service clerk?

A: It is the clerk's responsibility and, while you shouldn't have to ask, it is best to seek the clerk's assistance when you are faced with someone who has moved to close.

In a firm, but respectful way say, "Would you please ask the next customer to move back while I make my transaction?"

Many of the places you describe do have a sign or a line on the floor indicating where those in line should wait for their turn. The clerk asking them to wait there shouldn't be a problem. If they don't have such an indicator, they still have the responsibility to ask the person to step back and behind you.

To make sure space is given beyond the situation at hand, take the added step of talking to a manager after your transaction is complete. Tell them of your concerns and ask that the staff be reminded of their duty to protect their customers in these situations. If they don't have their customer service area organized to keep distance between the line and the customer at the counter, ask them to consider adding a sign showing where the line should start.

Dear Thelma: My son is purchasing his first home. He will be moving from our house to his own within the next few months. Is it okay for his parents to throw him a housewarming party at his new place?

A: Yes, you can throw your son a housewarming party or he can give his own. Buying a home, especially a first home, is exciting and a great chance to gather and celebrate. Friends and family will be eager to see it. Just be sure that your son wants to share it and is included in the planning and the guest list.

The party can be anything from a simple open house with drinks and hors d'oeuvres to an elaborate dinner party. People will expect to see the house, so let your son know he should plan to offer tours or allow people to wander through.

People may bring gifts, which your son can open as they're given or after the party. If everyone attending has brought a gift, he can open the presents as part of the celebration. He should be sure to send thank you notes for the gifts after the party.

Also, consider including the new neighbors on the guest list. Gestures of goodwill and good manners never go out of style.

Dear Thelma: I was taught never to begin eating until everyone at the table has been served. Some of my relatives, however, dig in as soon as they're served – something I find extremely impolite. Would it be rude of me as hostess to gently ask them to wait, or, more pointedly, to serve them last even though they are usually the elder members of the group?

A: In a home setting, the general rule is that you do not begin eating until your hostess or host sits down and begins. Also the guest of honor is served first, which doesn't necessarily mean the elder members of the group.

When I am hosting eight or ten people in my home, I serve the guest of honor first – the person celebrating a special event or accomplishment or someone visiting from out of town who we've gathered to see. I don't look at age in deciding who to serve first.

When everyone has been served and even if there are still things to do in the kitchen, I will sit down and start eating with them, signaling that they can begin. Then I may excuse myself to finish anything else that needs my immediate attention.

In your situation, you may say to your guests, "It will not take me long to serve. If you will wait a few moments, we can all start together." Also, if they are not the guest of honor, you may serve them last.

Dear Thelma: I am so offended by people who pierce or tattoo every part of their body. I defend their right to do whatever they want with their own bodies, but what about my right to have to look at them? I avoid a certain grocery store just because of this.

A: The sheer number of tattoos and piercings some choose to get certainly can be shocking and some of the images displayed can be repulsive to some people. But that is the wearer's choice. It is better for you to avoid that store than to pass judgment on the person with tattoos.

Some of my favorite people are tattoo fans and I've found that because I respect and care for them, the ink is not a distraction.

Dear Thelma: I work in a place where we don't really have our own desks and chairs. They are shared by different people during different shifts. My problem arises when I walk in and people have their feet on the chair or desk that I'm there to use. It bothers me to have to work in an area they've put their feet all over. What can I do?

A: Respect in the workplace should always extend to the people we work with and to the tools we're given to accomplish the work. And the closer the quarters, the more we have to pay attention to respect and privacy.

Placing your feet on the place where another must sit or work is not respectful. Although the office furniture is shared, a sense of privacy should still surround it. The chair next to you may not technically be someone else's property, but it's also not yours.

It sounds like there are multiple people causing this offense and that it has become habitual. Approach your manager at a time you're not feeling emotional about the problem, explain the situation and remind him or her of the need for privacy and respect in your shared workspace. The manager should then find a time to make an announcement to all employees about the concern. Then if you walk in and it's still going on, you can remind the offenders of what they should already know.

In close quarters, good manners never go out of style.

Dear Thelma: There is a nice trail around my neighborhood on which I run. Sometimes I take my dog. Many people use the trail for walking and running and a number of them bring their dogs along.

I always try to be aware of others on the trail and keep my dog on a short leash or even cross to the other side of the street when I am passing by someone. I do this because I am wary of dogs I don't know and I like to be assured that a person with the dog has some control over it. I try to show that to others by my actions.

Other people are not so concerned. One woman let her toy poodle rush my 50-pound mutt because, she said, if she pulled on the leash it would hurt the dog's neck. I had my dog on a short leash and under my control, but if my dog had decided to bite that poodle in half, I'm sure I would have been seen as the person with the out-of-control dog. Many people with small dogs don't have them on leashes at all. Many others do not clean up after their pets although there are plastic bag dispensers and trash cans all along the path.

Please share some dog-walking etiquette and I'll hope that my neighbors read it.

A: Respect for those around you is key to all manners. Keep it in mind when walking any size dog through the neighborhood. Train your dog to follow basic commands before you start walking in public so that you have the ability to control the dog and his interactions with other dogs and other people.

Don't leave your house without a leash and plastic bag with which to clean up after your dog. You may not be able to control when your dog has to go, but you can control where it ends up. This is your responsibility as a pet owner and in most places it's the law.

Keep your dog away from people's lawns, landscaping or mailboxes. Walk between your dog and other people's property, keeping your dog to the street side, so he can do his business there.

Realize that not everyone loves your dog, and it may be even better to assume that those on the trail with you don't like dogs at all. Some people are scared of dogs, even small dogs, or just not interested in being approached by them. Shorten the leash to keep the dog near you when you pass another walker. If a person wants to greet or pet your dog, they should ask you before they approach.

If you see another walker and her dog coming toward you, cross to the other side of the street to keep your walk on track or to ask from a distance if the other owner would like the pets to meet. Only then should the dogs be led close to one another.

Be a good neighbor by helping your dog to be one too.

Dear Thelma: Is it rude not to leave a tip at such places as coffee cafes? I'm offended by those tipping jars. We can see the prices for a cup of coffee, and we already expect it to be made for us. So for what extra service should the person making the coffee be tipped?

A: No, it's not rude. Tip jar contributions are optional and really should only be made if you feel you've received exceptional or added service. The cost of making those detailed coffee drinks should be reflected in their price. Nothing more is required.

A tip that's deserved and good manners never go out of style.

Dear Thelma: I sometimes find myself in the company of someone who receives a cell phone call and that person, rather than telling the person that he or she will call back, carries on a lengthy conversation while I am left to listen to that conversation. Is there a polite way to ask the person in my company to get off the phone?

A: This happened to me recently. When I realized a long conversation was starting, I said quietly, "Excuse me, I'll be back." The cell phone conversation stopped immediately and my companion told the person on the phone that he'd call back.

Respectful exchanges and good manners never go out of style.

Dear Thelma: I was in line with my young children to enter a public swimming pool. I was the only adult there among what seemed mostly to be middle-school-aged kids. The three boys in front of me were treating a girl terribly. They started by pulling her shorts down to her knees from behind. She just laughed it off. Rowdy behavior and bad language continued from there.

The final straw was one boy slapped the girl in the face. I could not let the behavior continue. For the sake of the girl unwilling or unable to get herself out of the situation and my own children witnessing it, I said loudly and sternly, "Cut it out." The kids were shocked, one boy said, "What did she say?" So I looked him and said, "I said, cut it out." Things settled down from there.

At what point do you think it is acceptable to play the disciplinarian among strangers?

A: First, let me thank you for having the courage to take control of the situation. What you witnessed was clearly harassment and bullying, which kids are getting away with too often today.

Regarding your question of timing, I think you could have stepped in even earlier. Any time there is blatant misbehavior it's appropriate and necessary to take a stand.

I hope that you talked with your children later about what they saw. I would have encouraged them to tell me what they thought was wrong with the situation and used it as an opportunity to stress the values that are important to the family. If these children had not been strangers to you, it would have been appropriate to talk to their parents about the incident as well.

I imagine after entering the pool behind these kids, you worried some about continued problems or retaliation. You may have needed to keep an extra vigilant watch over your kids during your pool time, but the good you did for the girl and the lesson you taught your kids was worth it to me. You may even have planted a seed in some of those kids about the importance of respectful behavior.

Obviously, the group needed that lesson. This didn't just happen at the pool. This kind of behavior points back to the home where they see it in person and where it is allowed to happen or to exposure to it at school or through television, music and the movies. It is my hope that your intervention caused these kids to think about just how mean their actions were.

Dear Thelma: My husband and I are invited to many weddings, showers, children's birthday parties and the like. We do not have children and are normally happy to share with our friends and their children. However, I'd like to know if there is an appropriate amount of money that is considered a nice sum without going over the top -- $50, $100? We're slightly older and what used to be considered a nice gift of $25 to $50, depending on how close an acquaintance, seems too little. What do you suggest?

A: There is no right or wrong amount to spend or give as a gift. It is obvious that you are happy to share and that you realize that by doing so you stay connected with important people in your life. Staying connected is not measured by the size of your gift, but by the sentiment behind it.

Trust your heartsense on this. There will be times when a gift of $25 feels right and other times and events when you will feel the urge to give more. The receiver should and will be touched by the affection you express and thankful for any gift you give.

In giving and receiving, good manners never go out of style.

Dear Thelma: I have had kid proof furniture most of my life. Now that my kids are grown, I have finally been able to buy a very elegant living room set. Is there a non-offensive way to ask one of my daughters to not let her three small kids (whom I love dearly), use my sofa and love seat as a trampoline when they visit? She was raised in a clean home and was never allowed to do this.

No amount of hinting seems to have an effect. When they are running wild through my home she just sits "comatose" while her husband just ignores the situation. I did get a mean look when I banned the three-year-old from taking corn chips to the sofa. I never ever want to cause a rift in my family, I have a friend who had the same problem and her son will not visit her anymore after it was mentioned.

A: First of all, congratulations on your grown-up furniture. You deserve it and you deserve everyone's help in taking care of it.

Talk to your daughter at a neutral time – not while the kids are running wild – about your wish to keep the furniture in top condition and the need to set some rules for its use for the kids. The conversation needn't be accusatory or demanding, but do go into it feeling confident about the stand that you want to take. It's my hope that your daughter will have enough respect for you to support you and to teach the kids show their respect by being obedient.

Then, talk with your grandchildren the next time they visit about your new furniture, how you want to keep it nice, and how you want them to play safely. Explain the new rules in your house and the consequences for breaking those rules – a time-out from the play or loss of something special, like dessert.

After that groundwork is done, allow your daughter the chance to step in when the kids break the rules. If she doesn't, it is perfectly acceptable for you to so.

As for your friend's son, I hope this column finds him and he realizes that his behavior is disrespectful.

Dear Thelma: I'm a member of a large church. I try my best, along with some others to get to Mass early. I enjoy sitting at the very end of a pew. There are some parishioners who stroll in 20 to 30 minutes late every Sunday and stand glaring at me to move to the middle. I have started standing up to allow them to pass so I may retain my seat. I recently saw one late comer roll her eyes at a man who stood also to let her pass. He arrives early too. Do people need to give up their seats for those who just pop in to receive Communion?

A: I smiled as I read your question as I have so frequently reserved that end spot for myself and refused to move over for those arriving after me. However, in asking myself why, I realize that for me to be present and participating in the Mass I don't have to sit at the end of the aisle.

There may be reasons someone needs to sit at the end – parents with small children who may need to leave or someone who's not feeling well – otherwise it's silly to be so territorial. Yes, the late-comers are a distraction and they should not be rude about getting into a seat, but focusing on love and service to others may help you see them and your need for that seat in a different light.

Bearing one another and good manners never go out of style.

Dear Thelma: This is not necessarily a question but more of a plea to encourage parents to teach their children cell phone etiquette. I understand that there may be reasons why 10- and 11-year-olds would need a cell phone. However, along with that comes responsibility. I have an 11-year-old daughter who does not have a cell phone, but has many friends who do. It is quite disturbing how these young girls text, answer calls and make calls at inappropriate times. They think nothing of texting during birthday parties (while we are singing "happy birthday"), answering calls during meals, and not even thinking of excusing themselves from the table.

If their parents think it is necessary for them to have a cell phone, I also think they should be aware of the etiquette factor. Some adults need to be reminded as well! I know you have printed cell phone etiquette in the past. Could you reprint and emphasize that responsibility and etiquette goes for the children too?

A: The behavior you are witnessing is very disheartening. While we know that kids sometimes fail to think of others first, what you describe sounds like kids who have never even learned what is proper or just don't care. Parents have to be very specific in the beginning to teach kids when and why to use a cell phone.

The very first thing parents should do is model proper behavior with every cell phone call or text they make or take. They should point out good behavior when it happens and assess with their kids situations in which cell phone manners have been ignored. These kinds of lessons can be taught far in advance of a child having a phone of her own.

Even with that groundwork laid, parents absolutely must instruct their children in cell phone manners before they hand over a phone. Cell phone etiquette is not necessarily intuitive, especially for the typically self-centered times of childhood and teen years.

Consideration for others is at the core of cell phone manners; kids have to be taught why that's important and why using the cell phone improperly is rude.

The guideline parents should start with is that the people in the room with you are always your first priority and they deserve your undivided attention. That means the friend you've gone over to visit or the cashier at the store. You should not make a call or send a text when you should be engaged with a person or a group and you should think very carefully about taking a call or reading a text. If the call is from your parents, you should ask your companion to excuse you while you take the call. If the call is from another friend, consider letting it go to voice mail so that you're not distracted from your current company. If you must take a call, always excuse yourself and move to a more private area. Don't force your companion to listen to your half of the conversation or to feel like you prefer the phone companionship to him.

Also remind kids to silence their phones in places like theaters, churches and restaurants, and to speak on cell phones at a natural volume. At a birthday party or a meal at a friend's home, avoid referring to it at all, unless you think your parents could decide to call.

After these points are clear, offer the cell phone with the instruction that impolite use will be grounds for confiscation. Then watch your kids and follow through if they ignore what they've been taught is right. Early etiquette lessons and good manners never go out of style.

Dear Thelma: I am a Filipina girl with a long-distance boyfriend in United States. He came to visit me for the first time in my country and then decided to stay for two more days. I was happy, but that meant he would have to reschedule his flight and pay another $600. He asked if I could pay for it and he would pay me back half slowly. I agreed. Now it's already four months later. We talk everyday but he only mentioned it once and said he didn't have money yet to pay me back. He also borrows money from me, $20 or $40, from time to time.

My problem now is how do I tell him without him getting offended that borrowing money from me is not okay. How do I tell him that I should be the last person that he should borrow money from because he says he wants to marry me? I love him but borrowing money from me shows a lack of responsibility and ability to take care of me even if he tells me many times that he can. It is very sad on my part because he is so nice to me and he loves me, but the problem is he is not aware of the etiquette of borrowing and lending when you're in a relationship.

A: I understand that your question is coming from the Philippines, but be assured this happens in many places.

I think you identified the heart of the issue when you said that borrowing money from you shows a lack of responsibility and ability to take care of you. You know in your heart what the problem is here. It's not that he doesn't understand etiquette. It's that you are allowing him to use you as a source of funds and that he is taking advantage of that.

Here's what you know: He's willing to borrow money on a regular basis that he knows he cannot pay back. And he does not have the income or the budgeting savvy to ensure that he meets his own expenses or he spends beyond his means. If your relationship with him continues, these are the habits and attitudes he will bring with him.

It's important that you have a frank discussion now about your attitudes about money. Set aside your worry of offending him and ask him why he must borrow from you so often. It is important to find out if your views of money are compatible. If they are not compatible, you have to consider finding a polite way to end the relationship as this issue, if left unresolved, will impact your entire life.

Dear Thelma: When I am shopping in the supermarket, standing in front of a shelf or at a produce section deciding on a product, sometimes people will reach right in front of my face to take an item, once a woman even bodily leaned against me to do so. I find this very rude and disconcerting – they act like you are invisible. I have no good response to this and would appreciate your advice as to how to handle this situation.

A: There really is no good response to this. What they have done is rude, but you don't want to answer rudeness with more rudeness. For those on the other side of this question who cannot wait for another shopper to make their choice, it would be most courteous to say, "Please excuse me," and then wait for the person to make some room before reaching.

Simple respect and good manners never go out of style.

Dear Thelma: A work area in which I find co-workers lacking in manners is conference calls. From my perspective, not keeping other participants waiting, muting the phone when you are talking to others or rustling papers, not talking over other participants, focusing on the call at hand, and setting an agenda for the call are just good manners.

Also, while in meetings or participating in conference calls, participants should put their cell phones on vibrate or silent. All those crazy ringtones are very disruptive and distracting. If it is necessary to take a call, please excuse yourself from the room or mute your phone.

A: Your points are beautifully made. As more businesses and organization are utilizing the conference call to connect employees or committee members and to facilitate decision making, these calls have become an important tool. Conference calls are proving to be incredibly beneficial in keeping people involved and committed to their work or volunteer opportunities. And I'm finding that it is a tool that is most successful when participants use the good manners specific to meeting in this way.

Particular attention must be placed on what you've described as "focusing on the call at hand." For a conference call to be a success, the manners that are not particularly observable to other participants must be grasped. An individual who allows him or herself to be interrupted during the call or distracted by other matters may not be observed by the rest of the group, but those disruptions do weaken the attention to and in most instances the quality of the conversation. If there are decisions to be made, quality attention must be given by all participants in the call.

An important way to ensure the success of a conference call is to make sure that the agenda and all accompanying materials reach all the individuals participating well in advance of the call. There is nothing more deflating that to spend precious minutes of meeting time waiting for the material to be faxed. In preparing for a call, participants should be sure the system they're using is one on which they can be heard clearly. Taking care of these logistics before the meeting will inspire more participation and ensure a timely decision.

The chair of the meeting should work to keep everyone involved by making a point to ask the opinion of members who have not entered the conversation. The chair also should establish a protocol that requires each participant to identify themselves before commenting, as in "This is Thelma and I suggest ..."

Placing focus on the manners of a conference call will always lead to greater productivity for the group and its individual members.

Dear Thelma: I read your column faithfully and usually agree with your responses and advice. Today's question about sitting at the end of the pew in church and moving for late comers is a rare exception.

When I arrive early, I choose the seat for the ability to view the service, to avoid being "compressed" in the middle of the row, for convenience in attending communion, or all of the above.

The late comer is rude to begin with and must have a highly developed sense of their God-given right to what they want when they want it. I say, stand up and let them move into the pew.

A: We don't know everyone's situation or their reason for being late, so as you stand don't let judgment cloud your attitude or your Sunday morning.

Compassion and good manners never go out of style.

Dear Thelma: I have several friends who can no longer drive, so I pick them up regularly to attend concerts or other events. Am I wrong in thinking they should have offered to share in the cost since they are unable to take turns driving? It took me a long time to summon the courage to ask for money. I felt very uncomfortable and used because I had to ask. I feel they were reluctant to contribute – one was quite rude about it. Now I feel awkward. How would you have handled this?

A: You did nothing wrong in this situation and you should not be made to feel bad about it. A rider who is regularly dependent on another driver ought to share in the responsibilities in any way that he or she can. The friends catching rides with you should have recognized their need to contribute and saved your feelings by offering to help.

I would have handled this by having a conversation up front, as soon as I realized that I was to be the go-to driver for this group of friends. I would start the conversation with how willing I am to be the driver and then ask how the others would contribute to the cause of us all getting out together. We could work out together whether we would take turns filling up the tank after our outings or whether everyone would contribute during each trip to a fund to cover expenses.

The fact that you waited to summon the courage to start the conversation doesn't matter. The response to it should have been the same – positive.

If you are a regular rider with someone and even if that person doesn't ask you to help with the transportation expenses, you should do something to show your appreciation. Offer gas money and if the driver refuses, then look for an opportunity to show your thanks in another way by periodically buying lunch or covering the entertainment costs. Shared experiences and shared input are what friendship should be all about.

Dear Thelma: I just got notice that my primary care doctor is moving out of state. I really like her and will miss her very much. I would like to send her a note to express how much I appreciated her and thanking her for the care she has given me over the years. Can you give me some suggestions on what to say?

A: Use this opportunity to speak from your heart. I think everything you have stated in your question can go into your letter. "I understand that you are leaving the state and so I want to express how much I appreciate you and the care you have given me over the years. I will miss you very much and wish you all the best." You might have a specific instance or memory that you want to mention or you may just keep it general. Either way, expressing your warm feelings will be appreciated by your doctor.

Everyone values being told they've touched the life of another. Anyone inspired to write a letter of appreciation or thanks should make sure they do it. Don't let yourself be intimidated or stymied by not knowing what to say. Say what's in your heart. In today's world, handwritten words carry added meaning. They carry the message that the writer took the time to do and say something special because the receiver was that important.

Honoring relationships and good manners never go out of style.

Dear Thelma: My husband and I are retired and live on a fixed income. We would like to discontinue the practice of sending and receiving holiday gifts with our relatives, who live out of state. The gifts we often receive are duplicates of items we already have or are not our style, and they add clutter to our very small home. We are often at a loss to figure out what to send the relatives, since we see them rarely. We would be willing to exchange gift cards, but adding more clutter to our home is becoming overwhelming.

Is there any polite way to broach this subject without hurting anyone's feelings? Would it be appropriate to suggest that we only exchange gift cards?

A: It's important for you to identify whether the issue is a need to scale back gift giving or if you're simply fed up with clutter.

Gift-giving is a personal and voluntary activity. It wouldn't be right to dictate what people may give you. What you choose to do with the gift is up to you. If you truly do not have room for it, you may try to return it for something else, you may regift it to someone in no way connected to the giver or you may donate it to a charity.

In the same way, what you choose to give is entirely up to you. A thoughtfully-selected gift card should always be appreciated. Making gift cards your gift of choice could even start a trend among the group.

If you need to scale back gift giving because of financial concerns or a rethinking of priorities, communicating from the heart as early as possible will be your best plan of action. If the group is small and you are in regular contact, consider conversations about your need to simplify and that you would like to end the customary exchange. By being forthcoming with the reason for ending the exchange, you diminish the risk of people feeling slighted or that you're interested in ending the relationship too.

If it's a larger group with which you need to communicate, you may want to write a letter to each of those on your list explaining your desire to simplify this year. Express your care and love for them and ask for their feedback.

Even if you don't exchange gifts, keep the relationships fresh with cards or phone calls during the holidays.

Dear Thelma: E-vite invitations seem to be gaining popularity. I have no problems with them for a casual barbeque with friends and family. However, I just received one for a baby shower for a niece having her second baby. It appears that the hostesses just downloaded her address book. Thirty-eight people have been invited, a good many are relatives living out of state and who generally communicate once a year through a holiday card. How can I inform these people that this type of invitation is not only inappropriate, it also makes it appear that it is a gift grab fest, which it probably is.

A: Technology is a tool in our lives that we shouldn't ignore and it often redefines what is appropriate. E-vites can be as creative and individual as a paper invitation and there is generally nothing inappropriate about their use. E-vites sent as individual email messages should be addressed individually and carefully constructed for look and content that honors the guest.

Even if they didn't get everything right, these hostesses should not be censured for using email or for who they invited. I'm sure many of the relatives living out of state appreciated being informed and may be interested in celebrating the new life.

If the invitation has truly upset you in a way that will taint the celebration, then it may be best for you to decline. Gifts are not expected from those who are invited but don't attend a baby shower.

Dear Thelma: I recently had an experience that left me puzzled and sad. I invited two couples to join my husband and me for an intimate dinner celebration at my home. Together we decided to share in providing the meal. One couple would bring an appetizer, the other a salad and I would provide the main course. On the night of the dinner, the salad arrived 45 minutes late and the appetizer 1 hour late. Everyone felt badly and apologized profusely, but the evening was a disaster.

I believe the same standards in accepting and honoring an invitation should apply whether it's a small event where you know everyone in attendance well or a more formal affair that puts everyone on their "best behavior." What do you think?

A: An intimate, friendly gathering requires the same respect, courtesy and promptness as a formal event – and maybe even more as these are your friends, the people to whom you are closest and who deserve your best.

We're often guilty of saying to ourselves, "Well, these are my friends. They'll understand. I can get away with being late or unresponsive." But following through with that kind of thinking leads to discomfort, guilt and hard feelings, things that don't sustain or strengthen friendship.

It is my hope that you are able to forgive your friends for their mistakes and move on from here. I also hope that your friends realize the importance of taking even a friendly invitation seriously and make their best effort to avoid ever being in this situation again.

Dear Thelma: I organized a potluck at work recently. I and a few people helping me asked everyone personally to bring a dish. However, the first person in line on the day of the potluck did not bring a dish, proceeded to fill his plate and then take it back to his desk to eat. Another guy went to the on-site cafeteria, bought six chicken strips, set them on our potluck table, and filled his plate with everything but chicken strips. The chicken strips were left untouched.

We organized this to celebrate a co-worker's birthday, not to provide a fast-food take-out opportunity. It is very frustrating for many of us. Do you have suggestions on how to make this work better?

A: If your group likes to plan potlucks on a regular basis, I would suggest that you gather a few people at lunch or on a break to develop a set of guidelines for potlucks that is appropriate for your work environment and culture. It should take a lighthearted tone – no demands or dictates – but still address the issues that will make for successful potlucks.

Your guidelines might include that everyone who wants to enjoy the potluck should contribute along with things like bringing enough to serve the group, taking home leftovers and dishes, and helping to clean up. Before each potluck, email the guidelines to the entire group so that everyone is informed and no one is singled out.

Once the guidelines are made clear, everyone should be able to police themselves. Even so, there will be people who forget or whose plans fall through. Organizers should be flexible and generous enough to help everyone feel welcomed.

If you are someone who ran out time and didn't prepare a dish or can't stop by the bakery before work, you should never be first in line to eat. After everyone has been served, apologize for being empty-handed and ask if there's enough for you too. But don't make it a habit, and next time, bring a dish.

A plentiful potluck and good manners never go out of style.

Dear Thelma: I am told I have a habit of cutting someone off (or as I call it interjecting) during conversations. When I hear something with which I strongly disagree my instincts are to say something about it before I completely forget. My boyfriend becomes highly agitated when I disrupt him. He convicts me of having no conversational manners at all. I feel a fool at times. Please help me understand why this is not acceptable.

A: It is not acceptable because it shows no regard or respect for the person speaking. It shows that instead of truly listening and making an attempt to understand the speaker, your concern is for making your own point at the expense of your partner in conversation.

Surely you are aware of the national attention disrespectful outbursts have gained in recent weeks – a congressman shouting out

"You lie!" during a presidential address and a disgruntled entertainer swiping the microphone during a teenage singer's award acceptance speech. Like you, these interrupters reacted instantly and emotionally to something with which they disagreed. Their outbursts were caught on film for the entire country to see, as were the apologies they had to make to those they had harmed and to the nation for their lack of civility. Their mistakes affected a wide web of people and will likely not be soon forgotten.

Your "interjections" may not have the same media coverage, but they do suffer from the same lack of judgment. A conversation is an exchange of ideas that requires listening and polite give-and-take. When you definitively cut your boyfriend off, you reject his premise and you reject him. You kill the conversation.

For the sake of all your relationships, I would encourage you to make a real effort to curb this behavior. You claim that you must interject so that you won't forget your point of disagreement, but if it truly is a strong and valid point you shouldn't need to worry about that. In a proper conversation, your opportunity to express your view shouldn't be long in coming.

Dear Thelma: I'm introducing a friend of mine, who needs an attorney, to an attorney I know. The friend is female and the attorney is male. What's the proper way to make this introduction?

A: First decide whether this is a social introduction or a business introduction. In social situations it is traditional to introduce a man to a woman. "Wanda, I'd like to introduce James Vigil, a friend of mine from college. James, this is Wanda Clark, my neighbor."

If your situation is more business oriented, the first aspect to consider is who holds the higher rank – the president of the company versus the new accountant. The person of lower rank is presented to the person of higher rank. "Mr. Richards, I'd like to present Jerry Reyes, our new sales manager in Las Cruces. Jerry, this is Douglas Richards, the president of our company."

Since rank is not a factor in your situation, you can move on to the next consideration – which person do you know better. Present the person you know best to the person you don't know as well. The person you know best is your friend, so you could properly say: "Mr. Sanchez, I'd like to introduce my friend Dr. Anna Hill. Anna is a trauma surgeon. Anna this is Alex Sanchez, an attorney with the Andrews Firm."

Keep it all straight by looking at or saying the name of the person who you've determined to be in the top ranking position, whether because of gender, professional rank or relationship to you. It's that person to whom you are presenting the other.

Carefully-considered introductions and good manners never go out of style.

Dear Thelma: School is in full swing and parent-teacher conferences at my son's elementary school are coming up soon. I do have some concerns, but I'm not sure they're appropriate to bring up because they revolve around the teacher's attitude toward her job. She is what I would call a bully. Her methods of instruction and discipline involve humiliating kids. She's notorious at the school and parents have complained about it to the administration before, but nothing changes. I worry about the example she sets for the class about how to treat one another. Do I go in swinging or lay low?

A: First let me address teachers. It is important to recognize that you are role models for your students. They are with you for almost as many waking hours per week as they are with their parents. Start each day with the realization that you are an extension of their families and important figures in their lives. How you dress, how you speak, and how you interact are important in setting the tone. All of those areas should reflect professionalism, competence and maturity, even when kids are your only audience.

I am not saying that it's easy. You may find that other role models in your students' lives are not living up to their responsibilities, but your career choice has put you into the position to make a positive difference. It is my hope that you will meet the daily challenge with grace and professionalism.

As to your question, I would make a separate appointment with the teacher to discuss the concerns you've brought up. Parent-teacher conferences often are scheduled in short blocks of time, typically just enough to go over the report card and get a basic idea of how your student is progressing. You may ask during the conference to schedule another meeting for a deeper discussion or call the school to schedule it in lieu of the conference.

As the time for this meeting approaches, work to take as much of your emotion and judgment out of the situation as you can. Approach the meeting with a desire to learn why the teacher uses the methods she does and how you can work together to help your son achieve success. Write down your values, expectations and concerns, and be ready to express them without sounding accusatory or defensive. Identify one instance that exemplifies the problem you see.

At the conference, let the teacher know you are there because you value your son's education and appreciate that the teacher is an important part of his life. Explain your values and expectations, and then describe the instance that you find troubling. Ask the teacher if you've understood the situation and the resulting discipline correctly from your son, and ask the teacher to explain.

Listen and engage in a conversation that helps you understand where the teacher is coming from and expresses your views. Keep the conversation non-confrontational and highly respectful. This is the person you trust to watch over your child for the majority of the day. She deserves your respect and consideration, even if you disagree with her.

This conversation may help her assess how she can improve the classroom experience, but be prepared for the possibility it will not change her methods. Even if it doesn't, it can open the door to collaborating with her on what you can do to help accomplish what is best for your child.

Dear Thelma: What is the proper way to address congratulations to the recently married? Is it congratulations to the groom and best wishes to the bride?

A: Contemporary etiquette does not require a specific address based on gender. Heart-felt expressions and good manners never go out of style.

Dear Thelma: I find co-workers seriously lacking in email manners. There are basic protocols to follow that really make life easier for the recipients and the sender. Things like using a subject line that is descriptive, not unnecessarily replying to all, and not unnecessarily forwarding attachments. Aren't these just common courtesies that everyone should know by now?

A: You are absolutely right. While email may be a more relaxed form of communication, we should not lose our sense of responsibility. Good manners are about thinking of others and treating them with respect and courtesy in all our actions – even those dominated by technology.

You've highlighted the most important basics of email etiquette.

Always use a descriptive subject line. It simply makes way for clear communication. More people are beginning to use the subject line as the first phrase of their message and then continue the beginning of the message with the rest of the phrase. This can be very confusing to people who aren't accustomed to that protocol. I suggest only using that very informal structure with someone you email regularly and who will appreciate your brevity.

Avoid the "reply all" button. Think carefully about who really needs to receive the message as you compose or reply. The same goes for forwarding attachments. By haphazardly sending everything in your mailbox along to the next person, or list of persons, you clog up inboxes unnecessarily and waste other's time. If you do send attachments, make sure beforehand that they are a format and size that your receiver can open and use.

Write messages that are clear, concise and have obvious meaning. Subtleties and sarcasm are easily misunderstood without the benefit of in-person dialog and facial expressions. Use proper grammar and punctuation even in brief communications and spell check before you send. Your written words are a reflection of you.

Dear Thelma: I just wanted to thank you for your excellent response in the recent column about a parent who wondered how to talk to her son's elementary teacher at the upcoming parent-teacher conference. The parent was concerned that the teacher seemed to be a bully.

As a retired elementary educator with 28 years in my own classroom and eight years working with teachers, I was very touched by your kind and highly respectful answer. Not once did you encourage the parent to remove her child from the class, or go directly to the principal. You helped the parent prepare to address her concerns to the teacher in a respectful way. It's perfectly possible that the parent has misunderstood or been misinformed about how the teacher behaves. It is also possible that the teacher isn't performing as we'd hope, as in the way you admonished all teachers to behave in the first part of your response.

In my experience, I believe that the teacher isn't likely to change her ways overnight nor in all situations as we would wish she would (if what the parent suspected is true), but I bet she'll listen to the parent who comes to her with a sincere desire to help her child and maintain a supportive relationship with the teacher.

I also believe that children learn more from sticking with challenging, less than perfect situations in school than from parents bouncing them around from teacher to teacher, school to school seeking to protect them from difficulties. They'll be better able to deal with difficult situations and superiors in the workplace when they're adults if they expect to adjust to and deal with challenges rather than expect the rest of the world to adjust to them.

A: Good teachers and good manners never go out of style.

Dear Thelma: When someone offers me a compliment I don't always know how to respond. Is "thank you" enough?

A: Yes, simply thanking the person for the compliment is all you need to do. Don't try to argue that the compliment is not deserved or somehow talk yourself out of the compliment, which many people try to do. You also don't need to struggle to find something on which to compliment the person who has complimented you.

Dear Thelma: There has been so much made in the media about the seriousness of the H1N1 flu and how to avoid its spread. With that in mind, I am shocked when I enter businesses and see sales people, waiters and other service providers coughing away or complaining about how ill they are. Isn't staying home the safe and polite thing to do when you are sick?

A: It really is best for those who are ill to stay home rather than expose those around them to the illness. That goes for children and teachers at school, office workers and those in customer service positions. It also may mean staying home from church, putting off shopping or declining social invitations until you are completely well. Taking such precautions shows unselfishness, respect and concern for those around you.

The current flu season has made most people much more aware of taking precautions to avoid infection, even to the point of avoiding the physical contact involved in shaking hands in greeting or introduction. I have written before on the importance of a handshake in building relationships and the positive energy the act conveys. We don't want to lose the respect inherent in that kind of greeting.

Someone I ran into recently asked me, "Shall we bump elbows or heads?" Well, neither. If you feel it's unsafe to shake hands, acknowledge one another by a nod of the head, a warm smile and other body language and words that convey the energy and respect that a handshake should. This lack of the traditional greeting may be awkward at first, but as we move though this flu season I'm certain we will find a way to accomplish a proper greeting.

If you are ill and know you shouldn't be shaking hands, do all you can to put the other person at ease if you have to refuse his handshake with a comment like: "I apologize for not shaking hands. I've been ill. But it is a pleasure to meet you."

Keep in mind that you will not become sick simply by touching another person's hand. If you are concerned, keep your hands away from your eyes, mouth and nose to avoid germs entering your system, and wash your hands every time you have a chance. To avoid spreading illness in the office or at home, disinfect phones, keyboards, remote controls, door knobs and any other commonly used items with disinfectant wipes or sprays.

Dear Thelma: I read your recent column on email etiquette and wanted to respond. Everyone should add to their email don'ts: Don't forward any rumors or stories without first checking someplace like www.snopes.com to verify their accuracy. Everyone I know receives at least weekly emails that are at best inaccurate, at worst actually dangerous.

A: Your point is an important one. You should verify any information you receive before forwarding it. Many of the emails that make the rounds are absolutely false, but they continue to circulate year after year. These sometimes elaborate hoaxes clog inboxes and raise blood pressure across the country. If you even slightly believe that Bill Gates is going to give you money for forwarding a message, check it out first rather than sending it to your entire address book.

Be diplomatic with "inspirational" forwards as well. Don't make a habit of sending such to all your contacts. Ask yourself who would actually appreciate the forward or has the time to appreciate it. Also concern yourself with the content. When it comes to off-color jokes or inappropriate images, let them stop with you. Sending them on could offend or create personal or professional problems for the receiver.

In person and on-line, good manners never go out of style

Dear Readers: As the holidays approach, I encourage you to get caught up in the true spirit of the season. This time of year gives us the opportunity to think about thankfulness and the value of the people in our lives. It's a chance to turn our sights outward to what we can do to honor others – those closest to us and those in need.

In preparation for the weeks ahead, I'd like to start thinking now about what we will do this season to bring peace to those around us and make a true effort to think outside the box of materialism and stress for which the holidays are known. With some thought we can enter this time of year with our hearts prepared.

With that in mind, I offer my top 10 tips for a holiday season to remember for its kindness and love.

10. Let thankfulness be your theme throughout November and December. As you gather with family and friends to celebrate your blessings on Thanksgiving, store up those thankful feelings to carry you through to New Year's Day. Even make a pact between yourselves or with one special family member or friend to keep reminding each other through calls or cards of the focus on thankfulness.

9. Use your Thanksgiving get-together to plan a family service project you can take on together during the holidays to benefit a charity or a family in need. You'll grow closer together through the effort and spread your blessings.

8. Talk with your family on Thanksgiving about ideas for a simplified gift exchange. If you are big family, consider each member drawing a name of the person for whom they'll find a gift. Plan to draw the names during the Thanksgiving gathering. You can even keep secret the names drawn to add to the excitement and fun.

7. Dispel the need for expensive gifts. Many of us are still in economic stress or have changed our lifestyles or ways of thinking about money over the course of a year, and our ideas about gifts have changed too. Instead of material value, focus on the things that connect people like time shared together during the holidays and beyond.

6. Restore a forgotten family tradition or create a new one. Family rituals provide the opportunity to reconnect with one another and solidify a family's values. The holidays create the ideal time for this. Give children special responsibilities that help them make the traditions their own.

5. Make a true effort to be fun and loving and to include as many people as you can in your holiday fun. Avoid the events, thoughts and situations that you know will counter this effort. If you lose a day of joy to stress, let it go and start again with the new day.

4. Regift the love that is offered to you. People always ask about the

propriety of regifting at this time of year. I can assure you that no one will ever mind you spreading love around or even returning it to the giver.

3. Resolve to be kind, courteous and respectful during the holidays and into the new year. Look for spontaneous opportunities to share an act of kindness. It will delight others and it will delight you.

2. Instead of tying it all up with a big, fuzzy ribbon, wrap it in heartsense – that feeling of knowing in your heart what is good and following that feeling where it leads.

1. Always remember, good manners never go out of style.

Dear Thelma: Children – my grandchildren included – get so caught up in getting during the holidays that it's hard to get them to focus on anything but that. How do you teach kids to be happy givers?

A: Much of the focus of the season is placed on letters to Santa and grabbing up the hot new toy to please a child. Lessons about giving come when more energy is placed on creating opportunities that allow children to give.

I know one family that sits down as a group and decides how they will give each year. Last year they chose to sponsor a family that couldn't afford much for Christmas. Their 11-year-old had $20 saved and ready to commit to the cause. Her six-year-old brother had $5. By participating in the discussion from the beginning the children were able to make helping those in need a focus of their own holiday celebration.

Whether you plan to head to the nearest Giving Tree or even try to get your kids to come up with gifts for each other, talk them beforehand. Encourage them to understand why giving is important and rewarding. Given the opportunity, I think they'll love having the chance to give.

Dear Thelma: I do not disagree with your advice in a recent column on a couple who wanted to discontinue the practice of the cross-country sending and receiving of holiday gifts. Here's what we did last year and will continue doing.

We also are at an age and point in life where we do not need or want additional "things." So, last year we sent an email to all of our friends and families (those who usually give gifts) and told them that because of the economy we were going to be making contributions to charities in lieu of giving gifts and that we would like for them to return the favor if they had planned to give us a gift.

Without exception, everyone was thrilled with the suggestion. I believe that a lot of people are turning away from consumption and wanting to give back to people in need (and animals too!).

A: Your clear and thoughtful communication with your family and friends helped make this new holiday tradition possible.

Sincere gifts and good manners never go out of style.

Dear Thelma: Recently my father and his wife were visiting from out of town and took our whole family (eight people) out to dinner. Everything went well until the end of dinner when I remarked to my father – who was paying the bill – that the waiter did a good job and deserved a good tip. I did not bring it up again and thought nothing more of the matter until my father let me know that he found my behavior to be very rude, that it was none of my business what kind of tip he left.

While I agree with him that the actual tip was none of my business, I did not feel I was rude in expressing my opinion of the service. Did I commit a social error that I am unaware of? My father is in his seventies and I am in my forties. Are there any generational differences that could explain our differing views on this issue?

A: Your father was right. While it would be fine for you to comment on the level of service, you didn't need to say anything about the tip. While it may not have been intended, your father may have taken your comment as a statement on his ability to assess the service and tip accordingly. No one appreciates that.

I see no generational gap here. When someone else is paying for the meal, you needn't discuss it. Think of it this way, would you have made such a comment to someone you were dining with for the first time? Would you have made such a comment to your employer buying you dinner? Your father deserves the same respect.

Dear Thelma: I have a brother-in-law who visits frequently. However, he will never speak directly to me. He directs everything to my husband. I feel it is rude, and it makes me not want to be around when he visits. How should I handle it?

A: He's your relative too, right? Stop the conversation and say, "I directed the question to you, can't you talk to me too?" This really is something that you have to address personally as it is happening if you want it to change.

Dear Thelma: I have a friend who I enjoy being with except when dining. Whether at a dinner party or lunch with the girls, after eating she has gotten into the habit of picking her teeth with her fingers at the table. She used to wipe her fingers on her napkin, but lately she has started using the table cloth. Maybe it's me, but I find this behavior so unappetizing. How can I tell my friend to please go to the bathroom and take care of this in private? Why do some people lose their manners once they retire?

A: I read your question and asked myself, "Is this for real?"

Retirement is not an excuse for losing your manners. All of the social behaviors you learn during your lifetime should become a part of you and who you are to the core. You shouldn't change dramatically from your true self upon retirement.

If this is your friend, then you must talk with her privately. Tell you that you are very uncomfortable with the change in her table manners and mention the particular problem. Say, "I'm comfortable enough with you to say that this should not take place in public." Be kind but very firm and explain to her that it is not only embarrassing to you but to everyone else as well and that it draws negative attention to her. At any age, good manners never go out of style.

Dear Readers: I've had two experiences this holiday season highlighting the worst and best in people and their manners.

As my sisters and I stood in line to see the latest holiday film released, we found ourselves behind a man and his family. He, his wife and his three children all had their hands full of popcorn, drinks and treats. With all hands full, he decided to present his tickets to the ticket collector from his mouth. Tickets clenched between his teeth, he offered his face to the poor girl. The girl looked at him in utter dismay. She made a concerted effort to barely touch the tickets and offer the part taken from his mouth back to him.

When I approached the girl I said, "You know what I would have done? I never would have taken them out of his mouth."

"I didn't want to," she said. "But I didn't think I had a choice."

The disrespect continued from there. The parents spread their kids' food out picnic-style in the theater walkway, while they sat up high and away from their crew. I didn't see them take any trash out of the theater when they left either.

This group showed no respect or courtesy for anyone. They were simply a force to be reckoned with and didn't care if they infected, tripped or disturbed anyone else. It was very disappointing.

On the other hand was my experience with a forgotten handbag. When I discovered after a shopping trip that I must have left it in the cart at Cost Co, I panicked, as everything important is in that bag. I already felt violated.

I went to the store and was politely directed to the manager. All I said was, "My name is Thelma Domenici."

"I have your bag in the vault," was her immediate reply. My bag was returned to me and not a thing was missing. The manager said an employee collecting carts had turned it in. I wanted to thank him or her, but she didn't know who specifically had returned the bag.

I felt so respected by that experience. I felt respected by the employee who returned the handbag, respected by the manager who asked me to immediately inspect the bag for missing items, and respected by the company for teaching its employees to provide such customer service.

I've said before that if I could start an epidemic, it would be a kindness epidemic. It's this kind of experience that when it infects us, it leads us to similar and greater acts of kindness. If you've experienced an inspirational act of kindness this holiday season, please share it with me. I'd love to share it with other readers.

Dear Thelma: What do you do when you frequently catch someone staring at you? There is an employee in our office who stares at me and others quite obviously, whether across the room or up close. It almost seems habitual. It's noticed by everybody and is a frequent topic of conversation in the office. It makes everyone uncomfortable. Can anything be done?

A: I've faced this situation too and it is very uncomfortable. It leads to people talking about it, wondering what is wrong with the person, and creates the beginnings of rumors and gossip.

My advice is to ask the co-worker closest to the person with the staring habit to talk with him or her about it from a work environment standpoint rather than a judgmental stance. That person can explain what appears to be happening and how that is making others uncomfortable. If there is not a co-worker who can have the conversation, talk to a manager about it.

Appropriate eye contact and good manners never go out of style.

Dear Readers: What is Christmas going to mean to you this year?

Is it different from past Christmases?

While you contemplate the answers for yourself, let me share what Christmas will be to me in 2009.

First and foremost, it will mean the chance to have the time to spend with family. I'm not diluting gift giving this year, but it's not a priority. Most important on my list is to listen to family stories, to share meals together, and absorb all I can during my time with family.

I'll be especially grateful for efforts made by family – especially those with little kids – to travel long distances to be together. I hope we'll all take responsibility for fostering the sense of awe that children have at Christmas while communicating the true meaning and heart-felt giving of the season.

This Christmas for me also highlights my gratitude for the gift of health. As I look around and see those less fortunate in this area, I realize that health is a gift I truly treasure. This year I hope we'll all make a point to visit those who suffer. Bring a bright moment to their day with a short visit, conversation and a smile. Run an errand for someone or give them ride to an appointment or to church. Along with that goes giving to those in need who we may not know personally, but who we can help with donations for clothes, food and shelter.

It's that giving of ourselves, making a deliberate effort to make others happy or making ourselves available to people who have no one, that brings the Christmas spirit alive. With that Christmas spirit comes joy. Joy finds its voice in our anticipation, our decorations, our gift-giving and our love. Decorating for Christmas is an explosion of joy for me. Friends laugh and say, "If you really want to know Thelma Domenici, come and see her house at Christmas time," as every surface is a canvas for my holiday joy.

Although we know that in our world turmoil exists and there are gigantic decisions to be made, my wish this Christmas is that we keep the Peace in our minds and the Love in our hearts that this season can open up to us. May we keep it today and throughout the new year.

Dear Thelma: You requested descriptions of acts of kindness. Here's what I like to do. When I am in line at grocery stores and have 10 or more items and the person behind me only has one or two, I always let them go in front of me – regardless of their age or sex. Unfortunately, the favor isn't returned very often. But I'm hoping if I continue to do this, more and more people will begin to spread it around.

A: Keep up the kind work. Although you aren't seeing a direct benefit to yourself, you are having an impact. People are often surprised that a person can be so giving in an age of "me first" and "hurry up." It can shock them out of a self-centered state.

You'll never know how that act influenced the rest of that person's day. They may not give up their place in line, but they may hold a door for someone or it may just put a smile on their face to share with someone in passing. Be aware that others are watching too – the store clerk, other shoppers, and children with their parents. All of these observers are touched too and are potentially motivated to advance the spread of the epidemic of kindness.

Good deeds – even those you don't see returned – and good manners never go out of style.

Dear Thelma: I'll be attending a New Year's party this weekend. The host is a good friend, but I don't know most of the other guests. Do you have advice on how to mix and mingle?

A: Your first task is to be open to new connections and relationships. Whether you are open or you aren't, it will come across in your body language and your conversations. If you set your mind on the task of meeting new people and plan to enjoy it, you'll have more success and more fun.

At an informal gathering, knowing how to introduce yourself, break the ice and engage in casual conversation are important. A smile and a "Hello" are all you need to get started. You already have something in common with this room full of strangers: you all know the host. A perfect entry into conversation is "How do know John?" Asking a question is a great way to get a conversation started or to keep it moving. Even "Have you tried the stuffed mushrooms?" will do.

Gather up upbeat or interesting topics of conversation before you leave for the party. Read the newspaper or check some online new sites for current events, sports stories or cultural events that people are likely to be discussing. Use your knowledge to add to discussions or start new ones.

When you do become involved in a conversation, listen actively. Look the person speaking in the eye, indicate that you're listening or understand with a head nod or a "hmmm," and ask questions. Make sure your body language indicates that you are listening too. Keep your facial expression interested, focus on the person speaking and sit or stand up straight with your arms relaxed. Never show signs of impatience or boredom – sighing, tapping your fingers, looking at the ceiling, crossing your arms – even if you feel these things.

When it is time to exit a conversation, do so politely. "Please excuse me. I'm going to go try those stuffed mushrooms you told me about."

Dear Thelma: I have been asked to "stand up for" my cousin who is getting married for the third time. Both she and her fiancé have had big weddings in the past and this is going to be a very small, simple civil ceremony with a small reception following. She is wearing a 1940s wiggle dress. What do I wear? What are my responsibilities? And since they have been living together and have a household, what do I give them for a gift? All I can think of is money, but that seems impersonal.

A: At any wedding, the bride should have the singularly most unique dress. It doesn't sound like that will be an issue here. Personally, I wouldn't look good in a wiggle dress, so I'm glad I don't have to consider wearing one.

You don't have to either. Since it seems to be a simple event and she hasn't selected something for you, you can choose something that is right for you and that honors the spirit of the celebration. Avoid white, since in traditional wedding parties that color is reserved for the bride. Consider how what you choose might complement the theme or the color scheme. Something simple might be the best accompaniment to your cousin's choice.

As to your responsibilities, ask your cousin what she expects. She may just want you as her official witness of the marriage or she may want your help with planning and executing the event.

Money is fine as a wedding gift. If you want something along that line but more personal, consider gift cards for dinner, a movie or an event for the newly married couple.

In relationships new and old, good manners never go out of style.

Ask Thelma 2010
You Are Who You Are All the Time

Dear Thelma: A friend's father recently passed away. I really only communicate regularly with this friend online through Facebook. When I heard about his dad, it was very natural to offer my condolences and support through Facebook. It felt a little weird though, like it was not respectful enough. What do you think?

A: I have a friend who recently lost her mother. While she wouldn't have expected it, Facebook became a source of comfort for her and her family as they dealt with their loss and received support from their extended circle of family and friends connected through the social networking website.

She reasoned that if she were sharing the sad news with her friends via computer connection, then it was fine for those friends to offer their support through the same connection. She received messages from long-time and far-away friends who may not have even heard the news if not through Facebook. The computer application also allowed family and friends to share beautiful memories that might not have surfaced without the forum. During this hard time, technology became as warm and personal as its users made it.

I don't think a computer message can delete the need for direct contact. When someone suffers a great loss, friends and family should do all they can and be as physically present for that person as possible. Cards, calls, visits and the presence of family and friends at the funeral service were still of vital importance to my friend's healing, but Facebook had its place too.

So while you shouldn't use Facebook to avoid other contact that the person needs from you, don't be worried that your kind sentiments left there won't be appreciated or will be frowned upon. I'd also suggest that you make sure the person is active on the Facebook site during their trials, as you wouldn't want your message to go unread. If they seem to be avoiding the site, try to reach them in another way.

As I've said before, technology does have a heart – it's yours.

Dear Thelma: I work for a local retail establishment with about nine stores. Our highest boss' wife was hired as an employee at my store. There is a dress code, which we all had to sign, that allows us to wear only the company supplied polo shirt and black or beige pants. This lady, who is well liked, wears jeans a few times a week, along with the company polo shirt. This annoys me, but I don't know to whom I should complain. All the "higher ups" in this company are related, so I don't want make enemies or seem petty. What can I do? Should I just let it go?

A: Do you want your job? If your answer is yes, you should let it go.

I don't condone the boss or his wife for their actions. This is clearly a "Do as I say, not as I do" situation. The boss and his relatives who are employees really should set the standard for the group and not act as if they have no respect for the company's model. That can easily poison a healthy work environment.

However, taking this on will not improve the situation for you. You will seem petty and could easily damage important work relationships. When you were hired, you agreed to wear the standard uniform. What anyone else wears doesn't change that for you.

If I were you I'd also avoid talking about the fact that the boss' wife is not abiding by the dress code with other employees. All it does is further damage morale and place focus on something other than doing your job well.

Good judgment and good manners never go out of style.

Dear Thelma: I spent time in two different hospitals recently. The difference between them was astonishing. I don't know if the level of care was different, but I felt so much better in the one in which the staff went out of its way to be kind. Do you think politeness and healing can be connected?

A: I know they can. When you hear you are going to spend time in the hospital it is not a good image that goes through your head. Your emotions and even fear begin to take over. Being in that kind of state certainly doesn't help you feel better.

I have had the same kind of experience as you. After a surgery I was moved from one facility to another. In the first facility I experienced consistent quality and kindness of service. In the second all of that was lacking and I was very scared. I knew I could not heal under those conditions and I had myself sent back to my original point of care.

Anyone who enters a hospital, whether it's for something major or minor, is afraid. It is so essential to experience kindness and graciousness in patient care. Medical staff must embrace the value of what they can do from a scientific standpoint, but also what they can do from the place of human connections. When a staff or a facility places value on the attentiveness and graciousness so vital to true patient care, their impact can be great.

Dear Thelma: I think it is wonderful to be a grandparent. But I listen to other grandparents whose own children take the joy out of grandparenting for them. They say they're told exactly what to do and how to do it. They seem to always be in conflict. Do you have advice on how to be a grandparent?

A: A grandparent I am not, but I too have observed relations between grandparents and their own grown children. I have seen grandparents who play an active role in the lives of their grandchildren as partners with parents. And I have seen grandparents and their children battle over everything.

The advice that I would give is the advice that strengthens all relationships. Make a real effort to treat one another with respect, courtesy and kindness.

Parents can lovingly set some rules and grandparents should respect them. They may be different from what you would choose, but they are important to your children. By joining with them in solidifying values and expectations for the children, you strengthen all the relationships involved.

Parents should show respect to their own parents by allowing them to make some of their own decisions in their relationships with the children. As long as it's not a safety or health issue that could truly harm a child, grandparents should have some latitude to do things differently. Kids can adapt to different rules in different homes. One mom I know doesn't allow food or drinks in her living room, but her parents do. The kids have no problem differentiating between the two and enjoy the special treat of eating on special little trays Grandma bought them to use when sitting on her living room floor.

Take the time to listen to one another. If your daughter explains how the never-ending river of chocolate milk at Grandma's house leads to no one eating dinner at home, limit the kids to one glass. If the kids are destroying your new sofa, expect your children to stand behind you when you discipline or set rules for the grandkids.

Kids learn respect, love and kindness as much from their grandparents as from their parents. All those relationships are important to establish and maintain.

Across generations, good manners never go out of style.

Dear Thelma: How do you tell employees that they are inappropriately dressed for the work place without angering them or becoming subjected to a law suit?

A: You sit down and talk to them about it respectfully and considerately. It's perfectly acceptable for you to say, "We're in a professional environment and there are certain professional standards we adhere to that include attire. The way we present ourselves sets the tone for our internal relations and our external contact with our customers."

If your company already has a workplace attire policy, it may be time to shine the spotlight on it. You may want to think about setting a time every year to refresh the group's memory and have them review their own choices in line with policy. If you don't have a policy in place, issue a memo outlining the standards you expect and set up a time when the group can meet to ask questions about what works and what doesn't.

When you need to speak to someone individually about his choices, let him know how much you value his contributions to the company and that with a more professional image he may have more of an impact. Help him to fully understand that he is helping to represent your business and that you need his look to match his value. When our look is too casual for a particular work place, it may send a message that we don't care, which is not the message we ever want to send.

As I like to say, you have one opportunity to make a first impression; it has to be a good one. You – and your employees – have to take full advantage of every first impression opportunity that presents itself.

Expecting employees to dress in the professional standards of the day should not lead to a lawsuit. Federal anti-discrimination laws can come into play for things like requiring or banning an article of clothing for one gender but not the other or violating religious beliefs, but expecting employees to wear clothing that is appropriate for their position should not be a problem.

Dear Thelma: Our son is getting married and the parents of the bride live far away. Should we call them and introduce ourselves on the phone or just wait until the wedding?

A: You should definitely call and introduce yourselves. This is the start of a vital relationship for your son and an important one for you. Friendly and open communication at the beginning will clear the way for better relations later.

Traditionally, the parents of the future groom contact the bride's family. Although in modern times either set of parents can make the first contact, the bride's family may be giving you the chance to honor that custom. So you should proceed quickly.

Your call doesn't have to be long, but should be friendly and casual. You already have something in common – children you love getting married. Express your wishes of happiness and blessing for the couple and talk about any plans being made or travel that will take place. If it's possible, you may even want to set up a time to meet in person before the wedding date.

After your phone introduction, I'd encourage you to keep the communication lines open with a short note or greeting card, an email or a call during the wedding planning stages. I hope the marriage of your children will mean a life-long relationship for you. Start now to build a solid foundation for that relationship, and quite possibly friendship.

Good family relations and good manners never go out of style.

Dear Thelma: If you receive emails that are religious or political and you feel they promote misinformation, anger and rumors, how should you tell a friend to cease? Won't it alienate them?

A: If this person is truly a friend, then you should be able to reply to him with something like, "I enjoy our friendship and our conversations on other topics, but I don't share your views on this subject. It would be best to take me off your email list for these kinds of messages."

That does not mean that in your response you should label what he's sent you as misinformation, anger or rumors. That's your opinion and assessment, which obviously is different than his, and it very well could alienate him.

Email is not a productive medium for debate. Too much of what is important in communication is lost over the internet. Things like body language, facial expression and tone of voice do not exist electronically and meaning is easily lost.

Your friend may feel embarrassed upon receiving your request, but he should respect your wishes and it shouldn't weaken your friendship. With a friend you should be able to be honest and open about things that could impact your friendship.

If you ask him to stop and he doesn't or becomes aggressive about it, then you can certainly block his emails from your in box.

Dear Thelma: I know you've written about this before, but if you are having a party and several people days before the event have not responded to the invitation's RSVP, should you call them or just assume they are not coming?

A: Sadly, Albuquerque has allowed itself to be labeled as a city that does not respond to invitations. Some have expressed to me that they believe these very late or non-existent RSVPs are a product of people holding back their decision until they know a better invitation is not on its way. I hope that's not true. If someone out there is doing such, they should stop.

As to your question, if your guests are part of an intimate group, I suggest that you call them. While I am in no way condoning late responses, the call would at least relieve stress for you during your planning and executing of the party.

With a less intimate group, you may still make the calls. If you don't want to spend the time calling, you can consider their responses to be "no." But as any host knows, those who haven't responded at all weigh heavily on you. You will continue to wonder if they might respond at the last minute or even just show up, both of which they shouldn't do out of respect for you.

For those receiving invitations, you really must respond as soon as possible after the invitation is received. Don't fall into a habit of setting invitations aside and don't let the demands of the moment interfere with their ability to make a phone call or send back a response card. Make a decision about whether or not you will attend as soon as possible and let the host know. That means you must contact the host even if you will not attend.

The habit I've developed and encourage others to form is to make a decision and respond within three days of receiving the invitation.

A considerate guest and good manners never go out of style.

Dear Thelma: My heart breaks every time I read a negative story about the University of New Mexico in the newspaper. My university is not the president and it's not the football coach. It is much bigger than those people making headlines.

I know that the actions of some make for great stories, but I also know there are wonderful things happening every day in the classrooms, the research labs and the hospitals of UNM. I can't help but think that all of these negative stories will make it much more difficult to raise the funds that are so badly needed for endowed professorships, scholarships and research to make UNM the very best that it can be.

How do those of us who have degrees from UNM, as well as current students, faculty and staff, best handle seeing our university diminished in this way?

A: First, you must not fall into the thinking that says, "I can't do anything to make it better." You can. What's needed at this time on and off campus are real ambassadors for the university who believe in it and its ability to fill a vital role. As an individual, take the time to learn how the university is continuing to live it mission of serving the state, nation and world through teaching, research, public services and health care. Don't allow yourself to become involved in rumors and critical judgments. When they arise – especially in your own circle – do your best to provide positive examples of the experiences you think exemplify the true spirit and importance of UNM.

I have had the opportunity to be involved at UNM and to learn how great a university it really is. Working with its very qualified staff, meeting students, and experiencing the commitment of the volunteers who give much to the university, I know there is a great deal of love, support and respect for UNM that goes beyond what's seen just by reading the newspaper. I've been told by students that UNM is a home away from home for them and I've seen that it is a place where our future leaders are learning to lead.

You worry that negative publicity will harm the university's ability to raise funds and to reach its full potential. I believe that when people understand the potential of the university and the far-reaching effect it has on the lives of those who study and work there, they won't pull away. I sincerely think they will desire to stay connected and continue their genuine commitment.

Dear Thelma: I am a single mother currently adopting a 12-year-old child. I am getting asked whether I am having a shower or if I need anything. My child came into my home as a foster child with very few possessions, but I also don't wish to share such personal explanations with everyone who asks. What are the appropriate answers here?

A: Whether it's a newborn or an older child, many people have a true interest in welcoming that child into a family and do so by their generosity. People who have raised children realize the expense involved in setting up a household for a child and they want to help. They don't need nor should they expect a detailed explanation in return. The fact that you've opened your hearts to each other is all they need to know.

You might want to consider an adoption celebration for you and your child. Let your child help with the planning and center the party around honoring the creation of your new family. When people ask, let them know the things your child would appreciate, like gift certificates for clothes or games, or let them know his or her interests like art, music or sports so they can choose something appropriate.

If you decide not to have a party, when people ask sincerely if you need anything, it's fine to mention things that your child needs and would appreciate. There also may be household items, bedding or furniture that you need. Many people may have extra that they can spare or will keep an eye out for good deals for you.

Above all, accept their generosity for what it is, the opportunity to play a small part in your family's success.

Dear Thelma: Graduation announcements will soon be mailed out for my daughter. I'd like to insert a note that no gift is required, just well wishes. What is the proper etiquette?

A: Those receiving graduation announcements are never obliged to send a gift and so your inserted note is unnecessary. It is appropriate to send a card of congratulations upon receiving a graduation announcement, but gift is not expected.

If your daughter also is having a graduation party, those invitations should be sent separately from the announcement and can include a line that reads, "No gifts please."

Dear Thelma: Please settle a dispute my wife and I have about whether or not to tip hotel housekeeping staff. A few years ago, we stayed at a hotel at Disney World. The management provided written suggestions for appropriate tips for every member of their staff, except housekeeping. I took that to mean that the housekeeping staff are compensated sufficiently so as not to rely on tips. But every time we are ready to check out of a hotel, my wife wants me to leave a tip on the table. We have agreed to let you settle this for us.

A: It has become customary to tip hotel housekeepers. The standard that many use is $1 to $3 per night per person and up to $5 per night per person in a luxury hotel. Leave your tip daily with a note or in an envelope labeled "Housekeeping" so that the person who cleans your room that day ends up with your tip.

Tipping housekeeping staff is new to many travelers. While not the same as tipping a waiter whose hourly wage is low and expected to be made up in tips, it is given simply in appreciation. Tipping of any kind should always be viewed as a reward for good service. If you're not pleased with the effort made by the service provider, decrease the tip accordingly.

Like good service, good manners never go out of style.

Dear Thelma: We have friends whose son has been arrested and his photo is often in the newspaper. We never mention it when we see them but it's the elephant in the room. What should we say to be supportive of them but not their son's actions?

A: If you approach them with true concern and support in mind, you don't need to say anything specific. You will easily show through your eyes, your body language and the way that you greet them that you want to show your support. A direct look in the eyes and a sincere and concerned, "How are you?" can show that you are aware of what they're going through and are open to discussing the problem if they are interested in sharing.

It is highly likely that these people know that their son did wrong. You shouldn't worry that being concerned and supportive of them would equate condoning their son's actions. Your relationship is with them, not their son. It's also important that these parents don't feel the need to seclude themselves from their regular group. They deserve and need the support of their friends.

Finally, if you don't know these people well, you shouldn't expect that they want to share the details of their troubles with you and you shouldn't pressure yourself to say anything about the situation. If they bring up their difficulties, then it's a clear indication that they want to talk about it and need your support.

Dear Thelma: I have been a professor for 20 years, and of course, there has been quite a change during this time in the way students communicate with faculty. Everything is done via email now. Few ever come to office hours any more, even though I have between 300 and 850 students per semester.

Lately I have noticed a strange trend. Students start their emails with my first and last name followed by a comma and then begin their message (Jane Smith, I am a student...). Obviously students know I am their teacher, so they know to address me as "Dr. Smith" or "Professor Smith." I wouldn't even mind "Ms. Smith" or "Mrs. Smith." I am not even a stickler for formality, and would not mind "Dear Jane." It's just this "First Name Last Name" formulation, sans "Dear" that strikes me as so odd, cold and very irritating.

Where did this come from and how can I get my students to stop doing it?

A: It is odd and I can't fathom where it came from. All I can deduce is that because of the extinction of the letter, children are no longer being taught by parents or teachers to correspond correctly in writing or they don't have enough practice at it to solidify it in their minds.

While it may not be completely relevant to your courses, I would suggest that you include a page in your syllabus each semester directing students on how to communicate properly with you and others and express in class how important it is. Let them know in cases of communicating with someone who they don't email regularly or don't know well or at all, a more formal letter-style format with a salutation (Dear Mr. Jones:), a closing (Sincerely or Best regards,) and their first and last name are necessary. These traditional components convey a message of respect and courtesy to the reader.

Even with a more familiar receiver, it's always kind during the initial email connection to offer a salutation, a closing and a signature. Not doing so can come across as abrasive. An ongoing email dialog may not require such conventions, but all who use email should make sure their messages doesn't lose clarity when they forego format standards.

Clear communication and good manners never go out of style.

Dear Thelma: Who's supposed to pay on a date? Should it always be the guy?

A: The person extending the invitation for the date should pay, and that could be a man or a woman. When you say, "Would you like to go out to dinner with me?" – especially on a first date – that's an indication that you will pay. Consider the inviter the host for what he or she has planned for the evening. If the person who is not paying suggests adding something to the evening, he or she should be prepared to pay for those additions.

If it's a more casual connection and you decide together to meet for dinner – "Let's have dinner." – or a date happens spontaneously, then you can plan to share the costs.

Once you've established a relationship it's appropriate to talk about expenses and decide how to split them. You might decide on always going Dutch treat or alternating who pays the full cost. I wouldn't encourage one or the other to incur all of the expenses under an attitude of "He earns less than me so I'll pay," or "I'm the guy; I should always pay."

Choosing things to do that are affordable to both parties is a good idea, as is thinking of a date as an opportunity to spend time with someone rather than to be treated.

Dear Readers: Over the course of 2010, I'd like to devote some time to thinking about the most important manners for people to learn and to practice. From kids to brides and professionals to grandparents, each group has a different focus and is faced with different issues. While all modern manners are built on respect, courtesy and kindness, the way we individually practice the day-to-day specifics covers a diverse range of behaviors.

Today I offer the first of my Top Manners Lists, the Top Manners for Little Kids. If you didn't learn these before entering elementary school, learn them now. They are the basis for functioning politely in the world.

5. Practice kindness. Even little children can learn to greet people properly and with a smile, to be helpful, and to think of others and their happiness.

4. Show respect. Teach children how to politely interrupt adults, waiting for a lull in the conversation or waiting patiently to be acknowledged. Have children call adults by a courtesy title and their last name, unless the adult asks to be called by a first name. Respect includes sharing with siblings and friends and should be practiced at home and away.

3. Apologize when necessary. "I'm sorry," is the first of four phrases that all children should learn to feel and to use. Even small children should learn the importance of making things right with

someone they've wronged.

2. Say "Please." When asking for something or for someone to do something, teach children to ask politely by including the word "please" in all their requests.

1. Use words of gratitude. Practice "Thank you," and "You're welcome," often with the children in your life and they will learn the sentiments behind them and how to use them.

Children learn by example and by doing. Parents, grandparents, relatives and friends should model these behaviors continuously from an infant's very first day at home. Encourage toddlers to follow the model as they begin to communicate and make choices. Expect small children to exhibit these behaviors in all their interactions and establish consequences for when they don't. With effort on the part of the adults in a child's life, these basic, but vital, manners can be firmly established by the time a child starts school – giving him a head start for future interactions. With consistent example, gentle guidance and appropriate expectations you can equip your children with skills and confidence to last a lifetime.

Dear Thelma: Would you date somebody who blew his nose on a cloth table napkin in a restaurant?

A: When I heard this question I just giggled to myself and wondered if it was real. For me personally, the answer is no. I would not be comfortable with a person who was not aware of how unsettling such behavior can be. If it is someone who you want to continue to see, I'd suggest you present him with a box of tissue, a smile and an explanation about cloth napkins at your next meeting.

A cloth napkin is different than a paper napkin; it should be treated as something lasting. A cloth napkin is strictly used to dab your mouth. It should not be used to remove lipstick or to blow your nose.

Blowing your nose can be handled quietly at the table as long as you face away from the table. If you do use a paper napkin to blow your nose, it must not go back on the table or be used for the rest of the meal. Ask for another napkin.

If blowing your nose will be a loud and drawn out event, it will be best to leave the table and take care of it in the restroom.

At all ages, good manners never go out of style.

Dear Thelma: I have recently remarried and am now blessed with two new children to add to my own. Together our blended family totals five of us and we are, as you might imagine, going through some good times as well as challenging ones. An issue that continues to come up for us is one of etiquette and it has caused some heartache.

My sincere desire is to raise all three of my children with the same level of etiquette that was required of me as a child, though I am met with great resistance from my two new children (ages 13 and 15) and from my husband with the response that most manners are antiquated. I disagree strongly and hope for a positive balance between what I believe to be a common sense foundation for everyday life and their mistaken belief that manners are pretentious and uppity. Please do help.

A: It saddens me to think that good manners would cause anyone heartache, but I'm sure your situation is not unique. Joining two families with two sets of ideas and standards is a challenge on many levels. However, it's difficult for me to comprehend that during the time that you were establishing your relationship there was not the opportunity to observe the manners of this family. If manners are important to you, then I believe you must have seen some during your courtship or you wouldn't have continued the relationship.

With that in mind, first you must really think about the essence of manners. The most important part of etiquette is the respect we show at all times to those around us, not how many rules we know. People – children and adults – can understand the importance of treating others with kindness much more easily than the importance of which fork to use at a formal dinner.

Next comes a conversation with your husband about respect and courtesy and why they are important to you. Give examples of respect you have shown each other and how it improves your relationship. Talk about what attracted you to one another and how those things relate to respect and kindness. Discuss how manners build the confidence of knowing how to act in any situation. Express that manners equip a person to fit into the world and become part of who that person will be all his life. Ask for your husband's support in teaching and modeling those important life lessons for the children. For your effort to work, it has to start with this conversation and with total understanding and commitment on both sides.

When it comes to the children, rather than focusing on rules and points of etiquette that would seem pretentious in their casual world, focus on respect and kindness. You may have grown up required to say "Yes, sir" and "No, ma'am" to every adult you encountered, but

314

if your 13- and 15 year-olds have never been required to use such terms you're unlikely to win that battle. Instead encourage them to look a person in the eye and smile when greeting someone or meeting for the first time. Teach that we don't use our cell phones at the table because putting them away shows respect for one another. Require that when you need to ask a question of someone in the home, you go find them and ask it, rather than yelling for them to come because it keeps the home peaceful and it's kind.

If you can make respect and kindness part of your family's daily life, etiquette will flow from there. And when it's time to go to the prom, they'll be ready for that lesson on which fork to use.

Especially in families, good manners never go out of style.

Dear Thelma: When I was growing up, I was always told there were two things one did not discuss in polite company – politics and religion. Today, in almost every gathering beyond my immediate family, I am deluged with political philosophies from both sides of the aisle. I am interested in our government, both state and national. I do know however, that no amount of discussion will solve the problems of our country while I am at the grocery store.

Recently, at a local school election, a man launched into a tirade which pretty much left me speechless. What an inappropriate place to loudly voice his opinions. I am never quite sure how to handle these situations. Can you suggest a tactful way to silence these bullies?

A: In the world we are living in today, you might as well put tape over your mouth and cotton in your ears if you hope to avoid political discussion. It definitely is growing more acceptable, and because of that we all must be more informed than ever. If you decide to enter a political discussion, you should be well informed. Handle any exchange respectfully and avoid becoming caught up on converting listeners to your position. Most importantly, remove as much emotion from the situation as possible. It's the emotion infusion that ends up causing the most distress.

I would agree that a school function is an inappropriate place to voice vehement political opinions. I envision what you call a school election to be something like a parent-teacher association meeting. Everyone at the meeting should be there because of a commitment to the school, its students or its staff. Opinions on anything outside of that realm are not appropriate for that gathering. If it continues, the school or organization itself might have to take a stand and form a policy that ideas not directly related to the business at hand are not to be discussed during meeting time. Then they'll have to enforce it.

I don't believe you're going to necessarily silence these bullies. You just have to be more informed than ever and sometimes have the courage to quell your own emotions and say, "Now is not the time for this discussion."

Political discussion is an important part of citizenship. The key to keeping it civil is the avoidance of inflammatory sound bites and unchecked emotion.

Dear Thelma: I recently received a thank-you note for sending a thank-you note. Do I now owe the sender a thank you for the thank you? At what point does this all end?

A: To thank someone for sending a thank-you note is totally unnecessary. As the receiver of a thank you for a thank you, you know that it made you feel uncomfortable and unsure as what is expected. That's the same reaction most people would have. The dialog should end with the first note.

I have faced a somewhat similar situation with host gifts. Host gifts are given to the host of a party or a dinner to thank the host for putting together the event and pulling together a group of friends. The gift is the thank you and a thank-you note from the host for that gift is not required. However, for a brunch that I host at Christmas time I have received gifts that are much more than typical hostess gifts. While I appreciate all the gifts that my friends bring, my common sense and my heartsense tells me that there are some that do require a note of thanks and they get one.

Proper appreciation and good manners never go out of style.

Dear Thelma: I have a dilemma I am hoping you can solve. It involves myself, my family, and my best friend. Whenever she is invited to be a guest at my home for a dinner, party and even my daughter's dance recitals, she always shows up with one or more of her friends who we barely know or have never met.

My husband and family consider it extremely rude and annoying. I feel anxious because I also consider it rude. I feel I have to spend time socializing with the uninvited guests, and my feelings are hurt because she ends up spending extra time with them trying to entertain them and make them feel at home.

I love and adore my friend. She is a kind and generous person who loves to help people. She is an extremely emotional person and I don't want to hurt her feelings, but any time I invite her I start to feel the anxiety of wondering who my unwanted guests will be. Please help me resolve this matter.

A: You have to sit down with this "best friend" and let your feelings be known. If she is as kind and generous as you say, then she should want to be kind and generous to you, not just at your expense. If she is your best friend, you should be able to say, "You are my best friend and I consider you a part of my family. When we invite you we want to spend time with just you."

Her behavior is not just rude and annoying, it's also inconsiderate and does not respect you as the person who issued the invitation. She needs to appreciate how disruptive it is to you as the host to not have control of your own guest list. All invitees must seriously consider who has been invited to any event. Whether it's a phone call saying come over for dinner or a wedding invitation, the invitation is always specific. Only if the person issuing the invitation specifically says you should bring a guest or a child or other additional people, is it appropriate to do so.

Don't be anxious, just talk to her as a friend. And when you do invite her to an event in which it would be appropriate for her to bring a guest, let her know that when you make the invitation.

Dear Thelma: As grandparents of three children ages 10 to 13 we have some suggestions to add to your recent column on grandparents that maybe our dear sons and daughters overlook when thinking about us and our grandkids.

1. It is OK to give us a small hug even though you're now an adult and a parent yourself. We miss the ones we got when you were tiny and not embarrassed. It's OK for your kids to hug us too.

2. Don't make fun of us in front of our grandkids as they will mimic you and disrespect us. Remind them how we can be important in their lives.

3. Please, maybe once a month, invite us for dinner. Hot dogs are great. I bet at least one serving goes down the disposal during the week. We only ask about one hour a month.

4. We would be thrilled if the grandkids actually dialed the phone once in awhile. Tell us what you bought with the birthday cash Grandma and Grandpa gave you.

We are bursting with pride over all of you, and never want to intrude. Please know though, we will not be around forever. Loving care and good manners never go out of style.

Dear Readers: It's time to consider the Top Manners for Big Kids. These elementary school-aged children should already have a good handle on the manners I suggested last month for little kids: kindness, respect, apologies, please and thank you. In fact, these should be automatic responses in most situations.

Big kids' next step is developing decision making skills. As a master's student at Michigan State University I surveyed children about decision making. My class studied the question of whether kids were too young to make some of their own decisions. We concluded given appropriate boundaries and supervision they weren't too young. I'll never forget the 9-year-old girl who said, "I really love my parents because they let me make decisions."

Decision making strengthens relationships and develops trust and honesty between children and parents. Decision making is important to big kids and plays a role in the manners and skills that they need to develop. Encourage them as they grow in these Top Manners for Big Kids.

4. Experience the joy of gift giving. Now is the perfect time to learn how to select or make a gift that someone will appreciate. Selecting a gift truly forces a person to let go of selfishness, consider another's preferences and be creative. Give a child a budget and these parameters and let her make her best decision. It may not be what you would have picked, but it will be from the heart.

3. Learn to use the phone. A child should be able to understand with whom a caller wants to speak and to ask who is calling before being allowed to answer the phone. Then she should be taught how to do it right. Chose a greeting like "Hello" or "Hello, Cordova residence" and teach her to quietly find the person the caller seeks rather than shouting out a name.

When your child wants to make a call, have him decide in advance what he's going to say. Teach him to greet the receiver with, "Hello. This is Alex. May I please speak to Dominic?" Also, teach him to leave his name, number and the name of the person he's trying to reach in a message. Always end a call with "Goodbye."

2. Practice table manners at every meal. Teach your child to place a napkin on his lap and use it. Require him to eat with a fork unless the food is meant to be eaten with fingers. Remind him to keep his free

arm and elbow in his lap while eating and not to rest them on the table. Teach him to eat slowly and with his mouth closed and to use "please" and "thank you" often at the table. Also show him how to arrange a basic table setting with a fork and napkin on the left, knife on the right, drinking glass at the upper right and plate in the middle. Then give him this task every evening.

1. Meet and greet. These aren't necessarily natural things for a child, but some basic instruction and expectations on introductions and conversations can take her far. Teach her to make direct eye contact and to smile at someone she is greeting. Show her what a firm handshake is and practice with relatives or with your priest or minister as you leave church. Let her know you expect her to answer Grandma's questions about school or activities with some real information and have her decide on at a story she could tell or a question she could ask Grandma before she arrives.

It may take the bulk of the Big Kid years to solidify, but with encouragement, deciding the proper way to act will become second nature.

Good decisions and good manners never go out of style.

Dear Thelma: I had to take my dad to an emergency room recently. We walked in and we were the only ones there. We went to the front desk area to check in. There were two employees talking to each other at the desk, and not once did they look up to greet us or find out why we were there. There was just a form for people to complete. While we were waiting, a few other people came in and, again, no one was greeted.

Then a young woman was wheeled into the area. She wheeled herself to these women behind the desk and asked if they would call a cab for a ride home. One of them loudly said the institution would be broke if they got cabs for everyone. The woman asked how she got there and the patient's response was by ambulance. The woman then said what about family and the patient said her mother is legally blind. The patient started crying and the woman continued to be so rude and nasty. She told her she could walk or take the bus. This young woman had on only a sweat shirt and we were having freezing temperatures. Someone in the waiting room finally jumped up and told her they would take her home.

How could any of this seem appropriate to the two employees of the hospital?

319

A: It's sad to say what you experienced does sometimes happen in emergency rooms. I must give you credit for writing it so well, as it leaves me with little to say except that it shouldn't be happening at all. Many of you know I've been a health care professional all my life. I almost feel I should apologize.

As I have said before, the manners we learn should become who we are all the time. People in a work setting never should be doing what these employees were doing. And in an ER, certainly the people assigned to be there to start the process should be attentive at all times.

It's very true that the ER is known as one of the busiest centers in a health care delivery system and patients coming into the ER recognize that. But inattention should never be a part of the culture of an ER. I know how tense, emotional and painful it can be to even know you have to go to the ER. If there is any place in the hospital where fear can be diminished and demonstrated respect can make an enormous difference, it's the instant you enter the ER.

I would encourage you to contact the hospital's management with your story. I was always very grateful when people made known to me areas that needed attention so that we could deal directly with the cause of the complaint and with the person making the complaint. Patients are always the primary clients and their needs should always have priority.

Dear Thelma: When I give a gift to a specific friend she always says how much she likes it. Then she asks, "Where did you buy it?" The response leaves me wondering if she is disappointed in the gift. Will my answer determine whether the gift is acceptable? It seems impolite. Am I being overly sensitive? How would you respond?

A: I think you are being overly sensitive and even mistrustful. While your friend's response is not the one I would use when receiving a gift, it sounds to me like it's just her way of being interested and excited about what you've chosen for her. I don't think her response is intended to leave you thinking that your friend is disappointed in the gift.

If it were me, I would just respond in a comfortable fashion and assume that this is a friend engaging me in conversation. I wouldn't assume she's making a judgment about me and where I shop.

Confidence in a friendship and good manners never go out of style.

Dear Thelma: As a 62-year-old woman with a disability, I need to walk with a cane. I try to stay out of people's way but find that people are clueless about respecting my space. At the Farmer's Market a young woman yelled at me when her dog tripped me. People bump into me and give me dirty looks as if I shouldn't be in public.

When I was growing up we showed respect for the elderly and disabled. Now it seems that people are so self-absorbed that they leave their manners at home. People no longer think, "There for but the grace of God, go I." Thank you for addressing this.

A: They've not only left their manners at home, they've left their hearts at home. Your experience displays every sad aspect of selfishness and unkindness, and as you've so aptly described, self-absorption.

I call every reader's attention to this situation. It's time to take an honest look at ourselves and make sure that our own busyness, stress and impatience are not causing pain and suffering to anyone else. Treating others as we hope to be treated means slowing down in a crowd and staying aware of the needs of those around us. It means offering assistance if we can and at least a smile when we meet another's gaze. It means consulting your heartsense and doing what you know is right.

Dear Thelma: When we are out with certain couples for dinner the man will often ask to order the wines. He will order very expensive wines without consulting my husband. Last time he ordered three bottles for six people and the bill was exorbitant because of the wines! My husband does not want to say anything. What would be proper to say without insulting our friends who are such wine connoisseurs?

A: So much uncomfortable and unnecessary tension can develop around what has the potential of being a nice social memory. Avoid that tension by talking about it.

The right time to talk about it is when you accept the invitation. You can say something like: "We thoroughly enjoy your company and respect your incredible selection of wines; however, at this particular time, like many people, we are taking a close look at our spending habits. We've decided that we'd like to spend money on the menu rather than the beverage. We hope you'll still want to spend time with us with less expensive wine or fewer bottles." If they are truly friends, they will agree and then watch the spending.

When the spending on alcoholic beverages is out of proportion it is a problem. When you describe your bill as exorbitant, I'd say that's out of proportion and a conversation is deeply warranted. The general rule is that the cost of a bottle of wine ordered at a restaurant should be equal to the average cost of an individual dinner there.

I experienced a similar situation and didn't have the courage to talk about it. On a group trip overseas, one-third of our entire food budget was spent on wine that I didn't drink, which I had not anticipated when I agreed to contribute to a food fund for the group traveling together. Every time the fund ran low everyone was expected to contribute equally to replenish it, but the reason it ran low was because of an individual's excessive wine buying. The situation really diminished my enjoyment of the trip and the experience.

So the next time this couple invites you, start with the conversation. An honest discussion and good manners never go out of style.

Dear Thelma: I have recently returned to the dating scene. The last time I was doing this was before everyone had voicemail at every number. What is the proper etiquette for leaving a message when one is calling for a date? I feel it is inconsiderate not to leave a message so I typically state in detail that I am calling to invite the recipient to join me for a specific activity with the date and time and asking that they call me back. What do you think of that approach?

A: Your approach certainly is polite, especially if you know the person well.

Before leaving this kind of message you want to be sure that you've made enough effort to talk to the person personally. You should know the person well enough to know if he or she is comfortable receiving that kind of information by phone. This isn't the kind of message you'd want to leave the very first time you call. It wouldn't be right for a first date or if you've just started dating.

You also want to make sure that you don't use voicemail to avoid having a real conversation.

If you are calling to ask someone out for the first time or early in the relationship and your call gets sent to voice mail, leave a message like, "I have something fun in mind for us. Call me back and we can talk about it." That will show the person you're calling that you want to get together and that there's room for discussion as to how that time is spent.

Hold off leaving a message with all the specifics until you've established a solid relationship.

Dear Thelma: My husband died a couple of years ago and I've had a wonderful financial manager who has really helped me and kept me from being afraid. He is married with three little kids, but he won't charge me anything for his help. He just provides it out of kindness and friendship to me. Is it OK to give him a gift to thank him? What kind of gift would you suggest?

A: You should absolutely give him a gift. A gift is a great way to show your gratitude and to express how special he is to you. What he's done for you sounds like it is done out of true friendship, and while he doesn't expect anything in return for that kindness, he will appreciate it.

In a world where it often feels like everyone is just out for him or herself, it's important to highlight the generosity of people who go above and beyond. Providing the advice and comfort that you have needed at a difficult time is a very honorable thing for this man to have done. Your desire to honor him is well placed.

When selecting a gift for him, think about what you know about him. Is there any activity or item you know he particularly enjoys? It could be a nice bottle of wine, a book or a gift certificate for a golf outing. You also might consider something he could share with his family, like a delivered fruit basket or a gift certificate to cover a family meal at a restaurant or a trip to a movie theater.

The amount you choose to spend will be left to you. Remember you are not attempting to pay him back for his services, so something extravagant is not necessary. You simply want your gift to honor him and show your thankfulness for his kindness that can't really be repaid.

Appreciation for generosity and good manners never go out of style.

Dear Thelma: I am part of a loosely organized group of military wives who get together every so often. Recently, one of the women invited me to a lunch she was gathering a group for. She asked me to invite any other wives I thought would like to come. I invited one woman who immediately accepted and said she would be brining her young son. Now I am worried that she might not be welcomed with her son. No one else is bringing children. I don't want the organizer to be upset with me and I don't want to hurt anyone's feelings. Is there any way out of this?

A: I don't think you should worry too much, and here's why: If the organizer had a strict guest list or strict criteria for guests in mind, then she would have and should have done all the inviting herself. She shouldn't be upset with any of the people she left the job up to. Also, this sounds to me like a casual affair in which everyone is welcomed, even a child.

If you are worried about the mother you invited feeling out-of-place, you could let her know that hers may be the only child there and let her decide what to do with that information combined with her knowledge of the group. Some young children handle a restaurant meal with adults with little trouble, while others can make things miserable. Leave it to the child's mother to decide where her little one fits. With her immediate acceptance, she is obviously interested and excited to attend. To retract the invitation could be very hurtful.

Your good intentions and good manners never go out of style.

Dear Readers: It's time to consider Top Manners for Teens. Our society needs teens who will become adults with integrity, commitment, honesty and love of themselves. Cultivating behaviors and habits that will lead to these qualities is a job for both teens and their parents. I'm not saying it's an easy job or that there won't be setbacks, but it will be worth the effort.

4. Communicate. Sometimes teens think that as they gain independence they don't have to communicate with their parents anymore. But because of the risks that come with newfound independence, communication at this time in life is more important than ever. Consistent and open conversation, even about the minutia of daily life, shows respect and concern for one another.

It is through communication that we build and solidify relationships. A relationship with a friend who you stopped talking to would quickly die. The same maintenance is needed with your parents and your siblings for strong ties when you really need them. Teens should make an effort to understand that questions from parents do not necessarily equate accusations but an attempt to understand and guide. Parents can work to create a structure at home that allows for regular interaction. Again, not easy, but worth it.

As far as modes of communication go, work to understand how to use a cell phone and its texting capabilities with respect and responsibility, making sure that the person with whom you are face-to-face takes priority over any phone call or message and that your messages are fit for the values expected by your family.

3. Don't forget what you've learned about safety. So many times I drive through a school zone outside a high school, and I am appalled at the risks students take crossing against the light, outside the cross walks, and at any time they please. Mostly, it's unsafe, but it's also rude to drivers. It's an easy example of the self-centeredness and dangerous behavior that is easy to fall into. Safety means protecting yourself from physical and emotional danger, which includes the dangers of alcohol and drug use and harmful sexual relationships. Taking the steps to independence means taking the responsibility to remember what you've spent your childhood learning and protecting yourself from danger.

2. Take decision-making seriously. By thinking seriously about the new daily decisions you now have the opportunity to make and by basing those decisions on respect for yourself and those around you, navigating the world may become smoother. Also, as you take more responsibility for yourself, be fully informed of the consequences of your actions when making decisions.

When a person takes his role as a decision-maker seriously, he begins to learn and appreciate the value of himself. For someone who fails to recognize that value, the consequences can be horrendous, not only on him but on those who love him.

Some of the first decisions you'll make will revolve around how you spend or save money. Think clearly and be wise about it. Another decision you'll control is how you choose to dress. You know that the way you dress communicates something about you. Avoid extremes in sloppiness or sensuality that send a negative message to the world at-large and boldly signify a lack respect for the majority of those around you.

1. Build relationships. That means make an effort with parents and siblings. These years are the final phase of your life where you are really at home and have the greatest opportunity to make these connections before a departure of some sort, whether it's college, a job or the military. Let your circle of friends into your family and let your family into your circle.

Strong connections and good manners never go out of style.

Dear Thelma: My young son has given up baseball because of the hostility of parents in the stands. He got yelled at so much that he told my husband and me that he was not going back. Having experienced the appalling behavior as well, we haven't made him. Is there some way to create a baseball league where parents aren't allowed?

A: The situation you describe is sad. Yes, we want kids to learn life lessons through sports, but at age 9, is learning to brush off verbal abuse really one of the lessons we're hoping to teach?

I doubt you could create a league without the help of parent volunteers, who do everything from coach to serve on the board to sell the snow cones – all for free. Before you give up completely, approach the team's coach or an assistant coach about the problem. Youth sports leagues often have rules regarding fan behavior and teams can be penalized when their fans break those rules. Most coaches don't want to risk that. The coach should call a parent meeting to remind his team's fans of proper behavior at youth events and let them know that he or an assistant or the team mom will be watching and reminding people to stay under control.

You also might explain the situation to the league president or a board member and ask him or her to observe one of your games. League officials can then remind the coach of his responsibilities concerning fan behavior.

Dear Thelma: Many of the charities I contribute to send me packets of greeting cards for various occasions. Some are very pretty with apropos messages, and of course, have their organization name and information printed on the back of the card. Since I obviously spent no time or money acquiring these cards, would it be considered cheap or soliciting to send these to persons I know?

A: They are fine to use. It's not cheap to use them since you did spend time and money supporting the charity. And, while by using the card you are publicizing your personal support of the effort, you're not making a solicitation or asking the recipient to make a donation. If they do take it upon themselves to ask you more about the organization or look it up online, that's good for the cause you support but it's their choice.

I've used the cards, particularly when I consider myself a supporter the charity. If it's something I'm connected to, I think it's nice to send to share my sentiments with my friend and to share a bit of something important to me.

Sincerity and good manners never go out of style.

Dear Thelma: My married daughter is one of five bridesmaids in a friend's wedding that is four months away. She received an email from the maid of honor stating that the bride did not want a "traditional" shower but wanted her shower to be an upscale cocktail party.

The maid of honor stated that she was making the arrangements at a nearby restaurant and would then let all the bridesmaids know the details. There has been no discussion about plans or budgets. The maid of honor is well-off but my daughter is afraid that plans being made are beyond her limited budget. She and her husband just purchased their first home and she has the expenses of graduate school.

She doesn't want to appear cheap and is willing to contribute, but dividing the expenses for such an event is more than she will be able to do. Not knowing the other bridesmaid very well, how can she comfortably approach this? I personally find it rude for a bride to dictate the type of shower. Am I just getting old and out of touch?

A: Anytime you're planning something as a group and will be paying as a group, the members should get together to discuss desires and budgets before anything is decided. When it comes to a bridal party, a bride should generally know the financial capability of those she's invited to stand up for her and make sure no one is pressured to take on more than they are willing to cover.

When the group meets, whether in person or over phone or email, they should be up front and realistic about costs. If a member of the group knows she can afford no more than a specific amount, she should make that clear from the beginning.

At this point in your daughter's situation and regardless of how well she knows the maid of honor, she should contact her as soon as possible and let her know the amount she is able to contribute. She should be honest and firm and expect the maid of honor to respect that. If she feels it necessary to do more, she could volunteer to help with the time-consuming tasks like addressing invitations or assembling party favors.

As far as planning the shower, a bride shouldn't dictate the type, but her wishes should be considered and accommodated if they can be.

It is important for brides to remember that going all out for your own wedding is fine, but asking your friends and family to make major sacrifices or create financial difficulties for themselves for your event is inconsiderate and it has the potential to place major stress your relationships. Even brides have to be considerate when it comes to their weddings.

Dear Thelma: Our stockbroker, "Bob," who lives in a neighboring state has three children who I have sent many lovely homemade gifts to. Since I had never met his wife or the children, she mentioned she would like to stop by and meet during a trip to New Mexico. Bob recently called to say they were coming and would drop by our rural home. Two days later he called and said he was not coming for financial reasons. I said that in that case I could travel to Albuquerque to meet his wife and kids and take them out to lunch. I was trying to be accommodating and considerate.

As the date approached, the wife called and said that the situation had changed and Bob would be driving in by himself after all and would join us. When they showed up at the restaurant it was not just her, Bob and the three kids, but also her mother.

When the bill came, it was set at mid table and Bob was suddenly very distracted with the youngest child. My husband took out his credit card and I picked up the check and his wife said, "Give it to him." But she made no move to pick it up and pass it to Bob. He looked at her and looked away at that point. There was no apology for adding himself to the mix, or bringing along an uninvited guest as well. There was not even an offer to pay the tip.

It is not the money that bothers me as much as how this was done. We feel it was tacky and low class and feel used and manipulated. I could not meet his eyes nor bring myself to make conversation with him when we all said goodbye. My husband says that he is sure that Bob knew at that point that he had "pushed the envelope"

Am I over reacting? Am I showing a bad attitude about this? I hope you can give me some feedback and advice on this.

A: All the way around I find this situation odd. It's odd that you as the client initially offered to take the family out to lunch. It's odd that Bob agreed to it.

By offering to "take them out to lunch," you set yourself up to host the wife and children. It may have been more appropriate to offer to meet them for lunch, which implies that everyone will pay their own way.

When more than the initial invitees arrived, Bob should have known that the original hosting duties should have shifted back to him. He should have insisted at that time that he cover the cost of the meal since the party's make up had changed. Is it possible that he was under the impression that you really wanted to do something special for him and his family and he didn't want to take your offer of goodwill from you? If not, his behavior was in error and obviously did nothing to improve his professional relationship with you.

Since you did not discuss the issue at the beginning of the meal, it would have been appropriate to start the conversation when the bill came. When the wife said, "Give it to him," it would have been appropriate to say, "Shall we split the bill?" That would have allowed everyone the opportunity to understand where the others were coming from.

There was definitely room for more communication in this situation. It could have taken place at each conversation when the plans changed or it could have taken place when the group arrived. The affair was left too open by both sides.

Clear, communicated intentions and good manners never go out of style.

Dear Thelma: Maybe you can use my situation as a warning and an etiquette lesson. My purse was stolen during lunch at a restaurant. My friend and I were sitting at the table almost ready to leave and a guy literally ran into the restaurant, grabbed my purse off of the empty chair at our table and ran to a car waiting for him. My friend said she saw the guy in the restaurant about 20 minutes earlier, so he must have been casing the place.

I am usually very aware of my surroundings and never dreamed that a guy would steal my purse that was sitting less than a foot from me at the table. The cops told me to have the car and house re-keyed since the thieves have my car keys and they know where I work and live – a $500 expense.

Where is the proper place to keep your purse when dining and is it safe?

A: Manners-wise, your handbag should never be on the table or hanging on the back of your chair, which makes sense safety-wise too as it could be an easy target from either of those locations.

Depending on the size and shape of your bag, you may place it in your lap or you may sit forward and place the bag on the chair behind you. You also may place it on the floor slightly under your chair, but make sure it is out of the way of servers and others passing by. Placing it in an empty chair would not be improper, but as you learned it's not the safest place. It seems that in your lap would be appropriate while offering the most protection from thieves, but I know this wouldn't work with all handbags. Each bag and each restaurant will have to be considered with safety and manners in mind.

Thanks for sharing your experience. I know it will make us all more aware.

Dear Thelma: We entertain frequently and at dessert and coffee time some woman will get up and start clearing the dishes and cleaning my kitchen. I protest over and over but they always say they are just trying to help. I know their intentions are good, but they break up the party, make the other women feel guilty so they generally get up and start helping, and I have to un-do most of what is done. I have a small kitchen and my husband and I both prefer to clean our own way on our own time, and we prefer to talk to the whole group during dessert. What more can be done?

A: A host's role always is to put guests at ease. Your friends with the penchant for cleaning up need their anxiety over seeing work to be done to be relieved.

When you say that you protest over and over, I assume that is within the entire group's hearing. And while that should be enough, it isn't with these particular friends. I suggest that as soon as a guest makes a move to start cleaning, follow her into the kitchen or to a private spot and tell her directly that you really want her to remain a part of the party. Let her know you appreciate her kindness, but that you and your husband plan to clean up together after all the guests have left. She should respect your wishes when they are made individually and directly and she should release her anxiety.

I'm sure she doesn't intend it, but your friend is creating anxiety for the rest of the group. Other guests do feel compelled to get up and help or they may feel badly to be enjoying themselves while others are cleaning up.

I believe every time I dine with others it's a celebration, and enjoying each other's company is part of that celebration. The host sets the tone for that by creating an ambiance of enjoyment and relaxation. Guests should use the opportunity to enjoy themselves. Guests can show their thanks in ways other than helping with the clean up. Bringing a host gift to the dinner or sending flowers or a note the next day are better ways to say thanks.

Dear Thelma: You've writing before about online dating. I would like to see a word of caution about scammers. While there may be love at first sight, trust is earned slowly on these sites.

I recently had an encounter with man who came on a little too fast and furious. He wrote me poetry and love letters and I started to melt. Then it happened. He asked me for money and when I refused, he called me some very unkind names and made some cruel statements. I ended the connection and reported him to the dating site.

I learned some valuable lessons and did not lose my money. Some people may not be so lucky. This can happen to men as well as women. So, please add the rule of "Buyer Beware." Do not give out your personal email address until you are absolutely sure of the person you are communicating with and do not send anyone any money on a dating site.

A: Thank you for your insights. Although technology can do much to help us establish and maintain all kinds of relationships, it also can, as you have experienced, be used dishonestly and with intent to harm. We must stay aware and vigilant in protecting ourselves and our personal information.

A healthy dose of caution and good manners never go out of style.

Dear Thelma: My niece and her fiancé are getting married sometime within the next two weeks. At this point, only one person in my extended family has received an invitation and we are unsure whether anyone else will receive one. Her dad says they haven't mailed the invitations out yet. A cousin says he got his two weeks ago. Her mom says they hung one up at the local fire department that covers my husband and me. My niece, her fiancé, and my husband are all members of the fire department. We've received conflicting reports on the date and the location.

My husband and I previously made plans along with our sons to go to a ticketed event during the supposed wedding weekend. We purchased the tickets before we were informed of the possibility of receiving an invitation or the date. What would be the appropriate thing to do if we should receive an invitation now, 11 or 12 days before the wedding? Also, are we required to buy a wedding gift if we do not receive an invitation?

A: Keep the tickets and enjoy the event you planned with your family without guilt or worry. However, don't play the same game of poor communication your niece has started. If you do receive an invitation, here is the conversation I suggest you have with your

331

niece: "I'm very sorry we have to decline the invitation to your wedding but we have had these tickets for some time and were not aware of the specifics of your wedding plans until very recently. I feel bad about the entire situation. As part of the family, I wish we could have had a conversation about plans and dates early on. In all honesty what's most disappointing to me is that I didn't receive a timely invitation."

If you do not receive an invitation, a gift is not required; however, you'll want to assess the situation carefully. While you may not appreciate the inconsiderate manner in which you've been treated, this is your family. Expressing your best wishes for the future of the new couple through a gift will be noticed and appreciated. A gift will may serve to end the whole affair on a high note.

As for the actions of the couple involved, the situation described is truly lacking in consideration of others and the main ingredient missing here is heartsense -- that feeling of doing what you know is right and doing it for the right reason. Sometimes couples get so wrapped up in themselves and their own planning that they forget to consider others. Yes, it is your wedding, but it's not a license to abandon all consideration for others. If you are truly interested in having people attend your wedding, invitations should be sent out 6 weeks before the date. Posting the invitation at the fire station should never be considered the appropriate way to invite individuals to a wedding. If you can't get your invitations out in the proper amount of time, then calls should be made to family and close friends who will want to plan to attend.

Dear Thelma: I was invited to a high school graduation party. When the adults arrived all the graduates disappeared. I asked where the grad was who I was there to honor and his mom said, "Oh, all the kids are upstairs having fun."

We all brought cards and gifts for this kid, and he was not to be seen. I was offended. What do you think of this?

A: I think this grad's mom did him a disservice by failing to teach him the responsibilities of an honoree at a social engagement. Of course, the guest of honor should be in attendance at the party. He should greet each person who has taken the time to come to the event in his honor and he should be available to his guests throughout the course of the event. If this grad strictly wanted to celebrate with his friends, then other guests shouldn't have been invited.

It is a parent's responsibility to coach a graduate ahead of time on how to interact with adults and what is expected as the party's honoree. A warm smile, a handshake and a polite answer to the guest's questions on his plans for the near future are really all he needs to have prepared. It is fine for his friends to attend too, but make sure he knows that his presence and attention to all his guests are expected throughout the evening. Learning that you can't just leave an event and do what you want to do is an important lesson in respect that he will need to carry forward.

A graduation party is a good place to begin to learn the importance of social interaction with adults, something that will be important as he advances his education and takes the first steps on his career path.

Dear Thelma: My kids want to buy a flag to display on the Fourth of July. I want them to understand the respect that goes behind flying it. What rules should I teach them?

A: First, talk with them about the flag as a symbol of our country and how we honor our national heritage by treating the flag with a special level of respect reflected in the rules of the U.S. Flag Code.

The code states that if you are displaying a flag on an angled or horizontal staff from the front of your home, the blue field of stars, called the union, should be at the peak of the staff. You also may hang the flag vertically from a window or a roof eave with the union to the observer's left. If you are displaying the flag horizontally against a wall, the flag also is positioned with the union to the observer's left.

The flag customarily is flown from sunrise to sunset. If you choose to display it at night, it should be illuminated to the point that its stars and stripes can be seen from a reasonable distance, which may be possible with your porch light. The flag should not be permitted to touch the ground, a floor or water.

As the years go by, watch that the flag you display remains in good condition. Have it dry cleaned and mended if necessary, but never hemmed to the point that it becomes disproportioned. If your flag is made of all-weather material, it may be flown during rain or other inclement weather, but if the weather will damage the flag, it should be brought down. Special care should be taken to protect the flag while it is in storage. When it becomes too worn to serve as a proper symbol it should be destroyed by burning in a dignified manner.

Our national symbol and good manners never go out of style.

Dear Thelma: I have a wonderful, lovely friend with an annoying behavior. She is smart, fun, and generous, but she is always late to everything. As an educated and professional career woman and mother, she is very capable of organizing her life. She is well-aware of her consistent tardiness and I am dumbfounded as to why she doesn't think this behavior is rude. Her good qualities out-shine this behavior by far, but she seems to be saying, "My time is more important than yours." Isn't timeliness a courtesy that should be extended to everyone?

A: She should definitely know better. This "educated and professional" person should know that consistent lateness is rude under any circumstances and she should be embarrassed with being labeled as consistently late. This behavior is not just mildly rude; it is extremely rude. And as a mother, she is setting an example that teaches her children that it's appropriate for them to do likewise.

Making the effort to be on time demonstrates respect for those around you. Perhaps this person needs to focus on what it means to be considerate of others and think about it as she plans the timing of her day.

At one time in my life, I had a boss who would rightly espouse that "To be on time is to be five minutes early." To arrive too early can cause problems for a host or hostess, but if you know you have a problem with lateness the best thing to do is adjust your behavior to get yourself there early so you can be on time.

You've indicated that this woman is a friend, not just an acquaintance. If this individual were my friend, I would take the time to talk to her about it. No one can change this behavior but the individual herself, but an honest conversation may help her realize its importance.

Dear Thelma: My middle school daughter really likes to wear bandannas. She uses them as an accessory to her attire in lieu of bows, ribbons, clips, and hairbands. Can you offer some etiquette tips for us regarding when and where bandannas are appropriate? For example, she views her bandannas as more of a hair accessory like a headband or clip and does not see the need for removal at, say, dinner. I see them as more like a hat in which they should be removed at appropriate times.

A: There's really no official etiquette regarding bandannas, but I agree with your daughter that a bandanna tied like a triangle scarf

334

over the head is more a hair accessory than a hat and shouldn't need to be taken off at dinner. Even a hat worn by a woman or girl as a fashion accessory is not required to be taken off at the dinner table, unlike a unisex cap that should be removed at meals.

If you and your daughter's taste in fashion has reached a divergence, that's different and you need think hard about what's important to you in terms of appropriate clothing and have a conversation about that. She's at a point in her life where she's ready to experiment with her own style. It's important to let her do that within the boundaries you set as a family. It seems to me a bandanna at the table is pretty harmless in the grand scheme of things, but that's for you as a parent to decide.

Thoughtful conversation and good manners never go out of style.

Dear Thelma: How can one go about encouraging proper attire for guests attending an evening wedding taking place this fall? Recently my wife and I have been totally appalled at what is considered proper clothing when one attends a wedding. Blue jeans, biker t-shirts, young women in very inappropriate wear – we have seen it all. Can or should a mention regarding attire accompany the invitation?

A: In addition to your question, I've also recently received a number of questions from readers asking me to assess their choice of attire for a wedding. I have been somewhat surprised by the confusion that people seem to have over dressing for a wedding. Perhaps because we don't often have the occasion to dress up, needing to do so throws us for a loop.

For me personally, a wedding is a very special event that requires special attire, the nicest outfit I have. The way you present yourself at a wedding shows your respect for the sanctity of the event and your honor for the couple and the families celebrating. What you wear should not distract from the wedding party by being overly revealing or just too casual.

Everyone's closet is different, but it's important to move at least a step or two up from your everyday casual wear when choosing what to wear. Even a six-year-old I know realized the importance of looking sharp at a wedding. He was asked to be the ring bearer, and was told he could wear what he wanted within the color scheme. When his mom asked him what he wanted to wear, he replied, "I want to wear a tux!"

Generally, cocktail dresses for women and dark suits for men are always a safe choice, especially for an evening wedding. Pretty pantsuits for women also are acceptable.

If you really feel it necessary to instruct guests as to the formality of attire you expect of them, it is acceptable to print "black tie" or even "cocktail attire" on the lower right corner of the reception invitation. The notations shouldn't be included on the wedding invitation itself, unless the ceremony and reception invitations are combined.

When you find yourself invited to a wedding, do your best to look your best regardless of whether the invitation is explicit about the dress code.

Dear Thelma, Recently I was invited to a lunch with just four women and we sat at a very small table. Two of the women talked the entire time to just each other about a club they belonged to. The other woman and I do not belong to that club. It was like the 7th grade all over again. What should have been said?

A: I don't know the nature of the relationships between the four you, but it is easy to assume that you each know each other well enough to handle this situation in a humorous way. I would have taken the initiative to bust this up. I like to use a "time-out" symbol, a T made with my hands familiar to sports enthusiasts. Then I would say, "We don't get together that often, is there a topic of conversation we can all get excited about?"

The behavior definitely is inappropriate and inconsiderate. The women may not have intended to be rude, but left unchecked, it sounds like they never did turn the conversation back to the group.

I don't know if I'd accept an invitation to lunch again with this group; however, if the opportunity presents itself, I'd find a way to talk about it early on.

An inclusive conversation and good manners never go out of style.

Dear Thelma: Facebook has gotten out of hand for me. I have accepted too many friends and really want to pare it down, but I don't want to offend anyone. How do I get myself out of this mess?

A: Facebook, the online social networking site, is creating a wide array of awkward social situations, but most can be handled with respect and consideration.

I have a friend who tackled the same dilemma you now face. She handled it by posting the following: "I'm checking out of Facebook for a while. If you really need to reach me, contact me directly." A day later she made serious cuts to her list of "friends," paring it down from about 180 to 35. By her post she let people know that a change was coming and that they shouldn't expect to see her.

A month later she's seen no social fallout from the change. No former Facebook friends have demanded to know why she dropped them. And she's much happier with her core list.

Another option is to "hide" those friends who you don't particularly want to see posts from on a daily basis. You'll only see when they write directly on your Facebook wall. You can also hide any Farmville, Bejeweled or other game updates you find annoying.

Dear Thelma: Recently while having dinner at a restaurant, the waiter serving beer at our table of six spilled a beer (or two) down my back. About three of the young waiters proceeded to mop up the spill with napkins and our waiter was very apologetic to me.

Very briefly, the manager came out and told my husband that we could have my leather jacket cleaned and present the bill to the restaurant for reimbursement. He never looked at me nor apologized nor mentioned any other compensation.

Later in the evening one of our party asked the waiter if my husband and I would be "comp'd" our meals. He said he had removed the charge for our two beers. Our friend told him that was not sufficient. He came back shortly and said that the best he could do was to remove the charge of my bill.

I felt that this was poorly handled. Having beer drench your back makes for a memorable evening and an uncomfortable dining experience. We did not leave because we had carpooled and did not want to inconvenience our friends. I would appreciate your opinion of how this should have been handled.

A: Although I'm sorry you had such a dismal evening, I feel the restaurant acted properly. The staff seemed in most respects to have handled the accident promptly, courteously and fairly.

However, it is apparent that their actions did not meet your expectations as a customer and that's something to which the establishment could have paid more attention. The manager's failure to acknowledge you is strange enough to make me think that it's possible that he thought your husband received the brunt of the spill.

If I felt as you did I may have carried on more of a conversation with the manager in private. I would have kept the tone as non-confrontational as possible. In the end, if I still was not satisfied I would have said, "Then we will not be back."

Dear Thelma: Regarding your recent column on timeliness, I also have a professional friend who is habitually late. In order to solve this situation, I now invite my friend an hour earlier than everyone else.

A: Positive solutions and good manners never go out of style.

Dear Thelma: I hosted a small dinner party and one guest, who has a reputation for being bossy, started acting as the hostess and ordering for others. I could not see the end of the table and with her interference was not sure some attendees had sufficient food and drink.

For some reason only half the number of desserts needed were delivered to the table and she called out to the waiter, "Cut them in half." I would not have ordered half portions of anything, but at this point I didn't know if she'd placed the order for the desserts.

At the end of the meal, she asked the waiter to box up the leftover salsa so she could take it home. I hardly knew how to check the bill when it arrived.

I feel there should be a polite way to deal with this kind of thing but I'd never faced it before and wasn't prepared. I would like to host these people again, but how do I politely avoid this situation?

A: You can avoid this situation by learning the responsibilities of a host. It is important to keep in mind that a host needs to be graciously assertive. The most important first step you can take in that direction is seating people, either individually or with place cards set out in advance. Seat yourself at the head of the table so that you can see the entire table and inform the restaurant that you are the host for the meal. The best way to control the bossy individual is to seat her to your immediate right where she can see by your position and your actions that you are in command of the meal.

As host you can have the restaurant put together a limited menu for your dinner a head of time, which could help with the difficulties of ordering.

If the bossy guest was not someone I was close to, I'm not sure I would include her next time. If you are close, then it is very appropriate to have a heart-to-heart talk with her. Let her know that you felt deprived of being host because of her actions. Tell her that in the future you will do your part to be the complete host and that she must allow you that opportunity.

Dear Thelma: I'm a teacher and it's back to school time. I would love my students and parents to read some advice from you on classroom manners before they arrive on the first day of school. How can we all have a well-mannered year?

A: I would propose everyone – students, parents and teacher – learn eight magic phrases and the attitudes that go along with them to create a positive atmosphere for learning and growing. Doing so may lead to your best school year ever.

1. Please. The word "please" is the simplest way to show that you are being respectful in making a request. It should be said often and with sincerity at home, at play and at school and by adults and children.

2. Thank you. A thank you recognizes the effort of another for your benefit and it shows that you are aware of the world outside yourself.

3. I'm sorry. We all know how important apologies are to us when we are wronged. We've got to recognize the reverse of that and be sure to offer ours when the time comes.

4. I'm listening. For true communication to take place there has to be an exchange. At school that means listening respectfully as well as talking whether the exchange is teacher-to-student, classmate-to-classmate, or parent-to-teacher. Show that you're listening by looking the speaker in the eye, giving a nod of your head to show understanding and asking appropriate questions.

5. Hello. Everyone you meet deserves a smile and greeting, whether they're your BFF or not. Be especially attentive to new students. The atmosphere of a place where people make an effort to connect is always positively charged.

6. Let's take turns – in classroom discussion, in conversation and in play. When everyone makes an effort to include everyone else, no one is left out.

7. I care. Making a conscious decision to care about others, their possessions and their feelings and saying that you do creates a space where people feel comfortable and ready for the task at hand.

8. I respect you. Give all those you encounter during the day the honor due them as human beings and treat them all with compassion, caring and consideration. Yes, sometimes it is hard. We have personality conflicts and there are people who just annoy us, but if we can focus on our own attitudes and the respectful people we want to be, it may be easier.

These are the heart of good manners for school and beyond.

Parents have the first responsibility of modeling these manners and instilling and expecting them from their children at home and at school. If you find yourself behind on these, start now. Choose one to focus on and keep it at the forefront until it's truly a part of your family.

As a teacher, you have the opportunity to model these attitudes for your students, teach them and expect them. You can set the tone with the way you speak, the way you interact and even the way you dress. All of these areas should reflect professionalism, competence and maturity, even when kids are your only audience.

I encourage you to start each day with the realization that you are an extension of the family and an important figure in the lives of your students. You may find that other role models are not living up to their responsibilities, and that will not make things easy. But your career choice has put you into the position to make a positive difference. It is my hope that you will meet the daily challenge with grace and professionalism.

Dear Readers: Colleges and universities opening their doors for the fall semester reminds us it's time to consider the next steps in building a well-mannered life – top manners for young adults. Building upon what should have been learned as a child and a teen, these years are a time to learn the manners of interviewing and employment. Whether you're in college, on your first full-time job search, or find yourself in the pool of job seekers for the first time in years, developing this social savvy puts you one step closer to landing that job and excelling at it.

4. Assess your on-line persona. Employers are going to Google you. If your Facebook profile and your blog are public, they are likely to create a first impression. If necessary, clean them up or make them private before you begin your job search. Use a site like LinkedIn to present your resume and other professional information.

When using email to communicate with prospective employers, use a simple address that incorporates your name and avoids references to your personality. Never use emoticons or text language in correspondence with someone considering you for a job.

3. Take cell-phone courtesy seriously. The person with whom you are face-to-face should always be your top priority. Going into a job interview or first time meetings with a new employer, turn your phone off completely as you don't want anything to distract you or

detract from you.

In meetings, keep your phone ringer silent. Once the meeting has begun only take truly vital calls after excusing yourself and leaving the room. Spending the entire meeting checking your email under the guise of "efficiency" and carrying on a text conversation when your presence and input are required show a lack of professionalism.

2. Dress for success. Observe what successful people in your chosen career field wear and look to them as guides as you interview and select a wardrobe. It may not be what you'd typically wear to class or hanging out with friends, but showing that you can fit in to a business' atmosphere and expectations improves your chances of receiving a job offer.

For men, a dark business suit – navy to dark gray of high quality fabric – with a starched, long-sleeved dress shirt and a tie that reaches the belt line is considered the most appropriate professional attire. Socks should be black, navy or dark grey and cover your shins even when you cross your legs. Wear black, cordovan or brown classic lace-up dress shoes and a leather belt to match.

Business suits, pant suits or dresses are the standard professional attire for women. Be extremely conscientious of skirt length, which should be no shorter than three inches above the knee. Hosiery your skin color or darker is required with skirts in the most conservative business environments. Heeled dress shoes should not be excessively high, look for something around two inches. Limit jewelry to two pieces at a time and conceal your cleavage.

1. Prepare and perform. Prepare for an interview well in advance. Review your achievements and qualifications and rehearse the best ways to articulate them. Practice answering questions about your professional goals and why you are interested in the job. Also analyze the organization and the position you're seeking. Know the company well and have questions of your own ready for the interviewer.

When you meet the interviewer, give a firm handshake, make eye contact and greet the person with their name. Don't sit down until the interviewer invites you to do so. When the interview ends, shake hands and establish a date for following up. Get the interviewer's business card so that you can send a thank-you letter 24 to 48 hours after the interview.

Lessons for life and good manners never go out of style.

Dear Thelma: I came from an area on East Coast where potlucks were held for school and church functions and large family gatherings where the hosts couldn't prepare all the food. When we moved to the Southwest we quickly learned to love the hospitality and more casual lifestyle including barbeques and informal gatherings where you were asked to bring your favorite dish or even theme potlucks. We found them a great way to make new friends and discover great recipes.

However, over the years I have notice that several friends *always* ask the guests to bring a dish for every party, including yearly family member birthdays; grades school, high school and college graduations; anniversaries and so on. At these gatherings etiquette seems to require a gift for the honoree as well.

These hosts are financially comfortable – more so than some of their guests. On some occasions the guest list is so large it would be difficult for the host to prepare everything; however, there are many delicatessens that specialize in great dishes to supplement a meal. Am I being fussy, or even lazy, to believe potlucks are not appropriate for some occasions?

A: No, you are being neither fussy nor lazy in your belief. You are correct that potlucks should be reserved for very casual social occasions like neighborhood barbeques and regular get-togethers among friends or for family holiday events where everyone shares in preparing the meal and one person offers their home as a place for everyone to gather on the special day.

If you plan an event centered on a specific person, like a birthday, anniversary or graduation, and especially an event to which the guests are expected to bring gifts, then you as the host are responsible for honoring the person of the hour and for providing for the guests.

As a host you have control of when and where the event is held, what is served and who is invited. It's even your prerogative to gain help by asking others to co-host with you. With all these things in mind you can create an event that falls within your time constraints and budget. To expect your guests to provide where you cannot or choose not to is improper.

The key when planning any event is to recognize that the people you are inviting are guests, in every sense of the word. Whether it is your sister-in-law, your dad, your neighbor or your boss, honor them with your invitation and with the care and effort you take to create a great event.

Dear Thelma: I recently received a thank you note for a graduation check. I am guessing that all the gift-givers received the same thank you: a photocopied general thank-you message taped to the thank-you note. There was no personal note to me or even a signature from the person sending the note. Am I right in feeling slighted?

A: This is the first time I've ever heard of this, but since it happened to you it's probably happening elsewhere. The saddest thing is that it's almost ungrateful. It doesn't express any real appreciation, but instead says, "I'm going through the motions of sending a thank you. I've done my duty." The fact that there is not even a signature furthers the insincerity. The person receiving such a document does not experience any appreciation for the gift they've given.

You have every right to feel slighted. Sadly, there's not really anything you can do about it aside from not giving gifts to this person in the future and doing your very best at every opportunity to show the world how a properly thankful thank-you note is written.

True appreciation for a kindness and good manners never go out style.

Dear Thelma: At a recent visit to a new doctor I was somewhat insulted when no one in the office – receptionist, nurse or doctor introduced themselves. The same thing happened a few days later at a consultation with a credit union employee. Is it not the most basic of courtesies to introduce yourself to someone you are meeting for the first time?

A: It definitely is a basic courtesy to introduce yourself to someone you're meeting for the first time. The people you've encountered this week seem to have lost sight of that within the context of their busy work environments.

Taking the time for introductions opens the door to more effective communication on both sides of the conversation, important in both the scenarios you present. Even at a restaurant I will ask the server's name and tell him or her mine, and I think my dining experience is better because of it.

If a receptionist or a nurse wears a name badge – which is always helpful to patients and clients – it's not a rule of courtesy that they introduce themselves. You can feel comfortable using their names when they've offered them via a badge.

When I find myself in your situation, instead of becoming insulted I like to take the lead with a simple introduction like, "My name is

Thelma Domenici. What is yours?" You have just as much right and responsibility to launch the introductions if they have been forgotten as do those you've come into an office to see. Personally introducing yourself serves the purpose of exchanging names and opening that flow of communication, which is worth the effort. Right the wrong and then feel glad that you have served as a good role model of protocol.

Dear Thelma: I have a friend who continually sends email and text messages and talks on his cell phone whenever we are eating at a restaurant, visiting in someone else's home, at his home, or at my home. It's as if he's bored with the conversation and rudely shuts everyone else out when he's playing with his electronic toys.

He's 47 years old and seems oblivious to what I consider his rudeness in the company of others. What is your take on his behavior? I've tried telling him that it's rude, but to no avail. I'd appreciate your opinion. Maybe your column would convince him that his behavior is inappropriate.

Thank you for your column. It seems as if some manners we take for granted as being the norm are beyond some people's comprehension.

A: From the way you describe this person I'm surprised you want to spend any time at all with him and I'm equally surprised that he bothers with spending time with anyone himself.

Here is the basic key to proper use of a cell phone that your friend must learn if he wants to maintain any face-to-face relationships: Give priority to the person or people in the room with you and to the task for which you've left the comforts of home.

Unless a person makes a conscious effort to follow this rule, the electronic distractions will draw him away. We have trained ourselves to respond to the urgings of a phone ringing or the electronic blip signifying a text or email. While only a small fraction of these communications are actually urgent or even important, we are easily drawn into the feeling that they demand our attention. By deciding to give precedence to them, we alienate the people in front of us.

Some calls or messages may need to be taken – a call you're expecting from a doctor or a call from your child's school. Make a mental list of those that you'll take and let the rest go to voicemail or save them to look at later. When those truly important calls do come through, apologize to those you're with and get up and move to another area to take them. Inconvenience yourself, rather than those you're with.

You say you've told your friend his behavior is rude, but nothing has changed. I think your next step, aside from avoiding his company all together, is to turn the tables in some way. The next time he begins what looks like a long phone or text conversation in your company, say quietly, "Excuse me, I'll be back." I've done this with success. The cell phone conversation that was threatening to edge me out stopped immediately and my companion told the person on the phone that he'd call back.

I hope your friend too will realize the value of your time and your company when faced with its loss and make an effort to change his habits.

Dear Thelma: I accepted a friend request from a guy at work and now I regret it. He is weird and creepy and now I catch him staring at me a lot. I want to de-friend him, but I'm a little scared. What should I do?

A: If you are truly scared for your safety, you should talk to your manager about the situation and work to resolve it. If you are worried about navigating the etiquette of Facebook, you don't have to be.

You've already learned the first lessons of Facebook etiquette the hard way: "Friend" only people you actually know and if you get an unwanted friend request, ignore it. Decide in your mind that having a Facebook page does not require you to share your life with everyone who requests it and consider that fact every time you encounter a possible "friend." Ask yourself, "Do I really want to share the details of my life with this person? Do I want him or her to know what I did last night or where I'm going on vacation?"

Next, realize it is acceptable to de-friend people, especially if you have no real connection to them even virtually or if you find their posts offensive, out-of-line with the way you want to use Facebook or just annoying. There are no bells and whistles when you de-friend someone. You just disappear and that's OK. It sounds as if this co-worker does not meet your definitions of a friend and even makes you feel uncomfortable. You should de-friend this person immediately.

Finally, for safety's sake, take a close look at your privacy settings, especially if you have a lot of marginal "friends." There's really no need to share your telephone number and email address, among other things, with everybody.

Dear Thelma: When traveling on an airplane, how can you let your seatmate know politely that you want to read and not talk the whole flight?

A: Interesting question, as it just happened to me on a recent flight from Missouri. I took out my Kindle, smiled and said, "I have so little time to read any more, I'm going to take the opportunity now."

You could also say, "It's nice talking to you. I'm going to listen to some music and close my eyes for a while." Politeness is key in easing yourself out of such a situation.

Some people look forward to making new friends on a plane, while others don't. Travelers should learn to recognize both. If someone is politely engaging in your conversation, it's important to read any non-verbal signs they give that they'd like some quiet time. Once they take out a book, computer or headphones, respect their need for privacy.

Dear Thelma: I have a second home in a beautiful city that people love to visit. Friends sometimes ask if they can use my home for a weekend get-away. I'm usually happy to allow them to, but I recently experienced a situation that left me upset. I agreed to let a friend and his wife and children stay at the home. Later he called back saying that two more guests and their children would be traveling with them.

I am very uncomfortable with this because I don't know these additional people. The home has a pool and I don't know how safe these extra children will be. I also don't know how well they will respect my property. Now I have to play the bad guy in saying no to the extra guests, while I feel my friend never should have put me into that situation. What is right here?

A: These guests have taken advantage of your kindness and failed to seriously consider the position in which they placed you. The bottom line is, if you ask a particular favor of someone, you don't get their assurance and then increase the level of the favor.

These guests have placed a bigger burden on you and on your property than what you originally agreed to. You remain polite by reiterating your original invitation and letting them know that you are not comfortable with additional people who you do not know staying in your home and cannot agree to it. Do this as soon as you can so that additional plans are not made by the travelers.

If your friend is truly a friend, he should do what is necessary to remedy the situation without causing you any more anxiety.

Dear Thelma: When invited to a friend's house is it appropriate to bring along your dogs? Many jump into the pool, cause my cats to disappear and conversations and games are interrupted with yelling and chasing after the dogs. Occasionally dogs roam the house, jump up on the furniture and cause damage and the owners do not clean up after their pets. These are nice people and good dogs, but I am having a hard time with the "love me, love my dog" attitude. What is the best way to deal with this?

A: Is it appropriate to bring your dog? Unequivocally, no. The invitation is not made to you and your dog. It is made specifically to you. Those of you who have pets absolutely know that if you bring that pet you are going to have to spend time caring for the animal and making sure it doesn't cause damage, which is totally disruptive to the socializing purpose of the invitation. Your host did not invite you so that she might enjoy your dog. She invited you so that she might spend time with you.

I recognize that many individuals consider their pet on the same level as a child, but in making an invitation, it is not the same. I can assume that the stay-at-home mom will bring her 2-year-old to a lunch date I arrange and I am prepared to deal with that. If I'm not prepared for that, I ask when she might be able to get a sitter so we can get together. I do not assume that your lab and your silky will be joining us.

It sounds like our questioner has dealt with the issue more than once. I'd say when you make your invitations, ask that the dogs be left at home because you'd like the evening to revolve around spending time with your human friends. When people show up with dogs, explain that you don't allow dogs in your house anymore because they scare your cats. Invite them to stay in the backyard or in the garage or offer them time to run the dogs home.

Dear Thelma: What is it with everyone having 2, 3, 4 or more baby showers. They are having baby showers for each and every child born not just the first. When I was younger it was you had a shower for your first child and not all of them. When did things change?

A: Things changed when showers became more a social event and celebration of the new life rather than strictly outfitting the new baby with the necessities. While showers for a first born often seem focused on equipping the new parents with the latest and greatest in baby gear, showers for babies following the first born tend to take on a different personality. They tend to focus even more on celebrating the new addition to the family and the world.

Close relatives and very close friends will definitely want to be included in any celebration, but generally for second showers and beyond the guest list should include people who weren't invited to the other showers.

For a second or later shower, it is appropriate to be very specific about the kinds of gift items you need. A diaper shower theme, in which diapers and baby wipes are suggested gifts, might be right. If you have boys and now are expecting a girl, people will want to know so they can shop for tiny rosebud prints and lace.

If second and third shower invitations are not cause for celebration to you, remember that showers are optional to attend and if you don't attend you aren't obligated to send a gift.

Sharing happiness and good manners never go out of style.

Dear Thelma: When a close friend's spouse died we didn't know whether to go over to their home or just call. Is there a rule of thumb in these awkward situations?

A: Your key words here are "a close friend's spouse." If it's a close friend, you go over. And it won't be awkward, it will be appreciated. If something precludes you from going over, make contact by phone as soon as possible.

Dear Thelma: When a meal is delivered to an individual or family following an illness, death in the family or a new baby, is a verbal thank you at the time appropriate, or should a note be written?

A: A verbal thank you at the time or a call later can be just as gracious as a note, especially during the times which you describe. Thank you notes are always welcomed, but everything does not have to be written. I must assume that a person delivers a meal during these types of life-changing situations because they understand the recipient's need for help and time. Continue the generosity and be satisfied with a sincere verbal thank you.

If you are the recipient of such kindness, give the very best thank you that you can at the time. It is always most gracious to send a note thanking those kind to you for their efforts. Your friends will be honored by it.

Continuing the kindness and good manners never go out of style.

Dear Thelma: I sometimes observe female business executives who attract totally non-flattering attention. From being pushy about being given the place of honor to being constantly late to wearing attire that is revealing and sensual with exposed cleavage, short skirts and high heels, none of it paints a professional picture. Can anything be done to encourage these executives to behave more professionally?

A: While we've had our successes, women as a group still have not reached the zenith of the corporate ladder. This kind of behavior from prominent business women doesn't help us.

When any CEO is in a position of increased visibility among the public and other business leaders, his or her behavior and attire play a very important role in how he or she is perceived, in how the company is perceived and in his or her future opportunities. There are so many incredible CEOs who play the role so well, admired for leading successfully with dignity and grace. They keep professionalism at the forefront, while favorite fashion trends and individual preferences -- such as the enjoyment of chewing gum or smoking -- take a back seat.

For women, pantsuits or dress suits are standard professional attire, with skirts no shorter than three inches above the knee. Heels should top out at two inches. For the most conservative look, wear nylons. Modesty is important here. It is possible to be attractive without showing cleavage or have your skirt rise to dangerous levels when you sit down. For the most professional look, nothing should distract from a beautifully refined and understated appearance. Add interest and complete the polished look with carefully-selected shoes, handbags and jewelry.

You ask what can be done. A close friend may have the opportunity to discuss with a particular female executive the impression her choice of attire is making in the community. Others will have to continue modeling appropriate dress and behavior and hope she notices. As for an entitled attitude and lateness, the business community can and should expect more. Start meetings on time, don't allow any latecomers to interrupt, and assign seats or tables at events and require that they be honored.

Dear Thelma: We have a supervisor who is showing signs of memory issues. He will tell someone to do something and get angry when he starts to do it himself while the person he told to do it is doing it. He also changes basic office rules so no one is truly aware of what to expect or do. Everyone is afraid to say anything because he can have a short fuse. How do we handle this situation?

A: To be handled correctly, your concerns should be taken to your company's human resources department or to the person charged with handling human resources issues. HR is a neutral entity and its hallmark is confidentiality for you and for the supervisor involved.

If the situation is a medical one, it will have to be handled respectfully by the top of the organization and may require contact with the person's family. If it is a personality trait that needs to be dealt with, that will be handled differently, also possibly by the top of the organization.

Work with your coworkers to end the perpetuation of anger and judgment among the ranks. Conversation about it should be stopped while time is taken by HR and the company to deal with the situation. Stay in contact with HR if you find the situation has not reached a resolution.

Addressing concerns respectfully and good manners never go out of style.

Dear Readers: One week into November, and the holidays are truly upon us. Before we become caught up in the hustle and bustle that comes with them, let's take a look at what we can do to make the close of this year its very best. When we embrace a set of attitudes based on heartsense and the manners that come with them, I believe we'll find the peace and joy the season promises. I hope you'll join me in this embrace and experience all the holiday season has to offer.

5. Recognize the importance of tradition. Researchers say that family rituals and traditions help make family life predictable and provide opportunities to reconnect with one another. Rituals also solidify and display what it is that we value. Honor the importance of your rituals by putting some extra thought into them this year. Remember how they started and who started them and pass along those stories to those participating in them with you. You might even think about starting a tradition of your own. Make respect for what has passed and what is to come the foundation.

4. Seek opportunities to serve. Whether it's an official volunteer project like serving at a soup kitchen or simply filling a need that you see in your immediate surroundings, find time during the holidays to focus on others. Help a loved one set up their Christmas tree or make it a point to hold the door for fellow shoppers at the mall. In turning

the focus away from ourselves we can find many opportunities to practice courtesy and spread happiness.

3. Be thankful. When a spirit of thankfulness fills my mind and my time, there are fewer opportunities for stress to play a large part in my day. When I am thankful, I am kind and that spills over into the manners I use with all those I encounter.

2. Share your time. Your time may be precious, but share it as often as you can. Whether it's time to organize a gathering for friends or time to attend the office holiday party, sharing your time with others builds relationships and strengthens important bonds. Also recognize the importance of sharing time with those closest to you. Deliberately setting aside time to spend in a special way with those living under our own roof may be the best show of respect and love we can offer.

1. Find the joy in giving. Rather than seeking the perfect gift, seek the perfect attitude of giving. What does your heart want to express by your gift? Love, appreciation, loyalty, friendship? Focus on that expression and the joy – as well as the perfect gift – will come to you.

All of these holiday attitudes revolve around recognizing kindness as the positive force it can be. The reverse of kindness can run rampant in our culture, often during the holidays and taking the forms of judgment or jealousy or apathy. We must work diligently to combat falling into the rut of those feelings.

If I could start an epidemic, it would be an epidemic of kindness. The kind act of one person infecting another with the inspiration to perform similar and greater acts. As kindness spreads it makes one more sensitive and aware of responding to other people in a similar way. If we could harness that, how much happier would we be and how easier would it be for all of us to embrace the tradition, service, thankfulness, sharing and generosity of the season. This year, let's try.

Heartfelt kindness and good manners never go out of style.

Dear Thelma: The holiday season means once-a-year air travel for many of us. It's a busy time of year at airports. People are often on edge and rude to each other and to those working in the airports. How can I get through the terminal with all this stress and not let myself fall into bad behavior?

A: People who travel know that the psychological issues surrounding air travel are so different today because of heightened security. Just walking into an airport can create anxiety and a negative attitude. It's up to individual travelers to neutralize that attitude in themselves and make an effort to promote peace.

That starts with deciding to embrace patience and respect as you leave for the airport. Think of it as an act of holiday service to your fellow travelers. Prepare yourself for the lines, the invasive nature of the security process, and even the possibility of encountering rudeness. Decide beforehand how you will respond to these infringements with patience and walk away from them unscathed.

If you arrive at the airport and are faced with unfamiliar computer terminals to handle ticketing, don't be afraid to find an airline representative to help you. It will keep things running smoothly for everyone. If you are faced with a long, snaking line to the ticket counter, don't crowd those ahead of you and be prepared for what's next. When you reach the counter, have your ID and flight information available and your bag ready to check.

As you approach the security checkpoint, have your ID and boarding pass in hand. Be ready to take your shoes off and to place your change, cell phone and plastic bag of liquids into the tray. You don't have to be in a rush, but do think ahead to what will be asked of you.

Show respect and courtesy for the employees handling security. Approach with the attitude that whatever is imposed upon us is done so for a reason. I recently had to walk through the metal detector four times before remembering that a newly reinforced knee was setting the thing off. Being rude or disrespectful to the screeners wouldn't have changed that.

Take the luggage restrictions seriously. Check with the airline beforehand on size and weight limits and number of pieces allowed. Also double check the rules on what is allowed in a carry-on bag. Following these rules to the letter will decrease delay and frustration for you and others.

Now that you're through security and waiting at your gate, limit your cell phone use to short and discreet conversations. If you really must conduct business or carry on a long conversation, find the bank of telephone booths or the area the telephone booths used to occupy when people used them. They're usually situated to provide space between phone conversations and waiting passengers. Stand there to make your call and no one will question your manners.

As it's time to board your plane, a little kindness goes a long way. Treat elderly or infirm passengers with patience and respect and be helpful when you can. Accommodate split parties. Be open to changing seats so the newlyweds or a father and son can sit together. If you notice someone struggling with their luggage, help them.

Your trip through the airport complete, you're ready to proceed to your destination. You've taken the proper first steps, may you carry with you the same thoughtfulness, patience and respect on your flight and throughout your holiday time with family and friends.

Airport awareness and good manners never go out of style.

Dear Thelma: The holidays bring a strange bit of awkwardness to the office. Navigating party invitations – official office parties and otherwise – and gift-giving seem to throw people for a loop. What are the best ways to avoid stress and hurt feelings and make it a true time of happiness?

A: It's during these holiday times that a spirit of exclusivity sometimes sneaks into an office environment. It's a sense that everyone is not included, and it has the potential to create turmoil if efforts aren't make to dispel those feelings.

It's important for the workplace to host one celebration that includes everyone. It's an opportunity to be together in a way that is different from the work day and allows for an added layer of relationship building among colleagues. Regardless of the year's profits or losses, the opportunity to share companionship and show appreciation for the people who work together toward a common goal every day is important to take.

At these kinds of events, it's good to focus on the personal side of the people you encounter. Ask questions about their interests outside of work and be ready to share yours. Use the opportunity to get to know people you don't typically spend time with or to meet someone in the company you haven't yet met. Approach the chance to make these connections with a positive attitude and use the time to build important bonds.

Those planning the office party should look for ways to put some added fun into the celebration. A white elephant gift exchange or a table decorating contest can be inexpensive ways to have fun and create shared memories.

Office gift giving also should focus on being inclusive. The spirit of the holidays can be celebrated without gift giving, but if a gift exchange is part of the office culture, drawing names and setting a price limit might help more people get involved.

Giving gifts should be a joyful extension of good feelings we hold toward each other. You never err when you are totally inclusive in gift giving in the office; however, never give a gift solely out of obligation. The insincerity will be apparent.

If you give a gift to an individual and do not have gifts for everyone else in your immediate area, give the gift outside of the office so that you don't cause others to feel neglected or not appreciated.

The gifts you give your co-workers don't have to be expensive or elaborate, just thoughtful and kind. A festive bow on their favorite candy bar and a holiday card with a personal message shows you've thought of them. Stationery, soaps, gift certificates for books, coffee or dinner, and baked goods – home baked or store bought – are always appropriate and appreciated gifts for colleagues.

Accept a gift in the spirit that it's given and receive with joy, even if you don't have a gift for the giver. Gift-giving is not meant to be a material exchange, it's an expression of the warmth we feel for people who bless our lives.

Always send a thank-you note for a gift received. It can be a thoughtful email, or it can be a note of thanks added to that holiday card you were planning to send out anyway.

The holidays in the office present a perfect opportunity to show thoughtfulness, kindness and respect for the people with whom we spend the majority of our day. Take advantage of the opportunity to reinforce those relationships.

Joyful working relationships and good manners never go out of style.

Dear Readers: When making your holiday purchases this year, consider the gift of time. A gift should always show someone that you value their place in your life and that you're thinking of them. Offering an outing during which you can spend time together may be the most valuable gift you can give.

Plan to give the gift of a lunch date with at least one friend or family member this season. Give the children in your life an outing to a unique place or experience – tickets to a sporting event, a musical or even the movies would be fun. One family I know ended their kids' usual gift exchange with another family and instead plan to spend a day during winter break together bowling and having lunch. Everyone is excited to share that time together.

Celebrate the relationships in your life by using this season's gift-giving opportunities to be truly present to those you love.

Dear Thelma: How much time and effort should be spent on wrapping gifts?

A: I feel really good when I see a pretty package. I think the receiver experiences an added dose of joy with a thoughtfully wrapped present. Whether it's extra attention to detail paid to a gift bag or wrapping paper, either way it shows thoughtfulness.

So, spend as much time and effort as it takes for you to express kindness with your gift inside and out.

Dear Thelma: If you are going to a party and take a gift for the hostess, do you include a card to express who it's from?

A: If you are one of many guests invited to a larger event, do include a card. A hostess is as gracious as she can be when accepting your gift at the start of her party, but she may not have the time to make all the connections at that moment and after the party she may not remember who put that great bottle of wine in her hands.

If your gift is wrapped, she is even more unlikely to be able to match the gift to you after the party. I have been a hostess in just this sort of situation and have been very disappointed to find that I have no idea who presented me with some beautiful things. I would love to send a note of thanks, but just do not know to whom I should send them. As a hostess, I truly wish they had included a note.

Dear Thelma: I gave my mailman a $15 gift card last year, and also purchased one for him this year. My husband said that he saw on television that you should not give your mail carrier a monetary gift at Christmas, or at any time. I still want to give him the gift card. Am I wrong in doing so? Also, I'm confused about the etiquette of giving a gift card to my newspaper delivery person. Is it proper to do so?

A: Postal carriers fall under federal standards of ethical conduct, under which cash and cash equivalents in any amount are considered prohibited gifts. The regulations also generally consider any item with a market value of more than $20 a prohibited gift. You wouldn't be wrong in offering the gift, but he would be wrong to accept it. I doubt you want to put him in that awkward position.

Newspaper carriers fall under no such federal regulation and are in the category of people who perform regular services for you during the year who can be tipped during the holidays.

The perfect gift and good manners never go out of style.

Dear Thelma: When my daughter came home from college for winter break last year I barely saw her. She was constantly busy with boyfriend and friends. I understand that she's an adult and can choose to spend her time as she wishes, but I also feel like she should show some consideration for her family. I plan to tell her that this year. Do you have suggestions on how to broach the subject?

A: I believe your situation is a common one. I know other parents of college students who bend over backwards to get their children across the country and home for the holidays. Everything in the home is focused on that college kid coming home. Then when he is home, his parents never see him. And in what seems like an instant, he's back at school. It would be nice if that college kid could just hang out with his parents a bit.

I would encourage college students coming home to recognize the anticipation that fills the hearts of those you're coming home to. Weave into your schedule balance and appreciation for those left at home while you're on your grand adventure. Your parents don't want to demand your time, but offering them some of it would be a respectful and loving thing to do.

Approach your daughter as the adult she is. Let her know before she comes home the events you have planned, invite her to take part and let her know how much you and others in the family would like to spend some time with her. Make some solid plans – whether it's a special family dinner in or out, seeing a movie together or a taking shopping trip. Get them into her schedule so that when the invitations start coming from friends the moment she walks in the door, some of her time is already set aside.

Treat her with love and respect and expect it to come back to you.

Dear Thelma: At this time of year so much seems to revolve around what material things kids want. How do we turn the focus to the importance of generosity?

A: The holidays are a great time of year to shine a spotlight on ideas like generosity and receiving gifts gracefully, but these really are things that we should strive to teach and exhibit throughout the year. Then we can use the holiday season to solidify what we've learned.

Many kids concentrate on what they're going to get at Christmastime, and that's OK. It's part of the tradition of being a kid at Christmas and we don't have to minimize that. However, we also can use those gift lists they come up with as an opportunity to talk about "wanting" and "needing." Those conversations can allow us to look at expectations and discuss what it means to be realistic, even under the magic of Santa.

Lessons can be taught in many family conversations. When we write letters to Santa, we can talk about how it feels to receive a great gift and how we can bring that feeling to others. Encourage kids to do things for each other, whether that means spending some hard earned allowance on your brother or spending time making a Lego creation for your sister. A surprise breakfast-in-bed is a treat everyone feels honored by. It could even mean going through your stuffed animal collection and picking out a favorite to give away to someone special.

Include kids in your own planning to do things for others. If you take a tag off a gift tree to buy for someone in need, let your kids experience the joy of shopping for that gift with you.

Kids can be surprisingly generous when given the opportunity to be. Bringing up the subject of giving as something they should be involved in and providing the opportunity is often all it takes to turn Christmas into as much a time for giving as for getting.

Dear Thelma: I am thinking about how to write a Christmas letter to tell people that you won't be sending them any more Christmas cards, that you're cutting your list. Not that I'm not interested in them, but it's been years since we saw these people and I don't want to hear about their passing by a returned Christmas card, or a note that says "By the way, Mother passed away several months ago. Sorry we never let you know." How would you handle the problem?

A: I wouldn't see it as a problem. If there are people you no longer want to send a card to, just don't send one. A letter to that effect is unnecessary. If they don't hear from you, they may end up not sending you card, but there is no polite way to ask someone to take you off their Christmas card list.

Dear Thelma: Our family Christmas celebration this year will include some new guests – my daughter-in-law's aunt and her new husband coming in from out of town. I'm a little worried about making sure everyone has the celebration they're looking forward to. How do we go about honoring our own family traditions and still make our new guests feel comfortable on Christmas day?

A: I'm sure your new guests are honored to be invited to your home and are ready to participate in whatever you have planned. That's what being a guest is all about. Rather than worrying about them, I would encourage you to include them in whatever you do, giving them the option to partake in as much as they desire. If you have a family gift drawing or a white elephant exchange, ask ahead of time if they'd like to take part. If you are going to church that morning before your celebration, tell them the time and place and let them know they are welcomed to join you. If everyone is bringing a dish, communicate that too and let them know what's needed. Even if they're coming in from out of town, they might like to pick something up or bring a favorite that travels well.

Opening your home during the holidays is a beautiful way to share the kindness and spirit of the season. Welcoming these new friends and introducing them to your traditions creates an intimate opportunity for sharing and building relationships that have the potential to carry on for years to come. Embrace the day and the opportunities that come with it.

Dear Readers: Are you making any resolutions for the new year? Now is a good time time to get our minds set for the coming year on a path of kindness and positive interaction. Our time can be impacted with so much negativity by the world we live in; it's up to us to counter it with the courtesy, kindness and respect of good manners.

I've said before that good manners are about who you are all the time. They are not just the behavior you put on when you get dressed up or are the in the company of certain people. This year let's resolve to make our best behavior our all-the-time behavior. Let's resolve to think about courtesy and kindness first and to show respect always.

I've also said before that if I could start an epidemic it would be an epidemic of kindness, where the positive feelings created for a person by one kind act inspire that person to repeat and create them in someone else. I would love for such a chain reaction to touch us all. Resolving to look for those opportunities is a start.

Finally, let's take care of our hearts this year. Let's focus on building and exercising our heartsense, that feeling of right and wrong at our cores that inform our judgment. We all should have it; it's often just a matter of deciding to follow it. In an every-day interaction or even an etiquette dilemma, ask yourself, "What is the kindest thing I can do?" What you come up with from your heart is probably the right answer.

Ask Thelma 2011
One Chance to Make a First Impression

Dear Thelma: I recently set up a LinkedIn account for business contacts. I soon received a request from a business acquaintance to post a recommendation of him on his LinkedIn page. I am not at all comfortable with this. I only know this person marginally and really don't have any knowledge of him that would make for a genuine recommendation. Not knowing him all that well, I also wouldn't want to have a recommendation come back to haunt me with my own clients or colleagues who may know him better than I do and may not feel positively about him. What are my obligations here?

A: Your obligation is to be honest, yet gentle. Respond that you don't feel qualified to offer a substantive recommendation and that you must decline. Keep it direct, yet light and open to future relationship building. That is all that is required.

To those who seek professional recommendations on LinkedIn, be selective. Don't send out a blanket email for recommendations to everyone to whom you're connected. Instead think carefully about who knows the quality of your work and reputation and ask those people. When you do ask, use a personal appeal rather than the form letter email generated by LinkedIn. Mention in your personal message the reasons you're seeking a recommendation from this particular person so that they know without a doubt they're not receiving a mass appeal.

LinkedIn can be a great networking tool. Use the manners of face-to-face networking to enhance the technological variety.

Dear Thelma: I had a wedding gift engraved and the name ended up being misspelled. I had no idea that it was wrong. The bride gave me another dish exactly like mine and asked that I get it engraved with the correct spelling, which she gave to me. The engraving was very expensive. Should I have agreed to do this the second time?

A: First, let's talk about engraving. If you are going to have something engraved, you must be absolutely certain that you supply the correct information and that it is spelled correctly. It is your responsibility as the giver to double check all your information, which probably means calling and asking the receiver or someone very close to her to verify the information. When you receive the item back from the engraver you also have the responsibility of checking the item for accuracy before you give it.

If you initially gave the engraver the wrong spelling, the mistake was yours and you should pay for the new engraving. If the mistake was the engravers, then the engraver should cover cost of the new engraving.

Dear Thelma: When I go to a restaurant by myself I often find that if I leave my table to use the restroom, when I get back the table has been bussed before I'm done eating or even have paid. I've had newspapers and books tossed away along with the meal. What's a polite way to inform wait staff that I plan to return to the table momentarily?

A: Get the attention of your server or another in the area and tell him directly that you are dining alone and indicate the table at which you are seated. Tell him that you'll be gone momentarily and wanted to let him know that you will be returning to your meal and to your belongings. Your server will appreciate the information and should keep everything in place for you.

Like a friendly and direct approach, good manners never go out of style.

Dear Thelma: I have recently joined the ranks of those who use the trails and I've discovered this to be an important and refreshing quiet time for contemplation and prayer. Occasionally I bring my children with me and instruct them to walk single-file in order to leave plenty of room for those walking the other way and to discourage much conversation out of respect for others who may want their quiet time as well.

While I applaud young moms for getting out and getting healthy with their friends and babies, I am hoping that those who walk in groups, those who have large jogging strollers, and those who like to visit loudly and walk astride will be gently reminded that they aren't the only ones to whom this walk-time is precious. Is there etiquette for walking the various trails in our city?

A: There is no formal etiquette for trail walking, but everything we ascribe to fits the bill with respect and responsibility at the forefront.

In my experience on the bosque trails, people do take care of their dogs, are aware of the space needed for their strollers, and are kind to fellow walkers. Most seem to understand that being outside doesn't equate to being rowdy, loud and not responsible. It's all part of being respectful to those around us so that we all can enjoy ourselves.

However, trail time is not a private prayer time for everyone and the trail is not a private labyrinth. Sometimes it is playtime for parents and kids, or an exercise session for a group of friends. It is important for you to realize and respect that as you set your expectations.

My worst experience on the trail was a time when we hid Easter eggs for the children in our family along the bosque. A man out walking got in our faces and yelled, "Get these eggs and these kids out of here!" I find that much ruder than the laughter and antics of well-supervised children, especially since he could have walked 20 yards past us and not been disturbed in the least.

Dear Thelma: I am an administrator for a large department with an office that opens to a main hallway. Several times a day either students, faculty, or staff stop by my office for help. People knock on the door, enter, sit down and start talking to me. Then someone else comes by and stands at the door waiting to see me.

What is the best way to handle this situation when someone needs to talk with me, but several other people are also waiting outside the door to see me? I would prefer to not close my office door.

A: It sounds like you are known for your kindness and wise advice to others. It also sounds like you should have an assistant who schedules appointments for you.

If an assistant is not a possibility, you need to make some changes. Require people to schedule time with you in advance. If that's not manageable, you might consider having a list outside your door and ask those waiting to sign in to hold their place in line. Then place a call to the next person on the list when you are available.

All of this comes back to you and your ability to communicate the system you're putting into place and stick to it. What those around you view as the norm can change, but it will take effort on your part.

Efficient procedures and good manners never go out of style.

Dear Thelma: I answer the phones for a large business very much in the public eye. People who call seem to feel it's OK to "vent" at the person who answers the phone. I have received all types of phone calls, many of them insulting to the business or to me personally if I can't give the caller the answer or provide the service he or she wants.

The hostility upsets me and I resent being spoken to that way. How should I respond to such callers in a way that won't cause further hostility and might even inspire them to become customers – without seeming to promise more than I can deliver.

A: I'm sorry that you are experiencing such rudeness. Try to keep your cool by keeping in the front of your mind that you are possibly that caller's first introduction to the face of the business. You are vitally important in creating, building or mending a relationship with that customer. While it's never right for a caller to be rude, realize that the he does not understand the nature of the business the way you do. Challenge yourself to be a gentle guide despite the caller's attitude.

When you get a strange request do your best to help the caller feel heard and offer to do what it is in your power to do. That may be to forward the call on to someone who can help or to offer another avenue of pursuit. Your kind direction alone may be enough to calm such callers and even win them over.

For those making calls that may be unpleasant, do your best to take reactionary emotion out of the call. If you have a problem, you can use your intellect to explain it calmly and without hostility. The person on the other end of the line deserves that courtesy from you.

Dear Thelma: In today's economy finding a job has become very difficult. My question involves employers who do not have the courtesy to respond to an applicant after having several phone conversations, a group interview with four members of the company, and two requests for references.

I followed all the recommended tips on follow-ups to interviews, thank-you emails, thank-you phone calls, follow-up emails and phone calls and still have yet to receive a response from this firm. Obviously I did not get the job, but they could at least have the manners to tell me that the job has been filled or been put on hold. I honestly thought that I nailed this job and feel like I wasted over a month pursuing this position. I don't want to become a pest but I would like to know why I did not get the job. Any advice?

A: In your situation, courtesy to those applying for a position is missing. Regardless of the number of applicants, all those interviewed should be notified of the decision by the company. It may be a call or a letter to the effect of "Thank you for your interest. We have selected another applicant for the position."

The firm isn't required to offer you a detailed explanation, but if you have a personal relationship with someone there, you can explore with them how you might have interviewed better.

When you interview for a job, you are right to send an immediate thank you. When the process is over, the company should show the same courtesy by sending an immediate letter or making calls to notify all of the outcome and to thank them for their participation. Good manners during the employment process should always flow both ways.

Dear Thelma: I am writing this in response to your recent column on etiquette for walking the various trails in our city. I thought I'd let you know that there is indeed a widely accepted guide for etiquette on Albuquerque's trails. The city's trail guidelines can be found at www.cabq.gov/openspace/rules.html

I think the person who asked you the question about how people should treat each other on trails would be interested in the section on public behavior. The city's guidelines state:

"Always be courteous when using trails. Everyone must yield to horses. Saddle and pack animals must stay on established trails. Mountain bicycles must stay on established trails and yield to hikers, and saddle and pack animals.

"Keep noise at a low level. The use of radios, tape or CD players, TV's or audio amplifying devices or instruments is prohibited."

Thelma, thank you for taking the time to help those who love our open spaces and trails learn the appropriate etiquette. Happy Trails!

A: Thank you for pointing out the city's guidelines. They are a good resource for all who use the city's open spaces. Like the recent column you mention, they encourage walkers to be courteous and respectful when encountering others on the trail. Also helpful is their instruction to hikers to stay on the right and provide enough room for faster walkers to pass on the left. Good advice for trails, and even for sidewalks and airports.

The key to all etiquette questions is respect and what I call heartsense. We know in our hearts the behaviors that will make the walk enjoyable for whomever comes along. When we keep those in mind and stay aware of our own impact on others, we won't make a mistake. A refreshing excursion and good manners never go out of style.

Dear Thelma: We have been asked to contribute money to a secret birthday fund for a friend who is giving a party but states on the invitation 'No Gifts.' We have given something, although we think this person will be upset when she learns that a friend created this birthday fund behind her back. We feel this is emotional blackmail. We don't want to be the only ones who do not contribute, nor do we know how much to give. What's the appropriate amount? What's insulting? How should we handle this in the future?

A: I'm highly inclined to agree with you that this could be perceived as emotional blackmail. It really is an inappropriate thing to do. When the invitation says "No Gifts" those wishes should be honored. If you are someone who chooses not to honor them, don't pressure others to join you.

I assume that in your situation everyone involved knows each other well and knows the birthday honoree well. No one should make the "No Gifts" request if they are not sincere about it. If I knew this friend well and were asked to contribute to this fund, I think I would realize how sincere the individual was in making the request that no gifts be given and I wouldn't contribute.

If I had made the request of no gifts and I arrived and there were gifts or one large gift, I would be upset and embarrassed. I'm not sure that I could conceal in a pleasant way my dissatisfaction that my request wasn't honored and embarrassment that a great deal of effort had been made to come up with the gift.

You ask what is the appropriate amount to give. My answer is that there is no appropriate amount. The appropriate thing is to respect and honor a sincere request.

If I were to receive a similar invitation in the future that I know will include the same group of invitees, I would prepare myself to politely refuse to contribute and be ready to explain that honoring sincere requests is more gracious than being the ultimate gift-giver.

Dear Thelma: My husband, who is in his late 30s, is finishing law school. I think of this as a tremendous accomplishment and would like to have a graduation party for him. It would be a great opportunity to celebrate with extended family and friends and also represents a good example for our children. He feels he is a grown man and such a celebration is more suited for a high school event. We both agree if we do have a party, we would request no gifts from any of our attendees. Can you please tell us if it is appropriate to have a sizeable get together for this occasion or if it's better celebrated quaintly by our immediate family?

A: Heavens, yes, celebrate. It is a phenomenal accomplishment and warrants as much celebration as you want to give it. You might ease your husband's worries by turning the focus towards sharing the celebration with the friends and family who have helped him reach his goals, rather than focusing only on him.

I think it is a great way to introduce the people you know well, like family and close friends, to the new people he has met through law school and his professional activities. It is wonderful that you are including your children in the celebration. It is important for kids to see what it means to have a network of family, friends and colleagues and to see how to behave in a social setting.

Joyful celebration and good manners never go out of style.

Dear Readers: As thoughts turn to romance this month I'd like to address engaged couples, newlyweds and those who love them. What a transition in life all of you are facing as you step into marriage, the marriage of your children, or even the remarriage of a parent.

A friend tells the story of being a young bride leaving the reception hall with her new husband. As they drove away they both unexpectedly began to cry. The emotion of the day was deeply felt, leaving life as they knew it with their families and starting something that was all their own. It was happy and sad, new and real, important and authentic.

Honor that authentic emotion in yourself and in your spouse by keeping respect, kindness and courtesy at the forefront. The etiquette of what I call the "marriage network" should do the same. When you marry, your relationship expands to a network of people who have the potential to connect or to divide. An extended family that works from all sides to provide emotional support, avoid critical judgment, and connect on a heartfelt level is such an asset to all involved.

An important piece of the network is a group of in-laws who can recognize and accept the creation of a new family unit connected to, but not under the control of, their own. Developing the in-law relationship takes time, energy and planning. It is an adjustment for parents, who may feel the hurt when Christmas can't be celebrated the way it has for years on end. And it's an adjustment for the newly married, who must juggle their own desires, the desires of a new spouse and those of parents or children. When all involved can recognize that change is part of the creation of this new family and and prepare to work together, the network will thrive.

With effort the marriage network can become a lifetime network and a complete familial connection. I felt the beauty of such a network when 25 nieces, nephews and their children showed up to honor a beloved aunt. The network stretched across generations and family units. Throughout a lifetime, that network capitalized on broadened traditions and inclusivity and created a strong web of support.

I'll admit that maintaining such a network is not without work and challenge. A simple birthday party may become a full-blown event-planning experience, but the rewards of those true connections are vast. Friction may raise its head at times, but with a commitment to a lifetime network built on heartfelt connections, difficulties are faced and overcome.

As you step out into a new adventure, do your part to make your network a strong one.

Dear Thelma: My daughter is about to become engaged to be married, and I have my grandmother's engagement ring that I would like to give the couple. I thought they could use the old diamonds out of it to make a ring, but I am now worried that this would be inappropriate or might encroach on the groom's role in some way. Please tell me if there is any appropriate way to volunteer this, or if we should wait for a different opportunity.

A: I would suggest that you let your daughter know about the jewelry and its availability. Then let her decide whether she is interested in it. She then has the option to present it and her wishes that it be used to her future groom. She will know best if the groom wants to surprise her with his own selection or would appreciate the sentimentality of the family connection.

Building the network and good manners never go out of style.

Dear Thelma: Please let me know if I am socially outdated. My friend and I attend many social dinner-dance functions. My date is quite social and everyone pretty much gets an earful during our dinners. I am outgoing, but do not share everything.

On three different occasions, a woman we know casually and two we barely met, mentioned that their husbands don't like to dance.

Then they stood up, grabbed my date by the arms, and dragged him out to the dance floor. I find this tacky and it humiliates me.

I have mentioned how his accommodating strange women's dancing needs makes me feel and he said he did nothing wrong. Since these women's husbands don't seem to mind their wives' neediness, I am feeling like I'm the odd one to be embarrassed.

What is the right thing to do without making a scene? Is my date supposed to just refuse, or am I supposed to ask the husbands to dance with their wives, or should I just sit there with a stiff, fake grin on my face? It just ruins the romance of a nice evening. Is this something women do these days, and I am not up to date?

A: It sounds like everyone likes your date, probably for the same reasons you do. He's a good conversationalist, a good dancer, and pleasant to be around. He's fun, and they see that.

At a such social dinner-dance as you describe, people do gather to mingle and have fun as a group. You may need to update your attitude toward these types of functions. You can dance with someone who you didn't arrive with and women can ask men to dance. While you might find yourself annoyed with your date's popularity, you needn't feel humiliated and embarrassed. These women are not asking him to dance to slight you and he's not accepting because he'd rather not be with you.

I would encourage you to have a conversation with this man away from the situation to let him know how you feel. Do not exaggerate the intent of the evening's activities or say things that only will make him feel bad. Take the opportunity to talk together and come up with a solution that ensures everyone will have a good time.

You may discover that you'd like to dance more frequently together so he's not often free for others. Or you may find that you don't like to dance as much as he does and that having additional opportunities to dance is something you want him to have the chance to enjoy. When he is dancing with someone else, don't sit with a stiff grin, get up and mingle.

If it remains a problem even after you discuss it, you might decide to avoid the crowd when you're looking for a romantic evening. But if you do choose a "social dinner-dance," that is what you're going to get.

Dear Thelma: My question is lengthy as I have to explain to you what I experienced recently at an evening birthday party at the home of friends of my husband. The couple are from another country. My spouse is from the same country, but I am not. The couple invited several people to attend the birthday party of their 4-year-old daughter at their home. The majority of the guests were of their nationality, but the hosts also had relations by marriage not of their nationality present at the occasion that evening.

The hostess made sure that she sat all those of her nationality in the dining room area and she had the relatives of her husband sit in the living room along with my spouse and me. Every time a dining room guest would go try to sit in the living room to visit with us, the hostess would get up from her area in the dining room and in her native language ask them to go back into the dining room.

The hostess did try to mingle a bit around the two rooms passing out appetizers to all of us, but finally at dinner time, she got up and instructed everyone in the living room that we should get up for dinner as we should eat first because the others tend to eat dinner much later in the evening. She had us serve ourselves and eat while the others watched and visited with each other. I was made to feel as if she wanted us out of there quickly so that they could begin their party once we were gone.

Please tell me what you think of the way our friend the hostess handled this event. I am reluctant to go back to future parties at her home.

A: Thank you for sending the question and sharing your experience. I will tell you first that the hostess' behavior does not represent the guidelines that I encourage hosts or hostesses to follow.

To be a hostess means using your heartsense to create an event during which all invited can enjoy the company of everyone equally. It should be an occasion for everyone to experience the evening in the same manner, and no one should ever wonder why they have been invited.

The top responsibility of the hostess is to prepare a guest list. The ultimate success of the evening is very much dependent on the combination of people invited. Develop a list of people who will enjoy being together and feel comfortable together. For the host of the party you attended, it would have been better to invite fewer people who could all experience the party on the same level, rather than making some feel isolated or separated from the group.

I use place cards to arrange seating at the dinner table for my guests, seating spouses away from each other and mixing up the group to allow people to socialize with someone new sitting near them. As host, I sit at the head of the table. From that spot I can initiate or consolidate the conversation if necessary. If two tables are used I ask in advance for a particular guest at the second table to exchange places with me at some point in the meal. I select someone I know will be comfortable doing this and plan it with him or her privately ahead of time. A host also should make sure everyone mingles and provide opportunities for that to happen.

As for going back if invited again, I would feel as reluctant as you, and it's likely I wouldn't go back. An honored guest and good manners never go out of style.

Dear Thelma: For many years I have entertained the same group of friends, numerous times, on many occasions. However, most of them don't seem to reciprocate. It's gotten to the point I'm thinking of finding new friends. Am I being silly?

A: No, I don't think you're being silly for feeling the way you do. If it's a repetitious thing, there is a responsibility to reciprocate. It doesn't have to be dinner party for dinner party, but an occasional social invitation of some kind is warranted. It's how we keep building and advancing our relationships. It keeps our friendships fresh.

Now you can't do a thing about it if they don't reciprocate, but you do have control of your own guest list. Don't be afraid to expand it. It's a real opportunity for a different kind of experience.

I'm the kind of person that believes that people's worlds expand as they make an effort to meet and increase their circle of friends. Personally, I'm always looking for opportunities to expand my friendship base. That seems best done by entertaining where I can create fun and celebration by mixing the new along with the old.

Dear Thelma: I love having house guests and want them to be comfortable. I am never sure if someone wears false teeth. What do I need to have available and put out in the bathroom for their use that is not offensive in case they don't wear false teeth?

A: It's kind of you to put so much thought into caring for your house guests. I would suggest you put out everything any person might need. That will include items that have nothing to do with false teeth. No one should be offended when they see you've provided for anyone who stays in your home.

For those who find themselves guests in another's home, plan to

369

leave behind a thank-you note and even a small gift as a token of your appreciation for their hospitality and generosity. Paying attention to all the details will help ensure many happy returns.

Dear Thelma: I read your recent column about the segregated dinner party and was very interested to see how you would respond. I was disappointed that you did not address anything about different cultures and how they have different communication styles, gender roles, social status frameworks, food traditions, and of course, languages. While the hostess should have explained (or had this person's spouse explain) the reasoning behind her approach, you cannot assume that someone from another country is going to just adopt an American approach to social gatherings. Especially in intercultural marriages and families, the socializing process can be very complex and is often somewhat uncomfortable for some attendees regardless of what special efforts the host or hostess makes. It is not as simple as controlling a guest list when it involves extended family who in some cultures would be very insulted if not invited.

Someone who is trusted by the hostess may be able to talk through how she thought the party went and perhaps make suggestions to employ some of the ideas in your column if they could be applied in a way that is culturally acceptable. In this way, future gatherings may be smoother for all concerned. Many cultures have a more indirect way of dealing with "constructive criticism" and sometimes it may take a while for changes to occur. It is important for people to realize that to reap the benefits of more diverse social circles, you will sometimes have a "learning curve" and occasions when you just have to relax and not have rigid expectations.

I have a master's degree in intercultural communication, have lived abroad, and am in an intercultural marriage so I speak from both formal study and personal experience. Thank you for considering an alternate response.

A: Thank you for your insight. While I agree that cultural differences are something we have to approach respectfully and seek common ground within, I contend that a host who invites group of people from varied backgrounds should attempt to make all of those people comfortable. That may mean explaining the differences a guest of another culture might expect to see or examining the guest list carefully.

As a guest, one should always enter a social situation ready to enjoy what is presented and as you say, "relax and not have rigid expectations." But on the flip side of that, no one should feel as the reader in the previous question did, as if the hostess "wanted us out of there quickly so that they could begin their party once we were gone." There was a disconnect there that made the event less than successful.

I come from a family in which both of my parents were born in Italy and immigrated to the United States, my mother as a child and my father as a teen. I grew up with my mother's Italian-speaking relatives living with us. Even though they could not speak English, they were always included with any company we entertained. Balancing the two cultures created the opportunity to learn from them and for them to learn from our guests. Since then I have been the kind of person who wants to learn about the world, especially from other people. To exclude them would have meant the loss of an incredible experience in life.

As our worlds expand and experiencing the diversity of culture becomes the norm, it is more important than ever to be cross-culturally savvy. The best way to do that is for those on either side of the cultural gap to stay respectful and work from both sides to meet in the middle.

A continuous search for knowledge and good manners never go out of style.

Dear Thelma: I like Facebook. My husband does not. He thinks it is rude to prowl around among people's personal information, photos and conversations. I say, if they've accepted me as a Facebook friend and put it out there for my consumption, it's not rude of me to look at it. What do you think?

A: Facebook, the social networking site that has quickly become a part of our culture, is designed as a place for people to put their information, photos and conversations out there. As you say, they've given you permission, so it's not rude for you to observe them there.

Where the rudeness may come in is in the way people use their own Facebook pages and in what they post on other's walls. The perils of less-than-thoughtful Facebook use show up all the time as people experience the growing pains of embracing a new technology. Facebook users have been disciplined at their jobs when irresponsible posts are viewed by superiors. Relationships on many levels have been damaged by careless posts or rash comments.

So be thoughtful in all your communications and be careful when sharing. If you are not discriminating in who you accept into your Facebook world, it's likely that many of your social connections will collide there. That includes your high school acquaintances, your relatives, your current friends, your significant other, your boss, your children and someone who requested friendship and has similar Facebook friends but you're really not sure you know. If you've allowed all these people to converge on your Facebook page, it's important that your behavior there – and even the behavior of these "friends" – meet the highest level expected. It's also important to realize that comments you make on other's walls or photos could be seen by anyone viewing their site, so comment accordingly.

Although on-line social networking is meant for fun and sharing, be sure that the respect and courtesy that guide your face-to-face relationships find a home on Facebook too.

Dear Thelma: I recently returned from visiting my son and daughter-in-law in California. We were there for a short three days and stayed at their home. My daughter-in-law is constantly texting on her cell phone. I did not say anything at the time, but I think this is rude and I feel she would rather stay connected to her friends instead of visiting with my husband and me for the short time we are there.

We went to a very fancy restaurant the last night and we sat across from each other. She again was on her cell phone texting. My son quietly asked her to please put the phone away. When I got home to New Mexico, I thanked my son by email for asking his wife to put the phone away as I thought it was rude. With that came a very quick email that my comments were totally unnecessary and he thought we had had a good visit so why ruin it by making a comment like that.

I now understand my mistake was sending the email. I should have talked to my son personally, but I still think this is rude when other people are around to constantly be paying attention to the cell phone rather than living in the moment with those around you.

How could I have handled this differently and what should I say the next time we are all together? I understand this is something this generation does, but it bothers me. Should I just accept it and move on?

A: The texting behavior you describe is rude. The most important text etiquette point that I teach and live by is that texting be done outside of your time spent with others. The person you are with face-to-face should always take precedence over a text message. That means the guest in your home or the cashier at the store. Texting in the presence of others is like carrying on a second conversation. It totally and very obviously, no matter how discrete you think you are being, takes your attention away from the people and activities at hand and keeps you from being present with what's going on in front of you.

Text etiquette requires that if you are expecting something urgent, you can inform the person you are with that you may have to attend to a text during your time together and apologize beforehand. Apologize again when the message comes through and use your text response to end the exchange until you are no longer occupied.

You've almost answered your own question concerning your email to your son. Any conversation that has the potential to raise emotion should be in person or by phone rather than by email. Tone, facial expression and body language – all things that help us read another person's intent and reaction – are all lost over email.

Thanking your son for a nice visit, especially for the special dinner and for any other attempt he made to honor you during your visit, may have been enough. He knows that his wife's texting is a problem, as it's probably a problem for him too. But to comment that his wife's behavior was rude, even though it caused him enough concern to ask her to stop, is bound to put him on the defensive. Although I can understand your sincere attempt to right a wrong, that is not your role in this relationship, which your son has made clear.

The next time you visit avoid putting a laser focus on the issue and work to be an example of impeccable cell manners any time you can.

Text savvy and good manners never go out of style.

Dear Thelma: When ordering a meal at a restaurant, if it does not meet your taste or order expectations (such as the chile is extremely hot), what do you suggest? I find myself continually ordering the food I have previously enjoyed without being as experimental as I'd like. Eating out is a luxury, but I still want to actually enjoy what is ordered without an uncomfortable confrontation. Please understand, I am not a particularly picky person, I just want enjoy my meal. Am I committed to paying for it if I don't like it? Is it proper to ask for a different meal? Your insight will be appreciated by others experiencing this same dining dilemma.

A: If you've experimented with your order and you don't like it, you are committed to pay for your meal. The restaurant has not made a mistake, and you are obliged to pay whether you enjoyed what you ordered or not.

However, if a mistake was made on the restaurant's part, such as bringing you the wrong meal or failing to cook your steak as ordered, they are typically willing to do what they can to get it right and see that you leave happy. In this case, you would get your server's attention, explain the problem and ask how it might be fixed.

So let your conscience be your guide. Is it that you don't like the meal your ordered or is there really something wrong with it? If it's wrong, the restaurant should fix it. It's always best to approach these types of situations with a pleasant tone and with an attitude that shows you are happy and willing to work with your server to resolve the problem.

Dear Thelma: I've been a vegetarian for a long time and have found that it sometimes makes people uncomfortable in a dining situation. So, when I need to attend a business function where food is served, I eat before I go. This way, I don't have to try and find something innocuous on the menu or draw any attention to my choice of diet. This makes for a comfortable environment for both me and the business associates I'm with. What do you think of this approach?

A: Thanks for exemplifying what it means to truly show respect for others by not calling unnecessary attention to yourself, especially in a situation that you've observed can make others uncomfortable. We are at our most mannerly when we do what we can to make others comfortable, even if it means an inconvenience to us. I applaud you for that.

But I hope you're not missing out on too many dining occasions. Most hosts of events and dinners have become aware that many people are vegetarians and they do what they can to show respect for all their guests. Most invitations I receive these days ask me for a diet preference or include a vegetarian choice. Many restaurants offer vegetarian options as well. When you have the opportunity, you may try to steer the selection of restaurants in the direction of such an establishment.

Good meals and good manners never go out of style.

Dear Thelma: My mother invited me out to dinner to celebrate my birthday with my sister and our husbands. We have gone to nice restaurants in the past to celebrate my mother and her husband's birthdays and my sister and I paid the bill, but I was reluctant to go out for my birthday dinner fearing I'd pick a restaurant that was too expensive.

I ending up deciding to go and chose a nice restaurant for dinner. I offered to contribute to the bill knowing the mid-range cost of the two bottles of wine we ordered. My mother refused my offer. When the bill arrived, her annoyance with amount was made obvious. She then made a sarcastic remark over my extravagance. The night was ruined. I will be sending a check for my and my husband's portion. My feelings have been incredibly hurt. Am I overreacting? And should I send a thank you card with the check?

A: It appears from your question that you have been to dinner with your mother before and you know what her reaction to expensive dining will be. While your mother's sarcastic remark was unnecessary and her handling of her shock over the final bill for the evening hurt your feelings, you failed to be as sensitive to your mother as you should have been.

Sometimes in a parent-child relationship, we forget to treat each other with the same courtesy we would use with someone not so closely related. We take for granted that we can express ourselves without restraint or remorse, and perhaps we're less thoughtful about what we expect from each other.

Would your mother have respond the same way when taking a friend out for a birthday dinner? It's not likely. Would you have ordered as much wine if an associate was buying? Probably not.

You do need to send your mother a thank you, but I don't know if sending a check is going to help or to hurt. I think a conversation is more in order. I would ask if she was truly upset by the event and talk about why. Then I would say that I was sorry that it happened the way it did and express that when we dine together again I will be more conscientious about my choices. There will be many opportunities for this group to be together again and there is a responsibility here to talk openly and candidly – but never sarcastically – about what's expected when this group gathers.

The bottom line is if you know that an expensive meal is a source of irritation for your mother you ought to respect that and choose accordingly when she is the host.

This is a relationship you must preserve. Do all that you can to understand and forgive your mother and create a new and better memory to replace this one in your mind.

Dear Thelma: How does one politely let newly-moved-in neighbors know that their little dog yaps almost constantly when left outside – especially at night – and that it is very annoying since their backyard is right outside our bedroom window?

A: I have the same problem. I haven't done anything about it because for me the little dogs have become like an alarm clock that tells me it's time to go to sleep.

Living in a neighborhood requires special patience for sounds and smells and sights that we'd rather not experience. I have found that simply talking to your neighbors can help in many situations. They have no way of knowing that what for their dogs might be routine is a source of annoyance for you. Faced with a friendly conversation, most neighbors are understanding and will do what they can to solve the problem.

Bearing with one another and good manners never go out of style.

Dear Thelma: Our son is getting married and we're thrilled with his wife-to-be. We have, though, encountered a dilemma concerning the wedding. The parents of the bride are only able to pay 40 percent of the wedding cost, forcing us to pay the remaining 60 percent, yet we can only include 10 guests out of the 100 guests planned for. We adore her parents and do not want to create any problems for anyone, but we feel this is unfair. How do we graciously deal with this situation?

A: It sounds from your question like a critical first step in this couple's wedding planning is lacking. That step is a friendly meeting including the bride, the groom and all the parents. Everyone should come to this meeting with a list of guests they would like to invite to the celebration and a thought as to why each guest should be included.

First consideration should be given to the bride and groom's lists. Next, equal attention should be paid to the lists of the parents. If at first glance the number of people on the lists far outnumbers the venue or the budget you have in mind, the lists should be whittled down equitably.

If this conversation has not taken place and you are already committed to paying for more than half the cost of the reception, you must stop the planning until this meeting can take place. Go into it with your complete list and work from there. This should be a case of making sure both families have the opportunity to include those with whom they wish to share the celebration. If the bride has 20 first cousins each with a family of their own who must be invited and the groom only has one, that shouldn't preclude from groom's parents from inviting other people who are important to them.

Listen and talk openly about affordability, responsibility, satisfaction and happiness. If cost is a barrier, cutting all the lists must be done, but those decisions should be made openly and candidly. If cuts can't be made by both sides, then new consideration should be paid to the type of wedding you're planning. It may be time to look at a new venue or a new menu or new expectations. Anyone insisting on a vastly unequal balance of guests should be willing to cover the expenses created by that imbalance.

If a lack of invitees lessens the happiness of the occasion, my advice is to not spend so much on the location, the flowers, the meal and any other cost you can control, and instead use your resources to include the people who you want to have there.

It sounds like the parties involved are happy with the match, and if you truly "adore her parents" as you say, you should approach them with courtesy and respect and they should respond in kind. This should be a happy and joyous event, the planning of it should avoid friction, stress and lack of listening. Deal with the situation graciously by reaching out and working together.

Dear Thelma: My mother introduces me as "the daughter." I feel it is rude, but my brother says don't sweat the small stuff. It isn't small to me – I am "her" daughter – and even though she is in her 80's, it doesn't make it right.

A: Have a conversation with your mother. Use phrases like "I want to tell you how I feel about..." rather than "You make me feel..." That helps keep defensiveness out and makes for a better conversation.

Personally, if my mom were alive she could call me anything she pleased. Even my funny nickname "Bombi" would make me happy.

Conversations and good manners never go out of style.

Dear Thelma: I'll finally graduate from college in May, a few years after most friends. Unfortunately, my university is several hours from my home. Because of the long commute to the ceremony and limited seating, I've chosen to celebrate my graduation with friends at home.

I've selected a favorite restaurant and bar where friends can gather and celebrate if they wish.

I'm quite sure that traditional etiquette rules state there is no proper way to ask for friends to pay for their own meals or drinks. Do you have any suggestions on wording? Also, is it improper to send a casual "invitation" on Facebook since most friends are recent grads themselves?

A: You're right that there is no proper way to ask people to pay for their own meals at a party you are hosting.

If you really do want to host a party, you should think about what kind of party your budget allows. If you can't afford to buy everyone food and drinks at a restaurant, which is very expensive, you should consider a gathering at home. There you can have it catered or make the food yourself. You can control whether you serve just appetizers and drinks or a full meal. It would even be fine to host it as a potluck, asking everyone to bring something to fit a menu you design or their favorite dish or drink.

Any invitation you send should honor your guests by its tone and presentation. Using Facebook to send invitations for parties such as those mentioned would be fine, provided that everyone you plan to invite is on Facebook and uses it regularly. If not all your invitees use Facebook, you should consider sending the invitation in a way that all equally could receive and respond to. An invitation to a casual event, by Facebook or otherwise, always includes everything that a proper invitation requires: purpose of the party, date, time, location, dress designation, and an RSVP or "regrets only" request.

If truly hosting a party is not what you have in mind, then you must be very clear in your communication to these friends you want to gather together. Talk in person or by phone to your closest friends and arrange to get together at the restaurant you've chosen, being clear that everyone should plan to cover their own expenses. Then if there's a larger circle you'd like to include, send your message on Facebook saying, "Hooray, I've graduated! A group of us are getting together to celebrate. I'd love for you to join us if you can. Here are the details."

A clear look at what you really have in mind and clear communication will make the evening you have planned a memorable and happy one.

Dear Thelma: How do I introduce Dr. Rubenstein as our mayor at the Citizen of the Year Banquet for the City of Saraland? Is it Mayor

Dr. Rubenstein or Dr. Rubenstein, the mayor?

A: Mayors are typically given "The Honorable" distinction before their names and the designation as mayor after their names when being introduced. This actually works well with the professional title: "The Honorable Dr. Larry Rubenstein, mayor of Saraland."

Because his professional title of Dr. may seem to put a hiccup in the normal introduction, it's always appropriate to ask the mayor or someone on his staff before the event how he prefers to be introduced.

Invitations, introductions and good manners never go out of style.

Dear Thelma: I am the parent of a daughter who is a member of a dance group. Their stated goal is "to help children develop discipline, a standard of excellence and a belief in themselves that will carry over in all aspects of their lives" through dance. Last year they performed at a large evening fundraising event held in a hotel ballroom. Unfortunately, during their performance, the audience never stopped talking or eating and were very loud. The students, ranging in age from 10 to 16, were quite disappointed by the rude reception. The sad irony didn't escape them that they were exemplifying the very discipline through their performance that the adults and wealthy donors in the audience were lacking through their inattention. Would you mind giving some advice how best to deal with such a situation if we encounter it again?

A: You can't force a rude audience to pay attention to you, but there may be some steps you can take to improve the response of a group who is gathered not specifically to see you. I'd suggest you tailor your performance so that it is of highest interest to the group, lasts an appropriate amount of time, and can be seen by everyone in the audience. At a large ballroom event, that may mean performing shorter routines than you would at a recital and positioning dancers throughout the room. Check your music beforehand for volume level and that it is properly cued. When it's time to perform, ask the master or mistress of ceremonies to get the audience's full attention and properly introduce your group before you begin.

You also should prepare your dancers for the situation into which they are sashaying. Explain that their performance is to a large group who are in the middle of dinner. Even if they feel they don't have the group's rapt attention, they should still focus on doing their very best and presenting a professional performance.

The people not paying attention to the entertainment are being rude to not show appreciation for the individuals who've worked to create a happy or memorable evening. Each member of the audience should do his or her best to focus on the entertainment provided. If they can't bring themselves to focus, they should at least be quiet.

If as a member of the audience you truly can't end your conversation to focus for several minutes on the entertainers, then you should leave the table before the performance begins and have your conversation in the foyer.

Dear Thelma: I was wondering if you know of proper etiquette regarding individuals who attend funeral or memorial services and then blog or YouTube about it without notifying or contacting family members. What do you think about that type of action or behavior?

A: The etiquette here does not rest upon the use of technology, but upon how it is used. Technology is as mannerly as its users make it.

Publication accurately describes what blogs and YouTube do. Publication of something as intense and emotional as the painful loss of a family's loved one should be done with care and forethought. Such publication without consulting or informing the family of the person who has died does show a lack of respect and it should be avoided.

I'd like to stress that blogs and YouTube are not to blame. This kind of technology is so easy to use and is an effective way to reach so many very efficiently. The key is to learn to use it with respect and always with the receiver of the message in mind.

Warm-hearted technology and good manners never go out of style.

Dear Thelma: Are there etiquette guidelines for dipping? My husband and I were at lunch with one of our teenage children, and the jokingly philosophical conversation (questioning the ingredients listed on a container of half and half) we were having was interrupted by a woman at an adjoining table who started to explain all the ingredients to us, and even offered to draw us a picture to show us the chemical makeup of one of them.

When we tried to explain that we really did know all this (my husband and I both have science degrees) and were just joking around, she informed us that she had a PhD, and even went on to ask us what we did for a living!

Needless to say, her condescending behavior put a real damper on what should have been an enjoyable family outing, and we ended up taking a good part of our meal to-go just to get out of there sooner.

Is there any way to handle this sort of unwelcome intrusion other than thanking the dipper and then ignoring her? I should add that we were speaking in normal conversational tones that wouldn't have easily carried to other tables, and were not discussing or saying anything inappropriate or offensive, or for that matter something so important that it required immediate correction.

A: I've never heard this kind of behavior called dipping, but I know that it does happen. I think a "thank you" to end the exchange would be best. Since you did engage her by explaining that you were aware of what she was explaining, she may have assumed that you were open to having a conversation.

I appreciate you pointing out that the conversation at your own table was not loud or inappropriate. Many times groups in restaurants are overly enthusiastic in their conversations, speaking at levels that are unnecessary for people sitting face-to-face and distracting to those around them. Those who want to keep their conversations personal, should keep them at a personal volume.

If this happens again and you think the intrusive person is going to continue to interrupt or make you feel uncomfortable, you may consider asking the server to move you to another table rather than taking your meal to-go.

Dear Thelma: I have a friend who always demeans email when anyone tries to use it to invite her for lunch or for any communication. She is the only one who demands a personal call, but with so much going on in our lives, we cannot spend time playing phone tag. It's sometimes easier to just skip over her. Any advice on how to ask her to keep up with the rest of us?

A: If she is a friend, you should talk to her. Express that time is a factor for all in your group. Tell her that it is hard to reach her by phone and ask if she'll consider accepting email invites. Let her know that you're worried that she may miss out if she continues to reject the use of email as a reliable and perfectly mannerly means of social communication.

Now, if someone simply doesn't have access to email, every effort should be made to contact that person by another means. A person in such a situation shouldn't find reason to "demean" email as you describe. They should make sure their friends have their best telephone number and check and return messages promptly. The same courtesy should be used by anyone responding to emailed messages as well.

Effective communication and good manners never go out of style.

Dear Readers: At this time of the year I experience both happy and proud conversations and anxious and emotional exchanges. They all revolve around the same event: A son or daughter graduating from college. I have participated in several of these conversations and the question always asked is, "Do you have advice for college graduates?"

As I seriously consider that question, I begin to realize how different the world has become since I grasped my college diploma and walked out into this wonderful world. I thought it was a wonderful world then, and I still think that it is today. While incredibly different and impacted seriously by a drastic increase in choices, this world is still very much in need of sincere, committed, courageous, honest and creative individuals. It needs individuals who desire to make a difference in their own lives and in the lives of those they meet on the journey.

My best advice for such people boils down to these, my top 10 tips for college grads.

10. Be grateful for your education and demonstrate that gratitude to those who were a vital part of achieving your educational goal. That may be your parents, professors, siblings and friends. Take time to fully recognize their impact and let them know how much you value their contribution to your successful education.

9. If the spirit of entitlement has become part of who you are – meaning you find yourself often dissatisfied with how much the world owes you but doesn't deliver – work to replace that with the choice to make the effort to do your part to improve yourself and the environment in which you will be working.

8. Make the pillars of your professional life respect for yourself and respect for each individual you will encounter that day, whether it's your boss, the colleague in the cube next to you, the drivers with whom you share the road or the cashier at your favorite coffee counter.

7. Establish personal goals for yourself. They will balance your life and allow you to use your talents to be an exemplary professional. Given proper consideration they can also helps you to become a role model exemplifying what it means to be a thoughtful, kind and humble human being.

6. Recognize that what you feel on the inside does show on the outside. Consciously develop a positive attitude toward the job you're seeking or the project you're working on that will effortlessly radiate into the environment and be evident for others to see.

5. Asses how what you are doing provides meaning and happiness to yourself and to those around you and maximize that meaning and happiness. Whether you're filing papers or building a bridge, seek the positive meaning of the task and gather happiness from that knowledge. Then share it.

4. Find the desire to run the extra mile and to appreciate every opportunity given to you. Then show it by your actions and your attitude.

3. Be who you are all the time. If you are authentic and true to yourself, you can develop and practice the traits of the positive person you know will make you happy and successful. Be that person all the time.

2. You have one chance to make a first impression. Make it a good one.

1. Use your heartsense – that feeling of right and wrong inside you. At the core of heartsense and at the heart of good manners are courtesy, kindness and respect. When you find yourself in a dilemma, ask yourself, "What is the kindest thing I can do?" What you come up with from your heart likely is the right answer.

Gracious grads and good manners never go out of style.

Dear Thelma: I love your column as it is time we had some manners in this country, however I certainly take exception to your answer on email invites. The writer of the question in your recent column was complaining that her friend "demands" a phone call, rather than responding to emailed invitations. Turn it around, she is demanding her friend access email when maybe she does not want to.

My cell phone is my main phone, it is with me everywhere and I return missed calls immediately. I also respond to text messages. However, I am not one to waste my time on the Internet all day long. I long ago stopped responding to email invites when I saw it was taking four to five emails to set up a luncheon date, something that can be accomplished in 60 seconds on the telephone.

We have been bullied into this Internet age and as a result have lost the art of personal communication. I consider email invites, like email birthday cards, email sympathy cards and email apologies to be tacky and showing little care for me on the part of the person who sends it.

I am surprised you don't agree with me. I consider email invites to be ill-mannered and I refuse to partake of the robotic culture that has become America because of the Internet. If one cannot take the time to call me on the phone, one obviously doesn't want me there bad enough, and that is certainly all right with me.

A: If we ignore technology as a tool in our lives, we run the risk of missing out on making real connections with real people. In addition, it is vitally important that we as people who care about good manners bring courtesy and respect to the technology so that we all learn how to use it with care.

The column you reference did address those who simply don't have access to email, saying that every effort should be made to contact that person by another means. What it didn't address is the importance when extending an invitation of never losing sight of being on-time, kind and gracious, no matter the medium you choose to use.

All invitations call for the same basic elements: the host's name, the occasion, the date and time, the location, guest attire, reply instructions and clarity as to who is invited. The email should be structured to evoke in guests the same feelings of style and grace they get from card stock and the message molded in a way that honors the receiver.

Composed this way, email becomes a substitute for postage but not for the grace behind extending the invitation. While there will always be a place for the polish of handwritten, printed and engraved invitations, the honor abundant in them can – and in our contemporary times will – be expressed via email.

Email loses its grace when it becomes obvious that the sender has used it as a quick fix. We can't let brevity or a "hurry-up" state of mind rule our interactions with email. Any invitation for a large event should be made four to six weeks ahead of time. Invitations to a casual dinner party should go out one to two weeks ahead. Even when a spontaneous get-together arises, the host must thoughtfully consider the best way to reach all the guests with all the information in the timeliest fashion, which, as you prefer, may mean a phone call.

While the written invitation may have been seen as the only gracious invitation in the past, it's up to us to make technology come through with same graciousness.

Dear Thelma: I have a friend whose daughter just graduated from college, with honors. I have been a close friend to the mom for years now, and I felt justified in mailing out a congratulatory card with a certified bank check for $50. I could imagine the graduate would be happy with a money gift. The enjoyment in giving is the thought of the girl's happiness in spending that money for anything she wanted because she had earned it.

After waiting two weeks, I had no word from my friend or her daughter. I asked my friend, if the card was delivered, as there is always the possibility of lost mail. A week or so went by and my friend emailed me with a message: "Yes, (daughter) has received it and she thought the card was really cute." Nothing else. In my mind I wondered, did she get the card, but the check was gone? Did the mother and dad keep the check? That was the only message I have had from mother or daughter.

So, I guess you can graduate with honors, capable and well educated, but still without manners. What do you think about this situation?

A: It was absolutely appropriate for you to ask politely if the card and check were delivered. As the sender of a gift, you want and need to know that it arrived safely. The fact that you had to solicit a response and the response you received were both lacking in courtesy and respect.

Failing to thank the giver of a gift is inexcusable. If the gift has come by mail, there's a greater responsibility to respond promptly so that the giver doesn't have to wonder about the delivery status of their gift. When you receive a gift in the mail, acknowledge it within a few days with a thank-you note or with a phone call or email followed by a written thank-you note. This is the case whether the giver is your grandmother, a friend or a friend of your parents.

Givers shouldn't shy away from contacting the receiver of a delivered gift directly. The more we make people aware of the need for thank-you notes, the more it will become part and parcel of receiving a gift. Part of giving a gift is sharing in the joy it brings to the receiver. A thank-you note lets the giver share in that joy.

Dear Thelma: We invited a family member to dinner. After dinner I handed her a container and told her to help herself to some leftovers. There was enough for two or three lunches left. She asked me if I was sure and I told her that only I would eat any leftovers. I then left the room and when I came back, I was shocked to discover that she had taken every morsel. I didn't say anything because I didn't want to cause a fuss, but I had to buy something for my lunch the next day.

My question is, what do I do when she returns the container? Do I say nothing and never offer leftovers again? Do I say, "Oh thanks, that is the container that carried away my leftover lunch"?

A: It seems to me there was a simple misunderstanding between you and your guest. There's nothing to indicate that she was trying to greedily harm you in some way. I don't see a need to say anything other than thank you when she returns the container.

I hope that you will let this go, and next time you have leftovers to share, package them up yourself and then offer those with which you are willing to part.

Clarity and good manners never go out of style.

Dear Thelma: Friends sent me an email to say they would be in town for a conference and would like to have dinner one of two days next week. I picked a day and sent it to them. They emailed back saying they wanted to invite another couple and would I make reservations, but I did not open this email until two days later. During those two days, three other people emailed asking me about the dinner I was arranging for the friends. I started reading the email train and it turned out my friends basically want to have a big party with as many as 16 people invited. The email insinuated they wanted me to do inviting and planning, all this before I even answered the email saying I would make reservations for the smaller dinner party.

I was pretty angry about it, but decided to just email and say I would make reservations but they needed to tell me what time and how many. I told them I couldn't be responsible for inviting the people they want there because I barely know them. Then I asked if they were planning to buy dinner for everyone or should they request separate checks because this is something that should be clear when reservations are made.

Well that got me an email lecture on how they are living on retirement and cannot afford to pay for dinner. Well, then I contend that they shouldn't have a dinner party. How do I get out of this mess?

A: This is a time when a telephone conversation would do everyone much good. Do not respond to what you feel is a lecture by email. Call your friends and tell them that the event has grown bigger than you can handle. Tell them that you still would like to join them for dinner on the day you planned if they are interested. Be clear about what you are and are not willing to do. Talking over the phone will let both sides respond naturally to the flow of the conversation and tone of voice, and avoid misunderstandings and assumptions.

Out-of-town guests who want to pursue a large dinner party with local friends should organize their own plans and guest list, how they will communicate with those guests and how the evening will be financed. If you want to gather this group but can't afford to buy everyone dinner, the fact that everyone will be responsible for their own dinner must be communicated to the friends and to the restaurant.

Organizing a dinner for a group takes planning and organization. No one should assume that someone who wants to see you on your visit also wants to plan an event for you. Wanting to have dinner with friends does not necessarily equal wanting to host a party for them.

Dear Thelma: Recently my daughter's boyfriend gave her what they are calling a "friendship ring." They are not engaged but are in a very committed relationship and believe they will marry in the future. She wants to wear it on the third finger of her left hand, which, as you know, is usually set aside for engagement and wedding rings. What is appropriate?

A: There is no set rule for friendship or promise rings. Many do wear them on their left-hand ring finger, but any other finger also is appropriate. What is most important is that the couple understand what the ring symbolizes for them.

If she does wear it on the traditional engagement ring finger and it looks like an engagement ring, people may assume she is engaged and congratulate her. She'll just have to be ready to explain her situation.

Heartfelt symbols and good manners never go out of style.

Dear Thelma: On two recent occasions I have been dining at restaurants and found that groups at quite a distance from me are talking and laughing so loudly that I can't carry on a conversation. It's as though they feel they are the only people in the restaurant and don't care that they are disturbing others. What can be done?

A: There are a few things that can be done. You can ask your server to approach the loud guests and ask for their cooperation in lowering their voices. You can ask the manager to do the same thing. Finally, you can ask to be moved to a new location.

Whether the server or manager will do this for you or be successful in doing so depends on the group causing the disturbance. Whether you can be moved and whether it will help or not may depend on the crowd out to dinner.

What will help is for all diners to be aware of how to behave. To that end I offer my top manners for restaurant dining – some timeless and some specific to our contemporary times.

10. Keep the level of conversation and laughter at a private level. Recognize the need of other diners to enjoy their conversations and keep your own in check. Don't think of it as stifling your rights, but of respecting others.

9. Once your silverware leaves the table, it should never return. When pausing during your meal, place utensils along the right-top edge of the plate or cross the knife and fork on the plate with the fork tines down. When you are finished eating, place the utensils diagonally across the plate. At no time during the meal or when finished should the handles of your utensils hang over the plate edge onto the table.

8. The napkin goes from the table to your lap when you sit down. If you leave the table, place it on to the chair. When you finish your meal, place it on the table to the left of your plate with no soiled spots showing.

7. If you drop a utensil on the floor, leave it there and ask your server for a new one.

6. Place handbags in your lap, in your chair seat behind you or under your seat. They should not be hung on the back of your chair where they can impede the wait staff, and they should never be placed on the table.

5. Be as gracious to the wait staff as you would be to a host. Get your server's name and use it respectfully. Use the words "please" and "thank you" liberally. Pull your chair in far enough so that the staff can maneuver.

4. Blot your lipstick before you come to the table so that you do not leave lip prints on your linen napkin, your silverware or your glass.

3. It is fine to share a taste from your companion's plate, as long as she's offered it. Give her your utensil so she can place a bite onto it and give it back to you. Don't reach across the table to feed someone and don't stretch your fork across and into your companion's plate for a bite.

2. Leave the table to blow your nose, use eye drops, comb your hair,

extinguish hiccups or coughing fits, and apply make up. If you can quickly and discreetly apply lipstick, you may. If you need a mirror, leave the table.

1. Cell phones are silenced and put away. Text messages are left for view and response later. Your first priority is to the person with whom you are face-to-face, and most especially when you've taken the time to have dinner out together.

At the table, good manners never go out of style.

Dear Thelma: This summer I am taking my three teen-age grandchildren on a tour through Europe. We will be traveling with families from all over the United States and Canada and with children of various ages. Can you suggest any guidelines for the kids to ensure that they make the best of this experience?

A: Congratulations on setting a wonderful experience into motion. I'm sure you've already accomplished the first step I suggest to anyone planning a vacation with travelers outside your immediate family: an honest assessment of how the assembled group will enjoy, accommodate and interact with one another. With that accomplished, the keys to your trip's success will be communication and consideration.

Well before the trip you'll want to meet together to openly discuss your plans and expectations. With a trip this extensive, this may be a series of meetings with the entire group and even some time spent with your grandchildren individually.

Start with a review of any material the tour company has provided. Get excited about the places you'll visit, talk about your expectations and review the rules of the tour. Let that naturally lead to a discussion of the issues anyone in the group believes could arise and how you will handle them. Talk about the opportunities to make new friends the trip will provide and about expected behavior towards each other and other travelers, which should include large doses of respect, courtesy and helpfulness. Talk about misbehavior and its consequences.

Discuss the importance of flexibility and prepare them for the fact that while each activity or destination may not be at the top of each person's list, everyone should show respect for the nature of touring as a group. Include a discussion on respecting the planned schedule and the importance of being on time for bus departures, events and meals. You'll also want to discuss personal expenses and budgeting for an extended trip, individual responsibilities, and care for belongings and living areas. Decide together how you will share decision-making opportunities while on the trip.

Plan as much as you can and make your compromises before you leave. By thinking about these things and having these discussions, you'll be prepared to step into the adventure together on the same foot.

This trip will create a learning experience without much effort, but you can encourage focused learning in many ways. My sister obtained permission to take her then 8- and 10-year-old sons out of school for a year to travel. They studied each trip in advance, wrote about each place visited and purchased one memorable souvenir from each stop. It was a combination of learning and fun they still talk about as adults. One of her sons even is repeating the experience with his three children this year.

You might encourage each member of your party to research a different place you'll visit or event you'll attend to share with the group while you're on the tour. It will be a great time to teach your grandchildren to keep a travelogue. It might even excite them to publish it for friends and family to see on Facebook or on a blog site if they will have access to a computer during the trip. Access to cameras, video cameras, sketch books and journals will encourage participation in recording the experience from each person's viewpoint.

Once the tour begins, everyone should be expected to be flexible, courteous and keep communicating. If difficulties arise, each traveler should remember that these are important relationships and strive to treat each other with the kindness and respect those relationship warrant. Speaking directly to the kids I'd add, have fun and don't forget to thank your wonderful grandparent.

Good travels and good manners never go out of style.

Dear Readers: Summertime often shakes up the routine of family life. Schedules fluctuate, trips are planned and taken, new ideas and activities are explored. Approached thoughtfully, summer can present great opportunities for growth and development of those all-important relationships with your children.

Turn up your listening ear. Car rides and meal times present good opportunities to listen and develop the ability to ask a question without it becoming an inquisition. One question that often doesn't get asked because we're all in such a hurry is, "Have you thought about ...?" Fill in that blank with the topic you'd like to hear your child explore.

I know one 7-year-old boy who is very concerned about his future career. He just can't decide whether he'll be an engineer, a pilot, a priest or film maker. He comes to Mom about once a week for a conversation to sort it out. He doesn't know what he should do, but he wants to talk about it.

Although his mom may be exasperated by the weekly replay of this conversation, she lets him talk, she asks questions, and she encourages him to explore the possibilities. I believe that if he experiences a parent listening every time he changes his mind, he will come back every time, even when those decisions are not still 10 years away. They are making a movie together this summer and his top college pick is the Air Force Academy, for now.

Take a hard look at media access. The Kaiser Family Foundation in 2010 reported that 8- to 18-year-olds spend an average of 7 hours and 38 minutes a day on entertainment media. By media multitasking they even add to that number, managing to pack 10 hours and 45 minutes of media content into those 7.5 hours.

Kids spend a lot of time plugged in. It's important that parents stay aware of the media being consumed and assess how it matches up with the values important to the individual family. Parents may struggle because they want to teach their kids how to make the right decisions, but media content is pushing them elsewhere.

Use the summer to talk with your kids about what's being watched or played. Explain the values important in your family and why some things presented in television shows or video games help advance those and others don't. Help kids begin to develop the ability to make their own judgments about how to behave and who's act to follow.

Encourage interests and potential. Potential is never stagnant and parents can take an active role in helping kids explore what they are capable of doing, make choices, and increase their confidence. A business-minded and crafty 10-year-old girl began making and wearing fabric flower barrettes to school. A friend asked for one. Seeing the opportunity, she replied, "I'll make you one for a dollar," and Bella's Blossoms was born. Mom and Dad encouraged her business pursuit with an investment and advice. Orders came in every week and she even established a retail presence at her mom's salon. By understanding and encouraging strengths, parents can help kids discover their potential.

Teach responsibility and respect. Throughout a summer of listening and encouraging, take time to find ways to challenge kids with new responsibilities. It might mean a new set of chores for the new age group they've grown into, work in the yard, or a job to do on the trip to the grocery store. Being trusted with new responsibility can build confidence.

Spend time thinking about respect for one another inside and outside your home. Work on manners at the dinner table, telephone skills, respectful communication with each other and thoughtfulness towards others. Remind when someone falls short and reward the success. Development of our future leaders and good manners never go out of style.

Dear Thelma: Recently you featured a letter from a woman who was having lunch with friends. They were bantering around a science question when a woman at a nearby table loudly inserted herself and her opinion into the conversation. Your reader asked you how she should have handled the unwelcome intrusion. You suggested if the intrusion continued that they have the waiter move them to another table.

Well, this letter really got me going. Many of us women have been trained since childhood to be "nice" and to avoid confrontations. However, I believe it is just fine to treat rudeness with rudeness! I would have told the woman at the next table that she had not been invited to insert her opinion and keep it to herself! And, if she persisted, I would have asked the waiter to move her to another table! Believe me, this type of behavior will continue forever unless we "nice" ladies speak up for ourselves!

A: Should you be a regular reader of this column, you know my consistent message of respect for others and the avoidance of critical judgment. You also know that I do not ever condone rudeness.

I also don't condone keeping this attitude going in your mind. I think you will find more happiness if you can replace it with peace and the understanding that situations like this do occur and that they can be handled respectfully, quietly and by the staff of the restaurant.

Nothing in our world improves when we dish out rudeness for rudeness.

Dear Thelma: Recently my mother-in-law sent out a retirement announcement. She talked about her career and some of the highlights. She also mentioned her family, two sons and their families (four grandchildren, two for each son). However, she forgot to mention me, her daughter-in-law, in her announcement. My feelings are hurt. My husband says that I'm just being too sensitive. My mother in-law is from England and is usually pretty big on etiquette. What is the standard for retirement announcements? Shouldn't I have been mentioned?

A: A retirement announcement is a personal communication by an individual to their colleagues and friends to let them know of the retirement. There is no standard for what should and should not be included.

I can see from your letter that you are hurt but thinking kindly about the situation. You say that she forgot to mention you but don't state that she was purposely trying to hurt or slight you. Continue that kind thinking. Focus on your relationship with your mother-in-law and the importance of its strength for the entire family, recognize the value you bring to each other's lives, and let go of your hurt over the announcement.

Dear Thelma: Last year, there was a question about how long the graduate should have to stay at the party given in her honor, when the guests were friends of the parents. My daughter had the perfect solution to this last year. She asked for our friends to come at the earlier hours of the set party, say 5:30 to 8:30 pm, and invited her friends to come from 8:30 on. It was the perfect solution. Everyone was happy!

A: This is an innovative solution and a good way to give the graduate the opportunity to focus on her guests. I would suggest, however, that there be some overlap in times segmented for each group of guests to allow socialization between them. Combining interesting groups of people makes a party fun.

Building relationships and good manners never go out of style.

Dear Thelma: What is your opinion regarding the seating of late arrivals at live theater performances? Over the last few years the number of late seatings at Popejoy Hall performances has been increasing. Recently, late arrivals were seated in the center section, near the front, approximately 10 minutes after the show started. What is the proper protocol or policy?

A: Latecomers are a distraction and disturbing to those theatergoers who have made the effort to arrive and be seated before the event begins. Out of respect and courtesy you should always plan to arrive at the theater well before the start time of the performance. If something delays your plans and you do arrive late, you should fully expect to stand in the back until the intermission.

The event venue should have policies in place to deal with latecomers that preserve the experience for those who arrive on time. Popejoy Hall's policy states that "each company performing in our hall sets its own late seating policy... If a company allows patrons to enter or re-enter during a performance, patrons might be seated at the back of the hall or in the balcony (until intermission) to disturb as few patrons as possible." Seating patrons in the center section 10 minutes after the show started does fall into the "disturbing to many patrons" category. I don't know why they chose to seat them.

An outstanding policy and enforcement example is the Santa Fe Opera, which will not seat you if you are late but instead offer you the opportunity to stand in the back until intermission. Its policy states: "Latecomers and those who exit the theater during the performance will not be admitted until the next intermission or an appropriate interval, as determined by the management."

The bottom line is, don't be late. And if you are, expect the consequences.

Dear Thelma: My niece sent a lovely, printed card with pictures and a magnet announcing her son's upcoming marriage. It read, in part, "Our desire would be to have you share this day with us in person. However, Susie and Johnny will be married in a small, intimate ceremony with only immediate family and a few of their close friends." In short, I am not invited. I have never heard of this before.

A: This was handled awkwardly. Your niece was trying to be nice, but she may have made things worse.

I have seen many questions from families who are struggling with guest lists and a limited number of invitations to offer because of budget or venue. They usually feel bad about the people they would like to include but just can't, and they struggle with what to do about it.

Rather than send a "non-invite," I suggest sending a wedding announcement. The announcement is designed to share the news with those the host isn't able to include on the guest list. The style and wording of the announcement matches that of the invitation and includes the date and place of the wedding. The sender of the announcement replaces the line that reads "request the honor of your presence at the marriage of..," with "have the honor of announcing the marriage of.. ." Typically, announcements are prepared for mailing before the wedding takes place so they are ready to send the day of the wedding or immediately after the event.

Those who receive announcements should feel honored by them. They may choose to send a gift, but they are not expected to. Sending a card of congratulations is proper.

Among invitations and announcements, good manners never go out of style.

Dear Thelma: I have an out-of- town gentleman friend with whom I have dinner a few times a year. He has had nerve-damage-related hearing loss since birth. It seems as we get older – we are now in our early 60s – it is getting worse. When we go out for dinner he reads lips pretty well, but when he responds it's like he needs to hear himself so he practically yells. It is making it very embarrassing to be out in public with him as I'm sure the other diners are not interested in our conversation. I have indicated he needs to use his "indoor voice" but have not discussed it directly with him as I don't want to make him uncomfortable. Suggestions, please?

A: I suggest you talk with him about it. To be honest with someone does not mean you're automatically going to hurt him.

If you are worried that he's not going to accept what you have to say, try anyway. I think that if you approach him kindly and with the mindset that he will accept, I think he will be grateful.

I have a friend who refuses to wear his hearing aid. We have talked about it, but he still won't wear it. I value his friendship more than I am troubled by his inability to hear. When we're out I sit next to him so we can communicate and I can share with him what's going on around us.

Your other option is to cook more of your dinners together at home.

Dear Thelma: A manager at our company is leaving for a position at another company. We are having a farewell event for him at a restaurant with about 30 employees in attendance. After I make a toast to him, do I ask if anyone else would like to offer their toast? Also do I tap on a glass to get the group's attention?

A: The kind of toast you are describing is so important. People do move on and it does provide an opportunity for you as company leadership to express appreciation. It also shows those in attendance that you respect employees in general.

When everyone has assembled and glasses are filled with any type of beverage, it's time to make the toast. Simply standing up at the table will get this sized group's attention. Tapping on glassware with a spoon isn't necessary. At a larger event you would ask for the group's attention over the sound system.

Make your toast simple and rehearse it beforehand. Face the person you're honoring and direct your words directly to him. As you conclude, look the person you're toasting in the eye and raise your glass high. Then take a sip and set your glass down.

While simply raising your glass is the most proper way to toast, clinking glasses is a very old custom and many people thoroughly enjoy it. I grew up in an Italian family where you said "Salute!", clinked your glasses and loved the sound of it. If someone does extend a glass in an obvious effort to clink, don't hold back. Just be careful with the glassware.

It is appropriate in this situation to ask if others wish to add their own toasts. It is a thoughtful gesture and demonstrates that management respects the importance of relationship-building in the organization. The guest of honor also may respond by returning a toast.

When you are toasted do not take raise your glass or take a drink with the others. Doing so would mean you are toasting yourself. Simply smile and nod or say, "Thank you." Leave your glass on the table and absorb the sentiments of the moment.

Warm farewells and good manners never go out of style.

Dear Thelma: Our last son is getting married and the wedding and reception will be in the bride's backyard. There is limited seating. Each family has an assigned number of guests permitted. We gave a list of very close friends to be included, but now there are about 10 other friends who assume they will be invited, to the extent that some have changed vacation plans to be here.

What to do? The list is full and save-the-dates cards have already been sent. Perhaps we should not have included any friends and kept it to just family, but that is hindsight. Is there a tactful way to explain the "small guest list" problem? We have not said anything to these friends yet, one way or another, about them not being included.

A: First, be assured that you have done nothing wrong. Do not ruin the celebration for yourself by regretting your guest list. Working within certain parameters, you created the guest list you wanted to create and that is your prerogative as a host of the event.

It is the presumption of your friends that has caused the difficulty. I don't know why they assume they're invited or how you've been informed of their plans. What I do know is that a conversation must take place before any more time passes. The tactful way to explain the problem is to be honest. Tell them that you've heard that they are making plans to attend the wedding and that you appreciate their kindness and value their friendship, but that the venue chosen by the bride and groom limited the number of people you could include on the guest list. Express that you are saddened by the situation, but you weren't able to include them.

If they are true friends, they will understand and you will end the conversation with the friendship intact.

Dear Thelma: Our son is getting married and the guest list is very limited. A couple of friends who are coming to the wedding want to give a bridal shower. They want to invite other good friends of ours who are not on the wedding list. They feel these guests would still want to come to the shower. What is the proper etiquette regarding this?

A: Any guest invited to a wedding shower should be included on the wedding guest list. The only exception is a large workplace shower where everyone in the office is included in the celebration.

Dear Thelma: I have a good friend with whom I like to have lunch, shop, and go to movies. I am married and she is in a committed relationship. The problem is neither I nor my husband care for the company of her significant other. Nothing against him personally, but we truly find that we have nothing in common with him. We have gone out with them a few times and have found these occasions to be awkward. They are constantly inviting us over for dinner and barbecues. How can I let my friend know that I value our friendship, but do not wish to socialize with both her and her partner? I don't want to hurt her feelings, but I don't wish to keep making excuses when they invite us to do things with them as couples.

A: If you truly want to decisively end the invitations, you must have a conversation with your friend. Avoid focusing on the shortcomings you perceive in her partner. Your feelings regarding outings together should be shared with kindness and respect, but be aware that she still may feel hurt and it may affect your relationship with her.

Gentle conversations and good manners never go out of style.

Dear Thelma: I have a colleague who has lost the use of his right hand. When I see him, we shake hands, me with my right hand and him with his left. We have another colleague who always offers his left hand. I've always thought that with disabled people, I do things normally unless the individual clearly needs help or asks for it; in this way I'm treating them like they are normally capable. Am I treating him with good manners, or is my other colleague?

A: Handshakes are important to building relationships. If they are performed properly, genuine positive energy can be exchanged through them. During a handshake, you should firmly clasp the hand of the person you're greeting so that your hands are palm to palm and with web between your thumb and index finger touching the web in his hand. Hold for three or four seconds while you pump the elbow two or three times.

Knowing the elements of a proper handshake, you know that a proper, energy-conveying one can't be given between your colleague offering his left hand and being given your right. What occurs in that situation is an awkward pinch of the fingers, likely to draw more attention to your colleague's disability and have little positive effect.

Although most of us feel natural extending our right hands for a handshake, the determination of which hand to use is made by the first person to offer their hand. If someone extends their left hand to you, offer your left hand as well.

If you extend your right and the other person gives you their left because they don't have use of their right, you may not have time to adjust to the other hand. But if you are fast-thinking and fast-acting enough and can make the switch seamlessly, it's worth it.

With your knowledge of your colleague's situation, the most respectful thing to do is to always offer your left hand for a proper handshake.

Dear Thelma: At a recent school buffet dinner I was seated at a table eating when a woman came and sat across from me carrying a dog. She spoke soothing words to it as we ate, petted it, explained it was really frightened.

I am aware people now think dogs are people, but so long as they still lick their private parts clean with the same tongues they use to lick us, I am not comfortable having them at the table while I eat.

What does one say, if anything? With this new "My Dog Is One of My Relatives" attitude spreading, is there a corresponding new set of etiquette rules for people to follow? Someone, probably me, needs help here.

A: I certainly respect the love that people have for their pets, but here's the bottom line: Do not bring them unless they've been invited. That means for the school buffet dinner or a barbecue at your brother's house or a visit to a friend. Never assume that your pet is welcome even if they're small and cute or large and well-behaved.

Social events are a time to be social with people. For many people dogs are a distraction to the personal interaction those social events are designed to provide. If you want to be social with your dog, go to places designed for that purpose like dog parks and restaurants with patios open to dogs.

I couldn't have sat through the dinner you describe. The options I would have considered are asking the host to speak with the dog owner about leaving the table, asking the host to move me to another table, or saying to the dog owner, "Please excuse me," and moving myself.

Thoughtful pet owners and good manners never go out of style.

Dear Thelma: I recently had a job interview at a well-known local company that works to create a sophisticated identity for itself. I subsequently didn't get the job. My beef is that when I received my "sorry, you're not the candidate we want to hire" email, not only was it addressed to "Dear Applicant," but also every other rejected candidate's email was included in the address field.

My biggest concern is that all of our names and emails were visible to every other rejected applicant, and I recognized two of the other people. On top of that, judging by the fact that there were only six other people, is it so hard to write my name? I spent an hour in the interview and another hour taking their aptitude test, but they couldn't find the time to insert my name into their form letter.

I find this in very poor taste and judgment, and extremely unprofessional. What do you think? Thanks, and still looking.

A: My first thought is, be thankful you didn't get the job. I wouldn't want to work for a company that shows such disrespect. From what you describe, there is nothing personal about this organization. A truly sophisticated organization would not reply in such a fashion.

You include the answer in your question. This kind of response to a job applicant shows poor judgment, is unprofessional and in poor taste. Every person a company interviews should be identified individually in a personal response.

Dear Thelma: We recently installed a swimming pool in our backyard. My kids love to play in it and they can get pretty loud. I've told them that while outside voices are fine to use, they still have to control themselves. They can't shriek incessantly at the top of their voices for the entire neighborhood to hear. My husband thinks I should just let them be. What do you think?

A: I do believe kids need the opportunity to let go outside, but self-control is always warranted. If their shrieking makes you take notice then it's probably annoying your neighbors. Tell your kids that while it's fine to laugh and yell and enjoy yourselves, you should be aware of times when the play makes it sound as if someone is being attacked or needs help. That can worry people around them. Also, an outdoor environment peppered with shouts and laughter is expected, but a constant din can bother.

I would advise you to set the boundaries as wide as you can, explain them to your kids and expect them to follow the rules. Then offer reminders when necessary.

Dear Thelma: Recently I attended a large luncheon meeting and a woman at our table constantly started side-conversations and it interfered with everyone's ability to hear the main speaker. I often see people do this and I really think it is unprofessional and rude. The woman was shushed a few times but still continued. What should anyone do in this circumstance?

A: This kind of behavior is rude. If you truly need to have a conversation during a presentation, leave the room. I have handled this kind of situation by seeking out a member of the wait staff to ask the person to refrain from conversation while the presenter is speaking.

During a large event people can gain a feeling of anonymity, that their behavior doesn't matter because it won't be noticed in so large a crowd. Anyone feeling that way should think again. You may think that your side conversation won't display rudeness to a speaker 15 tables away from you, but your behavior does affect those closest to you and won't be ignored.

Always and everywhere, good manners never go out of style.

Dear Readers: As we enter August the focus of many shifts back to school. For teachers, students and parents, now is the time for preparing for a new year. From fresh supplies to new interactions, back-to-school time is an opportunity to begin again. Teachers do a great deal to set the stage for that new beginning and to positively impact the entire school year.

If you are a teacher, you know that teachers influence not only how a student develops intellectually, but also how he develops as a total person. For the major part of a student's day, you are his adult role model. He is impacted by every detail you take the time to address – from the preparation of the classroom and the daily greeting he receives to your enthusiasm and mode of dress.

Teachers can advance their influence by striving to manifest an attitude centered on motivating students – even during those times that feel impossible. Teachers have the opportunity to allow and encourage creativity, which has the potential to give children a great deal of confidence. And teachers need to see that policies and rules are followed in a kind and respectful manner that avoids making students feel fearful.

When it comes to parents, show a desire to meet them and become a partner in their child's education and life.

Everyone who enters your classroom is impacted by how you interact with the world around you. Showing patience and understanding, listening carefully, offering praise for good work done, and giving consideration to one another – whether that other is a student, parent or teacher – creates positive energy.

One of the biggest things teachers as a group can do to contribute to a happy workplace environment is to avoid gossip of every kind. Some people really thrive on gossip. It's what gets them through the day like a cup of coffee or a candy bar in the afternoon. But gossip easily turns into critical judgment of others and that affects the morale of everyone, taking the place of respect and trust in the workplace.

If you find yourself in such a workplace, make a conscious decision not to participate in gossip. When gossip begins, walk away or gently say, "I don't wish to participate in this conversation." Your example will speak loudly.

Finally, I encourage teachers, students and parents to model the eight phrases for a successful school year I offered last year at back-to-school time:

Please. It's the simplest way to show that you are being respectful in making a request.

Thank you. It recognizes the effort of another for your benefit.

I'm sorry. It recognizes a wrong.

I'm listening. For true communications to take place there has to be an exchange.

Hello. Everyone deserves a smile and a greeting.

Let's take turns. When everyone makes an effort to include everyone else, no one is left out.

I care. Making a conscious decision to care about others, their possessions and their feelings and saying that you do creates a space where people feel comfortable and ready for the task at hand.

I respect you. Give all those you encounter during the day the honor due them as human beings and treat them all with compassion, caring and consideration.

Take every opportunity to model, teach and expect these phrases and attitudes during the school day and beyond.

Your career choice has put you in a unique position to make a positive difference in the world. Meeting the daily challenges of your teaching role with grace and professionalism will make a positive difference for you, your students, parents, fellow teachers and your workplace. Make it a great year.

Good teachers and good manners never go out of style.

Dear Thelma: We're having about 12 people over for a special 50th birthday dinner. That's all our dining room will seat. Is there a graceful way to invite 20 more friends to join us after, for dessert and drinks? I don't want the second shift to feel second class and can't think of an elegant way to say please join after the rest of us have had dinner. If there's no elegant way to do this, we'll go for two events.

A: If elegance is your goal, go for the two separate events or host the type of event that everyone can enjoy together. That may mean a buffet dinner with people eating in rooms other than the dining room. It also may mean a dessert event that can include everyone.

People always enjoy being invited, but when the invitation comes with a catch, it can put a damper on the festivities. From the way you've posed your question, it's obvious that you see there is problem that will lead some guests to feel less than honored by the invitation. Separate events or a single inclusive event will make for a more joyful celebration for everyone.

Dear Thelma: What is the proper etiquette for gift-giving in this wedding scenario: I had a dear friend decades ago. We slowly drifted apart over the years, and our last communication was a brief email several years ago. I have since sent Christmas cards and a few emails that went unanswered. I assumed my friend had since changed addresses.

Imagine my surprise when I received a wedding invitation after all these years. I considered going, but the timing, distance and a few other factors all prevent this. While I know I should consider myself honored to have been invited, I'm a little puzzled at the lack of communication for years preceding this.

Does the receipt of a wedding invitation necessitate a gift in this context? I'm not sure what to send, since I don't really know this friend at all anymore, and I wouldn't even know where to send it, since I'm not sure of the correct address. Thanks for your thoughts on my long lost friend.

A: There seem to be two issues that you are working through. The issue on the surface is whether to send a gift. The deeper and more important issue is whether to reconnect with this friend.

If you have no desire to reconnect, a wedding gift is not necessary. The etiquette tradition that says a gift should be sent for any wedding invitation received presupposes a relationship between the sender and receiver of the invitation. The level of relationship will vary. It will be a relationship that needs to be built, maintained or strengthened and the gift plays a part in that process.

Since so much time has elapsed, your "long lost friend" may have been making an effort to reunite with you and found the setting of a wedding celebration an appropriate venue to accomplish this. If you truly considered yourself honored by the invitation, you probably wouldn't question whether to send a gift. You would have tracked down that friend and her address, reconnected and happily sent a gift.

If the relationship causes you discomfort or emotional distress, there is no need to re-involve yourself. Sometimes when these relationships are over, they're over. That, along with whether to send a gift, is for you to decide.

Healthy relationships and good manners never go out of style.

Dear Thelma: I have a nearby neighbor who seems to be wanting me to become her new best friend. She is calling several times through the week to talk and to suggest doing activities together. My week is as full as I want it to be, and when I am home I don't want to be pestered by phone calls and dropping-by – she can see my backyard and thus knows when I am home. Subtle statements aren't getting through to her. How do I handle this without being rude?

A: First it's important to realize that while you don't have to be available to her all the time, it is difficult and usually ill-advised to turn neighbors off completely. That being said, however you do choose to handle the situation should be done with kindness and heartsense – that common sense of the heart that helps you act with grace.

While it's a sensitive situation, it can be taken care of with discretion. Take the time to accept one of her invitations or make one of your own. During that time kindly explain that you're happy to have the chance to talk to her about your situation. Explain your busy schedule and how it leaves little time for neighborhood socializing. Let her know that means you can't accept most of her invitations. If you have the opportunity, offer to introduce her to others in the neighborhood who might be seeking friendship and social activities.

I've found that neighborhoods are usually excellent places for friendships. In my situation, neighbor-to-neighbor conversations and help for one another has always been a nice part of living where I live.

Dear Thelma: I've had occasion to attend some funerals lately. As I'm in my late 60s, I suppose they will now demand my attention more frequently. Funerals seem to be more informal than they were some years ago. I notice that often there is less predictable ceremony and more *ad hoc* asking of attendees to stand up and share "stories" about the deceased. Sometimes there is an uncomfortable silence until some brave soul gets up to share. It surprises me that attendees would be expected to ad lib at a time like this.

Does it not seem better for the organizers of the funeral – the family or friends of the deceased – to arrange for three or four people close to the deceased to lead off the sharing? And for some kind of master of ceremonies to exert control over the process? Another issue is that sometimes a windy relative or someone with an agenda will get going and make for a rather uncomfortable situation.

By comparison, I attended a "traditional" funeral earlier this year and found myself to be relieved when the event was well organized and went off without a hitch. I wonder if, at such emotional times, all might be better off with better organized, more predictable ceremonies?

A: Funerals are entirely personal and there is no right or wrong format for them. The service in which you found yourself comfortable, others may not.

It's true that rituals surrounding a traditional funeral in most instances follow a format and are organized in such a way that people are asked ahead of time to participate. That can relieve tension. However, that's not the only way to celebrate a person's life. Spontaneously-shared memories can have their place too.

For me what is most important is how the family and those closest to the deceased want to honor the person. My role as an attendee at a funeral is to participate in that honor and support the family through the process they've chosen.

Proper honor and good manners never go out of style.

Dear Thelma: Recently I had guests that included two teenagers and their mother. We are not related but our families are close. Before they arrived I asked what they liked to eat and shopped for the things they mentioned. They were clearly disappointed with the food I bought specifically for them. I gave them two choices of meals I could make for dinner and they each chose a different one and argued over it. I went so far as to go out and buy another cut of meat for one of them. She then ate about three bites of it. Their mother did noting to control their behavior. Shouldn't they have been old enough to act civilly and shouldn't their mother have required it?

A: Yes, they should have been old enough to act civilly and their mother should have required it. I can see your dilemma as a host. You wanted to please and honor your guests, but they didn't offer the same in return.

Kids can and should be taught by their parents to behave respectfully in other people's homes beginning as early as their pre-school years. That includes in the homes of extended family and close friends. Grandma or your favorite aunt shouldn't be expected or required to teach those lessons, but it is in their homes where the lessons will first take place. Parents must require "please" and "thank you" and teach that food served by someone else must be assessed and tasted respectfully. You may not like it, but you should not make an obvious display of your displeasure or demand something else. Find something on the plate you can eat and stick with that if you have to.

Over the course of 10 years of such lessons, kids should reach their teen years with respectful behavior at the tables of others well established.

The family you describe took your graciousness for granted. They need to learn that even when you have close ties to someone, you must be courteous – maybe even more courteous because of those ties.

Before this family visits anyone again, they should learn several other things. Be graceful and willing to cooperate when you are a guest for a meal in a home. Be pleasant and nice, even if the meal being served is not your favorite. Don't let your behavior, attitude or conversation cause the host to say, "I'm sorry, can I get you something else?"

I don't buy the "kids are kids" excuse that seems to say that we shouldn't expect anything better from them. If a teen is taught how to be a gracious guest and expected to be one, no excuses will be necessary.

Dear Thelma: Regarding your answer to a question about asking members of a group if they'd like to make a toast following an official toast, I think asking others to make a toast without warning them ahead of time can create an awkward situation. I was at such an event once where attendance was obligatory and the person being honored was not liked by his employees. One person was designated to make the toast, but when others were invited to make their own no one had anything they wanted to say! Needless to say, it was very uncomfortable for all involved. Just something to think about.

A: The situation you describe is awkward. To avoid it the master of ceremonies for the celebration must be on his or her toes. It's fine to open up the floor for others to toast, but if no one volunteers immediately you must move along quickly to avoid the awkwardness.

An aware emcee and good manners never go out of style.

Dear Thelma: School has started and the kids are settled, but I have a concern. A group of girls in my daughter's fifth-grade class – who she has considered friends since kindergarten, who have attended all our parties, and who's mothers I have friendships with – have either been very insensitive in their actions and comments directed at my daughter or have simply gone out of their way to be mean. One rolled her eyes and flipped her hair in response to my daughter's hello on the first day of school. Another announced to the class that "student council elections are not a popularity contest because 'Kate' (my daughter) won last year and she's definitely not popular." My daughter was invited to half a birthday party that all the other girls were invited fully to. It's like they watched too much television over the summer featuring how happy mean little girls can be and are trying it out.

As I write this, I think it's time to get new friends, but we attend a very small school and it is likely these girls will all be in the same small class for the next three and half years. She has to at least learn to live with them and keep her self esteem.

Is my daughter overly sensitive? It's possible. Is my daughter hurt? She's done well until now, but it's starting to weigh on her.

I spoke briefly with the teacher, not making any accusations but letting her know there was unrest among the girls and asking her to be aware. From things my daughter has said, I know the teacher is addressing it generally and it seems to help for a period of time. But it is arising again and I'm considering taking more action.

Is it unmannerly to bring it up to a mother I consider a friend?

A: First let's untangle the girls' behavior from manners. While their actions indicate a lack of respect, it's more than poor manners. In what you describe I see the beginnings of bullying. Bullying is when people use their power – physical or social – to intentionally harm someone repeatedly.

I'm not a bullying expert and I'd direct you to the U.S. Government website stopbullying.gov for a solid base of information on the subject.

I do believe speaking early on with your daughter's teacher is a good first step. Keep in touch and let her know the things she has done or said that seem to have helped. If the behavior or the actions become more problematic, let the teacher know.

Also keep the lines of communication open with your daughter. While you don't need to dwell on every offense, let her know you empathize with her and that you will work together to find a solution.

The solution may be to find new friends, possibly from outside activities like soccer or dance who you don't go to school with but could look forward to seeing on weekends. If you have other children and it makes sense in your family, ask them privately to show their sister some extra care and attention during this rough time.

Finally, the government's website says not to contact the parents of a child who has bullied your child. However, if this mother truly is a friend, now may be a good time to talk about it. Keep the conversation general and start by asking if her daughter is having any similar difficulties this year. You might share the struggles your daughter is facing and ask if your friend has any suggestions that might help. Approaching it this way may create a positive outcome.

True friendships and good manners never go out of style.

Dear Thelma: Regarding your past columns on hat etiquette, in a restaurant just try to find a hat rack. They are no longer available. So where would you like me to put my hat? It may be a $100 Stetson. There may be an empty chair, or not. Surely you don't want me to put it on the table, so on the floor? No! Get real, sometimes etiquette needs to relax!

Dear Thelma: I was taught as a youngster: "take your hat off in the house or any building." I wear hats throughout the seasons, but restaurants make this difficult! Where are the hat racks? I have to put it on an empty chair if there is one. Same goes for live theater venues. They have no cloakrooms or coat checks. This is a real problem they are ignoring.

A: The topic of hat etiquette has hit a nerve with many of you and your responses have opened my eyes to the tug of war hat wearers find themselves in between current culture and traditional hat etiquette.

With fewer and fewer restaurants maintaining dress codes, people take a much more casual attitude toward dining out and toward what they wear at a restaurant. Restaurants, likewise, have done away with coat and hat checks and even racks, pushing contemporary hat etiquette even further away from hat removal indoors.

These realities do place hat wearers in a difficult situation, but I still believe removing your hat in a restaurant shows a proper level of respect for society and its traditions of civility. I suggest two things for those of you committed to that idea and struggling to find a place to put your hat.

The first is to take a good look at what restaurants do offer. A friend tells me her local bar and grill chain location does have hooks along the outer wall near each table for coats and hats, but she's never seen them used. And if sitting in a booth will provide a place for your hat, request one.

The second step to take is to ask the host or a waitperson where you might store your hat. The establishment may have a place for your hat of which you are unaware. If enough hat wearers begin to ask for a proper place to store a hat, they may get what they need. This also should be brought up with the live theater venues you visit.

If you've sought out a place and asked for one, and still find no appropriate place to put your hat, I would say you are justified in leaving it on in that restaurant. In a theater, you'll have to place it in your lap.

Dear Thelma: I was disturbed when Boy Scouts and their leaders held their sign-up campaign – with every member wearing hats – at my school here in the Pacific Northwest. When I reminded the boys (my students, so I know them well) of our "hats off in the building" rule, they replied that they were supposed to wear them all the time with their uniforms unless they were in church. I pushed the issue and told them that school rules and common etiquette required that they remove them. The adults responded with, "Our rules say that we wear hats all the time. They're part of our uniform."

A: This surprises me, as even those whose careers carry the strictest uniform requirements, like the military and law enforcement, remove their "cover" indoors unless they are carrying a weapon or are taking part in an official ceremony. I would encourage your scouts and their leaders to reassess their uniform rule.

Even in changing times, good manners never go out of style.

Dear Thelma: In her very first month of college, my daughter has had a terrible experience with her dorm roommate. The first week of school the roommate came back to the room at 3 a.m. and brought the party with her. My sleeping daughter had to endure several people celebrating loudly in her room until the campus police showed up. Nothing about their relationship got better after than.

She's now moving on to a new room and a new roommate. What can she do to have a better experience this time?

A: I'm not sure anything could have been done to make your

daughter's first roommate a considerate person. She obviously had no intention of monitoring her own behavior in order to get along with a roommate. It's good that your daughter has moved on. With this fresh start there are some steps to take that should improve her experience.

Open the lines of communication early and keep them open. Roommates do this well by making a point to talk casually at least once a week. Review plans for the coming days, when you'll be in or out, and whether you'll be studying for an exam in the room or in the library. Share anything that will help your roommate understand your needs in the room for the week and respect each other's space needs. If you both are working to understand and respect each other, compromise when necessary will be easier.

If you are accustomed to talking with one another, when a problem arises you can bring it into that regular conversation. "We've got to do something about that refrigerator. Maybe we should each clear out our inedible stuff once a week." Or "I'm sorry, but I can't sleep three feet away from your boyfriend every night. We've got to figure out another arrangement."

A good roommate also realizes that while this is her room, it's someone else's room too. Keeping a room neat means different things to different people. If your roommate makes her bed every day, she'd probably appreciate not having to look at your rumpled sheets and twisted blankets every time she walks through the door. But she also shouldn't expect military precision and 15 color-coordinated pillows from you. Find a happy medium that everyone can live with.

To get along well, roommates have to be reasonable about visiting hours and lights out. If it's 1 a.m. and your roommate is sitting on her bed dressed in her jammies glaring at you and your study group, break it up for the night. She doesn't want to have to ask you to be polite and she shouldn't have to.

Avoid borrowing. It's just good policy when you're already sharing so much of each other's personal space. If you do decide to borrow something, you must always ask and you must return the item promptly and in its original condition. If your roommate asks to borrow, it is your prerogative to say, "I don't think borrowing from each other is a good idea."

If you do find yourself faced with something you can't handle, get help from your resident advisor as soon as you can.

Dear Thelma: How do you tell someone they should not be

wearing very low cut tops or dresses to church?

A: Rather than confronting someone directly, take it in a general way to your pastor. Let he or she be the one to guide in the congregation in what is proper attire during services.

The right messenger and good manners never go out of style.

Dear Thelma: I host many holiday and celebratory meals for my extended family members and they are all very generous about contributing. My problem arises when those who volunteer to bring drinks or appetizers habitually arrive late. All the other guests arrive and I have no food or drinks to serve them because of the latecomers. What can I do to fix this but offend no one?

A: How wonderful that you have a family that enjoys sharing in the preparations for a meal. You want to do all you can to continue to encourage that.

For those who volunteer to bring drinks and appetizers, ask them before the event if they can arrive 15 minutes early so that you can get the drinks on ice or set up the appetizers. You might also ask them if they need you to pick up the items early if it's convenient. If you solicit contributions to the meal over email, you can include a note asking whoever volunteers to bring drinks and appetizers to arrive early. Put it into their minds in a gentle way that you need their contribution as close to the start time as possible.

If you're still worried, break up the drinks and starters among several different contributors or handle them yourself and make assignments from among other dishes.

We're often guilty of saying to ourselves, "Well, these are my friends or family. They'll understand. I can get away with being late or unresponsive." But following through with that kind of thinking leads to discomfort, guilt and hard feelings, things that don't sustain or strengthen relationships.

With our closest companions, good manners never go out of style.

Dear Thelma: I have a couple of people in my family who wait until two to 72 hours before an event to invite people and then complain if hardly anyone shows up. Quite a few times I was informed of birthday parties anywhere from two hours to the night before the party was to happen. There was a birthday party and a baby shower for which the host failed to get an invitation to me or orally invite me.

Would it be proper for me to give a gift in either of these situations? I don't feel I am expected to give a gift if I did not not receive an invitation. I believe not receiving an invitation was mainly due to poor party planning or maybe even an oversight. Should I give a gift for the party that was late in the inviting? We were not able to make the party because of the late invitation and my hubby and I had other plans already made for that day.

A: There are two aspects to your question that I'd like to address. While invitations should always be sent in a timely fashion and I realize that you are frustrated by the failure of your hosts to inform you properly, it's best to avoid judging the situation as poor planning or oversight. Just take the invitation as it comes and respond from there according to your own schedule.

A personal goal I work on every day is to avoid prejudgment, but it's not always easy. Recently I went to the pharmacy in a hurry. I took out my wallet and left my handbag in the car.

When I stepped out of the store, my car was in full view and I saw a woman standing next to it. Her ragged clothes and unkempt look startled me, and I didn't want her near my car. She caught my glance and motioned me over with a wave of her hand.

On my guard, I approached her and she said to me: "I saw that your car was unlocked and I saw two men walking around it. I noticed your purse inside thought I should stay nearby."

Well, I thanked her for her kindness but felt terrible about the prejudgments I had made. While we do have to be cautious in our current times and protect our selves and our property, we must also take time to assess before leaping to conclusions.

The dictionary defines prejudgment as the act of judging before sufficient evidence is available. Are we really aware of how much we prejudge people or situations even of the most innocent and simple kinds?

When we prejudge, we place a label on a person, preventing us from clear communication and causing us to focus on the label rather than on the content of a conversation. None of us is free of this and it's something we can work to avoid if we seek healthy communication as a part of our lives.

As to the gift aspect of your question, people have the idea that gift-giving is essential to specific events, but it should instead be thought of as essential to the relationship.

When you use your heartsense – that common sense of the heart –

you realize that you give a gift because you want to do something special for the person being honored. Gifts are always voluntary, and while they may be customary in certain situations, they are never mandatory. In the situations you describe, let your heart guide you as you maintain and build those relationships.

Gifts and good manners never go out of style.

Dear Thelma: I was at the mall recently on a crowded Saturday and experienced something I thought was very rude. Twice I was pushed out of the way by mothers with strollers. They basically used their strollers as a battering rams to get themselves through the crowd. One of the strollers didn't even have a kid in it – just a bunch of shopping bags. I realize strollers can be difficult to maneuver, but shouldn't they show some manners too?

A: Maneuvering in a crowded space always requires the courtesy of everyone assembled. For those converging with and without strollers, allowances must be made on both sides.

When you're pushing a stroller you realize you are going to have to move more slowly and more carefully in a crowed place. You also quickly realize that to get through it, you are going to have to move with purpose and sometimes ask those around you for the right-of-way. Barreling through with your "battering ram" shouldn't be your go-to option. Anytime you are trying to move through a crowd or against a flow of people with or without a stroller, looking people in the eye kindly and saying, "Excuse me," as you pass by will keep the peace and should get you where you need to be. Also be aware of where you park your stroller or stop for a rest or to help your child. Make an effort to keep your stops out of traffic areas.

When you're on the other side of the stroller, do your part to help things move smoothly. When it's obvious the stroller needs to get through, make some room for it. If a parked stroller is blocking your way, politely ask its navigator to let you pass. And if you have the opportunity to hold a door for a parent pushing a stroller, do so. It's a tremendous help.

Dear Thelma: Is the incorrect use of the "I" pronoun as widespread as I think it is? I hear very well-informed and well-educated people using it wrong. The rule for its use seems to be so simple. Evidently our schools are turning out students without any English grammar instruction. Is there a way to politely tell peers (and your grown children) they are incorrect when they say "She is going with Carlos and I"?

A: I think people overuse "Carlos and I" because in their young lives they were too often corrected by adults for using "Carlos and me" – whether it was proper form or not. They came to think that "Carlos and me" was always wrong.

But to your question, let's think first about whether you would find it polite to be graded on your grammar in public. Perhaps you regularly split the infinitive or end sentences with prepositions, which occur naturally in conversation but would earn you a red mark on an English paper. Would you appreciate that mistake being pointed out by your peers or your children? Most people would answer no.

So ask yourself if making the grammar mistake of using "I" when you should use "me" is going to cause harm? Is it going to cause more harm than that which will be caused by you pointing it out to people who may not appreciate your concern?

Unless your peers or children have asked you for critique or instruction, I believe it would be impolite for you to call it to their attention. Making a grammar mistake is not bad manners, but an overreaction to it may be.

Gentleness and good manners never go out of style.

Dear Thelma: When searching local stores for Halloween costumes for my kids, I made a sad discovery. It seems Halloween has simply become an occasion for women to dress provocatively. There are literally four times as many costumes for women than for children, the majority of them short, tight and low-cut with provocative themes or once innocent themes that have been twisted. Browsing the stores, my 10-year-old daughter came to believe that fish-net stockings were appropriate for Little Red Riding Hood. I think it's sad. Shouldn't adults grow up and let kids have their holiday back?

A: I've noticed the trend with disappointment as well, but adults are free to make their own choices. It's my hope that everyone would choose a costume wisely and pick something appropriate for the environment in which they plan to spend Halloween. Adults trick-or-treating with children or at a children's party should dress with care and choose a costume that will not scandalize anyone because it is too frightening or too provocative. Those attending an adult party, of which there are many at this time of year, should think carefully about the message that what they choose to wear sends.

Even on Halloween, good manners never go out of style.

Dear Thelma: My daughter is planning a wedding for the first week of April. It will include more than 200 guests. Our dilemma is this: She will complete medical school at the same time as she marries and at this time does not know where she will be for her residency. She does not know how she should register for wedding gifts. She feels that it is not appropriate to ask for money but feels it would be difficult to pack up a bunch of gifts and load them off to another location. She says there are some online registries that allow couples to ask for monetary gifts to help with funding a honeymoon or buying a first home. I had never heard of these. Are they appropriate?

A: These can be appropriate and a good way to solve your daughter's dilemma, but they must be communicated graciously and with the right attitude.

First, realize that gifts of any kind are always voluntary. While it may be traditional for wedding guests to bring gifts, it's not mandatory and guest should never be made to feel that it is. Gifts or gift registries are never mentioned in wedding invitations. Rather, they are communicated by family and the bridal party when asked by guests or through shower invitations. Guests who want to know where you're registered will make the effort to find out.

When asked, you, your daughter or a bride's maid can mention the impending move and let the person know about the honeymoon or house savings registry and its web address. The registry also can be included in a shower invitation and on the couple's wedding website if they choose to create one.

Such an arrangement will have an impact on the bridal shower. Showers are about showering the new couple with gifts. Part of the fun in those celebrations is seeing the gifts opened and admired. You'll have to be creative with the shower if you choose to focus on monetary gifts. Luckily, everyone attending should be close enough to know her situation and appreciate her need to keep the load light.

Your daughter also should consider a traditional registry for guests who will prefer to give a more tangible gift. She and her groom should be very selective in creating that registry so that the items on it are things they truly want and need and will be able to transport easily.

The bottom line is that a couple can't dictate what their guests bring to honor them, but most guests do appreciate the guidance of a gift registry.

Dear Thelma: What is a bread-and-butter letter?

A: A bread-and-butter letter is a thank-you note you write to someone who has shown you hospitality. It could be for a dinner, but is usually given for an overnight or weekend visit. If you've prepared ahead of time and brought stationery, you might leave it with your host at the end of your stay. Otherwise, send it in the mail immediately after your visit.

The letter thanks your host for his generosity and points out details of the visit you particularly enjoyed. It's a particularly pleasant way to to show your thankfulness for the hospitality and for the relationship.

As for the term "bread-and-butter letter," it has been found in print as early as the late 1800s. I speculate it was called such because in thanking a host for his hospitality you are essentially thanking him for proving you the essentials – the bread and butter – needed during your visit.

Essential thanks and good manners never go out of style.

Dear Readers: There are certain things that happen in life that act as a beacon, guiding us individually to reflect on thankfulness. For me this year that beacon is an event in which I participated with ARCA, a private nonprofit organization providing services for children and adults with developmental disabilities.

I joined with a group of Civitan volunteers to provide a tea and hands-on manners lesson for 60 clients and staff of ARCA. They arrived in hats and gloves. Their manners were already so incredible and yet they still so wanted to learn. I discussed the basics of holding a tea cup and the importance of conversation at a social event like a tea.

Though they faced difficult challenges, they had such happy hearts. While I taught them about tea, they taught me about the joy of their world. It was a lesson in appreciation for all of us and a live definition of what heartsense – that common sense of the heart – means. From the time the Civitan volunteers took to create a lovely and elegant event to the appreciation of the group, the day provided genuine beauty deserving of thankfulness.

I also point to the valiant woman who works with these individuals and was the catalyst for organizing something special for them. She found Civitan and me, and put it all together. It is hearts likes hers that constantly make people like those I met at ARCA know that they are special.

That event made an incredible impact on me and guides me to realize again the importance of thankfulness and of hope.

As we approach Thanksgiving, the thing lacing many conversations is fear. Fear that seems to permeate attitudes about everything as we reflect upon the state of the world, from the economy to jobs to boarding a plane. That fear can easily affect our minds, which ultimately affects our hearts and drives our behavior towards the world around us.

But if we can find that beacon of thankfulness and hope, like ARCA for me, we can take a realistic look at what we have to be thankful for. It may be family, friends, health, or simply the thing that brings a single smile to our face on a single day.

If we can allow that thankfulness to deny space for fear in our minds and hearts, we can truly find reason to celebrate on Thanksgiving.

Dear Thelma: I encounter some of the rudest behavior of the entire year at the mall during holiday shopping season. People seem to lose all sense when something stands between them and a 20-percent-off sale. How can we get people on track with the kindness of the season even while shopping?

A: The best we can do is to make sure that our own behavior reflects the courtesy and respect we hope to be shown by others. While it won't eliminate rudeness, it will make us more aware of courtesy when it does strike and maybe even more tolerant of other stressed-out shoppers.

Holiday shopping etiquette starts before you leave home. Allow yourself extra time than normal to do your shopping. Recognize that the stores will be crowded and the lines will be long. Realize that you are likely to encounter edgy people; be ready to counter that with kindness.

Decide that you will model respect and consideration toward other shoppers and toward sales clerks and do it. Greet everyone with a smile and "hello." Use the words and phrases "please," "thank you," and "you're welcome" abundantly. Make an effort to relax as you shop. Your decision to act in this way may rub off on another shopper or give a lift to an exhausted clerk.

When it is your turn at the register, give your full attention to the task at hand. Stay off your cell phone, and have your purchases and payment ready for a speedy transaction.

Of course, you will encounter delays and affronts to your considerate mindset. Cash registers will run out of tape, children will cry, busy people will jostle you. Meeting it all with the resolve to stay positive and polite should help you roll through your shopping trip with some measure of comfort and joy.

Dear Thelma: My family always draws names at Thanksgiving dinner for who we will purchase a Christmas gift for that year. This year two extended family members joined us for dinner. We invited them to join in the drawing and in the same breath invited them for Christmas, as you've got to attend in order to exchange your gift. They accepted and the drawing proceeded.

I immediately wondered whether we had done the right thing. We didn't really give them much time to consider what they were getting themselves into and they don't really know about half of the family very well. Potentially, they will have to buy a gift for someone they don't know and they are committed to our Christmas celebration. What do you think of this situation?

A: If we could rewind time, we would go back to the days before Thanksgiving and inform them of the drawing and invite them to consider participating. That would have included them and given them private time to make a decision. The next time we're in this situation, we will.

As for this time, I think you've done the kindest thing. They were made to feel a part of the celebration and probably appreciate that. If you phrased the invitation properly, they had at least a little time to think about it and the opportunity to accept or reject the idea. It's my hope, and you can make it yours, that they accepted because they wanted to.

A gift exchange like this generally is more about sharing kindness and fun among a group than the resulting gifts. If they have drawn the name of a person they don't know well, you can offer to help them with gift ideas if needed. Rest assured, your immediate kind actions in the situation were the right ones.

Kind actions and good manners never go out of style.

Dear Thelma: You wrote last week about behavior while holiday shopping. Personally, I think the parking lots can be scarier than the stores. Why don't you write about mannerly parking lot behavior?

A: Drivers' etiquette is important throughout the year; however, I agree that drivers seem to be at their worst during the holiday season. Or it may be that poor behavior is magnified when we're all trying to get into the same parking space.

Driving etiquette begins with following the law and respecting the safety the law seeks to provide. Using your turn signal properly, keeping to the speed limit, respecting traffic signals and following other cars at a safe distance are all required by law. But it's also simply considerate to let the driver behind you know you're going to turn. You would appreciate such a gesture from the car ahead of you.

As we get into the car to head to our favorite shopping center, we should do our best to lose the 21st century attitude that says getting there faster is better. It is inconsiderate to zip around other cars with obvious disdain or speed through neighborhoods and parking lots. It is absolutely rude to tailgate and to rush your left turn through the intersection after the signal arrow has turned red just because you know oncoming traffic will not pick up speed fast enough to hit you. Stop doing these things now.

It's important to keep the same courtesy you use face-to-face when you're bumper-to-bumper. Horns are reserved for emergency use only, not to express your frustration. Although you may be willing to risk your life crossing three lanes of traffic to make your left turn, the driver ahead of you may place more value on the lives of the three children in her car. Honking at her will not change that.

Now that we've arrived at the parking lot, we must acknowledge the fact that parking lots are designed for slow and cautious driving. Follow the traffic direction markings and be attentive to pedestrians. Never illegally take a handicapped parking space.

To claim a space that someone is backing out of, give the person leaving adequate room and use your turn signal to stake your claim. If you see someone near a space you want who has turned on his signal, consider the space taken. Do not attempt to race him for it. Finally, do not have your passenger jump out of your car to stand in the space you want but can't get to.

Once you've found a space large enough for your vehicle – remember that SUVs are not considered "compact" – park with care and consideration. Center your car between the lines. Be careful with your doors getting in and out of your car.

Finally, when drivers break these rules, don't take it personally and don't allow it to cloud your own judgment in making courteous driving decisions.

Dear Thelma: When you're invited to a potluck and bring a dish, should you also bring a hostess gift or bottle of wine? Or is the dish enough?

A: First let me say, you are free to bring a gift to someone any time you feel inclined to bring a gift. Nothing precludes you from honoring a person in that way. But when it comes to a potluck, I don't believe a hostess gift is expected, as it is for an event hosted entirely by a single person or couple.

For a potluck, the whole celebration is centered around everyone contributing. Your dish is your contribution and your way of assisting and honoring the host. Keep that in mind and bring your very best offering.

When sharing a meal, good manners never go out of style.

Dear Thelma: My 11-year-old daughter is a creative kid. She is very good at coming up with things that she can make herself and that her friends want. They are even willing to pay her for the crafts she makes out of duct tape. Is it unmannerly to sell things to friends? Would it be nicer to just give them the things she makes? I guess they'd make good Christmas gifts.

A: I believe it is vitally important for parents to encourage creativity in their children. When a child's creativity is supported at home, confidence, relationship-building skills and respect all increase for the individual child and in the home itself. All these things are what manners are all about.

I think you have to follow the lead of your particular child when it comes to selling items to friends. For some people the creativity is expressed in the craft itself and seeing other people take joy in it. That child might love to give her work away. For others, the entire process from gauging what a market wants, design and production, and finally sales hold creative interest.

I know a young girl in this latter category. She is also 11 like your daughter and her career goal is to be a business owner. She's getting her feet wet now selling fabric hair flowers. She made and wore her creation to school one day, other girls wanted their own and her business was born. The salon her mother goes to even took notice and bought a supply from her to sell there. Sales took a hit recently as the principal decided all proceeds earned at school should go to charity.

Undeterred and encouraged by her family, the young entrepreneur has sought out other markets, mainly on the sidewalk after school and at dance class.

So, no it's not unmannerly to be in business. Would it be "nicer" if she gave away her creations or sold them for charity? I'm sure her friends would enjoy receiving something for free, but it wouldn't do much for her creativity. She would probably just stop creating.

Her parents recognize that in her individual personality and encourage her to pursue what makes her happiest about the endeavor – creating something that she can develop a business around. And while it can be difficult, they have learned to be encouraging observers, offering the help she asks for but otherwise staying out of her way to let her creativity carry her forward and her personality grow.

Dear Thelma: We invite Jewish friends to our home for Christmas dinner. Is it inappropriate for us to say a Christian prayer?

A: They are your friends. They know it's Christmas. And they know why the celebration is occurring. You've asked them to celebrate with you and they've agreed. Because of all these things, I would not leave the blessing out.

It's very hard for me to sit down to eat and not offer a blessing. I don't water it down or require everyone to join me, but I do request that they do so. How they choose to is up to them.

If you wouldn't consider the group you are with to be actual friends, it's possible to be aware of who's in attendance and create a prayer that others might find more inclusive. You can address your prayer to our Creator. If you are Catholic and leading the prayer, you might not make the sign of the cross to demonstrate respect for the diversity in the room.

But in your case, I think you'd err in not offering a Christian blessing on the day you are celebrating Christ's birth.

Grace and good manners never go out of style.

Dear Thelma: For the past few years the adults in our extended family have drawn names for a Christmas gift exchange. We instituted it because when you add up parents, siblings, in-laws and adult children the list of gifts to buy was just too long for most of us. Everyone agreed to the exchange, but there is still one person who joins in the name-draw exchange but also brings an individual gift for everyone. He is driving me crazy.

So, do I stand on principle and stick with the exchange we all agreed upon, or do I make sure I have a gift ready to exchange with this person?

A: First, try to stop letting it drive you crazy. You can't control this person, only your reaction to him. Either of the options you've voiced are perfectly respectful and you can feel comfortable choosing either of them. Because the exchange with one person has been agreed upon, you can feel happy about focusing on that individual gift, and then receive the happy giver's gift graciously as well. Thank him for his generosity, but don't let it upset you. This path does more to maintain the integrity of the agreed upon exchange.

But if it makes you feel more at ease to have a gift ready for him, do so. Since everyone will be expecting to give and receive just one gift at your family exchange, individual gifts really should be given at a time separate from the main event and to the individuals alone rather than at another group gathering. This can be mentioned to the group when you draw names or in an email or phone call later.

Some people truly enjoy the opportunity to select a gift for all those they love, and they have the means to do so. To be told not to give is difficult for them. However, if a group has agreed to a particular plan for Christmas giving, that should be respected too. No one wants their actions to show disrespect for the decision or situations of their family members.

To the person giving additional gifts, I would suggest that he do so privately and in a way that doesn't stress or inconvenience others. He should speak to family members individually and let them know that he plans to buy them gifts, but that he doesn't expect anything in return. He should realize that some of them will feel pressured to give something in return, and he may undermine the gift-exchange decision.

Finally, don't let the pressure of gift giving squelch the heartfelt love and friendship that should always be behind a gift. Let an exchange of peace be at the forefront of any gift giving or receiving you do this year and your heart should stay merry and bright.

Dear Thelma: I loved your answer in the paper about my Christmas prayer said among non-Christians gathering with me for Christmas dinner. What do you think of the following prayer I wrote?

To our Creator of all, thank you for the fellowship around this table, for the good friends, and for the loving hearts and hands that prepared this wonderful feast. On this day observed by Christians world-wide as the birthday of Jesus, we honor all who come here today in the name of love and friendship. Bless us as we eat this bountiful food, for which we are grateful, and bless us as we gather in fellowship. In the name of God and in loving and respectful honor of our Christian brothers and sisters, Amen.

A: I believe your prayer will be much appreciated by all who gather with you for Christmas dinner.

Words from the heart and good manners never go out of style.

Dear Readers: During the Christmas season and as the New Year approaches we all make many wishes. It's an ideal time to both think back and to look ahead. My wish this year is that my mind will be filled with peace and my heart with love.

We can make this kind of wish come true by giving of ourselves. It's that deliberate effort to make others happy or to make ourselves available to people that brings the Christmas spirit alive. With that Christmas spirit comes joy. Joy finds its voice in our anticipation, our decorations, our gift-giving and our love. Decorating for Christmas is an explosion of joy for me. Friends laugh and say, "If you really want to know Thelma Domenici, come and see her house at Christmas time," as every surface is a canvas for my holiday joy.

I'll make that wish come true by spending time with family. Listening to their stories, sharing meals together and absorbing all I can during our time together. I will be especially grateful for those who travel long distances to be together.

I will treasure the gift of health and show true appreciation for those who make a point of caring for those who suffer. A short visit, a conversation and a smile bring such a bright moment to the day of anyone, but especially someone who is ill. How many of us can run an errand for someone or give them ride to an appointment or to church? When we can, we should. Along with that goes giving to those in need who we may not know personally, but who we can help with donations of clothes, food and shelter.

I'll make my wish come true by protecting my sense of awe. Awe, that potent mixture of amazement, respect and fear, is often what keeps us striving to be our best selves. Losing that sense of awe pushes us toward the cynical. Someone who is cynical believes the worst in people, has a sneering disbelief in the selflessness of others, and is doubting or contemptuous of the goodness of others.

Some people seem to pride themselves on being cynical. But after a close look at the word I can't imagine who really would want to be described as believing only the worst, or exhibiting sneering disbelief and contempt for goodness.

That's why it's good to be faced with Christmas once a year. Given the chance, Christmas can return us to a calmness and goodness inside ourselves. As we relive our childhood traditions or strive to create that sense of wonder for our own children, the importance of respect, kindness and goodness comes into focus.

The opportunity to highlight the importance of that respect and kindness is why I do what I do. Developing and exercising those qualities make them a part of you all the time. They are not a show you put on to impress the boss or to influence people. Learned correctly they become a part of you. Used wisely they can generate the feelings of generosity and peace we get at Christmas all year long. Properly formed, manners become who you are all the time.

I heard someone once say that it would be wonderful if we could credit to others the good will that we ourselves want to be credited with. Look for opportunities as the season comes to a close to find the goodness, sincerity and selflessness in others. Maybe they'll find these qualities in you too. And when we let that peace and love extend past Christmas, we'll make a positive impact year-round.

Peace, love and good manners never go out of style.

Ask Thelma 2012
You Act as You Think

Dear Thelma: I am often asked to volunteer for various community projects. I do so gladly. However, many times I feel that the entities asking for volunteers don't respect my "yes" or my time. I have often shown up to do what I have volunteered to do only to be told that there are already enough helpers. Or I sign up for something and am never contacted. This is very frustrating and it compels me to avoid working with that group again. I even feel it is rude. What do you think?

A: I love this question as our launch into the New Year. Volunteerism is so important to our communities and to our own lives. I'm also happy to answer because most of my life I have had a professional career and a volunteer career. One of my personal goals always has been to be highly involved in the volunteer community and to give back in a way that made a difference in the well-being of my community.

Volunteerism is a mutual endeavor. The organization must respect the volunteer and the volunteer must respect the organization. The situations you describe do not respect the volunteer. An organization has a responsibility to volunteers to fully understand that these people are volunteers and not staff. Their time must be honored as a donation to the organization.

Volunteerism is really the core of why so many nonprofit events are successful, and caring for volunteers is vital to keeping their time and talents working for the group. Effectively utilizing a volunteer force requires tremendous organization and communication. Staff should be involved in organizing and assisting volunteers and helping the volunteer to feel more connected to the organization. It's the organization's job to supply information to volunteers in advance about its project and goals. The organization also must show appreciation to volunteer, by the things it's leaders say and the support they show.

Volunteers must have the same level of respect for the

organization. Some people volunteer to build their resume. They shouldn't. Being a volunteer is not about increasing social status. It's about taking on responsibility to make a project successful. You become a volunteer in good standing by doing what you've committed to.

Qualities of a good volunteer include recognizing the time commitment required and being in full support of the mission of the organization and purpose of the event. In a sense volunteers are the real ombudsmen and the voice of the organization, an important responsibility. The volunteer must learn as much as possible so that he is better able to communicate and promote the message.

If a volunteer finds that she can't do everything that is expected, she should say so as soon as possible and the organization must respect that. For a person asked to volunteer who feels she can't make entire commitment, there's always a nice way to say no and still support the cause by what she says to other people. She can be a positive force without being active.

The rewards of volunteering are tremendous. For me, the successes that occurred because of my volunteer efforts were as fulfilling as accomplishing professional goals. I met some of the most wonderful people who became friends. And those connections were not just for the life of the project, but for life.

It is incredibly important to be a volunteer. So as we spend today thinking about New Year's resolutions, consider your volunteer life. In a time of economic struggle for individuals and for organizations, instead of the typical resolve to lose 10 pounds, put 10 pounds of effort into a cause close to your heart.

A gift of time and good manners never go out of style.

Dear Thelma: My husband and I recently adopted a baby obviously of a different ethnicity than ours and brought our total number of children to three. We are getting asked a lot of personal questions: Can't you have any more? Are they siblings? How much did she cost? I want to say, "It's really none of your business." What's a better way to let people know I'd like to preserve my privacy without being rude?

A: The simplest and most gracious way to answer confused on-lookers is to simply state, "We are blessed with three wonderful children that reflect the diverse world in which we live. Adoption has been a terrific option for our family."

Failing to address the more intrusive inquiries may go unnoticed, or better yet might hint at the inappropriate nature of the questions.

If all else fails, you could always respond "Why do you ask? Are you interested in adopting too?" It might get them thinking.

Dear Thelma: I have some questions about being a designated driver for a group of friends. When one person in a group of friends does a disproportionate amount of the driving and provides the vehicle as well, is it proper for the rest of the passengers to pay for their share of gas or other costs? Or is the driver a "host" who should assume all financial responsibility?

If a passenger makes a mess in the car, is it acceptable for the driver to ask him to clean it up? In the case where a passenger routinely "forgets" to clean up after himself or to pay his way, how can the driver politely correct the situation and avoid being used?

A: Those regularly sharing in the ride should always share in the responsibilities.

Anytime you officially accept to carry the driving responsibilities for a group, it's important to discuss guidelines and responsibilities with your passengers immediately. If you've suddenly found yourself in the driver's seat most of the time, have the same discussion as soon as you realize your role.

If you are sharing rides often, then it's likely you know each other well. Talk to the entire group to establish guidelines that include sharing expenses, cleaning up and being on time.

Friends who depend on a particular driver and his car for going out on the town should reimburse him for fuel and parking costs on a regular basis. Together you can come up with a fair rate that each passenger should pitch in when the evening begins – not when it ends and everyone is out of cash. Use humor to keep collections from feeling awkward, but don't use so light a touch that riders ignore their responsibility.

Adults really shouldn't have to be told to clean up after themselves, but some may. It is perfectly acceptable to ask your passengers to pack out everything they've packed into your car. Providing a container for trash may help. Or stop the car at a gas station trash barrel at the end of the evening and don't take anyone home until the car is clean.

Dear Thelma: My daughter and I were in a store recently and saw a person there with a service dog. My daughter is very friendly and approached the person and asked if she could pet the dog. The person was kind but said, "Not right now, the dog is working." My daughter was disappointed, but I explained that these dogs aren't just pets but special helpers. It got me thinking other people might not know how to act around service animals. There must be an etiquette to it, right?

A: Assistance dogs include guide dogs for people who are blind and visually impaired, hearing dogs for those who are deaf and hard of hearing, and service dogs for people with disabilities. Some assistance dogs may be identified by a cape placed around their midsection or a special harness.

I have had the opportunity to hear from people who use service dogs. They tell me people who approach to pet and talk to a dog while he's working can be an unwelcome distraction to the task at hand. Asking first is fine, but being told the dog can't interact at that time should be respected. Most states even have laws on their books prohibiting interfering with service dogs.

While it's very tempting to interact with these intelligent and beautiful dogs, it is proper to remember that they have an important job to do and allow them to do it without distraction.

Vital service and good manners never go out of style.

Dear Thelma: My husband and I have recently allowed our 13-year-old son to begin using text messaging to communicate with friends. He claims to be the last kid on earth to finally be allowed this "vital" form of social interaction. We've set limits on times and places he may text, and we've talked about improper subject matter. What other technology-specific etiquette can we share with him and expect from him?

A: The very first thing parents should do is model proper behavior. If you are not using text messaging yourself, you should start. Using the technology will help you to understand it and the behavior that should go along with it.

The most important text etiquette point for me is that text messaging be done outside of your time spent with others. The person you are with face-to-face should always take precedence over a text message. If you are expecting something urgent, you can inform that person that you may have to attend to a text during your time together and apologize beforehand. Apologize again when the message comes through and use your response to end the exchange until you are no longer occupied.

Next, if you've sent a text and the recipient doesn't answer, don't keep sending more messages. He's obviously unavailable. If your need is urgent, you can place a call. Otherwise wait until he's available to respond.

Most truly important matters shouldn't be handled by text. Text messages are informal and should be brief and concise. Anything more you have to express should be handled in a phone call or in person.

Users of any technology must take care to avoid replacing all in-person contact in favor their favorite device. Make sure your son knows he should avoid choosing the device over the people around him. Also address the feeling of anonymity that comes with using technological devices to communicate. Although your words will be displayed on a machine, they will be received by a live person. Don't send anything that could hurt, bully or damage anyone.

Other basic manners of using text messaging include selecting an alert tone that doesn't disturb and keeping its volume as low as possible – even silent in some instances. Don't confuse your reader with less than obvious abbreviations and double check the number before sending. And, while this doesn't apply to your son yet, for safety's sake, don't text while driving.

Make these points clear, and offer the instruction that impolite use will be grounds for confiscation.

Dear Thelma: My oldest child is a bright first grader. I get the feeling he is ahead of the teacher in terms of technology. He's very computer-savvy and he even wants to start a blog about dinosaurs. They don't do a lot with computers or technology in his classroom. Do you think I would offend the teacher if I brought it up to her?

A: Setting up a meeting with the teacher to talk about technology and her teaching philosophy would be fine. Your goal should be to find out her views and plans in the area and get suggestions from her on how to engage your child at home. If your conversation inspires her to do more, that's great.

As a parent, you are your child's teacher too and bringing more technology into your child's life may be up to you. That may mean maintaining a level of technological expertise you never thought you'd need, but supporting your child in that interest will foster and strengthen creativity. Start with the blog. They're free and easy to set up. Who knows where it will take you both.

In teaching technology, be sure to stress responsible computer use and respectful interaction. You can instill values even in cyberspace.

Thoughtful use of technology and good manners never go out of style.

Dear Thelma: I received an invitation to a 60th wedding anniversary celebration. The response card includes this statement: We have reserved two seats for you at the celebration. Then it also has spaces to fill in your name and indicate the number of adults and children attending. Isn't that confusing? What do you think?

A: I think this host is trying his best to be clear about who is invited and get a response from you on your acceptance. Your host knows that many people do not realize that the guests listed on the envelope in which the invitation is sent are the only people invited. So if Mr. and Mrs. Carter are listed, little Bobby Jr. isn't supposed to attend. I've heard of one instance where a couple invited to a wedding listed eight guests on their response card, which very much annoyed the bride.

Your host has invited two of you. Now indicate whether both or one or none of you will attend in the space provided. Yes, even if neither of you will attend, you should send in the card so the host knows he should not plan for you.

Good hosts, good guests and good manners never go out of style.

Dear Thelma: I was invited to a local bridal shower for a bride who lives overseas. The invitation stated that gifts that will not fit in her luggage "should be sent" to her address out of the country. I found this odd and even somewhat inappropriate to demand this on the invitation. What do you think?

A: It is very important that brides – and the friends and family members helping them – remember the importance of being thoughtful of the guests they invite to showers and to weddings. This invitation did not show that kind of thoughtfulness.

Although we all know that attending a shower presents the opportunity to give a gift, no mention of gifts should be included on the invitation itself. A separate insert can be included regarding gift registries and preferences, or family and friends can spread that information by word of mouth.

As all gifts are always voluntary, guests should never feel dictated to concerning their gifts. Wording surrounding gift preferences should come across as kind suggestions and should focus on the giver's convenience first and then the bride's.

While most guests do appreciate guidance when it comes to gift-giving, it must be thoughtful guidance. This bride could have avoided offending you, and perhaps other guests, by registering thoughtfully and planning to handle her own shipping concerns, or by expressing her need to have gifts shipped in a gentler way on a separate insert: "Guests wishing to ship gifts directly to the bride's home may send them to ..." Close friends and family members will know and understand her situation and probably be happy to help when asked graciously.

Dear Thelma: My son and his fiancée sent out 100 wedding invitations but between the time they were stamped and mailed, the price of a stamp increased. Now the invitations have been returned to us by the post office but we don't know whether to add the current postage to the returned envelope or start over with fresh envelopes.

A: I would add the current postage on to the original envelope so that people understand why they are receiving their invitations so late. If any of your guests are traveling to attend the wedding, you should consider calling them to let them know of the problem and provide any details they may need to finalize their plans.

Dear Thelma: A new friend had me, my husband and our baby over for dinner at her house with her husband and two children. We would like to return the hospitality, but our house is too small to have them all over. What should we do? Invite them to a dinner out somewhere?

A: You should return the hospitality, but how you return it is entirely up to you. Be sure to accommodate the same group of people who gathered in the first instance, which means the location and time you choose to host your friends should be fit for children and babies. That could be a family restaurant or it could be a special picnic in the park.

You also might reassess your own surroundings. While you might not all fit around your table, you may be able to make a special dining area for the children if they're old enough to eat on their own. If you have a yard and the weather is nice, you also may be able to create an appropriate space for entertaining there. Above all, be creative and don't let your small space constrict you from building important relationships.

Dear Thelma: What should you do when your baby makes a mess at a restaurant, specifically on the floor? I try to pick up the table as much as I can, but I don't know how far to take it when it comes to the floor.

A: Your baby is not the first to make a mess, nor will he be the last. Control the situation as much as you can by being attentive to your baby and how much food he has access to, but let the staff take care of anything that drops to the floor.

Dear Thelma: Recently at a dinner party my piece of meat cooked by the host was so tough and full of gristle that I couldn't eat most of it. I kept trying to hide taking it out of my mouth, but my plate didn't lie. I could see him looking at me. What is proper?

A: If you knew the meat was tough after the first bite, you shouldn't have tackled it. You could have felt fine about eating whatever else was on your plate and leaving the meat. It would have been less awkward than partially chewed bites returning to your plate.

Dear Thelma: My husband is in chronic pain so sometimes we have to cancel social arrangements at the last minute. Now, we feel we should not accept at all. What is the proper thing to do?

A: I assume most of the invitations you receive come from people who know you well and know your circumstances. In those cases, I would accept. If you have to cancel, do so as soon as you are aware that the condition will be a problem. If you don't know the people planning the gathering well and are afraid you will have to cancel, don't accept.

As the spouse of someone suffering with this problem, be careful not to isolate yourself. You could think about and talk to your husband about keeping some of these engagements by attending by yourself.

Maintaining connections and good manners never go out of style.

Dear Thelma: My college-aged daughter is preparing for a spring break trip with friends. We have traveled and we have had many conversations as she has grown up on how to behave properly and safely away from home. This is the first trip she is planning and taking with friends. I want to be able to comment and to be sure I feel comfortable with their plans. How do I engage in that conversation to be sure they stay safe?

A: The conversation you want to have is an important one and should take place as soon as possible. Start by approaching her as the young adult that she is saying, "Let's talk about your plans for spring break." During that time, make sure you're listening as much as talking. Ask questions, offer planning assistance and get excited with her about the trip. If you can start the conversation early and continue it through the planning process, you should be able to help her make good choices and decisions.

Make a point to talk frankly, but not accusingly, about safety. Encourage her to stay with friends at all times while traveling and to watch out for and take care of each other. Talk about the importance of you and other parents knowing the group's itinerary. Set specific times during the trip that she should contact you. Also discuss what to do if anyone gets into legal trouble on the trip. Let her know that you don't expect anything bad to happen, but that you want her avoid risky situations and know what to do if there is trouble.

Don't be afraid to start this conversation and to stay involved in her planning. Look for your relationship to grow as you and your daughter go through this process.

Dear Thelma: My former husband and father of my grown son is sick and may die soon. He was abusive to me during our marriage 30 years ago and we do not keep in touch. Should I attend his funeral?

A: I certainly recognize the deep emotion you face in making a decision like this. I would let your relationship with your son and your heartsense – that common sense of the heart – guide you in making it. If you and your son are close and he would appreciate your support on a difficult day, you can choose to attend for that reason.

You also may need to find your own closure to this part of your life and attending the funeral may be the best and only way to achieve that. There is no right or wrong in this situation. Your heart will be your best guide in making this decision.

Dear Thelma: I keep guest towels in both bathrooms and when a guest uses either one I expect them to use those towels and not touch mine. People rarely use those guest towels and I wonder why. Do they think they are being polite to leave them untouched? I think it is rude for people to presume to use my towels rather than those provided for them.

A: I doubt your guests are trying to be rude. They may just not realize that the hand towels laying on the vanity are guest towels. Perhaps they have a guest bathroom in which all the towels are for guests.

If you are a guest, you should be aware that typically guest towel design is different than the home's regular towels and they may even be very pretty paper towels. They sit on the vanity for your use.

Understanding and good manners never go out of style.

Dear Thelma: My sister and her husband recently moved out of state. My family and I will be going to visit and stay with them for spring break. Our families get along great and it will be a good time, but I'd like be sure we show how much we appreciate their hospitality. What's the best way to be great house guests?

A: It's great to think ahead in a situation like this. Doing so will ensure many happy returns.

First, make sure you're in good communication before the trip, sharing arrival and departure times and what you plan to do during the stay. Be aware of the daily or weekly schedule of the family with whom you'll be staying and accommodate it. Since you know your sister well, you'll be able to decide if individual family time is necessary or if you'll enjoy constant togetherness.

Talk to your family before you go and share the courtesies all should show during your visit. Throughout your stay, pick up after yourself. Make your bed and keep your living space clean. Help with the household chores where appropriate, and offer to make dinner for your hosts or treat them to a nice restaurant. Another courteous option is to offer to pay for the groceries. Finally, bring your own toiletries, as you shouldn't rely on your host like you rely on your local drug store.

Show your gratitude at the end of your stay with a sincere note thanking your hosts for their hospitality. In what's often called a "bread-and-butter letter," point out details of the visit you particularly enjoyed and invite your host to stay at your home in the future if it's possible.

It's also kind to leave a thoughtful gift. Considering this ahead of time will help make it special. Once you are spending time with your hosts, you may not have the opportunity to shop for a gift. If you can purchase the gift and wrappings before you leave home and take with you the card and envelope you'll need to write the note at the end of the stay, you'll be ready to leave the gift and note behind when you depart.

When considering a gift, think about your hosts' hobbies or things they enjoy. Do you know they enjoy wine? Add a bottle to their collection. Do they like to attend live performances? They might enjoy tickets to an event. A household item they can use, gift certificates or a basket of goodies from their former home state would also be appreciated.

If you aren't able to purchase a gift before or during your stay, have a flower arrangement or a potted plant delivered to them the next day as a special thanks.

Dear Thelma: I was at an event at a hotel last weekend with parking valets. What are a valet's duties? Is he to open door for the lady or does she wait for her husband or date to come around and open it for her upon arriving and leaving an establishment? Is the valet tipped if there is a charge for valet parking?

A: The parking valet should open the car door for the lady. The husband or date would then thank the valet for doing so. If the valet fails to open the door, the date should come around to open it or the woman may step out of the car on her own if she wishes.

Standard tipping for a parking attendant – whether the parking service is paid or free – is $1 to $2, given to the driver when the car is brought to you, rather than when you arrive. Merited tips above and beyond the standard are your choice.

Dear Thelma: I saw your recent column on good behavior for house guests and have a question from the host's point of view. We have changed our eating habits to a very healthy lifestyle which means no junk food, snacks or carbonated drinks. When having house guests, am I expected to have available food I normally don't use? Is it important for me to ask my guests for food requests?

A: If you have offered people a night or two in your home, then you are expected to offer them your best. That doesn't necessarily mean you must stock your pantry with all their favorites, but as a good host, you must provide something they can enjoy.

There is a middle of the road. All snacks are not junk food. You might have a wonderful fruit salad there for them, a bowl of nuts, or raw vegetables to dip in dressing and snack on. Those types of snacks could satisfy your guests and keep you from blowing your diet. They may even enjoy them more than that bag of chips you think they are so fond of.

If you know your guests particularly enjoy a certain soft drink, it would be very kind of you to have it on-hand during their visit. While it's not required, it would show a great deal of thoughtfulness. Only buy enough for them so there's none left over to tempt you once they've left.

Inviting guests to stay with you should mean planning for those guests. Asking them if they have any special requests would be very kind but not required.

Now, are you required to have an array of options on-hand for people who occasionally drop by? No, you aren't. Keep your healthy lifestyle on track and offer them what is now the regular fare in your home.

Dear Readers: Everything I've written about and try to express to you I recently experienced live at an Eagle Scout ceremony I attended for a young man named Marc Cogan.

Leadership, trustworthiness and respect for others all came across to me as I learned about the service project Marc planned and directed and saw the event that he organized for the ceremony.

Under Marc's management, he and his troop planted almost 20 medium-sized pine trees at the Albuquerque Museum Foundation offices to block unwanted views of a neighboring industrial complex. His project totaled 250 hours of community service.

"The Scouting program is an educational experience concerned with values," Mark told me. "Scouting activities are designed to build character, physical fitness, practical skills, and service to others."

Marc also completed about 325 other requirements including earning 12 required merit badges and nine elective merit badges, serving in troop leadership and participating in other service projects.

I experienced an unbelievable measure of team spirit as I watched Marc receive his award and say, "I didn't earn this by myself. We only succeeded as a team." I saw such appreciation for each other as his troop, its leaders, his family and his friends gathered to mark his accomplishment.

The organizational skills and confidence he gained through his scouting experiences, his service project and planning the ceremony amazed me as he and the other kids put the final touches on the event. Through this combination of personal development and civic duty, Marc learned to set goals and reach them.

It was also obvious that Marc's entire family was integral to the process and the accomplishment. Their love and support made an absolutely indelible mark on the life of this specific Eagle Scout.

Marc's father paid tribute to his son and talked about how proud he was of him. What I also experienced was how proud the son was of both his parents. When presented with his medal, he had a medal for each of his parents too.

"My uncle who is also an Eagle Scout finished the ceremony with the Eagle Charge," Marc said. "It basically explains my duties to continue to act according to the Scout Law and Oath, but furthermore remind me of the fact that I will always be held to a higher standard."

That day was a celebration of the Eagle Scout, but it was also a celebration for me of the hope, excellence and trustworthiness in our leaders of the future.

Dear Thelma: Have you ever been to one of those big community Easter egg hunts? I took my four-year-old and two-year-old to one last year and I was appalled. No one thought to instruct the children – or the adults, for that matter – on how to behave.

There was pushing and shoving and hoarding of eggs. It was not enjoyable and I won't go back, but maybe you could write about it so people can improve their behavior for this year.

A: I have attended such a hunt, and I'm aware that, with a large crowd, difficulties can arise. The most important thing for people to remember is to be considerate.

Before the hunt, parents should talk with their children about how to behave. Let them know that there should be no pushing or shoving to get to the eggs. Tell them that if they see that someone is bending down to pick up a particular egg, that egg is now that person's and shouldn't be swiped from them as they're reaching for it. Also, talk beforehand about an appropriate number of eggs to collect. Depending on the hunt and the crowd, that may be five per kid or a whole basket full. This shouldn't be an exercise of who can scoop up the most eggs. It's about having fun with a group and sharing what has been shared with you.

Adults should supervise the children they've brought to the hunt and they should be depended upon to follow the rules and make sure their own kids do. These large community hunts usually are divided into age categories and may have rules on how many eggs should be collected by each child. Parents are expected to make sure the rules are followed.

Finally, teach children the manners of being grateful for the things provided to them. Have your child personally thank an organizer of the hunt for planning the hunt and providing the fun and prizes.

Dear Thelma: I know you've written about the importance of family traditions in the past. I wanted to share with you one of our family's and how we're expanding it this year. I have four kids. Easter is a big celebration in our home and dying Easter eggs is a big event. My kids have talked about it to their friends and now all the neighborhood kids want to come over to dye eggs. We're excited to have found a fun and loving way to share our Easter tradition with those around us.

A: Easter egg dying in a family is a great connector that draws you closer through the sharing of the tradition. The fact that your kids enjoy it and want others to share in it is wonderful. Your willingness to share is wonderful too.

I'd suggest you make it an event that your kids can play roles in. Decide together when you will do it and those you will invite. You might want to ask each person to come with their eggs pre-boiled. Have the children put together an invitation with instructions and get it out to friends. Use the event as a way to teach your kids about party planning and being good hosts. At the event, assign big kids to help the younger ones who attend.

I'd love to know if you'll have a big neighborhood hunt with all the eggs or send everyone home with eggs for their own hunts. Either way it's a fun activity that will build closeness among you and your children and build community within your neighborhood.

Sharing traditions and good manners never go out of style.

Dear Thelma: I received a wedding invitation from a nephew and the dress designation says formal. The last time I went to a "formal" was prom in 1967. Am I expected to wear a floor-length gown and my husband a tuxedo or does this mean something else today?

A: I suspect that the bride and groom planning this wedding are trying to battle the casual dress epidemic that has taken over events across the country. They want guests to dress up for their special event, and, sadly, people seem to have an aversion to dressing up for anything.

While, formal is probably the most indecisive dress designation available to those planning events, it does signal that an elegant evening is at hand. The formal designation covers all types of formal wear and so is open to some interpretation. At the least it means dark suits and ties for men and cocktail dresses or dressy separates for women. At most it's tuxedos and white ties for men and floor-length gowns for women. If you know the bride and groom well, you may know their style and what they expect. If you don't know them well, it's fine to contact someone who does and ask.

For party planners, dress designations that leave fewer questions for guests are white tie, black tie, black-tie optional, and cocktail attire. White tie, sometimes called ultra-formal, requires men to wear full tuxedos with white ties, vests and shirts. Women wear long formal gowns to complement the formality of men in tuxedos and white ties. This is as formal as it gets.

A black-tie designation requires men to wear tuxedos with black bow ties. While black tie for a woman can mean a floor-length evening gown, it does not restrict her to one. Elegant cocktail dresses or sophisticated dressy pants designed for formal occasions can create a formal look. A woman can choose colors she enjoys wearing, lush fabrics and rich details that make the choice extra special.

The black-tie optional designation is a great way to let guests know that the event definitely is an occasion for dressing up. Men may choose dark suits with ties or tuxedos and women can choose from any of the black tie options of gowns, cocktail dresses or evening separates.

A dress designation of cocktail attire requires dark suits for men and cocktail dresses or dressy separates for women.

The host of an event has every right to decide the ambiance of his or her own party. A considerate guest will respect the dress request. As society gets more casual about everything and propagates an attitude of "it's all about me," more and more people are ignoring the dress designation in favor of their own contentment. This is unacceptable, especially when someone has gone out of their way to create an atmosphere and an event for your enjoyment.

Respect the dress designation and find enjoyment in fulfilling it.

Dear Thelma: Just a short note to thank you for your article on the Eagle Scout. Boy Scouts are often considered "not cool" or nerdy, yet they engage in activities from camping, river running, rock climbing, backpacking, canoeing, and other high adventure activities. Boy

Scouts provides values to live by, as in the Scout Oath and Scout Law.

I am an Eagle Scout (1961) with 60 years of continuous registration in the Boy Scouts. The Boy Scouts of America has maintained its dedication to providing values, and to developing character, personal fitness, and participating citizenship in all our members. Thanks again for your article.

A: Thank you for taking the time to write. Just like values, character, personal fitness and participating citizenship, good manners never go out of style.

Dear Readers: I love finding reinforcement that there are many good people out there in the world. People concerned with one another. People with the heartsense I often discuss in this column.

You've heard me tell how important volunteers are. That in society they are crucial. That they make miracles happen.

Their importance was validated for me again recently with the Presbyterian Healthcare Foundation Daffodil Days. It was a treat for me to be invited to see the preparation of more than 160,000 daffodils trucked-in for the annual project. For several days in March, 500 volunteers came together with the support of more than 150 local businesses to package and sell bunches and bouquets of daffodils to support Presbyterian Home Healthcare and Hospice. The funds raised provide for hospice patients with financial needs during a particularly difficult time of life.

For me to see the commitment of these volunteers to unpack, prepare, distribute, and then work at business sites to sell the flowers was precious. It was particularly poignant for me because I helped bring this event to Albuquerque more than 30 years ago when I ordered the first 5,000 daffodils to help support home healthcare patients in our city.

Volunteerism is the core of why so many nonprofit events are successful, and caring for volunteers is vital to keeping their time and talents working for the group. Effectively utilizing a volunteer force requires tremendous organization and communication. Staff must be involved in organizing and assisting volunteers and helping the volunteer to feel connected to the organization. It's the organization's job to supply information to volunteers in advance about its project and goals.

Effectively utilizing 500 people, Presbyterian Healthcare Foundation did its part to support the volunteers working in their community. The foundation provided breakfast and lunch during several days of volunteer work and truly showed appreciation for its volunteers, an important detail for an organization to address if it wants its volunteer efforts to be consistently successful.

After seeing this year's preparation process, I experienced the sales process: two children selling daffodils with their mother at a local business. I asked the children to explain what they were doing by selling the beautiful flowers. "We're helping sick people," the little girl told me.

It's a little miracle of the heart when people want to help each other. These kids experienced that miracle. They experienced the respect we can have for each other, the support we can show for each other, and a commitment to a cause.

The rewards of volunteerism are tremendous. From the communities benefiting to the volunteers giving their energy and effort, people come away fulfilled heart, mind and soul.

Dear Thelma: Not knowing if someone is a religious person is it still polite or even politically correct in this day and age for one to say "Bless you" or "Gesundheit" to someone sneezing when he or she is a stranger one is passing in public? I do not mind when someone blesses me and I always reply with a courteous smile and a thank you. And yes I am a religious person.

A: This centuries old practice may have originated as a prayer for the health and soul of the sneezer, but today these after-sneeze comments have become more cultural than religious. People say them as a matter of politeness.

I wouldn't worry about causing particular offense, and while it's fine for you to receive them as a blessing, others may not. There's no offense in that either.

Cultural niceties and good manners never go out of style.

Dear Thelma: My 16-year-old son says he wants a summer job and we are encouraging him to get one. The problem is getting him to approach the venture seriously. Instead of setting up his own interviews, he says others he knows just tag along with friends who land interviews and hope the restaurant or store will just interview them too. Can you give us some advice to share with him on making a good impression and landing a summer job?

A: The best way to land the summer job you want is to properly prepare. Be serious and diligent in your preparations and you'll have a better chance of making the best impression possible.

Encourage your son to make a short list of the type of summer jobs that interest him and where he'd like to work. Then he should do some basic research on those businesses and jobs. Are jobs available? What qualifications are necessary? What skills does he have that will fit those jobs? Imagine the questions that will be asked and come up with answers for them. Practicing his answers out lout to you may build his confidence.

When he lands an interview tell him that the person who makes the best impression on the interviewer is most likely to get the job. Make a good impression by wearing pants, a collared shirt and clean shoes – even if the job is with a landscaper or a fast food restaurant. Dressing neatly and with adult standards in mind shows seriousness and respect that can set him apart from other applicants.

Let him know the first few minutes of his interview may be the most important. He should be sure to look the interviewer in the eye, shake her hand with a firm grip and smile. When the interview ends, thank the interviewer for her time and shake her hand again.

This is a good time for him to take a close look at his email address and voice mail greeting. If he doesn't have a standard email address that incorporates his name, he should set one up for communicating with employers. He also should be sure his voice mail greeting clearly states his name and asks callers to leave a message.

Sometimes teens don't get excited about going through all the motions. It feels fruitless to them to make a lot of effort on the front end. It's not an exciting way to spend their time or the path isn't laid out for them so they balk at it. Sometimes they even may feel that they and their friends are a packaged deal in every other situation in their lives, so tagging along on a job interview makes sense to them. They also may be nervous or scared to get on the phone and make a call.

Take this time to inform him, set some standards you expect him to follow and reassure him that he can make that good impression.

Dear Thelma: My aunt and uncle are renewing their vows for their 50th wedding anniversary. What is the protocol for giving a gift?

A: Although gifts are always voluntary, an anniversary celebration typically is a gift-giving occasion. Use your heartsense to choose something to memorialize this special couple's 50 years together or to honor their commitment. What to give is up to you.

Some celebrating such a milestone indicate "No gifts, please" at the bottom of the invitation. If they have made such a note, do honor it. If you have something special you'd like to give them, bring it to them at another time, rather than to the party.

Loving respect for one another and good manners never go out of style.

Dear Thelma: We're approaching Mother's Day. My wife expects a certain level of pampering for Mother's Day, but I would like my kids to take on more responsibility in that. She is, after all, their mother. Is it proper to transition this gift-giving occasion to an 8- and 10-year-old?

A: I believe any opportunity you have to let children share in the joy of selecting and giving a gift should be taken, but they will need your guidance and possibly your wallet.

Mother's Day and Father's Day are great times to really get children involved the spirit of giving. Start by talking to your children about these holidays, what they mean to your family and how your traditionally celebrate. Talk about the importance of sharing time together and creating an atmosphere that shows love and respect for the person honored that day. Finally, have the children talk about their mother, what they know she likes and what they think they can do to show their love in a special way.

Children can be very creative in their giving when given a chance. Your children's ideas may lead them to make their mother something special or to plan and execute a special meal for her. They also may lead to a ride to the store and a budget from you. Lead and guide them in their selections, but let final purchase come from their ideas and hearts. What they come up with may not be what your wife is accustomed to receiving from you, but the love of her children should shine through.

Finally, even if your children do take on some gift giving, you are still right in honoring your wife as a mother and letting her know you appreciate what she brings to the family. If you're inspired to give her a gift too, don't hesitate.

Dear Thelma: Every year my husband and I go through the same situation. I expect him to take care of getting his mother a gift for Mother's Day as I do for my mother. Then he waits until the last minute and wants to show up without a gift or I have to come up with a gift. She's his mom, but I see showing up without a gift as a bad reflection on me. What do I do here?

A: I think your situation may be a common one. First you should ask yourself and your husband, how important a gift is to his mom. Do all the siblings show up with a gift? Does she do a lot of gift giving at other times of the year? Are gifts as an expression of affection important to in their family? All families are different. This assessment should tell you whether you're taking the gift-giving opportunity too seriously or if your husband is not taking it seriously enough.

If you decide that a gift is important, you have a couple of options. Volunteer to take on the purchase of all the Mother's Day gifts and pick up one at the same time you shop for your mom. This will give you control of the timing of the purchase and eliminate the frustration with your husband. If you and your husband decide to leave the gift-purchasing responsibility with him, let it go and leave it to him. You can always buy a Mother's Day card designed for mothers-in-law that will be your own personal expression of affection for her and give it to her discreetly that day if your husband shows up empty handed.

Good relations and good manners never go out of style.

Dear Thelma: I received two graduation announcements recently. Both contained self addressed envelopes. I sent each graduate a card and money. I did not use the self addressed envelopes and find it blatant. Is that how it's done now?

A: I like your choice of words. Blatant is exactly what it is.

A gift – graduation or otherwise – is always voluntary. Whether a gift for the specific occasion is customary or not, the giver makes the choice of whether to give and what to give.

These graduates and their families may have thought they were being thoughtful, but to include a self-addressed envelope puts all the focus on sending out the announcement as a means to receive a gift of money rather than on sharing the good news. That sends a selfish message that has the potential to offend many people.

Those sending out everything from graduation announcements to wedding invitations need to take a new look at the purpose of their mailings. Put your heart into what you are sending. Send an announcement of an achievement in your life or an invitation to an important celebration with love and expect nothing in return. You may be surprised to find that it's when you are sincere and act in love that you are most greatly rewarded.

Dear Thelma: Can you write about proper dress for summer college interns?

A: Interns will be taken most seriously and feel most comfortable if they dress in a way that meshes personal style with the expectations of the company. If you are an intern and the company hasn't already let you know their dress code, contact the human resources department for guidance. If they don't have a specified code, they should be able to tell you what's most suitable.

In many offices, women are expected to wear business suits, pant suits or dresses. Even for an intern, dress pants, a dressy top and dress shoes are likely the norm. Skirts should be no shorter than three inches above the knee and shoe heels no higher than 3 inches.

Men should find out if full suits are required or if dress pants, dress shoes and a collared shirt are standard dress.

Unless the highest levels of management show up in jeans, save them for the weekends. The same goes for flip flops.

An intern's goal should be to avoid distracting those around you, which may mean concealing tattoos and body piercing. Women should limit jewelry to a ring, one pair of earrings, one necklace, a bracelet and a wristwatch. It's also important to cover cleavage and make sure all undergarments remain concealed by clothes that fit properly.

Dear Thelma: I have some wedding related questions. Who is the one responsible for sending out announcements and invitations? How should the announcement or invitation be sent? By email, Facebook or postal? If one gives a gift at the shower, do they give one at the reception also?

A: All good questions for this time of year. The bride's parents traditionally sent the invitation since they traditionally covered the costs of the wedding. Today, a couple's parents may share the expense or the couple themselves may cover all or part of the costs. When that's the case, the invitation wording should reflect who's involved in the hosting the event. The task of actually putting the envelopes in the mail is up to the group. Announcements can be sent by any or all of those involved as well.

I believe all wedding announcements and invitations should be thoughtfully selected, worded and sent through the mail. This is an important event in the life of a couple and their families and the invitation should reflect that, even if the event the couple chooses to create is more casual than formal. The person receiving the invitation should feel honored to be a part of the occasion and the best way to ensure that is through an invitation sent through the mail. Email and Facebook are fine for save-the-date announcements or wedding plan updates, but if you're inviting more than your closest group of friends, a mailed invitation is best.

Anyone who does choose to use email or Facebook to send a wedding invitation should do so very carefully. The message should be sent to each individual with all of the information that would be included in a mailed invitation. The wording and the look of the invitation should create a feeling of honor in the recipient. A group message to everyone you know on Facebook will not create the kind of individual connection needed in this situation. Your very closest friends may be fine with it, but anyone outside of that tight circle may be put off by it.

Gifts are always a decision of a guest but are customarily given at both the wedding shower and the wedding. Generally, and especially if it's a question of budget, shower gifts can be less costly and less elaborate. For the wedding you can focus on a long-lasting gift for a new couple setting up their first home.

If you've already given a substantial gift at the shower, think about something more personal or creative you can share with the couple for a wedding gift – a book, a CD or a special photo album. The point of your gift is to let them know you share in their happiness and wish them well for the future.

Dear Thelma: How do you get the check away from a friend who always wants to pay the bill at a restaurant?

A: Tell your friend before the meal begins that you will take care of the bill rather than at the end of the meal when the check comes. Say to him, "I'm getting it now; next time you treat."

If he still goes for it at the end, just put your credit card down with his and ask the server to split the check in half. That will show how serious you are and next time he might just let you pick up the tab.

On either end of kindness, good manners never go out of style.

Dear Thelma: Are there any rules for wearing patent leather shoes? I've been told they are only to be worn during the summer months. Is that true?

A: Patent leather shoes only in summer falls into the realm of fashion rules that have become fashion folklore. If designers are making and selling patent leather accessories year-round, then it's appropriate to wear them year-round.

I bought a pair of patent leather shoes trimmed in white one winter – two supposed faux pas in one pair of shoes.

The prohibition against white before Memorial Day and after Labor Day is also a myth. White is appropriate all year in fabrics and in shoes. While the weight of the fabric or the shoe material may change based on the season, the color does not have to.

Sandals and slides also are sold and worn year-round, so they're not just for summer anymore.

And while some people wait for warmer weather to go without silk hosiery, many now go all year without it. That's not to say that it's improper to wear hosiery, most of us probably should, but your manners are in tact either way.

Fashions may change, but good manners never go out of style.

Dear Thelma: When writing an obituary, is it necessary to include an ex-spouse or partner if there are minor children? Or is it a matter of personal preference from the writer's point of view? I've seen this happening more often and quite frankly I'm not sure what to think of it. What are your thoughts?

A: Writing an obituary is a very personal experience for whomever the family of the deceased chooses to give that task to. It is up to that person and those who advise him or her to make the decision on what should be included.

Each family situation is different. What would be considered right to include in one person's obituary may be completely inappropriate in another person's. As a reader, it's not for us to judge. The information provided is what the writer believes is necessary to honor the life of the person and to inform the community of who has died and to whom that person is connected.

Dear Thelma: I read your recent column on paying a restaurant bill when a meal is shared with a friend with interest. An experienced server knows to present the check to whomever asks for it first. There should be no wrangling. It is unprofessional for the server if the matter is not resolved quickly.

As this is often not the case, there are several easy solutions. You can request the bill when the server first comes to the table. Also you can speak up when asked, toward the end of the meal, if anything else is needed – which is the server's nice way of asking if you're ready for your bill.

A more efficient way to pay for the meal is to take care of the matter away from the table, friend and other guests. Make an excuse to go to the restroom, make a phone call or whatever will allow you to leave the table politely. Find your server or a manager and ask for the check to be given to you. However, the best and most discreet solution is to give your credit card to the server/manager at that time. When the bill arrives, it has already been charged and will be presented to its holder for a signature. End of problem.

I am confident the last solution will work every time and if your friend catches on, you can ask for the bill when the reservation is made.

A: I like your ideas. They are especially appropriate when hosting a business meal or a large group.

However, in the previous question the reader wondered how to get the opportunity to share the bill or sometimes pay it when the friend refused let him. If that friend reads this, our poor reader will have to continue his fight. At the end of the day, clear communication between these two friends will be the solution to their problem.

Dear Thelma: Someone in my office recently had major improvements made to her teeth. Is it appropriate to tell her they look nice?

A: If she's someone you deal with often, I think it's fine during a regular interaction to say something like, "Your smile looks great." She knows there has been a change and she knows that people are going to notice. Don't expect a detailed explanation, but to be honest and move on will be less awkward than dancing around the issue uncomfortably.

A sincere compliment and good manners never go out of style.

Dear Thelma: My husband loaned a friend two beautiful table top photo books from Italy that I bought while we lived there. I love them because they remind me so of my wonderful time in that country.

Yes, you guessed it. It has been four months and he has not returned them. We have known this man for over a year, although we are not close friends. We belong to a social group with him and his wife. He's a professional and even though I wasn't there when my husband loaned him the books, I probably would have too.

So how do I go about getting them back? My husband has asked him twice. One time he acted as if he did not know what we were referring to and the other he ignored. I fear I cannot get them back and they are no longer in print so buying new is not possible. Is there an etiquette to asking for an item back? I am tempted to announce it at the group but I fear he will simply quit coming and that will be that.

A: Your borrower's failure to return the books to you before you had to ask for them is the etiquette lacking in this situation. Now, based on his reaction to your previous requests, your next steps must be firm and strategic. I see two possible courses of action.

You might consider approaching him and his wife while they are together in a social situation and asking to speak with them. You needn't announce it to the entire group, but hearing together about the need to return the books may help them motivate each other to get it done. Say, "We lent you two photo books on Italy and we need to get those back. Can we come by and pick them up this week?"

Another option may be to put it in writing. Send a letter addressed to both of them and express how important these books are to you and that you would like to get them back immediately. At the end of your request, include the statement: "If we don't hear back from you in a few days then we will call to talk personally with you because we do treasure these books and need them back. If something has happened to them, we would much rather hear about it than wonder about them."

Dear Thelma: Recently I picked up my new glasses at the opticians. While waiting for the clerk, I heard the murmur of a child's voice. I turned to find a very small boy, no more than 2 1/2 or 3, sitting quietly at the end of the room. One of the parents responded and then continued perusing the selections for new glasses.

Several minutes later, after completing my purchase and ready to leave, I noticed the tot was still sitting in the big chair. As I passed, I smiled and remarked that he was doing a great job waiting so nicely for his parents. He replied, "Thank you."

I was startled but only for a moment. I then turned and walked over to the Mom and Dad. I thanked them for bringing up such a well-mannered child. Their smiles made my day!

A: Thank you for showing your appreciation to the child's parents. Although all children are different and take different levels of parenting effort to get a child to the point of behavior you describe, these parents definitely had made the effort. I'm sure they appreciated hearing how their work impacted you.

Good behavior and good manners never go out of style.

Dear Thelma: I am facing a dilemma. A close friend has started and quickly advanced a romance with a man who I have reservations about. Before just a few months had passed they were building a house together, then contemplating a pregnancy, and finally saying they were getting married. No ring offered or official proposal made yet, but she's already asked me to be her maid of honor.

She and I have discussed my reservations about the man and I have told her that I feel she is proceeding too quickly. We decided not to discuss her personal life anymore because to do so upsets both of us. She knows exactly how I feel, but despite that she asks me to be in her wedding.

What am I to do? Do I place my reservations on a shelf and just be happy because she is happy? That's what she wants me to do. How do I stand up for the two of them if I'm not confident in the strength and quality of their relationship? Standing up for what I think is right may end our friendship.

A: It is obvious that you care about your friend. You have been honest about your observations and feelings out of your love and respect for her. Only the closest of friends can be that honest about a difficult topic and maintain their friendship. You have struck a rare balance.

Now it is your friend's choice to proceed as she sees fit, which may not match what you think is best. If she proceeds with the wedding, and it sounds like she will, you will have a choice to make. You will have to decide how important this relationship is to you. Is it important enough for you to set aside your reservations and support her as your friend. Or are your feelings about the couple so strong that to deny them would injure you emotionally and make maintaining the relationship even more difficult.

Only you can make that choice and that choice has to be right for you.

Dear Thelma: I have almost given up going to my beloved concerts

450

and opera. I am so afraid of coughing or having to clear my throat. I suck on drops – unwrapped before the performance – but I may need a sip of water. The venue is so staid and sanctimonious that if you take a water bottle to sip everyone around looks at you disapprovingly. No wonder attendance has dropped. Why is this so frowned upon?

A: I too am prone to coughing and it makes me very uncomfortable to cause such a distraction for the audience. Because I respect the audience with whom I want to enjoy a performance, I have taken to carrying a water bottle in my handbag. I only take it out when I need it and use it discreetly.

Just like the courtesy you show in unwrapping your throat lozenges before the performance, plan to carry a large enough handbag to fit your water bottle into easily and situate it in a way what you can access it when needed without causing distraction. Realize that anyone glaring at you would probably be glaring at you if you were coughing continuously so you may draw their ire either way. Don't let that keep you from enjoying the performances you love.

Managing the distractions you fear you are likely to cause is not rude. Not managing them is.

Planning courtesy and good manners never go out of style.

Dear Thelma: I serve on a board and there is a bully that is so bent on always getting his way that everyone has become afraid of him. I am sure he has been a bully his whole life. How do you handle an adult bully, and why do so many people on his level allow him to get by with it?

A: I too have experienced adult bullying diminishing a board. Through overbearing behavior this person rendered the board ineffective.

Adult bullying often is based on a need to control. That control is gained because of the power the bully has on the board, which the board has likely given to him. Adult bullies have a tendency in the beginning to lobby for their powerful position.

Once power is attained, it may be a lack of self-respect that makes it easy for bullies to take advantage of that power without regard for the people around them. When a person doesn't respect himself, he can't respect anyone else. That makes it easy for him to ignore his own bad behavior.

Coming from a place of power, the bully chooses to cause fear in others. Whether it's fear of being maligned or fear of confrontation, it

451

feels safer to let the bully have his way. At that point the board becomes separated. Each member is forced to take sides. Will you align with the bully or try to stand on your own?

The lobbying behavior is a red flag for me. When I observe a person lobbying for power on a board, I make a point to refrain from being judgmental but bring my observations about the behavior to other board members. Then I work to maintain my objectivity, ideas and commitment to the cause and avoid aligning myself with the bully.

A bully diminishes the strength of a board because he derails the membership from being attentive to the mission. Every meeting requires the energy to prepare for a battle with the bully rather than a focus on maintaining a strong commitment to support the mission and purpose of the board.

The more board members who can avoid aligning with a bully, the better. To be effective, board members must have their own power to get involved in discussions and decision making tasked to the board. It is their right and their responsibility as board members.

We have heard much recently of Apple CEO Steve Jobs and his behavior, much of which has been defined as bullying and worse. Even now, nearly a year after his death, people are aligning either for or against. Those who admire all aspects of Job's life see a man who let nothing get in the way of his vision. Those repelled by his behavior see a cruel tyrant.

I believe those who can advance their vision while maintaining respect and consideration for the people around them are the most successful in all aspects of their lives and the most admirable.

Bullying behavior includes embarrassing, intimidating, threatening and mocking others in order to preserve control or advance ideas. If you find yourself falling into these tendencies, take a step back and assess whether preoccupation with yourself has caused you to lose the ability to understand the feelings of others. Make changes now to make a positive impact on the world around you.

When faced with an adult bully, be confident, calm and clear. Name the behavior you find troublesome and state what is expected instead. It will take courage, but if more of us do it and support those who do, environments will improve for everyone.

Healthy relationships and good manners never go out of style.

Dear Thelma: Why do people invite you to a party with friends and then pay for a band that plays so loudly that you can't hear anyone around you? I think there is a time and place for music, but when you want to talk to your friends it becomes impossible when the music is so loud. Why are some hosts so unaware that this is a problem?

A: When someone hosts a party in his own home or for his own entertainment, he should consider the comfort of his guests. The volume of the music and how guests spend their time – whether in conversation or enjoying the band – are aspects of the evening a good host takes great pains to make perfect, but ultimately if a host wants loud music at his party, he can choose to have loud music.

I think the issue is magnified when planning an event for an organization. Great care should be taken when planning such an event and the ultimate purpose of the evening must be kept at the front of the planner's mind. That purpose changes from event to event. A fundraising dinner featuring special entertainment is one thing; a professional networking reception is another. Event planners have to think carefully about the atmosphere they are trying to create and select accordingly.

Dear Thelma: In the past, the "right" thing was to invite out-of-town guests to a wedding rehearsal dinner. Is this still true?

A: Yes, it is right to include out-of-town guests at wedding rehearsal dinners. If they have taken the time to travel to attend your celebration, you should show respect and courtesy to them by inviting them to the dinner. Otherwise, they are likely to spend the evening alone for the night in their hotel rooms

The traditional guest list for a rehearsal dinner includes the wedding party; the couple's parents, grandparents and siblings with their spouses or significant others; the officiate and his or her spouse; and any one else required to be at the rehearsal, like those doing readings. Spouses or significant others of the attendants are often included, as are out-of-town guests. Including these people makes for a gracious start to your special event.

Dear Thelma: I received an email invitation from a co-worker's daughter to celebrate her parent's wedding anniversary. I am not quite sure exactly who the invite is for. Yes, I know it is rude to ask for my husband to be invited, but I am not sure if the daughter realized just sending out emails to individuals omits spouses. Or does it?

I looked online and there seems to be very little on addressing etiquette for email invitations. "You're invited" could go either way on this one since in most cases an email belongs to one person. The event is to be held in a restaurant. Help!

A: I've always said it's perfectly fine to offer an invitation via email as long as all the elements called for by an invitation are covered: the host's name, the occasion, the date and time, the location, guest attire, reply instructions and clarity as to who is invited.

Who's being invited is an element that normally would be indicated by what's written on the envelope in a traditional mailing. Because of technology that subtle but important signal is missing in an emailed invitation that doesn't take the time to address it.

Those sending invitations via email can address it in this way. In the first line of your email message, write "To Carl and Kathy Baca" or "Mr. and Mrs. John Smith and Children." Then skip a line or two and proceed with the invitation wording.

As for your situation, I believe it would be fine to call the host of the event you've been invited to and say, "I'm not quite sure if your email intended to include my husband in the invitation."

Clarity and good manners never go out of style.

Dear Thelma: In May, my stepson and family asked if we'd like to take a whole family vacation up north. We live in different states. We said yes and he found a big vacation rental house we'd all fit in. My husband's health is poor and soon after they found this house, we began to doubt whether my husband would be able to make the trip. I asked my stepson about that possibility and he said if his dad couldn't go, they had some friends they'd ask to go in our place. The doctor said my husband definitely shouldn't go and about two and a half weeks before the vacation was to start, we gave my stepson the final word that we wouldn't be going. His friends weren't able to go either, so my stepson and his girlfriend were stuck with our $600 share of the rental.

I feel bad about it, but I don't know what is the right thing to do. I want to pay part of it, but it doesn't seem fully fair that we pay all of it. But then again why should they? What do you suggest?

A: I suggest that you pay the $600 incurred on your behalf. Your stepson was kind enough to go through the effort that it takes to research vacation rentals and plan an extended family trip like this, which you agreed to. In making those plans, he chose a location designed to meet the whole family's needs, not just his own. When you pulled out, he lost $600 along with all the time he spent planning the trip and accommodating the needs of all the travelers.

If you pulled out of a hotel reservation outside of their limits for cancellations, they would charge your credit card for that reservation without missing a beat. If you cancelled a cruise or a resort vacation, you would be stuck with the bill. If you left a friend with a large expense rather than a family member, you would feel obliged to cover that expense.

Your stepson is not going to charge your credit card or demand payment, but you shouldn't leave him with a significant bill on top of his own travel expenses just because you can. In family relationships it is important that we not take for granted those closest to us. It may be easy to get away with being less than courteous, but those kinds of injuries to a relationship can be damaging and long lasting.

The fact that he wanted to plan this vacation with you and your husband shows you have a close relationship. To maintain the health of that relationship, paying for the expense you caused would be the right thing to do. It shows that you respect his time spent planning the trip and understand the great effort he made to create a memorable experience for you.

Dear Thelma: Why does the press call Mr. Romney, Governor Romney, as he is no longer a governor? They also refer to former U.S. presidents Bush and Clinton as President Bush and President Clinton. Why do these titles stay with the person forever?

A: As a part of business and government protocol, certain titles accompany a person throughout their lifetime. This includes high-ranking officials who no longer hold office and high-ranking military retirees. It holds for presidents, ambassadors, U.S. senators and representatives, governors, judges, mayors and generals, who are all introduced and addressed by their former titles. We do it out of courtesy for the person and the office they held.

Courtesy – to those closest and furthest from us – and good manners never go out of style.

Dear Thelma: My niece, on the East Coast, recently passed away. Family and friends were aware that she was dying from cancer and that it was just a matter of time. Upon her death, her daughter sent emails notifying everyone rather than making phone calls. I was not on her email list and wouldn't have found out for days, but fortunately another niece knew this and thought to call me.

While email is expedient and reaches a broader audience more quickly than the phone, does this method seem way too informal or is it the new normal?

A: Email is an acceptable method of communicating timely information, even on the most delicate of subjects. Your niece's daughter, dealing with the emotions surrounding the death of her mother, got the information of her death to as many as she could as quickly as she could. While there may have been some people in her life that she felt compelled to contact directly with a phone call, it would have been up to her to make that determination.

Even in the days of more frequent phone calls, you may not have heard directly from the closest family member immediately upon a person's passing. Other relatives would have stepped in to bear some of the burden of making all those calls. Try to understand the situation your niece's daughter was in and feel grateful that you did receive the news even if it wasn't first-hand.

Technology can be as courteous and respectful as we make it. The email your relative had to compose and send needed to relay the sad information with honor and respect and reach as many family members as possible to start the chain of information flowing.

Those caught in the situation of communicating the news of someone's death by email might remember to include a line asking those receiving the email to share the news with others who may not have been included in the initial mailing.

While we'd all like to deal with this kind of information in person, it's not always possible. Quickly and in writing may be the next best thing.

Dear Thelma: A recent column suggested it was proper to include out-of-town guests at wedding rehearsal dinners. Although I find this thoughtful and generous, I have never heard this suggested as a tradition. Is it something unique to the Southwest? I would imagine, in today's world of far-flung families, it is a very expensive, sometimes impossible, requirement to meet. I am originally from New England, and have never heard of anyone feeling the need (etiquette-wise) to invite out-of-town guests to rehearsal dinners, which were always reserved for members of the wedding party where I came from.

A: In today's world, little is cut and dried when it comes to tradition. The column you reference noted that it is "right" to invite out-of-town guests to a wedding rehearsal dinner. It is a kind and thoughtful thing to do, and many couples and their families across the country choose to do it – even on the East Coast.

However, especially today when the lines marking what was once traditional are completely blurred, your guest list is your guest list and it can take whatever shape you give it. As a host of any event, the guests you choose to invite are up to you and are based on your desires for the event and your budget. Just be sure your invitations invoke feelings of honor and are as inclusive as they realistically can be.

Dear Thelma: My daughter was married this past summer in a beautiful wedding. Her reception was catered at a very nice golf course banquet room. She sent out her wedding invitations four months in advance. The banquet room arranged the food, drinks and decorations and charged a per person rate, which was not cheap. My daughter added her personal touch by taking care of the wedding cake, music and favors.

One month prior to the wedding RSVPs were received and plans finalized for 100 guests. On the wedding day, the banquet room was set up for the 100 guests and looked spectacular. However, we had a total of 40 guests who did not show up and offered no explanation or advanced warning. Even if we would have received cancellations on the day of the wedding, nothing could have been done. We were upset and disappointed, to say the least.

First of all, due to the no shows, we ended up paying for and wasting a good amount of food, as well as an expensive cake. Second, due to budget limitations, our initial guest list had to be limited to the number we could accommodate. Had we known that these individuals would not show up, we could have invited other guests that were over flowing on our waiting list.

Third, all of the no shows caused the bride, groom and family a great deal of embarrassment. It also caused a great deal of confusion with the seating arrangements since many of the tables were almost empty. As a result, guests were forced to shuffle around the room to join others and fill tables.

We feel that we gave our guest plenty of time to reply one way or another, so this situation should have never occurred. Also, most of our guests live in town, therefore transportation shouldn't have been an issue.

We found our "would-be" guests' behavior to be rude, disrespectful and hurtful. What's wrong with people? Don't they realize that they were specially selected to participate in this important celebration?

Hopefully this letter will remind invited guests of the importance of following through with a yes or a no when they receive an invitation. Remember, a host has gone through a lot of time, effort and expense to make guests feel welcomed and happy.

A: Your letter eloquently explains exactly what a host faces when guests do not honor the four most important letters in an invitation: RSVP. Whether your answer to an invitation is a yes or a no, you must respond quickly and you must honor that response so that the host can proceed with planning and can plan accordingly. To do otherwise dishonors your host and causes the waste, anxiety, embarrassment and disappointment described.

People have become very casual with their responses to invitations and almost indifferent to the fact that someone is working to create an occasion for their enjoyment. It's important that we reverse this attitude.

The habit I've developed and encourage others to form is to make a decision, mark my calendar if the date is available and respond within three days of receiving the invitation. In so doing, I avoid falling into a habit of setting invitations aside to be buried under a pile of "to dos" or letting the demands of the moment interfere with my ability to make a phone call or send back a response card.

I also suggest that we all seriously consider reviewing our guest lists to identify the people who habitually cause this inconvenience and consider not inviting them to the next event.

A proper response and good manners never go out of style.

Dear Thelma: I am a woman in my early 50s. My hair is rapidly becoming white, and I have no plans to color it. I have received a lot of comments, mostly from men, asking "Are you ever going to color your hair?" Do they not know their comments are rude and offensive? How should I respond?

A: I don't think they intend to be rude and offensive, and if they thought you were going to be hurt by their comments, they would hold their tongues. Some people, especially as they get older, are just blatantly honest. These men are surprised that you are one of the few women they know who do not color their hair and they're curious about it. They don't intend to hurt your feelings.

Those of you reading who are blatantly honest, take note. There are certain subjects that put people on edge: weight, aging and appearance are some of them. If you have to put in extra effort to be tactful on these subjects, you might just want to refrain from mentioning them.

I've never had this problem myself because I do color my hair, but I try to take comments like this that come my way lightheartedly. Put a marketing spin on it – "I'm all natural" or "I'm organic." It's your hair and your personal choice to do what you want with it. Keep your plans, be confident in them, and let the rest roll off of you.

Dear Thelma: There are many people with audible yawns. One man at work makes noise every single time he yawns. Is there a polite way to ask him to stop audibly yawning? It's disruptive.

A: The thing I focused on when I read your question was the fact that the man's yawns were repeatedly disruptive. I wouldn't call one yawn once a week a problem, but repeated audible yawns in a meeting setting or in an open office is a habit he should be asked to stifle. The person to talk to him about it privately is his supervisor.

It will be important to convey the idea that his audible yawns send the message that he's terribly disinterested in the meeting taking place or in his work and that he's sharing that sentiment with everyone around him – subordinates, colleagues and superiors. Let him know that it's disruptive to all and a signal that he needs to refocus his efforts and his energy.

Dear Thelma. At a recent gala dinner party, people at tables continued to talk while the MC and others were speaking at the podium. A friend told me that she has encountered similar rudeness. Have we forgotten our social amenities?

A: I doubt we've forgotten them, but as this example shows, we certainly do choose to ignore them and do whatever we want to at the moment. This behavior is rude.

During a large event people can gain a feeling of anonymity, that their behavior doesn't matter because it won't be noticed in so large a crowd. Anyone feeling that way should think again. You may think that your side conversation won't display rudeness to a speaker 15 tables away from you, but your behavior does affect those closest to you and won't be ignored.

Our best defense is to set the best example we can at our own table. Encourage those around us to end their conversations and pay attention and do the same ourselves. I have also asked members of the wait staff to ask people to refrain from talking during the presentation.

If you truly need to have a conversation during a presentation, leave the room.

Polite attention and good manners never go out of style.

Dear Thelma: Regarding your column on the man yawning excessively, this person may be suffering from a medical condition. He needs to see a doctor for a full medical workup, and soon.

A: According to the National Institute of Health's MedlinePlus website, you could be right. The NIH says that "yawning is a normal response to fatigue and drowsiness, but excessive yawning can be caused by a vasovagal reaction. This reaction is caused by the action of a nerve, called the vagus nerve, on the blood vessels. It may indicate a heart problem."

If you can't control excessive yawning, see a doctor. If you've made a habit of yawning so loudly that everyone around is distracted by it, exchange your rude behavior for a quiet, covered yawn.

Dear Thelma: I am applying for an in-house position change at the company for which I have been working for the last 19 years. The application requests a reason why you want to change. To me this is a "purpose-driven" career shift. How do I word this without sounding phony, self serving and insincere?

A: Since there is nothing phony about looking for a career change within your company, particularly with your record of tenure, you shouldn't have to worry about sounding that way. State clearly that you have had a clear commitment to the organization and you see the new position as an opportunity to continue being productive and effective as an individual and as an employee of the company. Your record of service will provide an opening to a discussion on the specific reasons why this particular career shift is good for you and for your company at this time.

You're not the first person to seek to change positions within your company. No one will be taken aback by it. You're simply looking for a new challenge, and there's nothing phony, self-serving or insincere about that. New challenges and good manners never go out of style.

Dear Thelma: We don't entertain in our home very often but I want to be a gracious hostess for a couple coming for an evening visit. I know we should take their coats and show them to the living room. But do we offer drinks right away? Do I offer snacks right away? Or do we sit and talk for awhile? What other things should a hostess be aware of? In this day of few home visits I guess I've forgotten how to take care of that special guest.

A: You've thought of many of the important aspects of being a good host. The way you carry them out will be unique to you and to that particular visit. Do bring them in and take their coats, then lead them to wherever is most comfortable for you and guests. That might be your living room, but it could be another sitting area, the backyard, or even a kitchen bar.

The most important thing to keep in mind is a goal of making your guests comfortable. Be present to them and spend the time focused on them. Don't let yourself be distracted by other things going on in your home – television, cleaning or projects. This is a time for sharing and getting caught up with each other. If your guests have just come from a long drive, you may want to offer something right away, but otherwise you don't have to serve drinks or snacks immediately. Do serve them near the beginning of the visit so that you don't get caught up in the conversation and run out of time.

While there may be fewer unscheduled drop-by visits because of people's busy schedules, I disagree that this is a time of few home visits. I find planned home visits to be very popular. They are wonderfully friendly and congenial times that help people stay connected or get reconnected. I find neighborhood home visits particularly gratifying as a neighborly home visit helps build a neighborhood community.

I hope your visit goes well and inspires you to plan more of them. Be sure to accept any invitations for visits that come your way too.

Dear Readers: Are you asking Santa for the latest and greatest in technology this year? Or are you surprising someone with such a gift? Today, it seems, everyone is buying up devices that are built to connect us with each other and with information like never before.

With this, our world is moving faster than ever. New technology is introduced every day; and we are constantly challenged to learn a new way of doing things whether by a new device or a new system or a new mode of operating. Some people fear it as an intrusion of

461

technology, but I don't. I see it as something to understand and embrace so that we all move forward.

Others wonder, is it time for new manners for these new times? My answer to that question is no. Technology is a tool which in our hands has the power to advance and encourage relationships and provide a mode of sharing the wonderfulness of who we are. It can impact the world for good. However, it also has the power to magnify the worst in us. Rude, caustic, confrontational, gossipy, revengeful – it provides the direct means for us to be all these things.

It's up to us. Technology becomes what you make it. If you're rude, it will be rude. If you are kind, it will be kind. Technology does little without a user. Plug it into the best in you – your heartsense, kindness and respect – and others will find the best in it.

There are three tenets I have always known and feel more deeply now than ever: you are who you are all the time; you act as you think and you only have one chance to make a first impression. These apply in every in-person situation you encounter, as well as every technological situation. When respect, courtesy and kindness are our guiding principles in every interaction – over Facebook, text or face-to-face – we need never worry about the etiquette of each. When our hearts and minds are in the right place, we will always do the right thing.

Think for a moment about those people you meet who genuinely make an effort to connect with you. The people who always greet you with a smile, a handshake, and a genuinely interested question or comment. Those people who make you feel like you're the only person in the room. Those people who are honestly personally connected.

Those people know that their actions – personal and technological – make a difference and they make an effort. While they may embrace technology, they're not plugged into it. It's plugged into them.

Balance will always be important. Users of any technology must take care to avoid replacing all in-person contact in favor their favorite device. They must also avoid choosing the device over the people around them. On the other hand, is the risk of ignoring technology as a tool in our lives. By failing to make use of what we can or absolutely rejecting technology, we may miss out on making real connections with real people.

Finally, it is vitally important that we as people who care about good manners bring courtesy and respect to the technology so that we all learn and model how to use it with care. We can't ignore the opportunities that are being created in this area by technology. We have the power to apply what we know is right to all that is new in the world. We just need to do it.

Moving forward and good manners never go out of style

Dear Thelma: It seems that now it is popular to bring a contribution to a meal and assume that the hostess does not want to keep the food. I have noticed in recent years that dinner guests take their food donation back home with them without asking. I was always taught that when you bring a dish to someone's home it becomes a gift for the hostess. Now people just start packing up what is left and bring it back home without asking the hostess if she wants to keep it. What is your opinion?

A: Always take any contribution to a dinner with the expectation that it is part of the party and that you will not be bringing it back home. If the host wants to send it back with you, he or she will offer it back.

Emptying any leftovers into a container of the host's so that the host doesn't have to worry about getting your dish back to you is fine. But again, offering the food back is up to the host.

Dear Thelma: My parents divorced when I was a small child and holidays for my family have two separate gift giving traditions – my mother and siblings all agree that holiday gift giving is for the children, and it ceases at age 18.

My dad and his wife believe that everyone should get and give gifts, so every year they provide all of us with a very specific wish list for Christmas. We also are required to provide him with our own wish list by Halloween.

Every year my husband and I make up packages for each family of goodies we've preserved from our gardens. Our gifts from our garden and orchard are incredibly labor intensive for us, and made with love. But every year I feel like we also have to buy more presents for my father and his wife because of their wish list.

More often than not, I ignore the wish list and purchase something for each of them that I feel reflects their personalities or my love for them. Every year they thank me profusely and tell me how much they love their gifts.

Is it appropriate for me to be completely ignoring these wish lists and would it be totally off base to stop sending them what I see as "extra" gifts? I want to "honor my father" but I feel like we are doing that when we make them beautiful gift baskets of our homemade goodies. Shouldn't it be enough?

I'll add one more thing: it's not the cost of the gifts to my father and his wife that bother me. It's the feeling that a store bought gift is expected and even not-so-subtly demanded from me that makes me feel like I'm not sincere in the loving act of giving.

A: Your question reflects a great deal of anxiety and a good deal of blame. You blame your father for your anxiety over gift giving, but I think it's time for you to let that go. Obviously your father enjoys the gift exchange. He provides a wish list and asks for one from you because it finds it helpful in the giving that he does. I don't think you should read any further into it.

As the giver of a gift, all the choices are yours. You decide to whom you will give, how much you will spend and what you will give. And you can feel perfectly fine about deciding to ignore the wish list.

Your homemade baskets are lovely and are made and given in love. Place all your focus on that and not on what you believe others are expecting from you.

Dear Thelma: I'm going to be in a wedding. We bridesmaids are planning on taking the bride out for her bachelorette party by going out for dinner and drinks, and then getting a hotel room to spend the night. The maid of honor just informed us that she's planning on bringing her newborn for the whole time, and she will be sleeping in the same room. She asked us if anyone objects. I do, and I want to communicate that, but I don't know how to say it. How should I respond?

A: I agree with you that this is not the type of event designed to accommodate a newborn and I think you must talk with the maid of honor about it. You can say something like: "We are here to celebrate the bride and offer her our love and friendship. Bringing a newborn along will distract from our plans. I'm not comfortable with it. If you can't get a babysitter and have to bring the baby, then we should plan a different type of event."

The right choices and good manners never go out of style.

Dear Readers: There's a wonder and excitement to this time of year makes it like no other. The feeling makes me want to dive in deeper and view Christmas through the eyes of a child. But which child? Each age and stage has something to appreciate and something beautiful to offer as we contemplate the warmth and love of the season sitting just under the surface waiting for us to draw it out.

I see in the infant's first Christmas, where the lights and sparkle are enough to captivate for the whole season, a precious opportunity to open my eyes anew and appreciate the simple beauty around me. In the 18-month-old's desire to touch and taste, and push and pull everything within reach, I find the joy in engaging to the fullest and appreciating each new experience offered. The 4-year-old, confident that all her wishes whispered in Santa's ear will come true, reminds me to hope and to dream. She also inspires me to share those dreams with someone dear to me and do what I can to make them come true.

Then there's the 9-year-old questioning the magic of the holidays. Although he's figuring things out, he still longs for the magic and isn't ready to give it up, even when it confounds logic and voices around him tell him to let it go. He wants to write another letter to Santa and be surprised by his empty cookie plate, filled stocking and wish come true on Christmas morning. His mom is not ready to give it up either and decides she won't ever, even when he's got it all figured out. That creation of magic, surprise and delight for one another is a worthwhile endeavor I'll gladly embrace.

I see the 12-year-old girl, a little sad she's not asking for a Barbie this year but excited for latest in sneaker fashion. She recognizes that change in interests and desires is a part of life and she's not afraid of moving on. She knows there are good things ahead. She's inspiration for joyfully letting go of things I love but no longer need to hold on to and looking to the future.

Finally the 14-year-old boy, pushing the bounds of childhood, who's anticipating his favorite Christmas foods and the latest gadget. He still loves the simple surprises found in his stocking – a pack of bubble gum or a funny toy that triggers a memory. He's beginning to recognize the love and care found behind every gift purchased for him. He's beginning to understand the call to share that love and care himself. Along with him, I appreciate the love that surrounds me and look for the opportunities to give it back.

We are blessed to have children in our midst, to slow us down and to remind us of what's important. They allow us to relive and recreate many of our happiest memories and traditions. They force us to step back and remember a simpler time, when wonder and awe were easy to come by. Awe, that potent mixture of amazement, respect and fear, is often what keeps us striving to be our best selves. A new dose of it would do many of us a world of good.

With these children in mind I'll appreciate the simple beauty, embrace new experiences, share my dreams, create magic, love and let go, and recognize and receive the love I'm offered. I'll carry the Christmas wonder forward and share it where I can.

Wonder and good manners never go out of style.

Ask Thelma 2013
Valuing Ourselves

Dear Readers: Many gifts have been given over the past several weeks. Gifts have been exchanged and accepted and treasured. We recognize during gift giving a sense of appreciation that may escape us during the day-to-day busyness of life. I hope that the season's good feelings bring to light an appreciation for the gift of our humanity. Our humanity is a lifetime gift we should highly value because when we value ourselves, we can properly value others. When we properly value others, we treat them with dignity, courtesy and respect.

With this value of ourselves in mind, I hope we can expand our New Year's resolutions beyond January and beyond the boundaries of specific habits we'd like to change or adopt. Perhaps we can expand our New Year's goal into being good to ourselves and see where that will lead us.

Nutritious eating and exercise, always popular in January, are part of being good to ourselves and we should adopt them. But don't stop there. Our valuable selves deserve healthy relief from stress, robust relationships, and regular opportunities to decompress. These should be regular parts of our lives as we work to be good to ourselves. It's good to allow ourselves time for those things and realize that in doing so, we take an active step in recognizing our value.

When we value ourselves, we can find happiness where it presents itself, we can seek activities that keep us healthy, and we can be fully responsible for ourselves. We'll avoid feeling sorry for ourselves and when when adversity comes along, we will be able to address it.

Valuing ourselves brings with it feelings of gratitude, appreciation and responsiveness to others. When we can place value on what we bring to the room, the family, the office and the world, we can be comfortable and effective in those places. Recognizing our value doesn't mean we become self-focused, but it instead allows us the insight and ability to value others and to help them find and understand their own value.

This can be most felt in our families. Despite the lingering effects of economic disruption and emotional uncertainty about the future, we can still be certain about what we mean to our family and what family means to us. When faced with crisis or tragedy, we clearly see that those relationships are all that truly matter in our lives. Don't wait for crisis to shine a spotlight on that reality. Recognize it now and respond accordingly. Respond to the needs we see in our immediate family and in our extended family. There may be someone there who needs extra attention and love. Give it to them.

The biggest gift we can give at any time of year is what's in our hearts. It's that heart connection that can heal, that can dispel loneliness, and that can shine a light on a person's value.

When we open our eyes to the value of ourselves and the value of others, we set the stage for good relationships and proper behavior toward one another. We see the importance of respect and courtesy. We avoid selfishness and behavior that will offend. And we strive to express and honor the value we find by all that we do and think and say. When we can do this, we've honored our humanity as a lifetime gift.

Use this year to find and express that value. It's a New Year's resolution that could bring about real change. A lifetime gift and good manners never go out of style.

Dear Thelma: In my office we have always known that our supervisor does not respect or like us. Administrative Associate days are always pay-your-own way events and birthdays have never been remembered or recognized.

We are given a gift at Christmas, but we are aware that these are regifted gifts. That's fine; however, this year, at least two us were given already burned candles with no card accompanying the gift. Even the wrapping had all obviously been used. I was given mine through an associate who said, "Here. (The supervisor) said to give this to you."

So, do I recognize this gift for what it is, pretend it is something that it isn't, or totally ignore it? This person retires early in 2013. I thought of giving it back as a retirement present. What do you suppose is the right thing to do?

A: I am sorry you have been treated this way. Most reading this will find it obvious that this supervisor is failing in more ways than just the gift-giving area, but I'll keep my observations focused on the specifics of your question.

Presenting such a gift in such a way completely negates the point of gift giving. Gifts are given or exchanged as a way of sharing good feelings and appreciation. They are a way of expressing positive sentiments in a very tangible way. They express how a giver feels without using words. If a giver has a negative attitude or is completely indifferent about the gift and its receiver, that's likely to come through too.

When gifts are given solely out of obligation, the insincerity is always felt by the receiver. When as little care is taken in selecting and presenting the gift as in your situation, it is not surprising that the receiver is offended.

This supervisor would have been better off giving no gifts at all. If this person did feel obligated to do something, he or she should have presented something for the entire office to share –- a fruit basket or bagels in the break room during the holiday season – rather than individual items that were so obviously used.

So what do you do now? This may be the one instance in which I don't encourage a thank-you note. You are offended and are not thankful for the sentiment expressed by the gift or by the gift itself. I think it is best to drop the exchange at this point so that you don't do or say something rude. If the supervisor asks you about how you felt about the gift, which I highly doubt he or she will, you can simply say, "It was quite a surprise. Thank you." Leave it at that. There is no reason to return the offense.

Although I chuckled at the thought of you regifting the candles back at your supervisor's retirement, I think you better stick to a carefully selected greeting card and congratulate yourself for staying above the fray.

Avoiding offensive behavior and good manners never go out of style.

Dear Thelma: There is a woman in an organization I belong to who always finds a way to not pay her way. We have tried several ways, including invoicing her, to budge her pocketbook. Other than expelling her, what can you do with cheap people?

A: Reading into your question, it seems that this woman is paying her organization dues or she wouldn't be included in the activities of the organization. So we can assume that she believes she can afford to be a part of the group and she should understand that she is required to pay for the activities in which she participates. If she can't afford to, then she shouldn't attend those activities.

I believe a conversation is in order between the group's leadership and this member. She may have simply developed a habit of not paying and now thinks it unnecessary or she may in fact be struggling financially. Either way, she must understand that for organizations to be effective, all members must meet the basics of membership.

In a private conversation, she should be shown what she owes for her activities and told how important it is to the organization that everyone cover their own expenses. If the organization offers some kind of official assistance, it can be offered. If she refuses it or if the organization doesn't offer it, then she should be clearly told that if she continues to ignore what she owes, she will forfeit her membership and its benefits.

Dear Thelma: I recently received a house-warming gift of art from a dear friend. I hung it and although the art is quite lovely, the frame doesn't work with my new home's decor. My friend visits all the time and will notice if the work is not hanging. If I change the frame the work will fit beautifully, but I certainly don't want it to damage our friendship. What can I do?

A: While it may make for good sit-com television, you certainly don't want to be putting the painting up and then taking it down between each of your friend's visits.

Since you have described the giver of this lovely piece of art as a dear friend, it really makes the solution to your dilemma quite simple. Dear friends may not share the same taste in gift selections, but most assuredly if someone fits into the category of dear friend other similarities are more important and more valued. Dear friends communicate in an honest, sincere and very open manner. At the core of their relationship is always mutual respect.

I would see no problem in talking with your dear friend about the issue. Show her where you want to hang this treasured piece of art and talk about the frame and why you don't feel it fits with the decor. Ask her opinion and ask her to share in your selection of a new frame. Having this conversation shows you value her gift, her opinion and her friendship.

If you decide not to ask her to help you select a new frame, you definitely should tell her you plan to reframe the piece and your reasons. If you reframe it without letting her know, her initial shock at the change will be awkward for both of you.

When situations like this occur and they are discussed, they can serve to strengthen an already wonderful friendship. This is an opportunity to use your heartsense, which is most important when it comes to dear friends.

Heartfelt conversation and good manners never go out of style.

Dear Thelma: My son has been invited to the wedding of his former college roommate. I told him to ask the young couple if they have a registry for gifts and he was emailed by the future bride that the couple would prefer to have no gifts for their wedding.

My son will be flying across the country for this wedding and the young couple will be helping with a place to stay and transportation, so he really wants to give them a gift. I told him a lovely card would be OK, but that I would ask you for your opinion as to whether a monetary gift would be OK to help with his stay and transportation costs. Any ideas?

A: If a host of a wedding, birthday or any other party where gifts are customary requests no gifts, you should always honor that request. A beautiful card with a sincere note is always appropriate, but you should not feel disturbed by arriving without a wedding gift. You should feel you've acted appropriately.

Now, your son's expression of his appreciation for the couple's hospitality is a different matter. This expression can take the form of a gift, but it will be different from a wedding gift as it will be the thank-you gift often left by guests for their hosts. It will come with a thank-you note and take the form of something they can enjoy together while they think of their guest, possibly a restaurant gift certificate, a bottle of wine, or a travel book.

Dear Thelma: As a health conscious person, I've noticed that some busboys use the same cloth to wipe down several tables and chairs at some eateries. Therefore, I've been reluctant to place my utensils on a table without a tablecloth. So my question is, if the fork and knife is wrapped in a napkin on table without a tablecloth, is it appropriate to place the utensils on your bread plate?

A: The proper place for the utensils before the meal has begun is on the table. If you truly feel your table has not been sanitized properly, you should ask your waiter to send someone over to clean it. If you feel the restaurant is unsanitary, you should think twice before dining there. If you feel you must put the utensils on the bread plate, you can, but it's not the appropriate place.

Once the meal begins and your utensils leave the table, they never return. If your knife and fork are set down once you begin eating, they are placed across your dinner plate. The spoon should remain on the table until you use it for coffee or dessert. Then it is placed on the saucer or on the dessert plate. The bread plate should be reserved for the butter knife.

Dear Thelma: You were spot-on in your answer to the woman who was given a gift of original art but worried about how changing the frame might hurt the giver of the art. May I add another suggestion? She should explain to the friend about her decor and ask her to help select a new frame, but she should also offer to give the old frame back to the artist. As an artist, frames are a huge consideration and an expense. Any artist would be happy to have the old frame back.

A: Thanks for adding your observation to the conversation. I think you are right that the artist would appreciate the frame back. And if the giver of the art is the artist, the action will go a long way in continuing to solidify and strengthen their relationship.

Thinking a situation through generously and good manners never go out of style.

Dear Thelma: We've heard a lot about the perils of online relationships in the national media lately. In your opinion is building a romantic relationship over the internet a proper thing to do?

A: Technology can do much to help us establish and maintain all kinds of relationships. It's used widely in business and in people's personal lives. However, it can, as some have experienced, be used dishonestly and with intent to harm. Because of the risk we must stay aware and vigilant in protecting ourselves and our personal information when building relationships that come with such an inherent element of anonymity.

When we engage in relationships that never allow for face-to-face contact, we lose the opportunity to read into more than just the written word or a person's telephone voice. We lose the opportunity to assess body language, facial expressions and tone of voice. These things, which are important to understanding a person and how we relate to them, do not exist electronically. Given the news of the day, we have no excuse to not see a red flag when the person with whom we have relationship finds a way to avoid ever being seen in person.

With these things in mind, I would suggest that people who want to meet others online, strike up relationships only with people in their immediate area. Those who craft deceptive psychological games to inflict over the internet must use avoidance to keep these relationships going, which comes easily if great physical distance keeps you apart. It's also wise to protect your personal contact information until you've met the person multiple times and decided this is a relationship worth advancing.

True and lasting relationships can be started over the internet. A friend's sister met her online match, dated "in-person" for two years and have been happily married for five. It was a relationship that began honestly and continued to grow honestly.

Are there people out there where who want to harm and do damage? Yes. But most do not. We can use our heartsense coupled with our common sense to seek out the difference.

Dear Thelma: My family and I will be visiting the White House, the U.S. Capitol and the museums of Washington, D.C., this spring. My son wants to know if there are special manners we need to use at these special places.

A: Respect and courtesy – the manners you practice every day – should be at the top of your list any time you travel. All of the sites you mention are likely to be crowded, so be prepared to interact pleasantly with those around you. When standing in line, don't crowd those ahead of you and be prepared for what's next. Expect to face the unavoidable snags with courtesy and a positive attitude.

Your tours of the White House and U.S. Capitol will have special requirements and restrictions as to what you can bring inside. Review those carefully and take them seriously. You don't want to be turned away or have to get rid of something valuable.

We can send a message of respect for the place we're visiting with what we wear to these important places. If you're lucky enough to secure a tour of the White House's West Wing, where the president works in the Oval Office, you'll be asked to wear business or business casual attire. That generally means a collared shirt and no jeans or shorts. While it's not required, you might consider dressing this way to visit other important workplaces in the city. Do wear comfortable walking shoes even when dressed up if you'll be walking between sites. And remember, you can be comfortable without wearing your most faded jeans and threadbare t-shirt. Take pride in your appearance.

When visiting the city's many museums, follow their rules. They usually include to not touch the works of art; to not eat, drink or chew gum; and to check large bags or backpacks. Different places have different rules on photography. These rules are designed to protect the art. To protect the experience of the museum's guests, turn your cell phone ringer off. If you must take or make a call, go to a lobby area to do so quietly.

Your trip to Washington, D.C., will bring you much fun and many treasured memories. It will also be tiring. Don't be afraid to take a break if you feel yourself unable to be considerate and respectful for one more minute. A rest or a quick snack may be all you need to keep the experience exactly on the level you want it to be.

Dear Thelma: I work for a radiation oncology company and receive voice messages from physicians. Some can sometimes be very hard to understand. How can I add, "please spell your name or provide your email address" to my outgoing voice message, without being offensive?

A: If you phrase your request for comprehensive information properly, I don't believe your callers will be offended. You may say something like, "In order to best serve you, please leave me your name and its spelling, along with your email address." You needn't explain the difficulty you've had in the past understanding some people. Simply state the information you need them to leave. When you are pleasant and clear in your request, you can hope for a pleasant and clear response.

Dear Thelma: Would it be appropriate to have a social gathering in the evening and invite all your male and female co-workers but no spouses or significant others?

A: The answer to your question depends upon the purpose of the gathering. A reception or event that is clearly held for work-related reasons or for relationship-building purposes within the organization can properly serve as an employees'-only gathering.

The waters get muddier as you move away from that scenario. A party held at someone's home or planned for an exclusive venue tends to be more social and people expect to bring their social companion when socializing. Companions also expect to be included.

As the host of a party you do have control of your own guest list; however, when it comes to partying, couples usually are a packaged-deal.

Dear Thelma: My friend's husband died six months ago. Last week would have been their 60th wedding anniversary and she admonished me for not sending her an anniversary card. She said her neighbor and sister remembered it. I didn't think it was necessary to send her a card under those circumstances. What is the correct protocol? Am I supposed to send her an anniversary card every year now?

A: To send such a card to your friend would be a very thoughtful thing to do, but be assured you did nothing wrong by not sending the card. By your question, it sounds like you are in regular contact with her during this time of grieving and are doing what you can to help her through it

Everyone deals with the loss of a loved one in their own way. You are learning that your friend wishes to continue marking those special occasions she shared with her husband and hopes others will do so as well.

With that said, I feel her judgment of you was very harsh. While receiving such a card is very nice, to expect one and to be critical of those who don't send one are wrong. Although a person may be grieving, they still should do what they can to show kindness and understanding to those supporting them.

How you proceed from this point is up to you. You may wish to send those special occasion cards you know she desires, or you may decide to send her a note of encouragement or give her a call during those times you know her grief will be most intense. Use your heartsense to show that you care in your own way.

Supportive friends and good manners never go out of style.

Dear Thelma: I have to take my 22-month-old son on a two-hour airplane trip next month. I have no choice, we have to go by plane. It is not going to be easy or fun for me, and I know that other travelers will be annoyed by us. My son will not sit still. What I can do to help them know that ruining their trip is not my intent?

A: Although you know the trip will be difficult, I would advise you to shift your attitude towards those people who will be understanding, rather than those who will be annoyed. Look for the people who give you that smile that says they've been there too or who offer a game of peek-a-boo or help with a bag. Recognizing that not everyone on the plane is upset with you should help you assess the situations that arise more calmly.

Beyond that, pay attention to your child. Many people become annoyed because they feel like the parent is not doing what he or she can to make the flight bearable. Little can be done about a child's excited squeals of delight or the cries that come from pressure changes. However, there are things parents can do to keep the flight as pleasant as possible.

As a parent, be prepared to be "on." If you expect to be constantly entertaining the little guy for the duration of the flight, it won't become a stress inducer. When the activities you brought get boring, get creative. Shop the Sky Mall catalog and tear out pages he likes or take a walk up the aisle. Produce a surprise item stashed in a carry-on. A whole roll of Scotch tape to himself could keep a two-year-old entertained for a few minutes.

When your son is older, you'll want to talk with him before a trip. Explain what's going to happen and how you expect him to behave. Help him choose toys or activities to bring and pack a few surprises as well.

Those without children should pack a little heartsense along with their noise-cancelling headphones. It's important to realized that sometimes the best efforts of parents do not lead to complete control.

Dear Thelma: My boyfriend complains that I have a bad habit of cutting him off during conversations. I call it interjecting. When I hear something with which I strongly disagree my instincts are to say something about it before I completely forget. My boyfriend becomes highly agitated when I disrupt him. He accuses me of having no conversational manners at all. Please help me understand why this is not acceptable.

A: It is not acceptable because it shows no regard or respect for the person speaking. It shows that instead of truly listening and making an attempt to understand the speaker, your concern is for making your own point at the expense of your partner in conversation.

Your "interjections" show a lack of judgment. A conversation is an exchange of ideas that requires listening and polite give-and-take. When you definitively cut your boyfriend off, you reject his premise and you reject him. You kill the conversation.

For the sake of all your relationships, I would encourage you to make a real effort to curb this behavior. You claim that you must interject so that you won't forget your point of disagreement, but if it truly is a strong and valid point you shouldn't need to worry about that. In a proper conversation, your opportunity to express your view shouldn't be long in coming.

Real conversation and good manners never go out of style.

Dear Thelma: My husband and I have been married for 32 years. We have no children of our own. He has two beautiful daughters from his first marriage, both of whom I love. We have one issue with them, however. They never learned basic manners such as "Please, Thank You, and I'm Sorry." Now, they are 38 and 42 years old, married with children, leading professional lives with incomes far above ours. We are generous in our gift-giving, especially to our three granddaughters. But, as in days past, they neither acknowledge receipt of the gifts we send, nor thank us for them.

What should our attitude be? We would at least like to know that our gifts have arrived safely. We have no idea whether or not they are appreciated or ignored. Do we just assume they have received and appreciate our thoughtfully-chosen gifts? We don't want to neglect our granddaughters because of their parent's social mistakes, but their negligence is very hurtful to us.

A: I believe that some children, whether young or old, take the generosity of their parents for granted. While this doesn't excuse your adult children's poor behavior, it may explain why they would treat you in a way that they likely would never duplicate with a friend or colleague.

Every gift sent by mail should be acknowledged by the receiver for just the reason you've stated. The sender needs to know that the gift arrived safely. A phone call to the sender the day the gift is received is a start. A handwritten thank-you note should follow within a few days.

Because it sounds from your question that you have a good relationship with these children outside of their failure to show gratitude, don't let their behavior spoil the love you enjoy showing through your generosity. Since you know their tendencies, when you send a gift and haven't heard from them a week later, call them up and ask in a friendly way if they received it and like it. Although it's not ideal, there is nothing improper about doing it and it takes advantage of an opportunity to open up a line of communication. It may even strengthen your relationship.

At age 38 and 42, these women know basic manners. It's my hope that they are so comfortable and confident in your love that they feel at ease getting away with not using them.

Dear Thelma: My husband is in the military and we move regularly. I often find myself in situations where I'm meeting people for the first time. What should you do when you introduce yourself and the other person doesn't? This happens a lot and is a pet peeve of mine.

A: Don't become insulted. After you've introduced yourself and given the person a chance to reciprocate, simply ask, "What is your name?" Remember the person you're meeting may not have experienced first-time introductions as often as you and may be nervous or not know how to handle them.

Personal introductions are important. They serve the purpose of exchanging names and opening the flow of communication, which is always worth the effort. It's best to complete the introductions upon first meeting, as you may feel more awkward as more time has passed without an introduction.

And what if you forget a person's name after you've been introduced? Remain poised, smile and say, "I'm sorry, but please tell me your name again." It's also fine to reintroduce yourself upon meeting up again with someone you've recently met, "Hello, we met at the school play. I'm Ann Johnson, nice to see you again." The person should reciprocate with their own name, but if he doesn't, you may ask for it again.

When playing the name game, good manners never go out of style.

Dear Thelma: How do you politely get away from negativity in conversations? I often find myself cornered by someone who wants to wallow in economic or political despair.

A: First, realize that everybody has been a part of those conversations involving the difficult times and situations faced by citizens of our country and of the world. We may not as individuals be able to do anything those negative issues, but we don't have to allow them to taint us as negative. In our own thinking we can look at negative issues without becoming negative ourselves and express our thoughts without further darkening the skies. Others' negativity over the topics may be unavoidable, but we control our response to them.

When you feel conversations turn to the negative or linger too long there, make an effort to introduce other topics or ask questions that veer onto another subject. If you truly feel cornered, you may need to say directly, "I think we've exhausted this subject. Let's talk about your plans for the summer."

Sometimes we also find ourselves part of negative conversations that spring from shared experiences at work, at school or in our social circle. Perhaps as parents we hear a complaint about a teacher that triggers a negative conversation over that teacher. It's important in a situation like this to avoid jumping on a bashing bandwagon, which doesn't solve any problems but tends to leave a negative cloud that's not easily dispelled. If that conversation must be had, stick to the facts and focus on solutions – a parent-teacher conference or a classroom visit. When facing those kinds of conversations, it's healthy to remember the saying: "You should always credit people with the goodwill that you want to be credited with."

Dear Readers: I wanted to share with you a tremendous experience I had last month sharing a day with a group of more than 90 sixth-through twelfth-grade girls from Sandia Preparatory School in Albuquerque. Planned by Sandia Prep students with the help of faculty and staff, the "Savvy Girls Empowerment Workshop" provided a day-long series of sessions designed to help girls grow in confidence and in their leadership skills.

This group of remarkable young women fully participated in lessons and activities with my team and me ranging from communications strategies to conflict resolution to social skills. Together we discussed self-respect, interpersonal relationships and traits of leaders, and we developed strategies to build on their strengths.

The program was made possible by Sandia Prep's Girls of Achievement and Leadership Fund (the GoAL! Fund), which since 2010 has raised $30,000 to support the development of leadership skills in girls through skill-building workshops and conferences, international travel for community service and tuition assistance.

It was refreshing to see Sandia Prep and its GoAL! Fund working to prepare these young women to fit into the competitive world in which they're going to live. And it was wonderful to see these young women participate so fully and gain all the knowledge they could from the experience, building confidence in their unique qualities and ability to make a difference.

The message that Sandia Prep and the Goal! Fund have paid attention to is one I wish more organizations and people would embrace – how important it is to respond to the leadership development needs of today's kids because it's their world and they want their place in it. We should prepare them well to take it.

Proper preparation and good manners never go out of style.

Dear Readers: The month of March marks the beginning of the tenth year of *Ask Thelma*. Together we've faced the simple and the complicated. We've explored heartsense and relationships. We've worked to do our best and to become our best selves. To celebrate this milestone, we'll take time this year to regularly explore the attitudes we face every day and how the adoption of the positive among them impact us and the people around us.

Forgiveness – that's where I want to start. There are times when we make mistakes that annoy or inconvenience others, and we need to seek forgiveness for those. Beyond those, there are times we truly treat each other unjustly or unfairly. We wrong one another purposefully. We hurt and we are hurt.

The most intense of these forgiveness situations always have a background story. Deep bonds are severed and emotional paralysis is the result. There is a flood of negative emotion that affects all aspects of life. I see a kind of cycle in these situations. There is anger, judgment, lack of respect, fear and separation. That's followed by an emotional paralysis that threatens our happiness, our peace and even our functionality.

The need to seek and give forgiveness doesn't come into focus until we experience it. About 20 years ago, my best friend was upset with me to the point that our relationship was severed. We had been friends since we were six years old and were like family to one another. I had unintentionally angered her. Her son, a car salesman, had worked with me on finding a new car. I found something on my own with someone else and bought it without a word to her. My friend felt betrayed, disrespected and hurt.

I hadn't communicated that I was looking in several places for a car and by my action of buying a car elsewhere, she judged me, maybe correctly, to have treated her son – and by association, her – unfairly. It was clear that I was out of her life until I took action to bring closure to the cycle.

I had to assess what had happened and find the courage and strength to say, "I'm sorry." I had to take the first step. My seeking her forgiveness and her granting it brought us back together again in a meaningful way.

What about the physical need to forgive? Harboring resentment puts us at risk for depression and health problems. In addition, I see the isolation created by unforgiveness as one of its most powerful injuries. Unforgiveness cuts us off from the person who has hurt us, but it also can bring bitterness into our other relationships and experiences. While full reconciliation with someone who causes harm is not always a possibility or even necessarily appropriate, forgiveness allows the release of the negativity we carry when we decide not to forgive.

In my own life I've experienced this through a painful divorce. It's an example of a time when the other party would never come to the table for resolution. My process of coming to a point of forgiveness was long. I finally came to it when I recognized the value of releasing unforgiveness in order to hold on to my own peace.

For forgiveness and full reconciliation to occur, there must be true communication. The connection that occurs during real communication – speaking, really listening and opening our hearts to one another – removes the critical judgment that keeps us from forgiving. The cycle of forgiveness is often a spiritual journey, and the core of forgiveness is always the heart. If you keep it all in your mind, forgiveness will never come.

Dear Thelma: As a high school graduation present, my husband and I decided to invite our nephew, who's also our godson, on our family summer vacation to Hawaii. His parents are divorced, so we first checked with his dad, my husband's brother, to see if it would be okay to invite him. His dad then checked with his mom, who was scheduling a graduation party for him around the same time it made sense for us to go. We looked into changing our dates, but found no other time that made scheduling and financial sense. We seriously considered moving the trip, but it just didn't work. So we decided to invite our godson and asked him to check with his mom. He said he didn't think the party plans were working out anyway.

Turns out his mom was pretty deep into her planning and for a while it looked like she was not going to be able to change those plans or let him travel with us. In the end, she decided the trip was a once in a lifetime opportunity and allowed him to go.

So do I apologize to her for messing up her plans? Do I thank her for letting us provide her son with an all-expenses paid trip? The whole thing has just become awkward.

A: You can imagine the dilemma your godson's mother faced when he came to her with your offer of a trip during the time she had planned for a party. Graduation parties are important milestone markers for kids and parents. I'm sure abandoning those plans was not easy. You also know that in divorced families emotions often run high, and this could have turned out much differently than it did.

Since you realize you did cause your godson's mother inconvenience and probably some stress, acknowledging that realization to her will help to soothe hurt feelings that she might have over being put in a difficult situation.

Also, you are obviously excited to provide this tremendous gift to your godson, but you do need the permission and blessing of both his parents. The fact that they are allowing you to take him is something for which to be thankful. I think it is appropriate for you to thank them for sharing their son with you.

To his mother you might say something like, "I know the timing of the trip caused some difficulties for you, and we are sorry about that. We're so very grateful that you are allowing us to take him. Thank you."

Dear Thelma: Please tell me how to control long-winded friends when phone calls go on too long. I value this friendship of many years, but dread the excessive time drain. What would be a gentle way of ending a conversation?

A: Politeness and directness go hand-in-hand in situations like the one you describe. At the beginning of the conversation you can say, "It's great to hear from you, but I only have about 10 minutes. Let's chat until then." When 10 minutes is up: "I've got to go now. Let's talk again soon."

If you need to end a conversation, at a stopping point say: "It's been great talking to you, but I have get going. Maybe we can get together soon and talk about this more."

Above all, remember that this is your friend who you value and who values you. Treating each other and each other's time as valuable – and being polite and direct when necessary – should not be a problem.

Polite direction and good manners never go out of style.

Dear Thelma: How do I address an employee's bad breath problem? This is a person who I supervise. I have noticed it and I have heard other employees talk about it. What do I do?

A: Because this is such a personal issue, you must handle it very sensitively. It can't be ignored because ignoring it can create a situation in which the employee could become isolated, and you don't want that. Ignoring it also could bring about criticism of your performance as a supervisor.

The causes of bad breath are not limited to food choice or a lack of hygiene. A mint or frequent tooth brushing may not help chronic bad breath, which can be a sign of health issues that the employee may need to address. If tooth decay, sinus infections or digestive problems are the cause, the employee may need to work with his or her doctor to solve the problem.

As the supervisor you have the ultimate responsibility to assess and handle the situation. The best way usually is to conduct the private conversation yourself, but the employee needs to know that this view you're expressing exists within the group. Begin with: "This is a difficult thing to say, but it has been brought to my attention that you may want to consider the freshness of your breath more carefully. I don't want you to be in any way isolated because of this and so that's why I wanted to let you know."

Dear Thelma: We have friends who have several animals. Every time we have dinner at their house our clothes are covered in dog and cat hair. It even makes the food unappetizing. We don't want to lose their friendship (and we would if we criticized their animals), but what can we do?

A: Personally, I would be as bothered by the pet hair as you are, and I would stop going to their home. Since they are your friends and you have a history of socializing, you need to give them a reason for turning down invitations you once accepted. Rather than criticizing them or their animals you can make the point but turn the attention away from them by saying, "I really enjoy spending time with you, but pet hair has become a problem for me. Can we meet at a restaurant instead?"

There are different ways your friends may react to this statement.

They may stop inviting you to socialize. They may limit their invitations to events outside their home. Or they may take action against the pet hair and tell you they'd like you to consider coming to their home again. Whatever they chose to do, you've been honest and polite in hopes of maintaining the relationship.

Dear Thelma: Recently we were house guests of a couple we have known for years. He used a terrible racial slur in political conversation, in which both my husband and I immediately told him we disapproved. It has changed our opinion of them. Now, they keep inviting us to join them but we don't want to. How do you handle something like this?

A: If you were house guests, then it would seem that you were close friends. You've been honest with them once about your reaction to the slur. You haven't indicated how the conversation played out, but since your opinion of them has changed I assume that you weren't satisfied with the outcome.

You no longer wish to join them, and that's your prerogative. Since you have a long-standing relationship, the next time they ask you over, you need to tell them that you can't accept their invitation and why. Tell them how the conversation you had during your last visit affected you and that you don't feel comfortable coming over anymore.

Being honest doesn't mean you are impolite. Honesty in this case clarifies what your values are and that you want to act in concert with those values.

I don't think political conversations can be avoided at this time in history, but they are one of the most sensitive conversations that can take place. They must be handled as such by everyone involved when they arise.

Dear Thelma: If someone you dine with has food on their face, should you tell them? If so, how?

A: This question reminds me of a time I was preparing to speak to a large group. Before I was to take the stage, a man I had met that day but really didn't know said, "I have to tell you something. You have lipstick on your teeth." It may have been difficult for him to bring it up, but I was grateful that he saved me and my lipstick from being a source of distraction to everyone else.

If you notice someone with a similar problem, it's always best to tell them because everyone around is seeing the problem but them. Yet they are the only ones with the power to solve it.

Use polite sign language to indicate they need to address ketchup on their cheek or quietly tell them they've got a piece of lettuce in their teeth. Gentle honesty and good manners never go out of style.

Dear Thelma: We have good friends who consistently pull out their smart phones and use them at meals. What can you say to people like this?

A: It's not clear in your question why these good friends are using their smart phones during your meals, but whether they are making and receiving calls or checking email and Facebook, what they are doing is deliberately drawing attention away from the meal with you.

The basic key to proper use of a smart phone is that you give priority to the person or people in the room with you and to the task at hand – a meal, a meeting, a movie. Unless a person makes a conscious effort to follow this basic rule, the electronic distractions will always draw him or her away every time. We have trained ourselves to respond to the urgings of a phone ringing or the electronic blip signifying a text or email. While only a small fraction of these communications are actually urgent or even important, we are easily drawn into the feeling that they demand our attention. By deciding to give precedence to them, we alienate the people in front of us.

We've also lost our ability to wait for information. If a thought comes into our mind, triggered by a conversation or an observation, we immediately seek the opportunity to fill our need for more information. We go straight to the smart phone to start our research, abandoning the person or event that triggered the thought.

Since you call these people "good friends," you should be able to talk to them about how you feel when they choose their phones over your company. Before they take them out, say, "I feel like we can't really visit when the smart phones are out causing distraction. Can we keep them put away until after dinner?"

Or you might choose to start your visit by saying, "I'm going to keep my smart phone out of sight while we eat together tonight. I don't want to be distracted from this wonderful company." If they're paying attention, they will keep theirs tucked away too.

Your last resort may be to turn the tables. The next time one of these friends begins what looks like a long phone conversation or an

Internet search in your company, stand up and say quietly, "Excuse me, I'll be back in a while." I've done this with success. The cell phone conversation that was threatening to edge me out stopped immediately and my companion told the person on the phone that he'd call back.

Dear Thelma: I must comment on your column regarding remembering anniversaries when one of the spouses has died. A few weeks after my father died, I sent my mother a letter commenting on their upcoming anniversary and regretting that my father and her husband would not be present. She responded with a scathing letter asking how could I be so cruel to mention their anniversary when her husband was no longer alive. It would be a very sad day for her, she said. Needless to say, I never mentioned their anniversary again.

Many years later, my mother criticized me for never remembering their anniversary and told me that my sister had been very thoughtful by giving her a red rose (her favorite flower) each year on their anniversary. When I reminded her of her letter of years ago, she denied having ever sent such a letter.

A: I'm sure this hurt you when you received the original letter and again years later when your mother criticized you. It seems that your mother was hurting at those times too. Grief is handled in many ways and sometimes not well.

The past is behind. To argue with your mother now over it will not change it or improve it. Focus now on the present and future. There have been feelings of anger, judgment, lack of respect, fear and separation on both sides. By replacing those with real communication – speaking, really listening and opening your hearts to one another – you may remove the critical judgment that has caused pain and that keeps both sides from forgiving.

Ask your mother how she feels now about talking about your father. If she's open to it, share your memories of your father with her or send her a note when the opportunities arise. Just a mention that you thought about him or that you're thinking about her may help her to feel less alone in her sadness and a greater connection between you may grow.

We can't always know how someone is going to respond to our gestures in times of grief. It's important to recognize that when our words and actions come from a place of kindness and sincerity in our heart, we've done our best. If those words and actions are rejected, we can learn from the experience but must try not to be hardened by it or let our damaged pride cause us to lash out or to withdraw. This isn't always easy. You've done your best with your mother, but don't stop now.

Dear Thelma: We learned about a great way to stop the smart phone obsession at restaurants with our friends. Everyone puts their phones in a pile on the table. The first person to reach for their phone has to pay the bill. It has worked great for us!

A: I love your idea. This is obviously a group that gets together to have fun, and avoiding the distraction of your smart phones is part of that fun. You've come up with a creative way to keep your social engagements social without anyone having to be heavy handed or becoming offended.

I always appreciate the opportunity to inject humor and fun into the difficult or uncomfortable situations in which we find ourselves. When you can lighten the mood over something that can cause discomfort or offence, you make great strides in building and strengthening relationships. The point of being out with friends is to build and strengthen those relationships. Anything we can do to facilitate that only improves upon it.

Especially with friends, good manners never go out of style.

Dear Thelma: Do you have advice for grandparents whose own children want to micromanage how they treat their grandchildren? Is there a way to avoid these battles?

A: I have seen grandparents who play an active role in the lives of their grandchildren as partners with parents, and I have seen grandparents and their children battle over everything. The advice that I would give is the advice that strengthens all relationships. Make a real effort to treat one another with respect, courtesy and kindness.

Parents can lovingly set some rules and grandparents should respect them. They may be different from what you would choose, but they are important to your children. By joining with them in solidifying values and expectations for the young children, you strengthen all the relationships involved.

Parents should show respect to their own parents by allowing them to make some of their own decisions in their relationships with the children. As long as it's not a safety or health issue that could truly harm a child, grandparents should have some latitude to do things differently.

Take the time to listen to one another. If your daughter explains how the never-ending river of chocolate milk at Grandma's house leads to no one eating dinner at home, limit the kids to one glass. If the kids are destroying your new sofa, expect their parents to stand behind you when you discipline or set rules for the grandkids.

Across generations, good manners never go out of style.

Dear Thelma: I have many business relationships where my clients are quite friendly with me; however, we do not socialize outside of work. I sometimes take them to lunch. If one of these people makes the suggestion that we have lunch or meet for a drink after work, should I still pay for everything?

A: No, you shouldn't be expected to. The person who makes the invitation, even if they are the client, is considered the host and should be prepared to pay for the meal or drinks.

As a client in that situation, it's important to say something like, "I'd like to take you to lunch," or "Drinks are on me this time," to make it clear that you intend to pay. If a client says, "Let's have lunch together," that may indicate that he'd like to share the expense. No one should ever invite a person to lunch expecting that his guest will cover the bill.

If you're unsure about the intention of your client's invitation but accept it anyway, it's fine to say, "Can I help with the check?" or "Would you like to split the cost?" before the meal begins. A good host will say, "No, I'm taking care of the bill today."

If the check comes and it's clear the client expects you to pick it up, go ahead and do so, and remember that the next time that client makes an invitation. Make your decision on whether to accept based on the realization you will likely – despite the impropriety – be expected to pay.

When you know your clients well and have established strong relationships with them they will want to reciprocate the kindness you've shown to them. Accept their genuine invitations graciously and let them honor you with a lunch or a drink.

Dear Thelma: What do you do when people ask you for gift ideas for your own birthday? I feel awkward when I get asked this question because I don't know what their price range is and it just feels funny. I usually tell them they don't need to get me anything, but they still want to get me a gift. How do I answer this question without coming across as greedy or rude?

A: If a person is asking you for gift ideas, it is because she wants to celebrate with you by giving a gift. She's asking because she wants to know. You shouldn't feel rude by answering her honest question. If she can't afford to give you a gift or if she just doesn't want to give a gift, it's unlikely she'd ask what you would like.

To answer these requests considerately, create a "mental registry." In your head have some ideas in mind to offer when people ask you what you'd like. Not a greedy list of things you expect, but a range of options to offer if someone asks.

If you know a person well, you can probably give an answer that fits his price range. You may really want a professional-grade kitchen mixer, but you know that a book you've been planning to read would be a better option for him. Let him know how much you want to add that book to your library. If you don't know him well, keep your answers in a range that you consider an affordable gift.

Dear Thelma: My sister called and invited herself and her family of five to our house for a long weekend. That's five extra mouths to feed for three days – not an insignificant expense. Money is tight right now, which my sister is well aware of. If we had invited them, I would never consider asking them to bring some of the food, but since they invited themselves, is it bad manners to ask them to help out?

A: It is perfectly appropriate to have a conversation with your sister about this before she arrives. Talk about how happy you are to have the chance to see her and explain the difficulty. You shouldn't have to say more than, "Money is tight for us right now. Can you help with the food? We can plan to shop for what you're family likes when you arrive."

Clear, honest and loving communication will do the most to ensure a happy visit and continued good relations with your family. It is better to have this honest conversation than to try to hint at it once she arrives, which will put her in an awkward and confusing situation, or to just sweep it under the rug, which will ultimately upset you. Both of these options have the potential to damage your relationship. Avoid them with an honest conversation.

Anytime you are a guest in someone's home you should be thoughtful about expenses. Offer to pay for the groceries, make dinner for your hosts or treat them to a nice restaurant meal. Show your gratitude at the end of your stay with a sincere note thanking your hosts for their hospitality and a thoughtful gift. A useful household item, gift certificates or a basket of goodies will be appreciated.

Dear Readers: I recently experienced the power of corporate culture during a visit to the University of New Mexico's Sandoval Regional Medical Center for an MRI. Many times healthcare workers are so preoccupied with their work that the "care" doesn't come through. This wasn't the case here.

My visit began with an unusual greeting, "Thank you for coming to us today," rather than a standard cursory "How are you?" – a greeting I find to be too frequently used in healthcare settings by those other than the nurse or doctor. The surprising, heartfelt statement set me at ease and did much to create a real connection for me with those to whom I was trusting my care.

When my test was over, I headed for the coffee shop. Upon being served I looked for a tip jar and asked the counter worker if they had one. Her reply was: "We don't need one here. They are so good to us, and we want to be good to our customers." Even in the coffee shop, which some might view as having nothing to do with patient care, I felt cared for.

Both of these brief and simple interactions made me feel welcome and as though I were not just one of many who would pass through the doors that day. I felt assured that the people in this place really were going to take care of me and it made a difference.

Dear Thelma: What do you say when someone continues to interrupt you and others in conversation? The interruptions are always wisecracks and attempts at humor, but the interruption is maddening. By the time I have the floor again, I've lost my timing for a story and just give up.

A: From your question it sounds like this happens within a group that knows each other well and that this is a situation that happens often. I suggest you approach the person before the group gathers and say something like: "We all appreciate your humor but I hope you'll let everyone have their say tonight. I'm sure you don't intend it, but sometimes I get cut off and don't get to finish what I'm trying to say."

If you can't get to the person beforehand, when the interruptions begin offer a lighthearted comment like: "Let's make sure everyone has their turn to talk tonight."

When a group gathers its members should respect one another enough to listen to each other. Constant interruptions and diversions from the conversation don't show the respect a group of friends should show to one another.

Dear Thelma: After the column regarding gift ideas, I thought I might add to your answer. As someone who often feels uncomfortable making suggestions of gifts for my birthday but has lovely and generous friends and family members, I started suggesting the types of things I like. For instance, I enjoy reading and short story collections are always welcome. In addition, I like kitchen gadgets, anything to do with tea, and hiking. This method of suggesting while leaving the specifics up to the giver means I receive gifts that remind me of that person and that leave the dollar amount negligible. This occurred to me when my children were young and just beginning to make gift selections. Since we always started with the question "what does the person like?" it came to me that this was the question friends and family members were really asking. The outcome is that I have received interesting, useful and beautiful gifts for many years as well as peace of mind so I can enjoy the real gifts which are my friends and family.

A: Your good manners never go out of style.

Dear Readers: Many times I am told that this column is regularly saved to share with grandchildren. I love to hear that because working with young people to explore their full potential is one of the things I love most. Having a solid understanding of how to interact with people and behave in social settings brings a kind of confidence that leads to success. The earlier children and teens can develop that understanding, the more opportunity they have to make it fully a part of who they are.

So today I'd like to play the role of grandmother and write a letter directly to your teens with the hope that you'll share it.

Dear Grandchild: As you make this short passage between childhood and your adult life, I have great hope for you. Our world needs teens who will become adults with integrity, commitment, honesty and love of themselves. You will fill that need in our world by finding comfort in being you and learning to relate to people in positive ways.

It is true that in learning etiquette you learn to be well mannered

491

and successful; however, when you come to a point where you are unsure of the rules you really need only to adopt one attitude, that of respect. In any situation ask yourself, does my action show respect for others and respect for myself? Asking this will always point you to the right path.

Think about the way you communicate. It is through communication that we build and solidify relationships. Sometimes you get frustrated by the feeling that adults aren't listening to you or are unable to understand you. Don't give up when you feel you're not being heard. Think it through and find another way or another time to say it. And always go into a conversation ready to listen as much as talk.

Work to understand how to use a cell phone and its texting capabilities with respect and responsibility. Make sure that the person with whom you are face-to-face is your only priority over any phone call or message. Only compose text messages that are fit for the values expected by your family.

Think seriously about the daily decisions you now have the opportunity to make. Base those decisions on respect for yourself and those around you. When you take your role as a decision-maker seriously, you begin to learn and appreciate the value of yourself. A decision you'll make every day is how you choose to dress. You know that the way you dress communicates something about you. Avoid extremes in sloppiness or sensuality that send a negative message to the world at-large and boldly signify a lack respect for the majority of those around you.

Don't forget what you've learned about safety. Safety means protecting yourself from physical and emotional danger, which includes the dangers of alcohol and drug use and harmful sexual relationships. Taking the steps to independence means taking the responsibility to remember what you've spent your childhood learning and protecting yourself from danger.

Finally, become a leader. It's important to realize that possessing leadership qualities doesn't necessarily mean that you want to be the captain of the soccer team or student council president. It may mean volunteering to take on a task when someone else backs out or leading yourself into the right decision when those around you have chosen poorly.

We all have qualities it takes to be a leader. Sometimes the best leaders are those who never ask anyone to follow them. In simply doing their very best, others want to follow them or they are asked to lead. Leaders work hard and inspire others to work hard with them.

Be happy, grandchild, and know that the inspiration you ignite and your good manners never go out of style.

Dear Thelma: A friend from another state called to say she and her husband are coming here to visit her father-in-law. I said we should make plans to meet for dinner. She explained how her father-in-law was "being a little weird" about them staying with him. I'm sure she was hoping for an invitation from me. I didn't offer one. Later she sent me a text asking directly if they could stay with us.

I really don't want them too. They are coming over a holiday weekend, during which we already have other plans. Secondly, they aren't good guests. The last time they came out and stayed with us we planned dinner for the two of them and after visiting their family they showed up back at our house with the father-in-law, his wife and four other people to join in the meal. And finally, we just aren't as close as we once were. I don't want to host them.

I feel obligated because she has invited us to stay with her in the past and we've taken her up on it. So I guess we owe her.

I'm not a mean spirited person. I would be perfectly happy to meet them for a meal to catch up on each other's lives, I just don't want them as houseguests. How do I refuse them without hurting their feelings?

A: Understand that you aren't obligated to host them and you aren't obligated to give a detailed explanation as to why you are declining to host them. To be invited to stay with someone, in which the control is the hands of the host, is different than asking to be a houseguest. Although you feel the pull of that past invitation extended to you, you aren't obligated to it.

Talk to your friend rather than sending a text. Say to her, "We can't host you on this visit. I'm sorry if that impacts your plans, but it's just not something we can do right now. We would enjoy meeting you for dinner while you're here. Can we make plans to do that?"

You know your friend and you can probably guess how she will respond. There's no guarantee that her feelings won't be hurt. She may see your refusal as a rejection and that is something you may have to risk.

Dear Thelma: I am planning a tea for a group of about eight friends and I think I made a mistake. I asked all of them to give me dates when they were and weren't available. Now there is not a single date available for the entire summer that doesn't conflict with one of their schedules. I am going to have to explain to one person that their conflicting date is the one I must schedule the tea for. How do I do that without making them feel like they don't matter to me?

A: These are close enough friends that you are planning a special event for them. They should also be close enough to be honest with and to count on to understand your dilemma.

Talk to this friend in person. Explain that you've decided to plan the tea on the date you have chosen for the event. You don't have to give details on the ratio of guests that could attend on one date versus another. Just say that's the day you have chosen. Express your disappointment in not being able to accommodate her schedule. Then invite her to join you for lunch or to get together for coffee on another day. At the end of the conversation, your friendship should be intact and your friend should still feel honored by you.

Polite refusals and good manners never go out of style.

Dear Readers: If you are regular reader of this column, you remember the story of my experience six years ago in a Dallas airport with our troops returning home from conflict in Iraq. As I was changing concourses, a voice over the public address system announced: "Attention. The airport manager would like to speak to you. In just a few minutes a group of our troops returning from Iraq is going to deplane. If you look up, you'll see a glass wall. That is the walkway you'll see them going through. Please join us in welcoming our soldiers back home."

As I looked up the doors opened and for the next 25 minutes these men and women moved through that walkway above us and for 25 minutes the applause never diminished. We couldn't hear each other, but the energy of connection was there. They threw back hugs and kisses and we waved and cheered. We could feel them and they could feel us.

It was the most profound, grateful, heartfelt, absolutely spontaneous reaction I've ever experienced. It gave me an incredible sensation as a cross-section of America sitting in this airport stood in unison to applaud our troops. In the entire concourse, no one was sitting and the applause never stopped or even faltered.

Then, after the last soldier went by, there was absolute silence.

Finally, the person next to me spoke: "Wouldn't it be wonderful if this were all of them."

The women and men who came home that day six years ago are today's veterans, and more return everyday. We know what they have done for us. Now is our time to see what we can do for them.

A friend and her husband, a Vietnam veteran, have taken this task to heart and view doing what they can for veterans as their job. Introduced to the modern challenges of today's veterans through a program for student veterans at the University of New Mexico, they have learned that most programs designed for vets help only a portion of them. My friends are especially concerned with bridging the gap between the GI Bill's 48 months of college financial aid and the actual time it takes vets to earn a degree while working full-time. The plight of women vets who return to civilian life as single parents with few resources is another of their concerns.

After committing their own resources, they began to ask friends for donations of computers, office supplies, gift certificates and business clothes. They also began matching veterans' groups with experts. A career counselor now helps vets turn military experience into workforce skills on their resumes. A bookkeeper donates her time to help women vets with accounting and taxes.

"We are thrilled to begin making a small difference," my friend says.

I believe concern for our veterans is in everyone's hearts today. Now is the time to turn that emotion and heartfelt thanks into a meaningful and personal response to the vets who come into our lives, our families, our businesses and our communities. We will all have the opportunity now and in the years to come to help veterans re-enter civilian society and it should be a focus of our attention. They fit in our homes, families and communities as important members and we need to let them know that.

Independence Day is a good time to examine the sacrifices made to win our nation's freedom and recognize the contributions and the needs of our country's military veterans. Many, like my friend, are already helping to honor and assist the men and women who have served, but there are many more we can reach.

Considering how you can help and good manners never go out of style.

Dear Thelma: Recently, during a doctor's visit, I was led into the exam room by the technician prior to the doctor coming in. In the small room, I was immediately taken aback by how much the technician reeked of cigarettes, which only worsened when she came closer to take vital signs. I felt assaulted by the smell and wanted to say something but didn't want to be too rude or judgmental. I thought I might say something to the doctor when he came in, but he arrived with another technician. How should I have handled this? Should I have said something to the doctor in private or ignored it, thinking I'm not going to change the technician's behavior anyway?

A: Your concern doesn't have to be with changing the technician's behavior, but instead improving the experience of patients coming into the office.

If I had been in your situation I would have looked for a way to speak about it with the doctor, either then or at a later time. I would share with him that when visiting a health provider's office, I have the expectation that I will encounter healthy habits and be encouraged to adopt them. I would tell him that the very strong smell of cigarette smoke on the technician who took my vitals disturbed me and I thought he should know.

You don't have to be irate or upset or demand that changes be made. Just let the doctor know what you experienced and how it affected you. It's his or her responsibility to take your input and use it to improve the practice.

Although cigarette smoke always lingers with someone who smokes, the technician who helped you can take steps to avoid reeking of cigarettes as you describe. As a member of the healthcare profession, she should make an effort to do so for the comfort and care of her patients.

Dear Thelma: I was to attend a dinner event with a friend. The night before I was very sick and could not attend. The friend took her sister but wants me to reimburse her for the $50 ticket. If she had not found a replacement, I could understand. Her sister enjoyed a nice dinner and the event. Is it reasonable to ask me to pay her back?

A: That depends on the agreement you had with your friend from the beginning and if the ticket was already purchased. If you had agreed to attend and to pay for your own ticket for the event and the friend just happened to pick up the ticket for you with the intention that you would be paying her back, then you should pay her back whether or not someone else used the ticket. In this situation the cost of the event was your responsibility.

In this case, you and your friend should have had a conversation about the ticket when you told her you could not attend. She should have given you first opportunity to find someone to give or sell the ticket to.

If your friend invited you as her guest, then she should have been prepared to pay for the cost of two tickets for the event. You not attending would not have changed what she was planning to pay and your friend should not ask you to reimburse her. If tickets were bought at the door, then the cost of her guest is not your responsibility.

Finally, put your friendship before the money issue and your heart will tell you the right thing to do.

True friendship and good manners never go out of style.

Dear Thelma: I am planning a rehearsal dinner in the banquet room at a hotel. There is a $300 room charge and a 20 percent service fee for the event. Is it also customary to tip and if so, what amount?

A: It is important that you have a conversation about the service fee with the venue's representative who is helping you plan your event. Ask specifically why the service fee is charged and what it covers. Typically, a charge labeled "service fee" does not necessarily go to the staff members who served you, while a charge labeled "gratuity" may.

If a gratuity is not included on your bill, it is customary to tip all the staff members who served at your event including the catering manager, waiters, bartenders and chefs. You can calculate 15 to 20 percent of the bill and give that to the manager in advance or at the end of the event to distribute to the serving and kitchen staff or you can offer a flat amount to each staff member in separate envelopes given to the manager. The amount you tip is up to you, but you should include that figure in your budget. If you feel you are going to be too busy during the event to get the tips to the right person, assign the task to a trusted family member or friend.

Take the time to understand what you're paying for, who is involved in making your event a success and the best way to get tips to them. A conversation with the venue manager going over the contract with you and helping you plan the event will help you determine these things with confidence.

Knowing where your money's going and good manners never go out of style.

Dear Thelma: For decades I've had season tickets to the NM Philharmonic at Popejoy and at the National Hispanic Cultural Center and to Simms and Placitas concerts. Now I am on oxygen full-time and the thought of a life without live music makes me sad. Do these venues make any provisions for the small puffing oxygen tanks that annoy other people? I admit to being very upset when a fellow on oxygen sat behind me at Simms, so I don't win a prize for compassion either. Maybe this is payback!

A: Rather than payback, I see that it has made you sensitive to both sides of the situation. You understand now that to deny the man whose oxygen annoyed you the experience of the concert would have been more damaging than you adjusting yourself to the puffs of his machine.

I encourage you to continue to embrace the things in life that bring you joy. Oxygen tanks are ordinary things that we all see and hear these days and most people have respect for those who use them.

You certainly can ask the venues you visit if they have seating options for people who use oxygen. They are aware of the issue and will have seats or suggestions for you. Otherwise, for your own comfort concerning the noise issue, choose your seats considerately. Try to seat yourself or get tickets that are on the end of a row where fewer people will be impacted by the sound, people can move past you easily and you can leave the row easily if necessary. Consider also whether being extremely close to the stage could cause the sound to be a distraction to the musicians.

People who find themselves annoyed by the sound of an oxygen tank have the options of asking the venue to reseat them or to provided them with an assisted listening device headset to block the noise.

The venues we visit want all of their patrons to enjoy their experiences and will do their best to give us every opportunity to do so. As patrons we must do our best to treat each other with consideration and respect and enjoy the music together.

Dear Thelma: Has something changed in how one addresses a letter to an individual? I continue to receive both business and personal letters at home and at the office addressed to "Linda Friedman" rather than using the salutation Dr. Linda E. Friedman. I find this very offensive. Am I just being an old fashioned "ninny" or is this the lack-of-respect du jour those of us over 60 have the pleasure of enduring?

A: I don't think a lack of respect is intended. Titles and their uses have changed dramatically over the past 60 years. At one point during that time, a married woman would only be addressed as Mrs. John Smith, which most women would be offended by today. Those 60 years saw the beginning of widespread use of the title "Ms.", an honorific that didn't tie the person to her marital status. With most correspondence today falling into the more informal realms of electronic communication, we've come to a time when the use of titles in addresses is simply not as vital as it once was.

While it will always be proper and even advisable to use titles in correspondence, it is important to realize the use or non-use of these conventions reflect the norm in society and not the level of respect the sender has for you. Avoid looking at how a letter is addressed as an act of disrespect and instead make your assessment based on what's inside. If you can get over the address, you may enjoy the fact that they wrote you a letter.

This said, I do believe a salutation in a piece of correspondence should coincide with the level of formal or informal connection the correspondents have with each other. The correspondence I would have with you should open with "Dear Dr. Friedman." I've identified myself to you as Thelma and invited you to "Ask Thelma." Greeting me with "Dear Thelma" is just fine.

Dear Thelma: Our son will return to school this month as a sophomore in high school. Last year he began a friendship with a boy who turned out to have opposing moral and political views as my son and our family. This boy is very vocal and confrontational about his views. He upsets my son when he goes on his rants, but my son has never countered him.

Last year was tough for my son. He was in a new school in a new city. He was happy to have any friend. Now he would like to get out of this friendship, but he doesn't know how. He's not interested in hurting anyone's feelings and he has found value in this friendship, but he feels trapped. Can he leave this friendship gracefully?

A: It is wonderful that your son has brought this situation to you, his parents who know him better than anyone else and can help him navigate the waters surrounding this relationship. It will be important for you to have a heart-to-heart conversation with him so that with your guidance he can figure out what he will do.

I see you discussing two options which may or may not end the friendship, but that will set your son on the solid ground he desires. First your son has to decide how he is comfortable standing his ground. Is he willing to take on this friend with respectful counterpoints of his own, and can he keep emotion out of it so that arguments don't turn to fights? This is difficult even for adults, but it something you and your son can consider together.

If he would rather avoid that kind of confrontation, he does need to be willing to respectfully say to his friend, "I don't agree with what you're saying. I'm not willing to argue with you, but I'm also not going to provide you with an audience." At that point he must get up and walk away.

Have this conversation or series of conversations with your son before school begins and have him prepare for how he will respond to the friend's very first confrontational display of the new year and for any that follow. Through your discussions it's likely you will develop other tactics together for dealing with the situation. Since it's your son who has to carry it out, it will be important that he decide the option he'll follow. No option will be easy, but thinking about it, having a plan and carrying it through will give your son a confidence that is being sapped by the current state of the friendship.

While the friendship can continue, your son's new approach will change it. The friend will have two options. He can decide to control what he has to say in order to sustain and maintain the friendship. He also can decide that voicing his own opinions to a receptive audience is more important than the friendship. From either situation, the friendship or lack thereof will develop naturally. And in either instance your son removes himself from the upsetting aspects of the friendship and can move forward knowing that he has dealt with the situation respectfully and maintained his own integrity.

This is an essential family conversation. It is important for parents to take the responsibility to help children understand how to work through a difficult relationship and feel strongly they've done the right thing for the right reason.

Can he leave this friendship gracefully? Yes, he can, and in doing so he can develop valuable skills he will use throughout his life; while you, as parents, have the tremendous opportunity to strengthen your connection as a family.

Dear Thelma: What do you do when friends you regularly go out to dinner with and split the bill with begin ordering expensive alcoholic drinks? They don't make any effort to pay for their own alcohol but instead expect my wife and I to pay for half of what they have drunk. What do we do?

A: Everyone who goes out with friends with the intention of splitting the bill should stay aware of how their orders match up with their companions. Use your heartsense – that common sense of the heart that steers you right from wrong. Of course no one wants to get stuck with more than their fair share of the bill. If you ordered prime rib and your friend ordered a salad, don't fool yourself into thinking that he'll find it acceptable to simply split the bill down the middle. If you drank a bottle of Champagne and your friend had water with lemon, no, she doesn't want to pay for half of your bubbly.

If your expenses total greatly over half of the bill, then you – the person who ordered the most – should contribute more than half to cover the added cost or ask the waiter for separate checks. Don't expect the friend who's been finagled to voice a concern as he's in a socially excruciating position. You yourself must realize that it's a concern and take care of it. That is the courteous thing to do.

If you are stuck in a pattern of paying more than your fair share with no end in sight, you must start a conversation with your friends that will resolve the issue so that you do remain friends. Before your next dinner out, say to your friends, "We need to discuss how to handle the expenses for our evening out. Beth and I aren't planning to order more than one drink each, so I thought we'd ask the waiter before the meal to give us separate checks. Is that fine with you?"

Your dinner companions should have no reason to disagree and asking for separate checks will be more simple than trying to sort out the bill after it comes.

Once you've had this one-time conversation, you can simply ask the waiter for separate checks before every meal. It should become your new pattern and may go a long way to enhancing and extending your friendship. Remember this the next time you start going to dinner with new friends and set the stage for separate checks from the beginning.

Fairness, friendship and good manners never go out of style.

Dear Thelma: Listen to my story and tell me if this is proper behavior for a grocery store line. I was in line behind one other customer. She was eating a muffin and drinking coffee while trying to unload groceries from her cart to the conveyor belt. I'm surprised she wasn't also on her cell phone.

Her cart was full of loose fruit, which she hadn't gone to the trouble to bag or separate as she put it onto the belt. The clerk was forced to sort a jumble of oranges, lemons and potatoes. Then she learned that if she had selected six bottles of wine instead of four, she would get a discount. She sent an employee to the back of the store for two more bottles. All the while holding up the line.

When it was time to pay, she wanted to put the bill on two different credit cards, but she could only find one of them. She went to her car to get the other while I waited in line behind her for a total of 28 minutes. Seriously? Shouldn't she have more respect for the rest of us or does the world truly revolve around her?

A: Most of us have had those times in the grocery store when we've forgotten something or left our wallet in the car, and some of us are slower or faster than others, but some of the poor behavior you describe sounds regular and practiced. Having a full basket and several coupons to use is one thing. A complete lack of concern for everyone around you is another.

Those in line at the grocery store should devote their attention to the task at hand as a courtesy to the clerk and other customers. Put the cell phone away and secure your drinks or snacks so that you can unload your cart efficiently. If you don't like the idea of taking home more plastic bags, group your fruit and vegetables on the conveyor belt so that each group can be weighed at once.

Slowdowns at the grocery store can't always be avoided, but as a courtesy to our fellow shoppers we should work to keep those to a minimum. We should be prepared for the tasks involved in buying our groceries and do our best to remember all our items and our wallets. We should do it because we are considerate in every situation and everywhere we go.

Dear Thelma: The recent column about the woman stuck in line behind the inconsiderate shopper reminded me of an experience I had. My parents were flying in for my daughter's wedding and were going to call me from the airport when they arrived. I realized I was missing one ingredient for our family dinner and thought I would have enough time for a quick trip to the store. I ran in a grabbed my single item and headed to the express line.

Only one elderly gentleman was ahead of me so I thought I'd be

OK. I soon realized that this man was a favorite of the cashier as she slowly scanned his items and chatted with him. I thought of my parents' confusion if they called me and got no answer. They hated travel and had already had to deal with a missed connection. When the cashier asked if he'd found everything he needed he told her he was looking for some spray to clean his shower head but couldn't remember what it was called. She said she knew what it was and left the register to go get it for him.

I fought to control my irritation as the gentleman turned to me and apologized for the delay. I smiled and told him I was in no hurry and thought it was nice of the cashier to go out of her way to help. He got tears in his eyes as he told me what a hard time he'd been having since his wife died a month ago. He was having a hard time learning to do things his wife had always taken care of. He said that only the kindness of people he met was keeping him going. My irritation was gone as I realized how lucky my family was and I was truly grateful that good manners had overridden my impulse to show my impatience.

A: I love your story. It illustrates that our kindness is always warranted, even when we are busy, late or annoyed. We really don't know what the stranger in front of us is going through, but maybe if we assume it is as hard or harder than what we're facing, we can temper our own emotions.

Approaching every situation with good manners doesn't mean you have to get stepped on or walked over. Instead it means remaining in control ourselves and choosing the kindest response.

Dear Thelma: We live in an old neighborhood with mature landscaping. Our neighbors are lovely people who seem oblivious to either the condition of their yards or to amount of work that we have to do as fallout from their inattention. This includes their trees dropping seeds en mass, or branches left from wind storms, weeds migrating from their yards to ours, and even total lack of landscaping which affects our property values. Please weigh in on this.

A: Everyone should take care of their own space, but you can't force your neighbors into yard work. What you can do is talk with these lovely people you describe. If their tree branch falls into your yard during a storm, go to them and ask if they will help you remove it. If you feel close enough to them, meet over coffee or over the fence to discuss your concerns.

If you feel the properties around you violate city codes for weeds or litter and don't feel you can talk with your neighbors about it, you can file a complaint with the city. The zoning department will notify them of the problem that needs to be fixed.

Dear Readers: In our tenth year of *Ask Thelma*, we're taking the time to explore core attitudes and behaviors we face every day and how the adoption of the positive among them impact us and the people around us.

Today my focus is leadership. I've had the opportunity to be mentored by and to work with exemplary leaders. The best of them have quietly inspired greatness in those around them. They have impressed me so deeply that I've asked myself, "How do they do it?"

I believe that they look at leadership as a form of service. They intuitively identify a set of responsibilities clearly tied to drawing success out of their team through their support regardless of the issue that sits before them.

They see a responsibility to create a particular kind of environment where everyone involved is part of the process and responsible for the success of the endeavor. They create that environment through the questions they ask, the resources they provide, the praise they offer, the creativity they encourage and the leadership they expect from others.

The best leaders know the mission of their organization and they make a commitment to it. They have the ability to clearly convey that mission and that commitment to those working with and for them. Through their work others understand the mission and the mission is strengthened.

These leaders see as a separate responsibility the need to make a difference in the lives of the people they work with. They find their own success in helping individuals explore their own potential and stretch beyond it. They trust people to be as valuable as they can be to the organization, and they give credit where the accomplishment takes place.

In the end, these leaders create an environment in which everyone involved feels the outcome was their accomplishment.

I clearly experienced the impact an altered form of leadership could have when I worked for the U.S. Department of Health, Education and Welfare in Washington, D.C. At that time Native American tribal leaders from across the country met twice a year in Washington to hear the department's ideas and plans for assisting them.

I was the newest associate executive secretary attending these meetings, but I left them with the feeling that these meetings lacked the give-and-take that would make them more effective. Through my own experience of visiting New Mexico's pueblos with my father and his wholesale grocery business, I knew that a better dialog could take place. I believed that we were telling them what was best for them, rather than listening to their needs.

I wrote a proposal asking if we could take the meetings to the tribes to find out what they needed and what they felt was best for them. My idea was embraced and I was allowed to take a management team across the country to meet with the leadership of each tribe. We found their priorities to be very different from those in Washington, and we found that as we began to listen as a department, they began to feel valued and trusted, and they began to initiate programs of their own. They also found that through their experience, they could help each other with shared issues and challenges. We found as a department that by our listening to them and trusting them, their decision-making ability grew stronger.

Leadership is at work every day in every corner of the workplace and the home. We are called as colleagues, assistants, instructors, parents and volunteers to show leadership in every task before us. How we approach it can inspire greatness.

Strong leaders and good manners never go out of style.

Dear Thelma: One of my husband's close friends is dating a married woman. My husband has told me about this relationship and his conversations with his friend mostly because he's scandalized by it and needs to get it off his chest. He has told his friend that what he's doing is wrong and stupid, but the friend "loves her."

My dilemma is that this friend, who we sometimes spend time with together, doesn't know that my husband has told me. I feel like whacking him upside the head when I know he's lying to me about where he's been and who he's dating. Do I let the charade continue?

A: At this point, I think you do. Your husband has come to you in confidence as his closest friend. The need to honor that relationship is more important than you expressing your opinion on the friend's questionable relationship. When the friend brings up his fictional dating life, don't engage him and steer the conversation elsewhere. If the friend opens the door to a discussion with you about the truth, then you're free to share your thoughts in a respectful way.

The other important thing to do is to talk to your husband about it. Find out how you revealing what you know will affect him, as your top concern should be the relationship between the two of you and doing all you can to honor that. Even if he says it doesn't matter or he doesn't care, you still might think twice about the effect it may have. If this is a friendship that is important to your husband, you don't want to be the cause of its end.

Dear Thelma: I must strongly disagree with your statement in a past column that a married woman may be properly addressed as "Mrs. Daniel Jones" and the like. It is not OK, under any circumstances, to address me as "Mrs. Ronald Gordon." Ever. On the rare occasions that it happens, it positively makes my blood boil and my stomach churn. I am not my husband! I believe many women feel this way, and in fact I've read that this is the prevailing view.

I'm 53 years old and have held this point of view since getting married 32 years ago. My husband agrees. My mother, who never married, thinks it's unimportant. I expect that if my daughter were to get married, and someone addressed her by her husband's name (if she ever took his name at all), she'd feel like punching their lights out. Which would be a breach of etiquette.

A: Having your own preference for what you'd like to be called is fine. Your blood need not boil. You can simply smile and say, "I prefer to be called Susan." When you receive a formal invitation traditionally addressed to "Mr. and Mrs. Ronald Gordon," I hope that you can find it in your heart to attend, while noting your full, preferred name on the RSVP card.

Since this has stimulated you to write to me and take the time to voice your opinion, I hope that you also will also take the time think more deeply about your reaction to attempts to address you with a traditional courtesy title. It's likely that those addressing you are doing their best to be gracious and do not mean to offend or demean you in any way. Leave judgment behind and approach the person who's addressed you with an open and happy heart. Thoughts of punching anyone's lights out should not even cross your mind.

Less prejudgment and good manners never go out of style.

Dear Thelma: I have a close friend whose brother recently passed away. She was keeping those of us who are close to her up to date on his condition via email and I wasn't surprised that she let us know of his passing through email. She also posted a message about his passing on her Facebook page. I don't have a problem with this. I think it is the easiest way to share the news with people you might not be in close contact with but who would still appreciate knowing. I do think a call is most appropriate to those closest to the person who has passed away.

My question revolves around the appropriate way to respond to the person who is grieving. Many people informed by email hit "reply all" and sent their condolences to the entire list of people who received the initial email. People also responded publicly to her Facebook post with lengthy posts of their own. I didn't feel that these were personal enough to give proper honor to the situation. What do you think?

A: In the situations you describe, I think we have to be careful to make sure that our expressions of sympathy and support put total focus on the grieving person. Whatever we do or say to express our condolences should center on our grieving friend and that should guide us.

In the case of email, I don't feel it is appropriate to publish sentiments of sympathy to an audience. There is no need for the members of the email group to know what an individual has personally said to express his or her sadness and support. That draws the attention to the writer rather than the person grieving.

Facebook may be handled in some ways differently. If the person has posted their loss on Facebook, they should be open to receiving Facebook responses. A short post acknowledging the person's loss and expressing sympathy in this space designed for public sharing may be appropriate, but I feel the most personal of sentiments should be made directly to the person through a private message. That direct contact is important at times of grief.

When a friend of mine lost her mother, she found that the public side of Facebook did become a source of comfort for her and her family as they dealt with their loss and received support from their extended circle of family and friends connected through the social networking website. The computer application allowed family and friends to share beautiful memories that might not have surfaced without the forum.

She reasoned that if she were sharing the sad news with her friends via computer connection, then it was fine for those friends to offer their support through the same connection. She received messages from long-time and far-away friends who may not have even heard the news if not through Facebook. During this hard time, technology became as warm and personal as its users made it.

In these days in which many expect everything to be public and instant, the value of one-on-one sentiment mustn't be forgotten. The warmth and sincerity of thoughts expressed directly to a person become more and more treasured as those direct expressions become fewer and farther between.

Computer messages are a fast and convenient way to express sympathy, but they don't delete the need for direct contact. When someone suffers a great loss, friends and family should do all they can and be as physically present for that person as possible. Cards, calls, visits and the presence of family and friends at the funeral service are still of vital importance.

Support in difficult times and good manners never go out of style.

Dear Thelma: As the restaurant hostess is leading a couple to their table, does the man precede or follow his lady friend?

A: Traditionally, the woman follows the hostess and the man follows his companion. The same holds true for a group, the women following the hostess together and the men following after them. This is a tradition that many people follow, and knowing it does make it easier to take a place line with ease and get to your table.

However, it also falls into the category of contemporary rules of courtesy that really have become non-gender specific. It would be just fine for a woman, who may be hosting a business lunch or who may have asked the man out for the date, to say, "After you" and offer the front of the line to the man.

Courtesies that may have been gender-based in the past are now inclusive. Any person should stand and extend his or her hand during any introduction or greeting. Whoever is the first to the door should hold it open for others. Any able person should offer to carry a package for anyone who needs help. The person at the front of the elevator exits first. A professional stands for a visitor to his or her office and remains standing until the visitor is seated. The person who invites another to dinner picks up the tab.

When the focus on gender ended, the importance of civility and consideration for each other expanded. We each have a responsibility to treat others with consideration and to help whoever is in need, whether we are a man or a woman. This new spin on the old rules doesn't negate the need for men and women to be gracious to each other. A man should not be afraid to hold a door for a woman and a woman should not be offended by his gesture. Being graceful means knowing how to offer common courtesies meant to show care for the other person's comfort or safety and how to accept those courtesies graciously. Anyone who offers a kindness or respectful action, should be greeted with a gracious thank you.

Dear Thelma: I can't find the answer to this one anywhere! Suppose a woman has remarried and her name has gone through changes. For example, a woman with the maiden name Paige Rita Calhoun married and changed her name to Paige Rita Calhoun Douglas. A second marriage then created the name Paige Rita Calhoun Douglas Anderson. If she wants to monogram something with three initials, presuming she uses her first initial "P" on the left, and her current married name initial "A" in the center, which letter would she use on the right?

A: Monograms are seeing a resurgence in popularity, so I'm sure there are others facing your question. However, I don't believe that there is a strict answer to it. I think that Paige can use whichever initial she is most attached to on the right side of her monogram. If she wants to use her first married name "Douglas," she can, but she might want to discuss with her current husband her reasons for that so that he's not hurt by it. Her maiden name and her middle name give a nod to the family that named her, and will each work just fine in her monogram. If she really wants to make it easy, she can just go with the two initial monogram. Whatever she does, she should choose what represents her best.

A monogram to be proud of and good manners never go out of style.

Dear Thelma: My next door neighbor lives alone, has no family nearby and has health issues that keep him from doing a lot of yard work. My son mows my lawn once a week and has no problem crossing over to the neighbor's small yard and keeping it mowed and trimmed. He wants to pay him for it and that's fine. However, for the past month, I have been mowing his lawn as my son has been busy on the weekends with football and school.

My neighbor called tonight to come by and pay my son. I told him I had been mowing and that he didn't need to pay, but he said he still wanted to pay. I didn't want to take his money, but he insisted. What's the proper thing to do here?

A: By paying your son for his work, your neighbor is able to manage his own landscaping affairs and not rely strictly on your kindness. It probably pleases him to give your son an opportunity to do some work and earn some money. It's also probably cheaper than hiring a landscaping company to maintain his yard.

Accept his payment to keep him from feeling like he's indebted to you for your kindness. Going forward, make sure your son gets the work done. Talk with him about his responsibility and how he can manage his time to fulfill it. If your son really can't fit it into his schedule, he needs to tell the neighbor and give him a chance to find another neighborhood kid he can employ.

Dear Thelma: My seventh grade daughter recently began attending a new school. It's a very small school where most of the kids have attended since kindergarten. She has fit in just fine. I, on the other hand, did not make a real effort to meet the parents of her classmates at the beginning of the year. We're often in a group as all the girls in the class play on a volleyball team together, but I feel I've let too much time pass to introduce myself. Can I fix this?

A: It's great that you're often in a group because that makes fixing it easy. The next time you're waiting for a game to start, sit next to a parent or group of parents and say hello. You can add, "I'm sorry to just be getting around to introducing myself, but I really wanted to meet the families of my daughter's new friends." The best way to get a conversation started is by asking questions and these parents should have a lot of information to share.

Dear Thelma: My boyfriend recently needed $500 from me to change some travel plans that included both of us. He said we could split the cost of the change, but he needed to borrow his half from me. He assured me he could pay me back his $250 share over time. I agreed and paid for the change. I have seen no attempt from him to pay me back or even mention the loan in four months. In that time, he has also "borrowed" smaller amounts of money from me that are quickly adding up.

I love him and we've even talked about marriage, but he shows a lack of responsibility and respect for me that I don't know if I can put up with long-term. I don't want to be the nagging girlfriend always whining about how he does or doesn't spend his money, but I'm pretty sure he's never going to pay me back. Is there a good way to fix any of this or avoid a fight?

A: You must have a discussion about the loan and the money he owes you. Tell him that it is important to you that he pay you back and ask him how and when he plans to start. Talk about how his not paying you back makes you feel.

Beyond that, I think you identified the heart of the issue when you said that borrowing money from you shows a lack of responsibility and respect. You know in your heart what the problem is here. It's not that he doesn't understand what a loan is and how it should be handled. It's that in you he has found a source of funds. He may not be malicious about it, but he is using it to his advantage.

Here's what you know: He's willing to borrow money on a regular basis that he does not pay back. Also he does not have the income or the budgeting savvy to ensure that he meets his own expenses or he spends beyond his means. If your relationship with him continues, these are the habits and attitudes he brings with him.

If you are serious about marriage, it's important that you have a frank discussion about your attitudes about money. Set aside your worry of offending him and ask him why he must borrow from you so often. It is important to find out if your views of money are compatible. If they are not compatible, you may have to consider finding a polite way to end the relationship as this issue will impact your entire life.

Dear Thelma: I live in a neighborhood where the school bus stops every few houses and at each stop parents feel the need to either talk with the driver or hand them a cup of coffee. Sometimes it's even several parents conversing with the driver and continually holding up traffic with the bus's stop sign out and red lights flashing.

If bus drivers must personally converse with parents after children are boarded and seated, shouldn't they should pull to the side and stop holding up traffic for those of us who need to get to our jobs?

A: The bus driver's protocol for picking up children is a matter of safety, and I don't know if pulling to the side is an option. But I agree that these parents are acting impolitely if it is their morning routine to delay the bus and the traffic behind it with conversation. A wave and a hello as the children board should be sufficient courtesy to the bus driver. Detailed conversation with the driver should be reserved for emergencies or scheduled for another time.

Even at the bus stop, good manners never go out of style.

Dear Thelma: Is there such a thing as Craigslist etiquette? I posted a Craigslist ad on a Monday, listing several household items that I wanted to give away for free. The ad stated that people could come pick them up the following Friday from noon to 2:00 pm on a first-come first-served basis. That was the most convenient time for me. I received over 40 replies, mainly from people asking for more detail about the items and others stating they would be there on Friday to take a look.

One reply was from a person who said he had a truck, and could take all the items off my hands on Tuesday, so I wouldn't have to deal with multiple people coming into my home on Friday. I agreed, he came on Tuesday and picked up all of the items.

Out of courtesy, I sent an email to the other 40+ people on Tuesday evening telling them that the items had already been taken by an early responder and that I would no longer be having an "open-house" on Friday.

Many of those people told me I was rude for advertising a Friday pick-up date and then letting someone else pick the items up before Friday. Was I wrong or rude? There was no money involved in this transaction.

A: Although I understand that convenience drove your decision to accept the offer of the responder willing to take everything, I also understand the other responders' reactions. They trusted your Craigslist ad and that you would honor it, just as they planned to do by not showing up at your house until Friday. Your failure to do that – whether money was exchanged or not – did lack courtesy. On a website like Craigslist, responsible courtesy and people's willingness to honor their commitments is all the control that exists.

In this instance it would have been most courteous to tell the person who wanted everything to show up at noon on Friday and load it up. This could have changed the outcome of the disbursement of your items, but you would have avoided the negative response you received.

I think you've learned a lesson, which is to be explicit in your ads and honor them. If you post a similar listing in the future, add a sentence that reads, "Anyone willing to take all the items listed immediately should contact me for an alternate pick up time." With that statement you've let everyone know of that possibility and given everyone a shot at taking you up on the offer. In that instance, the first to contact you should be the person you give the items to.

Dear Thelma: Following my husband's memorial service, I will be hosting a buffet reception. My niece suggested I lead the buffet line. Is this correct?

A: I would not advise it for two reasons. First, as the hostess of the event you would not lead the buffet line. Although you are a guest of honor in a sense, you are also the hostess. Graciousness and care for your guests is part of your responsibility. If you think it necessary to designate a leader, ask someone else to be it.

Secondly, people will want to speak to you personally and share their condolences and their stories of your husband at this reception. If you are the first to sit down at a table and begin eating, it will be awkward for those trying to talk to you and it will create continuous interruption for everyone at your table. Also, this will be a difficult time for you. Your emotions may be easier to deal with if you are not confined to one particular place but can easily circulate in the room. If you are hungry, eat, but you don't have to make partaking in the meal your primary concern.

Dear Thelma: I'm a newspaper carrier. I do my deliveries so well I've become invisible. My customers have forgotten I exist. I have several hundred customers and some customers receive two or three different publications every day – all reliably delivered by me. Newspaper prices have risen rapidly the last few years, and more customers have chosen to "skip" the carrier's tip option when renewing their subscriptions. They have also chosen to "forget" the carrier at Christmas. Every Christmas I purchase and send out calendar cards as a reminder I'm still around, but customers still don't acknowledge I was instrumental in their year's reading investment.

I tried to educate my customers on how little carriers actually earn, and how much it costs in supplies, gas and insurance to deliver their papers and I was anonymously told I had no class. I don't like whining or begging for recognition that should be given freely when I do good work. How can I and other newspaper carriers professionally connect with customers to remind them of this year's excellent delivery service and encourage them to tip?

A: You are in a difficult situation. Most people are in direct contact with their service providers who are tipped. They see the server bring their food to to the table efficiently or the stylist cut their hair as they want it. Even if it's brief, a relationship is established, an assessment is made and a tip is decided upon and given.

I imagine that the custom of tipping the newspaper carrier began when carriers did have a direct relationship with their customers. The carrier collected the subscription fees personally or the reader saw the afternoon paper delivered by a kid on a bike. Today, if a newspaper carrier is doing a good job, he is invisible and he is a stranger. He may only be thought of if the paper ends up under the car in the driveway or soaked by the sprinklers.

I think that placing a simple holiday greeting card in one of your delivered newspapers with your address is fine. It reminds customers that there is a person behind the paper on their porch and it gives them the information they need to send you a tip if they choose. People who are inclined to tip will need nothing more. But you must remember that while tips may be customary, they are always optional and at the discretion of the customer. As you found, trying to educate customers on how little you earn applies a pressure to which people don't respond well.

Dear Readers: This year I'm using Thanksgiving as a time dedicated to reflecting on my life, and I encourage you to join me and reflect on your own. Rather than just being thankful for the food, the people assembled and the year that has passed, I'm considering much more. I'm thinking about the journey that has been my life.

I'm starting with the family that formed me – parents, brother and sisters – and those very first relationships we formed. Each of them impacted me in a way that makes me who I am today. I am thankful that through the good and the bad times, they are mine.

From my family's safe embrace, I dove into the world of education. From the little girl who spoke only Italian and Spanish entering first grade to the homesick college freshman firmly set on not returning to Cincinnati after Christmas break, I overcame my difficulties and made the most of my opportunities. I am thankful for all that I experienced and learned and how I've been able to use it in a positive way.

My career path has not been a straight line but a winding road full of dips and turns. I joined the public sector at a time when women were just beginning to be counted on to bring in more than just the coffee. I retired as president of a home healthcare company and launched my own business. I am thankful for my career – every challenge faced and every contribution made.

Relationships have colored and sweetened the journey. The opportunities to build friendships and to share laughter and love are the glue binding time and experiences into a complete journey. I am thankful for each of those relationships.

I also must recognize my struggles. Whether in relationships, in health, in my career or in my education, the struggles and the difficulties helped to form me. I am thankful that I can see that.

When we are thankful and notice how much we have been given, our thoughts turn to how we can give. In my journey through life I have found there are two perfect gifts to be given: the gift of our time and the gift of our love.

Our time may be precious, but we must share it as often as we can. Whether it's time to organize a gathering for friends or time to attend a party, sharing our time with others builds relationships and strengthens important bonds. We should also recognize the importance of sharing time with those closest to us. Deliberately setting aside time to spend in a special way with those living under our own roofs may be the best thing we can offer.

Sharing our love lets people know that they are important to us. We should tell them that we love them and make every effort to give them the attention they desire and deserve.

So enjoy your Thanksgiving with a lovely meal and a beautiful celebration centered on fun, peace and love. Take some time to reflect on the gift of your life and think about what it means to be grateful, to appreciate others and to notice how much you have been given. Remember to embrace the opportunities you have to give the gifts of time and love.

This Thanksgiving I am thankful for the gift of my life. And I'm hopeful that each of you will find that your life too is a gift for which to be thankful.

Thankfulness and good manners never go out of style.

Dear Thelma: What is the best way to convey the message that my Christmas party centerpieces will not be given away and are not to be taken? Is it proper for me to make a verbal announcement? I do have an idea that doesn't involve a verbal announcement: placing a nicely made sign in the venue's restroom that reads, "Please do not remove centerpieces." No one has to know that I created them, and they don't know that I could have rented them.

A: First let me say that no guest should take a centerpiece off the table unless the centerpieces have been explicitly offered. No one should assume that the centerpieces are up for grabs at any event – party, wedding or shower – unless an announcement is made offering them. Even if this is a tradition in your culture or in your family, it should not be done unless an explicit offer is made.

Now to your worry, which I know is real, as many people will not have read the paragraph above. I think your sign in the restroom would be a gentle way to reach many of your guests without cluttering your tables with signs or placing labels on the centerpieces that may go unnoticed. A better option may be to have the centerpieces removed from the tables before people begin to leave. If there is a staff helping, you can ask them to do it as they clear the final dishes, or you can ask a small group of close friends to help you take care of it discreetly. Arrange for a safe area or containers in which to place the centerpieces after they've been removed.

Making a verbal announcement would be my last choice, but if you think it is necessary with this group, make it. At the end of your thank-you-for-coming remarks say something like: "Please leave the centerpieces on the tables as I will be using them again in the future."

I would say that you need to choose just one of these options. Using more than one will put too much emphasis on something that should not be the center of your celebration.

Dear Thelma: What's the appropriate level of tipping for services that aren't food related? I left a $5 tip for my dog groomer on a $45 bill, and afterwards I worried that was too cheap. It got me wondering, is there any kind of standard percentage for tipping our hairdressers, manicurists, massage therapists, dog groomers, etc.?

A: A good standard figure for tipping on most personal services we receive is 15 percent of the pre-tax bill. You can adjust up or down from there depending upon the level of service. While your $5 tip on the $45 bill was closer to 10 percent, I'm sure the groomer appreciated it and your business. Since this is someone you probably use the services of regularly, you can think about adding to the tip in the future.

Remember that tips are never mandatory and should always be merited. They are an expression of your satisfaction with the service.

At this time of year people also wonder about holiday tipping for the service providers they use regularly. While these expressions of thanks for a year's worth of good service aren't mandatory they are welcomed and appreciated. A holiday tip amount you might consider for these important people in your life is the cost of one regular session of their service.

Tips for good service and good manners never go out of style.

Dear Thelma: For the past several years the 15 adults in our extended family have participated in a gift exchange, each drawing one name for whom to buy a gift to give at our Christmas celebration. At different times people have chosen not to participate – a niece and her fiancé saving for their summer wedding, a nephew and his wife with a new baby. The exchange has gone on anyway among those who wanted to participate without a problem.

This year, one of the core members of the family is out of work and she and her husband said they would not participate this year. The family member coordinating the exchange thinks we shouldn't have the exchange at all because this couple is not participating, even though the couple opting out said they would not have a problem with the exchange going on without them. What do you think?

A: Every family would approach this situation differently and there's no purely right answer. I see the coordinator's dilemma. She doesn't want to create a situation where the family will be gathered to exchange gifts and these core members will be left out.

However, since you've had people who have opted out in the past and the exchange has still gone on, I believe that is what this couple probably expected when they chose to opt out. If they knew their action was likely to bring down the whole exchange, they might have considered their choices differently.

I think it's important for the core family members to talk about the situation. Be open to one another's ideas and feelings, and seek a decision that helps everyone involved feel comfortable and excited for the coming celebration. You also might consider asking the family member in distress if there's anything the family can do as a group to help her situation. Everyone in this situation wants to do the right thing. Talking about it will help identify what the right thing is.

Dear Thelma: In the past I've given holiday gifts to everybody I'm even remotely close to. This year that has to change as I just don't have the means to do it. But that doesn't mean that I don't cherish all of those people who won't get a gift from me. How do I do this right?

A: In the past, many of us have had no boundaries for our gifting. If we wanted to express the joy of the season to a particular person, we bought a gift and we enjoyed doing so.

This year may be different for some. People don't want to hurt the feelings of anyone, but they see the need to think differently. How do we go about this change without causing hurt feelings or confusion? I believe it's by communicating from the heart as early as possible. If the list of people you need to contact is small, consider a conversation. If it's a large group, you may want to write a letter. Express your care and love for your friends while telling them honestly that due to a need to simplify or financial constraints you would like to end the customary exchange. It is important for your friends to know the reason for ending the exchange so that they don't feel slighted or that you're interested in ending the relationship along with the exchange.

Stepping back and reassessing our gift-giving habits may be a positive exercise. It may make us look at how much we care, rather than how much we can give and will receive. And it may force us to be even more thoughtful than we were when we could easily swipe the credit card.

Expressions of the heart and good manners never go out of style.

Dear Thelma: I will be hosting a small dinner party during the holidays. My husband insists that, based on past history, some of my guests will be late. One showed up as dessert was being served the last time we gathered. How does one handle latecomers graciously?

A: Guests should always keep in mind the effort and timing that go into a successful dinner, and they should honor their host and his or her invitation by being on time. If that's not possible, latecomers to a small, intimate dinner should always notify the host in advance that they will be late and how late they will be. If they know ahead of time, they should let the host know as soon as they are aware of it. If something detains them that evening, they should call as soon as possible.

To help buffer the disruption caused by late arrivals, time your party so that the first 30 minutes are spent on introducing new friends and greeting one another. Serve drinks and light appetizers and use the time to connect with each guest. Waiting half an hour prior to seating everyone for dinner should allow for traffic tie-ups, wardrobe malfunctions and other obstacles that keep guest from arriving on time. When the pre-dinner activities start to dwindle and the food is ready to be served, it is fine to start dinner without the tardy guests who have been given ample time to arrive.

Seating can be quickly rearranged if you discover the latecomers won't attend at all, or you may leave it as is so they have places when they do arrive. Just don't leave any of your guest at the end of the table with too many empty chairs. Change the seating so that all are connected to the group.

When latecomers do arrive, graciously accept their apologies and welcome them to the table. Start them with the course the rest of the group is being served, even if it's dessert.

Despite all options available to deal with lateness, the bottom line is, don't be late.

Dear Readers: This time of year brings the realization that tradition has the power to draw us together as family, friends and community. It gives us the opportunity to build and strengthen those relationships and bonds. For me and for so many people, Christmas wouldn't be Christmas without the traditions surrounding luminarias. I can't remember a time growing up where luminarias weren't part of the celebration and the center of planning for our Christmas holiday.

Our family lived on Park Avenue west of Downtown where the Albuquerque luminaria tradition is strong. Luminarias were a family endeavor. My siblings and I began folding 800 brown paper lunch sacks with care and precision weeks in advance as we thought about lighting the way for the Holy Family. Each year Dad ordered a truckload of sand delivered to our driveway about a week before Christmas. We filled the bags with sand and a single votive candle each and lined our pathways and property in anticipation of lighting them on Christmas Eve.

Luminarias brought a unified spirit to our entire community. Everyone set them up. The unwritten policy followed by the neighborhood was that on Christmas Eve there would be no lights coming from our homes after about 4:30 p.m. At that time we would all begin to light our luminarias and fill our yards and the streets with their peaceful glow.

This tradition continues and hundreds of people come out on Christmas Eve to tour it. I did so last year when a very important person in my life wanted to spend Christmas Eve among the luminarias despite age and illness. We took him in a wheelchair, bundled up and in his knit cap along the sidewalks of my old neighborhood to see them. He relished the experience, which was to be the final Christmas Eve of his life.

Also in recent years I happened upon the beautiful Christmas Eve tradition of lining cemeteries with luminarias. My sister and I had gone to Mount Calvary Cemetery near dusk on Christmas Eve to remember our loved ones buried there. I was awed by the sight of hundreds of luminarias emanating their peaceful light. Families were gathered in prayer and song among the simple glowing lanterns remembering those who had died. We were all visiting the cemetery that night with love and respect for people to whom we wanted to pay tribute. The little luminaria for me represented a connection to that love and to that relationship. It touched and inspired me.

These recent experiences with our happy Christmas tradition deepen my thinking on the luminaria and give the humble lantern a new significance for me. The tradition that filled my hands and heart as a child has stayed with me and grown in importance. The luminaria on Christmas Eve is not just a pretty decoration, it's a spiritual tradition lighting the way to our homes for the peace promised by the Christ child.

I embrace Santa and the Christmas tree skirted by beautifully wrapped packages. They are all important traditions in a family, but the most meaningful for me is the luminaria. As we anticipate and prepare for the spiritual side of Christmas, one night filled with real candlelight is fitting for a season focused on tradition, giving and love.

As the luminaria candle burns it emits light and warmth in doing exactly what it was created to do. Burning throughout the night, it gives all of its beautiful self in fulfilling its purpose. As we look at that candle, our relationships and our purpose at this time of year, it's a good time to think about how we give of ourselves and how others give their precious selves to us. Are we like the candle, providing warmth and light and peace? I want to be.

Peaceful light and good manners never go out of style.

Dear Thelma: Most of my and my husband's friends are couples with children and so I'm hosting an all-ages New Year's Eve party. Do you have any advice on entertaining a group of mixed ages and interests?

A: What a wonderful opportunity you are creating for families to ring in the new year together. I know that your guests will appreciate your efforts to host a party they can all enjoy.

I have a friend who has hosted a similar New Year's party for several years. She first focuses on the children and teens when planning her party because if these groups are happy and entertained, their parents can relax and have a good time too.

Each of her three children's bedrooms is given a specific use. In one is moved the video game system that will be used for dance games or other group video games. One is outfitted with an air hockey table and pinball machine. The other contains a television and DVD player for watching movies. The kids are free to try it all.

In her invitation she lists times for a "Sleepy Heads Countdown" and a "Night Owls Countdown." At 8:45 p.m. she gathers everyone and hands out horns and hats and pours sparkling cider for the countdown to 9 p.m. She finds this to be the more exciting and vigorous of the two countdowns because by midnight most guests have left or are about to fall asleep.

Her menu includes soups and stews and lots of finger foods introduced throughout the night so there is always something fresh and new to eat. Since it is a family event, alcoholic drinks are downplayed. She will have some beer and wine available for the adults, but she concentrates her efforts on a fun, non-alcoholic cocktail that all her guests can enjoy.

While the kids are having fun, the adults are free to visit. At some point in the night she brings out the dominoes or cards to get a large group around the table for some competitive fun. Sometimes the kids join in or help their parents play.

Whether they leave before the first countdown or after midnight, everyone feels they've had a chance to take part in a celebration that's going on around the world, and they've done it with their family.

My friend started hosting the party because she wanted to do something fun with her family on New Year's Eve. It grew into an event that she, her family and all their friends anticipate every year. Don't be surprised if the same doesn't happen for your party.

Dear Thelma: Someone told me it is not appropriate to clink glasses with people after a toast. Is that true?

A: It is always proper to simply raise your glass, but for me, clinking glasses is a traditional social custom that I don't believe is going to disappear. I grew up in an Italian family where you said "Salute!", clinked your glasses and loved the sound of it. I have read, and I agree, that clinking glasses unites the listeners of a toast and makes them a part of the good wishes expressed.

If you are at a formal or business event, look to the host for guidance. If he or she clinks, feel free. If someone extends their glass to you to clink, return the gesture. If you are the person being toasted, don't clink or drink, just acknowledge the kind words with a nod or a thank you. And in a large group, reserve your clinks for those in your immediate area. You needn't stretch across a large table or move about the room to be sure to clink every glass.

A happy "ting" and good manners never go out of style.

Ask Thelma 2014
Defining a Legacy

Dear Thelma: I fear that my dad is becoming a grumpy old man. He's probably got another 20 years left on Earth but I'm afraid he is going to spend them all alone as he alienates himself with his negative attitude toward invitations and the events he is invited to. I hesitate to invite him to things because sometimes it just seems to make him mad to have to consider it. Do I talk to him about this?

A: I think you do. During my years working in home health care it was a topic we did help people deal with. When having a negative reaction to most things becomes a habit for someone, the effects of that attitude can harm their well-being.

At a calm and neutral time, speak to your dad gently about how his reaction to your invitations seems to indicate that he's upset to be invited. Tell him that you're worried that he will become isolated and ask him to think about how to express his concerns or disinterest in the invitation honestly, but without coming off as generally negative or grumpy.

It's my hope that he will listen to you and realize the need to make a change. If he doesn't, continue to invite him anyway. He can make the choice to attend, and you will have done right by continuing to include him.

A positive outlook and good manners never go out of style.

Dear Thelma: My wife and I are big on etiquette and try to do everything the proper way. We treat people how we would like to be treated. We have two best friends that we spend time with. They are a couple years younger and only boyfriend and girlfriend. He and I play golf and she and my wife go shopping. We love each other.

I have noticed recently that they come over a lot and use our stuff. We always have them over because we have a house with plenty of space. Lately it seems that we are always making dinner, cleaning, and providing wine and drinks. They never bring anything over and usually drink all of our wine. My wife and I are always cleaning up the house afterwards. I am getting frustrated with the lack of participation on their end. We are more fortunate but they both have jobs with hardly any bills. I feel like our relationship is starting to take a hit because we have slowly stopped having dinners and inviting them over.

I want to be firm with them about doing their share but I feel bad when they come over and I don't offer a glass of wine, especially when my wife and I are having a glass. How do we politely tell them to start bringing wine, bringing a side dish, or helping clean up?

A: This sounds like a relationship you all enjoy and a relationship that's worth putting in the effort to maintain. That maintenance comes not in trying to bury your frustration but in speaking honestly with your good friends. These are people with whom you feel genuinely comfortable so I think you can have a good and honest discussion about your concerns.

It's likely that they are having a great time enjoying your hospitality, which you're so good at providing they've become accustomed to thinking that it's easy for you. Since you get together regularly and you always host, I think your next invitation to them can properly include, "Can you bring some wine and a salad to go with dinner?" I don't think the good friends you describe will refuse and I think it will form new expectations for everyone.

If you think a more direct approach is necessary, invite them over and start by saying: "We love having you over. Spending time with you is so much fun, but we're starting to feel overwhelmed. Do you think you would be able to host our get-togethers sometimes or help with the food or drinks over here?" You don't have to be firm or accusatory. Just be honest. I believe they are good friends and they will say: "Of course! We're sorry you had to ask.

Important friendships need attention and periodic maintenance. Willingness to be honest with one another and to respect one another's time and effort goes a long way in preserving and building those relationships. Don't wait for frustration and resentment to set in. Talk to your friends.

Dear Thelma: On first contact with someone you want to do business with, is the proper way to address that person Ms. Thelma Domenici or Miss Thelma Domenici?

A. The title Ms. is always an appropriate business address for women. Miss and Mrs. are tied to marital status. If you don't know the woman well, you may not be able to determine that status. Ms., like the title Mr. for men, is not tied to marriage and so works for all women, precisely the reason it was created.

Respectful addresses and good manners never go out of style.

Dear Thelma: A year ago I attended a relative's out-of-state wedding. It was a nice affair except the bridal couple did not have a receiving line nor did they greet their guests at their tables during the reception. I have yet to meet the bride. Fast forward one year, a few days past their one year anniversary, they got around to mailing their thank-you notes.

I was very generous with the monetary wedding gift, and to be made to wait so long for a response is unforgivable. I was so incensed by their egregious behavior, I wrote them a letter expressing my anger and frustration. Evidently the groom's father heard about the letter and now is not talking to me. The letter was polite but instructive. Should I not have sent the letter?

A: I can understand your frustration and your hurt at the lack prompt thanks for your gift, but your letter was unnecessary and, as you can see, caused hurt to expand from you to the bride, the groom and his father.

From the tone of your question to me using words like "unforgivable" and "incensed," I suspect that your letter expressing "anger and frustration" was not as polite as you may think. A late thank-you is in no way unforgivable and to be incensed by one is an extreme reaction.

Here is the reality: The couple did send you a thank-you note. They knew it was late and they probably didn't feel great about that, but they did send it. To have you respond to their thank you with anger and frustration was probably upsetting to them rather than instructional, and I don't know how you can fault them or their family for feeling hurt.

Another thing you should have considered before sending the letter is that you may not know the circumstances that delayed the thank-you notes. To presume that they weren't prompt because of laziness or wonton lack of respect for their guests is unwise.

It is not always appropriate to instruct, even when we know we are right. Sometimes the politest thing we can do is to bear each other's mistakes and shortcomings with grace and patience.

Dear Thelma: I have experienced this at nearly every event that I attend. I will have a glass of water and perhaps an alcoholic beverage at my place, next to my purse and whatever other papers, trinkets and awards that my husband and I have collected throughout the evening. Even though I may be on the dance floor or visiting a friend at another table, to me it is obvious that these items should not be disturbed. However, inevitably the wait staff will clear off all of my beverages.

The last event I attended it happened twice and I twice had to run over to make them stop. When I have purchased a glass of wine, I expect to be able to finish it, even if it is close to the end time of the event. Sometimes we are staying at the host hotel, and I want to take it to my room after the event. How do I keep the wait staff from taking my drinks?

A: You typically can identify the servers assigned to your area of the banquet hall, and sometimes a specific server will even introduce him or herself to your table. Identify the servers who will be taking care of you, approach one of them and tell him you would prefer that your drinks not be cleared at all during the event. Explain that you plan to be mingling around the room or dancing throughout the evening and that you plan to leave your drinks at the table but will come back for them. Ask if he can let the other servers working in the area know of your request and thank him in advance for his help. I believe that if the servers know your intentions from the beginning of the evening, they will do their best to provide you the service you want and need.

Dear Thelma: My daughter told me to be at the chapel at 2 p.m. to help her into her wedding dress that I helped her shop for and bought for her. We were together all morning as she was getting her hair done. I was happy to pay for her hair and nails and we discussed in detail what time everything was to happen.

I don't see her often because we live in different states. The last time we were together was in September when I treated her to a mother-daughter cruise. When my husband and I visit her we stay in a hotel and pay for all the meals. We are happy to treat them when we can. At Christmas she and her boyfriend were sent nice gifts and my husband and I didn't even get a card.

I waited outside the chapel until my 2 p.m. time. She told me she wanted time to rehearse going up the aisle with her dad before I got there and I wanted to honor her wishes. I was there at 2, but to my surprise when I went to the bridal dressing room she was already dressed. One of the ladies that worked at the chapel told me she was very sorry that they just found out that it was my ex-husband's girlfriend who dressed my daughter.

I never went back to the bridal dressing room again. I felt that this is my daughter's wedding and if she chose to have this woman take my place that is her wish. All my daughter had to do was tell her that she was waiting for her mother who would be there at 2:00. My daughter is 33 years old, not so young that she would not know better.

My friends say they feel this was a setup between my daughter, my ex and his girlfriend. My husband and I were left to feel as if we were unwanted guests and this was done to humiliate us in front of everyone. My daughter has done these things in the past but now that she is older I thought she would grow out of this. Can you tell me what you think and what does this really mean?

A: It's hard to say what this means without understanding your daughter's side of the story. We don't know if she felt bad for her father's girlfriend and pressured to include her or if she is accustomed to your treating her very generously and operates from a sense of entitlement that makes her inconsiderate of you.

The only way to understand these things and to salvage your relationship is for you to talk honestly with her. Tell her that you were hurt when you arrived at the chapel to find her already dressed because you expected that to be a special time for the two of you. Tell her that you love her and want to be a part of her life, but that consideration for each other and each other's feelings has to be abundant on both sides. Listen to her, forgive and seek forgiveness if needed.

Children – even when they become adults – don't necessarily "grow out of" behaviors that are convenient and lucrative for them. Instead they may have to be asked to look honestly at those behaviors and recognize how hurtful and destructive they can be to their relationships.

I would abandon all concern for the motivations of your ex and his girlfriend. The most important relationship is the one with your daughter. Put your energy there.

Considerate relationships and good manners never go out of style.

Dear Thelma: A friend of mine wrote several posts on Facebook about the last days and death of her friend, mostly to share the information with other far-flung friends. Some people, who didn't know the deceased at all, responded to my friend's posts with condolences to her. It seems out of place to me to offer sympathy to the bearer of sad news about a stranger. I ended up doing nothing. Was I wrong?

A: While the people who expressed concern for your friend and her sadness weren't wrong, I don't think you were either. If you thought your friend was especially distraught, I believe you would instinctively reach out to her. You may want to talk to her about the loss the next time you see her, but formal or even Facebook casual sympathies wouldn't be expected.

Dear Thelma: I have met and talked with the parents of one of my son's good friends at least four times at school functions and at the football games they play in together. However, every time we encounter each other, these people act like they have never met me. It's just starting to feel like rudeness on their part and I feel like returning their snub. Should I be gracious and continue to introduce myself every time we meet or just stop even trying?

A: You absolutely should not return the snub. A kind greeting is always in order for anyone you meet. Despite your perception of anyone's lack of good manners, yours should never falter.

I would advise you to stop introducing yourself to them. When you encounter them say hello, inquire about their son so they can recognize the connection, and if the conversation ends there, move on. Avoid letting yourself become offended as you don't really know why they seem to forget they know you. Maybe they are bad with faces and names, maybe they are dealing with a difficulty in their lives and can't concentrate on peripheral relationships, or maybe they are shy and it comes across as stand-offish.

If you really get a sense that they are trying to avoid you or are not interested in a connection with you, let it go. Seeking them out will only make you uncomfortable and a confrontation with them would never be appropriate. When you are at school events, concentrate on those with whom you can share a conversation and make it a point to enjoy their company.

Dear Thelma: I just found out that my neighbor's mom died about six months ago. Is it too late to go to her and offer my condolences? Will my bringing it up now be worse than not bringing it up at all?

A: It's not too late to offer your support, and I don't believe bringing it up it will cause her greater pain. It's likely that she goes through some sadness daily; your remembrance of her mom may even help her feel less alone in that sadness.

Explain to her that you only recently learned the news and that you are sorry for her loss. If she wants to talk more with you about it, she will. And she will appreciate your show of concern and kindness.

Dear Thelma: What would you suggest is the appropriate response to a child who did not received a card or gift, much less a phone call from their biological mother over the holidays or for a recent birthday?

A: You don't say that the child is upset about this situation, only that he or she may need an explanation. I would suggest a response like this: "For some reason your mom hasn't been able to contact you. We don't know why that is, but we have to keep in mind what we do know, and that is that you love each other. We'll hope together that you do hear from her soon."

Children have a great capacity to love and to forgive, if we allow them to use it. By keeping our own prejudgments about the situation or the person to ourselves, we can help that child to preserve the good feelings he or she has concerning that important relationship.

When we prejudge, we place a label on a person. Often times, that label prevents us from clear communication, causing us to focus on the label rather than on the content of a conversation or the action. None of us is free of this and it's something we can work to avoid if we seek healthy communication as a part of our lives, even with people who frustrate us.

Dear Thelma: Could you please tell me how to deal with a coworker who is rude and is not polite? She does not use the words please and thank you when she wants me to do some work for her. How should I react to this person?

A: First of all, don't feel like this only happens in your work environment. Rudeness, which is a symptom of a lack of respect, is something that needs to be addressed in many workplaces.

The core of respect is mutuality. The respect we show by the civility of our interactions must flow both ways between individuals. You may have to start the process by modeling the behavior you would like to see from her, rather than reacting negatively toward her.

Then, if this is a person you work with closely, it would be proper to take the time to meet with her and say, "You may not realize it, but you rarely say please or thank you to me. I respect you enough to say please and thank you; I hope that you can do the same."

In any organization, this is an environment issue that must be addressed at all levels. Everyone must come to work expecting to treat people with respect and to be treated with respect. Respect and kindness should be modeled by the top levels of the organization and emphasized throughout.

Dear Thelma: I have a good woman friend who dresses horribly and is a business professional. Do I dare say anything?

A: Absolutely. If this person is a good friend, there is no way you'd be doing her a favor by keeping silent. To be a successful professional of either gender, professional attire is essential.

But before you say anything, you need to think through exactly what the issues are. Is her clothing revealing too much of her cleavage or her thighs? Is her clothing too casual for her workplace or her field? You should be able to identify and address a specific point of professional attire that she is missing. To simply think and say she dresses horribly won't be constructive or helpful.

For women, pant suits or dress suits are standard business attire, with skirts no shorter than three inches above the knee. Heels should top out at two inches. For the most conservative look, nylons should be worn. Modesty also is important. It is possible for a woman to be attractive without showing cleavage or having her skirt rise to dangerous levels when she sits down.

For the most professional look, nothing should distract from a beautifully refined and understated appearance. Women can add interest and complete the polished look with carefully-selected shoes, handbags and jewelry.

Once you've specifically identified the points you feel are important to discuss with your friend, engage her in a private and personal conversation. Talk with her in a friendly, gracious and honest manner about your care for her and what you've observed. Let her know how much you respect her as a professional and that you think that her tremendous work and potential can be highlighted with a more refined look. Recognize that your taste in clothing styles, colors and brands may differ, but that the standards of professional dress provide an outline within which to work.

She may need time to think about and process what you've said. Giver her that time, as well as your friendship and support regardless of what she chooses to wear.

Dear Thelma: My husband and I are in a difficult situation. What do you do when your friends divorce and the woman wants all her girlfriends to side with her, but we like her husband and don't want to discard his friendship?

A: This is not an unusual situation; couples almost always expect their friends to take sides in their divorces. You can most definitely choose not to, but unless the couple has an extremely civil relationship themselves, simply making that choice may drive one or the other of them away from you.

It sounds from your question that you value the husband's friendship as much as the wife's. For that reason I think you should continue to include both of them as your friends. You don't need to put the two of them in uncomfortable situations by planning things that include both of them, or discuss with one what you've done with the other, but you don't have to discard either of them.

Once you've made your choice to stand by them both, a choice you can express to them if you wish, they can then decide how they will approach the relationship with you. If one or both of them can't handle being friends with someone who is a friend to both of them, they may make the decision to end the friendship with you. If you have a chance to discuss it with them, talk with them honestly about your desire to support each of them.

Both parties to a divorce need encouragement and support to adjust to a new and different way of life. Friends helps to do that.

Supportive friendships and good manners never go out of style.

Dear Thelma: Leaving my 10-year-old son's basketball game last week, my 15-year-old son said he was going to write the rules on post-game etiquette for fans. My youngest was upset over the loss of the game. It was obvious from his face that he'd been crying and had taken the loss hard. Despite that, there were still people trying to engage him in conversation about the game. My oldest said people should follow these rules: 1. If the person you're talking to lost the game, give them time to cool off before asking them too much about it. 2. If they look really upset, just say, "Good job," and leave it at that. What do you think?

A: People do have to be sensitive to an athlete's feelings and state of mind after a game. We should all be able to empathize. Even if we aren't athletes, we've all had hard days or experiences that we need to process ourselves before we can do a lot of sharing or put on the happiest of faces.

Fans watching the game know the outcome and how individual players performed. It's not hard to assess how players might be feeling. I would agree with your son's suggestions. I'd add that time to cool off may be hours or days later depending on the strength of the emotion. It's natural for people to want to connect with players in some way after a hard-fought contest. A "good job" and a fist bump or a handshake may be all they should expect after a difficult game.

I would add one point of etiquette for the player to your son's list. Even when the player is feeling bad, he should give his attention those people who have come specifically to watch him – like Grandpa or Uncle Joey – with a hug or a handshake. He also should pull himself together enough to nod, offer a handshake and thank the people who want to acknowledge his effort.

Dear Thelma: What do you do when you are given a party and asked to create the guest list, then uninvited friends find out they were not invited?

A: I assume from your question that this is a retirement party or birthday party someone is giving in your honor and the host has asked you to compile the guest list. Your question doesn't mention that there is a limit to the number of people you can invite. If it did, you would gently tell the uninvited who approach you about it that the number of guests was limited by the venue or the host's preference. Then you might ask them if they'd like to get together at another time.

If there is not a strict limit to the number of people you can invite, I don't see why you can't include additional guests. You will have to judge whether these particular friends are likely be offended by a late invitation or will roll with it and will be happy to come and celebrate. To the later category who have approached you about it, you might say something like, "I'm sorry you weren't on the initial list. I would like to add you and I'd love for you to come."

The key word in your question is "friends." If these are truly friends, I would try to find a way to include them. If it complicates matters or would further upset them, then don't. If they ask for an explanation, say, "We just weren't able to include everyone this time."

Then think about a time you can get together with them and make plans for that.

Nurturing relationships and good manners never go out of style.

Dear Readers: I've had the opportunity in recent weeks to talk with three parents. Each in different stages of parenting teens and young adults, they face and have faced the common challenge of raising responsible, empathetic and grateful children who are true to themselves. In their examples many of us may find inspiration and support for nurturing our own parent-teen relationships.

Many parents wonder when their children are going to discover what's really great about themselves. The first friend I spoke with, a mother of three, struggles with that for her 13-year-old daughter. This mother clearly sees the interesting young woman this seventh-grader will become, but she also sees the weight of peers' perceived expectations keeping her guarded.

The girl decided this year that her annual friendship tea party would not be held. She worried that friends would find it too immature. Her mom was disappointed but understanding. When the classmates heard the news, they all protested, saying how much they loved the tradition of getting dressed up and going to tea. Buoyed by the love and support of her friends and her mom, she is happy to be once again planning the party.

My friend feels her job today is to encourage and protect her daughter's ideas and independence, while reminding herself how important friends can be. This girl is learning to become who she really is, and mom is working to create home where it's safe to do that.

My second friend will be sending her first-born to college in the fall and has frequently wondered if she raised her daughter well. There have been many times where entitlement, lack of gratitude and all-around snarky behavior sent her reeling.

Just when she thought she had failed, her daughter woke one morning with a new perspective. A school senior retreat opened her eyes to a much broader world where kids just like her suffer. Empathy for others became a visceral experience, and gratitude for the gifts and comforts of her life became her song.

Her daughter didn't suddenly become perfect, but my friend saw a transformation take place, and she came to believe that those life lessons taught over the last 18 years had found their way in. She now can confidently launch her into the world as a responsible, empathetic and grateful person.

My third friend has seen those lessons come full circle. He told me about the joy he found in the opportunity to speak at his daughter's wedding celebration and bring up her "Ten Ways to a Successful Life," which she wrote when she was 10 years old:

1. Believe in yourself.
2. Make reasonable, but high goals.
3. Be efficient as possible.
4. Don't procrastinate.
5. Don't make excuses.
6. Rely on yourself for what you think is right.
7. Remember that money isn't happiness.
8. Always be observant of what others around you are doing.
9. Work harder than anyone else.
10. Always have a smile on your face.

To share the insight and beauty of that 10-year-old – now an investment banker on the East Coast – with her peers and her family was one of life's golden moments for him. This father was able to tell this important group that she had stayed true to her guiding principles and that they were as much a part of her life now as they were then.

The lessons taught to our children are lasting. Although we have to let them work through on their own things we already have learned the answers to, there comes a time when all is illuminated and a mutual gratitude appears – a sense of thankfulness that fills the hearts of parents for their children and children for their parents.

Illumination and good manners never go out of style.

Dear Thelma: I am hugely annoyed at the side conversations that go on during conferences I attend. Why can't people just pay attention instead of acting like 13-year-olds?

A: During a large event people can gain a feeling of anonymity and think that their behavior doesn't matter because it won't be noticed in so large a crowd. Anyone feeling that way should think again. You may think that your side conversation won't display rudeness to a speaker 15 tables away from you, but your behavior does affect those closest to you and won't be ignored.

Our best defense is to set the best example we can. Encourage those around us to end their conversations and pay attention and do the same ourselves. I have also asked members of the wait staff to ask people to refrain from talking during the presentation.

If you truly need to have a conversation during a presentation, you should leave the room to do so.

Dear Thelma: A friend's wife has a terminal illness and we want to stay in touch but not interfere. What's the best way to do this?

A: Remember first that this is your friend. Recognize that these are people with whom you have a shared past and common interests. This is not a time to withdraw your friendship.

Call your friend. While the point of your call is to show support in this time of illness, the call will include conversation coming from both sides. It may even help your friend feel a moment of "normalness" in a time of turmoil.

It's fine to call and say, "I don't know what to say, but I want you to know I'm here for you." People are touched when someone reaches out to them with concern and respect. They can feel your sincerity, and those calls, in almost every instance, are viewed as support.

During your conversation it would be very appropriate to say, "Would you appreciate visitors?" Then he can tell you whether or not to come and when is the best time. You also can ask what help they may need or if you can make a trip to the store for them.

If you do visit, you should not stay long. It takes great energy to see visitors. Show your support and do what you can, but respect her need for rest and recovery. Take something like a card or small gift that you can leave behind for your friend and his wife to look at later or to leave if she is sleeping when you make your visit.

Dear Thelma: I believe that people should not forward emails that include rumors or warnings that they haven't checked out themselves. There are sites online where you can verify these things for accuracy and 100 percent of those I get are untruths. People should not be taken in by this stuff or spread it further.

A: Your point is an important one. You should verify any information you receive before forwarding it. Many of the emails that make the rounds are absolutely false, but they continue to circulate year after year. These sometimes elaborate hoaxes clog inboxes and raise blood pressure across the country.

Be diplomatic with "inspirational" forwards as well. Don't make a habit of sending such to all your contacts. Ask yourself who would actually appreciate the forward or has the time to appreciate it. Also concern yourself with the content. When it comes to off-color jokes or inappropriate images, let them stop with you. Sending them on could offend or create personal or professional problems for the receiver.

Dear Thelma: What do you say when a friend continually asks you about your finances, says "you must have a lot of money" to travel, or asks how much we have saved? We have no intention of telling him anything, but what could shut him up?

A: You call this person a friend. If he really is one, you should be able to say: "This is something that I don't discuss. It is private and is only for me to know and consider. Please don't bring it up again."

When people start to inquire about friends' or family members' finances, they are in a territory where no one should trespass. Finances are one of the most personal pieces of your life.

Despite the fact that we do all know this, there are many people who ignore it. They can be very intrusive and pass a lot of critical judgment based on what they think they know. Someone I know was approached and scolded for being the only member of a particular board who had not contributed sufficiently to the cause. The person approaching did not know her financial situation but took it upon himself to assume she was in a position to make a large contribution to a board she was already giving a lot of time to. This intrusive gesture may lose the organization a talented board member and any future contribution she may have considered.

We should not ignore the part of ourselves that knows that finances are a sensitive part of every person's life. They are not for public notice or public discussion unless the person whose finances are being discussed brings them up.

Dear Thelma: My family has members who hold grudges that are 60 to 70 years old and even go back to their parents. How can I get them to understand how damaging that is to the whole family? Why do people do this?

A: The definition I found of the word grudge calls it a persistent feeling of resentment resulting from a past insult or injury and its synonyms include bitterness, rancor, animosity and enmity. These negative feelings and expressions are definitely damaging. A family in this kind of situation faces a lack of sincere relationships. Those relationships simply cannot exist in a family that has surrendered the opportunity to grow its bonds.

The best way to resolve the issue is to face it, and sometimes you must put yourself in the place of trying to make a change even if you're not the one holding the grudge. Identify the family member who holds the grudge and have the courage and ability to respect that person while addressing the resentment in a way that is not accusatory. Say something like "I feel like we're missing so much by not dealing with this issue. Is there anything I can do to make things better for you and for all of us?"

The effort may or may not have the desired effect, but you'll know you worked toward establishing and maintaining your own peaceful mind and loving heart.

Dear Thelma: My brother and his wife and are not nice people and have not spoken to us for seven years. I'm at a loss when people ask me how they are? What do you say?

A: I know of someone who has faced this situation and her response to it seems most fitting. In an even and soft tone of voice she simply says: "I really haven't seen or heard from him in quite some time." No further explanation is needed.

Grace and good manners never go out of style.

Dear Thelma: Myself and five friends went out to dinner recently. We all know each other very well and enjoy getting together. However, on this particular occasion I was disturbed by how the evening played out. We were at a rectangular table with one person on either end and two each on the sides. Throughout much of the dinner, the person at the head of the table and the person to her right became involved in a whispered conversation that seemed very private. The person at the foot of the table and the person on her right were also having their own personal conversation. I and the person diagonal from me were completely left out, and we couldn't even talk to each other because there was too much distance between us. I didn't agree to attend just for a meal but for the company! What do you make of this?

A: A table of six is not so large that everyone can't be engaged in conversation, but it will take the attention of the group to be sure that everyone is included.

The two at your table that signaled through their hushed voices and probably their body language that their conversation was not up for group participation really should have saved that conversation for later or left the table to have it if it was of great importance. Their actions likely caused the rest of the group to feel very uncomfortable and disregarded the purpose of the evening, which was to gather with a group.

Sometimes when we know each other well, it becomes easy to take each other for granted and let consideration for each other slip. We have to guard against this if we want to keep our relationships strong and growing stronger. When you plan or agree to an evening like this, all involved should come ready to share the love and friendship that brought you together in the first place.

You know that these are your friends and that they are not making an intentional effort to leave you out. So if you find yourself in this isolated position again, I suggest using humor to bring the group back together. Say something like, "Hey, I'm over here!" to draw their attention and to subtly remind them that they are there as a group. And when you notice someone being left out, make an effort to fix it before they have to.

Consideration within groups and good manners never go out of style.

Dear Thelma: The way some people wear fragrance on a plane is really bad. I was on a flight where someone's strong fragrance – I don't even know if they were near me – made me sneeze repeatedly for the first half hour of the flight. There must be an etiquette to wearing perfume or cologne. What is it?

A: The etiquette of wearing fragrance applies all the time, not just when boarding an airplane. It is a matter of courtesy to others as well as a matter of health to be sure that your fragrance is subtle and appropriate, and it's also important to realize there are times when appropriate means going without your signature scent.

Some workplaces, health cubs and medical facilities have policies requiring a fragrance-free environment as people may be allergic or disturbed by scent.

Even if it's not official, visiting a newborn or someone who's ailing or is in the hospital is a good time to refrain from using a fragrance. I would include the close and enclosed quarters of an airplane as a fragrance-free zone. While you want to use deodorant and smell clean, your spritz of perfume has the potential to cause problems like sneezing, headaches or even nausea for other passengers. Avoid perfumes or cologne in these circumstances.

If it is permitted in your workplace, use fragrances cautiously. You don't want your fragrance to be distracting and there's no need for everyone in your general proximity to experience it. It should be subtle and light and apparent only to those who come within two feet of you. It shouldn't hang in the air after you've left the room.

Reserve heavy, musky scents for evening social occasions when a more glamorous look and scent are appropriate. When you do choose a heavier fragrance, don't be heavy-handed with it. A small spritz of any scent goes a long way and lasts long after you've stopped noticing it. Just because you can no longer smell it, doesn't mean you should reapply. Also even in an evening social situation, consider whether your scent is likely to compete with the event, like dinner or a wine tasting where aroma is part of the experience, and choose accordingly.

As with all personal grooming and hygiene, always apply fragrance in private and preferably at home.

Dear Thelma: Handshaking is very painful for me. How can I avoid shaking hands?

A: I'm sorry that pain keeps you from enjoying a handshake. Handshakes are important to building relationships and genuine positive energy can be exchanged through a handshake. I would advise a person to avoid them only if it's truly necessary. Even offer your left hand if you can.

If you really must avoid them because of pain or a compromised immune system, do all you can to put the other person at ease. As someone approaches, be the first to greet with a smile, bow of the head and a statement like, "It's such a pleasure to see you again."

If the person you're greeting places her hand out for a handshake first, you'll have to smile and say, "I'm sorry, shaking hands is very painful for me, but I'm very happy to see you today." Diffuse the awkwardness of the situation by keeping the conversation going with questions about the person or her family.

To those offering their hands, be understanding and be careful to avoid showing disappointment. Let your hand drop slowly rather than pulling it back defensively, and transfer the energy of your greeting into sharing pleasant comments.

Gracious greetings and good manners never go out of style.

Dear Thelma: I am a 13-year-old girl who loves to read. I buy many books and have lent them to my friends. My books make their way through about five of my friends before they come back to me. We talk a lot about books and about the next ones we'd like to read. They always want to know when I'm going to buy them so they can read them. Just once I'd like one of them to buy a book and lend it to me. I don't buy them because I have a lot of extra money to spend. I save up for them because they are treasures to me. It's really starting to bother me. I even made a decision to not buy a book because it's one my friends want to read. What is a good way to fix this problem?

A: I think you've found that sharing your love of reading and your love of books with your friends is a joyful experience. It's fun to escape to the world created by literature and share it with a person who can only understand it if they've read themselves to that world too. That kind of sharing is a great way to build and strengthen your relationships.

But the idea of the fairness of the acquisition of the books is stifling that joy. I do understand the way you feel. You want the people you are showing kindness to to reciprocate. It's a common feeling that arises in many types of situations. It's important to find a way to feel better about it so you can get back to enjoying your books.

I don't think your friends are trying to treat you unfairly, but they've developed a habit of counting on you for good books. So I have two suggestions for you. Talk to your friends about it gently. Say, "I've bought the last three books we've all read. Does someone else want to buy and share the next one?" See where the discussion leads in hopes that someone will take up the next book.

If no one is willing, head to the library and check out the next book on your list. When your friends want to read it, direct them to the library too. If the book is so great that you want to own it, buy it for your own collection but don't feel obligated to lend it if you don't want to.

I think that inserting a library book every once in a while will help you feel better about your contributions and put the focus back on all that you enjoy about reading with friends.

Dear Thelma: While attending a banquet at a hotel I stepped into the restroom. While there in the stall next to mine, a woman was having a work-related cell phone conversation. She was loud enough and animated enough that I could ascertain that she worked for the hotel. She was on the phone when she walked in and still on when she walked out. I'm all for advances in hands-free technology, but this was ridiculous. Was it up to me to pee quietly or was she completely out of line?

A: Attention all cell phone users: Do not use your phone in the restroom – public or otherwise. It makes everyone who can hear your conversation uncomfortable, and that's bad manners.

It's unpleasant for the other people in the restroom. Your broadcasting of the goings on there is a violation of their privacy. The enclosed space makes it impossible to ignore your conversation and creates a feeling of anxiety as they can't help but eavesdrop as they try to avoid offending your companion on the phone.

The person on the other end of the line will know where you are by the tell-tale sounds of a restroom and that person is likely to be offended. It would never be right to invite a person to have a conversation with you and then proceed to have that conversation from a bathroom stall. It shows a lack of respect.

Use your own good sense in this matter. End a conversation before you enter the restroom or let it go to voicemail while you're there. Having a cell phone conversation in a restroom is most definitely poor behavior. Do not do it.

Dear Thelma: Is it necessary to send written thank-you notes to those with whom you've exchanged gifts and thanked in person? I always write them to those who ship gifts as they were not here in person to see them opened and receive thanks.

A: No, you aren't required to write thank-you notes to people who have seen you open the gift and been thanked immediately in person. However, while it isn't required, you may do so if you want to add to your spoken sentiment. People feel especially appreciated when they receive a thoughtful note in addition to a verbal thank you.

If you receive a gift in the mail, call the sender promptly so they know the item they purchased and shipped has arrived safely. A written thank-you note should be sent quickly as well.

Thank-you notes and good manners never go out of style.

Dear Thelma: I visit my mother's grave at the cemetery regularly. I take new silk floral arrangements or fresh flowers. I see many graves nearby with very faded and weather-battered arrangements from long-past holiday seasons or dried-up flowers. Would it be alright while I am tending my mother's grave to clear up the graves around hers? Would that be appreciated?

A: As you know from tending your own mother's grave, gravesites are very personal spaces. People go to the cemetery to remember their loved ones and offer service to them by caring for their resting places. They also leave mementos that they don't want disturbed. Most people want to see that the last thing they left there is still there, even if it's the poinsettias they left at Christmas time and now it's Memorial Day.

I understand that you are thinking that the action will be a kindness, but I believe it would be best to allow families to take care of these things themselves.

Dear Thelma: I will be attending my husband's 20-year high school reunion this summer. We went to his 10-year and I met all his friends, but I'm not really going to remember them or their names when we connect again. Do we just start with introductions like we've never met or do I pretend to remember them and get my husband to clue me in to who they are when we're alone?

A: I don't think you should worry too much as you're all probably facing the same issue. They might remember meeting you, but they may not really recognize you or remember your name. Your husband will be the key to reintroducing you. He can introduce you as he normally would and then say, "You may have met at the last reunion." Everyone can then either remember the past connection or start fresh. Either way you're ready to proceed with the fun of the reunion.

If someone does remember you when your husband isn't around and you draw a blank, say, "I do remember meeting you. Remind me again of your name." Let the conversation flow naturally from there. It's most polite to settle it right away, rather than avoiding the name or the person.

If you remember someone who doesn't seem to remember you, remind her: "Remember, I'm Sarah Williams. I'm not in your class but my husband is Tom Williams." She'll appreciate you easing the way for her.

Reunions are about connecting and reconnecting with friends who share common bonds and common memories. When you're open to those connections, you can chuckle over forgotten names and get to remembering the fun times and creating new memories.

Dear Readers: I've been asked by several people for a refresher on the etiquette skills that lead to strong and successful business relationships. These skills are important for the teenager seeking his first summer job, the recent college grad establishing her new career, and the seasoned professional. Learning and practicing etiquette is important, but it is vital to first lay a solid foundation for using these skills. I find that foundation in three statements.

1. You only have one chance to make a first impression; make it a good one. Be prepared for new encounters by thinking about how to handle them before they arise.

2. You are who you are all the time. You can't live by one standard at work and another away from work. Positive or negative, your genuine self will always shine through. Make respect and courtesy part of your genuine self.

3. You act as you think. If you enter a situation with a positive outlook, your actions and attitudes will reflect positively even if everything doesn't go your way.

With the foundation established, we can proceed with our Summer Social Series, where we'll explore the key components to building your bank of business etiquette skills. Next week, the art of the business card and introductions.

Firm foundations and good manners never go out of style.

Dear Thelma: I'm 50 years old and have two adult children. Their mother and I divorced 15 years ago. Throughout my marriage to their mother, my ex-wife had affairs with many men. Five years ago, my son married a woman who has a very close relationship with my ex-wife. My son's wife has labeled me as a mental case to many family members, friends and acquaintances.

My son and I live about 60 miles from each other, and he now has a son who is almost 2 years old. I've only seen my grandson twice since he was born for a total of two and a half hours. I can count on one hand the number of times I have seen my son in the last five years. The few times I have seen my son, he has been extremely disrespectful. I believe my ex-wife has had a great influence, in a negative way, on the way my son has turned into a very cold and ruthless person. My son's actions have brought me much darkness and pain over the years.

I'm financially well-off and recently updated my will and only left my son $20 because of all the pain and anguish he has caused me. I prefer to distance myself from my son, but I would like to have a relationship with my grandson. Do you have any advice as I desperately want to have a relationship with my grandson?

A: I don't believe you can have a relationship with your grandson without healing the relationship with your son. Your son has control of who his child sees and with whom he spends time. He will be the key to the connection. Hearing your story, it seems that healing that relationship will not be easy. Seeking appropriate professional help to deal with your own pain may be a good first step.

Dear Readers: Personal introductions are important. They serve the purpose of exchanging names, opening the flow of communication, and establishing professional and personal relationships. The ability to perform them seamlessly while in a group is a skill that puts everyone around you at ease. And so we introduce our Summer Social Series with the art of the introduction.

Your introduction of two people should provide each person with the name of the other, their professional titles and some information that might help them start a conversation. In a business introduction, the first aspect to consider is who holds more authority. The person of less authority is presented to the senior person. Address the most important person: "Mr. Richards, I'd like to present Ms. Irene Reyes, our new sales manager in Las Cruces. Ms. Reyes, this is Mr. Douglas Richards, the president of our company." When it makes sense to use courtesy titles, use them.

In the case of a client, the client always occupies the position of most importance: "Dr. Chavez, this is Ms. Ann Honeywell, our chief executive officer. Dr. Dominic Chavez is a family practitioner in Phoenix and our new client."

When introducing people of equal rank, present the person you know well to the other. Start by addressing the person you know least: "Diana, I'd like you to meet Jerry Carlson. Jerry is a partner in my firm. Jerry, this is Diana Smith, a partner at the Hurst Law Firm."

In social situations it is traditional to introduce a man to a woman. Address the woman: "Emma, I'd like to introduce Tristan Clark, a friend of mine from college. Tristan, this is Emma Griego, my neighbor." Or introduce the person you know best to the other: "Sam, let me introduce Jay Moreno, my brother visiting from Alabama. Jay, this is Sam Morris, my neighbor with the Harley."

When you find yourself in a situation in which an introduction is necessary, but there's no one around to make it, introduce yourself: "Hello, I'm Melissa Park. I've just joined the accounting department here."

And what if you forget a person's name after you've been introduced? Remain poised, smile and say, "I'm sorry, but please tell me your name again." It's also fine to reintroduce yourself upon meeting up again with someone you've recently met, "Hello, we met at the school play. I'm Ann Johnson, nice to see you again." The person should reciprocate with their own name, but if he doesn't, you may ask for it again.

Once you've been introduced you may have the opportunity to present your business card. Although we live in a world that becomes more electronic every day, always carry your card and make sure it is in good condition, up-to-date and includes your name, email address and phone number. It should be of standard business-card size and clearly readable so that it can be easily scanned and transferred by a smartphone app. Present the card to a person face up and positioned so that the receiver doesn't have to rotate it to read it.

The way we meet and greet individuals makes a first impression and leaves a lasting one. It's a key component in your bank of business etiquette skills.

Starting relationships and good manners never go out of style.

Dear Readers: The cocktail reception is a networking mainstay in today's business world. These receptions provide the opportunity to establish and build important relationships for those who take them seriously and prepare well for them. Today our Summer Social Series takes a turn around the room at the business cocktail reception.

Prepare for a business networking event by dressing in business attire; carrying your business cards; keeping up on the day's news for conversation topics; and eating something beforehand. Yes, there will be appetizers at these functions that you are welcome to sample, but you don't want your stomach to be your primary concern. You are there to meet and greet, the food and drink are secondary.

Make an effort to arrive on time. If the host provides a nametag, wear it on your right shoulder as that is where the eye naturally goes when shaking hands. Plan to spend some time with at least one person before you head to the bar or the buffet, and start that interaction with a handshake.

As technology replaces much of the face-to-face contact we once shared in business, the importance of the handshake has never been so great. A good handshake conveys trustworthiness, openness and willingness to listen. Scrutinize your handshake as you would your wardrobe or your marketing materials.

When you are about three feet away, extend your right arm out at a slight angle across your chest with your thumb pointing upward. If you are sitting when someone approaches you, stand to greet him. Step or lean toward the person. Look directly into his eyes and smile.

Lock hands with the web between your thumb and index finger touching that of the person you're greeting. Firmly clasp her hand, avoiding a bone-crushing squeeze or an indifferent pinch with the fingers. From the elbow, pump her hand two to three times. A slight pause at the end of the handshake may express your sincerity and openness. A good handshake lasts three to four seconds. Greet the person you're meeting and use her name.

The simplest way to start a conversation is to ask a question. It could be about the person's business, how he's enjoying the event or the interesting lapel pin he's wearing. Small talk can continue over current events, cultural events or sports. Listen actively, using eye contact and the positive body language of a head nod, straight posture and relaxed arms that don't block people out or enclose yourself to show your interest and focus.

When sharing a business card present it with the information facing the person receiving it. Upon receiving a card, look it over and note the person's title or address for further conversation topics.

When it's time to exit a conversation, do so politely and considerately with a statement that includes, "Please excuse me..."

If you've done all this before making your way to the bar or buffet, you understand how convenient it is to meet and greet people without food and drink in your hands; however, enjoying these things together is also part of the event. Choose to either drink or eat so you can keep one hand available. Make an effort to choose foods that are eaten with a fork or a toothpick to keep your hands clean. Keep your food or drink in your left hand, so your right hand is free for handshakes.

Also take the time to mingle with groups of people. Assess the groups you see and approach those who appear to be engaged in casual conversations. Make eye contact and ask, "May I join you?" Introduce yourself with handshakes and an exchange of names with each member of the group. Successful networking and good manners never go out of style.

Dear Readers: During our Summer Social Series we've talked about taking your one opportunity to make a first impression to make it a good one. One key to making that good impression and maintaining it is dressing for success. Whether you're a business person or a summer job seeker, you want the look you present to the public to reflect self-confidence and professional competency.

The suit and tie best define professional attire for men. A heavy-starched, long-sleeved dress shirt, tie, belt and dress shoes with over-the-calf socks that match your pants are necessary accessories. A dark business suit – navy to dark gray – is considered most appropriate. The bottom button of a jacket or vest is left open.

Dress pants should have a slight break over the shoe in front and cover your socks. Socks should cover your shins even when you cross your legs. Choose a silk or high-quality blend tie that reaches your belt line in a print that fits with your industry and your own personal style. Dress shoes in black, cordovan or brown should be shined and in good condition. Choose a leather belt to match your shoes.

In general, a neatly trimmed hairstyle is best for business. If you do have long hair, pull it back into a neat ponytail. If you choose to sport a beard or moustache, assess it daily and keep it cleanly trimmed.

For women, business suits, pant suits or dresses with heels or flats in clean and good condition are standard professional attire. Women need to be conscientious of the skirt length they choose for professional settings. Skirts should be no shorter than three inches above the knee. Blouses should always conceal cleavage and heels higher than three inches should be saved for evening events or personal time.

In the recent past, hosiery was required with skirts at all times. If you're new to an employer or client, wear hosiery that is your skin color or darker until you can observe or ask about current views on hosiery in your workplace. Accessorize with jewelry, limiting selections to two pieces at a time. Style your hair and make-up neatly to complement your face and your professional look.

Men and women should cover tattoos and body piercings when dressing for business, and they should leave chewing gum at home.

When full business dress is not required at work, make a concentrated effort to create a business casual look that doesn't sway too casual. Avoid denim, t-shirts, sneakers and flip flops. You should still be dressed for business in collared shirts and pants for men, blouses and neat pants or skirts for women. Choose nice shoes that elevate your look and keep it on the professional side.

Dear Thelma: My husband and I are adamant that are children refer to adults as "sir" and "ma'am." Our problem is with some people who get downright rude at being referred to with a "sir" or "ma'am." We had one neighbor tell our sons that they couldn't come over and play anymore unless they quit calling him "sir." I understand that not everyone has the same standards as we do, but how do we deal with this with our kids?

A: We all at some point have to learn to deal with people who have different standards than we do without losing our standards. Your choices are to explain to your children why being called "sir" might bother this particular man and that they should to avoid it or you can stop letting them visit at the man's home. You know your children's maturity levels and which option will be best for them.

Despite challenges, good manners never go out of style.

Dear Readers: It's time to sit down to share a meal as our Summer Social Series progresses. Business meals expand the relationship building done at an appointment in the office. They offer the opportunity to connect on a social level while getting the work done. Breakfast and lunch meetings will be faster and to-the-point as most people need to get back to the office. Dinner meetings are slower-paced and offer more opportunity for social conversation and relationship building. They may even include spouses.

The next time you're out to eat, make an assessment of your table posture. Sit with both feet flat on the floor or cross them at the ankles. Women should place their purses on the back of their seat or on the floor under the chair. Avoid hanging a handbag from the back of the chair or placing it on the table. Keep phones, glasses and keys off the table as well. Keep your elbows close to your body and place your hands in your lap between courses. Place your napkin in your lap soon after sitting down. If it is a large dinner napkin, fold it in half with the fold toward your body. If you are with a large group and a host, wait for the host to place the napkin in his or her lap as a signal for you to do the same. Sit up straight as you eat and bring the utensils to your mouth, rather than bending close to the plate.

Learning and understanding the layout of dinnerware and utensils will save you confusion and frustration during a meal. The first rule to remember is solids on the left and liquids on the right. Some use the acronym BMW - bread, meal, water - to remember. The dinner plate centers the place setting in front of your seat. Your bread and salad plates are placed to the left of your place setting. Your water, beverage and wine glasses are placed to the right. Your napkin sits on the left of or on your plate.

Your forks are placed to the immediate left of your dinner plate. If you are given more than one fork, work from the outside in. The outside fork is used with your first course, maybe a salad. Leave that fork with the salad plate to be cleared when you are finished. Knives are set to the right of the plate. If you are given more than one knife, work from the outside for each course and leave the knife with the course's plate to be cleared. A beverage spoon or a soup spoon is placed to the right of the knives. If a soup spoon is included, find your beverage spoon above the plate, possibly with a dessert fork. Your coffee cup and saucer are placed to the far right, outside of the glasses and the utensils.

Wait until those around you have been served to begin eating. Chew with your mouth closed and take small bites so that you can be quickly ready to talk in between them. Use your napkin to dab your mouth. If you must leave the table, place the napkin on your chair seat. When your meal is finished and you are leaving, arrange the napkin neatly to the left of your plate.

Show as much consideration for the wait staff as you do for your host. Pull your chair in far enough so that the staff can maneuver comfortably around the dining room. It's nice to get the name of your server and use it respectfully. Finally, use common courtesy and the words "please" and "thank you" with those who are serving your meal.

Sharing a meal and good manners never go out of style.

Dear Readers: If you find yourself hosting a business or social dinner you may be called upon to select a wine. This can be a daunting task if you haven't ever considered the steps. This week the Summer Social Series offers tips to help you select with confidence.

It's fine to begin by passing the wine list around the table for others to offer recommendations. You may also enlist the assistance of your waiter or wine steward in making a selection. Be sure to tip him or her 10 to 15 percent of the cost of the wine.

Have a price range in mind before you order. As a guideline, spend about as much on a bottle of wine as you spend on a complete dinner at that establishment. A bottle of wine serves four to six glasses. If just one guest prefers white to red, you may suggest that he or she order an individual glass of wine and order a bottle of red for the others to share. If more than four guests are expected, you can order one white wine and one red wine.

When selecting wine, ask what your guests prefer and consider what everyone at the table is planning to order. Traditionally, red wine is selected with red meat and white with fish, poultry and pasta; however, even wine experts don't always adhere to the guidelines. Drink what you like or consider the general combinations that follow.

Light meat dishes like pork, poultry or salmon can go well with a red like pinot noir or French burgundy. A light white wine, such as chenin blanc, pinot grigio, or German Riesling, complements lighter fish and shellfish. Richer fish dishes like lobster go well with a full-body white wine such as chardonnay.

Chicken and pasta can work with either red or white wines depending on the sauce. Red pairs well with meat sauces and white with a vegetable or cream sauce. Heavy meats like beef, game and duck can be complemented with full-bodied red wines like cabernet sauvignon or zinfandel.

Once you've made a selection, the person who orders the wine will be asked by the server to inspect it. The server will bring it to your table and present it to you. Examine the label, making sure you received the wine and vintage ordered. The server will then remove the cork and place it on the table for your inspection. Feeling the bottle with your hand will determine whether the wine seems to be the proper temperature.

Next, your server will pour a small amount of wine into your glass. Consider the color of the wine. Red wines lose their color as they age, and white wines become deeper yellow or gold. Gently swirl the wine in the glass by holding the stem firmly while the glass remains on the table. Swirling provides oxygen to the wine releasing its full aroma or "nose." At this time, you may sniff the wine and taste it. If the wine tastes "off" or unpleasant, bring it to your server's attention. Usually, your server will bring you another bottle of the same wine or recommend a replacement.

When dining in a formal restaurant, you will find at least two wine goblets on the right side of your plate – a long-stemmed glass for white wines and a tulip-shaped glass for red. When you order wine, your server will leave the appropriate goblet on the table. Hold the stem of a white wine glass in order to keep the heat of your hand from warming the wine. Hold a red wine glass closer to the bowl because the heat from your hand releases the wine's flavor.

Confident selection and good manners never go out of style.

Dear Readers: Even when you plan and do everything properly at a business or social meal, the difficult and the unexpected can happen. Prepare for what you can with these dining tips from our Summer Social Series.

First come the hard-to-handle foods like cherry tomatoes and olives with pits. When a cherry tomato comes in a salad, pierce it carefully with your fork and cut it in half if it is large. If it's in a veggie platter, pick a small one that can be picked up with your fingers and eaten whole. Keep your mouth closed tightly as you chew.

Olives are finger foods when they come on an antipasti platter and it is proper to screen your mouth with one hand and use your fingers of the other to remove the pit from your mouth. Place it on the side of your plate or a provided dish. If a pitted olive comes in your salad, you can remove the pit with your fingers or use your tongue to push it onto your fork and then transfer to the side of the plate.

When shrimp, crab and lobster are steamed in their shells, use your fingers to de-shell them. Make sure you have a large napkin on hand and possibly a bib. The shells can be deposited in a bowl provided or in a neat heap on your plate. If you are served fish with bones, you can remove the bones from your mouth discreetly with your fork or with your fingers. Sushi can properly be eaten with chopsticks or the fingers. Eat sushi in one bite if you can. If it's too large, bite it into two.

Food served outdoors can be treated differently than when it is served indoors. Chicken, small birds, and ribs can be eaten with the fingers if outside. Inside, use a knife and fork unless your host invites you to pick it up or if you asked those around you if they mind. If chops are served with a sleeve on the end of the bone, you can use this as a handle to help in cutting with your knife. Don't pick up the chop to eat it off the bone.

If you use sugar or sweetener packets, tear off the top third of the package and place the wrappers under the edge of your plate or bread plate. Creamers, butter and jelly packages should be placed onto your bread plate or tucked under the edge also.

When things go wrong, keep cool and be discrete. If you drop a utensil on the floor, leave it there and ask the server for a clean utensil. If you're served a piece of food that is not cooked properly, call the server over and discretely explain the problem. You should receive a more properly cooked plate of food. If you find a foreign object in your food, discretely handle the situation with your server. Your meal should be promptly replaced and may be complimentary.

If you get food in your teeth, try to dislodge it by drinking water. If you can't, excuse yourself from the table and take care of it in the restroom. Also excuse yourself if you must use eye drops or blow your nose. If you can discretely apply lipstick after dinner, you may do it quickly at the table. But if you need a mirror, need to apply other make-up or need to comb your hair, excuse yourself to the restroom. If there is food on your companion's face, let him know.

Expecting the unexpected and good manners never go out of style.

Dear Readers: We conclude our Summer Social Series with communications technology. While email and texting may seem to be more relaxed forms of communication, we should not lose our sense of responsibility to communicating clearly and effectively when using them. Good manners are about thinking of others and treating them with respect and courtesy in all our actions – even those dominated by technological tools.

Always use a descriptive subject line in an email. It simply makes way for clear communication. More people are beginning to use the subject line as the first phrase of their message and then continue the beginning of the message with the rest of the phrase. This can be very confusing to people who aren't accustomed to that protocol. I suggest only using that very informal structure with someone you email regularly and who will appreciate your brevity.

Avoid the "reply all" button. Think carefully about who really needs to receive the message as you compose or reply. The same goes for forwarding attachments. By haphazardly sending everything in your mailbox along to the next person, or list of persons, you clog up inboxes unnecessarily and waste other's time. If you do send attachments, make sure beforehand that they are a format and size that your receiver can open and use.

Write messages that are clear, concise and have obvious meaning. Subtleties and sarcasm are easily misunderstood without the benefit of in-person dialog and facial expressions. Use proper grammar and punctuation even in brief communications and spell check or read the message over before you send. Do not type in all caps as it is perceived by readers to be a shout at them. Your written words are a reflection of you and your message includes more than just your words.

Text messages are typically informal and should be brief and concise. Don't confuse your reader with less than obvious abbreviations and double check the number before sending. Anything more you have to express should be handled in a phone call or in person. Most truly important matters shouldn't be handled by text.

With the proliferation of smart phones, email and texting can be done anywhere at anytime. The most basic manners of smart phones include selecting an alert tone that doesn't disturb and keeping its volume as low as possible – even silent in some instances. The most important etiquette point surrounding them for me is that their use be limited during your time spent with others. The person you are with face-to-face should always take precedence over your phone. If you are expecting something urgent, you can inform that person that you may have to attend to a message during your time together and apologize beforehand. Apologize again when the message comes through and use your response to end the exchange until you are no longer occupied.

Finally, think critically about your use of social media. Twitter, Instagram, Facebook and LinkedIn provide great ways to keep in touch and reconnect with friends, network with colleagues and get the latest news, but be smart about them. Don't forget that you are basically publishing the details of your life. Every post you submit sends a message that goes beyond just your words. Be selective about what you share. Recognize that through the way your "friends" or "followers" interact with your posts, your information may reach a much wider net than you expect. Make your sites as private as possible, but consider how them being viewed by a marginal acquaintance, a prospective employer or a complete stranger might affect you and post accordingly.

Even when embracing technology, good manners never go out of style.

Dear Thelma: I find myself in an uncomfortable situation. My daughter is in a feud with another girl at school. My daughter was initially in the wrong. She apologized and the girl did not accept so the bad feelings continue. Over the course of last school year and the summer, my younger son has become good friends with the girl's younger brother. The parents of this boy and girl are nice people. We chat at school often and when they have dropped the boy off to play. We have completely skirted the issue of our daughters' feud. I think the girls have to solve it themselves and I have no interest in hashing it out with the parents, but is it necessary to acknowledge it?

A: I don't think it's absolutely necessary. If they have allowed the boys' friendship to continue and grow, that tells me that they may be like you in thinking that this is something the girls have to solve for themselves. If you find the discomfort unbearable, in your next conversation you could say something like, "I wish the girls could figure out how to be friends again," but be prepared to handle with grace the backlash that might bring if the parents are critical of your daughter.

Dear Thelma: I have college-aged children who by any standard are clearly addicted to their cell phones. I was recently embarrassed by my son's rudeness at an important gathering of extended family – a reunion of family members from around the country celebrating a milestone. My son's absence was keenly felt as he stood outside the restaurant window in conversation on his cell phone for the entire event. I've tried everything and just don't know what to do anymore. What should I do?

A: If you haven't yet told him that his behavior is rude, you must do so now. It is definitely rude to accept an invitation to an event and then not show up, which is what he has done by withdrawing from the gathering to hold an extended cell phone conversation. He has, in a glaring way, demonstrated to the family gathered that this one conversation is more important than catching up with them.

He may have thought that taking his call outside was the polite thing to do. But he has missed the basic etiquette surrounding cell phone use, which is to give your attention to the people at hand rather than to a caller. You should be able to explain this to him and as a young adult he should be able to realize its importance and put it into practice.

Aside from the cell phone portion of your question, the idea of family reunions is important too. Family gatherings are more and more difficult to plan because of the busy lives of family members scattered across the country. These events become more important as time goes on. The older generation wants so much to get caught up with the younger generation's lives. They go with happy anticipation of making that connection.

Before you attend such an event with your children or teens, have a conversation with them about why the reunion is important and what is expected. Discuss showing the proper respect for their family. Talk about showing respect for members of the older generation attending through behavior, attitude and even attire and grooming. Include in your discussion the importance of being present in the moment, which means no cell phone conversations or texting.

I realize that being connected with cell phones is normal to young people. What we must teach them is that while it's OK to be normal, it's never OK to be rude.

Embracing the moment and good manners never go out of style.

Dear Thelma: I recently hosted a farewell party for a resident of the apartment complex I live in. This person is a friend to many and she is returning to her former home out of state. I think I fully understand the responsibilities of the hostess of such an event, but are there also responsibilities that the guest of honor should attend to? This party turned out to be very awkward when the guest of honor showed up 10 minutes late and then failed to mingle or introduce the three distinct groups of invitees to one another. I did my best as hostess to these people who didn't know me or each other, but I think the guest of honor should have stepped up too.

A: When a party is given specifically to honor a person or to recognize a milestone in their life like a move, a promotion or a retirement, that guest of honor does have to be more involved than just showing up at the party. There are important responsibilities that come with being the honoree.

Unless the event is a surprise, the guest of honor should be involved in creating the guest list. The list should fit the parameters set by the host, and the guest of honor should compile a list of people with whom she wants to celebrate and who will create a fun atmosphere by interacting together. The point of a party is to make new connections and solidify established ones. The people invited should advance that goal.

Again excluding a surprise party, the guest of honor should be on hand with the host to greet the guests as they arrive at the party, which means the guest of honor should be early to the party. The guest of honor should help the host with initial introductions. Once the party begins, the guest of honor should make an effort to speak with each of his guests and work to make introductions across already established social groups. The guest of honor should mingle constantly and work to spend some time with everyone who has come out to celebrate.

A surprise party won't have the input of the guest of honor before the event or as it begins, but once it has begun the guest of honor must make the same effort to mingle about the party, make introductions and share time with guests.

The guest of honor is the glue that binds everyone at the party together. That person must make a conscious effort to provide that connection for everyone in attendance. So if you are a guest of honor, show up early and be ready to make those social connections.

Dear Thelma: Interesting answer in the column about using cell phones instead of embracing the moment. In my view, talking to your kids about when to use a cell phone is not nearly as effective as the example you give them. Every day I see mothers or fathers with small children walking down the street pushing a stroller or in a restaurant or in a car in long conversations on a cell phone, totally ignoring the child. These small children inevitably grow up and repeat their example.

A: Example is a powerful force. We would all do well to exemplify the good behavior we want to see in others. Especially when it comes to cell phones, people have a difficult time at this. Their pull on us is strong. We must do all we can to make a conscious effort to choose the person in front of us – big or small – over the device.

Good example and good manners never go out of style.

Dear Readers: A close friend of many years has inspired me to think about our need to maintain our vital purpose in the world as we age. This friend, let's call her Angela, is 93 years old. She only recently left a long and successful career as an assistant to officials at the highest levels of the U.S. government. She has been and continues to be for me the model of a person who is truly vital.

Angela recently moved into a retirement complex where she's very happy swimming in the pool and walking in the garden. But taking up the majority of her time each day is visiting the sick and homebound of the complex. She visits five or six people everyday, sharing cupcakes and the stories she has collected over her lifetime and career. If people happen to be visiting at the same time she is, they tell her, "You come and see me too!"

"I'm not doing anything extraordinary," she says. "But everyday, when I leave these friends, I look up to the heavens and say thank you." She's thankful for the opportunity to share herself and what she has to offer.

Aging brings about its own set of freedoms and challenges. Continuing to see ourselves as vital is one of those areas that combines the two. How we approach the task of maintaining our vitality will be inspired and informed by the behaviors we've established, the manners we've made a part of ourselves and the relationships we've built over our lifetimes.

The older we get, the younger the world appears. As time and technology march on, we run the risk of feeling forgotten, isolated and less vital. When these feelings hit, the responsibility is on the individual to take action to stay vital and to recognize the difference between being alone and being lonely. I believe people often struggle with loneliness as they age when they don't value themselves enough and don't value what a gift it is to have time to spend.

By consciously valuing ourselves and the gift of our own time, we can turn our minds outward to the opportunities that exist for us today. We can find and create opportunities to stay connected with friends, and we can find and create ways to respond to the needs of others. All of these lead to that feeling of being vital and to maintaining a happy heart.

For younger generations, accomplishments are important to feeling vital. As we age, staying vital becomes tied to building essential relationships based on trust, mutuality, value in ourselves, kindness, and thoughtfulness to others. Our focus shifts from our current limitations to gratefulness for where we are at this point in our lives and what we have to offer.

Angela is vital. She recognizes the value of the time she can give to people who may only see her that day. She understands that being vital does not mean taking on huge tasks, but that it is in being available and continuing to help others. She doesn't think she's doing big things every day, but I find what she does to be extraordinary.

Take the time to continue making fun things happen in your life. And remember that you're likely to age in the same way you lived your entire life. Make sure that includes respect, courtesy and kindness in all life's stages. Successfully combined, it adds up to a peaceful mind and heart that loves.

The Angelas of this world and good manners never go out of style.

Dear Thelma: A co-worker sent me an email invitation to an anniversary party to be held at a restaurant. I am not quite sure exactly who the invite is for. It seems like a couples' event, but it's not clear my wife is invited. Does sending out emails to individuals omit spouses. "You're invited" could go either way on this one, but in most cases an email belongs to one person. I'm not sure what to do here. Can I contact my co-worker to find out?

A: I've always said it's perfectly fine to offer an invitation via email as long as all the elements called for by an invitation are covered: the host's name, the occasion, the date and time, the location, guest attire, reply instructions and clarity as to who is invited.

Who is being invited is an element that normally would be indicated by what is written on the envelope in a traditional mailing. Because of technology, that subtle but important signal is missing in an emailed invitation that doesn't take the time to include it.

Those sending invitations via email can address it in this way. In the first line of your email message, write "To Carl and Kathy Baca" or "Mr. and Mrs. John Smith and Children." Then skip a line or two and proceed with the invitation wording.

As for your situation, I believe it would be fine to call the host of the event you've been invited to and say, "I'm not quite sure if your email intended to include my wife in the invitation."

Dear Thelma: Recently I moved into an apartment complex that I describe as upscale. It has all the amenities: workout room, pool, sauna, Jacuzzi. Even after living in my own home for years, I'm finding that residing here has a very pleasant and at-home feeling. However, I have experienced that some residents do not do their share to keep this wonderful dwelling comfortable and safe for everyone. Do you have advice to give us?

A: I both appreciate and understand your question because I too have experienced living in an apartment complex. I have found when those in a shared living situation adopt two specific attitudes the living becomes more comfortable for all. The first is "Do unto others as you would have them do unto you." When all residents base their actions and decisions upon this golden rule, the living space is respectful and content.

The second attitude is one of ownership. Although the residents are not owners, their apartment is their home for whatever span of time they live there. When they take care of their apartments and shared space as if they were their own, respect for the space is heightened and living in it is more pleasant.

My first experience in apartment living was that the manager of the complex carefully reviewed the policies designed to make living together in this shared space more comfortable for everyone. Whether the policies are presented in person or on paper, plan to observe them from that day forward as you expect your fellow residents to do. Also, always show the respect you wish to receive to the manager and staff employed there to help you.

Respect your space by caring for your apartment and the things in it. When you move in and during daily living, take care to avoid damaging walls and carpets and care for your appliances. Do your part to maintain your dwelling, but report maintenance problems immediately so they can be addressed before they worsen.

Pay attention to cleanliness. Don't throw litter on the ground. There are always garbage cans nearby or even your own apartment to carry the litter to. In disposing of trash, be sure it's all in the dumpster and not outside of it for the next person to trip over. Where there is a pool available, do your part to keep the exterior patio area and the pool clean. The patio is not a place to leave food, towels or trash. You don't care to be faced with other people's trash, so make sure your own is properly disposed of.

Be aware of your own noise level. Apartments are not soundproof so be considerate with your television, musical instruments, conversations and parties.

Observe designated parking spaces. There are spaces designated for visitors, residents and future residents. Honor these designations so that everyone can find a place to park.

If the complex allows children, remember they are your children and must be supervised by you. You must be responsible for their behavior. That doesn't mean children can't enjoy themselves, but they must be the taught by you the respect required when living in shared space. They also must be taught to respect the property as if it were their own.

Total responsibility also must be taken of your pets if they are allowed in the complex. Always keep them secured and on a leash in common areas and clean up after them every time they create a mess.

When you're living in shared space, adopt or periodically recharge these attitudes of ownership and respect for those around you. Your good example and heartsense should influence your fellow residents.

Good living and good manners never go out of style.

Dear Thelma: I know you've written about it before, but it's worth repeating: Cell phone conversations do not belong in public restroom stalls! I was in an airport restroom recently and was appalled at the cell phone conversation going on in the stall next to mine. How do people who do this not get it?

A: Attention all cell phone users: Do not use your phone in the restroom. It makes everyone who can hear your conversation uncomfortable, and that's bad manners.

It's unpleasant for the other people in the restroom. Your broadcasting of the goings on there is a violation of their privacy. The enclosed space makes it impossible to ignore your conversation and creates a feeling of anxiety as they try to avoid causing offense.

And you're not fooling the person on the other end of the line. It would never be right to invite a person to have a conversation with you and then proceed to have that conversation from a bathroom stall. It shows a lack of respect. End a conversation before you enter the restroom or let it go to voicemail while you're there.

Dear Thelma: I don't like being taken to the exam room at a doctor's appointment and the nurse asking, "How are you today?" Half way out of the waiting room is obviously not the place to begin describing my medical condition, and if I'm at the doctor, I'm not fine. I would think some kind of sensitivity training would cover the inappropriateness of that question. What do you think?

A: I understand your frustration as I too have wanted to answer honestly to what really is a ridiculous question. How do I answer? I grit my teeth and say, "Fine, and you?"

There is a sense of congeniality that patients want and need to experience when they visit a doctor's office, and that is what the nurse is trying to create. She's trying to use a friendly greeting to make a connection with the patient. But because the question is tied so closely to health, it often does cause frustration rather than connection.

While the sentiment is right, the words may not be. I would rather a nurse give me a great smile and say, "Hello. It's nice to see you." This would create a connection I would appreciate.

Dear Readers: Some of you offered creative answers to last week's discussion of the greeting at the doctor's office of "How are you?"

Carole says: "I like to answer with an English expression which answers the question but gives little information and that is, 'Oh, bearing up under the strain, you know.' If questioned as to the meaning I tell them that all life can be a strain at times and like many others I am coping as best I can."

Richard says: "I always respond to the nurse's question, 'How are you?' with the standard, 'I'm here to find that out.'"

Honest answers and good manners never go out of style.

Dear Readers: Have you given much thought to the five senses? To see, taste, smell, hear and touch are daily occurrences for most of us and experiences we may take for granted. During the month of November and the winter holidays, when gratitude takes the forefront and when delighting the senses is often the aim, I think it's time to appreciate the gift of those senses and all they add to our worlds.

I'm sure that we have all encountered people who have made us acutely aware of our senses and highlighted the need for our appreciation of them. For me there are two very special people in my life who I'm aware have helped me both focus on and appreciate the five senses.

My own sister Karlene, who had an esophageal tumor and who passed away years ago, taught me the most important lesson on taste. My friend Leonard and I took Karlene to Hyde Park near Santa Fe to see the fall colors of the aspen. It had snowed very lightly so that the trees appeared to be covered with powdered sugar.

We enjoyed a brief walk around with her telling me that she felt like she was on her last vacation and that God's creation was so beautiful. At that time Karlene was was on oxygen and tube feeding. She had taken nothing by mouth for the previous three months. On the way home, she felt very thirsty. Although she could not swallow, I understood that she needed the sensation of relieving her thirst. We stopped and got her a Sprite, along with an empty cup. Karlene swirled the fizzy sweetness around in her mouth, not even minding that she had to spit it into the empty cup rather than swallow. She said to me, "You'll never know what it means just to taste this." For the brief time that remained in her life, this is how she savored the sense of taste, in her own way satisfying that need.

What Karlene revealed to me about taste, my new friend Michael Naranjo has shown me about sight and touch. Michael is a renowned sculptor recognized locally, nationally and internationally for his work created in clay and cast into bronze. Amazing about Michael is that as a young man serving in the Vietnam War in 1968, a grenade explosion took his eyesight and use of his right hand.

Despite the challenges, and maybe because of them, he became a sculptor. For more than 30 years he has created images of movement and beauty that express what he cannot see with his eyes, but what exists in his heart and his mind. What a personal privilege to know this individual and understand his sincere appreciation of the gift of life and the joy he experiences in creating sculptures that have made countless people happy. He found a way to see from within that benefits the world around him.

The efforts of Michael and Karlene to experience their senses and create value from those experiences inspires me. It inspires me to receive all the information my senses provide me with an open heart and mind, and use it to create positive effects in my own life and in the lives of those around me. And as I take the opportunity to pay tribute to my sister and my new friend, may we all be grateful for our five senses and all we experience through them.

Life experience and good manners never go out of style.

Dear Thelma: Friends and acquaintances I dine with sometimes will sit at the table and blow their noses. I've always be taught that this is rude. Shouldn't they leave the room to do this?

A: If you find it necessary to blow your nose with force, you should leave the table and go into a restroom or an empty room. The reason: a loud blow of the nose is sure to attract the attention of other diners, who will likely find it unappetizing to watch you go through this process. To show the most courtesy you can, it's best to leave the table.

Concern for the effect of our actions on others and good manners never go out of style.

Dear Readers: At this time of year we begin to think about the perfect gift. That gift that will exquisitely express our appreciation and our admiration for the receiver. Those gifts that will show just how thankful we are for the special people in our lives. In my journey through life I have found there are two perfect gifts to be given: the gift of our time and the gift of our love.

Our time is precious, and that is why it is such a valuable gift. We must share it as often as we can. We should first recognize the importance of sharing special time with those closest to us. Deliberately setting aside time to spend in a special way with those living under our own roofs may be the best thing we can offer them. Even making an effort to be more fully present during those everyday times together is a gift through which both the giver and receiver feel the benefits.

Time for those outside our closest circle also makes an impact. Making the effort to enjoy the company of a friend for the simple accomplishment of spending time together is a beautiful gift. Taking time to organize a gathering for friends or time to be a happy attendee at a party are other ways of gifting our time with others that build relationships and strengthen important bonds.

And the perfect gift of time is never limited to those you know best. As we call to mind the simple things we are truly thankful for, like shelter and food, we easily find opportunities to share with those in need. When we spend time reaching out to others, the intangible rewards of providing for tangible needs can bring a fresh perspective. You might even use your Thanksgiving get-together to plan a family service project you can take on together during the holidays to benefit a charity or a family in need. You'll grow closer together through sharing your time and spreading your blessings.

Our love is also a precious gift. Sharing our love lets people know that they are important to us and inspires confidence in that love. We should tell them that we love them and make every effort to give them the attention they desire and deserve as our loved ones. Express your love as a gift and it may take on new meaning for you.

I hope you'll let these perfect gifts guide you as you celebrate Thanksgiving and Christmas. Encourage those you see who do give these gifts and let them know you appreciate their efforts. When your sister-in-law volunteers to take on the family Christmas celebration, thank her profusely and then do everything you can to make it easier on her. When the stressed-out party host sighs that she doesn't know how she got herself into this mess, remind her that sharing her time creating an event where people can build relationships is a beautiful thing to do.

Open your heart this holiday season to also receive these perfect gifts. Look for the elements of love and time in all the gifts you receive. Recognize when these gifts are offered to you and rejoice in receiving them. Marvel at their perfection whether they are tied up with a sparkly bow or handed over humbly. These are the gifts that matter and that make a difference in people's lives and in the world.

Perfect gifts and good manners never go out of style.

Dear Readers: As the year comes to a close, many of us take stock of the recent past or even our lifetimes. Many will reflect on the possibility of a material downsizing in their lives. In recent years I faced the need to downsize, and it was one of the most difficult decisions I ever had to make.

It was my doctor who realized I was reaching a point where it would become more and more difficult for me to maintain my residence and continue my flower gardening hobby. I realized those kinds of responsibilities could become a burden, and I began the process of imagining a new way of living. Many couples go through similar assessments. Working together to create a new idea of home has been a beautiful experience for some couples I've known, but it's not easy.

Throughout a lifetime there are many enjoyable things that you want, that you obtain and that enrich your existence. Those things play an important and enjoyable role in your life; however, priorities do change over time. When my friend, Leonard, was faced with something to purchase that I found spectacular, he'd say, "That's just stuff." Or his response when I would suggest he replace a comfortable but tattered sweater would be: "I already have one and I don't need two."

Downsizing shines the spotlight on what you want versus what you need. In that glaring light you find you've accumulated a lot of stuff and it creates a kind of restlessness.

Faced with that restlessness, many take action as I did. I knew I needed to downsize my home and my possessions, but I also knew I absolutely would not downsize my life. The things I really needed became obvious to me – those things were the relationships and activities that keep me vibrant, happy and alive. I began to ask myself not only what do I need, but also what have I become. What do I really value? The answer was family, friends and the opportunity to participate in activities I enjoy. I would not downsize those.

I would not downsize the positive attitude with which I've lived my life, the spirit of generosity and friendship I have worked to nurture or the connections I had made and would still make with true friends. While the decision to downsize has to be made with the intellect, the heart plays its role too, seeking the beauty and emotion drawn out when possessions step to the background.

As I downsized, I found an essential thing in life to be how I used my time and my opportunities to love others. I let a focus on that time and opportunity become a driver of decisions in my life. I also found that throughout my life I had experienced many opportunities to joyfully do things for others. Now people want to joyfully do things for me and I must receive that love in the same spirit that I have often given it. The people in your life who anticipate what you need become deeply valued. Some people find it difficult to accept a selfless act on their behalf, but doing so builds connections and relationships that carry us forward.

We're told there is a time and a season for everything. When you reach the season of material downsizing, never downsize life. No matter the state of your possessions, remain alive socially, engaged publically and connected to the activity of the community in which you live. Keep yourself lively, engaged and valuable. Keep the spark inside you glowing. Vitality and good manners never go out of style.

Dear Readers: Have you ever given thought to what a life of unconditional love means? Have you ever thought of living that way?

For me a life of unconditional love is defined by several things. It includes the essentials of living peacefully, expressing compassion, and understanding one's own value. It is a life marked by mercy, simplicity and humility all of which create an overflow of generosity and gratefulness.

I have had the privilege of having someone in my life who by living a life of unconditional love has taught me so much about respect, courtesy, generosity and love. That person is my sister Nella.

At age 17, Nella entered the congregation of the Sisters of Charity. She knew at that young age that she wanted to dedicate her life to God. Throughout 67 years of service as an educator across Colorado, Ohio and 23 years as principal of St. Mary's School in Albuquerque, Sister Marinella taught the essentials of unconditional love and greeted every child in her universe with the pet name "Love Dove."

Nella has understood the privilege it is to make a difference in the lives the children and adults at her schools; she knows her value. Upon her retirement three years ago, her staff called her a faithful and tireless advocate of education offering positive, life-changing support.

By recognizing, valuing and utilizing the contributions only she could make, she made tremendous impact and grew St. Mary's from a school of 250 students to one bursting at the seams with 530.

On her path of unconditional love, she also lives her life giving without expecting in return, and that humility has made her a generous and grateful leader. And she has always had the keen ability to get out in front of disorder. She has managed problems before they existed and neutralized negativity before it could take hold.

On top of all that she's taught me how valuable a sense of humor is within a life of unconditional love. Recently we sat at the table eating a meal together and something caused her to begin to giggle. I decided to giggle along with her just to share in her joy. When we stopped, she looked at me with her sense of humor shining through and said, "Now wasn't that fun?"

Having shared the story of my sister with you, perhaps you can reflect on your own life, your own values, and the people who inspire you by their generous, peaceful and compassionate lives. Each of us has the opportunity and privilege to live a life of unconditional love. It's a life where we don't set boundaries or pass judgment on people. We reach out to respond to the needs of others. We value ourselves and those around us. We rely on our heartsense, that common sense of the heart that leads us to treat each other with respect, compassion and courtesy in every situation.

Look for those in your life who share these qualities and look for opportunities to share them yourself. The impact your unconditional love makes will be tremendous. A gracious impact and good manners never go out of style.

Dear Readers: More than a decade has passed since I first had the privilege of connecting with you, my consistent readers. You followed the column in the *Albuquerque Tribune* from March 2004 to October 2007. The first *Albuquerque Journal* column appeared Nov. 2, 2007. This is my 512th and final column.

This ending has me thinking about the word "legacy." The dictionary defines legacy as anything handed down from the past. I see it as more than that. Whether we have anything of monetary value or not, we all leave a legacy in our attitudes, our behaviors and our actions. We make an impact upon those around us. Our legacy defines us for the generations that follow. Whether that legacy is positive or negative is up to us and centers around how we live our lives and how we treat people.

This column is part of my legacy. The ideas, thoughts and instructions shared with you are my way of distributing what has been passed down to me combined with what I have learned over a lifetime. Through the column I have passed it into the future through you. You know this column was never just about etiquette. Here is what I hope you have taken from the column, made your own and have shared with those around you:

Kindness. It's so important to be kind. We often face critical judgment and cynicism, and it becomes easy to fall into adopting those attitudes. But they don't bring out the best in us or in others. Kindness is the antidote and it is contagious. When you share a kindness with someone, they are inspired to take the next opportunity to be kind. Being kind with your expressions, your actions and your time expands your heart, especially when there's no reward in return. Kindness is at the core of good manners. If you chose the kindest thing in any situation, you will always choose correctly.

Appreciation for life. With its celebrations and its challenges, life is meant to be lived. There will be questions and confusion at times, but the answers will be found. Seek them joyfully and live the now of your life, whatever stage of it you are in.

Mutuality. Life is an exchange, don't live it like you're at the tip of a top-down organization. Don't just show respect, but truly have respect for everyone with whom you come into contact, from those you consider the least to the greatest.

Heartsense. Frequently I have written about this term that really is my own. Heartsense for me is common sense of the heart. That internal awareness that leads you to what really is the right thing to do. I know you don't think with the heart, but its influence can be phenomenal in making decisions that influence your legacy. Heartsense has no boundaries, no prejudices, it lives the present moment, it does not judge others, and it wakes up every morning grateful for that day. It is my humble hope that this column has helped you to expand and to follow your heartsense.

I am grateful to the editors of the *Albuquerque Journal* for seeing the value of including kindness and manners within the pages of the newspaper. And I am so grateful to the readers of this column. You have been so open with me. Your questions and your personal comments to me, those you did and didn't want published, have motivated me. You have approached me with your praise, complaints and comments in the grocery store, at physical therapy and as we've gathered with friends. You have inspired me by the great attention you pay to being better equipped to handle personal and social situations in your lives. I have felt so connected with you. It's a reader relationship I take with me as a treasure.

I hope that you will consider your legacy as you think on this final column. As long as you're living you have the opportunity to affect what it will be. If there's something you need to change, change it. If there's forgiveness you need to seek, seek it. If there's love you need to give, give it.

And while you do it remember, good manners never go out of style.

Index

www.ingramcontent.com/pod-product-compliance
Lightning Source LLC
Chambersburg PA
CBHW031456270326
41930CB00006B/118